IT

for Cambridge International AS & A Level

COURSEBOOK

Ceredig Cattanach-Chell, Neil Rickus, David Waller,
Paul Long, Sarah Lawrey & Victoria Ellis

Third edition with Digital access

Shaftesbury Road, Cambridge CB2 8EA, United Kingdom

One Liberty Plaza, 20th Floor, New York, NY 10006, USA

477 Williamstown Road, Port Melbourne, VIC 3207, Australia

314–321, 3rd Floor, Plot 3, Splendor Forum, Jasola District Centre, New Delhi – 110025, India

103 Penang Road, #05–06/07, Visioncrest Commercial, Singapore 238467

Cambridge University Press is a department of the University of Cambridge.

We share the University's mission to contribute to society through the pursuit of education, learning and research at the highest international levels of excellence.

www.cambridge.org
Information on this title: www.cambridge.org/978100945284

First edition published 2017
Second edition published 2020

20 19 18 17 16 15 14 13 12 11 10 9 8 7 6 5 4 3 2

Printed in Poland by Opolgraf   .

A catalogue record for this publication is available from the British Library

Library of Congress Cataloging-in-Publication data

ISBN 978-1-009-45294-6 Practical Skills Workbook Paperback with Digital Access (2 Years)
ISBN 978-1-009-45298-4 Cambridge International AS & A Level IT Coursebook with Digital Access (2 Years)
ISBN 978-1-009-45300-4 Cambridge International AS & A Level IT Digital Teacher's Resource Access Card

Additional resources for this publication at www.cambridgeinternational.org/978100945284

CAMBRIDGE DEDICATED TEACHER AWARDS

2023

Teachers play an important part in shaping futures.
Our Dedicated Teacher Awards recognise the hard work that teachers put in every day.

Thank you to everyone who nominated this year; we have been inspired and moved by all of your stories. Well done to all of our nominees for your dedication to learning and for inspiring the next generation of thinkers, leaders and innovators.

CONGRATULATIONS TO OUR INCREDIBLE WINNERS!

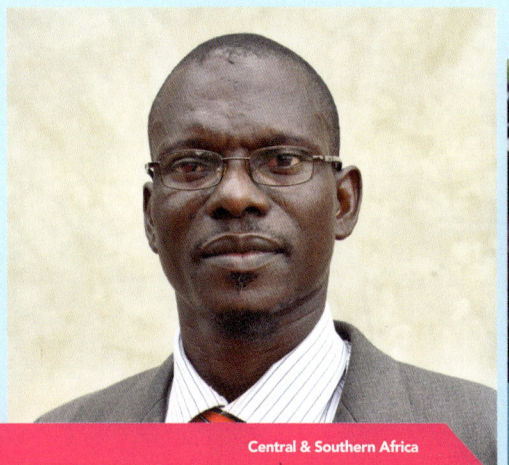

WINNER — Central & Southern Africa
Akeem Badru
St Michael R.C.M Primary School,
Ogunpa Lunloye, Nigeria

Regional Winner: **East & South Asia**
Gaurav Sharma
FirstSteps School, India

Regional Winner: **North & South America**
Nathalie Roy
Glasgow Middle School, United States

Regional Winner: **Australia, New Zealand & South-East Asia**
Goh Kok Ming
SJKC Hua Lian 1, Malaysia

Regional Winner: **Middle East & North Africa**
Uzma Siraj
Future World School, Pakistan

Regional Winner: **Europe**
Selçuk Yusuf Arslan
Atatürk MTAL, Turkey

For more information about our dedicated teachers and their stories, go to **dedicatedteacher.cambridge.org**

CAMBRIDGE
UNIVERSITY PRESS

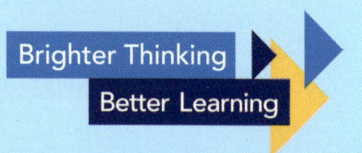

Brighter Thinking
Better Learning

Endorsement statement

Endorsement indicates that a resource has passed Cambridge International Education's rigorous quality-assurance process and is suitable to support the delivery of their syllabus. However, endorsed resources are not the only suitable materials available to support teaching and learning, and are not essential to achieve the qualification. For the full list of endorsed resources to support this syllabus, visit
www.cambridgeinternational.org/endorsedresources

Any example answers to questions taken from past question papers, practice questions, accompanying marks and mark schemes included in this resource have been written by the authors and are for guidance only. They do not replicate examination papers. In examinations the way marks are awarded may be different. Any references to assessment and/or assessment preparation are the publisher's interpretation of the syllabus requirements. Examiners will not use endorsed resources as a source of material for any assessment set by Cambridge International Education.

While the publishers have made every attempt to ensure that advice on the qualification and its assessment is accurate, the official syllabus, specimen assessment materials and any associated assessment guidance materials produced by the awarding body are the only authoritative source of information and should always be referred to for definitive guidance.

Our approach is to provide teachers with access to a wide range of high-quality resources that suit different styles and types of teaching and learning.

For more information about the endorsement process, please visit
www.cambridgeinternational.org/endorsed-resources

⟩ Contents

How to use this series   vii

How to use this book   viii

Introduction   x

1   Data processing and information   1

2   Hardware and software   33

3   Monitoring and control   55

4   Algorithms and flowcharts   70

5   eSecurity   105

6   The digital divide   125

7   Expert systems   138

8   Spreadsheets   148

9   Modelling   211

10   Database and file concepts   225

11   Video and audio editing   287

12   IT in society   312

13   New and emerging technologies   342

14   Communications technology   361

15   Project management   404

16   System life cycle   424

17   Data analysis and visualisation   463

18	Mail merge	481
19	Graphics creation	504
20	Animation	543
21	Programming for the web	580
Glossary		626
Acknowledgements		635

> How to use this series

This suite of resources supports students and teachers following the Cambridge International AS & A Level Information Technology syllabus (9626) for first examination in 2025. All of the books in the series work together to help students develop the necessary knowledge and critical skills required for this subject.

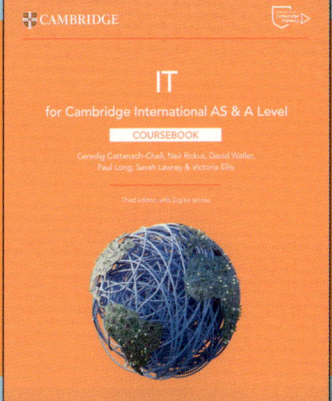

This coursebook provides 100% more activities than our previous edition and follows the same order structure as the Cambridge International AS & A Level Information Technology syllabus (9626). Each chapter includes questions to develop theoretical understanding or practical skills, and questions designed to encourage discussion. Practice questions for every topic help prepare students for their assessments.

The Teacher's Resource gives you everything you need to plan and deliver your lessons. It includes background knowledge at the start of each chapter, class activities with suggested timings, differentiation ideas, advice on common misconceptions, homework and assessment ideas.

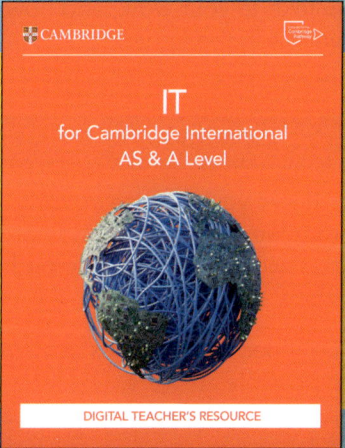

The Practical Skills Workbook contains worked examples and unique tasks to help learners practise core practical IT skills. With exercises increasing in challenge, it gives students further opportunities to undertake practice and refine their skills in the classroom or at home. It covers tasks for all of the practical chapters of the Coursebook that support many of the learning outcomes required in the syllabus.

> How to use this book

Throughout this book, you will notice lots of different features that will help your learning. These are explained below.

LEARNING INTENTIONS

Learning intentions, set the scene for each chapter, help with navigation through the coursebook and indicate the important concepts in each topic.

BEFORE YOU START

This contains questions and activities on subject knowledge you will need before starting this chapter.

REFLECTION

These activities ask you to think about the approach that you take to your work, and how you might improve this in the future.

ACTIVITY

These activities will give you practice in using technology and improve your understanding of the topics. Activities will ask you to do something, but won't tell you how to do it.

Answers are not provided for Activities as there are often multiple possible answers.

PRACTICAL ACTIVITY

Practical activities will teach you how to do something on a computer. These may require you to use supplementary source files, which you can download from the digital edition of this book.

DISCUSSION POINT

These boxes suggest interesting points for you to discuss with your classmates.

KEY WORDS

Key vocabulary is highlighted in the text when it is first introduced. Definitions are then given in the margin which explain the meanings of these words and phrases. You will also find definitions of these words in the Glossary at the back of this book.

UNPLUGGED ACTIVITY

These activities allow you to practise key skills and concepts without using a computer.

Answers are not provided for Unplugged activities, as there are often multiple possible answers.

WORKED EXAMPLE

Wherever you need to know how to approach a skill, worked examples will show you how to do this.

Questions

Appearing throughout the text, questions give you a chance to check that you have understood the topic you have just read about. You can find the answers to these questions at the back of the book.

TIP

Facts and tips are given in these boxes.

DID YOU KNOW?

These boxes will help you understand how the topics link to the real world.

PRACTICE QUESTIONS

Questions at the end of each chapter provide more demanding practice questions, some of which may require use of knowledge from previous chapters.

Answers to these questions can be found at the back of the book.

You can access answers for Questions and Practice questions on Cambridge Go, using the access code provided in the front cover of this book.

SUMMARY CHECKLIST

The summary checklists are followed by 'I can' statements that match the Learning Intentions at the beginning of the chapter. You might find it helpful to tick the statements you feel confident with when you are revising.

You should revisit any topics that you don't feel confident with.

PROJECT

The project at the end of each chapter gives you the opportunity to put into practice all the skills and knowledge you have learned in the chapter.

> Introduction

Welcome to the third edition of our IT for Cambridge International AS & A Level series.

This Coursebook has been written by experienced authors specifically for the Cambridge International AS & A Level Information Technology syllabus (9626) for examination from 2025.

The syllabus develops a broad range of IT skills. Throughout this Coursebook there are examples of IT in practice, practical activities that include extension activities for you to complete and discussion points to provoke further thought. There are questions that will test your knowledge and understanding. Whenever a task is presented, we would encourage you to carry it out before progressing further.

The key concepts for Cambridge International AS & A Level Information Technology (Impact of IT, Hardware and software, Networks and their role in the internet, Mobile wireless applications and Cloud computing, The internet, System life cycle, New technologies and how they may affect everyday life) recur throughout the syllabus.

This Coursebook has been written to reflect these key concepts, in particular in the following chapters: Hardware and software (Chapter 2); IT in society (Chapter 12); New and emerging technologies (Chapter 13); Communications technology, including networks and the internet (Chapter 14) and System life cycle (Chapter 16). It is not necessary to work through the book in order from start to finish.

The syllabus defines three assessment objectives: AO1 Recall, select and communicate knowledge and understanding of IT, AO2 Apply knowledge, understanding, skills and judgement to produce IT-based solutions and AO3 Analyse, evaluate and present reasoned conclusions.

The content of the syllabus focuses on current practice and practical applications of computers in everyday life. To reflect this, the practical elements of this Coursebook are not concerned with, for example, providing step-by-step advice on how to use particular software, but rather with helping you to discover what is available and having the confidence to apply your knowledge to different types of software. This will help you to prepare for the many different aspects of using computers that you will encounter in life, and not just in your exams.

This Coursebook makes reference to a variety of brand names. Note that marks will not be awarded for mentioning manufacturers' names in answers.

› Chapter 1
Data processing and information

LEARNING INTENTIONS

By the end of this chapter, you will be able to:

- explain the difference between data and information
- explain the use of direct and indirect sources of data and evaluate their advantages and disadvantages
- describe factors that affect the quality of information
- understand the need for encryption and describe different methods of encryption
- evaluate the advantages and disadvantages of different methods of encryption
- describe encryption protocols and evaluate their advantages and disadvantages
- explain how encryption is used
- describe the use of validation and verification methods
- explain the need for both validation and verification
- describe the advantages and disadvantages of both validation and verification.

CONTINUED

- describe batch, online and real-time processing methods and give examples of when each one is used
- write an algorithm to show the steps of each type of processing
- evaluate the advantages and disadvantages of different processing methods.

BEFORE YOU START

- Do you know the difference between input and output?
- Do you understand that when input data is processed it can be stored or sent to output?
- Do you understand the term encryption?
- Do you understand the term hacking?
- Do you know what a protocol is?
- Do you understand the structure of a table used in a database?
- Are you able to use a spell checker?

Introduction

We live in a world where we rely on data and information. It is important that data is accurate. Digital technology helps us to manage the input and transfer of data. Digital technology also helps us to make sure that data is fit for purpose and useful for the intended audience.

KEY WORD

data: numbers, letters, symbols, sounds or images without meaning

A picture without a description of what it shows is another example of raw data (see Figure 1.1).

1.1 Data and information

Data

Data are raw numbers, letters, symbols, sounds or images without meaning.

DID YOU KNOW?

The word data is plural. However, in English we often say 'a piece of data' as well, even though it is plural! Pieces of data or a piece of data are both correct.

Some examples of data are:

P952BR   @bbcclick   359   23557.99

Figure 1.1: Example of raw data.

The data P952BR could have several meanings. It could be:

- a product code
- a postal/ZIP code
- a car registration number.

Because we do not know what the data means, it is meaningless.

KEY WORD

information: data with context and meaning

Information

When we give data meaning or context, it becomes information. A person reading the data will understand what it means. We change data into information by giving it two things. First, we need to give it context. Context tells us what the data item represents, as shown in the examples of data in Table 1.1.

Data	Context	Comment
P952BR	A product code	This is a product code, but it is still not known what it is a product code for, so it is still data.
@bbcclick	An 'X' handle	This is an address used for X, but it is not information unless it is known to be an X handle or used within X software. It's also not known whose address it is.
359	Price	This is a currency value, but it is not known what the price is for, so it is still data.

Table 1.1: Examples of data being given context.

Second, we need to give the data meaning as shown in the examples in Table 1.2.

Data	Context	Comment
P952BR	A product code	A product code for a can of noodles.
@bbcclick	An 'X' handle	The X address for the BBC's weekly technology show, Click.
359	Price	The price of a mobile phone cover

Table 1.2: Examples of data being given context and meaning to become information.

Data + Context + Meaning = Information

Questions

A company creates websites using style sheets.

1. Identify one item of data that will be used by the company.
2. Describe how this item of data can become information.

Sources of direct data

Data collected from a **direct data source** (primary source) must be used for the same purpose for which it was collected.

KEY WORD

direct data source: data that is collected and used for a specific purpose

The data will often have been collected or requested by the individual or organisation who intends to use the data. However, data must not already exist for another purpose. The person collecting the data must know the purpose for which it is intended.

Imagine you want to find out how much a pair of shoes costs in different shops. This data can be collected from various direct sources. These could include:

- visiting shops and writing down the prices (see Figure 1.2)
- visiting shop websites and noting down the prices
- carrying out a survey of shop owners to ask about the prices.

Figure 1.2: Direct data source.

Questionnaires

Questionnaires can be used to collect specific data. Questionnaires are very useful when we may want to collect many responses (see Figure 1.3).

Questionnaires need to be designed carefully to:

- capture the information required
- enable effective data analysis
- be as quick to complete as possible.

Once the questionnaire is complete, we can enter the data into a database or spreadsheet to carry out statistical analysis.

Online questionnaires enable quicker analysis of data. An online questionnaire often stores data directly into a database. Storing data directly into a database will save time and money.

Questionnaire

Indicate your behaviour by ticking the appropriate box.

> you travel by car per week?

How many of your car journeys involve

Never

Daily

2 - 5 Times

mes per week

More than 5 times per week

you use Public Transport per week ?

How long is your average journey to your

Less than 1 Mile

1 - 5 miles

5 - 10 Miles

More than 10 Miles

Figure 1.3: A questionnaire.

Interviews

Interviews are another direct source of information. Questions are asked directly to respondents. The interviewer can then ask the respondent further questions, based on their answers.

Data logging

Computers can sense what is going on in the world by using sensors. Data logging is the process of automatically collecting data through the computer's sensors. The data is stored for use in the future. For example, a scientist may want to measure the quality of the water in the local rivers and streams (see Figure 1.4). They may be checking for oxygen levels or chemicals. They can use a computer sensor to log this data automatically on a computer. The scientist would then analyse the data in a laboratory.

Figure 1.4: A scientist using a laptop to measure the water quality of a river.

Observation

Observation is a way of collecting data directly. We can watch traffic go past and count the number of cars or buses. Or we can count the number of aeroplanes taking off from an airport every hour. We can also record a video of something, such as a sporting event, and watch it back to make observations.

Sources of indirect data

An **indirect data source** (secondary source) is data collected for one purpose but then used for something different (see Figure 1.5). The data may be collected by the same person who is using it, or it can be used by someone else.

> **KEY WORD**
>
> **indirect data source:** data that is collected for a different purpose (secondary source)

For example, you could use indirect sources to find out how much a pair of shoes costs at different shops by:

- looking at a sales catalogue which lists the prices of shoes. This is an indirect source because the initial data was collected for a wide range of shoes, not just the ones you want.

- looking at till receipts from the shop. This is an indirect source because the price on the till receipt is there to provide proof of purchase. It is not there to show the price of shoes in the store.

Figure 1.5: Indirect data source.

Question

3   Which of the data sources in Table 1.3 are direct data sources and which are indirect data sources?

Data	Reason collected	Reason used
a Names and email addresses of members of a political party	To record their membership and to be able to contact them.	To contact members by email to see if they will donate some money.
b Employee attendance dates and times	To identify when employees attended work and to calculate their wages.	To allow a police officer to check an employee's alibi if a crime has been committed.
c Flight times and prices from airline websites	To compare the prices and times for a trip to Florida.	To decide the best flight to use for a trip to Florida.
d Names, ages and addresses of people	For a national census.	To allow a marketing company to find out which areas have the highest population of children.
e Weather measurements from a weather station	To record the current weather.	To show the current temperature and rainfall on a website.

Table 1.3: Data sources.

Weather data

Weather data is often used as an indirect source of data. It is not possible for a single person to collect data from across a country or the world. Large weather data centres do this for us. They use lots of remote sensors from all over the world to collect data in real time (see Figure 1.6).

Figure 1.6: Remote sensors collecting weather data in Iceland.

Real time means that you can check on the weather at any time and know exactly what the weather is like in that place. Weather data centres collect many different items of data. For example:

- temperature

- humidity (percentage of water in the air)

- ultraviolet (UV) light levels (this tells us how intense the sunlight is)

- wind speed

- wind direction

- rainfall

- air pressure.

Collecting these pieces of data can be used to predict what the weather will do. This is called a weather forecast.

Census data

A census counts the number of people in a country. It also asks questions about aspects of their lives such as the jobs they do, their age, whether they have any qualifications and their general health. Census data may be used by governments to plan for hospitals and transport in certain areas of a country (see Figure 1.7).

Census data can also be used as a source of indirect data. A toy store may use it to see how many young people live in a region. They can then use this data to change the types of toy it sells.

Figure 1.7: A government census form.

Electoral registers

Governments often keep a register of people who are registered to vote. This register includes the names and addresses of each person who can vote.

Its main purpose is to enable those people to vote in elections. However, it could be used to check whether a person lives at the address. It could also be used to count how many people live in each household. Using the data in this way would make the electoral register an indirect data source.

Personal information collected by businesses

When you buy a product or service from an online company or sign up to a newsletter online, you may be asked to consent to the business collecting your personal information such as name, address and other details. If you give your consent, the business may then pass on your details to third parties such as other businesses and organisations, which will allow them to market their products and services directly to you.

Businesses that send out marketing emails or letters often purchase lists of email addresses or home addresses. This data helps them to direct their marketing at their target market. For example, a company selling school textbooks will benefit from a list of email addresses of teachers.

Different countries have different laws about how personal information may be used. Most countries have laws that require businesses to obtain consent from customers before the customers' data can be shared with a third party.

Figure 1.8: You will use a lot of indirect data at school or university.

Research

Have you ever used a library, textbook, journal or website to help you research something? This is using indirect data, or a secondary source (see Figure 1.8). You can use a website to help you research about spreadsheets. However, this website was not designed by you, or created just for this purpose. You are using someone else's information for your own purpose.

Advantages and disadvantages of direct and indirect data

Direct sources of data are more likely to be accurate and relevant than sources of indirect data. Table 1.4 compares direct and indirect data.

Direct data source	Indirect data source
The data will be relevant because what is needed has been collected.	Additional data that is not required will exist. This may take time to sort through. Some data that is required may not exist.
The original source is known and so can be trusted.	The original source may not be known, so it may not be trustworthy.
It can take a long time to gather direct data.	Indirect data is immediately available.

Direct data source	Indirect data source
A large sample of data can be difficult to collect for one-off purposes.	If statistical analysis is required, then there are more likely to be large samples available.
The data is likely to be up to date because it has been collected recently.	Data may be out of date because it was collected at a different time.
Direct data collection can reduce bias.	Indirect data may be biased.
The data can be collected and presented in the format required.	The data is unlikely to be in the format required, which may make extracting the data difficult.

Table 1.4: Comparing direct and indirect sources.

Questions

A builder uses the spreadsheet in Figure 1.9 to calculate the area of a driveway.

	A	B	C
1	**Area calculator**		
2	Length =	3	m
3	Width =	5	m
4	Area =	15	m^2

Figure 1.9: Part of a spreadsheet.

The builder using the spreadsheet needs to know the length and width of a driveway for a customer.

4   Identify one direct source the builder could use to find the length and width.

5   Identify one indirect source the builder could use to find the length and width.

6   Give one advantage of using the direct source instead of the indirect source to find the length and width.

1.2 Quality of information

The quality of information may be affected by several factors, including how accurate and complete the information is.

Accuracy

Data must be accurate to be considered of good quality. Imagine that a friend asks you to meet them at a large shopping centre. When you arrive at the shopping centre, you cannot find them. This is because you needed more accurate data, for example, 'Meet me outside <name of shop> at 17:00'. This would help you to locate each other far more easily.

Examples of inaccurate information include:

- decimal point in the wrong place, for example $90.30 instead of $903.00, could suggest a product is much cheaper than it really is

- spelling mistakes in words, or using the wrong words

- inaccurate context or meaning given about data, for example the wrong month of data could be used to predict the stock need of a shop.

Relevance

Information must be relevant to its purpose. Having additional information that is not required means that the user must search through the data to find what is actually required.

Examples of irrelevant information include:

- being given the colour of the bus you want to catch. You only need to know the time it arrives!

- being told the rental price of a car when you want to buy the car

- a user guide for a mobile phone that includes instructions on how to assemble a plug.

Age

Information must be up to date to be useful. Old information is likely to be out of date and therefore no longer useful.

> **TIP**
>
> When using indirect data sources, always check when the information was produced. There may be newer information available with more up-to-date results.

Examples of out-of-date information include:

- using census data from 40 years ago to find out how many people live in a town or city

- using the score from the start of a sports match when it is near the end of the match.

Level of detail

Good quality information has exactly the right amount of detail to be useful. Sometimes either too little or too much information may be provided. If there is too much detail, then it can be difficult to find the exact information required. If there is not enough detail, then it is not possible to use it correctly.

For example, a person orders a vegetarian pizza to be delivered. They forget to say what type of base they want or give the delivery address. The pizza company does not have enough information to fulfil the order.

Another example might be a passenger who needs to catch a train. The passenger phones the rail company to find out the time of arrival at their destination, the final station on the line. The rail company's automated phone message lists the times of arrival at every station on the route and the passenger must wait until the end of the message to get the information they wanted (see Figure 1.10).

Figure 1.10: The passenger must wait until the end of the message to get to the information they need.

Completeness

All information that is required must be provided for it to be of good quality. Not having all the information required means it cannot be used properly.

For example, a person has booked their car in to a garage for some repairs. The mechanic at the garage tells them the name of the street but does not give the building number. This information is incomplete – and the person may not be able to arrive at the right place to get their car repaired.

UNPLUGGED ACTIVITY 1.01

Come and Celbrate

Emmanuel's Bithday

11:00–1:30pm

18 Main Street

RSVP

There will be a magician. The magician was born on March 1st 1978 in Queen Elizabeth hospital in Birmingham.

Figure 1.11: Birthday party invitation.

Look at the invitation to a child's birthday party in Figure 1.11.

Describe how accuracy, relevance, level of detail and completeness affect the quality of information in the invitation.

Questions

7   Identify three factors that could affect the quality of information.
8   Describe the impact of using an old street map of a city to navigate your way around the city in a car.

1.3 Encryption

Encryption is when data is scrambled so that the data cannot be understood by people who are not meant to read it (see Figure 1.12). The purpose of encryption is to make the data difficult or impossible to read if it is accessed by an unauthorised user. For example, you may use a banking app on your mobile device. The banking app will encrypt the data you send to the bank. If someone intercepts the data, then it will be meaningless to them.

Encryption is important when sending or storing sensitive data such as personal data or a business's sales figures. Data sent across a network or the internet can be intercepted by hackers. Data stored on storage media could be stolen or lost.

Accessing encrypted data legitimately is known as decryption.

Figure 1.12: Many messaging services that you use on your mobile device use encryption to keep your messages safe.

DISCUSSION POINT

Encryption helps to protect data from being read by others. However, many criminals may use encryption to send data that is illegal, or to hide messages which discuss illegal activity.

Do you think that law enforcement agencies should be allowed to read encrypted data without a person's consent?

KEY WORD

encryption: scrambling data so it cannot be understood without a decryption key to make it unreadable if intercepted

Methods of encryption

DID YOU KNOW?

Original	A	B	C	D	E	F	G	H	I	J	K	L	M	N	O	P	Q	R	S	T	U	V	W	X	Y	Z
Encrypted	D	E	F	G	H	I	J	K	L	M	N	O	P	Q	R	S	T	U	V	W	X	Y	Z	A	B	C

A cipher is an algorithm to encode or encrypt data. Ciphers convert data into an encrypted form. Roman Dictator Julius Caesar created the Caesar cipher so that he could communicate in secret with his generals.

The Caesar cipher is sometimes known as a shift cipher because it selects replacement letters by shifting along the alphabet.

In this example the alphabet is to be shifted by three (+3) letters so that A = D, B = E and so on.

So to encrypt the word 'Hello', you would use:

H = K, E = H, L = O, O = R

which gives KHOOR.

While the Caesar cipher is very easy to use, it is also very easy to crack.

UNPLUGGED ACTIVITY 1.02

1 Using the Caesar cipher +3 example, write an encrypted message to a classmate. Ask your classmate to decipher it.

2 Choose how many letters you are going to shift by and write another encrypted message to a classmate. Don't tell your classmate how many letters you shifted by. Your classmate should try to decipher the code by working out which letters appear most commonly.

3 Look online for how to 'create a cipher wheel' and use it to encrypt and decrypt messages.

Symmetric encryption

Symmetric encryption is the oldest method of encryption. It requires both the sender and recipient (receiver) to possess a secret encryption and decryption key. This key is known as a private key. The sender creates the secret key and encrypts the data. They then tell the recipient what the secret key is. The recipient then uses the key to decrypt the data, as shown in Figure 1.13. But the private key may be stolen when it is sent to the recipient.

Figure 1.13: Symmetric encryption.

Asymmetric encryption

Asymmetric encryption is also known as public-key cryptography. Asymmetric encryption stops the problem of intercepting private keys. Asymmetric encryption uses a pair of keys. The first key is a public key that is available to anybody wanting to send data. The second key is a private key that only the recipient knows. Figure 1.14 shows how the process works.

Figure 1.14: Asymmetric encryption.

Here is an example. Tomasz sends a message to Helene. Tomasz encrypts the message using Helene's public key. Helene receives the encrypted message and decrypts it using her private key (see Figure 1.15).

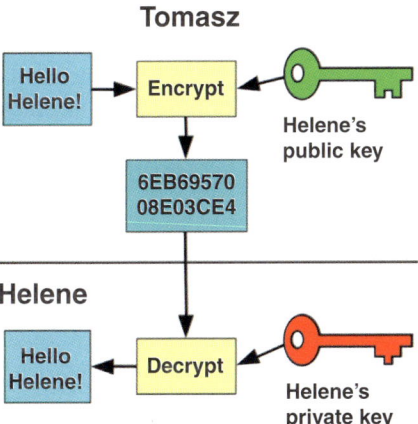

Figure 1.15: Example of asymmetric encryption.

Asymmetric encryption requires more processing than symmetric encryption. This means that it takes longer to decrypt the data. However, it is more secure than symmetric encryption. This is because the decryption key does not have to be sent to the other person.

A public key is unique to a user, or a server. Digital certificates identify the user or server and provide the public key. A digital certificate is unique to each user or server. A digital certificate usually includes the:

- organisation name
- organisation that issued the certificate
- user's email address
- user's country
- user's public key.

When encrypted data is required by a recipient, the computer will request the digital certificate from the sender. The public key can be found within the digital certificate.

Encryption protocols

Protocols are sets of rules. An encryption protocol defines a set of rules for encrypting data. This allows everyone to follow the rules to ensure that encryption is effective.

Asymmetric encryption is used for Secure Sockets Layer (SSL), which is the security method used for secure websites. Transport Layer Security (TLS) has replaced SSL but they are both often referred to as SSL. Once

SSL has established an authenticated session, the client and server will create symmetric keys for faster secure communication.

Internet Protocol Secure (IPSec) is a protocol like TLS. IPSec helps to keep data secure when it is sent over a network. It is often used in public networks. It can also be used to secure Virtual Private Networks (VPNs). Data is split into packets when sent over the internet or a network. IPSec uses the concept of keys to encrypt the data in each packet. IPSec authenticates packets before they are sent along a network. This means that the packets are secure, and the receiving computer can check that they are authentic. The computer that receives the encrypted packets uses decryption to reveal the data in each packet.

Most networking protocols are not automatically secured. Some protocols such as TCP/IP manage the sending and receiving of data. But TCP/IP does not secure the data with encryption.

TLS/SSL and IPSec are needed because basic communication protocols do not secure data. This means that data can be intercepted and read more easily. This would be like a doctor sending a confidential letter to a patient and not putting the letter inside a sealed envelope, or you accessing your bank account without needing to use a password.

TLS/SSL and IPSec add security to data before it is sent to other computers. This means it is far more difficult to access the data if it is intercepted by hackers.

> **KEY WORDS**
>
> **SSL:** Secure Socket Layer
>
> **TLS:** Transport Layer Security

Uses of encryption

Protection of data

Disk encryption encrypts all data stored on a storage device. This is different from encrypting single files. To access any file on the disk, the encryption key will be required. This type of encryption is not limited to disks and can be used on other storage media such as backup tapes and Universal Serial Bus (USB) flash memory (see Figure 1.16).

Figure 1.16: A USB encrypts stored data making storage more secure.

It is important that USB flash memory and backup tapes are encrypted because these are portable storage media and so are at risk of being lost or stolen. If the whole medium is encrypted, then anybody trying to access the data will not be able to understand it. The data is usually accessed by entering a password or using a fingerprint to unlock the encryption.

DID YOU KNOW?

Disk encryption software will often delete all the data on the disk if a password is entered incorrectly too many times!

Systems encryption

In addition to disk encryption, some systems have encryption to stop users accessing them.
Many operating systems have encryption systems. If you enter your password incorrectly too many times, the system will think someone is trying to hack it. It will then stop any more attempts at gaining access. This is called 'locking' the system.

Once a system is locked, it will require a Recovery Key to allow access again.

Systems encryption is often used on systems where very sensitive data is stored, such as banks or hospitals.

Most Wi-Fi access points and Wi-Fi routers use encryption protocols. This serves two purposes. The first is to allow only people who know the 'key' (usually a password) to access the network, so that any unauthorised users cannot gain access. The

second is to encrypt the data, so that it cannot be understood by unauthorised people looking to find out information ('snooping') on the Wi-Fi network. Wi-Fi networks are at risk of 'snooping' because no wires are required to connect to the network. The encryption protocols prevent unauthorised people from accessing the network.

DID YOU KNOW?

If you access a public Wi-Fi hotspot that is 'open' and therefore not encrypted, anybody with the right software can see what you are sending over the network, including your emails (see Figure 1.17). This applies to all mobile devices such as laptops, tablets and phones.

Figure 1.17: Your data may be at risk if using a Wi-Fi network in a public place such as a café.

Advantages and disadvantages of encryption protocols

Advantages	Disadvantages
Data is more secure during transmission.	If you forget the password or lose the encryption key, you cannot get access to the data.
Secure data can only be read by people with the correct key for decryption.	If you use simple passwords or keys then people may guess them and get access to your data.

Advantages	Disadvantages
Helps people feel more confident when sending personal data over the internet.	It takes time to encrypt data. This means that data transmission may be slower, especially when sending large amounts of data.
Protocols means people use the same rules and standards.	Some encryption protocols rely only on public keys. These may be easier to break.
Encryption protocols work across a range of digital devices.	Encryption protocols can increase the amount of network traffic, which can slow down a network.
It increases people's trust in using the internet and sending data.	

Table 1.5: Advantages and disadvantages of different protocols and methods of encryption.

Question

9   Why are encryption protocols needed?

1.4 Checking the accuracy of data

Validation

Validation is used to ensure that data is sensible and follows defined rules. Valid data meets the rules and is stored. Invalid data does not meet the rules and will be rejected.

For example, you may want to check that someone has entered an email address into a registration form and prevent them from entering a blank email address. You can validate the data using a check. This means they must enter something as an email address.

Despite the check, validation does not ensure that data is correct. For example, you can make sure someone enters an email address but this would not check that the email address is an actual address.

UNPLUGGED ACTIVITY 1.03

Create a flowchart to describe the process of validation. You should include the following:

- Start
- End
- Input of data
- Error message
- Data accepted
- Data rejected
- Validation decision

There are several different validation checks that can be used to check whether data is acceptable. These different checks are the different types of rule that are used.

Presence check

A presence check is used to ensure that data is entered. If data is entered, then it is accepted. If data is not entered, then the user will be presented with an error message asking them to enter data. Figure 1.18 shows a website that contains a presence check. The fields with the '*' mean that they are required. The website will display an error message if these fields are not completed.

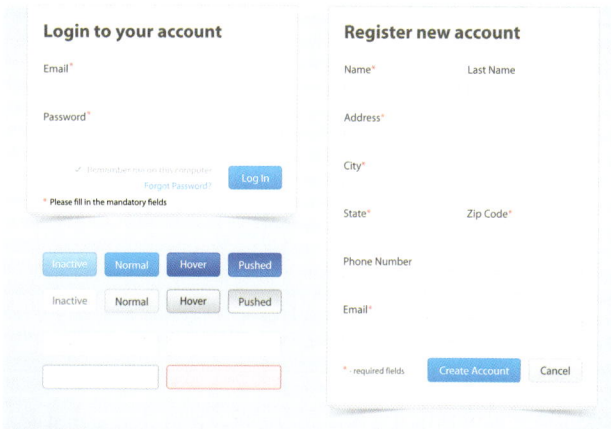

Figure 1.18: Required data on a website.

WORKED EXAMPLE 1.01

When filling in a 'contact us' form on a website, it is essential that an email address is entered. These inputs would be accepted by a presence check:

- a
- a@b
- abc@bc.com
- @
- 372823

Not all of these are actual email addresses, but they pass the rule that data must be present.

Range check

A range check ensures that data is within a defined range. A limit check has a single boundary. This could be the highest possible value or the lowest possible value. A range check includes two boundaries, which would be the lower boundary and the upper boundary. These symbols are used when comparing with a boundary:

> greater than	> = greater than or equal to
< less than	< = less than or equal to

WORKED EXAMPLE 1.02

1   You must be over 18 years old to join a club. The lower boundary is 18. There is no upper boundary, so this is a limit check. This could be written as:

Age > = 18

2   Letters representing grades for an exam are entered. Only the letters A–E are valid grades. The grade must be less than F. The upper boundary is E. The lower boundary is A. This is a range check and could be written as:

A < Grade < F

Data that is within the boundaries is valid. Data that is outside the boundaries is invalid.

But data that is valid may not necessarily be correct. For example, C could be entered when a grade A should have been entered. C is valid but incorrect.

Type check

A type check ensures that data must be of a defined data type. Examples of a type check include:

- If an age is entered, it must be an integer.
- If a grade is entered, it must be text with no numbers.
- If a price is entered, it must be numerical.
- If a date of birth is entered, it must be a date.

Data that is of the correct data type is valid. Data that is valid and of the correct data type is not necessarily correct. A date of birth of 28/12/2087 could be entered. The date is valid because it is a date data type. It is incorrect because the year is not yet 2087!

Length check

A length check ensures data is of a defined length or within a range of lengths. It is often used with text data. Examples of a length check include:

- A password must be at least six characters long.
- A grade must be exactly one character long.
- A product code must be at least four characters and no more than six characters.

Data that is of the allowed length is not necessarily correct. For example, a valid product code might require six letters. A code of WWDDWW would be a valid length because it contains six characters, but it would may not actually be a product that is sold.

Format check

A format check ensures data matches a defined format. It is sometimes known as a picture check or an input mask and the data has to follow a pattern.

WORKED EXAMPLE 1.03

An email address must include an @ symbol preceded by at least one character and followed by other characters. These data would be valid:

- john@bldef.co
- a@b.dek
- fdc@jb

Data that matches the pattern is valid. Data that is valid and of the defined format is not necessarily correct.

An email address of fdc@jb meets the rules above but is not a valid address.

Lookup check

A lookup check tests to see whether data exists in a list.

For example, students taking a qualification could be issued grades of pass (P), merit (M), distinction (D) or fail (F). When inputting the data, a validation rule could check that only 'F', 'P', 'M' or 'D' are entered.

Consistency check

A consistency check compares data in one field with data in another field that already exists within a record, to see whether both are consistent with each other.

> ### WORKED EXAMPLE 1.04
>
> A system that records whether a person is allowed a discount at a store will not allow a discount to be entered unless the person has a store membership number.

Check digit

A check digit is a number (or letter) that is added to the end of an identification number. It is a form of redundancy check because the check digit is redundant (not needed for the identification number, but just used for validation). Check digits are often used in barcodes. You can see barcodes on many things, for example

price labels in shops, parts on cars and invoices (see Figure 1.19).

When the identification number is first created, an algorithm (a series of calculations) generates a check digit. When the identification number is input, the same algorithm is run. The result of the algorithm should match the check digit. The data is valid when the result of the algorithm matches the check digit. The data is not valid when the result of the algorithm does not match the check digit.

There are a variety of calculations that can be performed to determine what the check digit should be. The important thing is that the same calculation used to create the check digit in the first place should be used to confirm the check digit when the identification number is input.

Figure 1.19: Scanning barcodes at the supermarket checkout ensures the correct price is entered for each item.

> ### WORKED EXAMPLE 1.05
>
>
>
> **Figure 1.20:** Unique product code check digit.
>
> The Unique Product Code (UPC) check digit is used with 13-digit barcodes (see Figure 1.20). It is the
>
> last digit shown on a barcode. The algorithm for calculating the check digit is as follows.
>
> 1   Add all the digits in even numbered positions together.
>
> 2   Multiply the result by **3**.
>
> 3   Add all the digits in odd numbered positions together.
>
> 4   Add results **2** and **3** together.
>
> 5   Divide the result **4** by 10.
>
> 6   Calculate the remainder (modulo 10) of result **5**.
>
> 7   Subtract the answer to **6** from 10.

CONTINUED

Valid example

In this example, the International Standard Book Number (ISBN) is 978095734041-1 in which the last '1' is the check digit. To calculate the check digit, this algorithm is performed on the ISBN (excluding the check digit).

1   Add all the digits in even numbered positions together (978095734041): 7 + 0 + 5 + 3 + 0 + 1 = 16.

2   Multiply result **1** by 3: 16 × 3 = 48.

3   Add all the digits in odd numbered positions together (978095734041): 9 + 8 + 9 + 7 + 4 + 4 = 41.

4   Add results **2** and **3** together: 48 + 41 = 89.

5   Divide the result **4** by 10: 89 ÷ 10 = 8.9.

6   Calculate the remainder (modulo 10, when the number is divided by 10) of result **5**: 89 MOD 10 = 9.

7   Subtract **6** from 10: 10 − 9 = 1.

The result of the algorithm is 1.

Invalid example

In this example, the ISBN has been entered incorrectly because two numbers have been transposed (7 and 3) accidentally: 978095374041-1.

1   Add all the digits in even numbered positions together (978095374041): 7 + 0 + 5 + 7 + 0 + 1 = 20.

2   Multiply result (1) by 3: 20 × 3 = 60.

3   Add all the digits in odd numbered positions together (978095374041): 9 + 8 + 9 + 3 + 4 + 4 = 37.

4   Add results **2** and **3** together: 60 + 37 = 97.

5   Divide the result **4** by 10: 97 ÷ 10 = 9.7.

6   Calculate the remainder (modulo 10) of result (5): 97 MOD 10 = 7.

7   Subtract result **6** from 10: 10 − 7 = 3.

The result of the algorithm is 3. The result 3 is compared with the check digit of 1 that was entered. They do not match. The ISBN entered is invalid.

ACTIVITY 1.04

1   Use a website to generate check digits for product codes.

2   The usual algorithm for UPCs is to multiply the odd digits by 3 rather than the even digits. It is only for 13-character barcodes that the even digits are multiplied by 3.

Find out how to calculate a check digit for ten-digit barcodes.

Verification and validation

Verification is the process of checking that the data entered matches the original source. Validation checks that data is of the right type. For example, when you enter your data of birth into a database:

- verification may ask you to enter the date of birth for a second time to make sure you typed the correct date of birth

- validation will check that the date of birth has a day, month and year.

KEY WORD

verification: ensuring data entered matches the original source

Visual checking

A visual check needs a person to read both the source data and the new data. They would then check that they are the same. This can be done by reading the data displayed on screen and comparing it with the original data. If the data matches, then it has passed the verification process. If it does not match, then it has failed the verification process and needs to be re-entered.

Figure 1.21: Visual verification check of paper records of stock levels in a warehouse against computer data.

Visual checking ensures that both data entries match (see Figure 1.21). However, if the original data is incorrect then this may mean that incorrect data is stored. For example, a sales assistant may write the price of $500.00 on a paper invoice for a customer. When the business owner enters the amount on the computer, they doublecheck the figure on the computer against the figure on the invoice to make sure the amounts are the same. But what if the sales assistant had meant to write $5,000.00 instead? This error would not be detected with visual checking.

Double data entry

Another method of verification is to input data into the computer system twice. The two items of data are compared by the computer system and, if they match, then they are verified. If there are any differences, then one of the inputs must have been incorrect. For example, when changing a password, most systems will ask the user to enter the new password twice. If the new passwords match, then the password will be changed. If the new passwords don't match, then one of the passwords must have been entered incorrectly.

It is still possible to pass double entry verification and for the data to be incorrect. If the data is entered incorrectly twice, then the two values may match. For example, if a person makes the same spelling mistake in their password, then the computer will still change the password.

Hash total

Hash totals can be used when entering a set of data. A hash total compares the sum of the values from one field against the sum of the values from the original data. Before starting, the person adds up the values of one field for all the records. Once input is completed, the computer will add up all the values from the same field. The computer then compares the hash total it calculates automatically with the hash total calculated manually before data entry. If the two totals are different, then a mistake has either been made during data input or in the manual calculation of the hash total.

WORKED EXAMPLE 1.06

A user inputs the following coursework marks for students.

Candidate number: 18292
Coursework mark: 74

Candidate number: 18264
Coursework mark: 38

Candidate number: 18279
Coursework mark: 82

The user adds up the total of all the coursework marks to give a hash total:

74 + 38 + 82 = 194

The user then inputs the coursework marks as follows:

Candidate number: 18292
Coursework mark: 74

Candidate number: 18264
Coursework mark: 83

Candidate number: 18279
Coursework mark: 82

The computer calculates the hash total to be 239. As 239 does not match 194 there was either a data entry error or an error in the manual calculation of the hash total. In this case, the error occurred with the input of candidate 18264 whose mark should have been 38 not 83.

A hash total is likely to find an error, but there are some occasions when an error would not be found.

WORKED EXAMPLE 1.07

A user inputs the following coursework marks for students:

Candidate number: 18292
Coursework mark: 74

Candidate number: 18264
Coursework mark: 38

Candidate number: 18279
Coursework mark: 82

The user adds up the total of all the coursework marks to give a hash total:

74 + 38 + 82 = 194

The user then inputs the coursework marks as follows:

Candidate number: 18292
Coursework mark: 73

Candidate number: 18264
Coursework mark: 39

Candidate number: 18279
Coursework mark: 82

The computer calculates the hash total to be 194. This matches the value needed. However, the errors of 73 and 39 were not detected.

Control total

Control totals are very similar to hash totals. Hash totals can be calculated from any field and may not have any meaning. Control totals do have useful meaning. For example, a control total could be the total number of items in a stock order for a shop, or the total of prices for individual items on an order.

Parity check

A parity check finds errors when transmitting data. For example, let's use a single byte of data to explain how a parity check works. One of the bits in each byte is used as the parity bit and the other 7 bits are used to represent the data. There are two types of parity check: even parity and odd parity.

With even parity, the total number of 1s in a byte must be an even number. If the number of 1s within the 7 bits is odd, then the parity bit will be set to one to make the total number of 1s even. If the number of 1s within the

7 bits of data is even, then the parity bit will be set to 0 (zero) to keep the total number of 1s even.

WORKED EXAMPLE 1.08

The following 7 bits of data are about to be transmitted:

1 0 0 1 1 0 0

There are three 1s in this byte, which is an odd number. The parity bit is therefore set to 1 so that the total number of 1s is an even number:

1 0 0 1 1 0 0 1

When this byte is received after transmission, the number of 1s are added up. If the total is even, then the data is accepted.

With odd parity, the total number of 1s in a byte must be an odd number. If the number of 1s within the 7 bits is even, then the parity bit will be set to 1 to make the total number of 1s an odd number. If the number of 1s within the 7 bits is odd, then the parity bit will be set to 0 to keep the total number of 1s as odd.

WORKED EXAMPLE 1.09

The following seven bits of data are about to be transmitted:

1 0 0 1 1 0 0

There are three 1s, which is an odd number. The parity bit is therefore set to 0 so that the total number of 1s is an odd number:

1 0 0 1 1 0 0 0

When this byte is received after transmission, the number of 1s are added up. If the total is odd, then the data is accepted.

Let's imagine that the data received is:

1 1 0 1 1 0 0 0

The total of bits in the received data is four. This is an even number so the computer system knows that an error occurred during data transmission. We can see that the second bit from the left should be a 0 but has been received as a 1.

Parity bits only check to see whether an error occurred during data transmission. They do not correct the error. If an error occurs, then the data must be sent again. Parity checks can find an error when a single bit is transmitted incorrectly, but there are occasions when a parity check would not find an error if more than one bit is transmitted incorrectly.

WORKED EXAMPLE 1.10

The following seven bits of data are transmitted using even parity with a parity bit of 1:

1 0 0 1 1 0 0 1

The data is received as:

0 1 0 1 1 0 0 1

The data is accepted by the even parity check because there are an even number of 1s. The parity check was not able to identify the error where the first two bits were transmitted incorrectly.

Checksum

Checksums are the result of a calculation on the contents of a file. The calculation is used to check whether a file has been transmitted or copied correctly. This can be useful to check that a hacker hasn't disguised a malicious file as a genuine one. Any slight change in a file will mean that a different checksum is generated. Figure 1.22 shows checksums for a Microsoft® Windows® file.

A checksum is usually represented as hexadecimal digits, which are the numbers 0 to 9 and letters A to F. Two hexadecimal digits represent a single byte. Different algorithms can be used to generate the checksum. Popular algorithms include SHA-256, SHA-1 and MD5. If the checksum at the start of transmission does not match the checksum at the end of transmission, then there will have been a transmission error.

Although it's very rare, MD5 and SHA-1 have been known to generate collisions. Collisions occur where the same checksum is generated for a different file. This can enable a hacker to disguise a malicious file as a genuine file, but this is unlikely to happen by chance. So, SHA-1 and MD5 are still suitable for checking for transmission errors. At the time of writing, there haven't been any reports of SHA-256 creating collisions. This means that it is currently the safest checksum method to use.

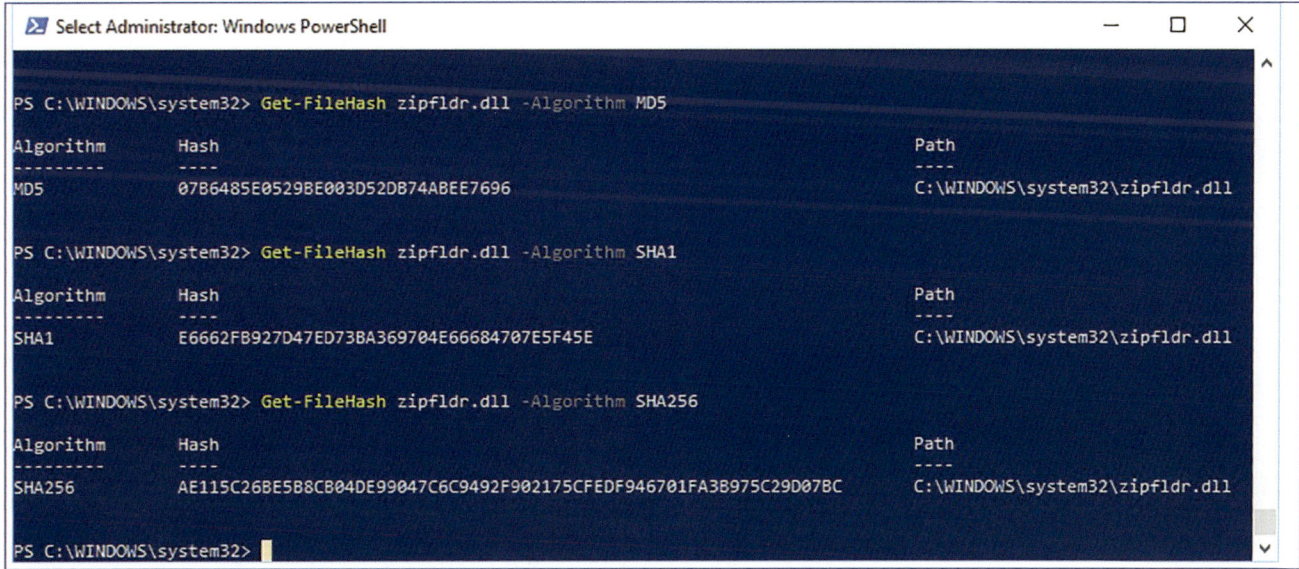

Figure 1.22: Checksums for a Microsoft® Windows® file.

ACTIVITY 1.05

1   Copy a file such as a word-processed document to a different folder.

2   Compare the checksums of the original file and the copied file using an online checker. What do you notice about the checksums?

3   Now make a change to the copied file.

4   Compare the checksums of the original file and the changed copied file. What do you notice about the checksums?

You can also see other checksums that would be created using other methods.

UNPLUGGED ACTIVITY 1.06

Perform a visual verification check on the following sentences. The sentences should be the same. The first sentence is correct. There are errors in the second sentence. Using a validation check, how many errors can you spot in the second sentence?

1   I was walking along the road yesterday when I spotted a dog without a lead. I called the dog, but it did not respond! The dog ran off.

2   I was walking along the road yesterday when I spottd a Dog without a lead I called the dog but it did not respond. the dog ran off.

The need for both validation and verification

It is possible to enter valid data that is still incorrect. It is also possible to verify incorrect data. By using both validation and verification, the chances of entering incorrect data are reduced. If data that is incorrect passes a validation check, then the verification check is likely to spot the error.

WORKED EXAMPLE 1.11

The validation rule for a test's results (fail, pass, merit, distinction) is that it must be a single letter: F, P, M or D. N is entered. This passes the validation check but is not an accepted grade (F, P, M, D). When verified using double entry, the user enters N first followed by M the second time. The verification process has identified the error. However, it is still possible that the user could enter N twice and both the validation and verification processes would fail.

REFLECTION

How will you remember the different methods used for validation and verification of data?

Questions

10   Describe the purpose of verification.

11   Identify three methods of validation.

12   Explain, using examples, why validation and verification do not ensure that data is correct.

Advantages and disadvantages of validation and verification

Table 1.6 lists the advantages and disadvantages of validation and verification.

	Validation	Verification
Checks data entered is of the right type	yes	no
Checks data entered is correct	no	yes
Ensures data entered is correct	no	no
Allows data to be stored in the same format	no	yes
Takes additional time to enter data	no	yes
Needs useful error messages to say what is wrong if the data is not accepted	yes	yes

Table 1.6: Advantages and disadvantages of validation and verification.

1.5 Data processing

Data processing is any activity that manipulates or carries out operations on data.

Data processing includes actions such as:

- collection and storage
- editing and updating
- sorting and searching
- output and sharing.

There are three different types of processing: batch processing, online processing and real-time processing.

Batch processing

Figure 1.23: Batch processing.

In a **batch processing** system operations or transactions are stored in a long queue (see Figure 1.23). They are not processed immediately. All the operations or transactions are processed by the system automatically at a later time. This is usually done when the operations or transactions do not need to be processed immediately. For example, an automated backup of a hard disk can be done overnight, or the processing of employees' wages could be done at midnight. The advantage to this is that it does not use CPU resources during busy times when many users may be logged into the system. This keeps the system running faster during peak use times.

Batch processing is usually used in systems where updates or processing of data are not crucially important to the operation of the business. In other words, processing does not have to be done immediately. In a similar way, running a washing machine only when there is a full load of laundry and operating it overnight when electricity may be cheaper.

Other examples of when batch processing may be used are:

- for preparing utility bills (for payment of usage of services such as electricity and water) to send out to customers
- updating credit card and debit card accounts
- updating information in customer accounts
- preparing a weekly weather forecast
- preparing and installing software updates to an IT system.

Master and transaction files

There are two main file types that are used to store data, **master files** and **transaction files**. A master file usually stores data about a thing such as a person, place or object. A transaction file usually stores data about an event, such as an order, electricity usage and travel expenses.

KEY WORDS

batch processing: sets of data processed all at one time without user interaction

master file: a table in a database containing information about one set of things, for example employees

transaction file: data that is used to update a master file

WORKED EXAMPLE 1.12

A business stores customer details such as name, address and the total money they have spent in a file. There is a record for each customer. Figure 1.24 shows an example of the master file.

In a payroll system, used for processing employee wages, the master file would contain details of each employee, such as their ID number, name, address, hourly pay, total earned for the year and the amount of tax they have paid.

Customer_Id	Customer_Name	Address	Postcode	Total_Spent (£)
01456	Webb	3 The Grove	CM6 4EW	132.65
03678	Rahman	13 Abbey Road	CB9 7FG	458.42
04632	Yang	6 Bath Terrace	DW9 13CA	1342.90
06342	Jenkins	9 Bridge Street	GS5 9RS	689.32
09763	Nkrumah	2 Cambridge Avenue	BR8 9GR	2954.56
13693	Hussain	28 Fenton Street	FC7 2BN	25.60
16936	Jackson	22 Grafton Street	MB1 1CP	193.87

Customer_Id is the primary key for each record. The data in the primary key field must be unique for each customer.

Figure 1.24: Example master file.

Whenever a customer orders a product, the transaction is recorded in another file called a transaction file. Figure 1.25 shows an example of a transaction file.

Customer_Id	Product_Ordered	Price ($)
16936	Sweater	25.00
09763	Blouse	30.50
06342	Jeans	60.75
03678	Shirt	35.60
04632	Jacket	100.00

Figure 1.25: Example transaction file.

After a regular interval, the complete batch of records in the transaction file are processed. In this example, invoices and delivery notes will be generated by merging the transaction and master files and the data in the master file is updated by recalculating the Total_Spent field.

At the start of the process, the transaction file is validated and any transactions that are invalid will be moved to an errors file.

The transaction file is sorted so that it is in the same order as the master file.

WORKED EXAMPLE 1.13

In Figure 1.26, the transaction and master files are sorted into ascending order according to the Customer_Id field.

Customer_Id	Product_Ordered	Price ($)
16936	Sweater	25.00
09763	Blouse	30.50
06342	Jeans	60.75
03678	Shirt	35.60
04632	Jacket	100.00

Unsorted.

Customer_Id	Product_Ordered	Price ($)
03678	Shirt	35.60
04632	Jacket	100.00
06342	Jeans	60.75
09763	Blouse	30.50
16936	Sweater	25.00

Sorted.

Figure 1.26: Transaction and master files.

The batch process moves through the transaction file and finds the corresponding record in the master file with the same Customer_Id.

WORKED EXAMPLE 1.14

The first transaction in the previous worked example has a Customer_Id of 03678. This transaction is merged with the customer master file to produce an invoice and delivery note and to update the Total_Spent field in the master file. In Figure 1.27, notice how the Total_Spent field of the second record has been updated.

This continues until all the records in the master file have been copied to the new version.

The new master file will now hold the information shown in Figure 1.28.

Customer_Id	Customer_Name	Address	Postcode	Total_Spent ($)
01456	Webb	3 The Grove	CM6 4EW	132.65
03678	Rahman	13 Abbey Road	CB9 7FG	494.02

Figure 1.27: Total_Spent field updated.

Customer_Id	Customer_Name	Address	Postcode	Total_Spent ($)
01456	Webb	3 The Grove	CM6 4EW	132.65
03678	Rahman	13 Abbey Road	CB9 7FG	494.02
04632	Yang	6 Bath Terrace	DW9 13CA	1442.90
06342	Jenkins	9 Bridge Street	GS5 9RS	750.07
09763	Nkrumah	2 Cambridge Avenue	BR8 9GR	2985.06
13693	Hussain	28 Fenton Street	FC7 2BN	25.60
16936	Jackson	22 Grafton Street	MB1 1CP	218.87

Figure 1.28: Updated master file.

One way of representing transaction processing as an algorithm could be as follows.

```
For each line in transaction file

   Repeat

Read next record in master file

   Until transaction file ID matches master
file ID

   master file total for current record =
master file total + transaction file value

Next line in transaction file
```

Advantages and disadvantages of batch processing

Table 1.7 sets out the advantages and disadvantages of batch processing.

Advantages	Disadvantages
It is a single, automated process requiring little human participation, which can reduce costs.	There is a delay as data is not processed until the specific time period.
It can be scheduled to occur when there is little demand for computer resources, for example, at night.	Only data of the same type can be processed since an identical, automated process is being applied to all the data.
As it is an automated process, there will be none of the transcription and update errors that human operators would produce.	Errors cannot be corrected until the batch process is complete.
There are fewer repetitive tasks for the human operators.	

Table 1.7: Advantages and disadvantages of batch processing.

ACTIVITY 1.07

Use presentation software, or flowchart software, to create a description of how batch processing works. Highlight the advantages and disadvantages of batch processing.

Online processing

We use **online processing** daily. We use online processing every time we search the internet or buy goods online.

KEY WORD

online processing: real-time processing using websites and digital forms

Online processing is used for transferring money between bank accounts. For example, a user may log in to their mobile banking app and make payments. Online processing is also used to pay for goods bought online. The customer enters their bank debit card details, the details are processed, and payment is then made from the customer's bank account to the retailer's bank account.

One method of online processing is to deal with data as transactions. A certain amount of data is input as a transaction. This amount of data is usually small. Once the data for the transaction is collected, it is processed and the next transaction can occur. For example, an online airline ticket booking system will process data in transactions. All the data about the customer, flight and seat number will be collected in the transaction. This will then be processed, and a ticket can be issued as an output. Because each transaction is processed in turn it stops a seat on the aeroplane being double-booked. Once a seat has been allocated to a transaction, the seat cannot be booked by anyone else. This is because transactions are processed in order. Concert ticket booking systems also use this system.

Electricity usage needs to be continuously recorded on a meter and meter readings regularly given to the electricity company so that accurate bills can be calculated. The readings are taken interactively using methods such as:

- an employee of the electricity company uses a PDA (personal digital assistant) or smart phone to read the homeowner's electricity meter

- the homeowner inputs the meter reading directly to the electricity company's website
- the homeowner phones the electricity company and enters the reading using the phone.

Electricity meter readings can also be taken automatically using a smart meter that does not require user interaction.

Electronic funds transfer

Electronic funds transfer is the transfer of funds (money) electronically to or from a bank account. Some types of electronic funds transfer payments include:

- Direct payments where money can be sent from one bank account to another. This can either happen immediately or within a given time frame or overnight. If it happens within a given time frame, then there is usually a batch process involved that processes a batch of direct payments at one time.

- Automated teller machines (ATMs) are used to withdraw cash from a bank account. The ATM will look up a customer's bank account in a database and, if there are enough funds, then it will allow a withdrawal to take place and deduct the amount withdrawn from the account balance.

Figure 1.29: Contactless payment is a method of electronic funds transfer.

- Debit cards can be used to give an instruction to your bank to take funds to pay for goods or a service. A debit card is linked to a bank account. When the debit card is used to make a payment, the transaction is sent to the bank. A customer confirms the card belongs to them by entering a PIN or through contactless payments (see Figure 1.29) without the use of a PIN up to a limit for each transaction. Once the PIN is confirmed, the account number and amount requested will be sent to the bank. The bank's computer system will check that the balance available to the customer is sufficient for the transaction amount. If there are sufficient funds, then the bank will return a message to the retailer confirming that funds are available.
  The retailer will then confirm the purchase and the amount to transfer from the customer to the retailer is sent to the bank. The bank's computer system will then create a transaction for the purchase, subtract the funds from the customer's account and add the funds to the retailer's account.

- Direct debits are used where regular payments need to be made. The owner of a bank account can authorise an organisation to take payments automatically. This is often used for paying utility bills that may vary each month.

Automatic stock control

Stock control systems ensure that shops always have enough stock (products) to sell. Stock control systems will try to keep stock within certain limits. They can also be used to ensure a business has enough parts available for a manufacturing process.

The main feature of a stock control system is a database. The database stores data about each product, the supplier of the product and the amount left in stock.

The system will also store the following data about stock:

- reorder level (the point at which more stock will be ordered)
- reorder amount (the quantity that should be ordered when the reorder level is reached).

Each time a product is purchased at the till, its barcode will be scanned. The stock control system checks the barcode number in the database and reduces the stock level by one item. The stock control system will order more stock (the reorder amount) when the number of items remaining reaches the reorder level. When the ordered items arrive at the shop, the database is updated with the number of products that have arrived.

Table 1.8 shows some examples of systems where the outputs affect the inputs of the system.

Microprocessor-controlled/computer-controlled system	Real-time processing	Output affects input
Greenhouses	Greenhouses use sensors to detect the temperature, or moisture in the soil (see Figure 1.33).	The inputs from sensors (like light, moisture or temperature) will mean outputs such as lights, watering or heaters may be used. The system will monitor the results of these outputs.
Central heating systems	A small processor detects the temperature around the house or building.	The output of the heater being turned on will raise the temperature. This output is then monitored as input to make sure that it does not get too hot.
Air conditioning systems	A small processor detects the temperature around the house or building.	The output of the air conditioning being turned on will lower the temperature. This output is then monitored as input to make sure that it does not get too cool.
Burglar alarms	A range of sensors (laser beam detectors, motion detectors, temperature sensors) are used to detect illegal entry.	The output of these sensors is monitored as input. If one changes it may indicate an intruder, and so the system will sound an alarm.
Control of traffic/pedestrian flow/smart motorways	Cameras monitor traffic flow of cars.	The cameras show how much traffic is passing. This may cause the smart motorway to lower the speed limit. The result of lowering the speed limit forms the input into the system so that the effect of the speed limit is measured.
Car park barriers	Sensors detect cars entering and leaving the car park.	The number of cars entering is detected and reduces the number of spaces available. When a car leaves, the sensors detect this. The sensor updates the system that a space is free. The car park can then allow another car to enter.
Traffic lights	Motion sensors or pressure sensors detect car movements.	The outputs of a motion sensor tell the system when cars are waiting at a set of traffic lights. This allows the system to change lights from red to green to manage the flow of traffic more effectively.

Table 1.8: Examples of microprocessor-controlled/computer-controlled systems.

Figure 1.33: Temperature and humidity sensors in commercial greenhouses ensure the best growing conditions for plants.

Wireless sensor and actuator networks

Sensors can also be wireless. Sensors can control actuators (type of motor that is used to move or operate another device) as output, like microprocessor-controlled/computer-controlled systems. (You will learn more about actuators and their uses in Chapter 3.)

Wireless sensors transmit their data directly to the microprocessor. The sensors do not need a physical connection. This is often useful where wires could be damaged, or weight needs to be saved. Cables are often very heavy. Examples of wireless sensor and actuator networks include smart homes, guidance systems and autonomous vehicles.

Smart homes

Many systems and appliances in the home such as lighting, entertainment systems, security systems, heating and air conditioning may be controlled remotely through the householder's smart phone.

The householder may set the central heating system to turn on the heating when the temperature in the home falls below a desired temperature, for example 20 °C. The central heating system constantly monitors the temperature of its surroundings (see Figure 1.34). When the temperature falls below 20 °C, the central heating boiler turns on the heating. When the temperature rises above the desired temperature, the central heating boiler turns off the heating.

Figure 1.34: A smart central heating thermostat displays the set and current temperature.

When the central heating boiler is turned on it generates heat, which will increase the temperature in the home. This increase in temperature affects the input to the system and therefore feedback has occurred because the output (heat) has affected the input (temperature). The same happens when the boiler turns off because the temperature in the room will fall and when it reaches a certain level the boiler will turn on again and generate heat. The feedback loop is shown in Figure 1.35.

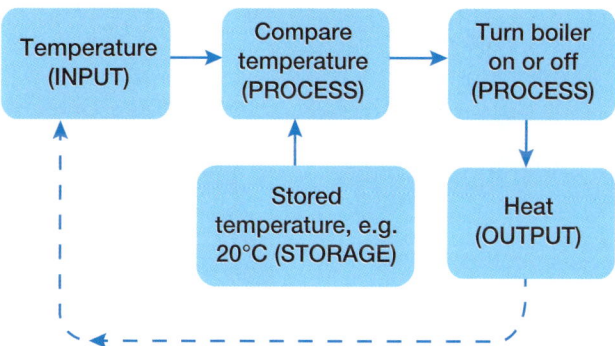

Output = Heat – directly affects temperature = input

Figure 1.35: Temperature control.

UNPLUGGED ACTIVITY 1.09

Draw a diagram like the one in Figure 1.35 to show how an air-conditioning system would work.

Guidance systems for space rockets

Space rockets use real-time processing for their guidance systems (see Figure 1.36). The delay in sending data back to Earth can be large. Data could take hours, or even days to reach a control centre on Earth. Then the response needs to be sent back to the rocket. The guidance systems need to react much more quickly than that. The rocket uses sensors to record data to tell it what is happening, and real-time processing to work out what to do with that data. The continuous loop allows the rocket to react more quickly and accurately. If the engine is overheating, it will reduce the thrust or turn it off. If the direction is wrong, it will make adjustments.

Wireless sensors allow sensors to be placed in areas where cables may be damaged, for example where they may be close to the engines, or in fuel tanks. The output (such as the amount of fuel required) allows the microprocessor to adjust the fuelling directly. It can also transmit this data to a central control centre for people to monitor.

Figure 1.36: Rocket launching a spacecraft on its way to the planet Jupiter.

Autonomous vehicles

Autonomous vehicles are self-driving and operate without human control. There are now autonomous aircraft, cars, drones and ships. Real-time processing is essential to the safe operation of autonomous vehicles so that their systems can react in real time to dangers such as other vehicles, pedestrians, birds and weather conditions. For example, an autonomous car would need to react to the bends in the road, pedestrians crossing the street, other vehicles and obstacles. Delaying this process would mean that the car is at risk of causing an accident.

Wireless sensors allow control and monitoring of the vehicle remotely. Sensors allow the vehicle to measure information like height, width, speed, traffic and fuel. The sensor outputs form the inputs for the calculations of the microprocessor. Like a space rocket, sensors can be monitored remotely by people to make sure everything is working properly. (There is more about autonomous transport systems in Chapter 13.)

UNPLUGGED ACTIVITY 1.10

List the advantages and disadvantages of real-time processing. Think about:

- why we would not make every processing system a real-time system

- what the impact would be if we did.

Question

14 Explain why real-time processing is required for a Microsoft Teams, Zoom or GoogleHangout meetings.

PRACTICE QUESTIONS

1   Using an example, define the term information.   [2]

2   Users can pay for premium services on a website using their credit card.

   a   Explain why the website uses https at the beginning of the website address instead of http.   [4]

   b   Explain symmetric encryption.   [2]

   c   The journalists working for the website encrypt their emails.
Describe how asymmetric encryption is used with emails.   [2]

   d   When the users subscribe to premium features, they have to choose a password.
Suggest how verification can be used when entering the password.   [1]

[Total 9]

3   There is a form on the website in question **2** that can be used to submit news stories.
When data is entered onto the form, it is validated.

   a   State what the purpose of validation is.   [1]

   b   Using an example related to submitting a news story, identify and describe one
method of validation.   [3]

[Total 4]

4   Describe the difference between an online and a real-time processing system.   [4]

5   Define the term 'master file'.   [2]

6   Describe three characteristics of a stock control system.   [6]

7   Describe how a stock control system maintains stock levels automatically.   [4]

SUMMARY CHECKLIST

- [ ] I can explain the difference between data and information.
- [ ] I can explain the use of direct and indirect sources of data.
- [ ] I can evaluate the advantages and disadvantages of direct and indirect sources of data.
- [ ] I can describe factors that affect the quality of information.
- [ ] I can understand the need for encryption.
- [ ] I can describe different methods of encryption.
- [ ] I can describe encryption protocols.
- [ ] I can explain how encryption is used.
- [ ] I can evaluate the advantages and disadvantages of different protocols and methods of encryption.
- [ ] I can describe the use of validation and verification methods.
- [ ] I can explain the need for both validation and verification.
- [ ] I can describe advantages and disadvantages of validation and verification.
- [ ] I can describe batch, online and real-time processing methods.
- [ ] I can give examples of when batch, online and real-time processing methods are used.
- [ ] I can write an algorithm to show the steps of each type of processing.
- [ ] I can evaluate the advantages and disadvantages of different processing methods.

PROJECT

Figure 1.37: Dubai's driverless metro system.

You are an intern helping to design a new autonomous train service which will connect many cities across the country , such as that shown in Figure 1.37. You have been asked to create a short report for the government about how the new train system will work. Your report must include the following:

1   The things that you might research to ensure the train system meets the expectations of the customers.

2   Which type of research (direct or indirect) is best for each thing you are researching, and why you chose each thing to research.

3   How you will ensure that your research data is accurate and of high quality.

4   The types of processing systems that will be needed to:

   a   Allow customers to book their tickets.

   b   Allow a factory to ensure it has enough parts to build trains when needed.

   c   Allow the trains to run without the need for human control.

5   The best encryption methods that may be used to secure customer data.

6   The best encryption methods to send your report to the government securely.

Present your report to the class and ask for feedback on your report. Improve your report based on the feedback you receive.

> Chapter 2
Hardware and software

LEARNING INTENTIONS

By the end of this chapter, you will be able to:

- describe the characteristics of mainframe computers and supercomputers
- give examples of the use of mainframe computers and supercomputers
- explain the advantages and disadvantages of mainframe computers and supercomputers
- describe types of system software and how they are used
- explain the advantages and disadvantages of system software
- understand the need for utility software
- describe types of utility software and how they are used
- explain the advantages and disadvantages of utility software
- describe the uses of customer written software and off-the-shelf software
- explain the advantages and disadvantages of custom-written and off-the-shelf software
- describe different types of user interfaces and their uses
- explain the advantages and disadvantages of different types of user interfaces.

BEFORE YOU START

- Do you understand the difference between hardware and software?

- Can you explain the purpose of input, output and storage devices?

- Do you know the purpose of internal hardware devices including the CPU, motherboard, RAM, ROM, graphics card, sound card, HDD, SSD?

- Can you evaluate applications software and choose appropriate software for a given task?

Introduction

Hardware **devices** are the physical components of a computer. Examples of hardware are the CPU, motherboard, RAM, graphics card, secondary storage, monitor, keyboard and mouse.

The programs and apps (application software) on a computer are called **software**. Examples of software include word processing, spreadsheet and anti-malware programs. The **operating system** is also software. The software programs give instructions to the computer to enable it to carry out a task. The instructions are sent to the CPU in binary, which is made up of ones and zeros (for example, 10101110 11101101).

KEY WORDS

device: hardware component of a computer system consisting of electronic components

software: program that gives instructions to the computer

operating system: specific software that manages the hardware within a computer system

2.1 Mainframe computers and supercomputers

Uses of mainframe computers

Mainframe computers can serve many thousands of terminals within an organisation. A terminal is a computer that is connected to the mainframe. Often, terminals have very little processing power and memory of their own, for example a basic computer or an ATM (automated teller machine). Mainframes often host business databases that are accessed by businesses and consumers simultaneously using a web interface. Mainframes also carry out large-scale transaction processing and batch processing. Other uses include industry statistical analysis such as analysis of census data and consumer statistics such as trends and spending analysis.

KEY WORD

mainframe computer: powerful computer serving several terminals

Uses of supercomputers

Supercomputers are designed to carry out large numbers of complex calculations very quickly. A supercomputer runs a few computer programs and executes instructions as quickly as possible for one purpose. The full power of the supercomputer is used to process data and solve single problems. It does this by using lots of **parallel processing**. Parallel processing allows many instructions to be executed at the same time.

KEY WORDS

supercomputer: large computer with parallel processing to complete highly complex tasks quickly

parallel processing: allows lots of instructions to be executed at the same time

Physics simulations

Quantum mechanics deal with the behaviour of matter and energy at the atomic and subatomic level. This is where classical physics breaks down. Physicists explore concepts such as superposition, entanglement, and wave-particle duality. These concepts are mathematically complex and computationally demanding to simulate. The huge processing power that supercomputers provide allows scientists to model these systems with great accuracy and detail.

Medical science

Supercomputers can be used to simulate the properties of new drugs and materials at the atomic level. The huge processing power of super computers help to support the development of more efficient medications and exploration of how to treat and identify both current and new medical conditions or diseases.

Environmental models

Creating sophisticated numerical models of the atmosphere, ocean and space takes a lot of processing power (see Figure 2.1).

The supercomputers will process billions of observations from weather monitoring stations, satellites, weather balloons, buoys and radar among others.

Figure 2.1: Sierra Supercomputer at the Lawrence Livermore National Laboratory.

DID YOU KNOW?

In 2022, the most powerful supercomputer reached 1,102 petaFlops. That is 10^{15} or 1 000 000 000 000 000 floating-point operations per second. That's more than 1000 times faster than an average home computer.

Characteristics of mainframe and supercomputers

Longevity

Longevity is how long a mainframe will last before it is replaced. Longevity is important because mainframes and supercomputers cost a lot of money and so they need to be used for many years. The ability to upgrade them by adding additional processors or memory is important to ensure they can cope with increasing demand.

Reliability, availability and serviceability

Mainframe computers need to have reliability, availability and serviceability (RAS) characteristics. This means that they are designed to be used 100% of the time. In a mainframe computer, the hardware components are capable of self-checking and recovering automatically in the case of failure. Software for use on a mainframe is tested extensively and can be updated quickly if problems are detected.

To remain available, the mainframe must be able to continue to operate at all times. Extra hardware components, such as storage and power supplies, take over automatically if an active component fails. This is called **redundancy**.

KEY WORD

redundancy: having spare components in readiness to take over in case another component fails

With redundancy, a failed component can be replaced without affecting the operation of the mainframe. This makes the mainframe serviceable. The term 'hot-swappable' is used to refer to hardware components that can be replaced while the system is still running.

Mainframes operate without downtime for many years. Serviceability measures how quickly a mainframe can be repaired if it needs to be shut down.

Mainframe security

As mainframes service many applications and thousands of users all at the same time, they require a multi-layer approach to security including identifying users, authentication and access control. Individuals and groups can be given permission to access different resources. Each resource will have different levels of access that can be granted. For example, web users would be allowed to see descriptions, images and prices of active products for sale, but only product managers would be able to see non-active products or make changes to the descriptions and prices. Security software will also monitor the mainframe for potential security threats and alert administrators if a threat is suspected.

Mainframe performance metrics

The performance metrics of a mainframe computer are usually measured by how many instructions its processors can perform every second. This is measured in **MIPs** (millions of instructions per second). However, MIPs is not considered an accurate measure of performance of the mainframe. Factors that affect processing speed make MIPs a poor way to measure performance include:

- a complex instruction can take longer to process than a simple one. CISC (complex instruction set computing) processors will have a single instruction doing many things at once whereas RISC (reduced instruction set computing) processors will have a single instruction that does very little but manages the instruction efficiently
- workload mix
- memory and cache sizes
- amount of input and output activity
- operating systems and software
- changes made to hardware.

Despite the shortfalls of MIPs as a measurement, the cost of mainframes is generally based on the maximum number of MIPs that can be achieved.

Another performance measurement is **FLOPS** (floating-point operations per second), or MFLOPS (mega floating-point operations per second). MFLOPS means mega FLOPS, which is one million floating-point operations per second. Floating-point instructions are used in scientific computational research and so MFLOPS are more often used to compare the speed of supercomputers. MFLOPS give a more reliable measure of performance than MIPS, but there are still discrepancies where some processors can carry out a single floating-point operation but others would require several floating-point operations for the same result. For example, the Cray-2 supercomputer has no divide instruction but the Motorola 68882 has divide, square root, sine and cosine functions. This means that the Cray 2 would require several floating-point instructions to carry out a division, but the Motorola 68882 would be able to do this as a single floating-point instruction.

> **KEY WORDS**
>
> **MIPs:** millions of instructions per second – used to measure the performance of supercomputers
>
> **FLOPS:** floating-point operations per second – used to measure the performance of supercomputers

Larger memory and cache sizes can make a significant difference to the performance of a mainframe computer.

Volume of input, output and throughput

A batch workload that operates sequentially will make efficient use of resources, but online activity such as web access will have a much more random resource requirement. Lots of input and output activity lead to less efficient use of processors with tasks being suspended (put on hold) while input/output interruptions are processed.

As the amount of input and output activity can seriously affect the performance of a mainframe, it is possible to include dedicated system assist processors (SAPs) that handle input/output requests. This frees up the main processors allowing them to operate without input/output interruptions.

Enhancements or bug fixes for operating systems and applications software can improve the efficiency of processing or can have an adverse effect on how efficiently processors are used.

As with desktop computers, there are many operating systems available for mainframe computers. Some operating systems such as z/OS are general purpose and offer a stable, secure and continuous environment for software that runs on the mainframe. Others such as z/VM specialise in offering virtual machines, each of which runs its own operating system. Some operating systems such as z/TPF specialise in transaction processing where there are a high volume of transactions taking place such as ticket sales. Most supercomputers run an operating system based on the Linux operating system, which is Open Source and so freely available for development.

Fault tolerance

How long should a server be able to run before parts of the server fail? This measure of how far a server is resistant to failure is called fault tolerance.

There are two parts to fault tolerance. One focuses on coping with hardware failure. The second focuses on software and data failure.

Hardware failure can be dealt with by using redundancy. Redundancy was discussed earlier in this chapter.

Software failure can be dealt with by copying the data to many different hard disks or storage devices. This means that the server can use the data on back-up disks if the main data store fails.

Operating systems

The operating system for a supercomputer or server is more advanced than a basic desktop computer. The operating system needs to be able to deal with fault tolerance and manage software processes across many more processors. Operating systems on servers are far better at managing computers on a client/server system.

Number of processors

The more processors a server has, the more processes it can run at the same time. It is also to know how many threads each core can run, and also the clock speed (how many instructions can be carried out per second) of the processors.

A server that uses more cores than another server will usually run faster and execute instructions more quickly.

Heat maintenance

Owing to the power and quantity of processors, mainframe computers and supercomputers generate a lot of heat, so cooling systems must be in place. One method is to use air cooling (see Figure 2.2).

Figure 2.2: Fans blow hot air away from the processors on the graphics cards to keep them cool.

Air cooling uses fans to blow the hot air away from the equipment, replacing it with cooler air. However, this uses up a lot of power. Many data centres are now being built in colder parts of the world where natural cold air can be circulated. A more efficient method is to use liquid cooling.

Liquid cooling is often used on processors. A plate connects to the back of the processor. The plate has cool liquid on the other side. This cools the processor down by transferring the heat from the processor to the liquid. The liquid is pumped around a system and through a cooling radiator.

Questions

1   State **two** purposes of mainframe computers.
2   Give **two** examples of uses of a supercomputer.
3   State what is meant by RAS in relation to mainframe computers and supercomputers.
4   Explain why colder parts of the world are a favoured choice as a location for many data centres.
5   Explain why you may use MFLOPS instead of MIPS as a performance measure for supercomputers.

Advantages and disadvantages of mainframe computers and supercomputers

Table 2.1 lists the advantages and disadvantages of mainframe computers and supercomputers.

Advantages	Disadvantages
They are designed to be reliable, available and serviceable, which makes them more reliable than regular computers.	The high cost of mainframes and supercomputers mean that they are only used by large organisations such as governments, banks and large corporations. They require specialist operating systems that are also very expensive.
They are scalable because processors and memory can be added as required.	A lot of space is required to install a mainframe or supercomputer and the temperature must be maintained so that it doesn't become too hot.
They are designed to last for at least 10 years.	Specialist support staff are required for maintenance.
They can store and process extremely large amounts of data.	The interface is command driven, which can be difficult to understand.

Advantages	Disadvantages
More than one operating system can be used at once, which can improve the overall performance of the system.	Supercomputers process 'big data' and so need massive external storage drives that are capable of reading and writing data quickly enough for during processing.
Hardware failures are notified immediately so that replacements can be made very quickly.	
Terminals only require input and output devices and can take advantage of the processing power of the mainframe. Desktop computers connected to a mainframe can use their own processing power for smaller tasks and the mainframe can perform more complex tasks.	

Table 2.1: Advantages and disadvantages of mainframe computers and supercomputers.

2.2 System software

Programs that are designed to maintain or operate computer systems are known as **system software**. The software that operates the computer hardware is known as the operating system.

Operating systems

An operating system manages the hardware within a computer system. When a computer is turned on, the Basic Input/Output System (BIOS) loads. This is stored on ROM on the motherboard. Then it loads the operating system. The operating system is the first piece of software that loads. The operating system links the hardware to applications software and manages communication between the two (see Figure 2.3).

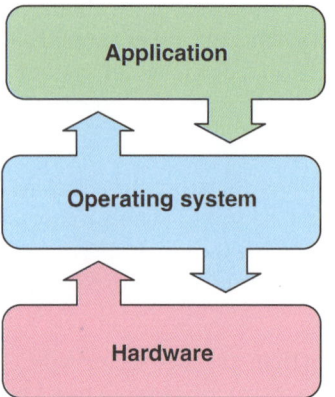

Figure 2.3: Operating system.

An operating system manages hardware by carrying out tasks such as:

- allocating memory to software
- sending data and instructions to output devices
- responding to input devices such as when a key is pressed
- opening and closing files on storage devices
- giving each running task a fair share of processor time
- sending error messages or status messages to applications or users
- dealing with user logons and security.

ACTIVITY 2.01

Microsoft Windows is an example of an operating system. Find at least two other operating systems used by desktop computers and at least three operating systems used by mobile phones or tablets.

Device drivers

Device drivers manage specific makes and models of hardware. A device driver is the software that comes with an external hardware component and sends customised instructions to the specific component. Operating systems often have common device drivers for hardware such as displaying basic graphics on a screen or allowing the user to use a printer. By using common device drivers, software applications can issue generic commands such as 'print' to the operating system without having to know the different instructions required for every different make and model of external hardware components (see Figure 2.4).

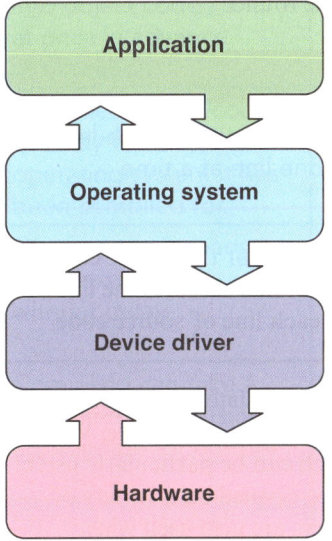

Figure 2.4: Device driver.

Translators

A translator translates a program written in a high-level programming language into machine code that a computer can understand.

Compilers

A **compiler** is a translator which creates a file containing the machine code known as an executable file because it can be executed by the processor. It can also be referred to as the object file. The original high-level programming language file is known as the source file.

KEY WORD

compiler: translates high-level programming language into an executable file in machine code

---

When a program is compiled, the whole source code is translated into the executable file at once and can then be distributed to resellers, customers and individual computers (see Figure 2.5). As it is in an executable format, it can only run on operating systems that the compiler has translated. For example, programs that have been compiled for Windows© will not work on Linux© unless they are compiled again for Linux. The same situation exists with mobile phone and tablet operating systems.

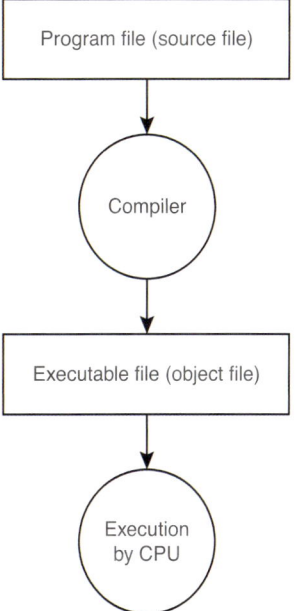

Figure 2.5: Compiler diagram.

The compilation process consists of three stages:

1   lexical analysis
2   syntax analysis
3   code generation.

Lexical analysis focuses on the words in the programming language. During analysis, any white space or comments will be removed, and the code will be broken down into tokens. Each token will represent a keyword, constant, identifier, string, number, operator or punctuation symbol.

For example, in Python, the following code displays a value to the screen:

```
print("Hello" + forename);
```

Advantages and disadvantages of system software

System software allows you to customise your device for many different jobs. Table 2.3 lists the advantages and disadvantages of system software.

Advantages	Disadvantages
You can choose many different types of software for the different tasks you need.	It may be hard to find software that does exactly what you need.
Many companies create programs for the same task, which gives you more choice. This can help with cost and choosing the features you need. For example, Microsoft and Google both create software for word processing.	You may need to do a lot of research to find the best piece of software for the right cost.
You can remove and update software depending on what you need.	You need to keep system software updated to ensure that it is secure and contains new features.
Many devices come with a range of system software for free when you buy it.	System software can be very expensive.
The range of system software you can get allows you to customise your device to your specific needs.	Free system software may not have the support and function that you need.
	Picking the correct software relies on you having a level of technical understanding.

Table 2.3: Advantages and disadvantages of system software.

Questions

6   Identify **two** functions of an operating system.

7   Describe the function of a compiler.

8   Describe **two** advantages of an interpreter over a compiler.

2.3 Utility software

Utility software is system software that performs maintenance on the computer system. Utility software does not include the operating system, but an operating system may come pre-installed with utility software.

> **KEY WORD**
>
> **utility software:** software that performs maintenance on the computer system

Anti-virus

Anti-virus software is sometimes referred to as anti-malware software, as it deals with other threats such as adware and spyware as well as viruses. It has two main functions. The first is an anti-virus monitor that is continually monitoring the system for viruses and malware. If the anti-virus monitor detects any unusual behaviour or signs of viruses or malware then it will prevent them from being executed so they cannot cause damage to files or programs. The second function is to check for viruses or malware that may already be on a system. This is usually known as scanning the system. If anything is found then the user will usually be given the option to disinfect the affected area, put it into quarantine or ignore it. Ignoring it is very dangerous because the virus or malware may be run and may have unexpected results. Disinfecting is the safest option as it completely removes the threat from the system, but it does mean that any data or program that had been affected would be deleted. The compromise is to put the affected area into quarantine. This is a safe area where the virus or malware cannot be executed, but the data or program remains isolated until it can be checked more thoroughly.

Back-up

Back-up utilities create a second copy of data and programs that are in storage. A back-up utility can be executed by the user, in which case the back-up takes place when the user asks it to, or it can be scheduled to execute at a predetermined time so that the back-up takes place automatically. The user is usually able to select which folders and files will be backed up and can usually decide where the back-up will be stored.

Data compression

Data compression utilities reduce the original size of files so that they use up less storage space. This can be achieved on a file-by-file basis or for a set of files or even a set of folders. It will be slower to open the compressed file than the uncompressed file, but as it is smaller it will use up less storage and can be transferred from one location to another more quickly.

Disk defragmentation

Storing data on a hard disk

A hard disk drive (HDD) consists of two main parts: the device that is the electronics that store the data, and the disk that is the medium onto which the data is stored. The device (or drive) includes a read-write head that sits at the end of an access arm and magnetises sectors on the disk (platter).

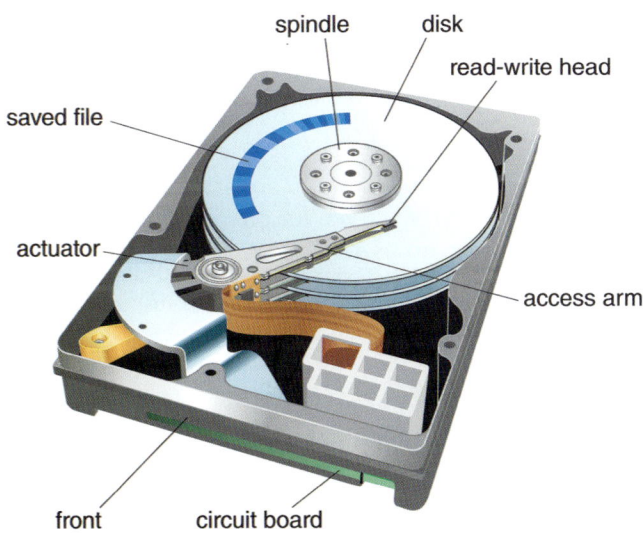

Figure 2.8: A hard disk.

There is usually more than one platter and therefore there will be several read-write heads for each side of each platter, as shown in Figure 2.8. Each platter has tracks and each track is split into sectors (see Figure 2.9).

The tracks that are in the same position on each platter form a cylinder. Wherever possible, a computer will attempt to store data in clusters on a single cylinder because this requires the least access arm movement. Moving the access arm is the slowest part of accessing data on the hard disk. Therefore, the less the access arm needs to move, the quicker the data can be accessed.

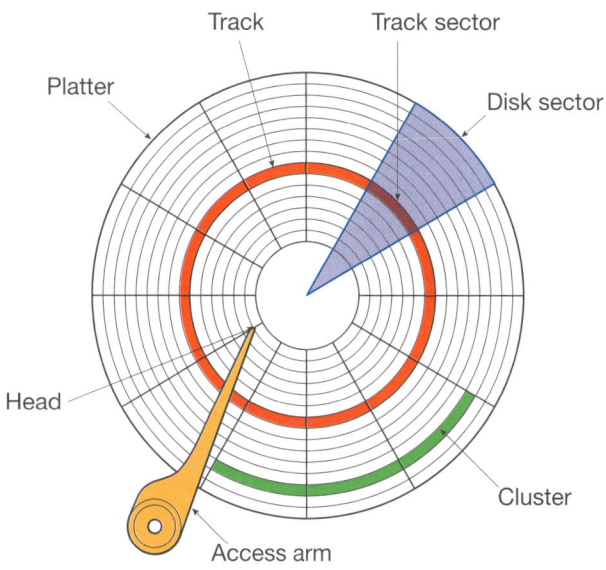

Figure 2.9: Structure of a hard disk.

REFLECTION

What ways can you use to remember the parts of a hard disk? Could you use those ideas to help you remember other things for example, the steps a compiler takes?

Fragmented files

As a hard disk gets used, files are kept together in storage on the same cylinder or adjacent cylinders. When files are deleted, gaps are left on the disk. If the size of a file increases, it uses up more space on the disk. Therefore, the file may be split across many clusters. When all the cylinders have been used, the only space to store files is within the gaps. If the gaps are not big enough, then files must be split across gaps, meaning that they become fragmented. The problem with this is that when opening the file, the access arm of the HDD must move to different locations to read the whole file. This makes opening the file a slow process.

WORKED EXAMPLE 2.01

In Figure 2.10, files have been neatly stored on the disk with file A, followed by file B, then file C.

A	A	A	B	B	B	C	C						

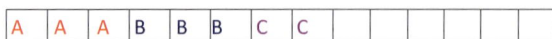

Figure 2.10: Non-fragmented files.

Figure 2.11 shows how each of the files has got bigger. First, file A got bigger with an extra two sectors, then a new file D was added, then file B got bigger by a sector, then file A again by a sector and finally file C.

A	A	A	B	B	B	C	C	A	A	D	B	A	C

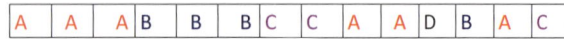

Figure 2.11: Fragmented files.

The files are fragmented and so they need to be defragmented as in Figure 2.12.

A	A	A	A	A	A	B	B	B	B	C	C	C	D

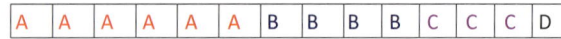

Figure 2.12: Defragmented files.

In Figure 2.13, files Q and S have been deleted.

P	P		R	R	R		T	T	T	T			

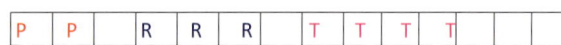

Figure 2.13: Non-fragmented files.

A new file U needs to be stored but it requires four sectors. It could end up being stored as in Figure 2.14.

P	P	U4	R	R	R		T	T	T	T	U1	U2	U3

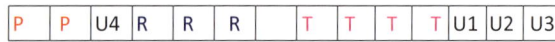

Figure 2.14: Fragmented files.

Defragmentation can solve this problem by temporarily moving U4, moving all of R next to P, moving all of T next to R and then moving all of U next to each other, as shown in Figure 2.15.

P	P	R	R	R	T	T	T	T	U1	U	U3	U4	

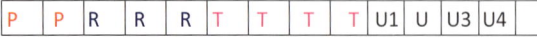

Figure 2.15: Defragmented files.

Defragmentation

A defragmentation utility will reorganise all the files so that each file is contiguous (kept together). It will do this by moving fragmented parts of files and small files to free space on the disk and creating space on whole cylinders or adjacent cylinders. It will then move the defragmented files to a place where the whole file is kept together. This can significantly improve the performance of a computer system, especially if program files have become fragmented and can be defragmented.

ACTIVITY 2.02

Open **2.01_Fragmentation_Defragmentation.gif**.

In the grid, each colour represents a file, and each cell represents an item.

- The red file is originally stored as items 1 to 7.
- The blue file is then stored as items 1 to 4.
- Additional items 8 to 10 are added to the red file, which are fragmented from the red file items 1 to 7.
- The green file is then stored as items 1 to 3.
- The cyan file is then stored as items 1 to 5.
- Additional items 4 to 5 are added to the blue file, which are fragmented from the blue file items 1 to 3.
- Additional items 4 to 5 are added to the green file, which are fragmented from the green file items 1 to 3.
- The orange file is then stored as items 1 to 7.
- The blue file is then deleted.

Now watch what happens as the purple file is added as items 1 to 2 where the blue file used to be and the green file items 6 to 8 are added in a fragmented manner.

Finally, watch how the file is defragmented by moving files into blank spaces and then reorganising them so each file is kept together.

Formatting

When a disk is prepared for first time use, it needs to be formatted. Formatting is the process of organising the tracks on the disk into sectors. Each sector is where data will be stored. A used disk can also be formatted, in which case all data will be lost and the tracks prepared again as if the disk was being used for the first time.

Low-level formatting

Low-level formatting completely removes the data from a disk drive. It recreates the file storage of tracks and sectors. Low-level formatting takes a long time because it overwrites the file storage system. It is also known as physical formatting as it makes marks on the disk. This means that data cannot be recovered from a disk that has had a low-level format. A low-level format is often known as resetting a hard disk to its factory configuration.

High-level formatting

High-level formatting is known as a 'quick format'. This is because it takes less time to complete when compared to a low-level format. High-level formatting does not delete all the data on the disk. Instead, it simply deletes the old file system and creates a new one. This allows software to save new data/files over the original data/files. It can do this because the computer does not know that data is stored there.

The disadvantage of a high-level format is that the original data will still exist on the disk until a new set of data/file overwrites the old data. Therefore, you can still recover the old data from a disk.

Partitioning

Each hard disk can be split into smaller parts. For example, a 300 GB hard disk could be split into three lots of 100 GB sections. Each section is known as a **partition**. A partition has its own file storage and file storage system. Each partition can be given a unique drive letter, for example, G or J.

Partitioning can be useful to create different stores of data for different people. For example, a teacher in a school may have access to the G drive, which may be where they store details of school policies. Students could then be given access to the S drive. This is where they save the work they do in class. The G drive and S drive can exist on the same secondary storage device.

> **KEY WORD**
>
> **partition:** a section on a hard disk with a unique file system, where data can be stored

File management

Files can be copied and deleted using features within an operating system's own interface. However, this can be slow and options are limited. File management utilities enable users to have more control over which files are copied and deleted, and how they are copied and deleted. For example, a user may only want to copy word processing documents that are within a series of folders and they may want all the files to be copied to a single folder on the destination storage. It is also possible to synchronise files across multiple storage locations or even multiple computer systems, so that when a change is made to a file in one location, it will then be updated in all other locations.

Some files become locked by an operating system and it becomes almost impossible to delete them. Some utility software can overcome this problem by deleting locked files and folders. When files are deleted using normal deletion methods, the data is still on the disk although the user is unable to see it. Therefore, another function of deleting utilities is being able to delete files permanently so that they cannot be restored or accessed. Some deletion utilities will remove temporary files that are no longer needed by the computer system, or files that are no longer used but have not been deleted when a program has been uninstalled or a user profile removed.

Disk management software

Disk management software allows a user to perform maintenance and operations on storage devices. The software will allow a user to partition and format the hard disk. It may also allow users to rename drive letters, scan for errors on the hard disk and change the file system on the disk. It will let users perform high-level formatting and low-level formatting.

Data compression software

Data compression software allows users to compress files or create compressed folders. This can be useful as each file will take up less storage space and means users can store more files on a hard disk. However, compressed files need to be uncompressed before they are edited. This can take time and means that a computer appears to run more slowly.

DID YOU KNOW?

People often refer to compressing files as 'zipping'. You may hear people use the term 'zip folder' or 'zip file' (see Figure 2.16). This is because compressed files were stored as a '.ZIP'. For example: MySmallFile.zip.

Figure 2.16: Zipping a file is like squeezing clothing into a small bag and 'zipping' it up to keep the clothing inside from bursting out!

ACTIVITY 2.03

Work in pairs. Look at the software installed on your school computer.

1   Make a table listing the programs on the computer. You could classify them as:

- anti-virus
- back-up
- file management
- disk management
- data compression.

2   Identify **two** advantages and **two** disadvantages of:

- disk management systems
- file management systems
- data compression utilities.

Add them to your table.

3   Compare your table with other pairs. Discuss any differences you may have. Add any advantages and disadvantages that you did not have to your table.

Questions

9   List two types of utility software.

10 Describe the role of anti-virus software.

2.4 Custom-written software and off-the-shelf software

Custom-written software

Sometimes we need software to carry out a specific purpose that may be unique. This means that the software will be written just for this purpose (see Figure 2.17). This is known as **custom-written software**. This is because it is customised to the needs of the client and will meet the requirements of the client. It would not be useful for other individuals or organisations, as it only carries out this specific task.

Examples of custom-written software for individuals or organisations are:

- Robots in manufacturing: an organisation may need specific software to control custom robots.

- Specific scientific experiments: a scientist may need specialised software to process the data from an experiment.

- Autonomous (self-driving) vehicles: custom-software is used to control vehicles from different manufacturers. For example, the software for a Ford car would not work on a Toyota or a Tesla.

Figure 2.17: Custom-written software is like buying clothes that are individually made to fit you.

Off-the-shelf software

When software already exists and is purchased online or from a shop, it is known as off-the-shelf software. The software is written for a general purpose that is likely to be useful to a large market. Any individual or organisation can purchase the software for a specified price. Examples include word processing software and financial software. It is likely that writing documents will always use similar features like spelling checks and changing fonts.

Advantages and disadvantages of different types of software

When choosing between buying custom-written software or off-the-shelf software, you will need to consider:

- The degree of testing: custom-written software may not have the same level of testing as off-the-shelf software. This is because fewer people use it, and so bugs may not be identified as quickly.

- Level of support: there is likely to be greater levels of support available for off-the-shelf software because more people buy and use it. This means the software manufacturer will have more money to spend on support for customers.

- Cost: custom-written software costs a lot more money than off-the-shelf software. This is because it is intended to be used for one specific task. Only one individual or organisation will want to buy the software. Off-the-shelf software has many customers, and so the cost to use the software is reduced.

- Adaptability of the software: both types of software can be adapted. However, custom-written software is more easily adapted. This is because

the adaptations are made for a small number of users. Off-the-shelf software has millions of users. Adapting the software will affect all those users. This means that the software may take longer to design and build, so that people are aware of what is changing and how to use the new software.

Table 2.4 summarises the advantages and disadvantages of custom-written software and off-the-shelf software.

Custom-written software	Off-the-shelf software
The entire development cost of custom-written software is met by the client for whom it is written, which makes it very expensive.	The development cost of off-the-shelf software is spread between all the customers who purchase it at a specified price, which means the cost is much lower.
Custom-written software takes a long time to develop, so the client will have to wait before being able to use the software.	Off-the-shelf software is immediately available, so the customer can start using it straight away.
The requirements of the client can be met precisely with no additional features that are not necessary.	Some tasks that the customer needs to carry out may not be possible and there will be many features that the customer never uses.
The developers of the software will ensure that the software is compatible with the hardware, software and data used by the client.	The software may not be compatible with existing hardware, software and data used by the customer.
As the software will not have been used before, apart from testing, it is likely that bugs will be found within the software as it is used by the client.	The software will have been used by thousands of customers and bugs will have been identified and fixed, and patches will be released as more bugs are found so that the software runs as expected.

Custom-written software	Off-the-shelf software
The client will have access to support from the company that developed the software.	Customers will be able to get support from a wide range of sources including telephone support, discussion forums and online training.

Table 2.4: Custom-written software versus off-the-shelf software.

Proprietary software

Proprietary software is owned by an individual or organisation who sells it for use under an agreed licence. Only the files needed to run the software are made available, with the source code used to create the software remaining with the owner. Different licences can be granted for the use of the software including freeware, shareware, single user, multi-user and site licence. For example, an office suite of software could be sold for use for business purposes on a single computer or it could be sold for use for personal purposes and allowed to be installed on up to five devices. Freeware and shareware can often be used free of charge, but some features might be restricted or it might stop working after a trial period until payment is made.

ACTIVITY 2.04

Research examples of shareware software and discover what restrictions are in place if the software may be used without making a payment. What different tasks can you find freeware or shareware for?

Open-source software

Open-source software has the source code freely available. This means that the source code used to create the software must be distributed with the executable version of the software. It can be freely accessed, used, changed, or shared. There is often a community of developers that contribute to the development of open-source software. Open-source software is often free but sometimes there may be a fee for use.

ACTIVITY 2.05

Visit the Open Source Initiative website and find out what defines open-source software.

Questions

11 Describe off-the-shelf software.

12 Describe two disadvantages of custom-written software.

2.5 User interfaces

A **user interface** allows a user to interact with a computer system or piece of software. A user interface represents the communication between a user and the computer system. This communication can take many forms.

KEY WORD

user interface: a way of communicating between the user and the computer system

Command line interface

A command line interface allows a user to enter text commands to tell the software/computer what to do. The computer system will respond by producing results in a text format.

For example, in Figure 2.18, the user has changed the directory (folder) to the logs directory ('`cd logs`'). Then the user has requested a listing of the directory ('`dir`'). Finally, the user copies the file directx.log to the root directory of the f drive ('`copy directx.log f:\`'). The user gets a confirmation message that one file has been copied. The only prompt that the user gets is information about which directory is currently active ('`C:\Windows\Logs>`').

```
C:\Windows>cd logs

C:\Windows\Logs>dir
 Volume in drive C has no label.
 Volume Serial Number is C8FD-8C85

 Directory of C:\Windows\Logs

29/01/2015  12:07    <DIR>          .
29/01/2015  12:07    <DIR>          ..
18/05/2015  03:12    <DIR>          CBS
09/12/2014  13:53           254,487 DirectX.log
17/10/2013  17:00    <DIR>          DISM
17/10/2013  18:10    <DIR>          DPX
22/08/2013  16:36    <DIR>          HomeGroup
23/05/2014  00:09    <DIR>          Paragon
23/05/2014  00:10    <DIR>          Paragon Software
22/08/2013  16:36    <DIR>          SettingSync
19/10/2013  10:17    <DIR>          SetupCleanupTask
08/06/2015  03:40    <DIR>          SystemRestore
29/01/2015  12:07    <DIR>          WindowsBackup
               1 File(s)        254,487 bytes
              12 Dir(s)   5,402,001,408 bytes free

C:\Windows\Logs>copy directx.log f:\
        1 file(s) copied.

C:\Windows\Logs>
```

Figure 2.18: Command line interface.

Command line interfaces use very little memory. They are useful in old systems or for maintenance of very small systems/devices (for example, engine management systems). They are also useful for technical users who need to carry out complex operations that cannot be performed using more user-friendly interfaces. However, command line interfaces can be difficult to learn and use because users must learn and remember all the commands. Errors can easily be made when entering those commands.

Graphical user interface

The most common type of interface is a graphical user interface (GUI), as shown in Figure 2.19. GUIs are found on desktop computers, tablet computers, mobile phones, televisions, set-top boxes, photocopiers and many in-car entertainment systems.

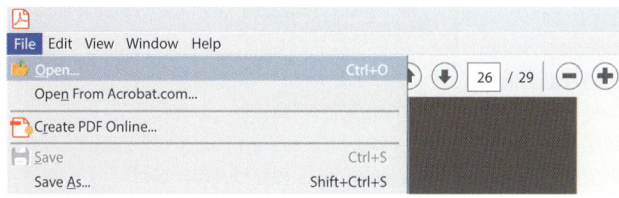

Figure 2.19: Graphical user interface.

GUIs can include some or all elements shown in Table 2.5. The acronym WIMP – windows, icons, menus, pointers – is commonly used to remember these elements.

Windows	An area of the screen devoted to a specific task, for example a software application, a file within a software application or a print dialogue box.
Icons	An image that is used to represent a program, file or task. The icon can be selected to open the program, file or task.
Menus	Menus are words on the screen that represent a list of options that can be expanded into further sub-menus.
Pointers	This is the method of representing movement from a pointing device such as a mouse or the human finger on a touch screen. The pointer is also used to select and manipulate objects on the screen.

Table 2.5: Graphical user interface elements.

Complex GUIs may require a lot of memory to operate. Simple GUIs can be used where memory is limited. Sometimes simple GUIs can be used instead of a command line interface in small systems such as embedded systems. Simple web-based GUIs are commonly used for the maintenance of devices such as routers, switches and printers.

GUIs are often easy to use. This is because commands are represented by pictures, and menus provide options that can be selected. However, they can be restrictive for some technical users. This is because you must navigate through menus to find the command you want. Technical users may know the command they want and prefer to type it because it is quicker. To help solve this issue, 'shortcuts' can be used. These are combinations of keys that load/run commands without having to use a menu. For example, many programs use Ctrl+C to copy and Ctrl+V to paste.

Within a GUI, form controls can be used. These include labels, text boxes, tick boxes, option buttons, drop-down boxes and buttons, as shown in Table 2.6 and Figures 2.20 to 2.25.

Control	Description	Example
Labels	Labels are used as prompts or instructions to enter data. They are text and cannot be edited by the user.	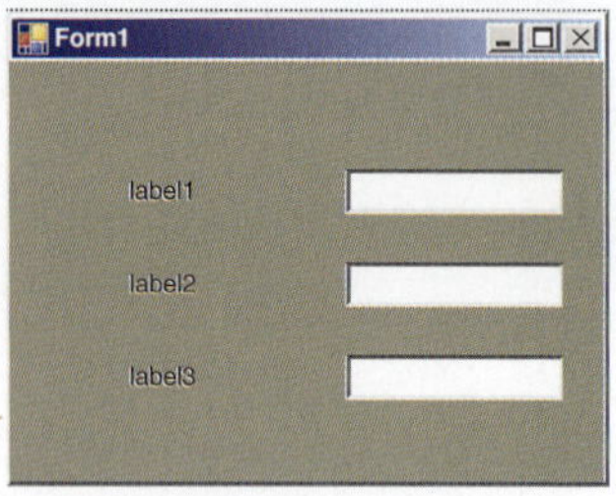 Figure 2.20: Label.
Text boxes	Text boxes are an area where the user can enter text such as their surname or credit card number. Errors can easily be made by the user when entering data into a text box, such as spelling things incorrectly.	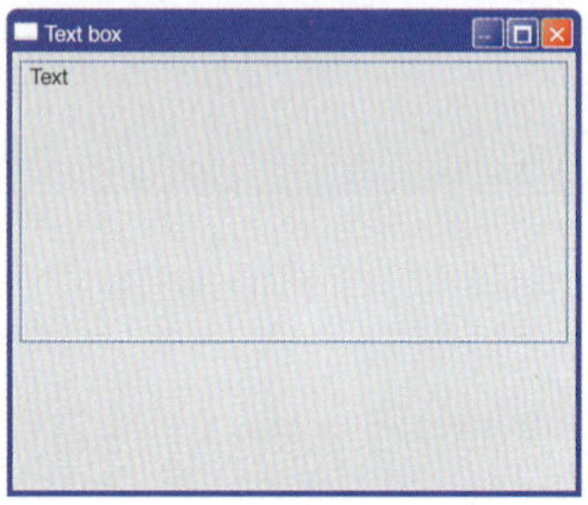 Figure 2.21: Text box.
Tick boxes	Tick boxes (also known as check boxes) allow the user to select from a set of options. The user can choose as many options that apply. For example, when printing, a user can choose to collate documents and to print on both sides.	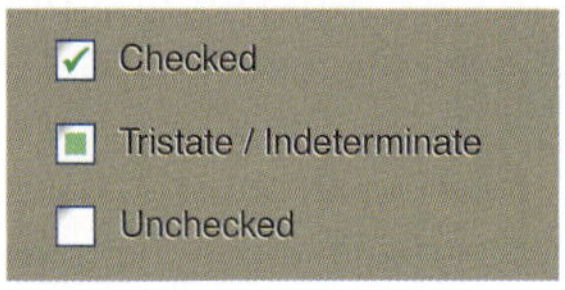 Figure 2.22: Tick box.
Option buttons	Option buttons (also known as radio buttons) differ from tick boxes in that only one option in a group can be selected at once.	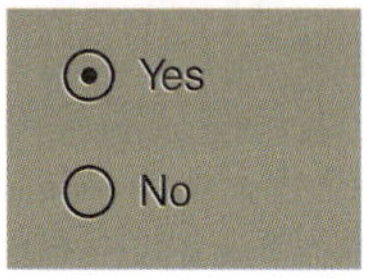 Figure 2.23: Option button.
Drop-down boxes	Drop-down boxes allow a user to select from a list that appears when the drop-down box appears on screen. Only one option can be chosen. The user can usually start typing the option so that it is found more quickly. Drop-down boxes are more appropriate than option buttons when there are many options to choose from, as the drop-down box doesn't take up as much space on the screen.	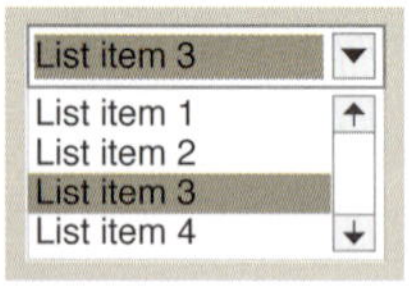 Figure 2.24: Drop-down box.
Buttons	Buttons can be used to navigate through an interface (forwards and backwards), to confirm that inputs have been completed, to clear inputs, to gain help and to access any other area of an interface.	 Figure 2.25: Confirm button.

Table 2.6: Form controls.

Dialogue interface

A dialogue interface allows users to speak to a computer system using their voice. The user gives oral commands and the computer system responds by carrying out an action. The computer may also respond using a synthesised voice.

Dialogue interfaces are very popular with mobile devices, including mobile phones and in-car entertainment systems. Some cars will accept commands such as 'Temperature 20' or 'Call home'. Mobile phones will accept commands and questions such as 'What is the time?' or 'Give me directions to get home' (see Figure 2.26). Some automated telephone systems will recognise a user's voice. This means that the user does not have to use the key pad on their mobile device to input information.

There is no need for a physical interface with dialogue interfaces, so they are suitable for systems such as home automation where voice commands can be given from anywhere to control equipment such as lights, entertainment systems and shutters. With entertainment systems such as televisions, the user does not have to find a remote control to use and anybody in the room can give the command to increase the volume or change the channel.

Dialogue interfaces may also be suitable for use in cars or when holding a telephone. In many circumstances, words can be spoken by a user more quickly than a user can type them.

Figure 2.26: Dialogue interfaces are often found on cloud-based voice services like Alexa or on mobile phones using technology such as Bixby.

The main problem with this type of interface is the computer system's ability to recognise a user's voice. Many things can make it difficult for the computer to understand, including accents, different voices, language and background noise (for example, a car's engine). Dialogue interfaces also require the user to know what commands are understood by the computer system otherwise the system will not know how to respond. Some dialogue interfaces will give prompts offering the user different options to choose from. Systems are not intelligent enough to simply understand requests in any format that the user chooses.

Gesture-based interface

Gesture-based interfaces will recognise human motion. This could include tracking eyes and lips, identifying hand signals or monitoring whole-body movement.

There are many applications of gesture-based interfaces. The original Nintendo Wii® enabled gamers to move their hands while holding a remote controller and that movement would be mimicked in games such as 10 pin bowling and boxing. Microsoft's Xbox® can track whole body movement without any devices being held or worn by the user. This enabled gamers to play a game using their whole body, so boxing could become kickboxing and 10 pin bowling could include a run-up.

Many computer systems, including mobile devices, may accept hand gestures as a way of controlling objects on screen. For example, a swipe of the hand across a screen may close a program, while pinching fingers together in front of a screen may zoom out on an image. Avoiding screen contact helps control infection in hospitals, for example in an operating theatre.

Gestures can be an essential form of interaction for some users who have physical disabilities that prevent them from using input devices. A person who has no control from the neck downwards could control a computer system with their eyes because the computer can track the movement of each eye.

One of the biggest problems with gesture interfaces is accuracy. For a gesture interface to be effective, it needs to interpret the movements made by the human user accurately. Tracking the movement of fingers, arms, legs and eyes requires highly accurate cameras or sensors. This is why many virtual reality applications still use sensors attached to various parts of the body to improve accuracy. It can also be very difficult to control a pointer when a finger is in mid-air rather than when firmly fixed to a touch screen or holding a mouse.

Advantages and disadvantages of different types of user interface

Table 2.7 lists the advantages and disadvantages of different types of user interface.

User interface	Advantages	Disadvantages
Command line interface	Very quick to use. Simple and cheap to design. Very low demand on resources as it just prints text to a screen.	Needs specialist knowledge. Can be difficult to know what to do. Format and layouts can be difficult to design well.
Graphical user interface	Clear and easy to follow. Suitable for people with low level of digital skills. Can represent more things more easily, for example using colours and layout to help understand what is happening.	Can take a long time to design. Takes up more resource (for example, graphics card).
Dialogue interface	Simple to use. Uses natural language. No specific commands to learn.	May not recognise certain voices or languages. User needs to be trained to operate accurately. May not be any screen or display to know what is happening. May be less suitable for users with disabilities.
Gesture-based interface	Simple to use. Uses body movement, which is easy to learn. No specific commands to learn.	May not recognise certain movements. User needs to be trained to operate accurately. Gestures and movements may be difficult to use, and many gestures may need to be learned. May be less suitable for users with disabilities. May need calibration to detect movements accurately.

Table 2.7: Advantages and disadvantages of different types of user interface

UNPLUGGED ACTIVITY 2.06

What sort of interface would you use for the following?

- aeroplane autopilot

- using a Wi-Fi router

- a self-driving car

- writing a presentation for school homework

- learning how to use a new program on a computer.

Compare your answers in pairs or as a group. Discuss why you chose each answer.

Questions

13 Give **two** reasons why a command line interface might be used instead of a graphical user interface.

14 Give **two** disadvantages of a command line interface.

15 Define the acronym WIMP.

16 Explain **two** advantages of dialogue interfaces.

PRACTICE QUESTIONS

1 A regional government uses a mainframe computer to host its databases and web-enabled applications.
   a State one measurement of processor speed used for mainframe computers or supercomputers. [1]
   b Explain the importance of reliability, availability and serviceability for mainframe computers. [6]
   [Total 7]

2 The accounts department has a new printer.
   Explain why the accounts administrator needs a device driver for the new printer. [2]

3 The administrator's laptop is running more slowly than usual. Disk defragmentation software shows the hard disk is 70% fragmented.
   a Explain how data is stored on a hard disk. [4]
   b Explain how the data on the laptop's hard disk may have become fragmented. [4]
   [Total 8]

4 The waste collection department needs new software. The software will link to the government's website.
   This will allow residents and businesses to log problems such as missed waste collections.
   Evaluate the use of a custom-written software solution for this purpose. [6]

5 The waste management software will use a Graphical User Interface (GUI).
   a Identify and describe three different form controls that could be used in the GUI, giving examples of how they could be used. [6]
   b Identify two other types of user interface. [2]
   [Total 8]

6 The software development team uses an interpreter for testing during development of software and a compiler to translate the final version of the software to machine code for government officials.
   Describe two differences between a compiler and an interpreter. [4]

SUMMARY CHECKLIST

- ☐ I can describe the characteristics of mainframe computers and supercomputers.
- ☐ I can give examples of the use of mainframe computers and supercomputers.
- ☐ I can explain the advantages and disadvantages of mainframe computers and supercomputers.
- ☐ I can describe types of system software and how they are used.
- ☐ I can explain the advantages and disadvantages of system software.
- ☐ I can understand the need for utility software.
- ☐ I can describe types of utility software and how they are used.
- ☐ I can explain the advantages and disadvantages of utility software.
- ☐ I can describe the uses of customer written software and off-the-shelf software.
- ☐ I can explain the advantages and disadvantages of custom-written and off-the-shelf software.
- ☐ I can describe different types of user interfaces and their uses.
- ☐ I can explain the advantages and disadvantages of different types of user interfaces.

PROJECT

Figure 2.27: A school computer lab.

Your school is buying a new computer to run a wide range of tasks for both staff and students in the school (see Figure 2.27). You have been asked to produce a report that will outline the type of computer the school should buy.

1 Write a short report recommending whether the school should buy a mainframe or a supercomputer. Explain the reasons for your choice.

2 Identify the tasks that you think the computer can be used for.

3 Discuss the need for longevity, RAS and security of the computer. What should the school be aware of when choosing the computer?

4 Write a summary of the types of software that the computer system may need. Consider the software required, and state why you recommend each piece of software.

5 What tasks will the software do, and why is this important?

6 What user interface will the computer system need? Explain your answer in your report.

> ## Chapter 3
> # Monitoring and control

LEARNING INTENTIONS

By the end of this chapter, you will be able to:

- recognise a range of sensors and understand how they are used in monitoring and measuring systems
- know what is meant by calibration and understand why sensors are calibrated
- recognise a range of sensors and actuators and understand how they are used in control systems
- write an algorithm to represent the process involved in a control system
- draw a flowchart to represent the process involved in a control system
- explain the advantages and disadvantages of different control technologies.

Introduction

You use monitoring and measurement technologies and control technologies every day. The technologies are an important part of our lives. **Monitoring systems** regularly check on systems to make sure that they are operating as expected. Monitoring systems use measurement technology to help them check that systems are operating correctly. Monitoring systems help with tasks such as making sure that the temperature of fridges or air-conditioning systems are at the correct level.

They also help keep workers safe in dangerous workplaces. A **measurement system** could use a heat sensor. The sensor would collect data about the temperature within the workplace so this can be reported. A **control system** can help keep workers in a chemical factory safe as it will ensure the production process is working correctly, so that workers are not exposed to chemicals for a dangerous amount of time (see Figure 3.1).

Figure 3.1: Monitoring systems ensure the environment in a chemical laboratory stays safe.

KEY WORDS

monitoring system: a system that observes and often records the activities in a process

measurement system: a way of measuring data, either at set times or continuously

control system: a system that manages or regulates a process by physically changing aspects of the system depending on collected data

It is important for you to learn how these important technologies operate and how they benefit many aspects of daily life.

3.1 Monitoring and measurement technologies

Sensors

A **sensor** is an input device. It collects data about the physical environment. Sensors can be used automatically by control systems or directly by a human. Automation with a control system removes the need for a human to collect the data manually. Data collected by a sensor is input into a system and any necessary action required is taken.

KEY WORD

sensor: an input device that collects data from the surrounding physical environment

There are several advantages of using sensors to collect data:

1 Data can be repeatedly collected 24 hours a day. This means that a human does not need to be present all the time and can rest.

2 Data can be collected remotely in harmful and dangerous environments. This means that the lives of humans are not endangered to collect the data.

3 The data a sensor records is likely to be more accurate. A human is more likely to make mistakes, which lead to errors in data samples (see Figure 3.2).

Figure 3.2: Sensors in smart devices can help people monitor their health at home.

If you look at the environment around you, you will see that it has many different elements.

Question

1 What kind of things can you see, hear and feel in your environment?

When answering Question 1, you may have noticed things such as:

- the temperature
- the level of sound
- the level of light
- movement.

There are also many more things that are changeable about the environment, such as:

- humidity (humidity is the level of moisture in the air)
- electromagnetic fields (a field created by moving electrical charge)
- pressure.

Many sensors are designed to be small. This means that they can fit into many devices that are portable. Smart watches have many sensors in them. For example, some smart watches have sensors that can detect:

- heart rate
- body mass composition
- electrocardiogram (ECG), which checks your heart's rhythm
- air pressure sensors
- location on the planet using GPS
- temperature (body temperature and air temperature)
- motion.

There are many types of sensor. Each sensor is designed to collect a specific item of data. For example, there are sensors for:

- light/UV (a wavelength of light)
- temperature
- pressure
- humidity
- pH (the level of acidity in water)
- gas types (detects the different levels of gas in an environment, including oxygen, carbon dioxide, carbon monoxide and oxides of nitrogen)
- sound and **ultrasonic**
- magnetic fields/**induction loops** (often used in car parks)
- infrared (a type of light that gives out heat but cannot be seen)
- touch
- electromagnetic field
- proximity.

KEY WORDS

ultrasonic: sound waves that cannot be heard by humans

induction loop: a system that uses magnets to create an electrical current in a wire

Questions

2 It may be obvious what some of the sensors collect data about, for example light and sound. What data do you think the following sensors collect?

a infrared sensor

b induction loops

c pressure sensor

d proximity sensor

3 a Think of two situations in which a sensor may start to provide incorrect readings.

b What detrimental effect could this have?

You have learned that there are advantages to using sensors, but there can be disadvantages too. The biggest disadvantage is that a sensor can malfunction (fail to work normally). The sensor may provide incorrect readings. This might have a big impact on the control system. For example, if a sensor does not detect the height of an aeroplane correctly, it can cause an accident.

Calibration

It is important that the data a sensor records is accurate. To make sure that the data is accurate a sensor is **calibrated**. This process is called calibration. Calibration tries to make sure that the data a sensor logs is as accurate as possible.

> **KEY WORD**
>
> **calibration:** the process of testing and modifying a device to make sure that it is taking accurate readings

Calibration needs a calibration reference. This is a fixed standard to calibrate against. A simple method of calibration is to test readings against another sensor that you know is calibrated. If the readings from both sensors are the same, then we know our sensor is calibrated. Another way to calibrate a sensor is by using another physical reference. For example, a ruler or measuring tape could be used to find out if an item that should trigger the proximity sensor does so from the correct distance set.

Each sensor has a characteristic curve. This curve maps the sensor's response in comparison to an ideal response. There are three main categories of result that can be given by a sensor. These are:

- level of offset: the readings are higher or lower than the ideal reference (see Figure 3.3)

- sensitivity: the readings change over a range at a different rate from the ideal reference (see Figure 3.4)

- linearity: the readings are directly proportional to the ideal reference (see Figure 3.5).

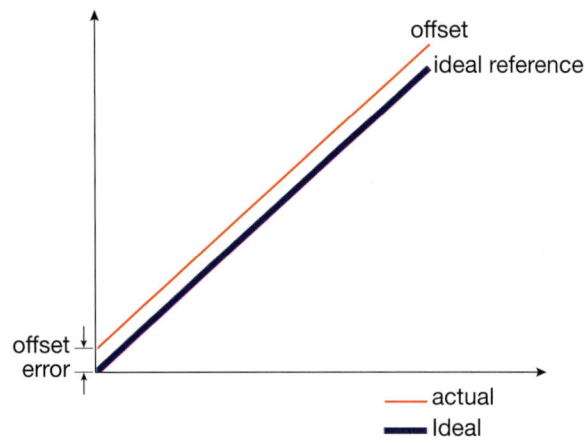

Figure 3.3: Offset.

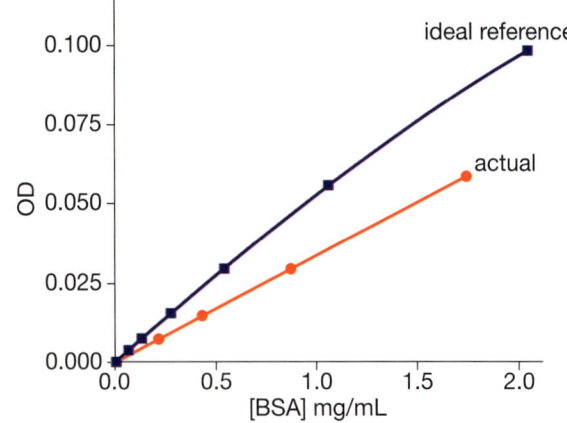

Figure 3.4: Sensitivity.

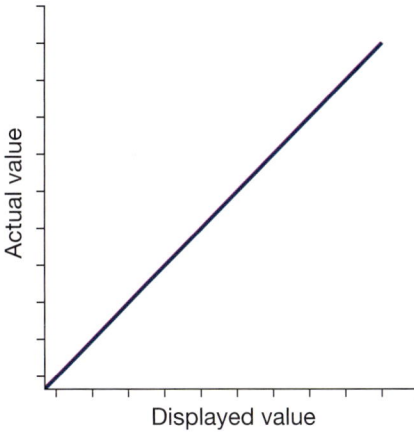

Figure 3.5: Linearity.

Methods used to calibrate devices

There are three different types of calibration that can be used for a sensor. These are:

- one-point calibration
- two-point calibration
- multipoint calibration.

One-point calibration

One-point calibration is the simplest form of calibration. It corrects an offset calibration curve. Remember, offset calibration means that a sensor measures too high or too low consistently. Therefore, we can calibrate the sensor based on a single reading. This will then bring the sensor's measurements closer to the ideal reference.

For example, we know a sensor always measures consistently higher than the current temperature. We use a single reading to check how high the sensor reads. We find that the sensor is reading 2 °C higher than it should. We can calibrate that sensor by adjusting all of the data it sends by −2.

Here is an example of the process steps:

1 Take a reading with the sensor.
2 Compare the reading with a device measuring at the ideal standard.
3 Subtract the reading from the reference to get the offset.
4 Add the offset to every reading to get the calibrated value.

For example, if a thermometer (see Figure 3.6) tells you the temperature of a room is 22 °C, but the reading from your sensor tells you that the room is 20.5 °C, the calculation would be:

$$22 - 20.5 = 1.5$$

This means the offset that needs to be added to each reading from the sensor is 1.5.

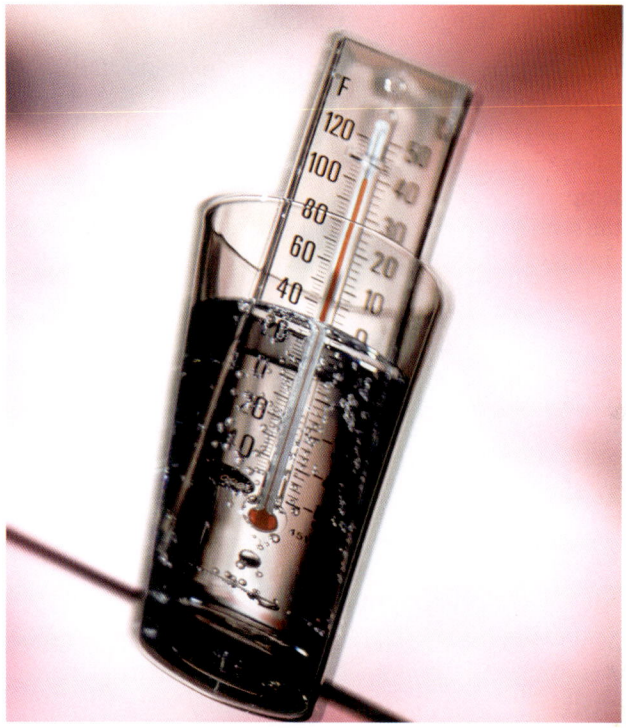

Figure 3.6: Thermometer.

Two-point calibration

Two-point calibration can be used to correct a data set that is both offset and contains sensitivity. It rescales the output to do this. It is often a more accurate method of calibration than one-point calibration.

There are different methods used to perform a two-point calibration check depending on the sensor. One method could be:

1 Take two different readings with your sensor. It works best if you take a reading at the lower end of the scale and a reading at the higher end of the scale.
2 Compare the readings to readings from a device measuring at the ideal standard.

3 Calculate the range value for the sensor readings by subtracting the low reading from the high reading.

4 Calculate the range value for the ideal standard by subtracting the low reading from the high reading.

5 Use a formula to calculate the correct value for each reading such as:

CorrectValue = (((SensorCurrentValue – SensorLowValue) * IdealRangeValue) / SensorRangeValue) + IdealLowValue

For example, if a temperature sensor measures the temperature of an iced water bucket as 0.75 °C and a boiling kettle as 98 °C, you can use this two-point calibration method to get a correct reading for the temperature sensor. You can use a current reading from the sensor of 37 °C. You can use a set of common ideal standard readings for iced water (0.01 °C) and boiling water (100 °C).

SensorRangeValue = 97.25

IdealRangeValue = 99.99

CorrectValue = (((37 – 0.75) × 99.99) / 97.25) + 0.01 = 37.28 (2 dp)

Therefore, the correct value for the sensor reading of 37 °C is 37.28 °C.

Multipoint calibration

Multipoint calibration is similar to the other calibration methods but is performed using at least three different readings. This further increases the accuracy of the calibration and can help calibrate sensors that would produce readings that do not naturally form a linear line.

This means that the computer can adjust the readings more accurately. For example, a sensor may read temperatures between 0 and 10 °C accurately. However, it reads temperatures between 10 and 30 °C by +2 °C too high. Above 30 °C, it becomes more inconsistent. At 40 °C, the sensor is accurate. At 50 °C it is inaccurate by −2 °C, and at 60 °C it is inaccurate by +1 °C.

The computer can calculate the adjustments needed to remove the inaccuracies with multipoint calibration.

Uses of monitoring and measurement technologies

A monitoring system collects the data and stores it for later use. For example, data may be collected about the temperature in a garden over a period of 24 hours, for a week. The data could then be analysed later to see which day was the warmest and what time of the day the warmest temperature was recorded.

The main technologies used in a monitoring system are sensors. Other technologies that may be used are storage devices to store the data collected. Graphing software could also be used to create visual representation of the data to make it easier to interpret.

An example of this type of system could be a monitoring system for the level of chlorine in the water of a swimming pool (see Figure 3.7):

- a pH sensor is placed in the swimming pool

- the pH sensor takes readings at regular intervals, such as every minute

- the readings are sent to a storage device

- the readings are put into a graph by the manager so that they can see the level of chlorine in the water throughout the day.

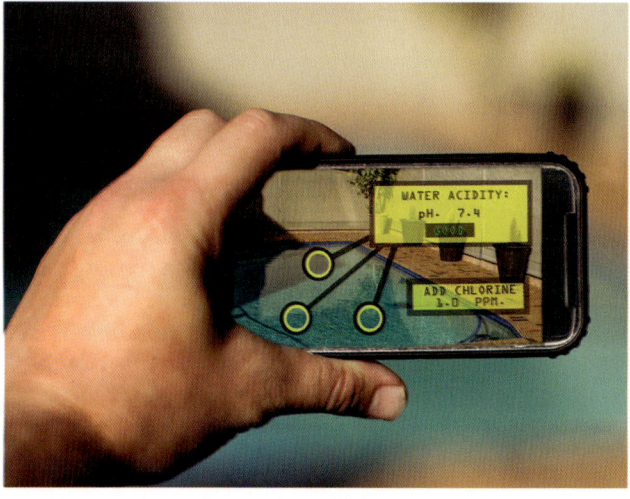

Figure 3.7: Sensors monitor pH levels in a swimming pool.

Environmental monitoring

Environmental monitoring checks the state of the world around us. For example, it can measure the levels of water pollution in rivers and streams. Environmental monitoring allows us to respond to changes in the environment more quickly, which could mean we avoid a natural disaster. For example, environmental monitoring could identify whether a small increase in chemicals in a river may have resulted from a leak from a nearby factory. Safety checks could then be performed at the factory to find and stop the cause of the chemical leak.

Real-world example – weather stations

Weather stations use many monitoring systems to provide everyone with daily information about the weather in their area, and all over the world. We can use weather station data to plan a day trip. Farmers can use the weather data to help with growing their crops for food (see Figure 3.8). For example, weather data shows that strawberries grow well between March and June but might need to be grown in a greenhouse in colder or warmer weather.

Figure 3.8: Farmers use weather data to decide what to grow, where, and when.

A weather station uses lots of sensors that are spread across an area or country. These sensors take data samples regularly. The data samples are stored at the weather station. The data can then be sent to a computer for analysis. This data can then be used in many ways, for example to report the current temperature.

Modern weather stations use sensors to measure:

- local temperatures (the ambient temperature) throughout the day and night

- the change in atmospheric pressure

- the humidity of the area – including absolute humidity (the amount of water that is in the air) and relative humidity (the amount of water in the air compared with the greatest amount of water the air could hold at that temperature)

- the amount of sunlight.

UNPLUGGED ACTIVITY 3.01

Draw a large poster that shows how a weather station makes use of different sensors.

Question

4   A textile factory is about to open. The factory is near a river. The local environmental department is worried that chemicals used to dye textiles may leak into the river. They decide to set up a monitoring system to check the pH level of the river at regular intervals. Explain what sensors could be used and how they could be used in this system.

Monitoring patients

Sensors and monitoring systems are also used in hospitals to enable medical staff to monitor the functions of the body (see Figure 3.9). For example, sensors may measure a patient's:

- pulse

- blood oxygen levels

- heart function

- lung function

- levels of chemicals in the body

- brain activity

- sugar levels in the blood

- blood pressure.

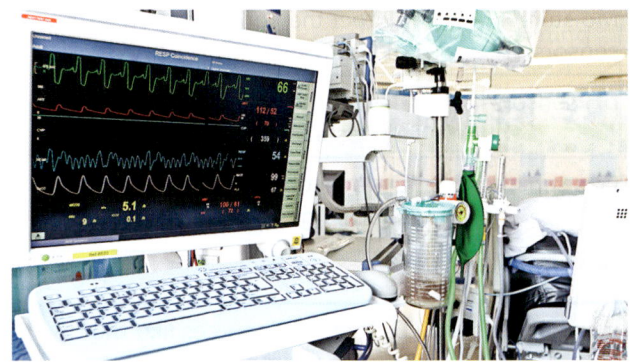

Figure 3.9: Sensors are used to monitor the health of patients in hospital. The data are displayed on screens.

DISCUSSION POINT

In groups, discuss the following:

1   What could be the impact of uncalibrated sensors when monitoring hospital patients?

2   What sort of calibration could you use for these sensors?

3   How often would you run calibration of the sensors? Are some systems more important than others?

Advantages	Disadvantages
Can move devices without the need for human interaction.	Pneumatic actuators can be noisy.
Can operate devices that humans cannot use due to weight or location.	The cost of hydraulic and electric actuators is relatively high.
Can operate more quickly than humans (faster reactions).	Fluid leaks can be a problem in hydraulic actuators and prevent operation.
Can make very accurate movements.	Need calibrating to ensure accuracy.
Can operate continuously with little maintenance needed.	May need to be replaced – causing the system to stop.

Table 3.3: Advantages and disadvantages of actuators in control technologies.

Microprocessor-controlled/ computer-controlled technology

A **microprocessor** is an electronic component that can perform similar functions to a central processing unit (CPU). It can process instructions and perform mathematical comparisons and calculations. Microprocessors also have small areas to hold data called registers. Microprocessors are normally a single integrated circuit.

KEY WORD

microprocessor: an integrated circuit that is used in monitoring and control systems

Table 3.4 identifies the advantages and disadvantages of using a microprocessor in control technologies.

Advantages	Disadvantages
They can be programmed to execute several different tasks.	There is a limit on the size of the data they can process.

Advantages	Disadvantages
They are small so can be easily built into different technologies.	They can overheat if too much demand is placed on them and may need cooling.
They can process data immediately.	They may break and the control system stops working.

Table 3.4: Advantages and disadvantages of microprocessors in control technologies.

How does a control system work?

Sensors, microprocessors and actuators are programmed to interact with each other to create a control system (see Figure 3.12).

There are several stages in the process of a control system:

1 The sensor collects the data at set time intervals, for example once every minute.

2 The data is sent to a microprocessor.

3 The microprocessor will analyse the data. This could involve comparing it to a pre-stored value or range of values.

4 If the data does not match the pre-stored value, the microprocessor will send a signal to an actuator or device.

5 The actuator or device will trigger any action that needs to be taken.

An example of this type of system could be an air-conditioning system (or a central heating system).

Figure 3.12: Air conditioning is an example of a control system.

1   The user sets the temperature to 22 °C.

2   The value of 22 °C is stored.

3   A temperature sensor collects data about the ambient temperature in the room.

4   The data collected by the sensor is sent to the microprocessor. The data is converted from analogue to digital.

5   The microprocessor analyses each data sample sent to see whether it is equal to the stored value of 22.

6   If the data sample is greater than 22 °C, the microprocessor sends a signal to an actuator, triggering the system to increase the cooling function.

7   If the data sample is less than 22 °C, the microprocessor sends a signal to an actuator to trigger the system to increase the heating function.

8   If the data sample is equal to 22 °C, no action is taken.

9   The whole process is then repeated at a set time interval, for example, once every minute.

This list represents an **algorithm**, which is a set of instructions or steps to be followed to achieve a certain outcome, for this example of a control system.

KEY WORD

algorithm: a set of instructions or steps to be followed to achieve a certain outcome

This system could also be represented as a flowchart, as shown in Figure 3.13.

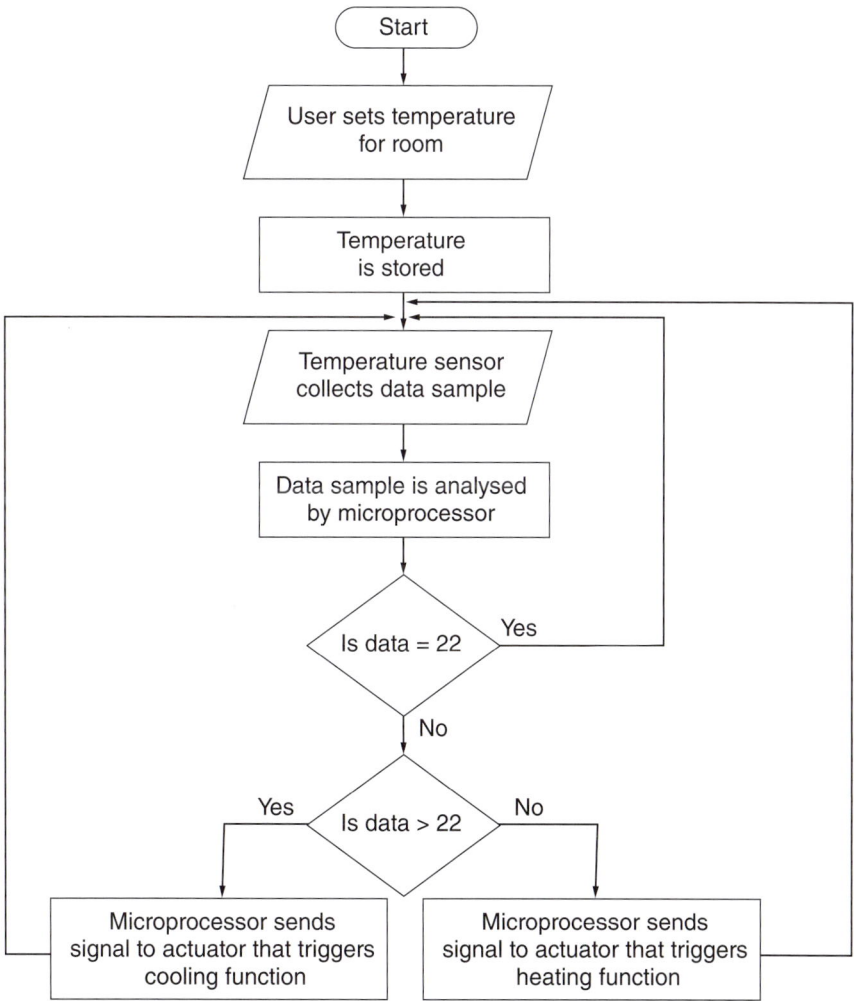

Figure 3.13: Temperature control flowchart.

Real-world example of a control system – growing crops

A farm that grows fruit and vegetables makes use of many different control systems. The farmer relies on these systems to make sure that the produce is kept in the correct conditions to ensure they grow. It would be a huge task for a farmer to constantly check their produce, so they rely on control systems to do this (see Figure 3.14).

One control system could control the conditions within the greenhouses. The correct level of light and temperature needs to be maintained. The control systems will incorporate light sensors, temperature sensors, microprocessors and actuators to maintain the correct conditions. The farmer wants to make sure the temperature is between 22 and 25 °C:

1   The control system uses a temperature sensor to regularly read the temperature within the greenhouse.

2   The readings are sent to a microprocessor. They will need to be converted from analogue data to digital data to be processed by the microprocessor.

3   The microprocessor compares the reading to the set range.

4   If the reading is within the range, no further action is taken.

5   If the reading is greater than 25 °C, the microprocessor sends a signal to an actuator that could drive an action, such as open a window to the greenhouse to allow cooler air to enter and lower the temperature.

6   If the reading is less than 22 °C, the microprocessor sends a signal to an actuator that could drive an action, such as turn on a heater in the greenhouse to warm the air temperature.

7   The whole process is repeated.

Question

5   a   Draw a flowchart to demonstrate how the environment control system in the greenhouse will operate.

    b   The control system is missing two vital processes. What do you think they are?

Figure 3.14: Farmers check the growth of the lettuce crop in an environmentally controlled greenhouse.

Real-world example of a control system – detecting a burglar

A jewellery store uses three main control systems to keep its stock safe and secure when the business is closed. The first security control system detects if a burglar enters the store through a door or window. Infrared beams of light are run across each doorway and window. If one of these beams is broken, an alarm will sound and metal bars will close every door and window, trapping the burglar inside the store.

Question

6   Write an algorithm to demonstrate how this entry detection control system will operate.

The second security control system detects if a window is broken by a burglar trying to enter the store. The sound of breaking glass is measured. If the sound of breaking glass is detected, the alarm will sound again.

Questions

7 Draw a flowchart to demonstrate how the broken glass detection control system will operate.

8 Either write an algorithm or draw a flowchart to demonstrate how the glass cabinet control system will operate.

The jewellery store's third security control system detects if any of the jewellery glass cabinets are opened by a burglar. The weight of the glass for each cabinet is 5 kg. If any of the glass is lifted up the alarm will sound and the bars will close every door and window.

ACTIVITY 3.03

1 In a group of five, each choose one of the following control systems where microprocessor-controlled/computer-controlled technology is used:

- control of traffic/pedestrian flow, including smart motorways
- car park barriers
- traffic lights (see Figure 3.15)
- wireless sensor and actuator networks
- smart homes.

2 Describe.

- The sensors used in the control system
- The processing or analysis that the microprocessors carry out
- The actuators and outputs of the system

3 Share the information you have found with your group. As a group, check any flowcharts and make corrections if you need to.

Figure 3.15: Traffic lights control the flow of vehicles and pedestrians on this busy street.

Advantages and disadvantages of control technologies

Control technologies automate many things. Table 3.5 lists some advantages and disadvantages of using control technologies.

Advantages	Disadvantages
Operate continuously with little need for humans.	Can be expensive to build.
Can operate in dangerous or remote places.	Can lead to people being too trusting of them and ignoring when things look wrong because the control system says everything is functioning correctly.
Can take accurate measurements repeatedly without a break.	It may be unclear who is responsible if things go wrong.
Can process data very quickly and react instantly.	Can be expensive to maintain.
	Often need back-up systems to ensure safety in critical systems, for example aeroplanes.

Table 3.5: Advantages and disadvantages of control technologies.

REFLECTION

What were the most difficult parts of control technologies to learn about? How did you come up with strategies to remember them? Why did this work well for you?

ACTIVITY 3.04

1   Copy Table 3.5. Research additional advantages and disadvantages to using control technology and add them to your table.

2   Create a presentation on the following:

    a   an example of where a control system has benefited humans, for example it has kept humans safe, prevented loss of life, or stopped a natural disaster

    b   an example of where a control system has led to a serious incident, for example a plane crash or explosion.

3   Hold a class debate on the following question: Should we fully trust microprocessor/computer-controlled technologies? Refer to the list of advantages and disadvantages that you have researched and your examples.

PRACTICE QUESTIONS

1   Define the role of a sensor. [1]

2   Define the role of a microprocessor. [1]

3   Define the role of an actuator. [1]

4   Describe how a sensor is calibrated using two-point calibration. [3]

5   State two advantages of using a microprocessor in a control system. [2]

6   Explain the difference between monitoring technologies and control technologies. [4]

7   Describe how a control system using touch sensors can be used to make sure the level of cooling liquid in a nuclear power plant is maintained at a certain level. [5]

8   Draw a flowchart to represent a control system with the following requirements:

- A proximity sensor is used in a mobile phone.
- The proximity sensor measures the immediate environment, using infrared (IR), to see if it is close to a human ear.
- If an IR level of 12 microns is detected, the screen on the mobile turns off. The screen will immediately turn back on again when the IR level reduces. [6]

SUMMARY CHECKLIST

☐   I can identify a variety of different sensors and explain how they are used in monitoring systems.

☐   I can identify a variety of different sensors and actuators and explain how they are used in control systems.

☐   I can explain how sensors are calibrated, using different types of calibration.

☐   I can draw a flowchart to represent a control system.

☐   I can write an algorithm to represent a control system.

☐   I can explain at least two different advantages and disadvantages of control technologies.

PROJECT

Figure 3.16: A view of the Earth from the surface of the moon.

You are part of a mission to live on the moon. You will use monitoring and control systems to ensure that the astronauts are safe as they travel to the moon. You will also need monitoring and control systems to make sure they are safe when they are living on the moon.

Create a presentation for the head of the Space Agency and:

1   List three monitoring and control systems you will use on the flight to the moon.

2   List three monitoring and control systems you may need for living on the moon. Try to pick different systems.

3   Determine what sensors each system will use.

4   Determine what calibration you will use. How often will you calibrate the sensors?

5   Determine what types of actuators will be used in the control systems.

6   List the advantages and disadvantages for each control system.

7   Write flowcharts or algorithms for the control systems that you have used.

› Chapter 4

Algorithms and flowcharts

LEARNING INTENTIONS

By the end of this chapter, you will be able to:

- write and edit a given algorithm
- write an algorithm using pseudocode to solve a given problem
- draw a basic program flowchart to solve a given problem
- edit a basic given flowchart
- identify errors in an algorithm/program flowchart.

BEFORE YOU START

- Do you have experience of following instructions and creating sequences of instructions for someone to follow?
- Do you have any experience of block programming in languages such as Scratch, or of controlling a turtle on screen such as through Logo?

Introduction

In this chapter, you will learn how to develop algorithms to solve problems in a form that a computer could follow. All computer programs are a series of algorithms that are written in a specific way that the computer's processor can then follow one at a time.

KEY WORDS

flowchart: a set of symbols with commands used to represent a problem

pseudocode: a simple language used to write an algorithm

4.1 Algorithms

An algorithm is set of steps, or commands. We write algorithms to solve problems. Algorithms can be very complicated, such as those that control a spacecraft. Algorithms can also be very simple, like following a recipe to make a cookie (see Figure 4.1).

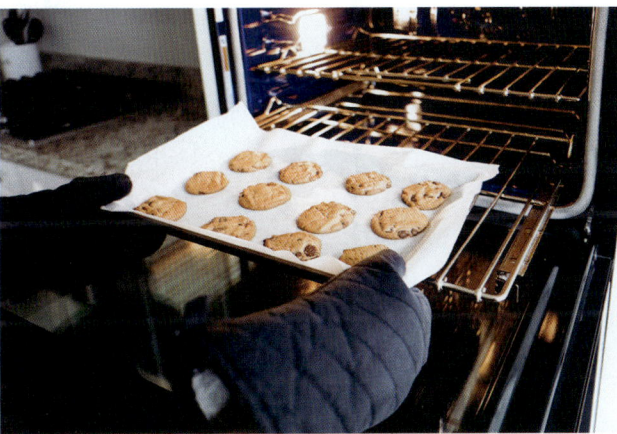

Figure 4.1: Baking cookies is an algorithm because you have to follow a set of instructions in a specific order.

We design algorithms using a **flowchart** and we may also use **pseudocode**. Pseudocode has no specific syntax. It doesn't have to follow a set format, but it is more structured than English sentences. We usually design an algorithm before creating it as a computer program.

We can use an algorithm to show the steps needed to walk through a maze. The instructions you might use are:

FD Move forward a number of spaces – for example, FD 5 would move forwards five spaces

BK Move backward a number of spaces – for example, BK 4 would move backwards four spaces

RT Turn right 90 degrees

LT Turn left 90 degrees

You start in the space labelled 'Start' in the maze shown in Figure 4.2, facing to the right.

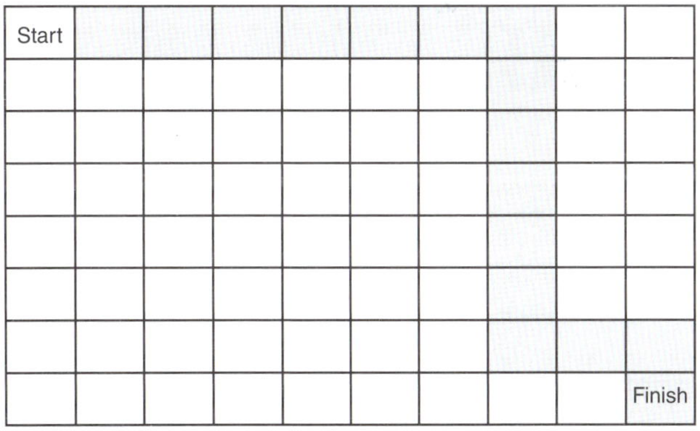

Figure 4.2: Maze 1, start.

To get to 'Finish' you would need to follow these steps:

Step 1:	FD 7	**Step 5:**	FD 2
Step 2:	RT	**Step 6:**	RT
Step 3:	FD 6	**Step 7:**	FD 1
Step 4:	LT		

WORKED EXAMPLE 4.01

You are on Start, facing to the right.

You need to move from Start to Finish. Let's write an algorithm for the maze shown in Figure 4.3.

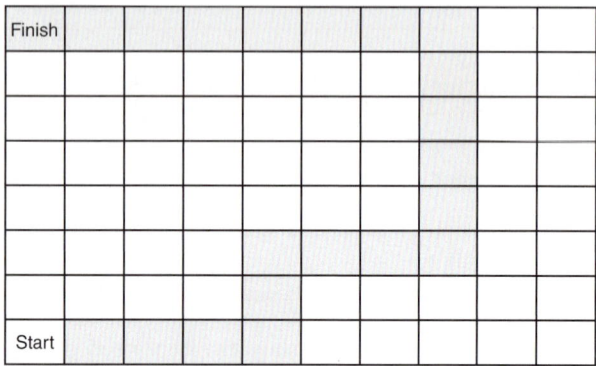

Figure 4.3: Maze 2, start.

You are facing to the right so need to count how many grey spaces there are until you need to turn. There are four spaces, so the command is:

FD 4 (see Figure 4.4).

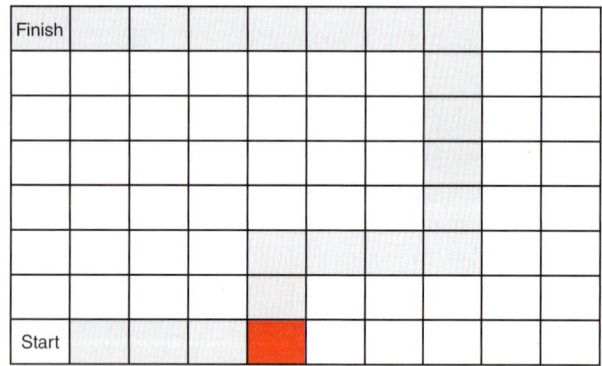

Figure 4.4: Maze 2, FD4.

You need to turn so you are facing up – this means turning to the left, 90 degrees.

The command is

LT

How many spaces forward? 2

FD 2

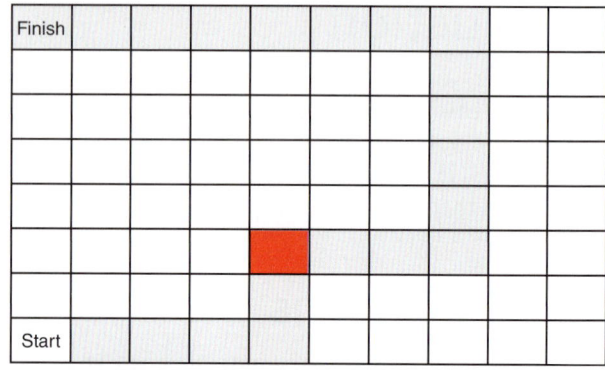

Figure 4.5: Maze 2, FD 4, LT, FD 2.

You have reached the red square shown in Figure 4.5. You need to face to the right again, so:

RT

The next turn is three spaces to the red square in Figure 4.6:

FD 3

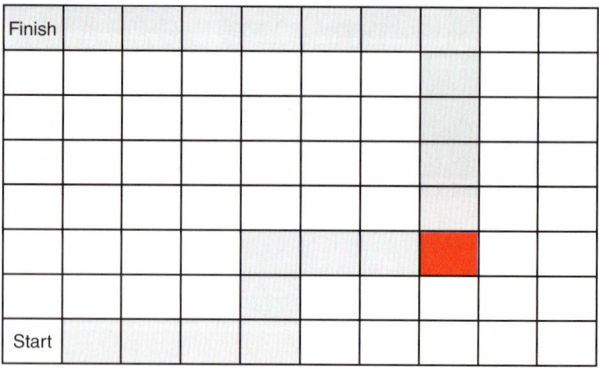

Figure 4.6: Maze 2 – FD 4, LT, FD 2, RT, FD 3.

CONTINUED

You need to face up, so you are turning left again:

LT

Now you need to move forwards five spaces:

FD 5

You've reached the red square shown in Figure 4.7.

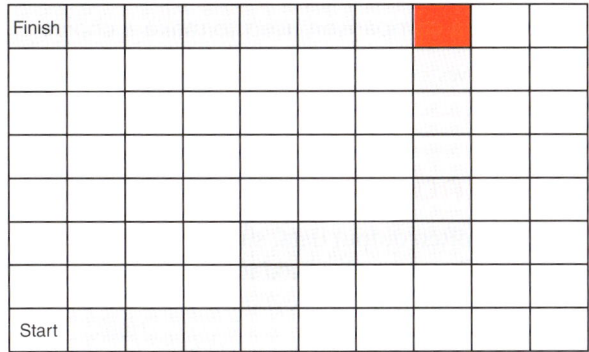

Figure 4.7: Maze 2, FD 4, LT, FD 2, RT, FD 3, LT9, FD 5.

To get to the Finish in Figure 4.8, you need to turn left:

LT

Then move forward seven spaces:

FD 7

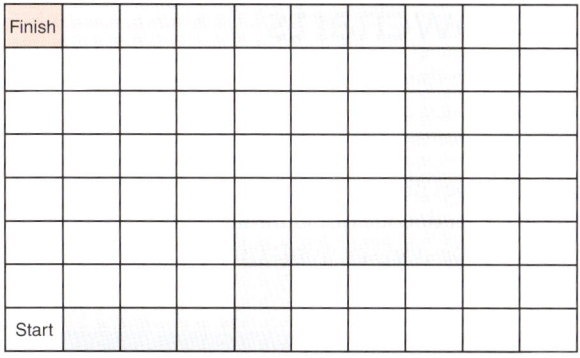

Figure 4.8: Maze 2, finish.

Together, the algorithm becomes:

FD 4, LT, FD 2, RT, FD 3, LT, FD 5, LT, FD 7

Questions

1   What is meant by an algorithm?

2   How can an algorithm be represented?

UNPLUGGED ACTIVITY 4.01

Write an algorithm to move from Start to Finish in the maze shown in Figure 4.9.

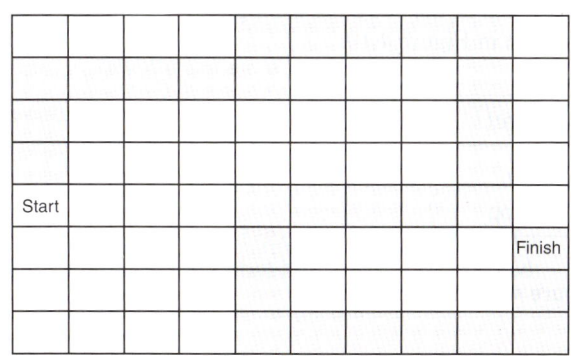

Figure 4.9: Maze 3, Start.

WORKED EXAMPLE 4.02

An algorithm needs to ask a user to enter their name. It should take their name as an input and then welcome them by name, for example 'Welcome Sasha'.

Let's draw a flowchart for the algorithm.

Start by identifying the steps required.

Step 1: Ask them to enter their name.

Step 2: Take their name as input.

Step 3: Welcome them by their name.

Then identify what type of symbols these steps need.

Step 1: Ask them to enter their name.

   Output

Step 2: Take their name as input.

   Input and store in variable

Step 3: Welcome them by their name.

   Output including variable

CONTINUED

Draw the flowchart following the steps identified (see Figure 4.18).

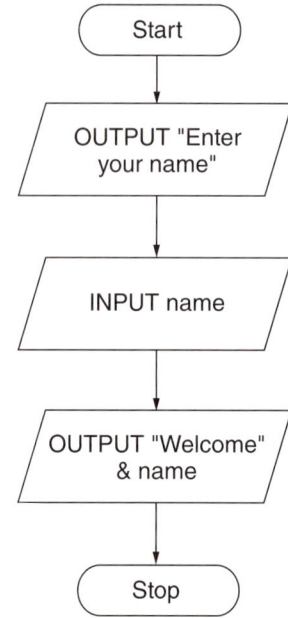

Figure 4.18: Flowchart 'Welcome'.

WORKED EXAMPLE 4.03

Convert the flowchart in Figure 4.18 into pseudocode.

Take each statement from within the flowchart and write it on its own line.

```
OUTPUT "Enter your name"
INPUT name
OUTPUT "Welcome" & name
```

Questions

3   Draw the symbol for Start and Stop in a flowchart.

4   Describe the stages in the flowchart in Figure 4.19.

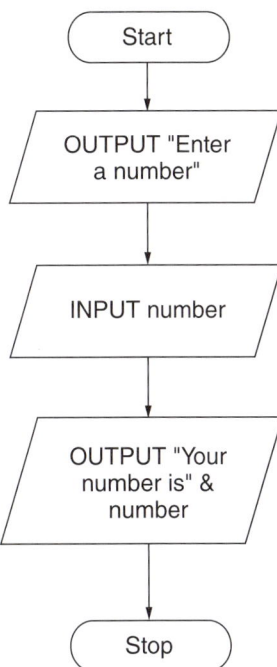

Figure 4.19: Flowchart: enter a number.

Operator	Description	Example
+	Addition	`myNumber = 10 + 3`
–	Subtraction	`myNumber = 10 – 3`
*	Multiplication	`myNumber = 10 * 3`
/	Division	`myNumber = 10 / 3`
^	Power of	`myNumber = 10 ^ 3`
MOD	**Modulus division** (gives the remainder)	`10 MOD 3 = 1` `20 MOD 8 = 4`
DIV	**Integer division** (gives the whole number)	`10 DIV 3 = 3` `20 DIV 6 = 3`

Table 4.1: Arithmetic operators used to perform mathematical calculations.

KEY WORDS

arithmetic operator: a symbol, or symbols, that perform a mathematical calculation

modulus division: when the remainder is given from a division

integer division: where only the whole number is given from a division

---

UNPLUGGED ACTIVITY 4.02

1 Convert the flowchart in Figure 4.19 into pseudocode.

2 An algorithm needs to take a word as an input, and then output the same word.

   Draw a flowchart for this algorithm.

3 An algorithm needs to tell a joke. It should output the joke, and let the user give an answer, before outputting the actual answer.

   Create a pseudocode algorithm for the problem.

Using flowcharts

Processes are shown in rectangular boxes (see the example in Figure 4.20).

```
Process
```

Figure 4.20: Process box.

Processes

A process is an action that is performed. For example, you might add two variables together, or subtract a number from a variable.

There are different types of mathematical processes that may be performed. Table 4.1 shows the **arithmetic operators** used to perform mathematical calculations.

The mathematical calculations can make use of numbers, and/or variables. For example:

`myNumber = 10 + 3`	`myNumber` now stores 13
`myNumber = myNumber + 3`	`myNumber` now stores 16 (it already had 13 in and now has another 3)
`myNumber = myNumber + myNumber`	`myNumber` now stores 32 (it already had 16 in it, and it was added to itself, so 16 + 16 = 32)

Putting a value into a variable is called **assignment**.

In the process box shown in Figure 4.21, two numbers are multiplied together and stored in a variable.

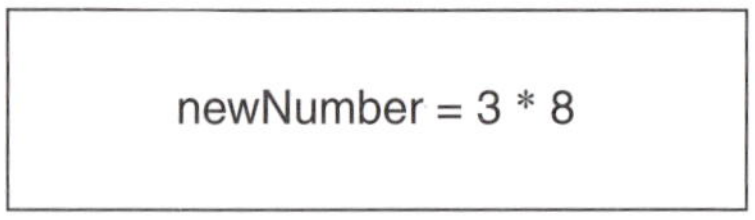

newNumber = 3 * 8

Figure 4.21: Assignment in process box.

Figure 4.22 shows a flowchart in two parts. Sometimes, flowcharts are long and may not fit on one page, or it may be clearer to split them into parts. To do this, we need to show where part of the flowchart stops, and the next part starts.

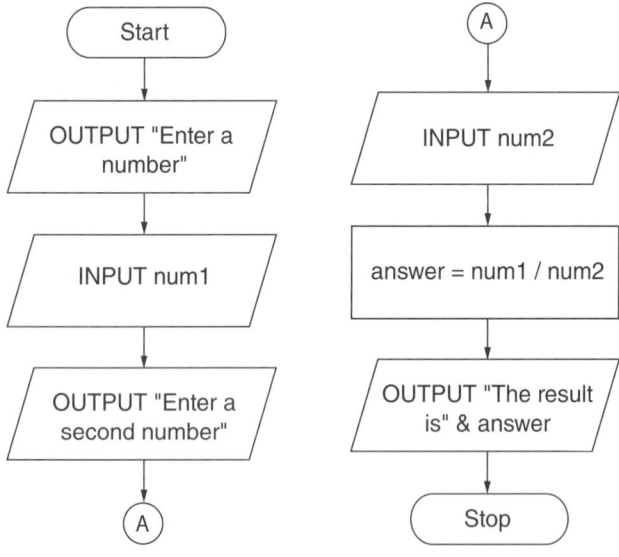

Figure 4.22: Flowchart: arithmetic calculation.

When flowcharts get too long, we can split them into parts. In Figure 4.22 we have split the algorithm into two parts. We use a **connector symbol** to join them together and show which parts of the flowchart are linked.

The algorithm in Figure 4.22 takes in two numbers (`num1` and `num2`), divides `num1` by `num2` and stores the result in `answer`. It then outputs the message 'The result is' and the value in `answer`.

Using pseudocode

Processes use the same structure as in a flowchart, but without the box. The process is shown in Figure 4.23:

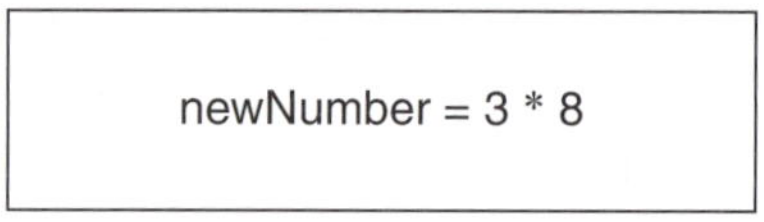

newNumber = 3 * 8

Figure 4.23: Assignment in process box.

would become this:

```
newNumber = 3 * 8
```

WORKED EXAMPLE 4.04

A program needs to ask a person's age, then tell them how old they will be in 50 years.

Let's draw a flowchart for the algorithm.

Start by identifying the steps required.

Step 1: Ask them to enter their age.

Step 2: Take the age as input.

Step 3: Add 50 to their age.

Step 4: Output the new age.

CONTINUED

Identify what type of symbols these steps need.

Step 1:   Ask them to enter their age.

> **Output**

Step 2:   Take the age as input.

> **Input and store in a variable**

Step 3:   Add 50 to their age.

> **Add 50 to the variable and store the result**

Step 4:   Output their new age.

> **Output variable**

Draw the flowchart following the steps identified (see Figure 4.24).

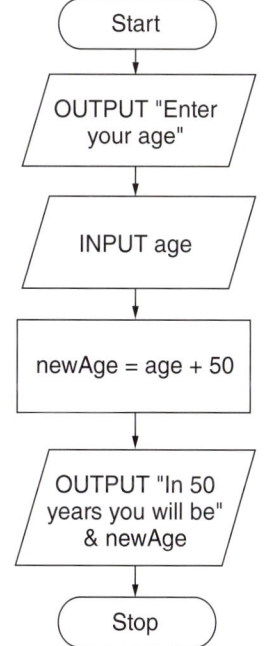

Figure 4.24: Flowchart: new age calculator.

WORKED EXAMPLE 4.05

Let's convert the flowchart in Figure 4.24 into pseudocode.

Take each line and write it on a separate line.

```
OUTPUT "Enter your age"
INPUT age
newAge = age + 50
OUTPUT "In 50 years your will be" & newAge
```

Questions

5   What is a process?

6   What action does the operator ^ process?

7   Write a statement to multiply 3 by 7.

8   Describe the stages in the flowchart in Figure 4.25.

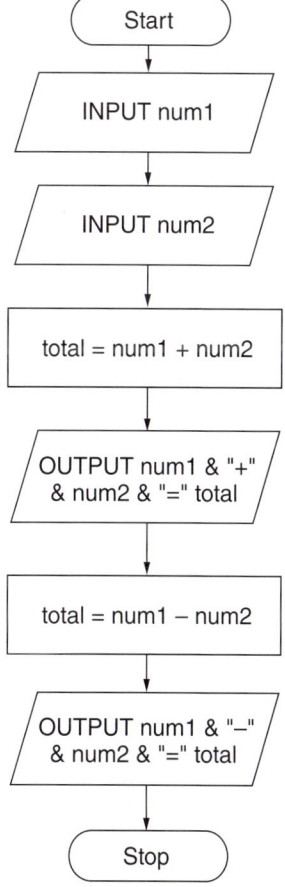

Figure 4.25: Flowchart: arithmetic calculation.

UNPLUGGED ACTIVITY 4.03

1 Convert the flowchart in Figure 4.25 into pseudocode.

2 An algorithm needs to take three numbers as input. Add them together and output the result. Then divide the total by the quantity of numbers and output the average.

Draw a flowchart for this algorithm.

3 Convert your algorithm from task 2 into pseudocode.

Decisions

A decision is also known as **comparison** and **selection**. Comparisons are either true or false. For example, 100 is greater than 20 is TRUE. 20 is less than 15 is FALSE. The result of the comparison will lead to a selection. If the result is true, then we will select one set of instructions to follow. If the answer is false, we will select another set of instructions to follow.

KEY WORDS

comparison: comparing two items of data resulting in true or false

selection: use of a conditional statement to decide a course of action or which section of code to run

A comparison needs two sides of the argument and a comparison symbol. Table 4.2 shows common comparison operators.

Operator	Description	Example
>	Greater than	10 > 5 is true
		5 > 10 is false
<	Less than	10 < 5 is false
		5 < 10 is true
>=	Greater than or equal to	10 >= 5 is true
		10 >= 10 is true
		5 >= 10 is false

Operator	Description	Example
<=	Less than or equal to	10 <= 5 is false
		10 <= 10 is true
		5 <= 10 is true
=	Equal to	10 = 5 is false
		10 = 10 is true
!= or <>	Not equal to	10 != 10 is false
		5 <> 10 is true

Table 4.2: Comparison operators.

Either side of the operator can be a number or a variable.

Using flowcharts

Flowcharts often use **conditional branching**. Sometimes a flowchart may make a single decision on its own. For example, if a price is greater than a certain amount then we will apply a discount.

However, some flowcharts need to make more than one decision after another. For example, if the price of the item is greater than a certain amount AND if the person buying the item is a member of the shopping store.

Single selection is where one decision is made on its own. Multiple selection is where a decision is followed immediately by another decision.

KEY WORD

conditional branching: using comparison operators to make decisions in flowcharts, which affect the flow of logic

Single selection

The selection must be in the form of a question, for example 'is 10 > 5?' This is because it has two results: true and false.

The selection flowchart symbol is a diamond (see Figure 4.26).

Figure 4.26: Selection box.

There are two options from a selection box: True and False, or Yes and No. This means selection has two arrows (two flow lines) that need to be labelled, as in the example in Figure 4.27.

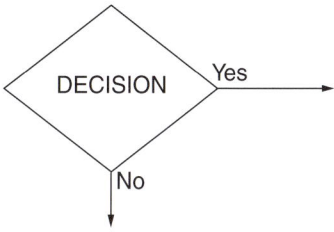

Figure 4.27: Selection box with options.

Figure 4.28 shows a flowchart with a single selection. It checks if someone's age is over 18 and then prints a message, depending on the answer.

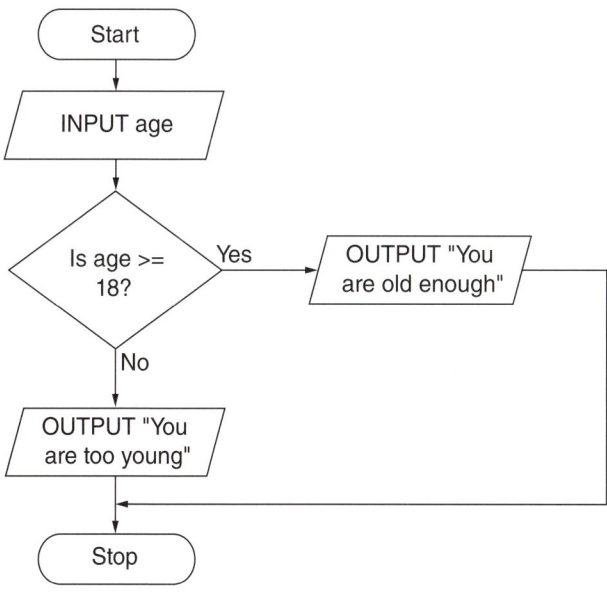

Figure 4.28: Flowchart with selection box.

This flowchart starts by the user inputting an age. The decision statement asks if age is greater than, or equal to, 18. If the result is Yes, then it outputs 'You are old enough'; if it is No it outputs 'You are too young'.

Multiple selection

If you have multiple options, then you will need multiple decisions, as shown in the example in Figure 4.29.

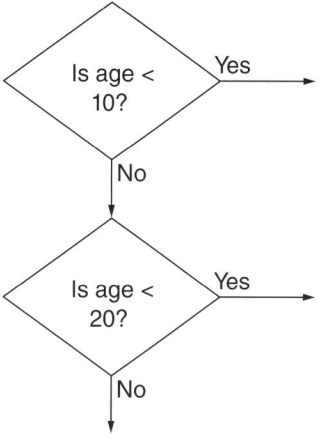

Figure 4.29: Flowchart with multiple selection boxes.

The first decision is 'If age is less than 10?' If it is not, then it goes straight to another decision and asks whether age is less than 20.

Using pseudocode for decision making

IF...ELSE...ENDIF

Selection uses the keyword IF and THEN. The question 'Is' in the flowchart is replaced with IF, and the '?' with THEN. All the code that runs when the condition is true goes beneath the IF and this is finished with an ENDIF to show where it ends.

For example, if the value in age is more than 18, then the output message will be displayed.

```
IF age > 18 THEN
    OUTPUT("You are old enough")
ENDIF
```

An IF statement can have an ELSE. This is what happens if the condition is true. For example, if the age is not more than 18, then 'You are not old enough' will be displayed.

```
IF age > 18 THEN
    OUTPUT("You are old enough")
ELSE
    OUTPUT("You are not old enough")
ENDIF
```

CASE...END CASE

This is a different selection statement. This is used when you are checking the value of one variable and you have many different values you want to check it against.

CASE uses the keyword SELECT, followed by the identifier of the variable you are checking. Then it has the keyword CASE followed by the condition.

For example, if you are checking if a menu choice is 1, 2 or 3:

```
SELECT menuChoice
    CASE 1: OUTPUT "You chose 1"
    CASE 2: OUTPUT "You chose 2"
    CASE 3: OUTPUT "You chose 3"
```

A CASE statement can perform comparisons other than equals to, but this time you need to include the variable name to make it clear what the comparison is.

There is also a default keyword for CASE, where the code in this will run if none of the conditions have been met.

```
SELECT symbol
    CASE "+":
    result = value1 + value2
    CASE "-":
    result = value1 - value2
    CASE "*":
    result = value1 * value2
    CASE "/":
    result = value1 / value2
    CASE DEFAULT:
    OUTPUT "Invalid symbol"
```

WORKED EXAMPLE 4.06

An algorithm needs to take two numbers as input, and output that which is the largest.

Let's draw a flowchart for the algorithm.

Start by identifying the steps required.

Step 1: Ask the user to input two numbers.

Step 2: Input two numbers.

Step 3: Check if the first number is larger than the second.

Step 4: Output the first number if it is.

Step 5: Output the second number if it isn't.

Identify what type of symbols these steps need.

Step 1: Ask the user to input two numbers.

Output

Step 2: Input two numbers.

Input and store in a variable

Step 3: Check if the first number is larger than the second.

If first > second

Step 4: Output the first number if it is.

Output first number

Step 5: Output the second number if it isn't.

Output second number

The flowchart is shown in Figure 4.30.

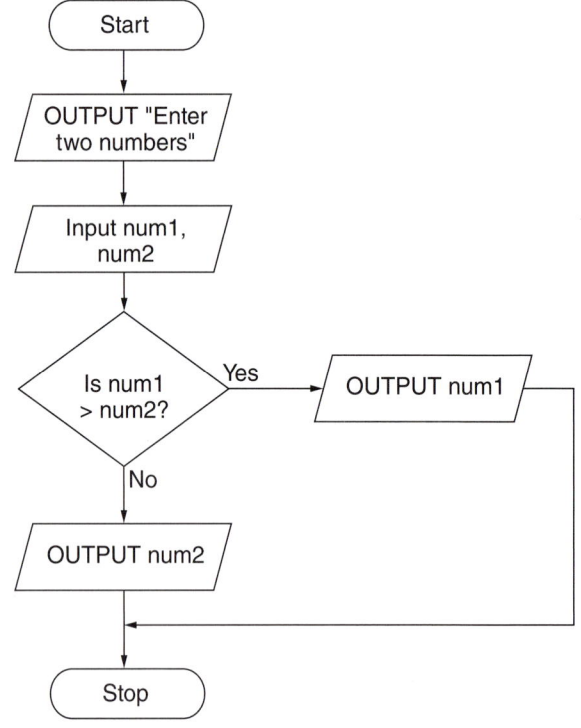

Figure 4.30: Flowchart: compare two numbers.

WORKED EXAMPLE 4.07

Convert the flowchart in Figure 4.30 into pseudocode.

Write each line separately. Only one value can be input at a time.

Replace Is with an `IF` statement.

```
OUTPUT "Enter two numbers"

INPUT num1

INPUT num2

IF num1 > num2 THEN

    OUTPUT num1

ELSE

    OUTPUT num2

ENDIF
```

DISCUSSION POINT

Which system is easier to show multiple decisions in: flowcharts or pseudocode?

Questions

9   How many arrows must come out of a selection symbol in a flowchart?

10   Define selection.

11   What is the Boolean value of 956 > 856?

12   What is the Boolean value of 123 < 123?

13   Is 55 = 66?

ACTIVITY 4.04

This activity may be completed using either flowchart software or paper and pen.

1   Describe the stages in the flowchart in Figure 4.31.

2   Convert the flowchart in task 1 into pseudocode.

CONTINUED

3   An algorithm needs to take three numbers as input, and output the smallest.

   Draw a flowchart for this algorithm.

4   Convert your flowchart from task 3 into pseudocode.

5   An algorithm needs to take two numbers as input, then subtract the smallest from the largest.

   Create a pseudocode algorithm for the problem using an IF statement.

6   Replace the IF statement in task 5 with a CASE ENDCASE statement.

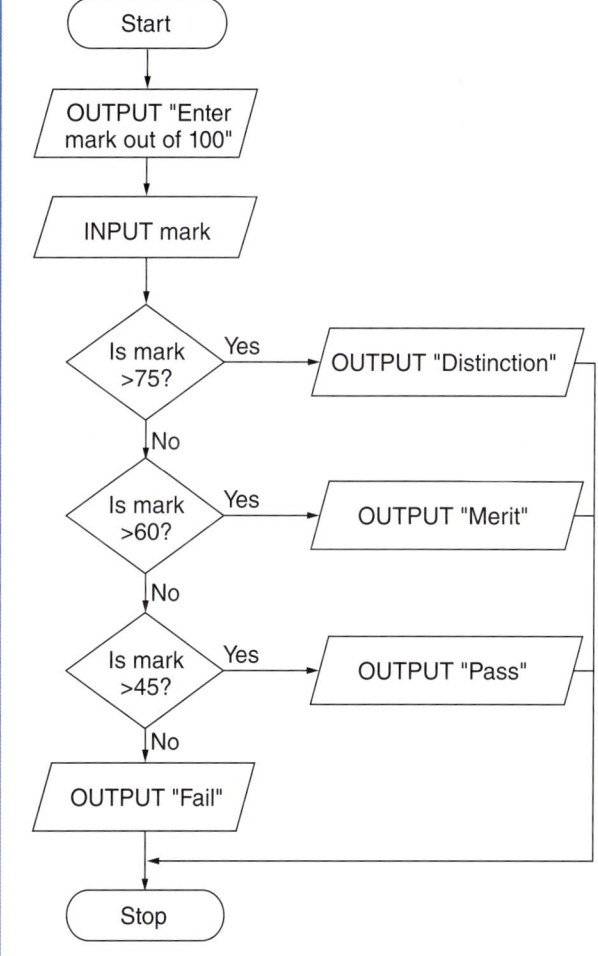

Figure 4.31: Flowchart with comments.

Looping

Looping is another word for repetition. Looping is doing the same thing several times. It is often called **iteration**.

Loops are often used in two scenarios:

1   You want to iterate a fixed number of times (for example, four times). This is a **count-controlled** loop.

2   You want to iterate until something happens (for example, a specific condition is reached). This is a **condition-controlled loop**.

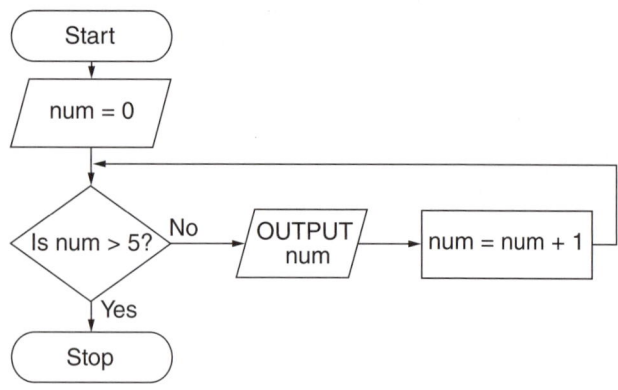

Figure 4.32: Flowchart with counter.

In the example in Figure 4.32, the counter variable is num. num is set to start at 0. Following the arrows, it keeps increasing by one until num is greater than five, at which point the algorithm stops.

Using pseudocode

A **FOR...NEXT loop** is a count-controlled loop. You need to know what number to start with, and when you will end. The loop increments the number each time through.

> **KEY WORDS**
>
> **iteration:** repeating a section of code for a fixed number of times or until a required outcome is achieved
>
> **count-controlled loop:** a loop where you know the number of times it will run
>
> **condition-controlled loop:** a loop that runs based on a condition, not the number of times it will run

Count controlled

Using flowcharts

A count-controlled loop needs a counter to keep track of the number of repetitions you have done (the number of loops). The counter is a variable. Before you start the loop, the counter needs to be set to the starting value (usually 0 or 1). We then **increment** the counter (this means add 1 to it) each time the loop runs.

> **KEY WORDS**
>
> **increment:** add 1 to something
>
> **FOR...NEXT loop:** a count-controlled loop

In this example, the variable counter starts at 0 and continues until it is 9.

```
FOR counter = 0 to 9
    OUTPUT counter
NEXT counter
```

WORKED EXAMPLE 4.08

An algorithm needs to ask the user to input the 10 marks of its students, and then output the average.

Start by identifying the steps required.

Step 1: Repeat 10 times.

Step 2: Ask the user to input a mark.

Step 3: Input the mark.

Step 4: Add the mark to a total.

Step 5: After all the marks are entered, calculate the average.

Step 6: Output the average.

Identify what type of symbols these steps need.

Step 1: Repeat 10 times.

> **Loop 10 times**

Step 2: Ask the user to input a mark.

> **Output**

Step 3: Input the mark.

> **Input and store in variable**

Step 4: Add the mark to a total.

> **Add input to total**

Step 5: After all marks are entered, calculate the average.

> **Total divided by 10**

Step 6: Output the average.

> **Output**

The flowchart is shown in Figure 4.33.

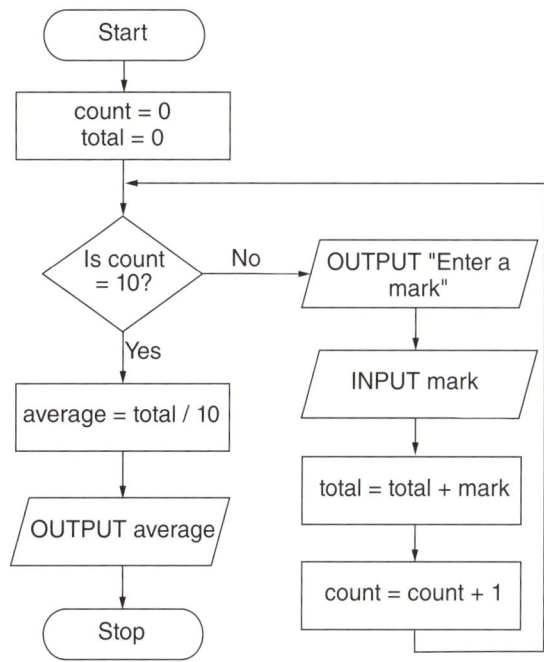

Figure 4.33: Flowchart: calculating average.

WORKED EXAMPLE 4.09

Now let's convert the flowchart in Figure 4.33 into pseudocode.

Write each line separately. Replace the count and selection with a `FOR` loop.

```
total = 0
FOR count = 0 TO 10
    OUTPUT "Enter a mark"
    INPUT mark
    total = total + mark
NEXT count
average = total / 10
OUTPUT average
```

Questions

14 What is iteration?

15 What is a count-controlled loop?

16 When is it appropriate to use a count-controlled loop?

17 What three elements do you need in a count-controlled loop?

UNPLUGGED ACTIVITY 4.05

1 Discuss each stage in the flowchart in Figure 4.34 with a partner and describe what happens. Make some notes.

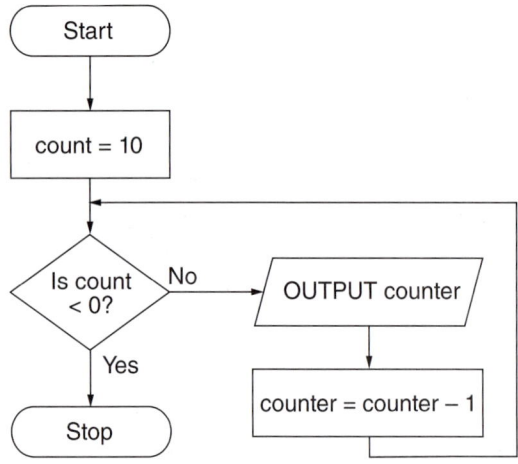

Figure 4.34: Flowchart with counter.

2 Convert Figure 4.34 into pseudocode.

3 An algorithm needs to output the 12-times table using iteration. Create a flowchart for the algorithm.

4 An algorithm needs to ask the user how many numbers to output. The algorithm should then print out the numbers from 1 to that number input.

5 Create a pseudocode algorithm for the problem.

Condition controlled

A condition-controlled loop looks like a count-controlled loop. But it doesn't need a counter. It uses a variable to hold a condition. This could be a number, a word or a TRUE/FALSE. Once the value it is comparing is the same as the value in the variable, the loop stops. Or, once the variable does not equal the value, the loop stops.

Using flowcharts

Figure 4.35 shows an example of a condition-controlled loop.

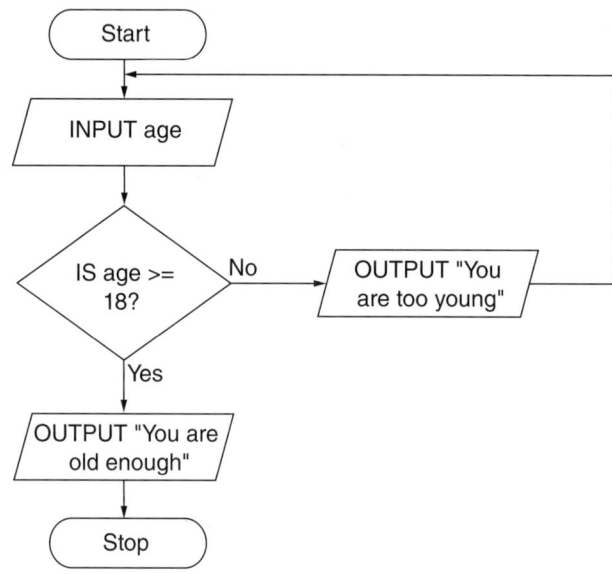

Figure 4.35: Flowchart with condition-controlled loop 1.

Figure 4.36 is an example of a **REPEAT...UNTIL loop**. This is a type of condition-controlled loop. It is also called a **post-check loop**. The code inside the loop will always run once because the condition is checked at the end (post-check) of the code. This means that the flowchart will always ask for the INPUT age. The statement value = value * 2 repeats until the value is = 100.

KEY WORDS

REPEAT...UNTIL loop: a condition-controlled loop that runs until the condition is true

post-check loop: the condition controlling the loop is checked at the end of the loop; therefore, the loop will always run at least one time

---

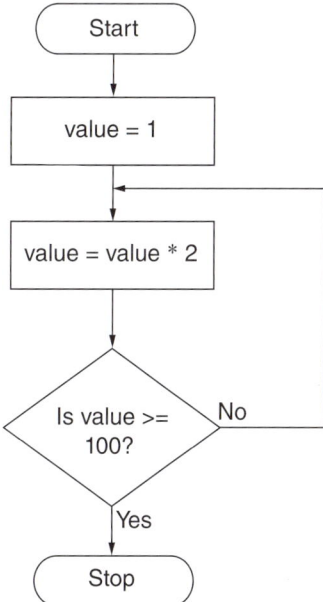

Figure 4.36: Flowchart with condition-controlled loop 2.

In this example, the loop keeps on going until the number in the variable value is greater than 100.

Using pseudocode

A **WHILE...ENDWHILE loop** is also a condition-controlled loop. It keeps looping while the condition is true. This is an example of a **pre-check loop** condition. In this example the loop checks to see if the age is less than 18 at the start of the loop. If it is, it will run INPUT age. If the value of age was set to 30 at the start, the loop would not run as the condition of age < 18 would be false.

```
age = 0

WHILE age < 18

    INPUT age

ENDWHILE
```

In this example, the loop continues until `value` is 100 or greater.

```
value = 1

WHILE value < 100

    value = value + value

ENDWHILE
```

DID YOU KNOW?

The word *post* means after. The word *pre* means before. It has links to Latin! You may recognise these in other words such as post-match and pre-match.

WORKED EXAMPLE 4.10

An algorithm needs to continually ask the user to input numbers, and add them to a total, until the total is more than 100, then output the total.

Start by identifying the steps required.

Step 1: Repeat until the total is more than 100.

Step 2: Ask the user to input a number.

Step 3: Input the number.

Step 4: Add the number to the total.

Step 5: When total is more than 100, output the total.

Identify what type of symbols these steps need.

Step 1: Repeat until the total is more than 100.

Loop until total > 100

Step 2: Ask the user to input a number.

Output

CONTINUED

Step 3: Input the number.

Input

Step 4: Add the number to the total.

Process – add number total

Step 5: When total is more than 100, output the total.

Output

The flowchart is shown in Figure 4.37.

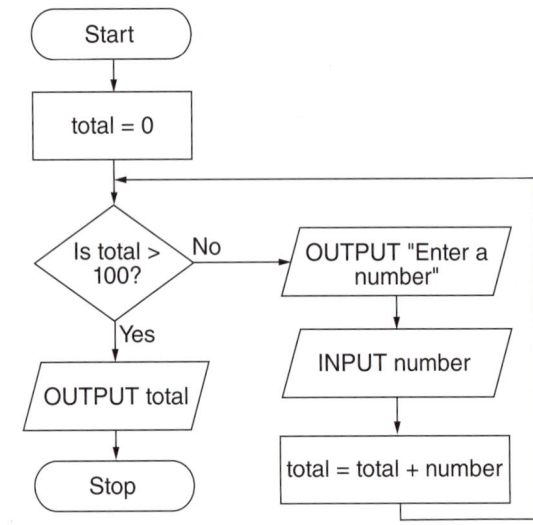

Figure 4.37: Flowchart: totalling number with control loop.

WORKED EXAMPLE 4.11

Now let's convert the flowchart in Figure 4.37 into pseudocode.

Replace the selection condition with a `WHILE…ENDWHILE` loop.

```
total = 0
WHILE total < 100
    OUTPUT "Enter a number"
    INPUT number
    total = total + number
ENDWHILE
OUTPUT total
```

Question

18 When should a condition-controlled loop be used?

ACTIVITY 4.06

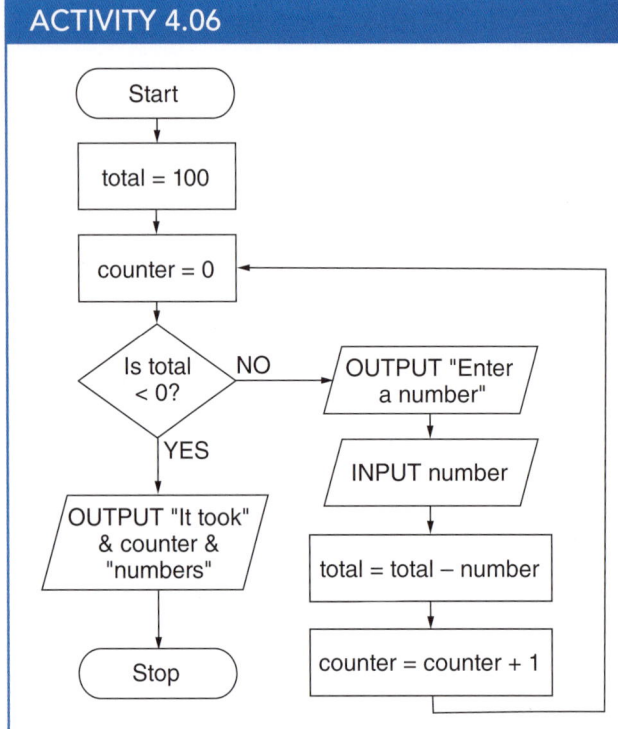

Figure 4.38: Flowchart with control loop.

1 Discuss each stage in the flowchart in Figure 4.38 with a partner and describe what happens. Make some notes.

2 Convert the flowchart into pseudocode.

3 An algorithm needs to ask the user to input a number between 100 and 200. Keep asking the user for the number until it is valid. Draw a flowchart for the algorithm.

4 An algorithm stores a number. The user has to guess what this number is. They keep guessing until they get it right. The algorithm then outputs the number of guesses the user took. Write a pseudocode algorithm for this problem.

FOR …NEXT…STEP

The `NEXT` command word moves to the next item. This is useful if we want to go through 10 items in a list.

```
FOR item
    PRINT item
NEXT item
```

However, sometimes we want to move through a list in a different way. For example, if we want to do addition by three:

```
FOR x = 0
    PRINT x
STEP 3
```

This would print 0, 3, 6, 9, 12. The STEP command increases X by three each time the FOR loop repeats.

Subroutines and procedures

A **subroutine** is a set of instructions which are not part of the main program. However, they can be 'called' from the main program. Calling a subroutine means the program runs that set of instructions. Subroutines have an identifier (a name). When a subroutine finishes running, the main program code carries on running from the same point that the subroutine was called.

There are two types of subroutine, a **procedure** and a **function**. A procedure performs a set task and then ends. A function performs a set task but also returns a value to the main program. You do not need to know about functions, or use them in this chapter, but it is useful to understand that a procedure is not the only form of a subroutine.

KEY WORDS

subroutine: a set of instructions that have an identifier and that are independent from the code; it is called from another part of the program and returns control when it has finished

procedure: a type of subroutine that does not return a value to the main program

function: a separate piece of code that has an identifier and performs a task; it can be called from elsewhere in the code and returns a value

---

Using flowcharts

A subroutine design is created in a separate flowchart. The separate flowchart starts with a 'Start' symbol, but we replace the name 'Start' with the name of the subroutine or identifier (see Figure 4.39).

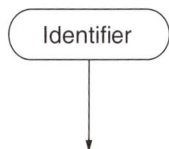

Figure 4.39: Subroutine identifier.

In the example shown in Figure 4.40, the subroutine is called OutputText. The symbol to call a subroutine is like a process box, but it also has parallel vertical lines on each side. The algorithm in Figure 4.40 begins at Start. There is then a subroutine symbol. The name of the subroutine we want to call goes in the box. This subroutine symbol tells the flowchart to go to Output. The subroutine Output runs. This outputs the word 'Hello' and then stops. When the subroutine ends, we go back to the first flowchart, and the main flowchart also then stops.

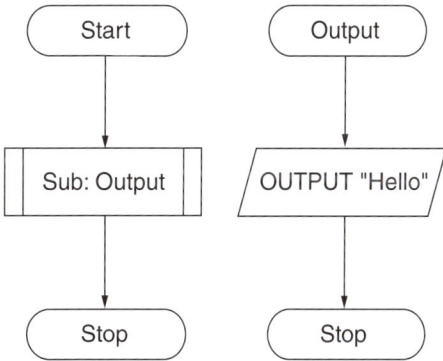

Figure 4.40: Flowchart calling subroutine.

Using pseudocode

In pseudocode, a subroutine needs an identifier or a name. It starts with the command `PROCEDURE` or `PROC` and ends with `ENDPROCEDURE` or `END PROC`.

In this example, the procedure is called `outputMessage()`. The brackets identify it as a subroutine. The procedure outputs the words `"Hello World"` and then returns control.

```
PROCEDURE outputMessage()

   OUTPUT "Hello World"

ENDPROCEDURE
```

A procedure is called by using the name of the procedure, for example:

```
OUTPUT "Calling procedure"

outputMessage()

OUTPUT "Finished"
```

Procedures are usually declared at the top of a program. Then the main program is written after. This makes it easier to see what procedures have been written in the program.

Parameters

You can send data to a subroutine; this data is called a **parameter**.

Using flowcharts

In this example, the main flowchart calls a subroutine. The subroutine calculates and outputs the variable 'number' (see Figure 4.41). The flowchart then carries on and checks if the number entered is greater than 10. If TRUE, the program stops. If FALSE then the program loops back and starts again.

However, in this program, there is a decision. If the number entered is 10 or less, it loops back to the start; or else, if the number is greater than 10, the program ends.

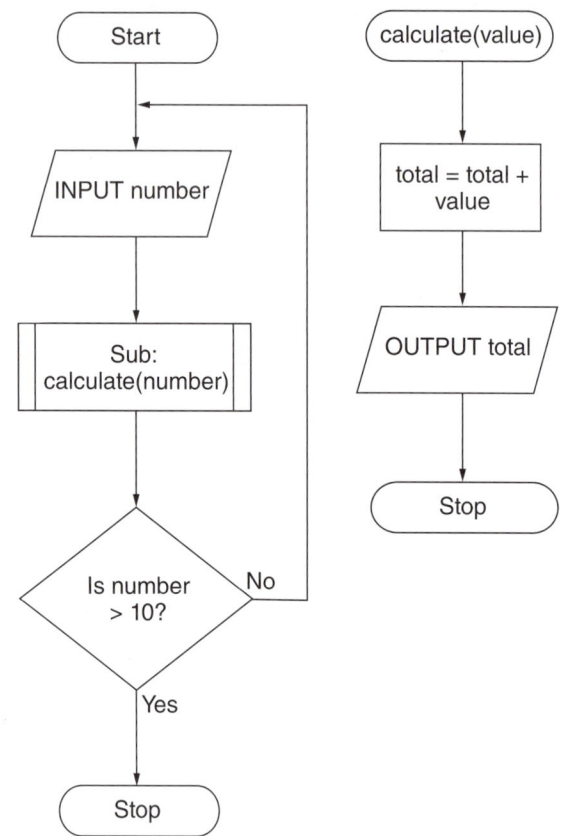

Figure 4.41: Flowchart calling calculate subroutine.

Using pseudocode

Parameters are identified within the brackets.

The procedure 'calculate' multiplies the number by two and then outputs the number before it ends.

```
PROCEDURE calculate(number)

   number = number * 2

   OUTPUT number

ENDPROCEDURE

INPUT number

calculate(number)
```

WORKED EXAMPLE 4.12

A program asks the user to input a number. It loops that several times. Each time through the loop, if the number is even, it calls a subroutine to output the number multiplied by itself. If the number is odd, it calls a subroutine to output the number to the power of itself.

Let's draw a flowchart for this algorithm.

As always, start by identifying the steps required.

Step 1: User inputs a number.

Step 2: Set the counter to 1.

Step 3: Loop until the counter is the number entered.

Step 4: If the number is even, call subroutine.

Step 5: Else if the number is odd, call subroutine.

Create a subroutine taking number as parameter.

a Multiply the parameter by itself.

b Output the result.

Create a subroutine taking number as parameter.

a Calculate the parameter to the power of itself.

b Output the result.

Identify what type of symbols these steps need.

Step 1: User inputs a number

> **Input number store in variable**

Step 2: Set counter to 1.

> **Process counter = 1**

Step 3: Loop until counter is the number entered.

> **Loop until counter = number**

Step 4: If the number is even call subroutine

> **If counter is even call multiply()**

Step 5: Else if the number is odd call subroutine

> **else call powerof()**

Create a subroutine taking number as parameter.

multiply(number)

a Multiply the parameter by itself.

> **Process number * number**

b Output the result.

> **Output result**

Create a subroutine taking number as parameter.

powerOf(number)

a Calculate the parameter to the power of itself

> **Process number ^ number**

b Output the result.

> **Output result**

Draw the flowchart for the subroutines.
The flowchart is shown in Figure 4.42.

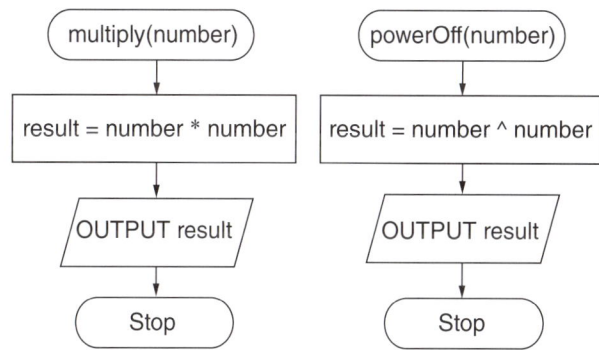

Figure 4.42: Subroutine flowcharts.

CONTINUED

Draw the flowchart for the main program. The flowchart is shown in Figure 4.43.

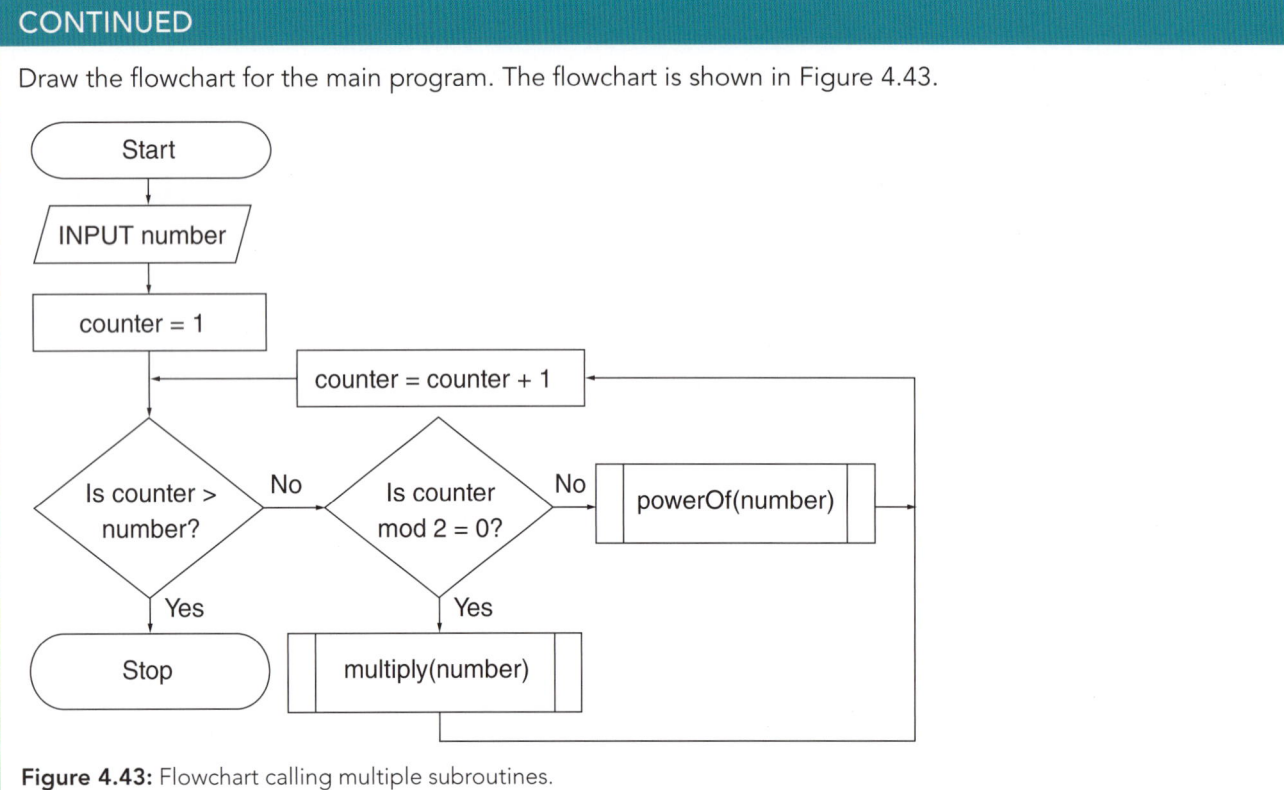

Figure 4.43: Flowchart calling multiple subroutines.

WORKED EXAMPLE 4.13

Now we can convert the subroutines and main program to pseudocode.

Write each subroutine first, then the main program.

```
PROCEDURE multiply(number)
   result = number * number
   OUTPUT result
ENDPROCEDURE
PROCEDURE powerOf(number)
   result = number ^ number
   OUTPUT result
ENDPROCEDURE
INPUT number
Counter = 1
WHILE counter < number
   IF counter MOD 2 = 0 THEN
      multiply(number)
   ELSE
      powerOf(number)
   ENDIF
ENDWHILE
```

Questions

19 What is a subroutine?

20 Why are subroutines used in programs?

21 What is a parameter?

UNPLUGGED ACTIVITY 4.07

1   Describe what the flowcharts a–d in Figure 4.44 show.

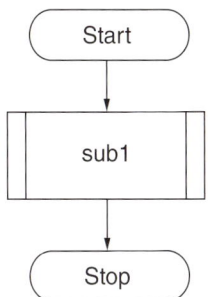

Flowchart **a**

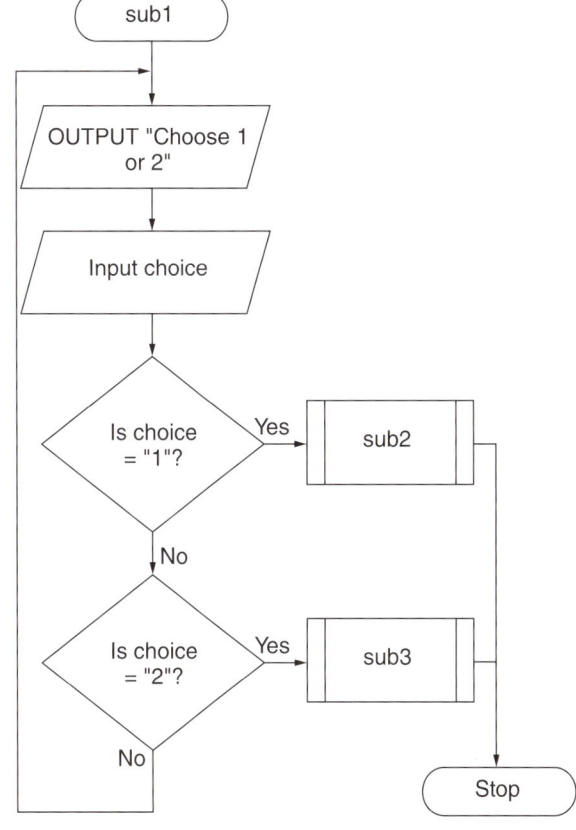

Flowchart **b**

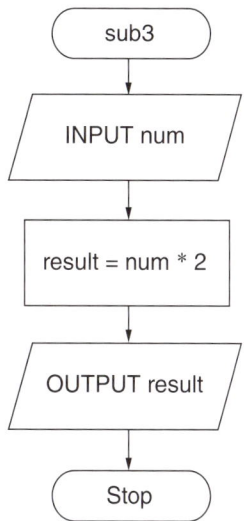

Flowchart **c**

Flowchart **d**

Figure 4.44: Flowcharts a–d.

2   Convert the flowcharts in task **1** into pseudocode.

3   Create a program that asks the user whether they want to make a word uppercase or lowercase. Create a procedure to turn a word uppercase and output it, and a second procedure to turn a word into lowercase and output it. Call the appropriate procedure for which choice the user inputs. Draw a flowchart for the algorithm.

4   Convert the flowchart from task **3** into pseudocode.

WORKED EXAMPLE 4.15

Let's convert the flowchart into pseudocode.

Each loop is count controlled so replace with FOR NEXT loops.

```
FOR studentNumber = 1 to 101

    total = 0

    FOR result = 1 to 11

        OUTPUT "Enter " & studentNumber &
        "'s result " & result

        INPUT studentResult

        total = total + studentResult

    NEXT result

    OUTPUT "Total is" & total

ENDWHILE
```

Question

22 What is a nested statement?

UNPLUGGED ACTIVITY 4.08

1 An algorithm should ask the user if they want to perform a calculation and should continue asking this until they say Yes. Then the program should ask them how many numbers they want to add together. The program should input that quantity of numbers, add them together and output the result. Draw a flowchart for the algorithm.

2 An algorithm should take a word as input from the user. Then take each letter in turn, and output it the number of times of its position in the alphabet. For example, 'a' would be output once, 'b' would be output twice, and so on. Create a pseudocode algorithm for the problem.

Editing a basic program flowchart

You need to be able to read an algorithm or flowchart, and be able to identify how to make changes to it.

To do this, you need to work out what the algorithm does first. Do this by using test data to run the algorithm, follow each step and write down what happens. Then look at the difference between what the algorithm did, and what you need to make it do.

UNPLUGGED ACTIVITY 4.09

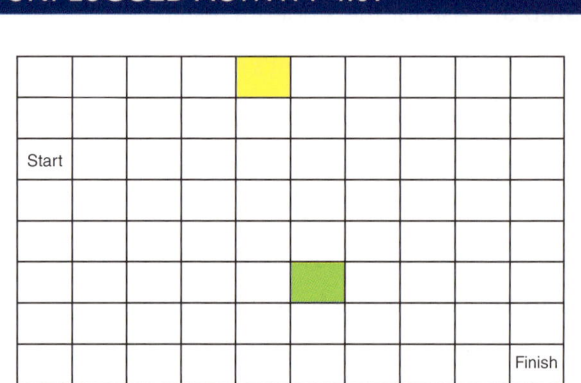

Figure 4.47: Maze 4.

Write an algorithm for the maze in Figure 4.47 in pseudocode. You start at the 'start sign' and end at the 'finish sign'. You must pass through the yellow box and the green box.

Compare your algorithm with another classmate. Do you have the same algorithm? Which do you think is better, theirs or yours? Why is this?

Questions

23 The flowchart in Figure 4.48 takes 10 numbers as input, adds them together and outputs the total.

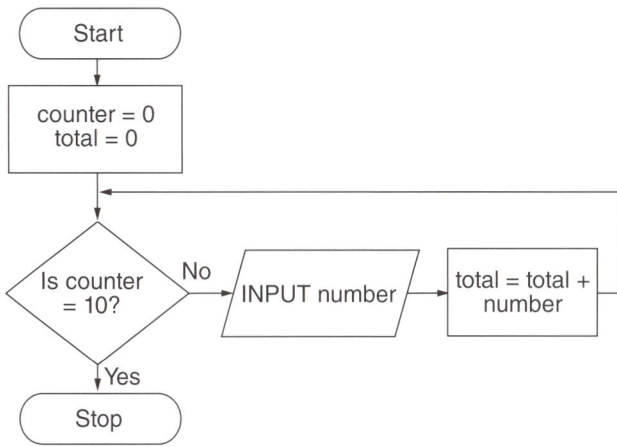

Figure 4.48: Flowchart: total 10 numbers.

Change the flowchart so it inputs 20 numbers and adds them together.

24 The following algorithm asks the user to input 50 numbers. It finds the smallest number and multiplies it by itself before outputting it.

```
smallest = 9999

FOR counter = 0 to 50

  INPUT number

  If number < smallest THEN

    smallest = number

  ENDIF

  NEXT counter

  answer = smallest * smallest

  OUTPUT answer
```

Change the algorithm so it finds the largest number and multiplies this by itself before outputting it.

Identifying errors in an algorithm/program flowchart

You may need to find an error in an algorithm such as a program flowchart. To do this, you need to follow each step of the algorithm, performing the actions it instructs to find where it goes wrong.

WORKED EXAMPLE 4.16

An algorithm should take three numbers as input, it should add together the two largest, and output the result.

Find the error in the algorithm in Figure 4.49.

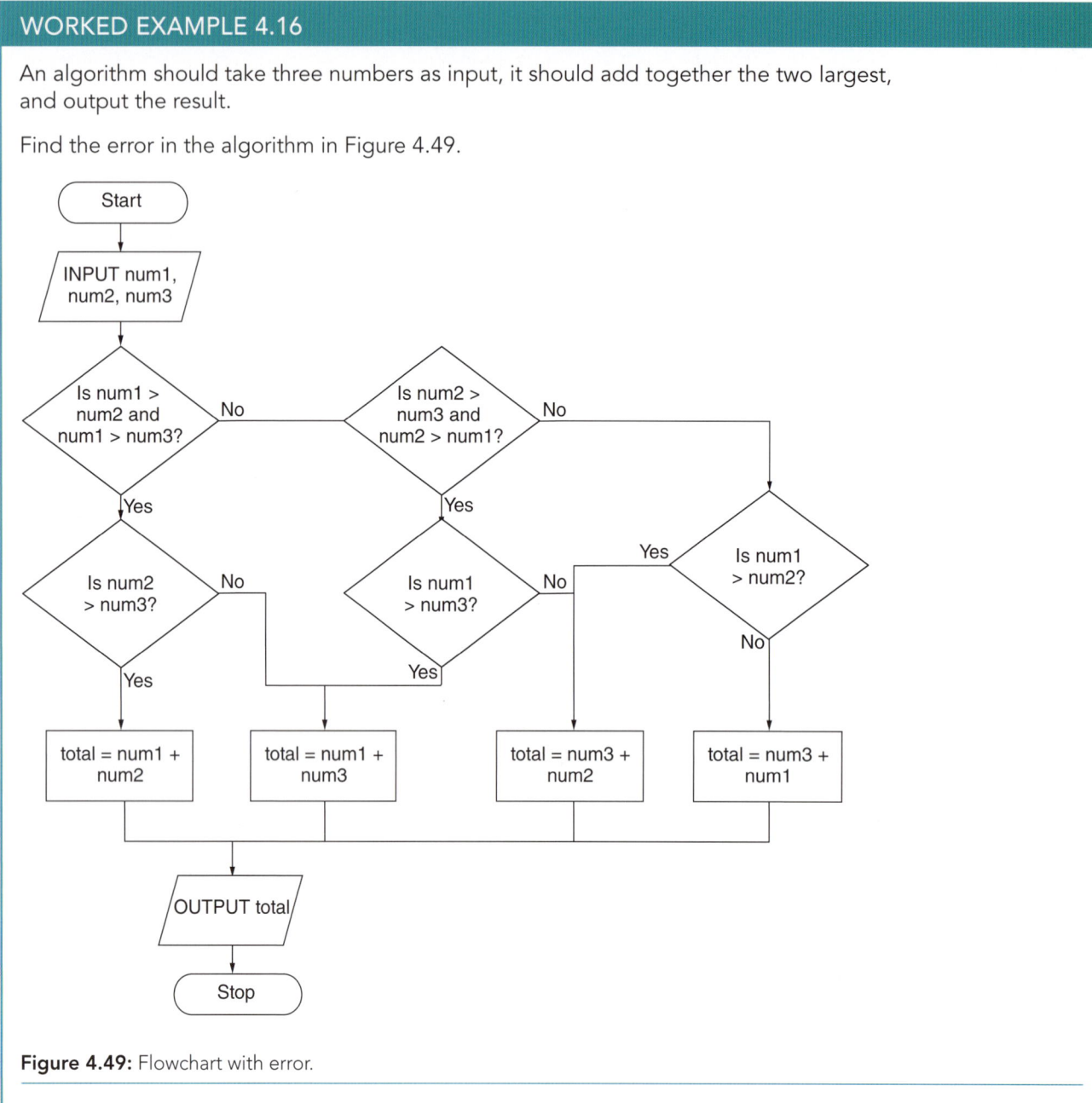

Figure 4.49: Flowchart with error.

CONTINUED

Run the algorithm with all possible different types of example data, for example:

Test 1: num1 = 10, num2 = 5, num3 = 3 (num1 and num2 are the largest), Output should be 15

Test 2: num1 = 5, num2 = 3, num3 = 10 (num1 and num3 are the largest), Output should be 15

Test 3: num1 = 3, num2 = 10, num3 = 5 (num2 and num3 are the largest), Output should be 15

Test 1

Is num1 > num2 and num1 > num3? Yes

Is num2 > num3 Yes this is true, total = num1 + num2 = 10 + 5

OUTPUT 15 – correct

Test 2

Is num1 > num2 and num1 > num3? No

Is num2 > num3 and num2 > num1? No

Is num1 > num2? Yes, total = num3 + num2 = 10 + 3

OUTPUT 13 – This is incorrect. It should have carried out total = num3 + num1.

The yes and no from the Is num1 > num2? boxes are in the wrong order; they need swapping.

Test 3

Is num1 > num2 and num1 > num3? No

Is num2 > num3 and num2 > num1? Yes

Is num1 > num3? No total = num3 + num2 = 5 + 10

OUTPUT 15 – correct

UNPLUGGED ACTIVITY 4.10

1   The algorithm should ask the user how many letters they want to enter, then let them enter that many letters. All the letters should be concatenated and output. Find the error(s) in the algorithm in Figure 4.50.

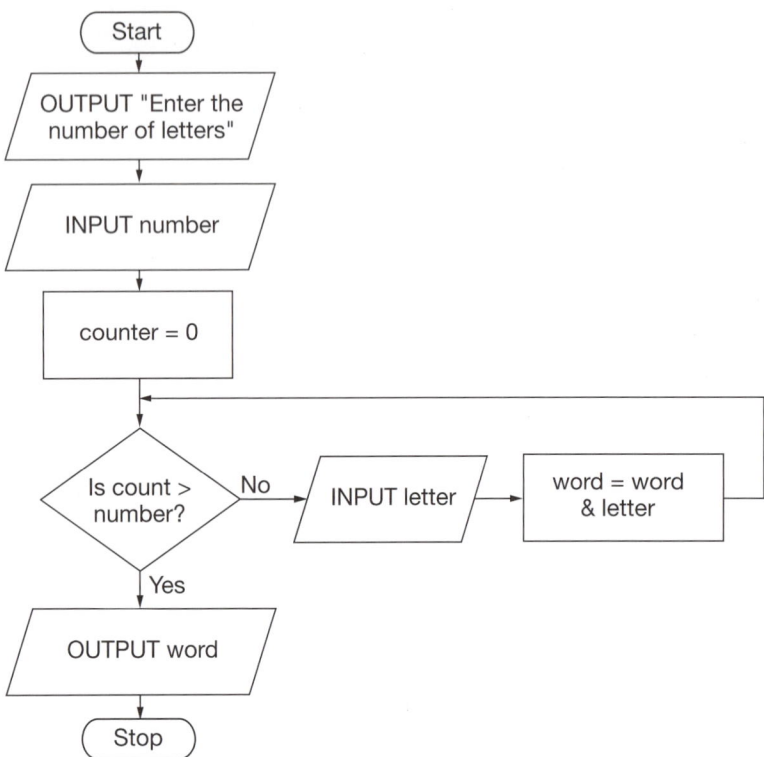

Figure 4.50: Flowchart with errors.

2   The algorithm should repeatedly ask the user to input a number. The difference between that number and the previous number should be added to the total. This should continue until the total is more than 1000. Find the error(s) in the algorithm.

```
total = 1

previousNumber = 0

WHILE total < 1000

  INPUT number

  total = total + (number - previousNumber)

  previousNumber = number

ENDWHILE
```

PRACTICE QUESTIONS

1 Identify two ways in which an algorithm can be expressed. [2]

2 Name the actions for these flowchart shapes.

[3]

3 State what the output will be when this algorithm is run when the data input is 10. [1]

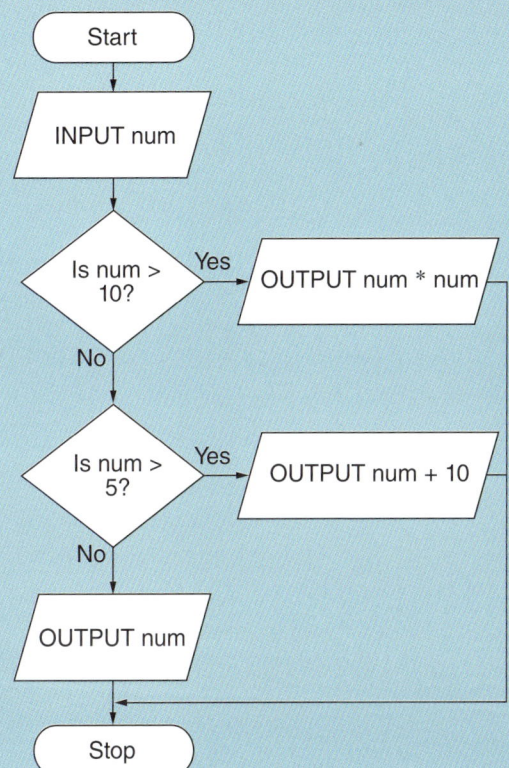

4 Change this algorithm so it outputs the 9-times table.

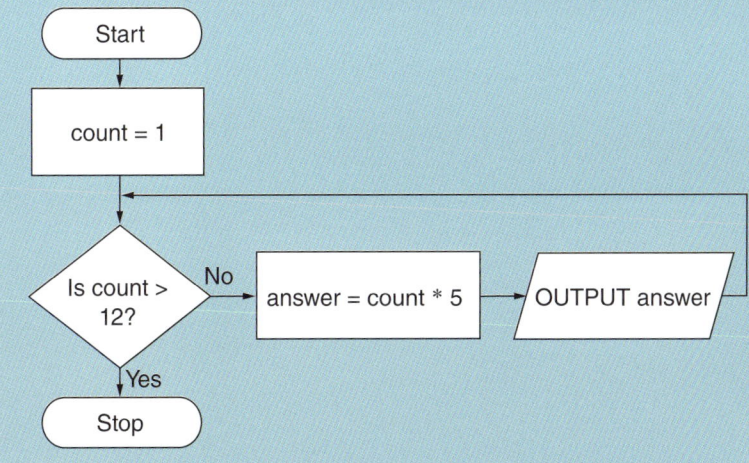

[3]

CONTINUED

5 This algorithm should loop until the user enters something other than 'Yes' or 'yes'.
Each time through the loop, it adds the two numbers the user inputs to the total.

Find and correct the error(s) in the algorithm. [1]

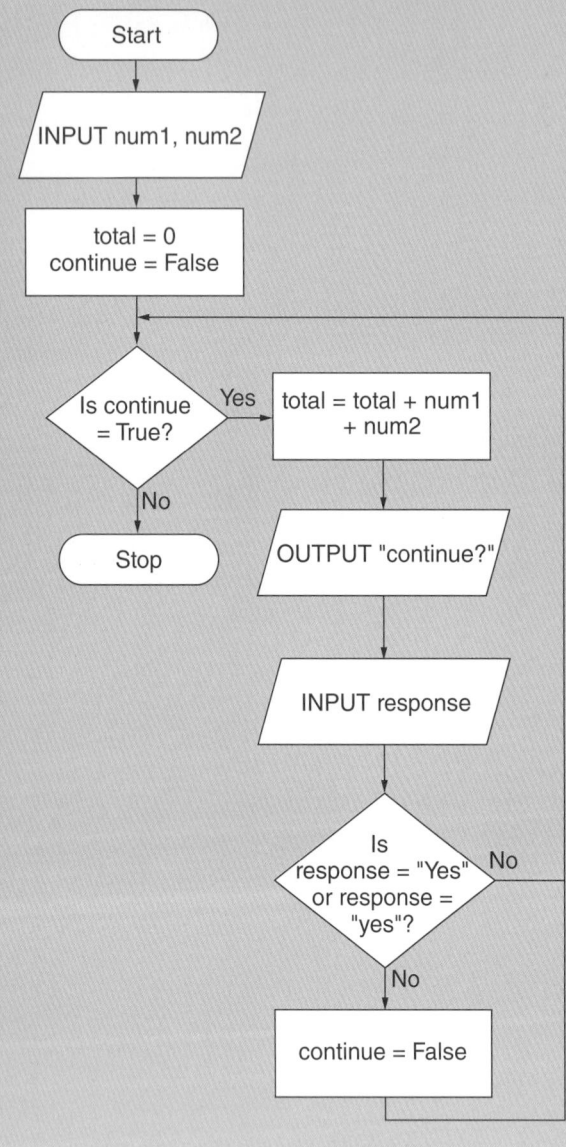

CONTINUED

6   Follow this algorithm.

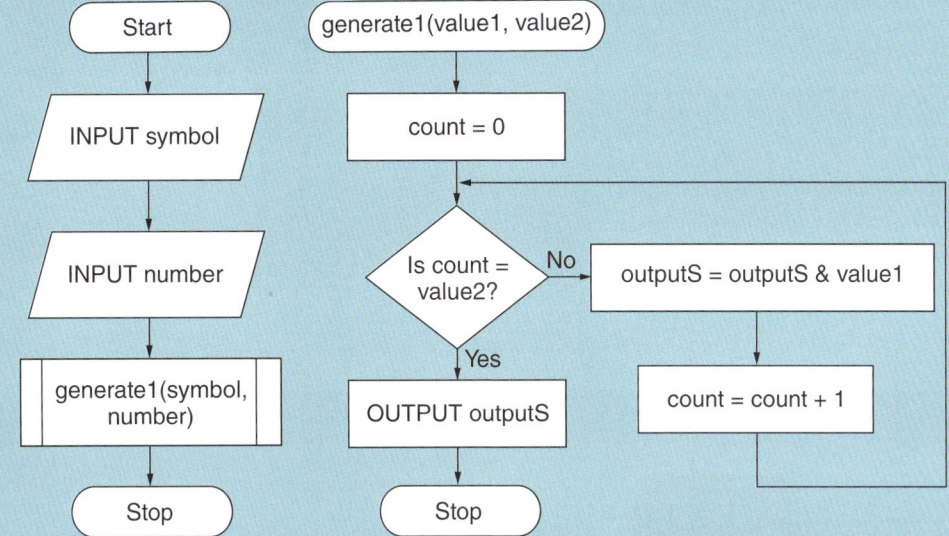

a   State the name of the procedure in this algorithm.   [1]

b   State the number of parameters that are passed to the subroutine.   [1]

c   State the name of two variables in the algorithm.   [2]

d   State what will be output from the program if the inputs are: "*" and then 5   [1]

[Total 5]

7   An algorithm is needed to output the odd numbers from 0 to 100.

Draw a flowchart for this algorithm.   [6]

8   Write an algorithm for a calculator. The user should be able to input two numbers and
a symbol (+ or –, or * or /). The algorithm should use subroutines for each of the calculations
and output the result.   [9]

SUMMARY CHECKLIST

☐ I can write and edit a given algorithm.

☐ I can use conditional branching, looping, nested loops and procedures/subroutines.

☐ I can write an algorithm using pseudocode to solve a given problem.

☐ I understand how to use comparison operators and arithmetic operators.

☐ I can draw a basic program flowchart to solve a given problem.

☐ I can draw a basic program flowchart using flowchart symbols that demonstrates a decision-making process using symbols.

☐ I can edit a given basic program flowchart that demonstrates a decision-making process.

☐ I can identify errors in an algorithm/program flowchart for a given scenario.

PROJECT

Figure 4.51: Creating a podcast episode.

You have been asked to create a podcast episode for your local community centre's digital skills course (see Figure 4.51). Your podcast will introduce the basic ideas covered in this chapter to do with algorithms and flowcharts.

You will work in pairs to design and create a script for the podcast.

Your podcast will cover the following ideas:

1   The benefits of creating algorithms

2   The symbols you may find in flowcharts

3   The common keywords in pseudocode

4   The different types of loops

5   Why subprograms are useful

6   A guide to finding errors in algorithms and how to correct them

Listen to another pair's podcast. Note some feedback to share with them. Base your feedback on:

• Identify three positives about the podcast.

• Can you spot any mistakes?

• Can you give them two ways to improve their podcast?

Act on the feedback you get from another pair. Develop and improve your podcast.

> Chapter 5
eSecurity

LEARNING INTENTIONS

By the end of this chapter, you will be able to:

- recognise and understand what is meant by personal data, how to keep it secure and prevent its misuse

- recognise types and uses of malware, their consequences for organisations and individuals and methods of prevention.

Introduction

The world of Information Technology can be fun and exciting. However, it also comes with its dangers and it is important to be aware of these and how to safeguard against them.

There are people online who try to harm others, for example by stealing personal data to commit fraud. To keep yourself and others safe when online, it is important to know what preventative measures to take to make sure your data stays private.

5.1 Personal data

Personal data is any data that relates to an individual. This includes data such as:

- name
- date of birth
- address
- telephone number
- email address
- bank details
- medical records
- salary
- political opinions
- membership of online communities or services.

Why personal data should be kept confidential

Through sharing personal data with another person or organisations, especially online, individuals can be exposed to a range of dangers, including identity theft, fraud, bullying and blackmail. Issues relating to identity theft and fraud are often the result of individuals having their personal information shared without their permission, which is then used to withdraw money from a person's bank account, take out loans, or gain access to online accounts. Blackmail and bullying can take place when an individual has personal information they wish to keep private, such as medical conditions or political views. Alongside financial losses and a possible loss of reputation, sorting out such issues can be challenging and extremely worrying for individuals. It is therefore important to consider how information is shared online, as well as considering how data stored and transferred can be kept secure.

How personal data can be kept confidential

When sharing data online, particularly when using social media, personal data could be viewed by other people and organisations (see Figure 5.1). It is therefore important to consider what needs to be shared and, when personal data is shared, how it can be kept confidential. Steps that help to keep personal data confidential include:

- Remove **geotags** from photos/videos, which means the location details for where the content was created cannot be seen, as this could reveal an individual's home address, place of work or school. Other location services can also be disabled, including checking in at places visited.

- Check information shared on social media profiles carefully, particularly if part of a profile is public, as this can often still be used to view some personal data, such as photos or information related to hobbies/interests.

- Ensure the personal data shared with friends or contacts on social media platforms is appropriate. For example, a social networking platform only accessed by close friends and family might be used to share different personal data from a business networking platform.

Block and report users unexpectedly asking for personal data online, such as asking for your phone number within a direct message on a social media platform.

Use a non-recognisable username rather than your real name where appropriate, for example when online gaming.

Figure 5.1: Personal data shared using social media needs to be carefully considered.

Anonymising information involves changing data so the individual it relates to cannot be identified, such as by replacing their full name with a unique numerical code. Anonymised information is used by many organisations to keep personal data confidential, such as when analysing how people use social media or collecting information that may be sensitive. However, it is still important to examine what data is being collected and how it is used, as the data collected could still lead to an individual being identified. For example, a person sharing their date of birth and the street they live on may be easily identifiable if someone lives in a place containing a small number of properties, which might affect their privacy if other personal data has been shared.

Problems with keeping personal data confidential often arise due to **aggregating information**. Aggregate data

Figure 5.2: A smart watch may contain information about an individual's health and fitness.

combines specific data related to an individual, which may lead to personal data being revealed. This could be from information explicitly shared online, or from devices, such as those connected to the IoT (Internet of Things). For example, an individual's purchases on an online shopping site could be compared with data from a smart watch, which might provide information about an individual's health or medical conditions (see Figure 5.2). This data could then be used to target advertising at the individual, or the data sold to other organisations.

Organisations have a **duty of confidence** when personal data is shared, which means it cannot be disclosed to others without an individual's consent. However, when registering for a service, the user may be presented with several options requesting that data be shared beyond the organisation. These options need to be carefully considered to ensure personal data is shared as expected by the individual and not made available to others without the individual's consent. This is particularly important when considering how data may be aggregated.

KEY WORDS

geotag: an electronic tag that assigns a geographical location

anonymising information: changing data so the individual it relates to cannot be identified

aggregating information: combining data about an individual from multiple sources

duty of confidence: an agreement between an organisation and an individual that data cannot be disclosed to others without an individual's consent

How personal data can be kept secure

We may take a number of measures to keep ourselves safe in daily life, such as locking doors, not talking to strangers and checking carefully before crossing the road. However, when people go online, they may not be aware of the safety measures they should take or how to behave in a safe manner.

There are several guidelines that you can follow to keep your personal data secure and prevent its misuse.

For example, when accessing digital devices and online services:

- Set strong passwords on any account that holds personal data, which means they cannot be easily guessed by individuals, or by automated password cracking tools. Stronger passwords include characters, numbers and symbols and are not a recognisable word, such as those found in the dictionary.

- Ensure passwords used for each service are unique. This ensures that if a password from one account is shared or compromised (an unauthorised person accesses your password), it cannot be used to access another account. Password managers can be used to help generate unique, hard to guess, passwords for all accounts used by an individual.

- Make use of **biometric** devices where available. Biometric devices use a person's unique biological data, such as a thumbprint or the iris in the eye, to quickly access systems and authorise transactions (see Figure 5.3). Biometric data can be used in place of other authentication methods, such as passwords.

Figure 5.3: A biometric device recognises the individual's thumbprint.

Use **two-factor authentication**, often referred to as 2FA, which uses an additional means of accessing a service before allowing a user to login. Two-factor authentication often involves combining a username and password with another authentication method on a smart phone. For example, the user might need to enter a code sent to them as a text message or viewed on an app, answer an automated phone call from the service, or use an app to verify they have the phone in their possession. A security key can also be used as a form of two-factor authentication and must be inserted into a laptop / desktop computer, or held nearby for a tablet / smart phone, to access the device.

UNPLUGGED ACTIVITY 5.01

Alex is opening an online bank account. They have heard about strong passwords but are not sure what strong passwords are. Alex was born in 2006. They have a pet cat Beth and their favourite colour is purple. Advise Alex on what is a strong password from the following list:

Alex2006

AlexandBeth

BethCat?

ALeX06!

U75jSweet0

Beththecat2006

purpledaisies17

DID YOU KNOW?

Stolen personal data could be used to trick a mobile phone operator into sending a new SIM card for a user's phone to an unauthorised user, which is then inserted into a criminal's phone and used to gain access to online services using two-factor authentication.

It is also important to ensure digital devices, such as laptops, tablets or phones, are protected:

- Use **encryption** where available, which converts data stored on the device into a secret code. For example, encrypted text might be stored as a random combination of letters, numbers and other characters, so that it cannot be read if the device is stolen. Data cannot be accessed without the use of a private key, which is only available to certain users, such as the owner of the laptop when they log onto the machine. (You can find out more about encryption in Chapter 1.)

- Install **anti-virus software**. Anti-virus software scans the computer to identify and remove viruses and **malware**, which can steal personal data. Anti-virus software, also known as virus checkers or anti-malware software, can also actively monitor a digital device while it is being used. This will help ensure viruses and malware do not infect the machine.

- Keep the operating system and application software up to date by installing updates regularly. Updates often resolve security issues, which can be used to steal personal data.

Finally, when using the internet:

- Ensure web-based content and apps used are trustworthy. Websites should be checked to ensure they use SSL (secure sockets layer), which is an encryption-based internet security protocol and often indicated by displaying a padlock symbol in a browser's address bar. (You can find out more about SSL in Chapter 1.) URLs (web addresses) and a page's content should be checked to ensure they are correct and not mimicking another site.

- Check messages, such as emails or direct messages, carefully to ensure they are from a genuine source. Avoid opening links to webpages and attached files unless you know they come from a trustworthy source.

KEY WORDS

biometric: data related to a person's physical character, such as a fingerprint

two-factor authentication: an additional device is required to log on to a service

encryption: converting data into a secret code so it cannot be accessed by unauthorised individuals

anti-virus software: software that is used to check for and identify viruses on a computer and remove them

malware: malicious software designed to gain unauthorised access to, or to disrupt or damage, a computer system

Network security measures

Public Wi-Fi networks, such as those found in coffee shops and gyms, often have limited security in place. This means care must be taken when using a device, as personal data could be intercepted or the device accessed by other people using the network.

Instead, use a **virtual private network (VPN)** to encrypt your data. A VPN ensures your data cannot be viewed by others connected to a network. It is safer to use a VPN when using online services that require you to enter personal data, such as passwords or bank details.

KEY WORD

virtual private network: an encrypted connection that can be used to send data more securely across a network

DISCUSSION POINT

How many of the guidelines within this chapter do you currently follow to keep your personal data confidential?

UNPLUGGED ACTIVITY 5.02

Create a plan to implement any of the guidelines that you do not currently follow to keep your data confidential.

How personal data can be gathered by unauthorised persons

There are several ways that an unauthorised person can try to collect personal data. They include:

- phishing
- smishing
- vishing
- pharming.

Phishing

Phishing involves a person sending a realistic looking email to a user to steal their personal data. The email contains a hyperlink to a website that also looks real, such as an internet banking login page. The user is encouraged to click on the link and to input personal data into a form on the website, such as being prompted to login using their username and password. Instead, the email could simply ask the user to reply to the email with their personal data. The user is tricked into giving their personal data as they believe it is from a genuine source, although both the email and the linked website are from a fake, unauthorised source.

The personal data input is then collected by an unauthorised person. This person can use the data for criminal acts, such as to commit fraud or steal the user's identity.

Phishing emails often pressure or intimidate the user to act quickly, such as by threatening the user that they must click the link and correct a situation immediately, or there will be a further issue.

> ### DID YOU KNOW?
>
> Phishing is a respelling of the word 'fishing'. But instead of looking for fish, a person who is 'phishing' is fishing for data (see Figure 5.4).
>
>
>
> **Figure 5.4:** Individuals fish for fish. They may also 'phish' for data!

How to recognise a phishing email

It's essential that you can recognise phishing emails to help keep your data secure and prevent it from being misused. Here are some measures you can take to protect data:

- Check the sender's name and subject line before opening the email. If the name appears fake or the subject line looks suspicious, it could be a phishing email. It may be safer to delete the email without opening it.

- Does the sender's email address look fake? Trustworthy businesses will use their own domain name.

- Check the opening line of the email. Does it address you in an impersonal way, for example 'Valued customer' or 'Dear Client'? An email from a trustworthy business will usually address you by name.

- Is the message well written? If it contains spelling mistakes and poor grammar, it may be a phishing email. It may be safer to delete the email.

- What is the content of the message? Does it ask you for personal data? Does it use aggressive language to get you to reveal your personal data such as 'Your account will be suspended if you do not act now!' Trustworthy businesses would not ask for your confidential data in this way.

- Does the message ask you to click a hyperlink? Hovering over a link allows a web address to be checked to ensure it is genuine. Trustworthy businesses use their domain name, so don't click on the link unless you are confident it is safe to do so.

- Check the signature on the email. The person named at the end of the message should include their contact information. If there is no name and no contact information, then the email is likely to be fake.

- If you think an email is phishing for data, then delete it. It may also be possible to report the phishing email to the organisation involved, which could enable the organisation to monitor communications with their customers.

> ### DID YOU KNOW?
>
> Many organisations regularly send fake phishing emails to their employees to test whether employees spot them and know what action to take. Employees are encouraged to report phishing emails, both real and fake. It is part of organisations' IT awareness training.

Smishing

Smishing (SMS phishing) is similar to phishing. Smishing uses mobile phone text messages to trick the mobile phone user into providing personal data, such as bank details and passwords or credit card numbers (see Figure 5.5).

The user's mobile phone receives a text message from what appears to be a genuine business, such as their bank or an online retailer. The text message may contain a link to a website, or it may ask the mobile user to call or text a telephone number to resolve an urgent issue. Mobile users will then be asked to reveal personal data, such as their login details.

Mobile phone users should be suspicious of unexpected text messages that appear to be from real companies. Banks do not contact customers asking for information in this way. The phone user may check if the website link is genuine by typing the address into their web browser rather than clicking on the link in the message. The safest way to deal with a smishing message is not to respond, block the caller's number to reduce the risk of receiving another smishing message and then delete the message.

Figure 5.5: Smishing uses text messages to obtain data illegally.

Vishing

Vishing (or voice phishing) is another type of phishing aimed at obtaining a user's personal details. The user receives a telephone call that could either be from an automated system, or it could be a real person (see Figure 5.6).

An automated voice usually speaks to the user and advises them of a problem, for example suspicious activity on their bank account. The user may then be asked to call another number, or to simply press a number on their phone and be directed to another automated system. This system will ask them to provide their bank account details to help resolve the problem. The bank account details have then been obtained by the unauthorised user and can be used to commit a crime against the user, such as transferring money from their bank account.

Sometimes, a real person may try to convince the user that there has been an issue with an account they have, then ask them to provide the login details or PIN (personal identification number) for the account to verify their identity.

To avoid becoming a victim of vishing, users should remember that no organisation will ever call and ask an individual to provide login details or PIN details over the telephone. They may ask you to provide other personal information, and if in doubt, it is advisable to end the call, and then using another phone, if possible, call the organisation back on their phone number that you may already know or can obtain.

Figure 5.6: Vishing tries to obtain data through a phone call.

Pharming

Pharming is when an unauthorised person installs malicious code on an individual's device or network hardware, such as a server. The aim of a pharming attack is to steal a user's personal data.

The malicious code is designed to redirect a user to a fake website when they type in the address of a real one. The fake website is designed to look like the real one, so they are unaware that their request has been redirected. The user will then enter their personal details into the fake website, believing it is genuine and the unauthorised person will now have their personal data.

A common technique used in pharming is domain name server (DNS) cache poisoning. This technique exploits vulnerabilities in the DNS system and diverts the internet traffic intended for a genuine server towards a fake one instead.

To carry out pharming, the unauthorised person needs to find a way to install the malicious code on the computer. They often hide the malicious code in an email attachment or link. When the user opens the email attachment or clicks the link, the malicious code is downloaded.

A real-life example of pharming

In 2007, 50 different companies all over the world were subject to a pharming attack. Over a three-day period, hackers managed to infect over 1000 personal computers a day with a malicious pharming code.

When users who had been infected visited the websites of the different companies, they were redirected to a real-looking version of the sites that were designed to steal their personal data.

The original email containing the malicious code was set up to look like a shocking news story. Users were encouraged to click a link in the email to find out more information. The code was downloaded when the user clicked the link. It is not known how much money unauthorised persons were able to steal because of this fraud.

How to prevent pharming

All of the measures to help recognise phishing, smishing and vishing attacks can be used to spot pharming. There are other things that can be done to prevent pharming attacks. These include:

- Have a firewall installed and operational. A firewall monitors incoming and outgoing traffic from your computer. It checks this traffic against set criteria and will flag and stop any traffic that does not meet the criteria. A firewall could detect and block suspicious traffic, such as a malicious code trying to enter your system. Firewalls can be implemented as software installed onto individual machines and are often part of a device's operating system, or can be a dedicated hardware device which monitors traffic for the whole network.

- Have an anti-virus program installed that is designed to detect malicious pharming code, which includes the ability to check for any malicious code. It is advisable to set up an automatic scan once a day at a time when the computer will normally be switched on.

- Be aware when using public Wi-Fi connections. A hacker could look to directly access your computer and install the malicious code if you are connected to a public Wi-Fi connection. As mentioned earlier, it is often advisable to use a VPN when using public Wi-Fi.

Smishing can also be used as a form of pharming. A mobile phone user is sent a link which downloads malware onto their mobile device when clicked. To protect against this, security software should be installed on mobile phones and the device scanned regularly to detect any presence of malware.

Question

1   Investigate the use of a VPN. Find out what benefits it may have, along with any drawbacks.

Advantages and disadvantages of methods of preventing misuse of personal data

Table 5.1 shows a number of advantages and disadvantages to the various methods available to prevent the misuse of personal data. While each method helps keep personal data secure, its use should be carefully considered to ensure the benefits outweigh the risks. For example, a method that is time consuming to use and has a negative impact on the user is unlikely to be widely used.

Method	Advantages	Disadvantages
Strong, unique password	Can be entered quickly by the user. Requires no additional items to be used, such as a smart phone or biometric data.	Multiple passwords can be difficult to remember. Depending on the complexity of the password and the security measures in place, the password could still be compromised.
Biometrics	Always with you, so no need to remember a password or to have access to another device. Can enable almost instant log on.	Initial setup can be time consuming. Biometric data cannot be altered, unlike a password, which could be an issue if compromised.
Two-factor authentication	More secure than passwords or biometrics, as access to an additional device is required. Range of options available to authenticate, including voice calls, text messages, apps and physical security keys.	Can slow down the login process. Can be difficult to change or reset login information, particularly if a device is lost or stolen.
Encryption of data stored on a digital device	If a digital device or the storage media is stolen, the user's data cannot be accessed. Once encryption is enabled, no further action is required by the user.	Initial setup can be time consuming. If the user forgets their password/encryption key, the data cannot be accessed if the storage device needs to be moved to another computer.
Use of anti-virus software	Constantly checks for a range of viruses related to data security. Automatically kept up to date.	Can slow down using a device, such as when accessing files. May require a subscription for updates or more comprehensive protection.
Firewall	Blocks access to specific ports / services on a computer (software) or a network (hardware). Can monitor and report on unusual activity.	Can prevent all network traffic if it malfunctions or is incorrectly configured. Unable to block all unauthorised access.
Encryption of data when using a network, including Wi-Fi	Data cannot be intercepted while being transferred. Once setup by the user, functions without further intervention.	Initial setup can be costly and require technical knowledge. Can slow down network communication.

Table 5.1: Advantages and disadvantages of different methods of preventing misuse of data.

5.2 Malware

Malware (or malicious software) refers to any software that is designed to disrupt or damage a computer system or gain unauthorised access. Malware is used to steal personal data or financial reward.

There are various types of malware. These include:

- virus
- trojan
- worm
- spyware
- adware
- rootkit
- malicious bots
- ransomware.

It is important to understand how each type of malware operates and how to minimise the risk from each.

The consequences to the individual or to a business will depend on the type of malware. Some malware may simply cause a nuisance, such as slowing down a computer. Other types of malware may have more serious consequences, for example making data inaccessible or theft of personal data. This can lead to identity theft, corruption of data or blackmail.

Virus

A virus is a common type of malware and is the only type of malware that infects existing files on a computer system. The virus attaches itself to an uninfected file and modifies (changes) it, which means the file is now infected. The virus then replicates (copies) itself and attaches to another uninfected file. This process is repeated, with computer viruses designed to spread like a human virus.

Once a virus has infected a file, it may begin to replicate immediately, or it can lay inactive until actions performed by the computer cause the virus to start working. If an infected computer is part of a network, it may also begin to infect other computers on the network. A virus can be especially dangerous if it infects files on a server that are accessed by many different computers.

There are several signs that a computer has been infected with a virus, including:

- slower system performance
- files multiplying or duplicating automatically
- files being deleted without the user's knowledge.

The aim of a virus is to corrupt and disrupt data in a computer system.

> **DID YOU KNOW?**
>
> The first virus to infect PCs, named 'Brian', was created in 1986 and intended as an anti-piracy measure to stop people copying software. The virus was transferred via copied floppy disks (see Figure 5.7) and, instead of an infected machine starting normally, it displayed a message asking the user to call the virus's author to discuss how to obtain the software legally.
>
>
>
> **Figure 5.7:** Floppy disks were used to store files and programs. Computers used to have floppy disk drives to read these, which worked in a similar way to CD, DVD and Blu-ray drives.

Preventing viruses

If a virus infects a computer system, it can be very difficult to remove. Anti-virus software should be installed on a computer to prevent the risk of infection by a virus. The computer should be regularly scanned for viruses. Most modern anti-virus software runs in the background scanning the computer for viruses while it is switched on. If the anti-virus software doesn't scan automatically, it is best to set up a daily automatic scan of the computer at a time when you know that the computer is likely to be switched on.

Any files the anti-virus software believes contain a virus will be **quarantined** and the user alerted. The user can then select to delete these files or investigate further.

Alternatively, the anti-virus software can be configured to automatically delete all quarantined files.

The anti-virus software can detect a virus in a file by comparing the code to a database of known virus codes. If it finds a code that matches it will quarantine the file.

One weakness of anti-virus software is that it is dependent on the database it holds. If a system is infected with a virus not in the database, it will not be recognised and removed. The virus could cause significant damage, so it is important to regularly update anti-virus software to ensure it includes the latest known viruses.

Some anti-virus software can be set for real-time checking. This means that all programs that are requested for download are immediately checked for viruses. If the anti-virus software detects a virus, it will alert the user and tell them not to download the file, as it contains a virus.

A firewall can be used to minimise the impact and likelihood of being infected by a virus through filtering and monitoring incoming and outgoing traffic from a computer system. If the firewall detects malicious software trying to enter the system, it can stop it before it is able to enter. As with anti-virus software, a firewall again relies on the rules and filters to be kept up to date to detect the malicious traffic in the first place.

Care should also be taken when sharing resources using portable storage devices, such as a USB memory stick or external hard drive. USB memory sticks inserted into a computer should be scanned immediately, even if it is an individual's own storage device, as it could have been unknowingly infected by another machine. Some organisations do not allow the use of employees' personal memory sticks in work computers. This reduces the risk of viruses entering the network.

Trojan

A trojan is a type of malware that disguises itself as a genuine file or software. A trojan can also be contained in software that may have been infected. A trojan is typically downloaded from an infected email or website. It hides within a malicious program. When the program is opened, it will often release another type of malware such as a virus, or attempt to steal personal data.

Preventing trojans

It can be difficult to prevent trojans, as they disguise themselves as genuine software, which is unexpectedly run by the user. Anti-virus software can typically check for all types of malware, including trojans. Dedicated malware removal tools are also available, which could be used to remove a specific malware infection. In addition to using a firewall, the main way to reduce the risk of a trojan is to only open files and run software that you know is from a trusted source, such as from reputable software companies and trusted websites.

Question

2   Find out what is meant by a backdoor trojan.

UNPLUGGED ACTIVITY 5.06

Imagine that your friend does not have any security installed on their computer. They think that no one will bother to hack into their computer. They do not realise that they could download a virus at any time. You need to convince your friend that they should take action to protect their computer. You could also advise them on what security measures they could take to prevent a virus being installed.

Write a one-minute speech to convince your friend. In pairs, practise the speech. Give your partner feedback. Say one positive thing about their speech and one thing that could be improved. Listen to your partner's feedback and improve your speech.

Worms

A worm is a type of malware that acts in a similar way to a virus, but with a major difference. A worm is a program that replicates itself, like a virus. But unlike a virus it does not need to attach itself to another program or file to cause damage. Worms can enter through security holes and issues in a computer, such as those within an operating system.

A worm replicates itself and typically aims to fill up all the free space on a computer to slow it down and stop it working (see Figure 5.9). Usually, the first sign for a user that their computer has been infected with a worm is the computer starts to run slowly and space on the hard drive begins to rapidly decrease.

A worm usually also tries to spread to other computers on a network. If a worm is able to spread throughout a network, it can block up bandwidth and slow down the whole network.

Worms are normally downloaded and spread through email attachments, peer-to-peer file-sharing networks or using a link to a website. Once downloaded, they will replicate.

A well-known example of a computer worm is Stuxnet, which was used as a cyber weapon in 2010. It was discovered by two security researchers who recognised that the worm was a great deal more complex than any they had previously seen. The worm was being used to attack a power plant and security experts believed the aim was to sabotage (stop) the production of nuclear weapons.

Figure 5.9: A worm can slow down the entire network.

Preventing worms

Worms often enter a computer through security weaknesses in the operating system or software installed by the user. It is important to regularly update the operating system and software to prevent worms. The update process can often be set to take place automatically, which removes the need for the task to be completed by the user.

Like phishing, a worm may be sent using an email, either as an attachment or through a hyperlink. Unless the email is from a trusted source, never open an attachment or click the link. Instead, delete the email to reduce the risk of the computer being infected with a worm.

Anti-virus software usually checks for worms and, as they can be spread throughout a network, disconnecting a computer from a network when the network's resources are not required can help keep it safe. However, this may be impractical, as computers increasingly rely on a network connection, including to the internet, to use applications.

Spyware

Spyware describes malware designed to gather information about human interactions with a computer, such as key presses. As the name suggests, the aim of spyware is to spy on the user. Spyware is normally used to gather personal and sensitive data that can be used in fraudulent and criminal activity (see Figure 5.10).

A common example of spyware is a key logger. A key logger is installed on a user's computer, normally without the user knowing. The key logger will then record any key presses that are carried out by the user. All this data is sent to a third party, such as the person or group who created the spyware, to be analysed to establish any patterns in the data. The patterns are then examined to see if any of them look as though they could be personal or sensitive data, such as a password.

Figure 5.10: Spyware may gather information about you.

However, spyware can perform actions beyond key logging, such as:

- obtaining specific data within a system, such as contact lists or email addresses

- monitoring emails sent or websites visited

- obtaining audio, photos and videos taken on the device.

Spyware is often unknowingly downloaded while using the internet. It can be embedded into pop-up adverts offering a prize or a free product which entices the user to click them. It can also be embedded into the download of a video, music or application file, particularly if they are illegally made copies. Sometimes, this may involve the user unknowingly given consent to the spyware to be downloaded, as the agreement can go unnoticed within the terms and conditions.

Preventing spyware

As with other types of malware, it is important to check what is downloaded, especially when downloading software that is free of cost, or obtaining files from video and music sharing sites. Downloads should only be obtained from reputable (trustworthy) sources. In addition, links or offers in pop-up adverts should not be visited, no matter how enticing they may seem.

Terms and conditions (T&Cs) should be checked, along with user agreements, to ensure spyware is not included as part of software being installed. T&Cs could contain clauses about sharing data with third parties, which could also be obtained by spyware.

Anti-virus software can be used to scan a computer to remove spyware. If a key logger is found, it is advisable to change all passwords immediately, as this personal data could have been stolen.

ACTIVITY 5.07

1   How has the UK General Data Protection Regulation (GDPR) affected the use of spyware?

2   Find out about mobile spyware.

   a   How are mobile phones infected?

   b   How is spyware used in mobile devices?

Adware

Adware (advertising supported software) is a type of software that displays advertisements and pop-ups on a computer's browser. Adware collects data about a user's browsing habits. It then uses this information to customise advertisements targeted at the user's buying patterns and interests (see Figure 5.11).

Adware may be installed on a user's computer when software is downloaded. It may be present in the download without the user knowing. A user may only realise adware has been installed when they notice an additional task running on their device or search bar in their browser, or pop-ups start appearing. Adware may not be easy to delete, as there may be no uninstall option.

Some businesses use adware as a method of advertising, or to prompt users to use their search function. Adware used in this way may raise revenue for the business that, they argue, keeps down the cost of their products. Some users are happy to receive this type of targeted advertising. Adware can also be used maliciously causing the browser to keep displaying unwanted pop-ups and banners.

Figure 5.11: Adware uses browsing data to target advertising at individual customers.

Preventing adware

The most effective measure to avoid being infected with adware is to check exactly what is being downloaded and installed onto a computer. This could include examining the list of components that are included in the download and ensuring that any parts that could be adware, such as a search bar or task bar addition to the browser, are not installed.

As malware often does not have an uninstall option, it can be challenging to detect and remove, so a dedicated malware removal tool may need to be used. When a computer has multiple users, or forms part of a network, the system administrator may be the only one allowed to install software. This should help to prevent additional components being accidentally installed by non-specialist users.

> ### DISCUSSION POINT
>
> Should organisations restrict users' access to certain software or tasks on the organisation's computers, such as downloading software or using USB memory sticks? Or is it more beneficial to train users on appropriate behaviour when using digital devices and accessing online services?

Rootkit

A rootkit is a computer program that enables an unauthorised person to gain administrator access to a victim's computer. A rootkit is designed to stay hidden on a user's computer, allowing the computer to be controlled by the unauthorised person from a remote location. A rootkit allows the unauthorised person to carry out criminal acts with the computer, such as hiding illegal files on the computer, using the computer as part of a larger cyber attack or to steal personal data (see Figure 5.12).

Rootkits can get installed because the user's device password is cracked or the security of a computer system is weak. The person controlling the rootkit can then use the access to stop the computer recognising that the rootkit is installed, so the victim will not know that someone else has complete access to their computer system. The rootkit will normally be hidden within the operating system, which makes it difficult to detect by anti-virus software. Other malware can be incorporated into a rootkit, which may be concealed on the computer to cause harm.

A rootkit may be installed on a computer by an individual purposely leaving USB memory sticks, infected with a rootkit, in places they believe they will be found. The individuals are relying on the curiosity of another user to insert the USB memory stick into their computer and therefore inadvertently install the rootkit.

DID YOU KNOW?

An early rootkit example is NTRootkit, which appeared in 1999. It was designed to access Windows operating systems. A rootkit that was designed to do the same with Mac operating systems didn't appear until 10 years later.

ACTIVITY 5.08

Rootkits can be used a positive way. Research how rootkits are used in connection with Digital Rights Management (DRM). Make notes of your findings.

Figure 5.12: Never insert a USB memory stick into a computer unless you know it comes from a reliable source: it may be infected with Rootkit.

Preventing a rootkit

Here are some measures you can take to reduce the risk of infection by a rootkit:

- Set a strong password on your device to reduce the risk of it being cracked by an unauthorised person. Change the password regularly in case it has been discovered.

- Only download software from reputable sources.

- Never insert a USB memory stick into a computer system unless you trust the source.

- Removing a rootkit from a computer once it has been installed can be extremely difficult. It is software that is designed to be hidden and heavily relies on this feature. A rootkit may be detected by some anti-virus software or malware removal tools, although it may be necessary to completely reinstall the operating system.

Malicious bots

Bots (short for robots) are automated applications. A bot may be used to carry out simple, repetitive tasks that humans might find dull and time consuming, such as indexing a search engine. Malicious (intended to harm) bots are used by cybercriminals. This type of malware includes:

- Spam bots, which are used to bombard people's email inbox with spam (unwanted) emails, including those used to carry out other types of malware attacks.

- Zombie bots, which are used to create a bot network. The bot will lay hidden on a computer until an attack is launched. The computer will then connect to lots of other computers that have been infected with zombie bots to launch a large-scale attack on an organisation, such as a Distributed Denial of Service (DDoS) attack. Bots connected in this way are often known as a botnet.

- Malicious chatter bots, which pretend to be humans on certain websites or online services, such as social media platforms. They try to mimic human interaction, with the goal of obtaining personal data.

- File-sharing bots, which provide a fake link for a user's online search request. When clicked, the link downloads malware on to the user's computer.

- Malicious bots, which are like worms, as they can replicate and spread themselves.

DID YOU KNOW?

Large DDoS attacks can see networks hit with more than 300 million requests per second using infected machines across the globe, which makes computers and online services unusable.

Preventing malicious bots

Malicious bots are often embedded into links or software downloads. They are often spread in the same way as phishing attacks. So, the same measures used to protect against phishing can be applied to bots. Users should avoid clicking on any suspicious or unknown links, particularly if they are not from a reputable source.

As bots are often used by chat or messaging services, users should be careful when sharing personal data with a chat bot. Bots can even be used to mimic conversations with a user's contacts, such as family or friends, so individuals should still be careful about sharing personal data requested by others, particularly if the request is unexpected, or within a service not typically used.

If a user suspects they have downloaded a bot, anti-virus software can be used to detect and remove it. A firewall can also be used to detect the activity of malicious bots as it may recognise suspicious email traffic created by the bot. However, more sophisticated bots can disguise their communications as genuine network communications, so will go unnoticed by a firewall.

Question

3 a State **one** way a bot can be used positively.

   b State **two** ways a bot can be used maliciously.

Ransomware

Ransomware is a type of malware that restricts a user's access to their computer system and files. The ransomware will normally demand that the user pays a ransom, usually by transferring money so as to regain access to their computer system (see Figure 5.13). Some ransomware programs will completely lock a user's system, while others will encrypt all files on a system in a way that makes them useless. Ransomware will often enter a system in a similar way to a trojan. If the user doesn't pay the ransom in a set amount of time, they risk losing their data forever.

The likelihood of a person paying a ransom relies on the importance of the data to them, along with whether uninfected backups are available. Users that do pay the ransom can often be exploited further and asked for additional payment to release their data.

Figure 5.13: A Ransomware demand.

DID YOU KNOW?

A well-known example of Ransomware is WannaCry. The unauthorised person demands that the infected user pays a ransom. If the user does not pay within a certain period of time, the amount is increased. If payment is not made shortly after the amount is increased, the unauthorised user will delete the infected user's files forever.

Preventing ransomware

As ransomware is distributed in a similar way to trojans, the same measures used to prevent trojans can be followed. Users can also limit the risk of losing data in this type of attack by making sure they have a copy of their data. If a separate back-up is available, which is kept up to date, then the risk of losing data in a ransomware attack becomes greatly reduced. This means users have a copy of their data if it is deleted during an attack.

The risk of losing data during a ransomware attack can also be reduced by storing data remotely in the cloud. Cloud servers often have a facility that allows the user to roll back to a previous version of the data, so it can be restored if lost.

> ### ACTIVITY 5.09
>
> An organisation can use a practice called principle of least privilege (POLP) to help keep data safe and secure. Research POLP and make a list of ways it can help keep data safe and secure. Share your list with a partner, and add more ways to your list.

Uses of malware

Malware is often used to carry out a number of illegal activities. These include:

- fraud
- theft
- industrial espionage
- sabotage.

Fraud

Fraud involves deceiving an individual or organisation into thinking a person is someone they are not. The aim of fraud is to obtain money or property. Malware can be used to make a user believe they are interacting with a reputable organisation when visiting their website. Instead, they are being deceived into using a fake website which is being used to gather personal data. The user may also be deceived into purchasing inferior quality products or services.

Personal data gathered through malware can be used to steal a person's identity. The theft of online banking details or credit cards may be used to purchase goods or apply for financial products, such as loans or benefits. Personal information can also be used to illegally obtain identification documents, such as passports or driving licences, which can be used to deceive others, for example to give false information when fined for a traffic offence.

Theft

As malware is often used to obtain an individual's online banking details, money can be stolen by an unauthorised person logging into the individual's account, then transferring money to another account. Stolen credit or debit card details may be used to create a copy of a card to get cash out of an ATM or to purchase goods and services at a shop or online.

Unauthorised persons can also use malware to steal intellectual property from a computer, such as artistic or literary works. Physical items can be stolen if a user's personal data such as an entry keycode to a warehouse is used to gain access to a building (see Figure 5.14).

Figure 5.14: Personal data such as door entry password codes stored on a computer may be stolen.

Industrial espionage

Industrial espionage involves spying on organisations to gain an advantage in business (see Figure 5.15). Malware may be used to steal secrets from an organisation, such as product specifications, creative designs, upcoming releases, or contract information. Using this information, the unauthorised person could enable another organisation to gain a competitive advantage. This could include being able to launch or enhance products before their competitors, being the first to offer new services to customers, or having improved terms within contracts.

Industrial espionage may lead to the discovery of unethical or illegal business practices, which could be damaging for an organisation and could be used as part of a ransomware attack.

Figure 5.15: Industrial espionage can be used to gain improved terms within contracts.

Sabotage

Sabotage occurs when equipment or buildings are deliberately damaged or destroyed. Malware may be used to purposely delete or damage files, or make computers difficult to use, such as through disrupting network traffic.

Malware is increasingly used to target industrial equipment and infrastructure, such as power stations and electricity grids. Sabotage can be particularly dangerous if safety critical systems are targeted, such as those in nuclear reactors, or life support systems in hospitals.

Consequences of malware for organisations and individuals

While malware can sometimes be a nuisance, such as adware pop-ups and banners, the consequences of a malware attack can be severe:

- An organisation's operations may be badly disrupted or stopped. The organisation may be unable to serve its customers, which will lead to financial loss as well as a possible loss of business reputation. Customers may choose to buy from the organisation's competitors instead. There is also the time and cost of removing and resolving issues caused by malware. The consequences of a malware attack may only be evident in the longer term. For example, a competitor gains a business advantage when they launch products based on stolen product designs.

- Malware attacks take time and money for individuals to resolve as they may lack the expertise to fix any issues themselves. Not having access to a functioning digital device may limit an individual's ability to work and earn money, or mean that educational tasks, such as completing assignments, cannot be completed. Personal data stolen through malware and used for identity theft can be particularly difficult to resolve. The stress may cause the individual to suffer health issues.

Malware prevention software and physical prevention methods

Both anti-virus software and malware removal tools can be used to prevent malware attacks. The system can also be scanned for malware and infected files quarantined or removed. The technologies outlined above should also be used as required, including firewalls, VPNs, software updates and only authorised users allowed access to computer networks.

Malware attacks often result from a user's actions on a device, so it is important individuals are aware of appropriate behaviour when online and using digital devices. Organisations may provide training on malware prevention for employees. Users should be made aware of the dangers posed by email links and attachments, using USB memory sticks to transfer data and the need to check what is included as part of downloaded software.

Individuals and organisations should also react quickly should a malware attack occur, including disconnecting any infected computers from a network and using appropriate software to remove the malware.

Advantages and disadvantages of the methods of malware prevention

Many of the advantages and disadvantages of the methods used to prevent malware are outlined earlier in the chapter. Table 5.2 identifies additional advantages and disadvantages.

Method	Advantages	Disadvantages
Regularly update software and operating system.	Patches known bugs and security weaknesses used by malware. Can take place automatically, without user intervention.	Users may be unable to use the machine while the update takes place. Updates might unexpectedly alter other parts of the software or operating system.
Limit user access to a computer, including downloading software and using USB memory sticks.	Reduces the likelihood of a device being infected through downloading and / or installing malware. Malware may only be able to access data stored on a user's account, rather than the whole computer or network.	Initial setup can be time consuming, with a computer's administrator required to install software or make changes to the computer. Users can become frustrated about not being able to use the computer how they want.

Table 5.2: Additional advantages and disadvantages of malware prevention methods.

PRACTICE QUESTIONS

1 Identify three guidelines that can help keep personal data safe. [3]
2 Explain one difference between phishing and pharming. [1]
3 Explain two similarities between phishing and pharming. [2]
4 Identify four different types of malware. [4]
5 Describe how a firewall can be used to help prevent a virus infecting a computer system. [5]
6 Describe how spyware can be used to obtain a user's password for an online account. [5]
7 Rootkits can be used to allow an authorised person to hide illegal files on a user's computer.
   a State what is meant by a rootkit. [1]
   b Explain how the risk of rootkits can be minimised. [2]
   c Identify two other malicious ways that rootkits can be used. [2]
   [Total 5]
8 Ransomware can be used to prevent a user gaining access to their data.
   a State how ransomware prevents the user gaining access to their data. [1]
   b Explain two measures that can be taken to reduce the risk of ransomware. [2]
   [Total 3]

SUMMARY CHECKLIST

- [ ] I can identify what is meant by personal data.
- [ ] I can understand the importance of keeping personal data confidential.
- [ ] I can describe several guidelines that can help keep personal data confidential.
- [ ] I can explain how personal data is collected by unauthorised people, using practices such as phishing, smishing, vishing and pharming.
- [ ] I can describe the advantages and disadvantages of different methods of preventing misuse of personal data.
- [ ] I can describe how a range of malware operates.
- [ ] I can identify a range of consequences of malware to organisations and individuals.
- [ ] I can explain what measures can be taken to reduce the risk of each type of malware.
- [ ] I can describe the advantages and disadvantages of different methods of malware prevention.

PROJECT

Figure 5.16: A debate allows both sides of an argument to be discussed.

Working in pairs or small groups, hold a debate with another group about the most effective way to prevent the misuse of personal data and malware infection (see Figure 5.16).

Before the debate, choose two or three approaches you believe are the best methods for preventing misuse, and ensure you are familiar with their advantages. You should also examine the disadvantages of each method and consider whether there are any counter arguments.

During the debate, clearly outline the advantages of each method and listen carefully to the arguments from the other groups. As required, put forward counter arguments and justify why you believe the approaches selected are the best.

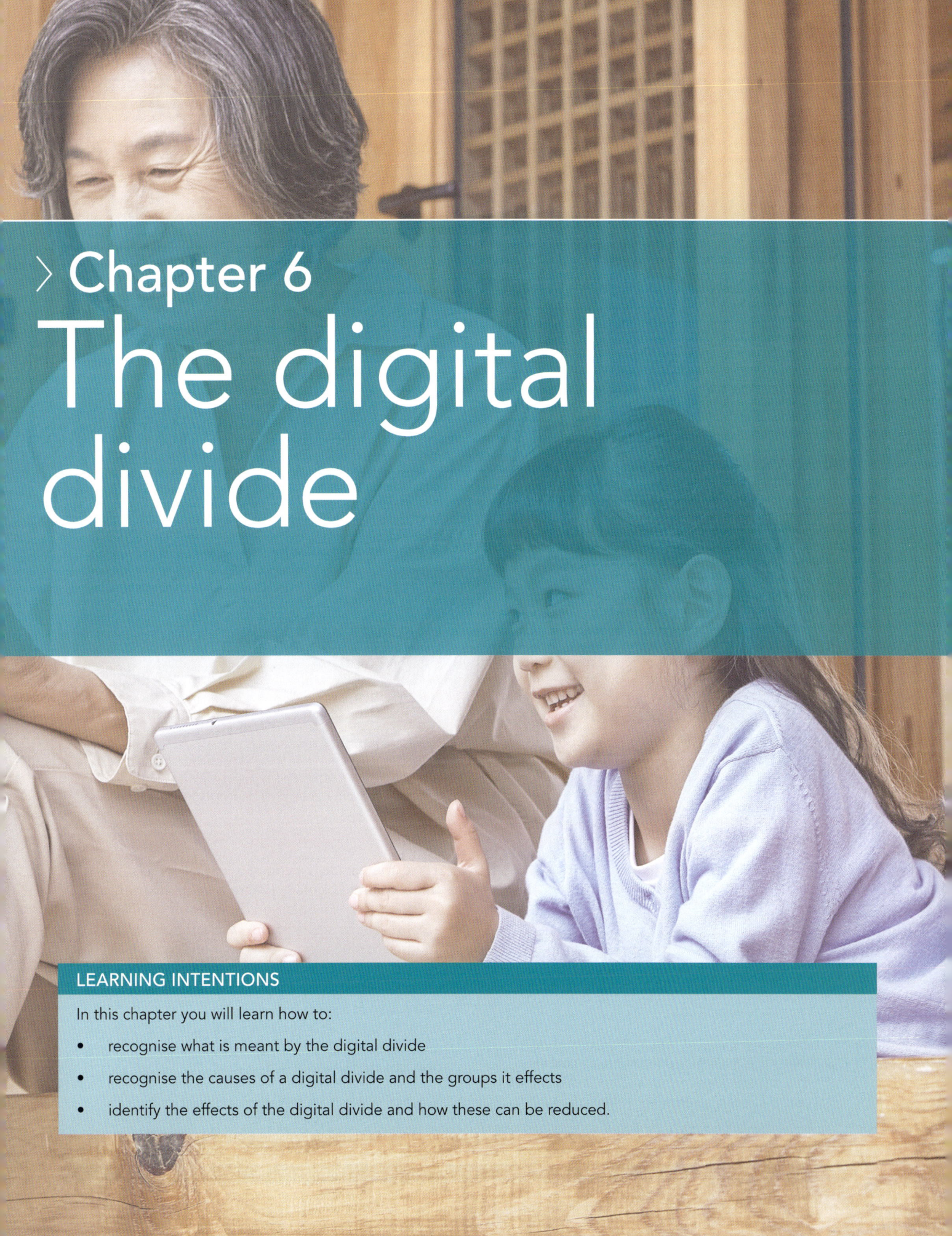

> Chapter 6
The digital divide

LEARNING INTENTIONS

In this chapter you will learn how to:

- recognise what is meant by the digital divide

- recognise the causes of a digital divide and the groups it effects

- identify the effects of the digital divide and how these can be reduced.

Introduction

The range of tasks that we rely on technology for is growing rapidly (see Figure 6.1). In 2021, the number of mobile devices worldwide was estimated at 15 billion. In 2023, the number of internet users was more than 5 billion – that means around 62% of the global population had access to the internet.

Figure 6.1: A passenger uses electronic check-in at an airport.

DISCUSSION POINT

Discuss the following in a group:

- Why do you think that around 40% of the world's population do not have access to the internet?

- What challenges may people experience if they do not have access to the internet or modern technology?

- There are plans to beam the internet to remote places that do not have access. Is this a good idea? What are the advantages and disadvantages of this plan?

6.1 What is the digital divide?

The **digital divide** refers to the differences in people's ability to access technology, such as smart phones, personal computers, tablets, laptops and TV, and the information and communications services they provide. A digital divide exists between those who have full access to technology and those that have restricted or no access. There can be a digital divide between countries, different **demographic** groups (particular sections of the population) and different **economic** areas (areas defined by their production and use of goods and services). The digital divide can be judged by several factors, such as a person's age, income and location.

KEY WORDS

digital divide: the difference in ability to access modern technology

demographic: a particular section of a population

economic: considering a country in terms of their production and consumption of goods and services

The digital divide is a complex and growing issue. Information technology generally brings many benefits to people. For example, you can interact with your bank account from a smart phone. You can place orders for goods/shopping using a computer and the internet. You can access knowledge and learning from a wide range of places using the internet. A lack of access to technology is seen as a disadvantage. It may lead to inequality. People who are not able to access technology may miss out on opportunities, both in their personal lives and in the workplace.

For a country, the digital divide may describe the difference between those who have regular access to modern technology and those who do not. At an international level, a digital divide may describe the difference between countries with access to the latest technology and those countries that have less access to modern technology.

DISCUSSION POINT

What do you think are the main causes of digital divides in your country?

Understanding the digital divide matters because access to modern technology can bring many benefits to people and countries.

It is important to remember that digital technology also has challenges. Some people may choose to avoid modern technology because of these issues, for example some people might not trust the development of **artificial intelligence (AI)** . Other people might experience a negative effect on their health because of social media.

KEY WORD

artificial intelligence (AI): the use of computer programs that can simulate human intelligence

Figure 6.2: Some people might not have access to a computer, smart TV, mobile phone, or tablet.

6.2 Causes and effects of the digital divide

The digital divide describes the gap between people who have the latest technology and those that do not. There are many causes of the digital divide.

Access to electricity

Technology requires electricity. Devices can run on battery or directly from mains electricity. Even if a device uses a battery, it still needs to be recharged.

It can be difficult to install electrical cables in remote parts of the world. It is expensive to build cables and install them in places many hundreds of miles away from power stations. Examples of places like these include deserts, mountains and remote villages or towns.

Solar power can help reduce the impact of being in a remote place. However, solar power is expensive to install.

Without access to electricity, people cannot use digital devices effectively.

Cost of technology

New technology is very expensive. Old technology is cheaper than the newest technology but will not be able to perform the same functions, access new programs or be as reliable. People from poorer areas of the world may not be able to afford new technology, or they may not be able to afford electricity to power the technology. They may not be able to pay for repairs if the technology breaks.

The cost of technology can create a digital divide in big cities. Cities have shops that sell the new technology. But if people have low paid jobs, they may not be able to afford to buy or rent new technology.

Ability to repair devices

Digital devices often need repairing or upgrading. Upgrades could include adding storage or updating software. If a person is unable to find a way to repair their device, for example by a local computer or phone technician, they will not be able to use their digital device (see Figure 6.3). A person with a particular brand of mobile device may not be able to get their device repaired locally. This may mean they need to buy a new device.

Figure 6.3: One cause of the digital divide is a lack of easy access to repair devices.

Access to the internet and wireless connections

Access to the internet is important as many services are only available by using the internet. For example, video conferencing, email/messaging apps and websites all require internet access. However, certain things like using word processing apps and printing may not need the internet.

Remote places make it difficult to install internet connections. The use of mobile phone networks and satellites removes the need for physical connections. However, satellite connections cost a lot of money to use. Satellite connections can also be slow and unreliable. Because the signals travel through the atmosphere into space, and back again, they can be disrupted by weather conditions like thunderstorms. Mobile phone networks only have a limited range and may not reach remote locations.

Very slow connections to the internet, or a total lack of connection adds to the digital divide. Lack of internet is probably one of the biggest factors when discussing the digital divide.

Availability of technology

The availability of technology refers to how many digital devices there are compared with how many people want them. For example, there may be 10 000 people who can afford a digital device, have access to the internet and are able to use these devices. However, if there are only 5000 devices available, then 5000 people will still not be able to access a digital device.

The COVID-19 pandemic meant that manufacturing of many things was disrupted. Prices of digital devices increased significantly at this time. This is because the microchips needed to manufacture these devices were not produced in the numbers that were needed.

New technology may need new manufacturing processes or better robots to build. This may limit the quantity of high-performance technology that is available. This increases the price for the technology.

6.3 Groups affected by the digital divide

Here are some examples of ways in which we can compare the digital divide:

- people in different age groups
- people in cities and people in rural areas
- people with differing levels of education
- people in different social-economic groups
- people with accessibility barriers
- people in more and less industrially developed nations.

People in different age groups

Technology is developing at great speed. New technology is released every year. For example, mobile phone companies may release new mobile phones every two years. People born in the 1960s grew up with very limited information technology. Business and personal communications relied on landline telephones (connected to wires and cables). Letters were typed or handwritten. Letters were sent by post or fax machine (see Figure 6.4, using a phone line) rather than using email. Groceries, clothing and other goods were bought at the shops.

Figure 6.4: A fax machine is used to copy and transmit a document down a phone line. The receiving fax machine prints out a copy of the document.

DISCUSSION POINT

Have you ever seen or used a fax machine? Do you think you would know how to use it? Would you just guess? Or would you want to see the user guide?

People born in the 1980s saw new technology emerging. This included simple mobile telephones, the ability to send short text messages, basic low-speed access to the internet using telephone lines, simple websites and downloading items from file storage.

By the beginning of the 21st century, wireless technology and almost instant communication became available. For example, smart phones, using wireless technology, allow instant access to online banking and shopping, the ability to book healthcare appointments, social media, messaging services, email and streaming services.

Many people today have grown up using this technology. They have been taught the IT skills required to use new technology in school or college. Younger people are better able to learn new skills as new features are introduced. On the other hand, some older people may find it hard to learn the new skills needed to use digital devices and the new technology. This is because the technology works in a very different way from the technology that they grew up with.

A person's ability to learn about and use technology effectively is called **digital literacy**. A lack of digital literacy may prevent a person from benefiting from online services. Lack of digital literacy can affect people from any age group. For example, an older person may lack digital literacy because they live in a rural area and do not have access to a local community college to learn about new devices. Without digital literacy, they will lack skills to access digital services or communicate with people effectively using digital devices. A younger person may lack digital literacy because they cannot afford technology and are less confident using it.

The term digital divide describes the difference between people who have and use technology and those who may have difficulty accessing and using new technologies.

KEY WORD

digital literacy: the skill level of a person to use digital technology to find and create information, and communicate with others using digital technology

ACTIVITY 6.01

Choose an activity that you use a digital device for, such as playing an online game, or creating and sending a short video.

Create a short video or presentation that explains how to do to this activity on your digital device.

The video or presentation should teach someone who has never used this technology what to do.

Real-life example

Mohammed is an independent 75-year-old living in his own home. He has a mobile phone so that he can contact his daughter who lives in another town. He doesn't know how to use the mobile phone's other features. He only knows how to phone his daughter.

Mohammed has regular hospital appointments. He used to receive a letter from the hospital reminding him of his appointments, but the hospital no longer does this. Instead, it sends Mohammed text messages, reminding him of the date and time of his appointment, and asking him to confirm by text if he will attend. Mohammed doesn't know how to send a text message. He knows his daughter is very busy and doesn't want to phone and ask her what to do. Instead, he worries that he will lose his hospital appointment (see Figure 6.5).

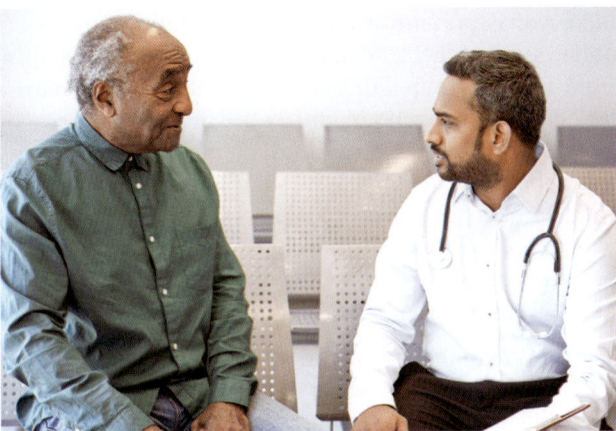

Figure 6.5: People who lack digital literacy skills may be at a disadvantage.

UNPLUGGED ACTIVITY 6.02

Design a poster to show how technology in a shopping centre may affect people with low digital literacy. Include:

- the technology used

- the challenge faced by someone with low digital literacy

- the benefits of this technology to the shopping centre or store.

Reducing the digital divide between different age groups

One of the biggest barriers to people using technology is fear of new things. They may be more comfortable doing things in ways that are familiar to them. For example, they may prefer to visit different shops to look for an item that is difficult to find, rather than search the internet to find the item they need. A person may believe that they are not clever enough to learn how to use digital devices. Quite often, older people feel more scared learning about new technology. Technology changes so fast that they feel they 'cannot keep up' with all the changes.

DISCUSSION POINT

Imagine you have been asleep for 100 years. You wake up and technology has developed. The following technologies have been developed:

- teleporters

- fully automatic robots to help you in the home

- flying cars

- machines that make all your meals

- headsets that read your thoughts to operate things such as the television, your car and write emails.

Discuss with a classmate:

- How would you feel?

- What challenges would you experience?

- What things would you need to help you adapt to the new technology?

- How does this relate to how older people or those with low technology skills feel in today's world?

People often choose to learn new things when they see the benefits of learning the new skill. People are more likely to learn to use new technology if they see that the benefits will be greater than the challenge of learning the new skill. For example, learning how to use social media may allow people to communicate with family and friends and prevent them from being socially isolated and combat loneliness. Many countries support older people to help them appreciate the advantages of technology and teach them how to use it.

DISCUSSION POINT

Discuss the following idea as a class.

Would you choose to learn a new language to speak to new people? What would be easier for you? Would the benefit of being able to talk to all the other people who use that language be useful? Discuss the advantages and disadvantages of both learning the new language, and not learning the new language.

infrastructure for the availability of high-speed internet connections is far more developed in city locations.

KEY WORD

infrastructure: the facilities that are needed for the operation of a society, such as roads, buildings and utilities

Real-life example

Retirement villages (places with houses or apartments intended for older people) are built using several different technologies to show how the technology can benefit their lives. Sensors can monitor a patient's health and doctors can take advantage of high-speed broadband to make video-conference calls to check in and look after older patients. This helps people who find travelling to a clinic more difficult.

Libraries and community centres may offer short IT sessions to help people get started with computers, tablets and using the internet (see Figure 6.6).

Figure 6.7: Providing high-speed internet to places in remote locations can be a major challenge.

Figure 6.6: Technology can be accessed by different age groups.

People living in cities and rural areas

The place where a person lives affects their access to technology. One aspect of this is whether they live in a city or a small town or village.

One of the main services affected by location is access to the internet. Access to high-speed and reliable internet connections are more often found in cities than small villages and towns (see Figure 6.7). This is because the

Because many people live in a city there is a greater demand for high-speed internet connections. There are also many hundreds of people living close to each other. Connecting people living in cities to the internet takes less resource (for example, you could connect 300 people to the internet with 100 m of cable). This means that it is cheaper for internet providers to deliver services in cities.

Some people live in rural areas, many kilometres from larger towns and cities. There may be only 300 people in a village. A city may have many hundreds of thousands of people. Providing a connection over a large distance for a small number of people is not very profitable. So, internet providers may try to avoid investing in high-speed internet in rural areas.

People who do not have high-speed internet access may struggle to access the services available on the internet, which may include online shopping and services offered by some online television broadcasting companies. This would happen if they cannot stream films or TV reliably or consistently and could result in a person feeling isolated.

Questions

1   a   How could a lack of high-speed internet access affect a person's ability to use online learning platforms?

   b   How could this affect the digital divide between those living in a city and those living in a rural location?

2   a   How could a lack of mobile phone internet services affect a person's ability to communicate with others?

   b   What kind of services might they not be able to use?

   c   How might this lack of ability to communicate in certain ways make them feel?

The issue of a lack of access to high-speed internet can extend to mobile telephone internet services. In a rural location, a person may find that they have limited connection to mobile networks, or may not get any connection at all.

Real-life example

Sofia lives in a rural area of Spain. Access to high-speed internet in her village is very limited. She is a furniture designer who works from home. Sofia currently creates her designs and sends them to clients using the internet. She wants to make video calls to her clients to have meetings (see Figure 6.8).

However, Sofia's internet connection does not allow her to use video-conferencing technologies effectively. Sofia's internet connection puts her at a disadvantage compared with furniture designers who have access to high-speed internet connections.

Reducing the effects of the digital divide in rural areas

To reduce the effects of the digital divide in rural areas, there are two main issues:

* the access people have to digital devices and technology

* how they connect devices to the internet. This could be via the internet or by mobile networks.

Building infrastructure for high-speed internet or mobile networks can be very challenging. For example, a village could be hundreds of kilometres from the nearest city, or a village may be up in the mountains, or in a remote inaccessible area. One way to provide internet access to remote locations is to use satellite technologies. This reduces the amount of infrastructure needed, while still providing access to the internet.

Real-life example

BharatNet is an initiative of the government of India that focuses on developing infrastructure in rural India to provide affordable internet. They are planning to do this through increasing the infrastructure based on fibre optic cabling (see Figure 6.9). They are also planning to deliver access through satellites in approximately 5300 locations.

Figure 6.8: Video-conferencing technologies help rural businesses to connect with clients.

Figure 6.9: Building digital infrastructure.

ACTIVITY 6.03

Imagine you are a government technology representative for your country. You have been tasked with improving internet access in rural areas of your country.

Work with a partner and create a presentation that highlights your plan for improving internet access in rural areas of your country.

Your presentation should also include the advantages that such access will provide.

UNPLUGGED ACTIVITY 6.04

Reflect on a time when you needed to increase your digital literacy, for example, to learn a new technology or a new way of using technology that you were already familiar with.

- What concerns did you have about learning the new skill?

- Did you use any learning techniques that you already knew?

- How did you apply your current level of digital literacy to help develop the new skill?

- What was the outcome of learning this new skill?

- How would you change your approach if you had to learn a new skill again?

People with differing levels of education

Using technology can be complex. Different types of technology have different interfaces and are used in different ways. Without a certain level of education in how to use technology, it can often seem challenging.

DID YOU KNOW?

In the UK, 6.3% of adults said they had never used the internet in 2020. That's an estimated 3.4 million people.

Many businesses have online systems to allow people to buy products, book tickets or use services. This is very useful for people who are educated in using technology and are confident in using the systems. But people who are not educated in using these systems may find it frustrating and miss out on opportunities.

There are many different reasons why people are not technologically educated. For example, they may not have access to technology and therefore do not have experience in using it. Some people simply do not have an interest in using technology. Some people may struggle to keep learning about all the new developments in technology and so 'give up'.

Question

3 Think of two advantages that people who are educated in using technology may have over those who are not educated in using technology.

Real-life example

A person wants to buy tickets to see their favourite band. Tickets are only available online. The person has never used an online ticket booking system before and feels very nervous about doing so. They usually call the concert location and purchase tickets over the telephone, but this option is not available.

When the person tries to use the online system to buy the tickets, they are confused and do not know how to operate the system. By the time they work out what to do, the tickets have all sold out. The person now cannot buy the tickets to see the band because they did not have the education in technology and experience needed to navigate the ticket booking system.

Reducing the digital divide by improving digital literacy

One effective way of reducing the digital divide is through digital literacy teaching by providing access to technology courses in local communities. Digital literacy courses for adults are often offered by colleges, schools and libraries. Courses can be offered for free, or at a low cost. This allows people to improve their knowledge of how to use technology. Courses allow people to learn with other people of the same skill level. This helps people feel more comfortable about learning new skills. Local face-to-face courses have a teacher or a leader to help them with problems. People often find face-to-face courses more useful. This is because they may need to learn about skills to access online learning courses. People can then use the skills they learn to use technology more confidently in the future.

Real-life example

A country offered a 12-week course to its citizens for learning skills in everyday software. The course was provided by a virtual university. The course provided basic knowledge on using software and how to use the internet for communication (see Figure 6.10).

This education provided people with a basic education in the use of technology. It allowed them to feel more comfortable and confident in their skills. The country believed this helped people to be more competitive in the digital world.

Figure 6.10: Virtual education can provide essential digital literacy skills.

People in different socio-economic groups

The digital divide between different socio-economic groups often revolves around cost. Richer people can afford higher-speed internet connections and expensive advancements in technology. This improves their standard of living because they have better access to:

- information and learning
- entertainment
- online services such as shopping
- worldwide communication.

Lack of access to information tends to have a greater impact on people with lower levels of education. The lack of access to services like free education can create a greater digital divide between the rich and the poor. Ensuring access for all to education and information is an important way of improving the socio-economic circumstances.

Questions

4 How could the ability to access free online learning platforms support people in poorer communities?

5 How could access to high-speed internet connections for entertainment purposes improve the lifestyle of a person?

Real-life example

Taliya is a film studies student. She has high-quality recording equipment, a 4K monitor and a high-spec computer system at home. She really enjoys recording scenes for her film projects and editing them on her computer system at home.

Jaz is also a film studies student. He is becoming increasingly frustrated as he only has a low-spec mobile phone to film and edit all his film projects. He knows that he could produce much better work, and enjoy his studies far more, if he had access to a better computer system to edit his films with.

Reducing the digital divide in different socio-economic groups

Many countries try to provide technology at lower cost (or even for free) to those in poorer communities. This helps close the digital divide by giving access to the advantages that the technologies can provide.

Large organisations, such as Facebook and Google, are working with internet service providers. They help to build infrastructure to bring internet access to areas or countries that cannot afford it. For example, they help to reduce the costs of installing Wi-Fi access points. Organisations collaborate in this way because it means more people have access to the internet. This means that more people may use the services that these organisations provide.

People with accessibility barriers

The digital divide can affect people who may have specific challenges in accessing a particular technology. For example, someone living with vision loss will not be able to use a digital display effectively (see Figure 6.11).

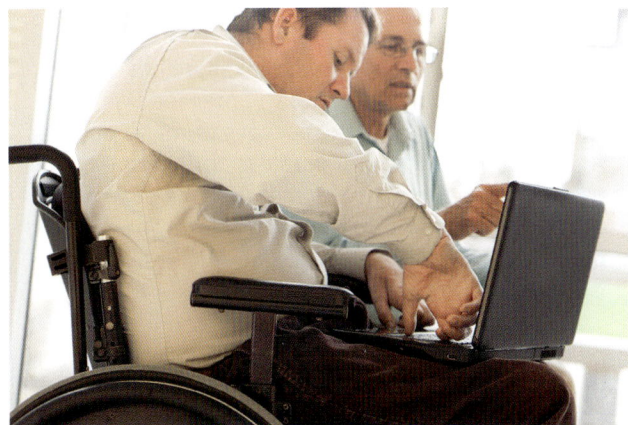

Figure 6.11: A person with a spinal cord injury overcomes accessibility barriers by using their thumb to access and use their laptop.

Support for people with accessibility barriers is important when digital technology is developed. Many digital devices have some support included. For example, there are screen readers that convert the text on the screen into sound. Effectively, a person can hear what is on the screen as the digital device reads it out to them. Voice input/commands can be used to help those who may not be able to operate keyboards or touchscreens effectively.

People in more and less industrially developed nations

The parts of the world that have greater access to modern technology are the USA, Europe and northern Asia. These areas mostly consist of more industrially developed countries. Areas where technology access is more restricted include parts of Africa, India and southern Asia. These are areas that are less industrially developed. Access to technology may be less in these areas because the countries may need to use their financial resources to provide other important services. They may not have the money to spend on the development of their technology services.

The costs for countries to build the infrastructure for technology use are very high. However, not having access to technology and the internet could put them at both a competitive and economic disadvantage. Lack of technology may limit trade opportunities and therefore they may fall behind financially when compared to more industrially developed countries. It may also affect the level of education that can be provided to the country's citizens. They may not be able to access the learning and information available to them on the internet. This can have an impact on both the education and the skill level of people in those countries and prevent them from competing on an international level.

DISCUSSION POINT

Business and education are two areas where the digital divide can restrict the industrial development of a country. Work with a partner. Think of one other area that could be affected and discuss what impact this could have on the country.

ACTIVITY 6.05

How aware are you of the technological infrastructure in your country?

1   Make a list (without a computer) of the technology facilities that you think the government of your country provides to its citizens.

2   Use the internet to research the list of facilities the government provides.

3   How many did you get right? Were there any you are surprised by?

4   Do further research using the internet to find out any future plans your country has to improve its technological infrastructure.

Real-life example

A village cooperative in Kenya makes hand-beaded necklaces that it sells to local people and tourists. The members would like to expand the business and sell their necklaces to a wider market. This would increase the cooperative's income and benefit everyone in the village (see Figure 6.12). The cooperative sets up an online business, but internet access to the village is poor and it is unable to run the website effectively. The lack of infrastructure has put the cooperative at a competitive disadvantage.

Figure 6.12: Internet access allows people across the world to see a business's products and place orders for them online.

The village cooperative wants to improve access to the internet in their village. Developing internet access is expensive and the cooperative may not be able to pay for this without help. Local communities often create campaigns to help raise awareness of the local facilities, and what they want in the future. The campaign will be sent to the local government, or maybe even the national government. They would create a campaign to ask for better services, and show how these services could impact their community. It is important to remember that the members of the cooperative may have a low level of technology awareness. They may not know about the best digital technology or how to use it. Part of the campaign may involve a consultation with IT specialists from the government. This would allow the government to show what technology is available, and for the members of the cooperative to see how they can use the technology. A plan can then be put in place that balances the technology and costs against the impact on the cooperative.

Reducing the digital divide in less industrially developed areas

The internet has become essential to global infrastructures. Those with limited access to the internet may not be able to access all the benefits of the internet. Satellite technology may assist remote areas to access the internet. Large companies plan to use satellite technologies that allow such areas better access to the internet.

DID YOU KNOW?

A company called Starlink is aiming to provide high-speed internet connections to the world using satellites in space. Starlink launches satellites into space that beam internet signals to Earth. This allows internet access to many places where cables and other wireless connections cannot reach. This means that millions of people could soon be able to access the internet without the need for local infrastructure. The challenge is that satellite technology is expensive to run. This means that the cost to access the internet by satellite is quite high when compared to using ground-based access.

Governments in many less industrially developed regions try to promote the business and products that they could offer if they had better infrastructure and high-speed access to the internet. They are keen for more industrially developed countries to invest and help them to build the necessary infrastructure. These coordinated efforts can benefit the world on a global scale.

Real-life example

Microsoft has an initiative called the Microsoft Airband Initiative. The aim of the initiative is to close the global digital divide by working with its partners to provide internet access to millions of people worldwide whose communities have limited or no internet access. The initiative uses a range of wired and wireless technologies. One part of the initiative uses Television White Spaces (TVWS) technology. TVWS is fixed wireless technology that uses radio frequencies which currently broadcast television. Internet access can be provided using these radio frequencies that are often unused and unlicensed. This technology is giving internet access to people in countries where the cost of adding ground-based infrastructure is either very expensive or would take a long time to build.

PRACTICE QUESTIONS

1   Define the term 'digital divide'. [1]
2   Identify two aspects that can create a digital divide. [2]
3   Explain the impact of the digital divide on a person's geographical location. [4]
4   Explain how a person's education can be affected by the digital divide. [4]
5   Explain two strategies that can be implemented to reduce the digital divide. [4]

SUMMARY CHECKLIST

☐   I can explain what is meant by the digital divide.

☐   I can explain the causes of the digital divide.

☐   I can discuss the effects of the digital divide and what measures can be taken to reduce the digital divide among different groups.

PROJECT

Figure 6.13: People using a range of digital devices.

You will create a magazine story about the digital divide in your area.

1   Research your local area or city.

- Find out what technology is available for people to use.

- Do you have infrastructure to access the internet? How reliable is it?

- Who has access to the technology? Is it shared fairly for all?

- Think about the age of the people around you.

2   Create a magazine story that discusses:

- the differences in technology in the area you live

- the socio-economic challenges in your area

- what plans or schemes there are to reduce the digital divide in your area

- what you feel needs to be done to help reduce the digital divide even further.

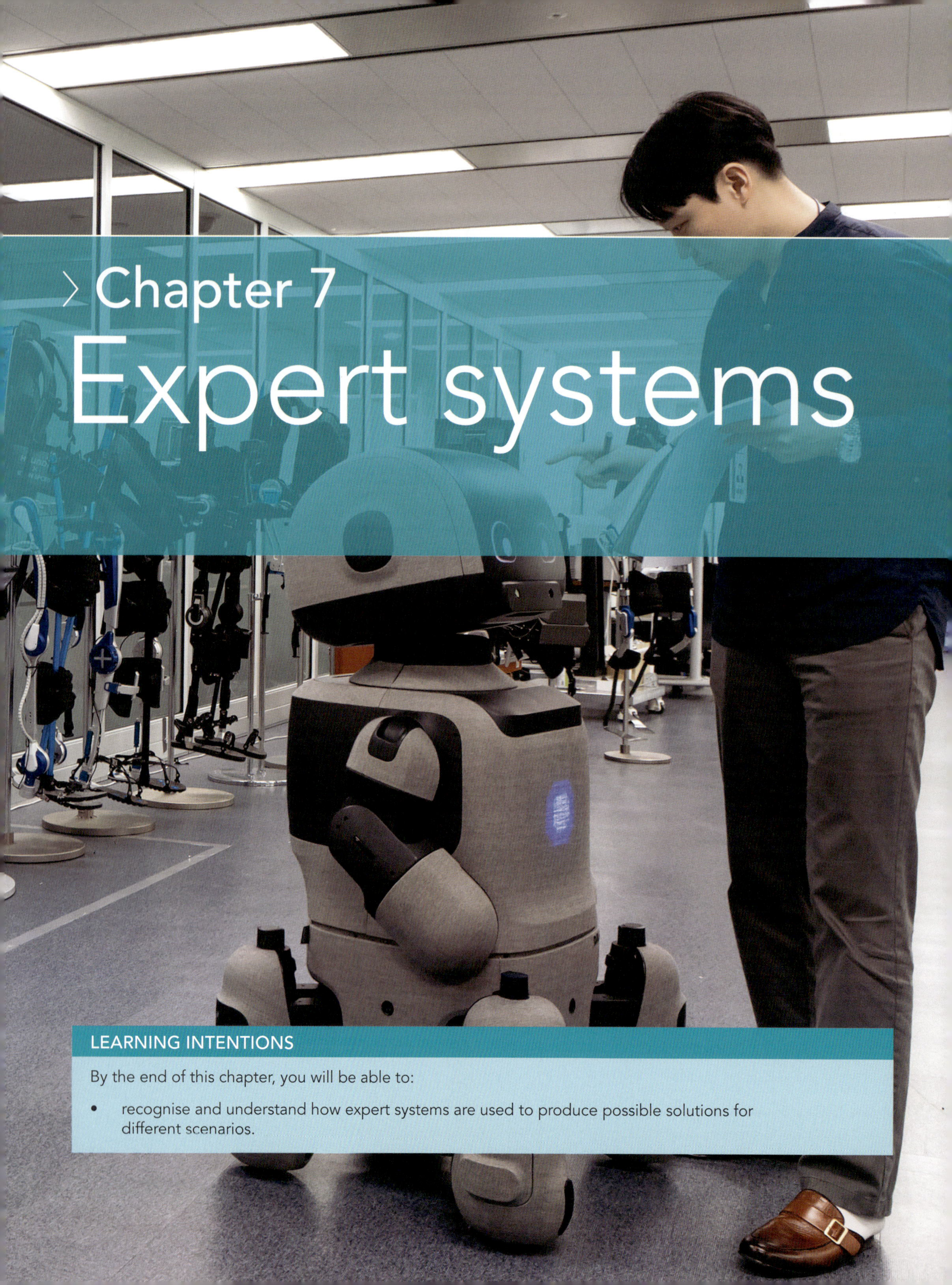

› Chapter 7
Expert systems

LEARNING INTENTIONS

By the end of this chapter, you will be able to:

- recognise and understand how expert systems are used to produce possible solutions for different scenarios.

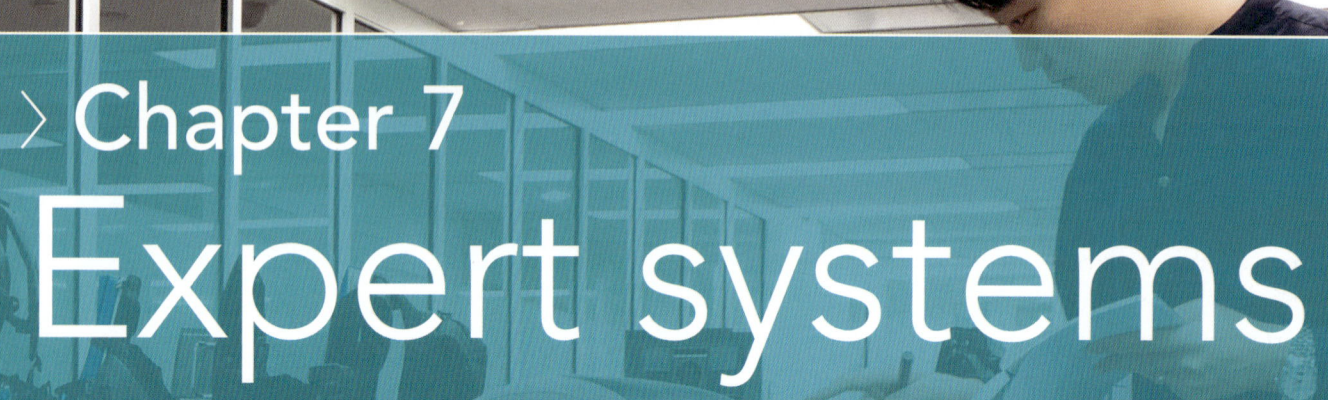

Introduction

You spend time every day developing your knowledge, thinking and making decisions (see Figure 7.1). It is possible to develop systems to aid decision-making processes. These are called expert systems.

An expert system is a computerised system that attempts to reproduce the decision-making process of an expert human being. Expert systems are designed to try to replicate the judgement of a human that has expert knowledge in a certain field. By doing this, expert systems can be used to replace or assist a human expert. The person who designs and develops an expert system is called an expert system engineer.

An expert system operates by prompting the user to enter certain data using the user interface, referring to the knowledge base and using the inference engine to aid the decision-making process it is designed to support.

Expert systems can be used in many different scenarios – settings where expert systems are used for specific tasks. Expert systems can be used as a diagnostic tool, such as in financial planning and risk analysis. Expert systems can even be used for a more fun purpose, such

Figure 7.1: A touch screen interface can form part of an expert system's user interface.

as playing Scrabble online against a computer. They are also a form of artificial intelligence, which is a computer system designed to simulate human intelligence.

7.1 Components of an expert system

An expert system consists of several components. These components include:

- a user interface

- a knowledge base (as a database of facts and rules base)

- an inference engine

- an explanation system

- a knowledge base editor.

User interface

The user interface is the way that a user interacts with the expert system. This could include using a keyboard to enter data into text query boxes, or choosing options by pressing offered choices on a touch screen.

The user interface will prompt the user for the data they need to input into the expert system and will then display any output from the expert system. Other output devices may also be available, such as a printer to produce a paper copy of results.

Without a user interface, a user would need to know how to program each of the interactions they want to make with the expert system. The quality of the design of a user interface is important to the usefulness of an expert system.

Question

1   What could happen if the user interface for the expert system is poorly designed?

Knowledge base

The **knowledge base** is a database of related information about a particular subject. It allows the storage and retrieval of the knowledge required for an expert system to operate.

When an expert system is developed, several experts will be interviewed and asked to provide the knowledge they have of a given field. This knowledge is then used to build a **database of facts**, which is the knowledge base for the expert system.

The developers will want two types of knowledge from the experts: factual knowledge and heuristic knowledge. Factual knowledge is knowledge that is widely shared among experts in the field. Heuristic knowledge is knowledge that is built on personal experiences and reasoning.

Part of the knowledge base is the **rules base**. The rules base is a set of rules that will be used to produce a decision by the expert system. These rules are used by the inference engine as a base for reasoning, to obtain a solution to a problem or a decision. Each rule will contain two parts, IF and THEN. A rule can also have multiple IF statements, which are joined together by Boolean operators, including AND and OR.

A simple example of a rule could be:

IF a > b AND a > c THEN highest = a

> **KEY WORDS**
>
> **knowledge base:** a component of an expert system that stores the knowledge provided by experts
>
> **database of facts:** all information that is known about the subject within the knowledge base
>
> **rules base:** a part of the knowledge base that contains all the rules to be analysed by the expert system

The knowledge base should be regularly updated. So, the expert system needs to have a **knowledge base editor**. The knowledge base editor allows the knowledge base to be edited and added to when necessary.

Question

2   What could happen if the expert system did not have a knowledge base editor?

Inference engine

The **inference engine** is the part of the expert system that makes judgements and reasoning using the knowledge base and user responses. It is designed to produce reasoning based on the rules base and the knowledge base.

The inference engine will ask the user questions and, based on their answer, it will follow a line of logic. This may then lead to further questions and, eventually, to a final result.

Explanation system

The conclusion or decision the expert system provides may not always be an obvious choice to a user. The user may therefore want to gain an understanding of how the conclusion or decision was made. To provide this information, some expert systems have an **explanation system** built into them. This will provide an explanation of the reasoning process and show how the output given by the system was reached.

> **KEY WORDS**
>
> **knowledge base editor:** a component of an expert system that is used to change or update the knowledge base
>
> **inference engine:** part of the expert system that makes judgements and reasoning using the knowledge base and user responses
>
> **explanation system:** a component of an expert system that provides an explanation of how an outcome was reached

Questions

3   Think of a scenario in which an expert system would be useful.

4   Think of a scenario where an expert system would not be suitable.

7.2 How are expert systems used?

Expert systems are used in a range of scenarios by individuals and organisations to support decision making. Expert systems may be used in:

- medical diagnosis
- car engine fault diagnosis
- providing financial planning and investment analysis
- providing insurance planning advice
- plant and animal identification
- scheduling routes for delivery vehicles
- mineral prospecting.

Medical diagnosis

The organisation WebMD has a website that offers a medical expert system called 'symptom checker'. It asks the user a series of questions about their symptoms and then provides possible conditions that match the symptoms. It lists the possible conditions in order, starting with the one it finds to be the closest match.

Questions

5   What could be the benefits and the disadvantages of people using online self-diagnosis systems?

6   Why might a doctor use an expert system to aid a diagnosis?

Car engine fault diagnosis

Most modern cars have lots of technology built into them. The technology includes an on-board expert system, known as the on-board diagnostics system. The on-board diagnostics system monitors the car's engine performance. If the engine develops a fault, the diagnostics system turns on a warning light on the dashboard to alert the driver. When the driver sees the warning light, they should take the car to a garage. At the garage, a mechanic will connect a diagnostic tool to the on-board diagnostics system (see Figure 7.2). The expert system will provide the mechanic with a code that will help them to find and fix the fault.

Figure 7.2: A car mechanic checks the on-board diagnostic system to find the source of the fault in the engine.

ACTIVITY 7.03

Figure 7.3: In 1997, the expert system Deep Blue beat the world champion chess player Garry Kasparov.

Find out about:

- the expert system Deep Blue (see Figure 7.3)
- the chess playing system, AlphaZero.

Create a slide explaining the key features of the chess systems and significant victories against human opponents.

Financial planning and investment analysis

Expert systems can be a useful tool in financial planning for both individuals and businesses. They can create a financial plan or assess what financial actions need to be taken to achieve a desired outcome.

They can help people to:

- manage their debt
- reduce their outgoings
- reduce their taxes
- plan for retirement.

A user enters information about their financial situation and personal circumstances. The expert system will then produce a financial plan, or a list of possible outcomes, based on this information.

Expert systems can also be used to analyse investments and help maximise returns on funds invested. They can help people to:

- Monitor stock markets and suggest when to buy and sell shares.
- Determine how much risk is involved with certain investments.
- Make decisions based on the amount of money they wish to invest.
- Examine options on the period of time to invest their money, for example 1–5 years.
- Decide whether to move from one type of investment to another.
- Using such systems, sometimes with the support of a professional financial adviser, can enable people to make informed decisions based on the information provided.

Insurance planning

Many insurance company websites use an online expert system, so that users can quickly see if the company has a policy that would be suitable for them. Such systems will ask the user for relevant personal information and it will then provide a result to say whether the insurance company would be willing to give the user an insurance policy. If the expert system is able to match their data to a possible policy, it will then inform the user with details about the policy, such as how much it will cost and what benefits it will provide.

Question

7   An insurance company offers life insurance policies. What kind of questions do you think the expert system will ask to check whether an insurance policy can be issued to a user?

Plant and animal identification

The Native Plants Database, provided by the University of Texas in Austin, allows users to enter a range of characteristics about a plant. It mostly covers native plants in North America.

The website takes the data input about the plant and analyses it against its rules and knowledge base. It then tells the user what kind of plant it could be, with further options provided to offer more specific results if required. A user could find out what kind of plant is growing in their garden, or try to discover the type of plant they have seen when on a walk (see Figure 7.4).

Expert systems are also available to enable users to identify animals. For example, the user could input data based on an animal's characteristics to determine what animal it might be.

Figure 7.4: Using an online plant finder to identify a plant.

Route scheduling for delivery vehicles

Delivery companies can use expert systems to find out the best route for a delivery driver. The expert system helps determine the most efficient route, such as the shortest distance or quickest time, for all the deliveries the driver has on a given day.

Each of the deliveries the driver needs to make is put into the system. The system then outputs a route that will be the most efficient route for the driver to follow. It may request further information, such as the type of delivery vehicle and how long each delivery will take. The system may make further recommendations about how many drivers are needed to deliver all the items that day and what kind of vehicle each driver will need to take for the packages they need to deliver.

It is likely that an expert system could work out this type of outcome quicker than a human, due to the amount of data it is likely to handle, especially in large delivery companies where multiple vehicles are being used at the same time (see Figure 7.5).

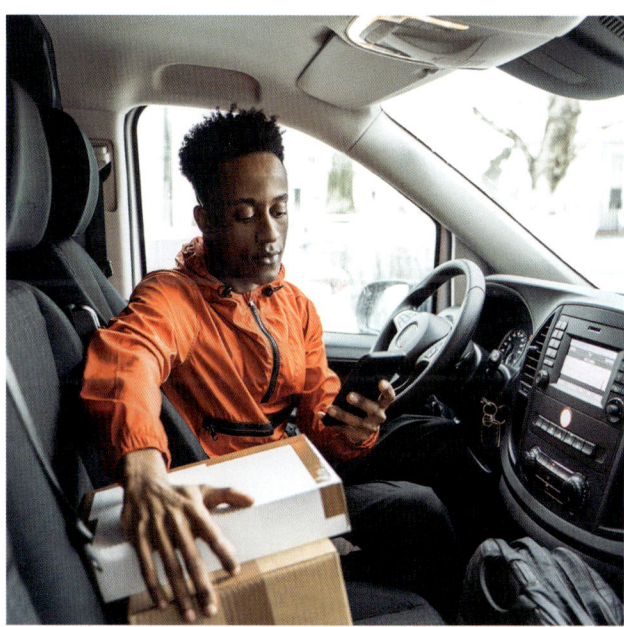

Figure 7.5: Expert systems help make deliveries more efficient.

Question

8 What kind of questions would an expert system ask in order to identify a type of animal?

Mineral prospecting

Minerals, like ruby, emerald and iron, can be very precious, and geologists can spend a long time trying to source them (see Figure 7.6).

Figure 7.6: A raw emerald stone before it is cut, polished and used to make jewellery.

An expert system called PROSPECTOR was one of the first expert systems developed to aid geologists in exploring for minerals. Digging for minerals can be very expensive, so companies want to be sure that minerals will be present when they break ground (see Figure 7.7). PROSPECTOR can be used to calculate the probability of minerals being present in a certain location by examining data related to factors such as the soil type and topography of the land.

Figure 7.7: Prospecting for minerals.

7.3 Backward chaining and forward chaining

There are two main methods that an inference engine can use to simulate reasoning. They are **backward chaining** and **forward chaining**. IF…THEN constructs are used to determine whether a rule is true when using these methods.

Backward chaining

Backward chaining is based on **goal driven** reasoning where reasoning is dependent on finding a desired goal. This type of chaining is used when the possible outcomes are limited and clearly defined. In backward chaining, the system takes a goal and repeatedly splits it into sub-goals that are simpler to achieve. This type of system moves backwards from the goal to be achieved, using the sub-goals to inform the next piece of data that is needed by the system, to reach a goal.

For example, within a video game, an expert system might be used to determine whether a player can progress to a certain area (the goal). Backward chaining could be used to check IF the player has collected certain items, such as a key, AND IF they have defeated a specific enemy, such as a robot spider (sub-goals). Should both these facts be true, THEN the player can move on to the next part of the game. Figure 7.8 shows the process of backward chaining.

KEY WORDS

backward chaining: breaking a goal down into sub-goals that allow the system to work backwards from the goal

forward chaining: a system that moves forward from rule to rule until it reaches a possible outcome

goal driven: a system that is dependent on finding a desired goal

---

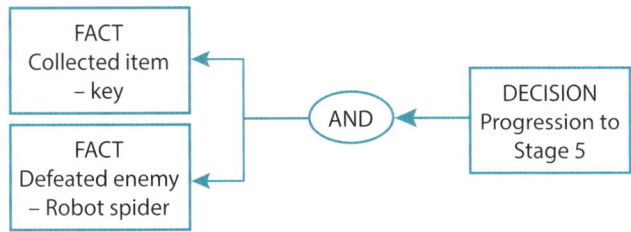

Figure 7.8: Example of backward chaining used in gaming.

Forward chaining

Forward chaining is based on **data driven** reasoning and is dependent on the data that the expert system is provided with. This type of system is used when a problem is more open ended, and the outcome is not always clearly defined. The system will take data input by the user and move forward from rule to rule to suggest possible outcomes where the rule for the data input is true. It will then ask the user for more data and repeat this process until it can suggest an outcome.

> **KEY WORD**
>
> **data driven:** a system dependent on the data that it is provided with

For example, when a doctor is deciding on a diagnosis for a patient, they will input data prompted by the expert system, such as IF the patient is over a certain age. Should the patient be older than the age specified, such as over 65 years, THEN further questions will be asked appropriate to that age group, such as if they have mobility needs. Different questions could be asked if the patient is the same age or younger than the age specified.

Figure 7.9 shows the process of forward chaining.

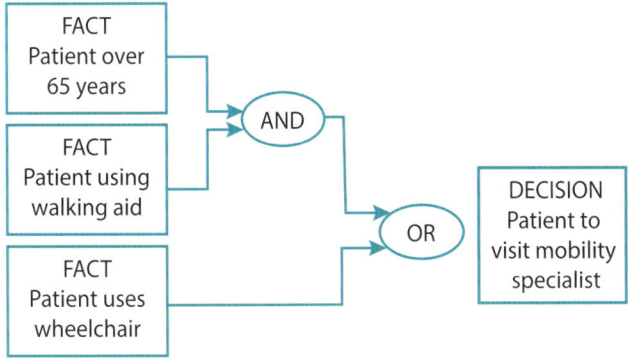

Figure 7.9: Example of forward chaining used in diagnosis.

Artificial intelligence

Data driven artificial intelligence (AI) may be used to manipulate social media. Social networking platforms can use data related to the user's behaviour, such as videos viewed, group membership and adverts clicked on, to change the content provided to individuals. Through manipulating the content shown to a user, AI can be used to ensure only certain viewpoints are presented, which may influence the user's point of view and decision making. Using data in this way may result in users being presented with false or misleading information, potentially allowing their views to be manipulated.

7.4 Advantages and disadvantages of expert systems

Table 7.1 shows possible advantages and disadvantages of using an expert system.

Advantages	Disadvantages
Can provide answers to questions that are outside the knowledge that you currently have.	Do not have the intuition that humans have. This means that their response can only be a logical one and may not be useful.
Can aid professional people by prompting and guiding them to look at areas of knowledge they may not have considered or remembered.	Are only as good as the rules and data they are provided with. If there are errors in the data or rules, such as if the data or rules need to be updated, then this will produce incorrect results.
Are consistent in the responses they produce as they are arrived at in a logical way.	Are expensive to create and maintain. Many experts need to be consulted and a high level of skill is required to build the component parts, along with keeping the system up to date.

> Chapter 8
Spreadsheets

LEARNING INTENTIONS

By the end of this chapter, you will be able to:

- create page/screen structures to meet the requirements of an audience and/or task specification/house style

- create and edit spreadsheet structures

- control data input using validation techniques

- protect cells and their content

- freeze panes and windows

- create and use formulas

- use absolute reference, relative reference, named cells, named ranges

- understand why absolute and relative referencing are used

- use functions

- use appropriate input and error messages

- format cells

- format cell emphasis

- appreciate the requirements, purpose and use of a spreadsheet

- test a spreadsheet structure

CONTINUED

- test data
- extract data
- sort data
- summarise and display data
- import and export data
- create a graph or chart appropriate to a specific purpose
- apply chart formatting.

BEFORE YOU START

- Do you know that spreadsheets can be used to manipulate numbers, perform calculations, present summary data and make predictions?

- Are you able to create a basic spreadsheet structure using cells, rows and columns?

- Do you understand the purpose of cells, rows, columns and ranges within worksheets?

Introduction

A **spreadsheet** is a software application that organises data in rows and columns. There are many actions that a spreadsheet can perform on the data, including carrying out calculations, organising the data and creating graphs (see Figure 8.1).

KEY WORD

spreadsheet: software that can organise, analyse and manipulate data, which is organised in a grid of rows and columns

Figure 8.1: Charts made with a spreadsheet may be used to examine an organisation's performance.

8.1 Creating a spreadsheet

Creating page and screen structures

When setting up a spreadsheet, you will need to think about its purpose, that is the task you want it to do. You will also need to consider the spreadsheet's target audience, the people who are going to use the spreadsheet. For example, it may be better to spread the data across multiple pages if fitting all the data onto one page will make it too small to read when printed. An organisation might have specific rules or guidance around the presentation of the spreadsheet, known as the house style. For example, there may be a requirement to have the title of the document and the page number in a header or footer, which will help the audience understand the structure of the document.

The formatting options that follow will help you to present the spreadsheet in the most appropriate way. Each of the options can be found in the File menu, then Page Setup.

Page orientation

The orientation of the page refers to the direction the document is displayed. The orientation can be set to portrait, where the shorter edge of the page is horizontal, or landscape, where the shorter edge of the page is vertical.

Page size

The size of the page can be set to common paper sizes, such as A4 or Letter. Alternatively, custom page sizes can be specified. Further options are available when setting the page size, such as deciding whether to print gridlines.

Fit to page

Sometimes, large spreadsheets cover several pieces of paper when printed. To save paper and format the data as required, it is possible to set the spreadsheet to fit on a single page when printed. Alternatively, the number of pages to use when printing can also be set by specifying the printed spreadsheet's width and height.

Margins

The top, bottom, left and right margins can be adjusted to provide space at the edges, such as to punch holes or write comments, or to reduce the space at the edge and provide more space on the paper for printing.

Header and footer

Information can be included at the top and bottom of each printed page. This could include the title and author of the document, page number, file name and date, or simply custom text entered by the user.

> **TIP**
>
> A different header and footer can be used on the first printed page of a spreadsheet if required.

ACTIVITY 8.01

Open the spreadsheet **8.01_Page Formatting.xlsx**, which currently requires 20 pages to print.

1   Add a header of 'Chapter 8 figure list'.

2   Remove gridlines from printing.

3   Remove row and column headings from printing.

4   Add a footer of 'Page # of *n*', where # is the current page number and *n* is the total number of pages.

5   Change the settings described so that the document fits onto just three pages.

Creating and editing spreadsheet structures

Data within a spreadsheet is stored within **cells**, which are organised into rows and columns. Each cell has a unique name, known as a cell reference, which starts with a letter to represent the column, such as 'B', and ends with a number to represent the row, such as '4'. The cell reference would therefore be 'B4'.

Insert and delete rows and columns

It is possible to add rows and columns by inserting them using the Insert menu, or by clicking with the right mouse button on the cell and selecting Insert. Rows are inserted above existing rows. Columns are inserted to the left of existing columns. Rows and columns can also be deleted by using the Edit menu and selecting Delete, or by clicking with the right mouse button on the cell and selecting Delete.

> **KEY WORD**
>
> **cell:** a single unit/rectangle of a spreadsheet formed at the intersection of a column and a row where data can be positioned; its reference (name/address) is based on its column and row

Questions

1   What different methods can be used to insert rows?

2   What different methods can be used to delete rows?

Hide rows and columns

It is possible to hide a row or column. Rows or columns are hidden as they may contain data that does not need to be seen by the user, or they may contain private or confidential data that should not be viewed.

To hide a row or column, select the required rows or columns, then click with the right mouse button and select Hide.

Resize rows and columns

Rows and columns can be resized. Rows can be made taller or shorter, and columns can be made wider or narrower. Rows are resized to enable different sizes of text to fit, or to allow multiple lines of text within one cell or row. Columns are resized to allow more data to fit in the column or to save space by narrowing the column.

To resize row and columns, go to the Format menu and select either Row, then Height, or Column, then Width.

Merge cells

Sometimes it can be useful to merge two cells, for example where a large amount of data needs to be stored in a cell. Merging multiple cells will create a single cell, with the cell reference being the original upper-left cell of the merged cells.

To merge cells, select the required cells, then click the Merge and Centre button on the Home toolbar at the top of the screen. The drop-down menu to the right of the Merge and Centre button has further options related to the merging of cells, including Unmerge Cells (see Figure 8.2).

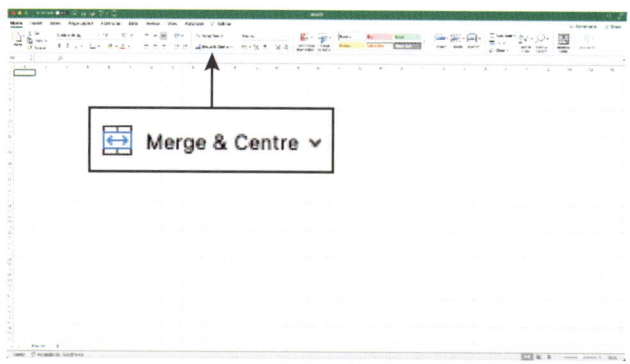

Figure 8.2: Merging cells.

WORKED EXAMPLE 8.01

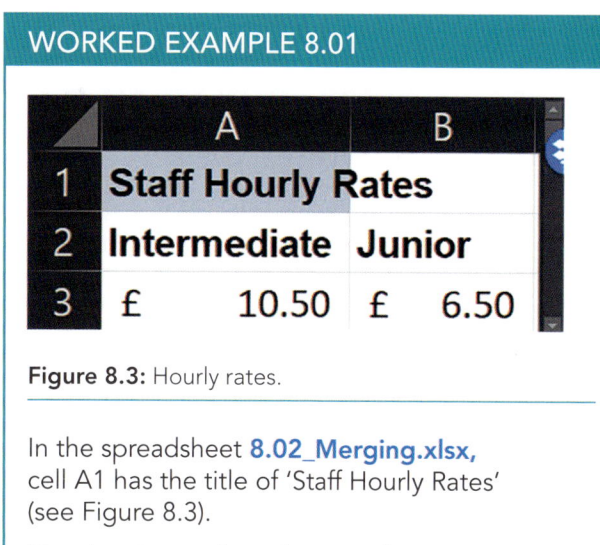

Figure 8.3: Hourly rates.

In the spreadsheet **8.02_Merging.xlsx,** cell A1 has the title of 'Staff Hourly Rates' (see Figure 8.3).

The data is in cell A1, but overflows into cell B1. Cells A1 and B1 have been shaded. Cells A1 and B1 can be merged so that it is one single cell, as shown in Figure 8.4.

Cell B1 no longer exists as the space is used for the larger cell A1.

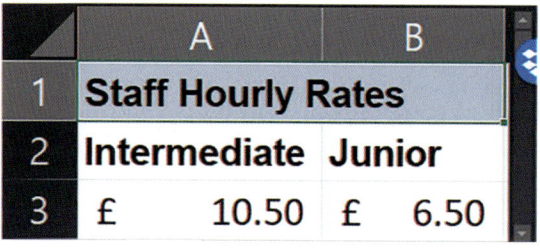

Figure 8.4: Hourly rates merged.

ACTIVITY 8.02

Open **8.03_Rows and Columns.xlsx**.

1 Insert a row above row 5.

2 Delete column C.

3 Increase the height of row 1.

4 Decrease the width of column B.

5 Hide rows 2 and 3.

6 Merge cells A4 to C4 to become a single cell.

Controlling data input using validation techniques

Spreadsheet software can apply validation rules to data that is input. If data passes the validation rule, then it will be accepted. If data fails the validation rule, then it will be rejected and an error message shown.

To validate the data input, select the Data menu, then Validation. The validation rules that can be used in spreadsheet software include looking up values in a list, range, type (integer and real) and length. A range check can be set up with the following properties:

• between two values

• equal to a value

• not equal to a value

• greater than a value

• greater than or equal to a value

• less than a value

• less than or equal to a value.

To enable the user to select from a drop-down menu, select List from the Allow menu, then enter the allowable data that can be entered into the Source box. Alternatively, allowable input options can be specified by defining a cell range within the spreadsheet. For example, to allow all data from cells A4 to B6, A4:B6 could be entered into the Source box.

WORKED EXAMPLE 8.02

In this spreadsheet, the user is asked to enter the company head office they are based at. They have two valid options: 'Mumbai' or 'Toronto' (see Figure 8.5). The user has accidentally entered 'Mal', which is not a valid option (see Figure 8.6). An error message has appeared telling the user what to do to fix the problem (see Figure 8.7).

Figure 8.5: Toronto.

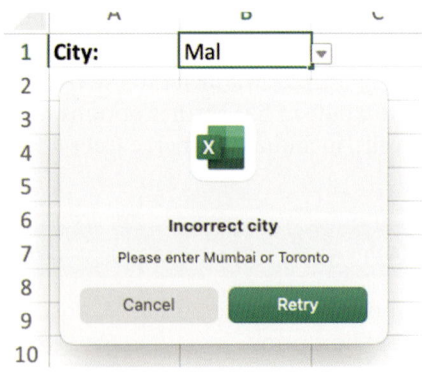

Figure 8.6: Mumbai/Toronto validation fail.

CONTINUED

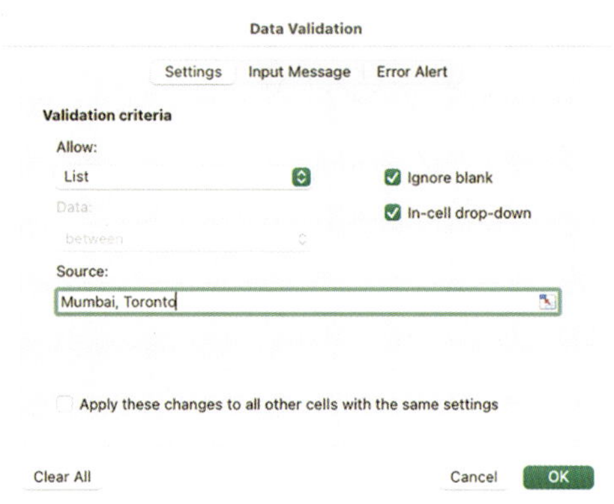

Figure 8.7: Mumbai/Toronto validation setup.

This is the rule that had been set up:

The rule ensures that the only data that can be entered must exist in the list that contains 'Mumbai' and 'Toronto'.

When setting up Data Validation, Input Messages and Error Alerts can be defined by clicking on the relevant tab in the Data Validation window.

An input message is used to explain to the user what they should enter in the cell and provide additional guidance if required.

Error messages are displayed if incorrect data is entered. Error messages should clearly tell the user what they have done wrong and what they should do to correct the error. For example, an error message stating 'Error' or 'Invalid Data' is unlikely to be helpful to the user.

WORKED EXAMPLE 8.03

In Figure 8.8, the validation rule is a range check that checks input data is a whole number between 1 and 99.

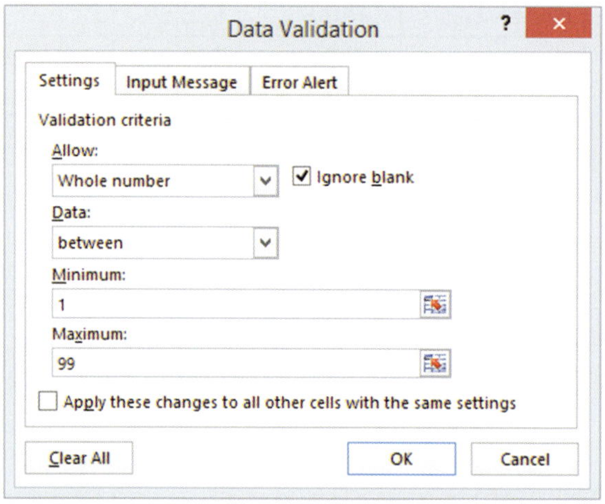

Figure 8.8: Range validation.

ACTIVITY 8.03

Open **8.04_Physics results.xlsx**, which is ready for students' marks to be entered for tests 1, 2 and 3.

1 Create validation rules that only allow the entry of marks up to and including the maximum marks for each test.

2 The validation rule should also ensure that negative numbers cannot be entered.

ACTIVITY 8.04

Create a new spreadsheet.

1 Create a validation rule that will only allow the entry of 'Junior', 'Intermediate' or 'Senior'.

2 Set up an appropriate error message.

Question

3 The data below is an extract from a spreadsheet.

Customer	Product Code	Price	Quantity
K&N Motors	QRV58N	$28.50	2
Cosmic Flavours	PWC48H	$19.23	1
Boldmere Carpets	GEV28X	$218.29	1

a Using the example shown, describe **three** types of validation rule that could be applied to the Product Code.

b Using the example shown, describe **two** different types of validation rule that could be applied to the Quantity.

Protecting cells and their content

Different parts of spreadsheets can be secured in a variety of ways, which means certain sections cannot be viewed and/or edited.

Worksheets and workbooks

The simplest form of security is to protect a whole **workbook**, which is a spreadsheet file containing one or more **worksheets**.

A whole workbook can be protected from having any new worksheets added or existing worksheets removed. To protect a workbook, select the Review toolbar and click Protect Workbook (see Figure 8.9).

KEY WORDS

workbook: a spreadsheet file which contains one or more worksheets

worksheets: a collection of rows and columns of cells, used to store and manipulate data

---

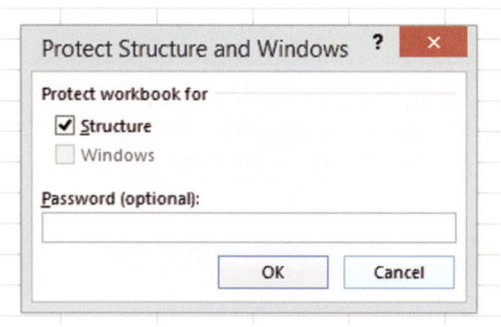

Figure 8.9: Workbook protection.

In addition to a whole workbook, it is possible to protect a worksheet from having any changes made to it. To protect a worksheet, select the Review toolbar and select Protect Sheet.

WORKED EXAMPLE 8.04

In Figure 8.10, the worksheet is protected to the extent that no changes can be made to any data and no data can be selected. No columns can be added and no rows can be added. Cells and rows cannot be formatted. This is useful if the whole worksheet contains only output data, or is a data table used for calculations elsewhere within the spreadsheet.

Figure 8.10: Worksheet protection.

Cells, rows and columns

It is also possible to protect a worksheet but allow the user to only edit certain cells within that worksheet. For example, all cells containing titles could be locked, although the user is still able to enter and change input data.

By default, once a whole worksheet is locked, all cells become locked. To unlock specific cells, rows and columns:

1 Unlock the worksheet using the Unprotect Sheet button on the Review toolbar.

2 Once the worksheet is unlocked, select the cells required, then click the right mouse button and go to Format Cells.

3 Click on the Protection tab and untick the Locked box.

4 Press OK, then lock the worksheet again. This will lock the remainder of the worksheet but ensures only those cells specified are unlocked.

WORKED EXAMPLE 8.05

In Figure 8.11, the commission and prices can be changed by the user so those cells have been set to be unlocked.

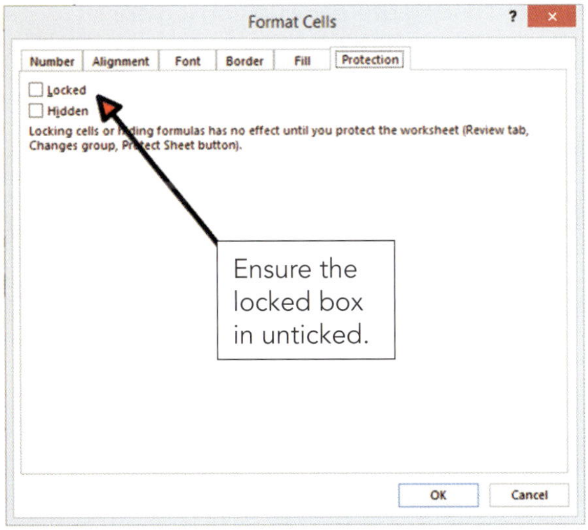

Figure 8.11: Unlocked cell.

CONTINUED

Now that those cells have been unlocked, the sheet can be protected and only the unlocked cells can be selected, as shown in Figure 8.12.

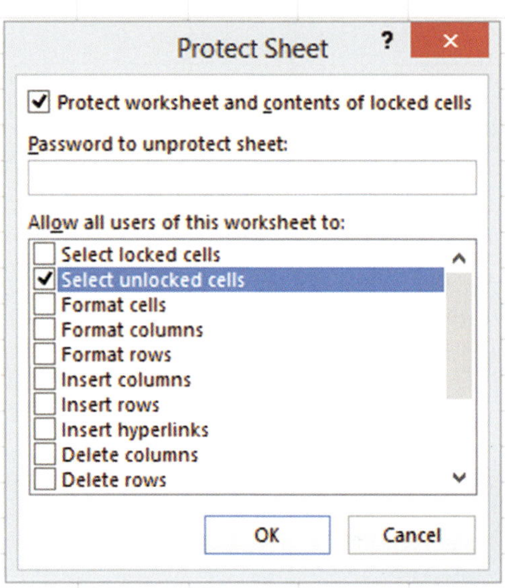

Figure 8.12: Worksheet protection with unlocked cells.

Cells can also be protected so that the **formula** cannot be seen by a user. This may be used to prevent users from seeing how certain confidential calculations are made but still letting them see the results of the calculation based on changing input data.

KEY WORD

formula: a mathematical calculation using $+, -, \times$ or $\div$

To hide a formula, click with the mouse button on the required cells and selected Format Cells. Click on the Protection tab and ensure the Hidden box is ticked. Press OK, then lock the worksheet as outlined previously.

WORKED EXAMPLE 8.06

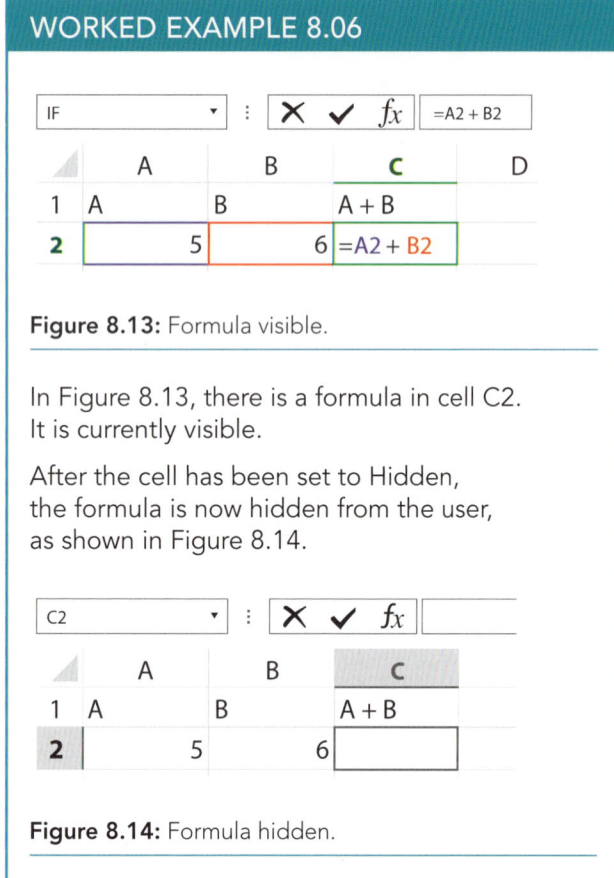

Figure 8.13: Formula visible.

In Figure 8.13, there is a formula in cell C2. It is currently visible.

After the cell has been set to Hidden, the formula is now hidden from the user, as shown in Figure 8.14.

Figure 8.14: Formula hidden.

Freezing and unfreezing panes and windows

Spreadsheets can sometimes become so large that they cannot fit visibly onto a single screen. It is possible to freeze specific groups of cells, known as panes, so that the top row remains on the screen as the user scrolls down the spreadsheet. Similarly, the first column can be frozen so that it remains on screen as the user scrolls across the spreadsheet.

To freeze panes, click on the View toolbar at the top of the screen and select Freeze Top Row or Freeze First Column (see Figure 8.15).

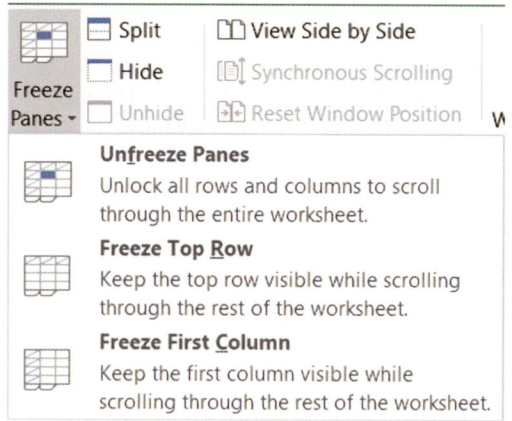

Figure 8.15: Freeze pane options in Microsoft Excel.

To freeze additional rows or columns, select the first cell that should not be frozen and then select Freeze Panes. This will freeze all rows above and all columns to the left of the selected cell.

To unfreeze panes, select the View toolbar and click on Unfreeze Panes.

WORKED EXAMPLE 8.07

In the spreadsheet **8.05_Freezing panes.xlsx,** cells that will be frozen when cell B4 is selected and freeze panes is applied are shown in Figure 8.16.

	A	B	C	D	E
1	Physics				
2	Student	Test 1	Test 2	Test 3	Test 4
3	*Max Marks*	*40*	*30*	*50*	*20*
4	Matthew	3	27	5	12
5	Elijah	6	21	10	2
6	Caleb	36	8	34	18
7	Joshua	32	7	29	12
8	Sheila	30	29	17	20
9	Junayna	4	28	41	4
10	Jordan	21	11	38	11
11	Sharon	39	29	26	17
12	James	12	15	7	7
13	Naomi	38	27	49	20

Figure 8.16: Cell selected for freezing panes.

CONTINUED

As the user scrolls down and across the screen, rows 1 to 3 and column A remain visible as shown in Figure 8.17.

	A	D	E	F	G
1	**Physics**				
2	**Student**	**Test 3**	**Test 4**		
3	*Max Marks*	*50*	*20*		
4	Matthew	5	12		
5	Elijah	10	2		
6	Caleb	34	18		
7	Joshua	29	12		
8	Sheila	17	20		
9	Junayna	41	4		
10	Jordan	38	11		
11	Sharon	26	17		
12	James	7	7		
13	Naomi	49	20		

Figure 8.17: Panes frozen as user scrolls down and across.

PRACTICAL ACTIVITY 8.05

1   Open the spreadsheet **8.06_Worksheets.xlsx**. The spreadsheet contains four worksheets.

   a   Try to add or delete a worksheet. The workbook has been protected to prevent this from happening.

   b   Unprotect the workbook using the password 'openme'. Now try to add a new worksheet.

2   Select the **Invoice** worksheet.

   a   Try to select any cell. This worksheet has been protected completely to prevent this from happening.

   b   Unprotect the worksheet using the password 'payment'. Now try to select cells and make changes to data.

3   Protect the **Breakdown** worksheet so that no changes can be made at all.

CONTINUED

4   Open the **Prices** worksheet.

   a   Try to change one of the titles in column A. These cells are locked so that you cannot edit them.

   b   Now try to change the prices of the photos. These cells have been unlocked so the prices can be changed.

   c   Now try to change the commission rate in cell B2 (10%). Notice how an additional password is required to do this. This is because this cell has been set to allow users with that password to change it.

   d   Enter the password 'special' and then change the rate of commission.

5   Open the **Purchases** worksheet.

   a   Lock the cells in columns A, B and C. Unlock the cells in columns D and E. Then protect the worksheet and see what you can and cannot change.

   b   Scroll down the Purchases worksheet and across to the right and notice how the top row and first two columns remain in place.

   c   Unfreeze the panes and then try scrolling again. Notice how all the data moves, including the top row and left-hand columns.

   d   Freeze the top row. Scroll down and across. Which cells remain on the screen?

   e   Freeze the first column. Scroll down and across. Which cells remain on the screen?

   f   Freeze the panes so that columns A, B and C and row 1 remain on the screen. Which cell did you click on to achieve this?

Creating and using formulas

A formula enables mathematical calculations to be performed with a spreadsheet.

Formulas are entered into a spreadsheet by clicking on a cell, then typing '='. The data within certain cells can be used within the calculations, such as B5, or specific values, such as 6.5. For example, the following formula would add together the data in cell B5 and B6: =B5+B6.

The following operations are typically used in spreadsheets:

Operation	Symbol used in formula
Addition	+
Subtraction	-
Multiplication	*
Division	/
Indices (or powers)	^

There is no limit to the number of calculations that can be included within a formula, such as: =(B5+B6)*3/100-(D1-D2).

WORKED EXAMPLE 8.08

The spreadsheet shown in Figure 8.18 is used to calculate the cost of broadband, TV and phone packages. The formula in cell B9 adds up the monthly costs of line rental (B6), TV (B7) and broadband (B8) then multiplies the result by six. Finally, it adds any setup costs from B3.

	A	B	C
1		Broadband 1	Broadband 1
2		Original	Family
3	Initial cost	$ 15.00	
4			
5	1st 6 month		
6	Line rental	$ 15.40	$ 15.40
7	TV	$ 10.75	$ 16.50
8	Broadband	$ 20.00	$ 20.00
9	Total 6 months	=6*(B8+B7+B6)+B3	

Figure 8.18: A formula.

To calculate indices, or powers, the ^ symbol can be used. For example, =6^3 would raise 6 to the power of three. Alternatively, a function, as outlined in the Using functions section next, can be used. The POWER function uses the syntax =POWER(number,power). For example, =POWER(6,3) would raise 6 to the power of 3.

WORKED EXAMPLE 8.09

The spreadsheet shown in Figure 8.19 raises the numbers in column A to the power given in row 1.

	A	B	C	D
1	Original number	Power 2	Power 3	Power 4
2	4	=POWER(A2,2)	=A2^3	=POWER(A2,4)
3	3	=POWER(A3,2)	=A3^3	=POWER(A3,4)
4	7	=POWER(A4,2)	=A4^3	=POWER(A4,4)

Figure 8.19: Powers.

ACTIVITY 8.06

Open the spreadsheet **8.07_Powers.xlsx**, which contains random values for the number to be raised and random values for the power.

1   Create a function in B8 that raises the value in A4 to the power given in B7. Do not use any numbers, only use cell references.

2   Use cell references to enter functions in cells C8, D8, B9, C9, D9, B10, C10 and D10

Using absolute, relative and mixed referencing to replicate formulas

Relative cell referencing

When creating formulas in a spreadsheet, **relative cell referencing** is used by default, which means a cell is referred to by its relation to its row and column position. When formulas are replicated, such as if the same formula is copied into other cells within a column, relative cell references change based on their position in relation to other cells.

WORKED EXAMPLE 8.10

	A	B	C	D	E
3	Job	Hours	Cost	Quantity	Total
4	A5 Leaflet	1	$ 12.50		3	=C4*D4
5	A4 Leaflet	1.5	$ 18.75	1	
6	A3 Leaflet	2.5	$ 25.00	2	

Figure 8.20: Replication 1.

This spreadsheet lists the number of hours it takes to produce a promotional leaflet, the cost to be charged for the leaflet and the quantity to be produced. The total to be charged is then calculated by multiplying the cost (C4) by the quantity (D4), as shown in Figure 8.20.

One way of entering the formula in E5 for the total cost of A4 leaflets is to type it in again but changing row 4 to row 5 so the formula would be =C5*D5. However, it is much quicker and more accurate to replicate the formula by copying it from E4 and pasting it into E5 and E6 (see Figure 8.21).

	A	B	C	D	E
3	Job	Hours	Cost	Quantity	Total
4	A5 Leaflet	1	12.50	3	=C4*D4
5	A4 Leaflet	1.5	18.75	1	=C5*D5
6	A3 Leaflet	2.5	25.00	2	=C6*D6

Figure 8.21: Replication 2.

The cell references used in the formula in the previous example were relative cell references, as the cell references point to another cell in a position relative to the current position. When referring to C4, it is pointing to a cell that is two columns to the left of column E. When referring to D4 it is pointing to a cell that is one column to the left of column E. Therefore, when the

formula is replicated down to rows 5 and 6, the references continue to point to the same columns, but the row reference is increased.

WORKED EXAMPLE 8.11

The same process happens when copying formulas across a spreadsheet. The formula in B3 calculates the number of kilometres travelled. When it has been replicated to columns C and D, instead of the row numbers changing, the column letters change. B2 is referring relatively to one row above and B1 is referring relatively to two rows above (see Figure 8.22).

	A	B	C	D
1	Start distance	38029	38098	39273
2	End distance	38087	39137	39410
3	Distance travelled	=B2-B1	=C2-C1	=D2-D1

Figure 8.22: Replication across.

If required, formulas can be used to retrieve a value from another worksheet. To do this you should include the name of the worksheet before the cell reference.

WORKED EXAMPLE 8.12

To use the value in cell B4 in a worksheet called 'Data source', use the following formula:

='Data source'!B4

The inverted commas are only required if the name of the worksheet includes a space, but the exclamation mark must always be used.

The following formula will multiply the value in B4 on the 'Data source' worksheet by C15 on the current worksheet:

='Data source'!B4 * C15

Relative cell referencing is useful when the same calculation needs to be repeated within multiple rows of columns, for example multiplying the total of a number of items sold at differing prices by the number of units of each item sold.

Absolute cell references

Absolute cell referencing is used when a cell reference should remain the same within a spreadsheet, such as when replicating formulas. Either a row, a column, or both can be set to use either relative or absolute referencing.

To prevent both the column and row being altered, a $ symbol should be added before both the row and column values, such as $E$6.

Absolute referencing is useful when a specific cell needs to be referred to by a number of other cells within a spreadsheet, such as whether tax or commission needs to be calculated based on a fixed rate.

To stop only a row from being changed, a $ symbol must be put before the row number. So C5 would become C$5. This makes the row an absolute reference, but leaves the column as a relative reference. Similarly, to stop only a column being altered, a $ symbol is placed before the column letter, such as $D4. This is known as **mixed referencing**, as part of the cell reference is relative and part is absolute.

KEY WORDS

absolute cell reference: a cell reference that does not change when it is copied into other cells

mixed reference: a cell reference that uses both relative and absolute referencing

---

ACTIVITY 8.07

Open the spreadsheet **8.08_Absolute References.xlsx**. The spreadsheet contains two worksheets: **Absolute 1** and **Absolute 2**.

Use worksheet **Absolute 1**, which is similar to the example used for relative cell references. The cost is calculated by multiplying the hourly rate in B1 by the number of hours in B4.

1 Replicate (copy) the formula from C4 to C5 and C6.

2 What has gone wrong?

CONTINUED

3 Why has it gone wrong?

4 Change the formula in C4 to be =B$1*B4.

5 Replicate (copy) the formula from C4 to C5 and C6.

6 Examine the formulas in C5 and C6.

7 Which cell references have changed and which have not?

Use worksheet **Absolute 2**. This worksheet is used to calculate the wage bill each month.

8 Look at the formula in C4 which calculates the cost of workers in week 1 month 1.

9 Make any changes necessary to the formula in C4 before replicating it for months 2 to 4.

10 Try copying the formula from C4 to E4 for week 2 workers.

11 What has gone wrong?

12 Why has it gone wrong?

13 Change the formula in C4 so that when replicated both across and down it will still work.

14 Now replicate the formula down column C and across to columns E, G and I.

15 Complete the spreadsheet with formulas in column J.

Named cells and ranges

A named cell is when a name is used instead of a cell reference. A named range is when a name is used instead of cell references to a group of rows and or columns. Both named cells and ranges can make formulas easier to understand, as it is evident what an absolute reference refers to.

Named cells can be used as an alternative absolute cell reference. Whenever a formula containing a name cell is replicated, the formula will still point to the same named cell.

To name a cell in a spreadsheet, click on the cell name in the top left-hand corner of the worksheet, which is known as the Name box. Delete the existing cell reference, then type a specific name, followed by pressing the enter key.

WORKED EXAMPLE 8.13

	A	B	C
1	**Tax rate**	0.15	
2			
3	**Product**	**Cost**	**Tax**
4	6 × 4 frame	12	=B4*TaxRate
5	5 × 7 frame	15	=B5*TaxRate
6	10 × 8 frame	18	=B6*TaxRate
7	12 × 8 frame	21	=B7*TaxRate

Figure 8.23: Tax rate named cell.

The spreadsheet **8.09_Tax Rate.xlsx** contains a named cell of 'TaxRate', which is cell B1 (see Figure 8.23). The formula in C4 is =B4*TaxRate.

When this formula is replicated down column C, the reference to TaxRate remains the same, as it is an absolute reference.

Named ranges can also be used within formulas. To name a range in a spreadsheet, highlight the required cells and click on the Name box in the top left-hand corner of the worksheet. Delete the existing cell reference, then enter a name for the range, followed by pressing Enter.

WORKED EXAMPLE 8.14

In **8.09_Tax Rate.xlsx**, cells C4:C7 have been named as 'TaxCharged'. Instead of using a function of =SUM(C4:C8) for the total tax charged, the named range can be used instead (see Figure 8.24).

CONTINUED

	A	B	C	D
1	**Tax rate**	15%		
2				
3	**Product**	**Cost**	**Tax**	**Cost inc tax**
4	6 × 4 frame	$12.00	$ 1.80	
5	5 × 7 frame	$15.00	$ 2.25	
6	10 × 8 frame	$18.00	$ 2.70	
7	12 × 8 frame	$21.00	$ 3.15	
8	Total tax charged:		=SUM(Tax Charged)	

Figure 8.24: Total tax charged name range.

ACTIVITY 8.08

Open **8.09_Tax Rate.xlsx**.

1   Change the formula in C4 so that it uses a named range for the cost.

2   Replicate this formula to C5:C7.

3   Use a named range to calculate the total cost in B8.

4   Name the range for cost including tax.

5   Use a named range to calculate the total cost including tax in D8.

ACTIVITY 8.09

Open the spreadsheet **8.10_Times Table.xlsx**, which will be used to show the times table.

1   Create a formula in B2 that will calculate the value in B1 multiplied by the value in A2. Do not use numbers, only use cell references.

2   Change the formula so that it has absolute references where needed so that you can replicate the formula across and down. You should only need one formula.

Named ranges can be used across multiple worksheets within the same spreadsheet. When referencing a named range in a different worksheet, it is not necessary to reference the name of the worksheet.

Using functions

A **function** is a predefined formula used to perform a range of calculations, such as calculating the total or average.

> **KEY WORD**
>
> **function:** a ready-made formula used to perform a calculation

Using functions that perform calculations

Table 8.1 shows some of the available functions to perform calculations.

Function	Purpose	Example
SUM	Calculates the total of values within a range.	=SUM(B3:E3)
AVERAGE	Calculates the average of values within a range.	=AVERAGE(B3:E3)
MIN	Calculates the smallest value within a range. Only numeric values are considered.	=MIN(B3:E3)
MAX	Calculates the largest value within a range. Only numeric values are considered.	=MAX(B3:E3)
MINA	Calculates the smallest value within a range. Numeric, logical values and text are considered.	=MINA(B3:E3)
MAXA	Calculates the largest value within a range. Numeric, logical values and text are considered.	=MAXA(B3:E3)

Table 8.1: Functions to perform calculations.

Questions

4   Which function calculates the total of all numbers within a specified range?

5   Which function calculates the maximum value with a range of only numerical values?

> **WORKED EXAMPLE 8.15**
>
> The spreadsheet **8.11_Student Marks.xlsx** calculates the total, average, minimum and maximum mark that each student scores in a set of four tests (see Figure 8.25). In row 2, the total has been calculated by adding up each cell individually using a formula. In row 3, this has been done using a function that requires much less effort. In row 2, the average has been calculated using a formula, but it is necessary to know how many marks there are to complete this calculation. In row 3, this has been done using a function that does not require knowledge of the number of values to be averaged and will allow extra values to be added in the future by inserting columns.

CONTINUED

	A	B	C	D	E	F	G	H	I
1	Student	Mark 1	Mark 2	Mark 3	Mark 4	Total	Average	Minimum	Maximum
2	Name 1	98	40	36	84	=(B2+C2+D2+E2)	=F2/4		
3	Name 2	31	67	61	77	=SUM(B3:E3)	=AVERAGE(B3:E3)	=MIN(B3:E3)	=MAX(B3:E3)
4	Name 3	62	58	29	38	=SUM(B4:E4)	=AVERAGE(B4:E4)	=MIN(B4:E4)	=MAX(B4:E4)
5	Name 4	64	83	85	27	=SUM(B5:E5)	=AVERAGE(B5:E5)	=MIN(B5:E5)	=MAX(B5:E5)
6	Name 5	87	45	64	42	=SUM(B6:E6)	=AVERAGE(B6:E6)	=MIN(B6:E6)	=MAX(B6:E6)
7	Name 6	93	58	43	73	=SUM(B7:E7)	=AVERAGE(B7:E7)	=MIN(B7:E7)	=MAX(B7:E7)
8	Name 7	99	29	55	92	=SUM(B8:E8)	=AVERAGE(B8:E8)	=MIN(B8:E8)	=MAX(B8:E8)
9	Name 8	57	58	44	93	=SUM(B9:E9)	=AVERAGE(B9:E9)	=MIN(B9:E9)	=MAX(B9:E9)
10	Name 9	45	43	98	55	=SUM(B10:E10)	=AVERAGE(B10:E10)	=MIN(B10:E10)	=MAX(B10:E10)

Figure 8.25: Summary functions.

SUBTOTAL function

The SUBTOTAL function can be used to find a subtotal of a range of cells. The SUBTOTAL function uses the syntax:

=SUBTOTAL(type, range)

A number of different subtotal types can be calculated, which either include or exclude hidden rows, as outlined in Table 8.2.

Type (includes hidden rows)	Type (excludes hidden rows)	Function
1	101	AVERAGE
2	102	COUNT
3	103	COUNTA
4	104	MAX
5	105	MIN
6	106	PRODUCT
7	107	STDEV
8	108	STDEVP
9	109	SUM
10	110	VAR
11	111	VARP

Table 8.2: SUBTOTAL types.

For example, the formula = SUBTOTAL(1, H6:H8) will calculate the average of the values in cells H6 to H8.

The SUBTOTAL function is useful when hidden rows are to be excluded, or formulas need to be quickly changed to see certain calculations. In addition, unlike other functions, when results are filtered, as outlined later, filtered cells are not included in the calculation. Finally, when using SUBTOTAL to perform calculations within a column, any other uses of the SUBTOTAL function within the column are automatically excluded from the results.

ACTIVITY 8.10

Open **8.11_Student Marks.xlsx**. Use functions to calculate the average, minimum and maximum mark for each of the four tests.

Rounding functions

Numbers can be rounded to whole numbers or to a specific number of decimal places. Table 8.3 shows the functions that can be used.

Function	Purpose	Example
INT	Returns the whole number, or integer, value of a decimal number (the value before the decimal point). The INT function effectively rounds the number down to the nearest whole number.	=INT(A2)
ROUND	Rounds a number to the number of decimal places specified. This example rounds the value in A2 to three decimal places.	=ROUND(A2,3)
ROUNDUP	Rounds a number up to the nearest decimal place specified. This example rounds up the value in A2 to two decimal places.	=ROUNDUP(A2,2)
ROUNDDOWN	Rounds a number down to the nearest decimal place specified. This example rounds down the value in A2 to four decimal places.	=ROUNDDOWN(A2,4)

Table 8.3: Rounding functions.

WORKED EXAMPLE 8.16

In **8.12_Rounding.xlsx** you can see how the functions in Table 8.3 have been used (see Figure 8.26).

You can also see the results of the calculations made by the functions (see Figure 8.27).

	A	B	C	D	E
1	Original number	Integer	Round	Round up	Round down
2	25817.32817	=INT(A2)	=ROUND(A2,3)	=ROUNDUP(A2,2)	=ROUNDDOWN(A2,4)
3	3852.876985	=INT(A3)	=ROUND(A3,3)	=ROUNDUP(A3,2)	=ROUNDDOWN(A3,4)
4	928.2341	=INT(A4)	=ROUND(A4,3)	=ROUNDUP(A4,2)	=ROUNDDOWN(A4,4)
5	0.03256	=INT(A5)	=ROUND(A5,3)	=ROUNDUP(A5,2)	=ROUNDDOWN(A5,4)

Figure 8.26: Rounding functions.

	A	B	C	D	E
1	Original number	Integer	Round	Round up	Round down
2	25817.32817	25817	25817.328	25817.33	25817.3281
3	3852.876985	3852	3852.877	3852.88	3852.8769
4	928.2341	928	928.234	928.24	928.2341
5	0.03256	0	0.033	0.04	0.0325

Figure 8.27: Rounding values.

ACTIVITY 8.11

Create a new spreadsheet and experiment with the four rounding functions using different values for decimal places.

DID YOU KNOW?

If you change the number of decimal places when using a rounding function with a negative number, −1 rounds to tens, −2 rounds to hundreds and −3 rounds to thousands. The minus number relates to rounding to the power of 10 rather than rounding to a set number of significant figures.

Using functions that count the number of cells that meet a criterion

A range of functions can be used to count how many cells meet specific criteria, as outlined in Table 8.4.

Function	Purpose	Example
COUNT	Counts the number of cells that contain a number in a specified range	=COUNT(B4:B7)
COUNTIF	Counts the number of cells that meet a certain in a specified range, such as whether they are less than a value	=COUNTIF(B4:B7,"<10")
COUNTIFS	Counts the number of cells in multiple ranges that meet multiple criteria	=COUNTIFS(B4:B7, "<10",C8:C23,">20")
COUNTA	Counts the number of cells that are not empty in a specified range	=COUNTA(B4:B7)
COUNTBLANK	Counts the number of empty cells in a specified range	=COUNTBLANK(B4:B7)

Table 8.4: Functions that count the number of cells that meet a criterion.

Using functions that look up data

Lookup functions will find a specific value, then return another value in a corresponding row or column. The vertical lookup, or VLOOKUP function, is used to look for a value in a column and return a value from the same row. Horizontal lookup, or HLOOKUP function, is used to look for a value in a row and return a value from the same column.

VLOOKUP function

The VLOOKUP function uses the syntax:

=VLOOKUP(Search Value, Lookup Table, Column, Match)

Search Value is the value being looked up in the table. Lookup Table is the range of cells that define the location of the table. Column is the number of the column that should be returned as the result in the matching row of the value that was found. Match is optional and defines whether an exact match should be found: TRUE for approximate match (the default value if Match is not specified) or FALSE for an exact match.

For example, the following formula looks for the value of 'Banana' within the table A2:B5, then will return the value within column number two of the table. An exact match is required, as the last argument in the formula is FALSE:

=VLOOKUP("Banana", A2:B5, 2, FALSE)

WORKED EXAMPLE 8.17

	A	B	C	D
1	**Number**	**3 Letter**	**Month**	**Francais**
2	1	Jan	January	Janvier
3	2	Feb	Febuary	Février
4	3	Mar	March	Mars
5	4	Apr	April	Avril
6	5	May	May	Mai
7	6	Jun	June	Juin
8	7	Jul	July	Julliet
9	8	Aug	August	Août
10	9	Sep	September	Septembre
11	10	Oct	October	Octobre
12	11	Nov	November	Novembre
13	12	Dec	December	Décembre

Figure 8.28: Lookup table.

The spreadsheet **8.13_Months.xlsx** contains two worksheets: **Months** and **Number**.

A table in the worksheet **Months** lists the numbers that represent months, the three-letter shortened version of each month's name, the full name of each month and the French name of each month (see Figure 8.28).

The worksheet **Number** asks the user to enter a number that represents a month and it will then look up that number in the table and return the three-letter code, full month name and French month name, as shown in Figure 8.29.

CONTINUED

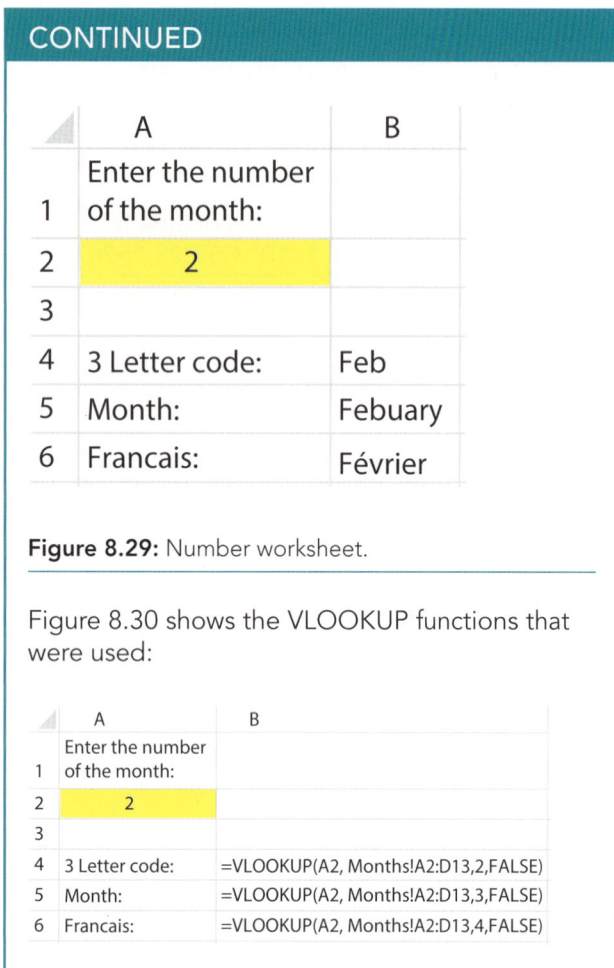

	A	B
1	Enter the number of the month:	
2	2	
3		
4	3 Letter code:	Feb
5	Month:	Febuary
6	Francais:	Février

Figure 8.29: Number worksheet.

Figure 8.30 shows the VLOOKUP functions that were used:

	A	B
1	Enter the number of the month:	
2	2	
3		
4	3 Letter code:	=VLOOKUP(A2, Months!A2:D13,2,FALSE)
5	Month:	=VLOOKUP(A2, Months!A2:D13,3,FALSE)
6	Francais:	=VLOOKUP(A2, Months!A2:D13,4,FALSE)

Figure 8.30: Lookup functions.

VLOOKUP functions can also be replicated in the same way as any other function. However, the lookup table cell references will change as they are copied down the rows.

ACTIVITY 8.12

Open the spreadsheet **8.14_VLookup Price Categories.xlsx**, which calculates the prices of tickets purchased for a show.

1   Look at the lookup table on the **Ticket Categories** worksheet. It shows the prices for each category.

2   Look at the function in C2 on the **Ticket Sales** worksheet. Describe what this function is doing.

CONTINUED

3   Replicate the function from C2 down the column.

4   What has gone wrong?

5   Why has it gone wrong?

One way of overcoming problems with cell referencing when using VLOOKUP, is to change all the cell references in the lookup table, but not the lookup value, to be absolute cell references. It may be beneficial to make the lookup table a named range, as outlined in the Named range section before.

ACTIVITY 8.13

Continue using **8.14_Vlookup Price Categories.xlsx**.

1   Name the range containing the lookup table on the **Ticket Categories** worksheet.

2   Change the VLOOKUP function in C2 to include the named range instead of the range 'Ticket Categories'!A1:B5

3   Replicate the function from C2 down the column and it should find the correct prices for each category of ticket.

So far, the VLOOKUP function has been used to find an exact match within a table. However, there are occasions when an exact match is not required, but the closest value below or equal to the search value should be found.

WORKED EXAMPLE 8.18

The spreadsheet **8.15_Exam Results.xlsx** includes a lookup table of the minimum mark required to achieve each grade. This table has been called 'GradeBoundaries' as the named range (see Figure 8.31).

CONTINUED

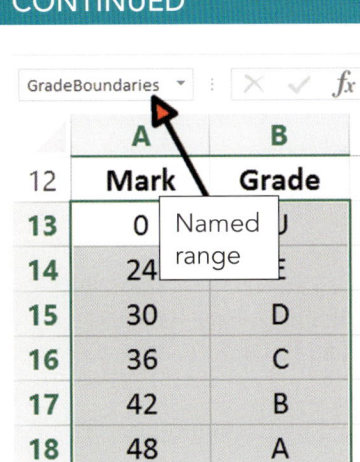

	A	B
12	**Mark**	**Grade**
13	0	U
14	24	E
15	30	D
16	36	C
17	42	B
18	48	A

Named range

Figure 8.31: Non-matching VLOOKUP table.

Each student's marks are entered in cells B2 to B10, which has been named 'Mark'. The VLOOKUP function is then used to look up the Mark in the GradeBoundaries table and return the second column, which is the grade. Not many of the marks are an exact match and so the TRUE element at the end of the function means that the closest mark below or equal to the student's mark will be found and the grade returned as the answer, as shown in Figure 8.32.

It is essential that the lookup table's first column is in order from lowest to highest for this to work as described.

	A	B	C	D
1	Student	Mark	Grade	Function
2	1	5	U	=VLOOKUP(Mark,GradeBoundaries,2,TRUE)
3	2	30	D	=VLOOKUP(Mark,GradeBoundaries,2,TRUE)
4	3	35	D	=VLOOKUP(Mark,GradeBoundaries,2,TRUE)
5	4	22	U	=VLOOKUP(Mark,GradeBoundaries,2,TRUE)
6	5	49	A	=VLOOKUP(Mark,GradeBoundaries,2,TRUE)
7	6	47	B	=VLOOKUP(Mark,GradeBoundaries,2,TRUE)
8	7	48	A	=VLOOKUP(Mark,GradeBoundaries,2,TRUE)
9	8	39	C	=VLOOKUP(Mark,GradeBoundaries,2,TRUE)
10	9	25	E	=VLOOKUP(Mark,GradeBoundaries,2,TRUE)

Figure 8.32: Non-matching VLOOKUP function.

HLOOKUP function

The HLOOKUP function works in a similar way to the VLOOKUP function, but instead of searching for values down a column in the table, it searches for values within a row across the table.

The HLOOKUP function uses the syntax:

=HLOOKUP(Search Value, Lookup Table, Row, Match)

Search Value, Lookup Table and Match are the same as in the VLOOKUP function. Row is the number of the row that should be returned as the result in the matching column of the value that was found.

WORKED EXAMPLE 8.19

The spreadsheet **8.16_HLookup.xlsx** lists products and their prices and the discounts that are currently being applied to each of those products. The function used in D2 for the Discount Rate is:

=HLOOKUP(C2,DiscountRates,2,FALSE)

The discount rate code (C2) is looked up in the named range DiscountRates (B13:F14) and the corresponding rate in the second row of the table is returned as the discount rate (see Figure 8.33).

	A	B	C	D	E	F
1	Product	Price	Discount Rate	Discount	Discounted Value	Discounted Price
2	Product 1	£ 124.81	B	30%	£ 37.44	£ 87.37
3	Product 2	£ 242.44	A	40%	£ 96.98	£ 145.46
4	Product 3	£ 203.72	C	20%	£ 40.74	£ 162.98
5	Product 4	£ 197.12	B	30%	£ 59.14	£ 137.98
6	Product 5	£ 178.24	D	10%	£ 17.82	£ 160.42
7	Product 6	£ 127.98	B	30%	£ 38.39	£ 89.59
8	Product 7	£ 109.83	E	5%	£ 5.49	£ 104.34
9	Product 8	£ 162.22	A	40%	£ 64.89	£ 97.33
10	Product 9	£ 178.88	C	20%	£ 35.78	£ 143.10
11	Product 10	£ 233.96	E	5%	£ 11.70	£ 222.26
12						
13	Code	A	B	C	D	E
14	Rate	40%	30%	20%	10%	5%

Figure 8.33: HLOOKUP.

XLOOKUP function

XLOOKUP provides a more flexible alternative to VLOOKUP and HLOOKUP. Values can be searched for both horizontally and vertically, so values can be looked up in both rows and columns. The corresponding data to return can also be in either rows or columns.

TIP

XLOOKUP is only available in Excel for Microsoft Office 365 and Excel 2021 or later.

XLOOKUP uses the following syntax:

XLOOKUP (Search Value, Lookup Table, Return Table, If Not Found, Match Mode, Search Mode)

Search Value is the value being looked up in the table. Lookup Table is the range of cells that define the location of the table. Return Table is the range of cells that should be returned as the result in the matching row or column of the value that was found. If Not Found is optional and enables text to be displayed if a valid match cannot be located. Match Mode is also optional and defines whether an exact match is required. Match can take the following values:

0 – Exact match (default). If not found, display #N/A.

–1 – Exact match. If not found, display the next smallest item.

1 – Exact match. If not found, display the next largest item.

2 – Match using wildcards, which enable partial matches to be found, using *, ? or ~.

The final value, Search Mode, is optional and can take the following values:

1 – Start searching at the first item (default).

–1 – Start searching in reverse order from the last item.

2 – Assumes the lookup table is sorted in ascending order and performs a binary search.

–2 – Assumes the lookup table is sorted in descending order and performs a binary search.

(Please note, for the binary search options above, invalid results will be displayed if the lookup table is not sorted into ascending/descending order.)

For example, the following formula looks for the value of 'Apple' within the table C3:C11, then will return the value within the corresponding column of table F3:F11. If a match is not found, 'No matches found will be displayed'. An exact match is required. The search will begin at the last item in the lookup table and take place in reverse order:

=XLOOKUP("Apple", C3:C11, F3, F11, "No matches found", 0, -1)

REFLECTION

Lookup functions contain a range of complex syntax. How might you remember what needs to be specified when using VLOOKUP, HLOOKUP and XLOOKUP? Share your approach with a partner.

INDEX function

The INDEX function will find a value based on its position within a table. The INDEX function uses the syntax:

=INDEX(Lookup Table, Row, Column)

Lookup Table is the table where the value will be found. Row is the number of the row to use within the table and Column is the number of the column to use within the table.

WORKED EXAMPLE 8.20

	A	B	C	D
1	**3 Letter**	**Month**	**francais**	
2	Jan	January	janvier	
3	Feb	February	février	
4	Mar	March	mars	
5	Apr	April	avril	
6	May	May	mai	
7	Jun	June	juin	
8	Jul	July	juillet	
9	Aug	August	août	
10	Sep	September	septembre	
11	Oct	October	octobre	
12	Nov	November	novembre	
13	Dec	December	décembre	

Figure 8.34: Table of months.

The spreadsheet **8.17_Months index.xlsx** includes a table of months in short form, full word and the French translation (see Figure 8.34). The table has been called 'Months' as the named range.

To find the French word for June, this INDEX function would be used:

=INDEX(Months,7,3)

Months is the name of the table used to look up the value. The number 7 is the row where the month of June is to be found. The number 3 is the column where the French translations are to be found.

ACTIVITY 8.14

Open the spreadsheet **8.18_Days index.xlsx**

1 Create an INDEX function in C10 to find the full name of the 5th day of the week.

2 Create an INDEX function in C12 to find the three letter version of the 2nd day of the week.

3 Create INDEX functions in B16, B17 and B18 to find the three letter version, full name and German names for the day number input by the user in cell F14. The INDEX function should work for any value between 1 and 7 that is input in F14.

MATCH function

The MATCH function will find the position of a value in a list. Its MATCH function uses the syntax:

=MATCH(Search Value, Lookup Table, Type)

Search Value is the value to be found in the list. Lookup Table is the table to find the value. Lookup Table must contain values in one row or one column only. Type is a type of search, which can be one of three values, as shown in Table 8.5.:

Type	Description
0	Finds the position of the value that is EQUAL to the Search Value. The Lookup Table can be in any order.
1	Finds the position of the largest value that is less than or equal to the Search Value. The Lookup Table must be in ascending order.
−1	Finds the position of the smallest value that is greater than or equal to the Search Value. The Lookup Table must be in descending order.

Table 8.5: Type values.

WORKED EXAMPLE 8.21

	A	B
1	**Product**	**Price**
2	Clock	₺30.80
3	Water bottle	₺6.50
4	Crisps	₺3.70
5	Calculator	₺59.50
6	Ring binder	₺13.20
7	Telephone	₺95.00

Figure 8.35: List of products and prices.

The spreadsheet **8.19_Match.xlsx** includes a list of products and their prices in Turkish Lira. Figure 8.35 shows the list of products and their prices.

To find the position of crisps in the list of products, the following function can be used:

=MATCH('Crisps', A2:A7,0)

This will search for Crisps in the Lookup table A2:A7 and find the position for an exact match.

Amir has 10 Lira available to spend. To find the most expensive product that he can buy with his 10 Lira, he needs to find the position of the largest value that is less than or equal to 10 Lira. First, the table needs to be sorted into ascending order of price, as shown in Figure 8.36.

Now a MATCH function can be used:

=MATCH(10,E2:E7,1)

The number 1 indicates that the largest value that is less than or equal to the search value should be found. This will return the value 2, which is the position of the largest value that is less than or equal to 10 (6.50).

	D	E
1	**Product**	**Price**
2	Crisps	₺3.70
3	Water bottle	₺6.50
4	Ring binder	₺13.20
5	Clock	₺30.80
6	Calculator	₺59.50
7	Telephone	₺95.00

Figure 8.36: Product list in ascending price order.

CONTINUED

	G	H
1	**Product**	**Price**
2	Telephone	₺95.00
3	Calculator	₺59.50
4	Clock	₺30.80
5	Ring binder	₺13.20
6	Water bottle	₺6.50
7	Crisps	₺3.70

Figure 8.37: Product list in descending order of price.

To find the cheapest product that Amir could not afford, the list needs to be sorted into descending order, as shown in Figure 8.37.

The MATCH function can then be used to find the position of the smallest value that is greater than or equal to 10 Lira:

=MATCH(10,H2:H7,−1)

The number −1 indicates that the smallest value that is greater than or equal to the search value should be found. This will return the value 4, which is the position of the smallest value that is greater than or equal to 10 (6.50).

ACTIVITY 8.15

Open the spreadsheet **8.20_Match marks.xlsx**

1   Create a MATCH function in E11 to find the position of Balraj in the list of names.

2   Create a MATCH function in E12 to find the position of the highest mark that is below 90. (Remember to sort the list.)

3   Create a MATCH function in E13 to find the position of the lowest mark that is above 50. (Remember to sort the list.)

4   Use an INDEX function and the result in E13 to find the value of the lowest mark that is above 50.

Using functions that make decisions based on certain criteria

Many functions within spreadsheets enable comparisons to be made between values based on certain criteria, known as a condition. Depending on whether a condition is true or false, different values can be displayed.

IF function

WORKED EXAMPLE 8.22

The spreadsheet **8.21_IF functions.xlsx** contains a simple quiz that asks users what the capital city of a country is. If the user gives the correct answer in cell B1, then they are told 'Well done' in cell B2, otherwise they are told 'Oops' (see Figure 8.38). The formula in cell B5 is incorrect and the error will be fixed in Activity 8.16

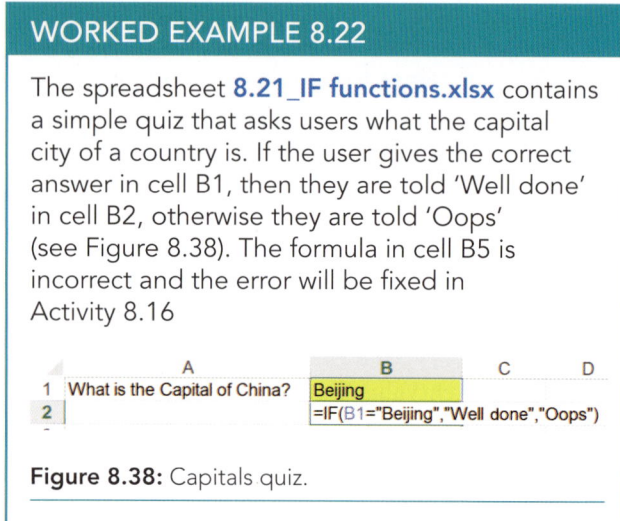

Figure 8.38: Capitals quiz.

An IF function has three arguments, as shown in Table 8.6.

Element	Purpose	Example
Condition	Specifies the rules to be checked.	B1 = 'Beijing'
True Value	Specifies what to display if the condition is met.	'Well Done'
False Value	Specifies what to display if the condition is not met.	'Oops'

Table 8.6: IF function elements.

PRACTICAL ACTIVITY 8.16

Open **8.21_IF functions.xlsx**. The spreadsheet contains two worksheets: Capitals Quiz and Mark Book.

Use the **Capitals Quiz** worksheet.

1 Why does the spreadsheet say 'Oops' when the answer for the capital of France is correct?

2 Fix the IF function for the capital of France so it works properly.

3 Test your function by entering an incorrect answer.

4 Add another question in row 7 and write an IF function to give feedback to the user.

This is quite a slow way of creating a quiz. Try this more efficient method:

1 Put the answers to each question in column C next to where the user will put their answer in column B.

2 Change the IF function in B2 to be =IF(B1=C1,'Well done','Oops')

3 Now replicate this to the other two questions and write another two so you have five in total.

Notice how much quicker it is now to add the new questions because you don't have to keep editing the IF function. However, the user can see the answers. Use security measures such as hiding columns and worksheet protection to hide the answers from the user.

Use the **Mark Book** worksheet.

1 Students need to get 75 marks or more to pass maths, otherwise they fail. Write a function in D4 to display Pass or Fail.

2 Replicate this function for the other maths results.

3 Students need to get 60 marks or more to pass English, otherwise they fail. Write a function in D12 to display Pass or Fail.

4 Replicate this function for the other English results.

Nested IF and IFS functions

It is possible to have an IF function nested within another IF function. This can be useful if there are two or more alternative outputs.

WORKED EXAMPLE 8.23

The spreadsheet **8.22_Nested IFs.xlsx** contains a mark book in the **Mark Book** worksheet. Students who get a mark of 80 or above get a distinction. Those who get a mark below 40 get a fail. All other students get awarded a pass. Notice how a nested IF has been used to show the grades (see Figure 8.39).

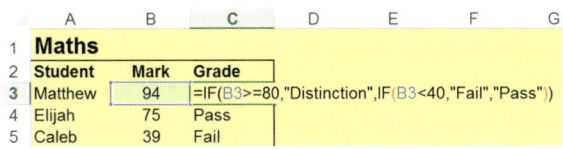

Figure 8.39: Nested IF example.

WORKED EXAMPLE 8.24

The spreadsheet **8.23_Photo frames.xlsx** shows the charges for a photo frame with a standard embossing or a gold embossing. The user can select Standard or Gold embossing and the quantity to purchase. The price can be determined by the algorithm shown in Figure 8.40.

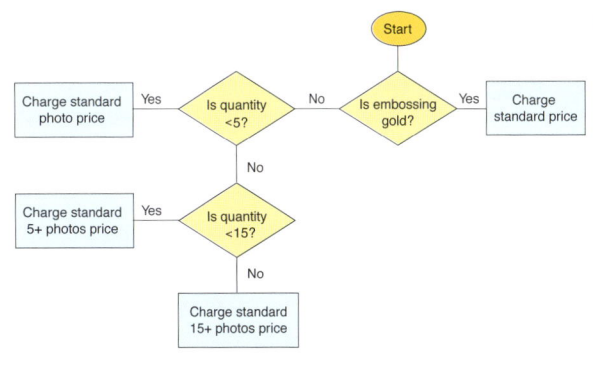

Figure 8.40: Flowchart algorithm.

CONTINUED

A nested IF function is used to determine the price by following the same algorithm (see Figure 8.41).

	A	B	C	D	E	F	G
1	Embossing	Photo price	5+ photos	15+ photos			
2	Standard	$ 1.00	$ 0.80	$ 0.70			
3	Gold	$ 1.80					
4							
5	Embossing	Standard					
6	Quantity	5					
7	Unit price:	=IF(Embossing="Gold",B3,IF(Quantity<5,B2,IF(Quantity<15,C2,D2)))					
8	Total price:	$ 4.00					

Figure 8.41: Nested IF for unit price.

A nested IF can become quite complex and difficult to follow. To overcome this, IFS can be used instead. IFS works by using pairs of conditions and outputs:

=IFS(condition1, output1, condition2, output2, condition3, output3 …)

WORKED EXAMPLE 8.25

The spreadsheet **8.24_IFS instead of nested IF.xlsx** contains a different mark book for the same students used in Worked Example 8.23. The nested IF has been replaced with the IFS function. Notice how the condition and output pairs are used and also how an extra condition has had to be included for 'Pass', because there is no ELSE option (see Figure 8.42).

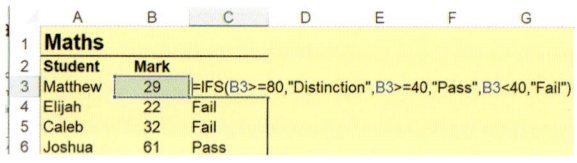

	A	B	C	D	E	F	G
1	**Maths**						
2	Student	Mark					
3	Matthew	29	=IFS(B3>=80,"Distinction",B3>=40,"Pass",B3<40,"Fail")				
4	Elijah	22	Fail				
5	Caleb	32	Fail				
6	Joshua	61	Pass				

Figure 8.42: IFS instead of nested IF.

ACTIVITY 8.17

Open the spreadsheet **8.25_Photo Frames.xlsx**.

Replace the nested IF function in B7 with an IFS function.

AND and OR functions

If needed, more than one criterion can be checked when using IF, IFS and nested IF. AND can be used within an IF function to check if both conditions are true. For example, the formula below will check if A2 is greater than 0 and B2 is less than 100. If both conditions are true, 'Great' will be displayed. If one or both conditions are false, 'Not today' will be displayed:

=IF(AND(A2>0,B2<100),"Great","Not today")

Alternatively, if either condition can be true, OR can be used within the condition element of the IF function. For example, the formula below will check if A4 contains the word 'Yellow' and B7 contains the word 'Pink'. If one or more conditions are true, 'Colourful' will be displayed. If both conditions are false, 'Wrong colours' will be displayed:

=IF(OR(A4="Yellow",B7="Pink"), "Colourful","Wrong colours")

Using functions that insert, extract and calculate with date and time

Calculations can be used to insert, extract or calculate dates and times. Once in a suitable format, comparisons using conditions such as IF statements can then be used with dates and times, as shown in Table 8.7.

Function	Purpose	Example
DAY	Extracts the day part of a date.	=DAY(B1)
MONTH	Extracts the month part of a date.	=MONTH(B1)
YEAR	Extracts the year part of a date.	=YEAR(B1)
DATE	Combines given values for a year, month and day to enable a date to be inserted. As the date is stored as a value, calculations can then be performed using the date if required.	=DATE(B4,B3,B2)
HOUR	Extracts the hours part of a time.	=HOUR(B8)
MINUTE	Extracts the minutes part of a time.	=MINUTE(B8)
SECOND	Extracts the seconds part of a time.	=SECOND(B8)
TIME	Combines given values for hours, minutes and seconds to enable a time to be inserted. As the time is stored as a value, calculations can then be performed using the time if required.	=TIME(B9,B10,B11)
NOW	Inserts the current date and time.	=NOW()
weekday	Extracts the number of the day in the week, such as 1 for Sunday.	=WEEKDAY(B1)

Table 8.7: Date and time functions.

Using functions that extract numeric values from strings, concatenate strings and test cell contents

A range of functions can be used with text to extract parts of text, such as numeric values, and join text together.

Extract numeric values from a string

Text strings will often contain both text and numeric values, such as a car registration plate or a product code in a supermarket. It can be useful to extract the numeric values, which then enables calculations to be performed using the values.

If the numeric values are located at the start or end of a string, the LEFT or RIGHT functions, as examined in the 'Extract characters from strings' section below can be used. For example, if a car registration plate is 'RTYH578' and located in cell C3, the number '578' could be extracted with the function =RIGHT(C3,3) as the number is located within the last three characters of the string.

The flash fill tool can also be used to extract numbers from strings. Flash fill automatically detects the data that should be extracted by using an example provided by the user. Once the example has been provided, copy the example to the clipboard, then click on the row below and press Ctrl and E to perform a flash fill.

WORKED EXAMPLE 8.26

Figure 8.43 shows an organisation's Product IDs.

Product ID	Number
sfg1246dd	
fdfg213hjk	
178gfh	
1299lljj	

Figure 8.43: Product IDs containing numeric values.

To extract the numeric values, manually enter the numeric values within an adjacent cell (see Figure 8.44). For example, within the first product ID, the numbers 1246 need to be extracted. Enter 1246 into the adjacent cell, then copy the data to the clipboard.

CONTINUED

Product ID	Number
sfg1246dd	1246
fdfg213hjk	213
178gfh	178
1299lljj	1299

Figure 8.44: Example of required numeric data to be extracted.

Click in the cell below the number entered, then press Ctrl and E together to perform a flash fill. The numeric values will be automatically extracted from the product IDs and placed in the adjacent columns, as shown in Figure 8.45.

Product ID	Number
sfg1246dd	1246
fdfg213hjk	213
178gfh	178
1299lljj	1299

Figure 8.45: Numeric values automatically extracted from other product IDs.

Concatenate strings

Concatenate means to join things together to form a single item. The CONCAT function can be used to concatenate text strings.

Function	Purpose	Example
CONCAT (or CONCATENATE)	Joins together text strings	=CONCAT (A1,B1,C1) Joins together the text in cells A1, B1 and C1 to create a string.

Functions can be used to determine whether data is of a particular type or even if a cell is blank (see Table 8.8).

Function	Purpose	Example
ISTEXT	Returns TRUE if a value is text	=ISTEXT(A1)
ISNUMBER	Returns TRUE if a value is a number	=ISNUMBER(A1)
ISNONTEXT	Returns TRUE if a value is not text	=ISNONTEXT(A1)
ISBLANK	Returns TRUE if a cell is blank	=ISBLANK(A1)

Table 8.8: Functions to test cell contents.

Questions

6 What method could be used to extract the numerical data from the following strings: 'FCVB124' and 'TYHJ387'?

7 What method could be used to extract the numerical data from the following strings: 'RF45GH' and 'TY41QW'?

WORKED EXAMPLE 8.27

	A	B	C	D	E
1		ISTEXT	ISNUMBER	ISNONTEXT	ISERROR
2	Hello	TRUE	FALSE	FALSE	FALSE
3	012 555 555	TRUE	FALSE	FALSE	FALSE
4	BD54QRT	TRUE	FALSE	FALSE	FALSE
5	258	FALSE	TRUE	TRUE	FALSE
6	19.32	FALSE	TRUE	TRUE	FALSE
7		FALSE	FALSE	TRUE	FALSE
8	#DIV/0!	FALSE	FALSE	TRUE	TRUE
9	#VALUE!	FALSE	FALSE	TRUE	TRUE

Figure 8.46: Data type results.

The spreadsheet **8.26_Data type functions.xlsx** uses the ISTEXT, ISNUMBER and ISNONTEXT functions, along with the ISERROR function, as outlined in the Perform error trapping section in Figure 8.46.

Figure 8.47 shows the functions that were used in the previous example.

	A	B	C	D	E
1		ISTEXT	ISNUMBER	ISNONTEXT	ISERROR
2	Hello	=ISTEXT(A2)	=ISNUMBER(A2)	=ISNONTEXT(A2)	=ISERROR(A2)
3	012 555 555	=ISTEXT(A3)	=ISNUMBER(A3)	=ISNONTEXT(A3)	=ISERROR(A3)
4	BD54QRT	=ISTEXT(A4)	=ISNUMBER(A4)	=ISNONTEXT(A4)	=ISERROR(A4)
5	258	=ISTEXT(A5)	=ISNUMBER(A5)	=ISNONTEXT(A5)	=ISERROR(A5)
6	19.32	=ISTEXT(A6)	=ISNUMBER(A6)	=ISNONTEXT(A6)	=ISERROR(A6)
7		=ISTEXT(A7)	=ISNUMBER(A7)	=ISNONTEXT(A7)	=ISERROR(A7)
8	=A6/0	=ISTEXT(A8)	=ISNUMBER(A8)	=ISNONTEXT(A8)	=ISERROR(A8)
9	=FIND("b",A2)	=ISTEXT(A9)	=ISNUMBER(A9)	=ISNONTEXT(A9)	=ISERROR(A9)

Figure 8.47: Data type functions.

The spreadsheet **8.27_Using data type functions. xlsx** contains some examples of using some of these functions in practice. In the next section, the FIND function is examined, which searches for a value. It returns an error if the value is not found, as shown in Figure 8.48.

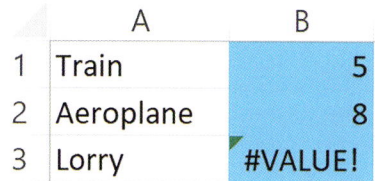

	A	B
1	Train	5
2	Aeroplane	8
3	Lorry	#VALUE!

Figure 8.48: Find function causing error.

We can fix this by using the ISERROR function to check if an error has been found. If an error is found, then the value 0 could be returned, or something else like 'Not found' (see Figure 8.49).

	A	B
1	Train	=IF(ISERROR(FIND("n",A1)),0,FIND("n",A1))
2	Aeroplane	=IF(ISERROR(FIND("n",A2)),0,FIND("n",A2))
3	Lorry	=IF(ISERROR(FIND("n",A3)),0,FIND("n",A3))

Figure 8.49: Removing an error.

The ISNUMBER function could be used to check a value is a number before performing a calculation on it. This could avoid errors. In Figure 8.50, ISNUMBER is used to check a value is a number before trying to divide it by two.

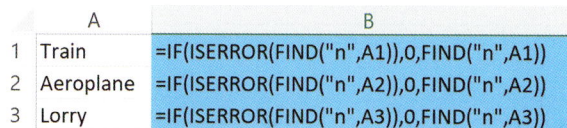

	A	B
5	one	=IF(ISNUMBER(A5),A5/2,"")
6	1	=IF(ISNUMBER(A6),A6/2,"")
7	1.5	=IF(ISNUMBER(A7),A7/2,"")

Figure 8.50: Avoiding errors.

If the value in column A is a number, then it is divided by 2, otherwise a blank value is displayed.

Using functions that extract characters from strings

A number of functions can be used to find and extract characters from text,
along with performing conversions to upper or lower case text, as shown in Table 8.9.

Function	Purpose	Example
LEFT	Extracts the furthest left characters, based on the number of characters specified in the section argument.	=LEFT(A1,4)
RIGHT	Extracts the furthest right characters, based on the number of characters specified in the section argument.	=RIGHT(A1,2)
MID	Extracts characters from a starting point, based on the starting position in the second argument and the number of characters in the third argument.	=MID(A2,4,6)
LEN	Calculates the length of a string.	=LEN(A1)
UPPER	Converts text into upper case.	=UPPER(A1)
LOWER	Converts text into lower case.	=LOWER(A1)
FIND	Searches for a substring within a string and returns its position.	=FIND('@', A2)

Table 8.9: Text functions.

WORKED EXAMPLE 8.28

	A	B	C	D
1	Mr	Minjun	Park	Mr Minjun Park
2				Mr Minjun Park
3				
4	Apples	Bananas	Strawberries	Pears
5	App	as	awb	5
6				
7	APPLES	BANANAS	STRAWBERRIES	PEARS
8	apples	bananas	strawberries	pears

Figure 8.51: Extracted data.

In the spreadsheet **8.28_Text functions.xlsx**, text functions have been used to extract data. Before looking in detail at how each function works, can you predict which function has been used in each of the cells D1, D2, A5, B5, C5, D5, row 7 and row 8 (see Figure 8.51)?

We can now look at each of the functions that have been used. Experiment by changing values and looking at what difference it makes (see Figure 8.52).

	A	B	C	D
1	Mr	Minjun	Park	=(A1 & " " & B1 & " " & C1)
2				=CONCATENATE(A1," ", B1, " ", C1)
3				
4	Apples	Bananas	Strawberries	Pears
5	=LEFT(A4,3)	=RIGHT(B4,2)	=MID(C4,4,3)	=LEN(D4)
6				
7	=UPPER(A4)	=UPPER(B4)	=UPPER(C4)	=UPPER(D4)
8	=LOWER(A4)	=LOWER(B4)	=LOWER(C4)	=LOWER(D4)

Figure 8.52: Extracted data functions.

Notice how D1 and D2 return the same values. These are two different methods of concatenating data.

For apples, the first three characters from the left are extracted, which are 'App'. For bananas, the last two characters from the right are extracted which are 'as'. For strawberries, the three characters starting at character 4 ('a') are extracted which are 'awb'.

For pears, the length is shown, which is the number of characters in 'Pears' that is '5'.

Row 7 converts the data from row 4 into upper case and row 8 converts the data from row 4 into lower case.

ACTIVITY 8.18

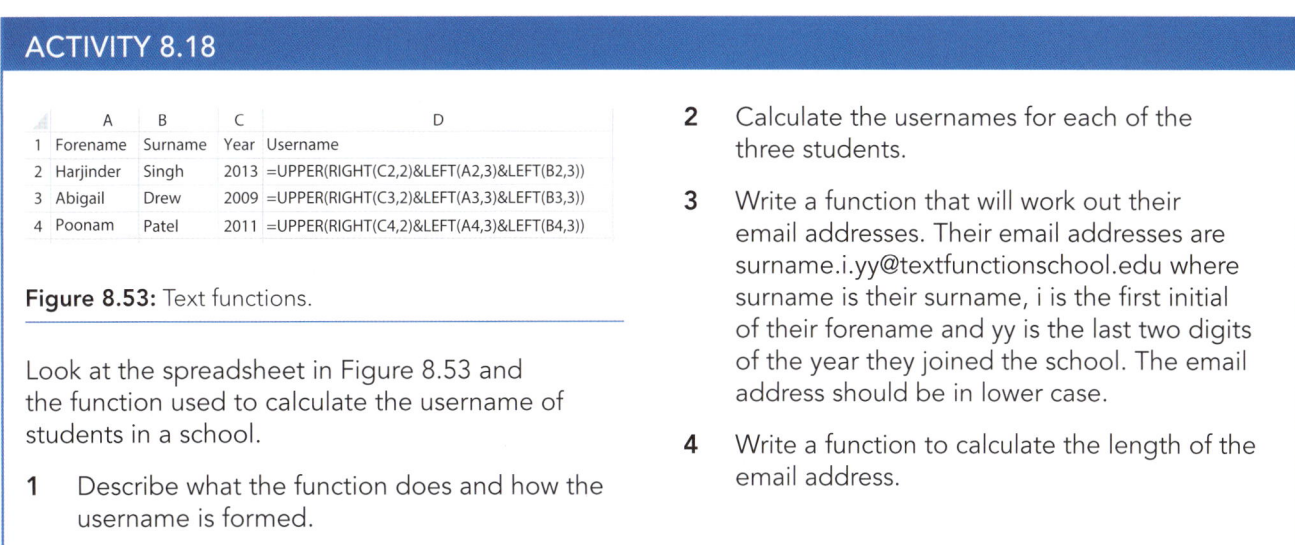

	A	B	C	D
1	Forename	Surname	Year	Username
2	Harjinder	Singh	2013	=UPPER(RIGHT(C2,2)&LEFT(A2,3)&LEFT(B2,3))
3	Abigail	Drew	2009	=UPPER(RIGHT(C3,2)&LEFT(A3,3)&LEFT(B3,3))
4	Poonam	Patel	2011	=UPPER(RIGHT(C4,2)&LEFT(A4,3)&LEFT(B4,3))

Figure 8.53: Text functions.

Look at the spreadsheet in Figure 8.53 and the function used to calculate the username of students in a school.

1   Describe what the function does and how the username is formed.

2   Calculate the usernames for each of the three students.

3   Write a function that will work out their email addresses. Their email addresses are surname.i.yy@textfunctionschool.edu where surname is their surname, i is the first initial of their forename and yy is the last two digits of the year they joined the school. The email address should be in lower case.

4   Write a function to calculate the length of the email address.

FIND function

The FIND function can be used to find the position of a substring within a string. For example, FIND('@', 'username@domain.com') will return the number 9 because the @ symbol is in position 9.

WORKED EXAMPLE 8.29

	A	B
1	Train	5
2	Aeroplane	8
3	Lorry	#VALUE!

Figure 8.54: Finding a character.

In the spreadsheet **8.29_Find.xlsx**, the FIND function has been used to calculate the position of a specific character in A1, A2 and A3. Can you predict which character the FIND function is looking for (see Figure 8.54)?

In this example, the FIND function was being used to find the value 'n' (see Figure 8.55). As 'n' does not exist in 'Lorry', it returned an error. Later in this chapter you will find out how to manage errors in spreadsheets.

	A	B
1	Train	=FIND("n",A1)
2	Aeroplane	=FIND("n",A2)
3	Lorry	=FIND("n",A3)

Figure 8.55: Finding a character function.

The next part of the spreadsheet uses the FIND function to find the @ symbol in an email address and then returns the characters after the @ symbol. These characters form the domain name of the email address (see Figure 8.56).

	A	B
5	mpark@dmail.com	
6	Domain:	dmail.com
7		dmail.com

Figure 8.56: Extracting a domain name.

CONTINUED

In cell B6, the RIGHT function is used to extract data from the right-hand side of the email address. However, to do this the number of characters to extract needs to be calculated. This can be done by subtracting the position of the @ symbol from the length of the email address (see Figure 8.57).

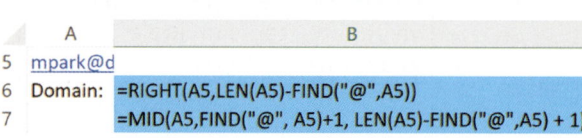

	A	B
5	mpark@d	
6	Domain:	=RIGHT(A5,LEN(A5)-FIND("@",A5))
7		=MID(A5,FIND("@", A5)+1, LEN(A5)-FIND("@",A5) + 1)

Figure 8.57: Extracting a domain name functions.

Notice how cell B7 uses the MID function instead of RIGHT to return the same result. Can you explain how this function is working?

ACTIVITY 8.19

1   Create a function to find the position of the phonetic sound 'igh' in a word.

2   Create a function to extract the part of a word that comes before the phonetic sound 'igh'. For example, for 'bright', the function should extract 'br'.

Using functions that apply conditional formulas

Many functions that perform calculations, such as SUM and AVERAGE, also have conditional functions available, which enable function calculations to only take place based on certain conditions. Conditional functions are shown in Table 8.10.

Function	Purpose	Example
SUMIF	Adds up all values within a range that meet a specific condition.	=SUMIF(J3:J200,"<5") Only calculates a total for numbers less than five in the range J3 to J200.
SUMIFS	Adds up all values within a range that meet multiple criteria.	=SUMIFS(A5:A9,B5:B9,">10",C5:C9,"Apple") Only calculates a total for the values in A5 to A9 if their corresponding value in B5 to B9 is greater than 10 and the corresponding value in C5 to C9 is "Apple".
COUNTIF	Counts all values that meet a criterion within a range.	=COUNTIF(H3:H200,"Yes") Only counts cells that contain "Yes" in the range H3 to H200.
COUNTIFS	Counts all values that meet criteria within multiple ranges.	=COUNTIF(H3:H200,"Yes",J3:J200,"No") Only counts cells containing "Yes" in the range H3 to H200, along with cells containing "No" in the range J3 to J200.
AVERAGEIF	Calculates the average of all values that meet a criterion within a range.	=AVERAGEIF(J3:J200,">0") Only finds the average of numbers greater than zero in the range J3 and J200.
AVERAGEIFS	Calculates the average of all values that meet criteria within multiple ranges.	=AVERAGEIFS(J3:J200,J3:J200,">65",J3:J200,"<85") Only finds the average of the numbers in the range J3 and J200 that are greater than 65 and less than 85.

Function	Purpose	Example
MAXIFS	Calculates the largest numeric value that meets multiple criteria in a range of values.	=MAXIFS(A3:A9,B3:B9,23) Only finds the maximum value in the range A3 to A9, where the corresponding cells in B3 to B9 have a value of 23.
MINIFS	Calculates the smallest numeric value that meets multiple criteria in a range of values.	=MINIFS(A3:A9,B3:B9,"<7") Only finds the minimum value in the range A3 to A9, where the corresponding cells in B3 to B9 have a value less than 7.

Table 8.10: Conditional functions.

Questions

8   What function is used to calculate the average of all values that meet certain criteria?

9   What function is used to count all values that meet criteria within multiple ranges?

WORKED EXAMPLE 8.30

The spreadsheet **8.30_Maths results.xlsx** results shows the marks and grades awarded to students taking a maths test. In cell C13, a COUNTIF function is used to count only those students who achieved a Pass (see Figure 8.58).

	A	B	C
1	**Maths**		
2	**Student**	**Mark**	**Grade**
3	Matthew	12	Fail
4	Elijah	76	Pass
5	Caleb	12	Fail
6	Joshua	26	Fail
7	Sheila	44	Pass
8	Junayna	77	Pass
9	Jordan	98	Distinction
10	Sharon	76	Pass
11			
12	Total Students		
13	Passes		4
14	Fails		
15	Distinctions		

Figure 8.58: Maths results COUNTIF.

ACTIVITY 8.20

Open **8.30_Maths results.xlsx**.

1   Use a function to count all the students in cell C12.

2   Use a function to count all the students who failed the test in C14.

3   Use a function to count all the students who achieved a distinction in cell C15.

4   Use functions to calculate the average distinction mark, pass mark and fail mark in cells C17 to C19.

Open the spreadsheet **8.31_Member ratings.xlsx**, which shows how many meetings each member of a club has attended. Members who have attended 50 meetings or more are awarded 'Gold member' status.

1   Use a function in B13 to calculate how many members have Gold member status.

2   Use a function in B14 to calculate the total number of meetings that have been attended by Gold members.

Questions

10   Describe the purpose of a named range of cells.

11   Describe the difference between a formula and a function.

12   Compare absolute cell referencing with relative cell referencing.

13   Using an example, describe how absolute cell referencing could be used in a spreadsheet.

Using functions that perform error trapping

Table 8.11 identifies functions that can be used to identify, or trap, errors and display suitable error messages if required.

Insert nested functions

A nested function involves using more than one function at the same time. For example, the average of a range of values could be calculated using an AVERAGE function, then a message displayed if certain criteria were met, using an IF function.

Each function is surrounded by brackets, with the function within the brackets undertaken before the function surrounding it is used.

Function	Purpose	Example
ISERROR	Returns TRUE if a cell contains an error.	=ISERROR(A1)
IFERROR	Check to see if a calculation gives a result or an error. If there is an error, the message specified is displayed. If there is no error, the result of the calculation is displayed.	=IFERROR(A7/B7,"Calculation has an error") Checks for an error when dividing the value in A7 by B7 and displays the result of the calculation if there is no error, or "Calculation has an error" if there is an error.

Table 8.11: Functions to trap errors and display error messages.

WORKED EXAMPLE 8.31

The spreadsheet **8.32_Nested Formula.xlsx** calculates the average mark using separate total and average functions in columns F and G (see Figure 8.59).

In column H, a nested formula has been used to calculate whether each student is above or below the average mark. It examines the average mark for the student in column G, then divides the total of all the average marks by the number of average marks to see if column G is higher. If column G is higher then 'Above' is displayed, otherwise 'Below' is displayed.

	A	B	C	D	E	F	G	H	I	J	K	L	M
1	Student	Mark 1	Mark 2	Mark 3	Mark 4	Total	Average						
2	Name 1	98	40	36	84	258	65	=IF(G2>(SUM(G$2:G$10)/COUNT(G$2:G$10)),"Above","Below")					
3	Name 2	31	67	61	77	236	59	Below					

Figure 8.59: Nested IF.

ACTIVITY 8.21

Open the spreadsheet **8.33_Profit calculator.xlsx.**

1   Create a single nested formula for E2 that will calculate the total profit made for product 1.

2   Replicate this formula for products 2 and 3.

3   Without using the AVERAGE function, create a nested formula to calculate the average total profit in E5.

Using functions that rotate data from columns to rows or vice versa

Sometimes, data has been entered into a spreadsheet in columns, but needs to be rotated so it is arranged in rows instead, or vice versa. For example, it may be a user has decided data should be presented in a different way, or data being copied into a new spreadsheet needs to be rotated to fit the existing structure.

To rotate data, first select a new location for the data to rotate by highlighting the required cells. For example, if the data is currently arranged so it is stored in 10 cells, with two rows across and five columns down, then 10 new cells should also be selected, but with two columns down and five rows across (see Figure 8.60).

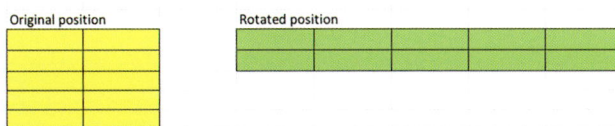

Figure 8.60: Original and new location for rotated data.

Once the cells have been highlighted, the TRANSPOSE function can be used to rotate the data. For example, to rotate the data held in the range B4 to C9, the TRANSPOSE function can be used as follows:

=TRANSPOSE(B4:C9)

Using appropriate input and error messages

Input and error messages are examined in the controlling data input using validation techniques section previously.

Formatting cells

Cells can be formatted to ensure the data entered into the cell appears in a specific way. To format cells, highlight the cells required, then select the Format menu, then Cells. Alternatively, click with the right mouse button on the required cells and select Format Cells.

Date and time

Cells within a spreadsheet can be formatted for an appropriate data type. Dates can be formatted in a variety of ways, such as dd/mm/yyyy where dd is the day, mm is the month and yyyy is the year. Other ways of presenting the date include displaying the month as text, using leading zeros for days and months, and using either four digits or two digits for the year. Times can be formatted to include hours, minutes and seconds, or just hours and minutes. Time can be formatted to show a.m. or p.m., or to use the 24-hour clock.

DID YOU KNOW?

In the USA, the date is often written in the form mm/dd/yyyy, so dates need to be formatted in a manner that is suitable for the target audience.

Text and numeric

Cells can be set to contain text, such as names or address information. This is particularly useful if a set of numbers needs to be entered that start with zero (known as a leading zero), as these may otherwise be removed by the spreadsheet software.

Numeric cells can be set to include a specific number of decimal places, including no decimal places.

Currency

Currency can be set to include a specific number of decimal places, and the currency symbol can also be chosen.

Percentage and fractions

Cells formatted as Percentage multiply the value of the cell by 100 and display the result with a percent symbol after a number. For example, 58% would be displayed for the value 0.58.

Decimals can be entered into a cell and turned into fractions. For example, entering 0.25 would give a fraction of ¼.

ACTIVITY 8.22

Open the spreadsheet **8.35_Data Types Task.xlsx**.

1 Format cell B2 to be a date with no leading zeros for the day and month and two digits for the year.

2 Format cell C2 to be a date with leading zeros for the day, the full name of the month and four digits for the year.

3 Format cell B3 to be a time with AM/PM.

4 Format cell C3 to be a time with hours, minutes and seconds.

5 Enter the value 0382 in cell B4. What happens?

6 Format cell C4 to be text and then enter the value 0382. What is different from B4?

7 Format cell B5 to have two decimal places. What happens?

8 Format cell C5 to have one decimal place. What happens?

9 Format cell B6 to be currency in euros with two decimal places. What happens?

10 Format cell C6 to be currency in Japanese yen with two decimal places. What happens?

11 Format cell B7 to be a percentage. What happens?

12 Format cell C7 to be a percentage. What happens?

13 Format cells B8 and C8 to be fractions up to one digit. Are they both correct? What do you think needs to be done to fix this?

Text orientation

It can sometimes be difficult to fit all the necessary text into a column title without the column becoming too wide. In these circumstances, the text **orientation** can change, so the text is displayed either diagonally or vertically.

KEY WORD

orientation: the direction of text, for example horizontal or vertical

To change the orientation of text, highlight the required cells, then click the Orientation button on the Home toolbar at the top of the screen. Alternatively, click on the Alignment tab in the Format Cells window.

WORKED EXAMPLE 8.32

The spreadsheet in Figure 8.61 shows the scores between international football teams. The number of goals scored by the team is shown in each row and the number of goals scored against a team is shown in each column. You will notice that the columns are too narrow to fit in the full team name. In Figure 8.62, the columns are too wide.

	A	B	C	D	E	F
1		Japar	Mace	Unite	Pakis	Ukrai
2	Japan	■	3	2	4	1
3	Macedonia	2	■	3	0	0
4	United States of America	1	0	■	0	2
5	Pakistan	2	3	2	■	0
6	Ukraine	0	1	2	5	■

Figure 8.61: Columns too narrow.

CONTINUED

	A	B	C	D	E	F
1		Japan	Macedonia	United States of America	Pakistan	Ukraine
2	Japan		3	2	4	1
3	Macedonia	2		3	0	0
4	United States of America	1	0		0	2
5	Pakistan	2	3	2		0
6		0	1	2	5	

Figure 8.62: Columns too wide.

To overcome this problem, the text can be orientated vertically, as shown in Figure 8.63.

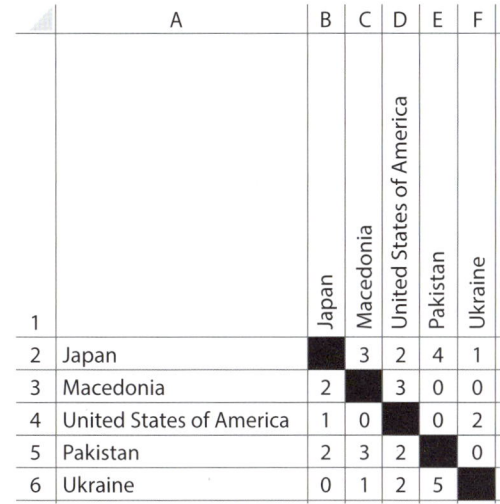

Figure 8.63: Columns rotated vertically.

Alignment

By default, the horizontal **alignment** of text is to the left, with numbers aligned to the right. However, it is possible to change the way that data is aligned within cells, such as by having all data aligned to the centre of a cell. The vertical alignment of cells can also be altered. By default, data is vertically aligned to the bottom of a cell.

To change the alignment of text, highlight the required cells, then click the relevant Align to… button, such as Align to Right, on the Home toolbar at the top of the screen. Alternatively, click on the Alignment tab in the Format Cells window.

> **KEY WORD**
>
> **alignment:** positioning text so that it is in line, for example on the left, right or centre

---

WORKED EXAMPLE 8.33

One problem that often occurs is when different numbers of decimal places are used in the same column. The numbers are aligned to the right of the cell rather than by the decimal point, as shown in Figure 8.64.

	D
3	87.23
4	18.5
5	23.56
6	34.23472

Figure 8.64: Decimal point alignment problem.

Unlike a word processor, it is not possible to change the alignment to be on the decimal point. Therefore, the number of decimal places needs to be made equal (see Figure 8.65).

	D
3	87.230
4	18.500
5	23.560
6	34.235

Figure 8.65: Decimal point alignment solved.

ACTIVITY 8.23

Open the spreadsheet **8.36_Alignment.xlsx**. This shows the election results for three areas of the UK in 2015.

1   Change the names of the parties in C2 to P2 to be vertical orientation.

2   Increase the height of row 2 if necessary.

3   Change the names of the parties to be centred vertically.

4   Change the number of votes in C3 to I5 to be right aligned.

5   Change the number of decimal places for the percentages in K3 to P5 to be one decimal place.

6   Change the titles in B2 to B5 to be right aligned.

Formatting cell emphasis

Cells can be formatted to appear in different ways, such as emphasising certain values or heading. There are several ways cells can be emphasised, such as changing the size, style and colour of text, or the background colour of a cell. Options to change cell formatting are available on the Home toolbar, or in the relevant section of the Format Cells window, as outlined next.

Size, style and colour

The font used to display text can be altered by clicking on the Font tab in the Format Cells window. The font, font size and font colour can be changed, along with changing the font style to be bold, italic or underlined.

Shading

The background colour used within a cell can be altered by clicking on the Fill tab in the Format Cells window. Different colours and patterns can be selected, with a sample displayed at the bottom of the window.

Merge

Merging cells was discussed in the Creating and editing spreadsheet structures section previously.

Borders

Borders around the edge of a cell can be added by clicking on the Borders tab in the Format Cells window. Different thicknesses, colours, locations and styles of line can be selected.

Question

14   What different formatting options are available to highlight important cells within a spreadsheet?

Comments

Spreadsheets can contain a large amount of data. Some data may require additional information to explain what it is used for or what it represents. In addition, it can be useful to comment on the structure or data within a spreadsheet when giving feedback to others. Comments can be added to cells, which are displayed when the user selects the cell. To add a comment, click with the right mouse button on the required cell and select New Comment.

ACTIVITY 8.24

Open the spreadsheet **8.37_Emphasis.xlsx**.

1 Change cells A2, A4, A11 and A15 to be bold and font size 14.

2 Add borders to the bottom of cells B4, C4, B11, C11 and D11.

3 Add a thick blue border around cells A1 to D19.

4 Shade A1:D1 and A1:A19 in yellow.

5 Shade C13 and D13 in black.

6 Add a comment to cell B2 to read 'This is the commission a school will earn'.

Conditional formatting

Cells can be formatted based on certain conditions being met, which is known as conditional formatting. Conditions can include:

* values in a cell that are equal to a set criterion (e.g. = 'Good')

* values in a cell that are greater or less than a set criterion (e.g. >5)

* values in a cell that are between set criteria (e.g. between 2 and 10)

* values in a cell that are duplicated elsewhere in the worksheet

* values that are above or below average

* a scale of values from lowest to highest.

To add conditional formatting, select the cells required, then the Format menu, then Conditional Formatting. Alternatively, click the Conditional Formatting button on the Home toolbar at the top of the screen. The Conditional Formatting button contains a number of conditional formatting rules available for use, including those listed above, which can be customised to use the formatting required.

WORKED EXAMPLE 8.34

In the spreadsheet **8.38_Conditional Formatting.xlsx**, a questionnaire has been sent out and respondents have had to give a priority to each question from 1 to 5 or x if they disagree completely.

The average response, total x responses and total blank responses has been calculated. The following conditional formatting rules have been used:

* Respondent reply = 1: white text with green shading

* Respondent reply >= 4: white text with red shading

* Respondent reply = x: white text with red shading

* Respondent reply between 2 and 3: yellow shading

* Average response < 2: white text with green shading

* Average response >= 4: white text with red shading

* Average response between 2.0 and 2.9: yellow shading

* Total x >= 4: red text with light red shading.

ACTIVITY 8.25

Open the spreadsheet **8.39_Member List.xlsx** and conditionally format cells according to the following rules:

1   Basic members: orange shading

2   Premium members: white text, blue shading

3   Full, junior or patron members: green text

4   Lapsed members: red text

5   Do not email = TRUE: yellow shading with red border

6   Number of years >=10: green text

7   Number of years between 5 and 9: purple text.

Spreadsheet requirements, purpose and use

In addition to considering the page and screen structure when creating a spreadsheet, the requirements of the spreadsheet's functionality for a specific audience should also be considered. For young children, simple formulas could be included to ensure they are able to understand the calculations required. Older children might wish to use a spreadsheet to automatically calculate certain values, such as averages, so a spreadsheet's functions could be used.

For scientists, the complex formulas that can be created within a spreadsheet enable them to analyse results and make predictions about the outcomes of experiments, along with producing charts to display data. Administrators often use spreadsheets to keep track of finances, with formatting used to highlight important values, such as an organisation's available funds. Other audiences, such as artists, can also use spreadsheets to keep track of materials and equipment, along with orders and sales.

Finally, some individuals also use spreadsheets for creative purposes, such as producing pixel art (see Figure 8.66)!

Figure 8.66: Pixel art created with a spreadsheet.

8.2 Testing a spreadsheet

Testing a spreadsheet involves ensuring that both the spreadsheet structure and the data it contains are robust and will meet the requirements of users.

Test a spreadsheet structure

All formulas, functions, validation rules and conditional formatting need testing within a spreadsheet. To test a spreadsheet, input data that will be used should be identified and the expected output recorded. For example, the result of a calculation could be recorded, along with the appearance of a cell based on an expected result. It is therefore necessary to work systematically through the spreadsheet to identify where formulas, functions, validation rules and conditional formatting need testing, then to identify appropriate test data, as outlined next. The required tests will often be recorded within a test plan, which provides evidence of the tests completed. A test plan also enables tests that have failed to be easily identified and retests performed once errors have been corrected.

Test data

Appropriate test data needs to be selected to test the spreadsheet. It is not possible to test every possible input value, so a range of normal, extreme and abnormal data should be selected, as outlined in Table 8.12.

The expected output for formulas and functions should be calculated without using the spreadsheet and then compared with the result from the spreadsheet.

Type of test data	Purpose
Normal (valid/acceptable data)	Test using data typically used with the spreadsheet, which should pass validation rules.
Abnormal (erroneous/invalid data)	Test using data that will not be used with the spreadsheet and should therefore generate an error message.
Extreme	Test using data on the boundary of data that can be used with the spreadsheet, which will only just pass the validation rule, as it is on the boundary of acceptable data.

Table 8.12: Types of test data.

WORKED EXAMPLE 8.35

Test data input value	Type of test data	Expected result
A6 = 5, B6 = 8 on Addition worksheet	Normal	C6 = 13 on Addition worksheet
A6 = 30 000 000, B6 = 80 000 000 on Addition worksheet	Extreme	C6 = 110 000 000 on Addition worksheet and is fully visible
A6 = 0, B6 = 0 on Addition worksheet	Extreme	C6 = 0 on Addition worksheet

This test plan tests the formula = A6 + B6 located in cell C6 on the worksheet named Addition.

When a tester runs a test plan, there will be an additional column called 'Actual result' where the results of the test will be entered.

UNPLUGGED ACTIVITY 8.26

Generate test data that will test the rules below. Using paper away from the computer, you should use a table with three columns: test data value, type of test data and expected result. Ensure you cover all four types of test data.

- input value is a whole number <1000
- input value is a decimal >25
- input value is between 100 and 200
- input value = PASS or FAIL (there are no extreme tests for this)
- input value exists in list Junior, Intermediate, Senior (there are no extreme tests for this)

ACTIVITY 8.27

Open the spreadsheet **8.40_Testing Task.xlsx** and run the tests from Worked Example 8.35.

1   Record the results in **8.41_Test Results.docx**.

2   If a test fails, record what happened.

ACTIVITY 8.28

Open the spreadsheet **8.42_Invoices.xlsx** and **8.43_Test Plan.docx** and complete the test plan below with at least six other tests. Calculate the expected result away from the computer and then enter the input data and compare with the actual result.

Test data input value	Type of test data	Expected result	Actual result
Quantity for Product 3 on Invoice worksheet = 31 Cost for Product 3 on Invoice worksheet = $1,345.00 VAT rate on data worksheet = 20%	Normal	VAT for Product 3 on Invoice worksheet = $9,684.00	

Question

15 The data below is an extract from a spreadsheet.

Customer	Product Code	Price	Quantity
K&N Motors	QRV58N	$28.50	2
Cosmic Flavours	PWC48H	$19.23	1
Boldmere Carpets	GEV28X	$218.29	1

To validate data, the following validation rules have been setup in the spreadsheet:
- customer name should always be present
- a product code should be exactly six characters long
- the quantity must be an integer above zero.

Using the example shown, copy and complete the test table below.

Test data input value	Type of test data	Expected result	Reason for choosing data
Customer = Null			
Customer = _____	Normal		
Product Code = XYZ12AB			
Product Code = _____		Error: 'You must input a product code with 6 characters'.	
Quantity = 'a'			
Quantity = _____	Extreme	Value accepted	It's the smallest allowable quantity.
Quantity = _____		Value accepted	

8.3 Using a spreadsheet

Extracting data

When there is a lot of data stored in a spreadsheet, users may want to view only some of the data. Specific data can be viewed by extracting, or filtering, the data that is required by searching for data that meets certain conditions.

WORKED EXAMPLE 8.36

In Figure 8.67, people with a title of 'Dr' in column A have been filtered.

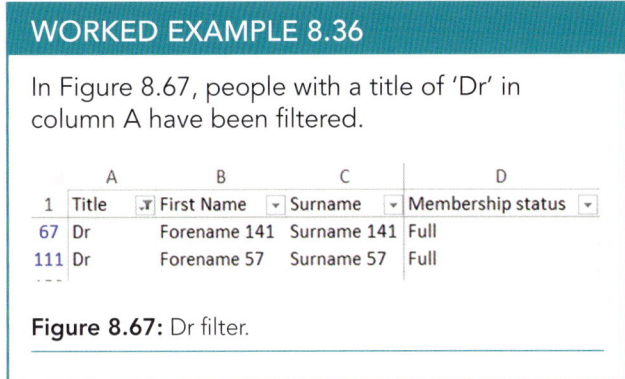

	A	B	C	D
1	Title	First Name	Surname	Membership status
67	Dr	Forename 141	Surname 141	Full
111	Dr	Forename 57	Surname 57	Full

Figure 8.67: Dr filter.

Searching using text, numeric and date and time

To filter data, highlight the data that is to be filtered, then select Sort & Filter from the Home toolbar at the top of the screen, followed by Filter. Drop-down arrows will appear within the column headings. Click on the drop-down menu containing the text Choose one, then select Equals to find cells containing the data entered in the box to the right of the menu.

Text, numeric and date and time data can all be filtered, with the available filter options to altered to reflect the data within the column. For example, if filtering data containing dates, an option to filter by dates next week is available.

ACTIVITY 8.29

Open **8.39_Member List.xlsx** and apply the following filters:

1   People with a membership status of Full.

2   People who do not want to be emailed.

3   People who have been a member for one year.

Boolean operators (AND, OR, NOT) and comparison operators (>, <, =, >=, <=)

The Boolean operators AND, OR and NOT can be used when filtering data to find data meeting multiple criteria.

Once a single filter has been entered within the Filter window, a drop-down box for additional filters to be entered appears. The AND option should be selected to only filter data where both conditions are true, or the OR option should be selected to only filter data where one or more of the conditions are true.

To use the Boolean operator NOT, an option to find data not equals to a specific value is available within the Choose one drop-down menu, as shown in Figure 8.68.

WORKED EXAMPLE 8.37

In Figure 8.68, the filter shows members who have NOT lapsed their membership.

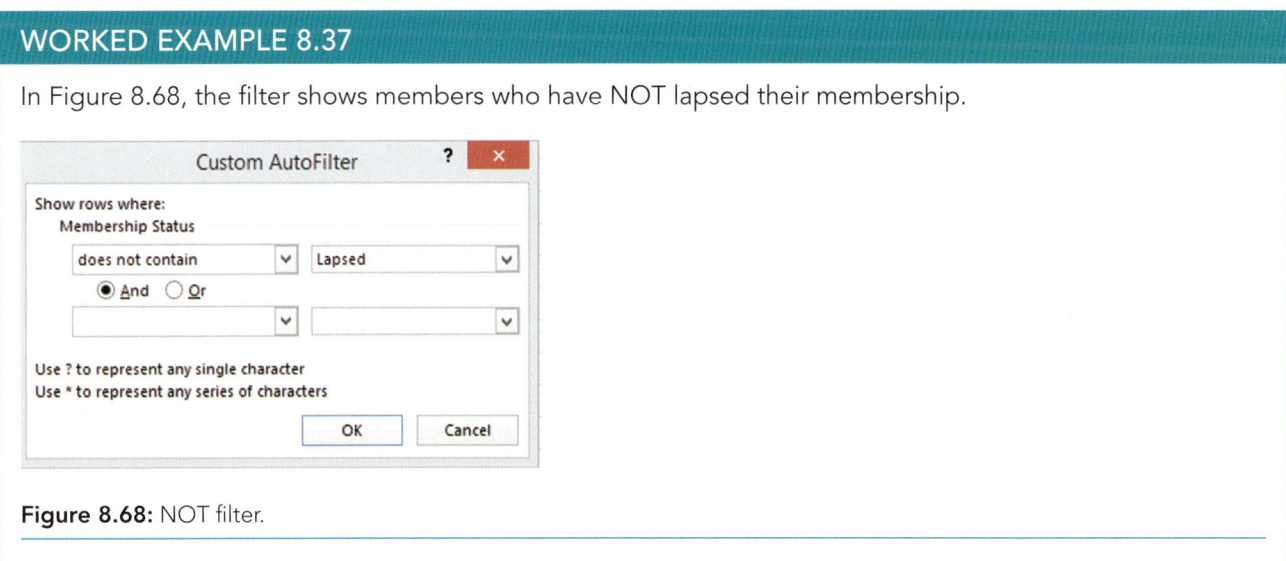

Figure 8.68: NOT filter.

CONTINUED

In Figure 8.69, the filter will show members who have five or more years of membership AND less than seven years of membership.

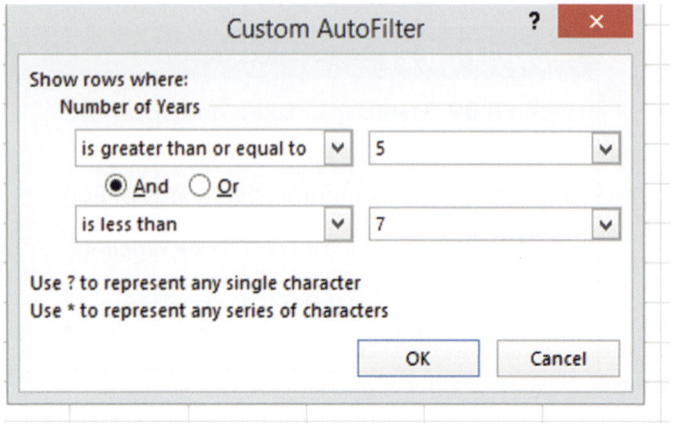

Figure 8.69: AND filter.

Figure 8.70 shows the result of the filter:

	A	B	C	D	E	F	G
1	Title	First Name	Surname	Membership Status	Membership Type	Do Not Email	Number of Years
13	Mrs	Forename 3	Surname 3	Full	Basic	FALSE	5
23	Mr	Forename 50	Surname 50	Full	Premium	FALSE	5
24	Mrs	Forename 7	Surname 7	Full	Basic	FALSE	5
37	Mr	Forename 90	Surname 90	Lapsed	Premium	FALSE	6
38	Miss	Forename 10	Surname 10	Full	Basic	TRUE	6
39	Mr	Forename 110	Surname 110	Full	Basic	FALSE	6
50	Ms	Forename 24	Surname 24	Patron	Basic	FALSE	5
52	Mr	Forename 69	Surname 69	Full	Premium	FALSE	6
53	Mr	Forename 15	Surname 15	Junior	Basic	TRUE	5
58	Mr	Forename 129	Surname 129	Lapsed	Basic	FALSE	5
61	Mr	Forename 133	Surname 133	Patron	Basic	FALSE	6
74	Mr	Forename 122	Surname 122	Lapsed	Basic	FALSE	5
78	Mrs	Forename 14	Surname 14	Lapsed	Basic	FALSE	6
83	Mr	Forename 108	Surname 108	Patron	Premium	FALSE	5
88	Mr	Forename 37	Surname 37	Full	Premium	FALSE	5
114	Mr	Forename 48	Surname 48	Full	Premium	FALSE	5
128	Mr	Forename 89	Surname 89	Lapsed	Premium	FALSE	5
132	Mr	Forename 78	Surname 78	Full	Premium	FALSE	6
146	Mr	Forename 70	Surname 70	Full	Premium	FALSE	6

Figure 8.70: AND result.

Filters that use comparison operators, such as greater than, when filtering numbers, dates and times, are shown in Table 8.13.

Filter	Purpose	Example
Greater than	Selects data in a column that is greater than the value specified.	>10
Less than	Selects data in a column that is less than the value specified.	<10
Greater than or equal to	Selects data in a column that is greater than or equal to the value specified.	>=10
Less than or equal to	Selects data in a column that is less than or equal to the value specified.	<=10

Table 8.13: Filtering for a range.

ACTIVITY 8.30

Open the spreadsheet **8.44_USA Addresses. xlsx** and apply the following filters:

1 State is Arizona 'Az' OR California 'CA'.

2 City starts with 'San'.

3 Company ends with 'Inc'.

4 Company includes '&'.

5 Position is <=10.

6 Position is >10 AND <=50.

7 State is NOT = 'FL' AND NOT = 'OH'.

Searching using contains, starts with and ends with

A range of text filters can also be used when filtering data, as shown in Table 8.14.

Filter	Purpose	Example
Contains	Selects data in a column that includes the text specified.	Contains 'CH' will select all data in a column where CH exists anywhere within each data item. Chicken, Reach, Church and Ache would all be included, but not Card.
Starts with	Selects data in a column that starts with the text specified.	Starts with 'CH' will select all data in a column where the data starts with CH. Chicken and Church would all be included, but not Reach, Ache or Card.
Ends with	Selects data in a column that ends with the text specified.	Ends with 'CH' will select all data in a column where the data ends with CH. Church and Reach would be included but not Chicken, Ache or Card.

Table 8.14: Text filters.

Sorting data

Ascending and descending

It is possible to sort data into ascending or descending order, such as in numerical order from the lowest number to the highest number.

To sort data, highlight the data to sort, then select Sort & Filter from the Home menu toolbar at the top of the screen. The available options are altered depending on the data selected. For example, if text data is selected, the options will be given to sort either Sort A to Z, or Sort Z to A.

Applied to single or multiple columns

If only a single column is highlighted, then only the data within the column will be sorted based on the criteria specified. However, this can mean data in adjacent rows becomes out of order, as its position in relation to other cells has changed. Therefore, when sorting only a single column, a Sorting warning window appears to check whether all data within a table should be sorted (see Figure 8.71). Select Expand the selection to sort all columns based on the original sorting criteria specified.

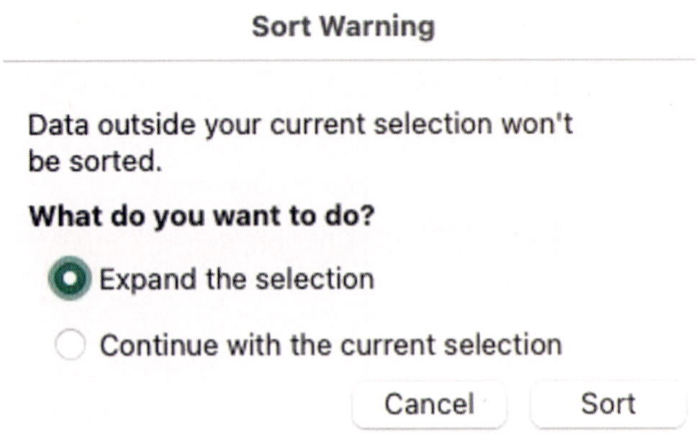

Sort Warning

Data outside your current selection won't be sorted.

What do you want to do?

⦿ Expand the selection

◯ Continue with the current selection

Cancel   Sort

Figure 8.71: Warning message highlighting the need to expand the selection of selected cells.

To sort data based on the order of data in multiple columns, it is necessary to specify the sort order for each column and which column should be sorted first. For example, to sort by surname and then to sort any matching surnames by forename, by surname would need to be sorted first.

To sort data using more than one column, select Sort & Filter and choose Custom Sort.

ACTIVITY 8.31

Open **8.44_USA Addresses.xlsx** and sort data into the following order:

- Position from 1 to 500.

- Position from 500 to 1.

CONTINUED

- State in alphabetical order from A to Z.

- City in reverse alphabetical order.

- Surname in alphabetical order from A to Z with Forename as the secondary sort.

Summarising and displaying data

There are several methods you can use to summarise and display data.

Pivot tables

A pivot table enables data within a spreadsheet to be analysed and summarised, such as providing totals and averages for a data set. Pivot tables are especially useful as they can replace the need for several functions. Summary data can also be sorted and filtered as required.

To create a Pivot table, highlight the data required, then select the Insert toolbar from the top of the screen and click Pivot Table. Ensure the correct range of cells has been selected, then click OK to create a new worksheet for the pivot table, as shown in Figure 8.72.

WORKED EXAMPLE 8.38

The file **8.39_Member List.xlsx** contains a list of members of a club including their membership status, membership type, whether they want to be contacted by email and how many years they have been a member. There are 148 members in total. Figure 8.72 shows an extract of the data.

	A	B	C	D	E	F	G
1	Title	First Name	Surname	Membership Status	Membership Type	Do Not Email	Number of Years
2	Mrs	Forename 6	Surname 6	Full	Basic	FALSE	13
3	Mr	Forename 32	Surname 32	Full	Premium	FALSE	11
4	Ms	Forename 22	Surname 22	Patron	Basic	FALSE	1
5	Mr	Forename 144	Surname 144	Junior	Basic	TRUE	14
6	Mr	Forename 101	Surname 101	Patron	Premium	FALSE	15
7	Mr	Forename 85	Surname 85	Lapsed	Premium	FALSE	4

Figure 8.72: Extract of members list.

CONTINUED

The Pivot Tables worksheet of the file includes some more pivot tables. One of the pivot tables shows the average number of years of membership for each type of member and membership type, as shown in Figure 8.73.

Average of Number of Years	Membership Type ▾		
Membership Status ▾	Basic	Premium	Grand Total
Full		7.9	9.2	8.9
Junior		9.6	8.8	9.4
Lapsed		7.1	5.5	6.6
Patron		6.5	9.6	7.8
Grand Total		7.6	8.8	8.3

Figure 8.73: Pivot table.

Figure 8.74 shows how the membership status has been selected as the row, the membership type as the column, and the average number of years as the value to display.

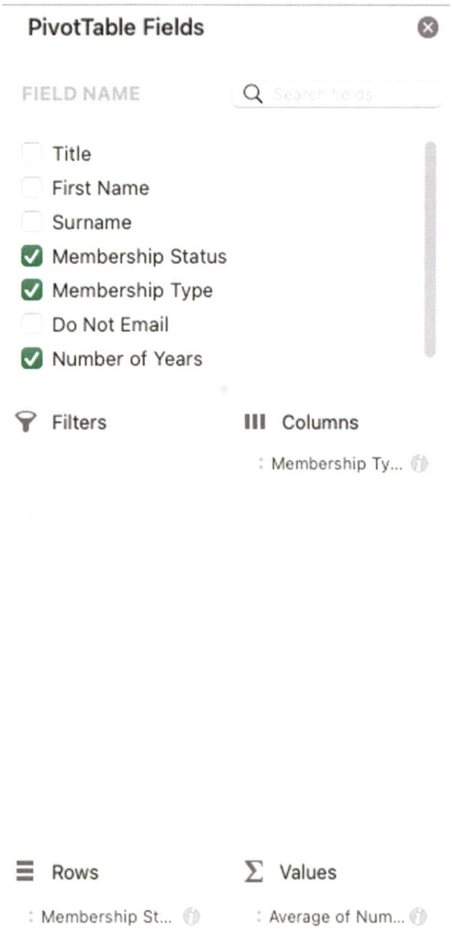

PivotTable Fields ⊗

FIELD NAME   🔍 Search fields

- ☐ Title
- ☐ First Name
- ☐ Surname
- ☑ Membership Status
- ☑ Membership Type
- ☐ Do Not Email
- ☑ Number of Years

▽ Filters   III Columns

⋮ Membership Ty... ⓘ

≡ Rows   Σ Values

⋮ Membership St... ⓘ   ⋮ Average of Num... ⓘ

Figure 8.74: Pivot table configuration.

A pivot table can summarise data based on any row or column in the data source. Summary data can use a range of functions, including calculating the sum, count, average, maximum, minimum and standard deviation.

The data to include within the pivot table can be selected and arranged within the PivotTable Fields section on the right-hand side of the screen.

WORKED EXAMPLE 8.39

Figure 8.75 shows the number of years for each status of member, grouped by membership type as a percentage of the total number of years of membership. For example, 4.3% of all members are junior premium members.

Sum of Number of Years	Membership Type		
Membership Status	Basic	Premium	Grand Total
Full	12.26%	44.64%	56.90%
Junior	8.60%	4.30%	12.91%
Lapsed	10.88%	3.57%	14.45%
Patron	7.95%	7.79%	15.75%
Grand Total	39.69%	60.31%	100.00%

Figure 8.75: Pivot table showing percentage of total.

Pivot charts

A pivot chart works in a similar way to a pivot table but shows the data graphically.

To create a pivot chart, ensure your pivot table has been setup as required, then select the Pivot Table Analyse toolbar from the top of the screen, then click Pivot Chart. The chart will appear within the pivot table worksheet.

WORKED EXAMPLE 8.40

The pivot chart in Figure 8.76 shows the number of members in each membership category and if they are basic or premium members.

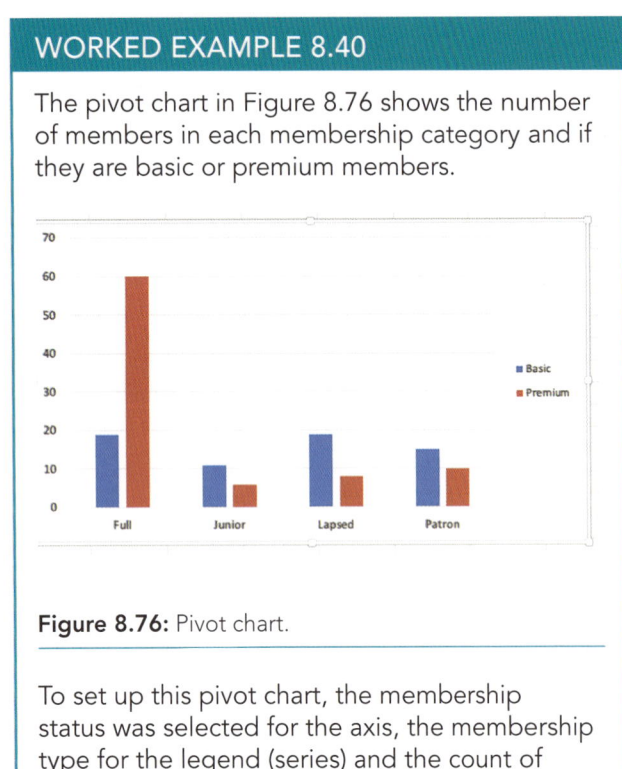

Figure 8.76: Pivot chart.

To set up this pivot chart, the membership status was selected for the axis, the membership type for the legend (series) and the count of membership type for the values (see Figure 8.77).

CONTINUED

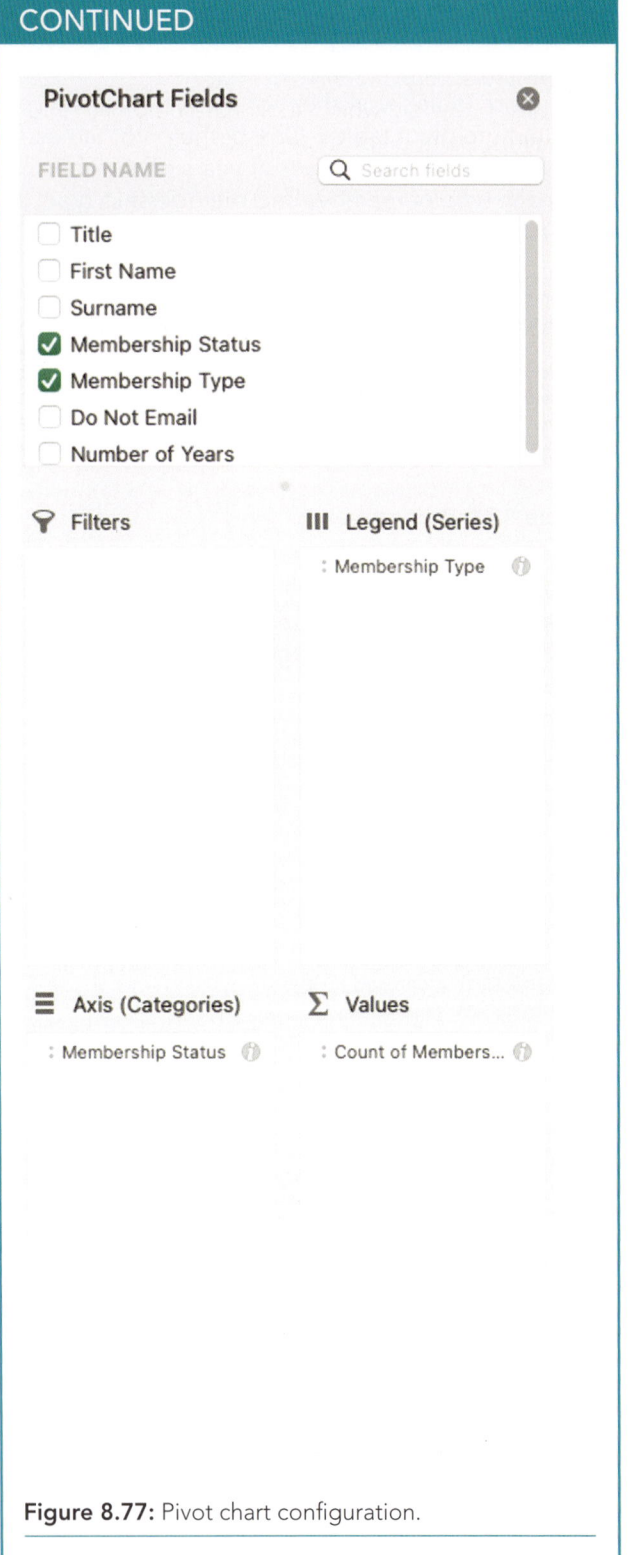

Figure 8.77: Pivot chart configuration.

ACTIVITY 8.32

Open the spreadsheet **8.45_Height in centimetres.xlsx**, which shows the height of 500 people. Create pivot tables to show:

1   The number of people in each state.

2   The number of people in each age group in each state.

3   The number of people in each county of the state of Arizona (AZ). <Hint: use a filter for the state.>

4   The average height for each state.

5   The average height for each age group in each state.

6   The number of people and the average height for each age group in each state.

7   Create pivot charts to show the data in tasks 1, 3, 4 and 5.

8   Create a pivot chart to show the number of people in each age group in the state of New York (NY).

Subtotals

Subtotals are described within the Using functions section previously.

Groups

Worksheets containing a large amount of data can be challenging to view, so data can be organised into groups, with each group shown or hidden as required. For example, if a large amount of data is used to calculate a subtotal, all the data used to calculate the subtotal could be hidden until it needs to be modified, or is required for further analysis.

To create a group in a spreadsheet, highlight the data to group, then select the Data tab at the top of the screen, then click Group. The data can be hidden and shown by clicking the minus and plus symbols next to the row numbers and/or the column letters.

Importing and exporting data

Data can be **imported** into a spreadsheet from other formats, such as a comma separated values (CSV) file, text (TXT) file or from a database.

To import data, go to the File menu and select Open. Select the file type to import, then choose the file to import, followed by OK.

KEY WORD

imported: to bring in data from another application

TIP

If using a Mac, go to the File menu and select Import, rather than Open, to import a CSV or TEXT file.

ACTIVITY 8.33

Within your spreadsheet software, open **8.46_ Instructor.txt** and select options that will cover the following:

1   This is a delimited file that is separated by commas.

2   The file has data headers in the first row.

3   The Date of Birth should be in date format with no time.

4   The charge should be in currency.

5   Use the find and replace option in the Weekends column only to replace 1 with 'Yes' and 0 with 'No'.

Try to open **8.47_Lessons.docx** from your spreadsheet software. It is unlikely that your spreadsheet software will recognise how to import this data. It is essential to ensure that the data being imported is structured in a way in which the spreadsheet software can understand it by using rows of data and separating columns with a special symbol such as a comma.

Data can also be exported so that it can be used in other software. If it is exported in a common format such as CSV or TXT, then other software will be able to recognise the rows and columns. Formats such as portable document format (PDF) will enable the data to be viewed by a wide variety of users but not manipulated, so is a suitable file format showing output data.

Graphs and charts can also be exported as an image file, which can then be used in other applications if required. To export a graph or chart as an image file, right click on the graph or chart and select Save as Picture.

KEY WORD

exported: to prepare data for use another application

ACTIVITY 8.34

Open **8.44_USA Addresses.xlsx** and export it to the following formats:

- csv
- txt
- pdf
- Open Document Spreadsheet (ODS) – works with Open Office
- Web page (HTML).

View the files that you have exported the data to and note how the data has been stored.

8.4 Graphs and charts

You can use your spreadsheet to present data visually through graphs and charts.

Creating a graph or chart appropriate to a specific purpose

A range of different graphs are available within spreadsheets.

To create a graph or chart, highlight the required data to include, which will be used to represent the various data points on a graph, known as a **data series**. For example, all data in the spreadsheet could be selected, or data from a specific range(s). Select the Insert tab from the top of the screen, then choose the required graph or chart from the toolbar. Formatting options for graphs and charts, including details of those show in the worked examples, can be found in the Apply chart formatting section below.

Graphs and charts can be created from **contiguous data**, where a range of cells are next to each other, or **non-contiguous data**, where the cells are located in separate columns within the spreadsheet. To select contiguous data, click and drag to highlight the cells. To select non-contiguous data, hold Ctrl (Windows) or Cmd (Mac) while selecting the required cells.

KEY WORDS

data series: data used to represent data points on a graph

contiguous data: a range of cells that are next to each other, without any rows or columns between them

non-contiguous data: a range of cells that are not directly next to each other

Bar charts, including comparative bar charts

A bar chart is a diagram in which numerical values are represented by rectangles of equal width. Bar charts can be used to show one set of data. In addition, bar charts can show more than one set of data, which are known as comparative charts, as one set of data can be compared against another set of data.

WORKED EXAMPLE 8.41

In this spreadsheet, the worksheet **Monthly Sales** contains a bar chart showing the monthly sales over a period of 12 months. Notice how a chart title and x-axis title have been included (see Figure 8.78).

The comparative bar chart on the worksheet **Monthly Worldwide Sales** compares the sales of different continents for each of the months in 2015, as shown in Figure 8.79. Notice how a legend is used to show which continent is represented by which colour.

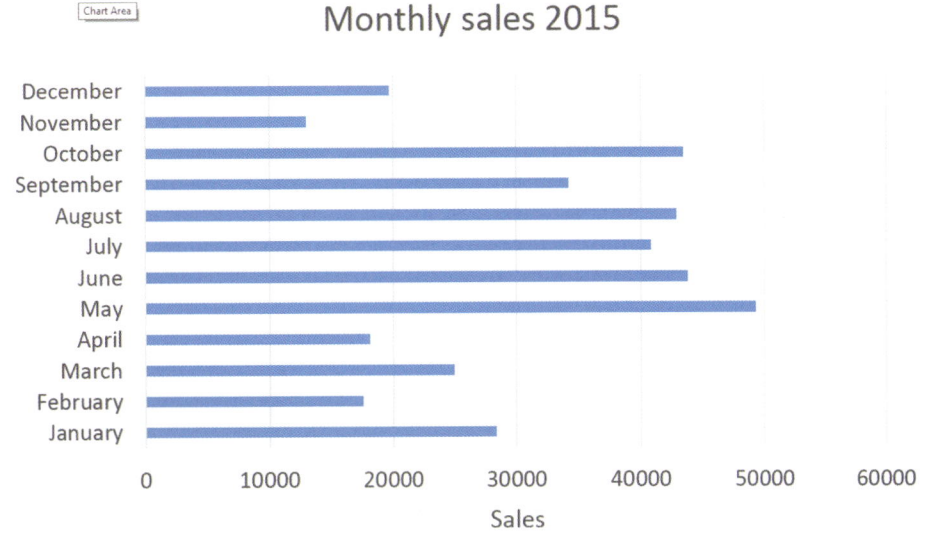

Figure 8.78: Monthly sales bar chart.

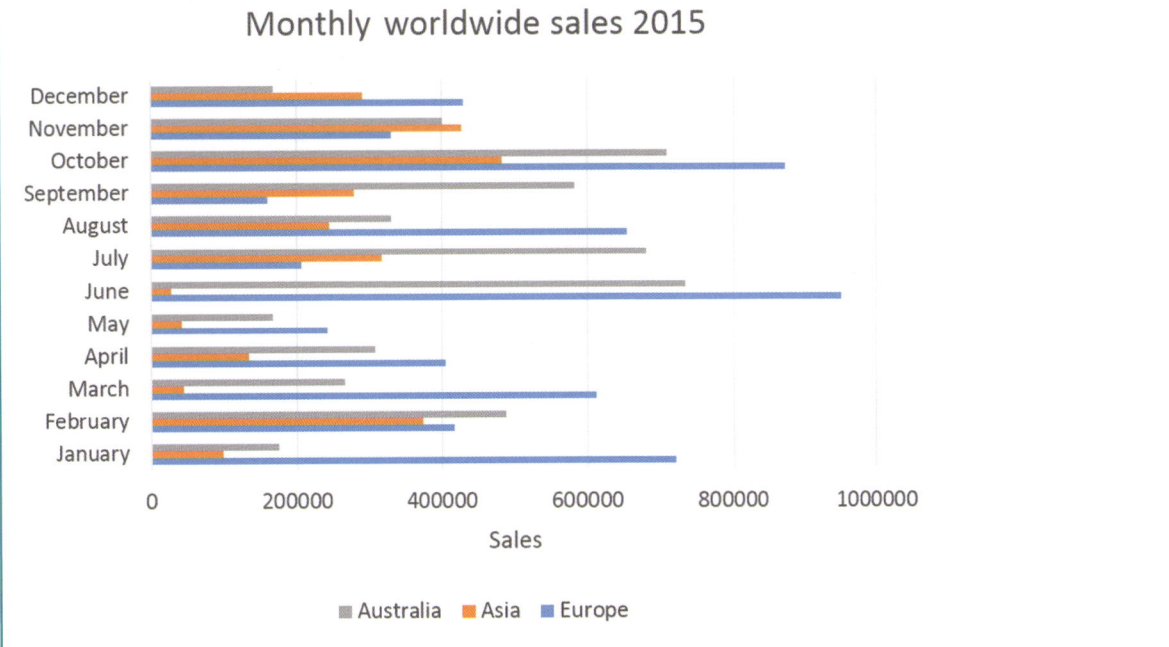

Figure 8.79: Worldwide sales comparative bar chart.

CONTINUED

	A	B	C	D
1	Monthly Sales	Europe	Asia	Australia
2	January	767784	153710	444583
3	February	845619	483590	495572
4	March	547861	10578	537289
5	April	487561	122980	513220
6	May	876780	470416	454170
7	June	719862	46656	534387
8	July	258994	156400	648415
9	August	527236	340102	542103
10	September	790027	175028	782983
11	October	683973	370258	244798
12	November	843379	438223	656699
13	December	395084	288689	667735

Figure 8.80: Selecting non-contiguous columns.

The chart currently shows sales for Australia, Asia and Europe, but it may be that only the sales for Europe and Australia need to be shown. Australia and Europe are in non-contiguous (non-adjacent) columns. One way of creating the graph would be to select only the columns that are required (see Figure 8.80).

Note that this method can be used to select any specified range of data. Alternatively, the Asia data series could be removed from the chart (see Figure 8.81).

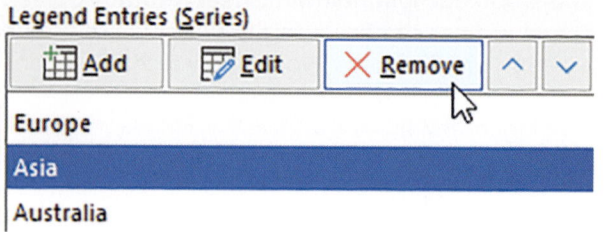

Figure 8.81: Removing Asia data series.

The chart is also only showing the sales values at intervals of 200 000. This can be changed to a different data interval by setting the major units. In Figure 8.82, the data intervals (major units) have been set to 100 000 and, to enable more space on the graph, the display units have been set to Thousands.

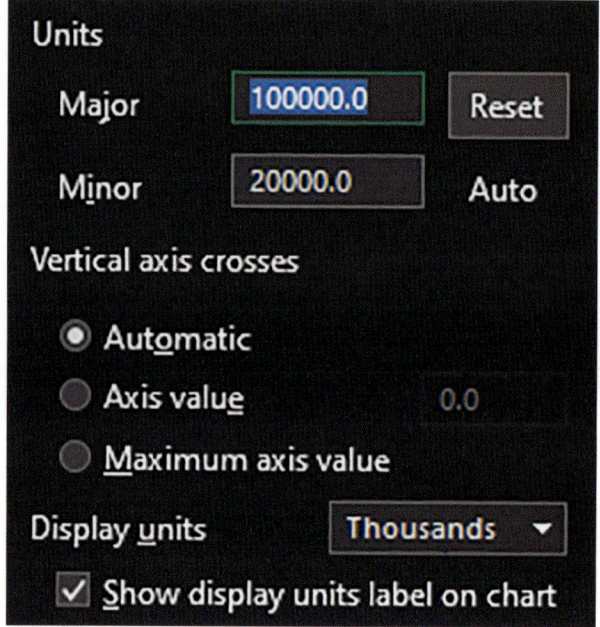

Figure 8.82: Changing data interval.

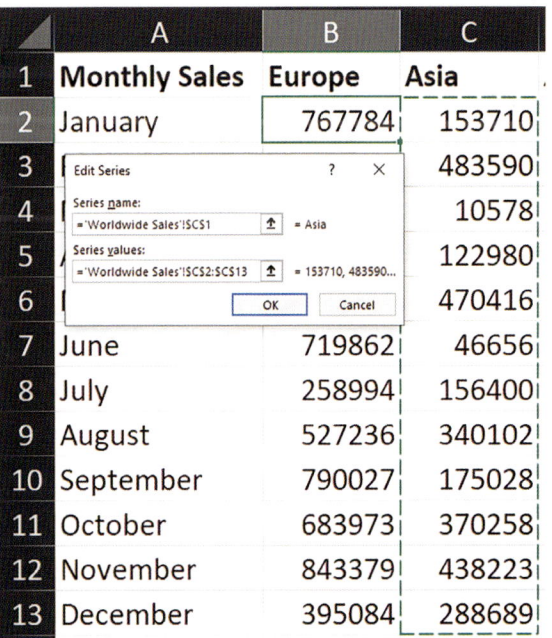

Figure 8.83: Monthly worldwide sales bar chart.

The graph now looks like the one in Figure 8.83.

If we wanted to add the Asia series of data back again, then we could add a new series and specify the range of data to use (C2:C13) and the name of the series (C1 = 'Asia') (see Figure 8.84).

	A	B	C
1	**Monthly Sales**	**Europe**	**Asia**
2	January	767784	153710
3			483590
4			10578
5			122980
6			470416
7	June	719862	46656
8	July	258994	156400
9	August	527236	340102
10	September	790027	175028
11	October	683973	370258
12	November	843379	438223
13	December	395084	288689

Edit Series
Series name:
='Worldwide Sales'!$C$1 = Asia
Series values:
='Worldwide Sales'!$C$2:$C$13 = 153710, 483590...
OK   Cancel

Figure 8.84: Adding Asia data series.

CONTINUED

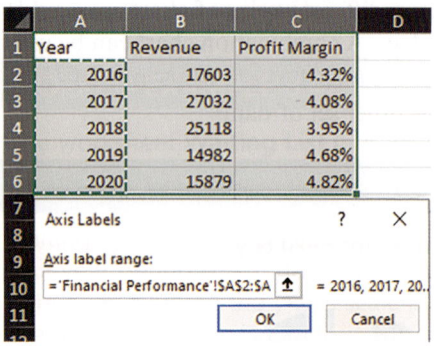

Figure 8.90: Editing horizontal axis labels.

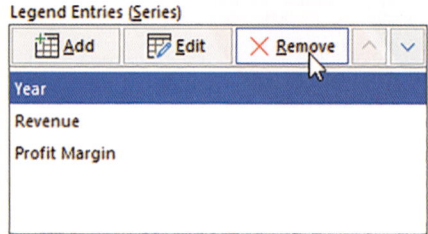

Figure 8.91: Removing the Year.

The Year can also be removed from the legend and series data (see Figure 8.91).

In Figure 8.92, the graph now includes the revenue and profit margin, but the profit margin is so small compared with the revenue that it is not visible.

Figure 8.92: Chart with revenue and profit margin.

A secondary axis is required for the profit margin data series. The chart type can be changed to a combination (combo) chart with the Profit Margin as a Line Chart and having its own secondary axis, as shown in Figure 8.93.

Finally, the chart title, axis labels and units can be added (see Figure 8.94).

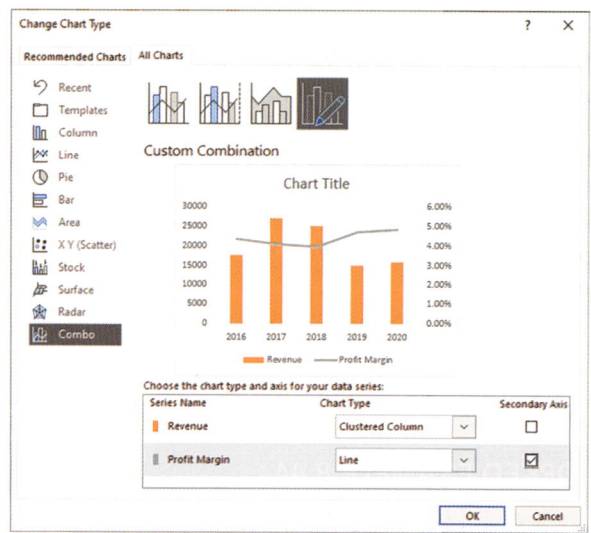

Figure 8.93: Combination chart.

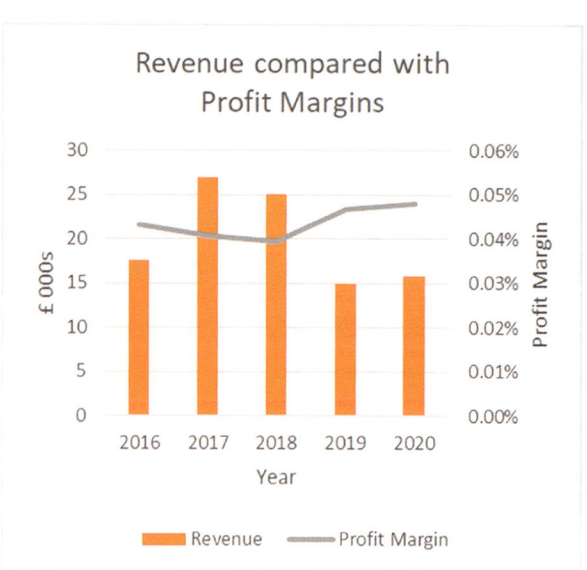

Figure 8.94: Final chart.

When selecting which type of graph or chart to produce, an appropriate type should be selected, as outlined in Table 8.15.

Type of graph/ chart	Purpose
Bar/column chart	Used to show a single series of data in columns or rows.
Comparative bar/column chart	Used to compare more than one series of data in columns or rows.
Line graph	Used to show how a single series of data changes over a period of time.
Comparative line graph	Used to compare how more than one series of data changes over a period of time.
Pie chart	Used to show the proportion that is used by each item of data.
Combination (combo) chart	Used to show more than one series of data using a combination of a column and line chart where there is a secondary axis.

Table 8.15: Rules for selecting type of graph or chart.

Questions

16 When would a bar chart be used to display data?

17 When would a pie chart be used to display data?

Apply chart formatting

When creating a graph or chart, different formatting options are available to alter the appearance of each part, as shown in Table 8.16.

To format each part of the graph or chart, click with the right mouse button on the relevant part and select the related menu item. For example, to change the title, select Format Chart Title from the menu.

formatting	Purpose
Title	A brief description of what the graph or chart shows.
Legend	A key to show what the colours used represent.
Series label	The name given to a series, which can be used on a legend.
Value axis label	Each of the axes (usually x and y) should include the values, including any units.
Category axis label	Each of the axes should include a title to state what the data represents.
Add secondary axis	A second axis used to show data for a different set of values to the primary axis, such as when creating a combination chart.
Percentages	When using a pie chart, the percentages can be displayed for each segment.
Segment label	Instead of a legend, each segment in a pie chart could be labelled with its description.
Segment value	As well as, or instead of, the percentage, each segment in a pie chart could be labelled with its quantity.
Extract pie chart sector	Extract one sector of a pie chart from the rest of the pie chart by moving its position.
Scale	The scale of the y-axis can be set to a normal or logarithmic scale.
Data interval/ major units	The interval between values on an axis.
Axis scale maximum	The maximum value to be used on an axis.
Axis scale minimum	The minimum value to be used on an axis.

Table 8.16: Labelling graphs and charts.

ACTIVITY 8.35

Open **8.30_Maths results.xlsx**.

1 Create a bar chart to show the marks for each student.

2 Include a title and axis titles.

Open **8.04_Physics results.xlsx**.

1 Enter some marks for each student for each test.

2 Create a comparative bar chart to show the marks for each student in each of the tests 1, 2 and 3.

3 Include a title and axis titles.

4 Include a legend for the tests.

5 Change the y-axis maximum scale value to be 50.

6 Change the y-axis scale to have intervals of 5.

Open **8.49_School attendance.xlsx**.

1 Create a comparative line graph to show the attendance of each of year 1 and year 2 over the period of the year compared with the target.

2 Label the chart appropriately.

3 Adjust the y-axis scale and maximum scale values appropriately.

4 Include a legend.

5 Change the line type of the target series to be dashed.

Open **8.39_Member List.xlsx**.

1 Open the worksheet **Pie Chart**.

2 Create a pie chart to show the proportion of members for each status.

3 Give the chart a sensible title.

4 Add the percentages and membership statuses to the pie chart segments.

Open **8.16_HLookup.xlsx**.

1 Create an appropriate chart to show the products, original price and discounted price.

2 Label the chart appropriately.

Open **8.48_Graphs and charts.xlsx**.

1 Copy the graph Monthly sales 2015.

2 Open a word processor or presentation software.

3 Select the option to paste as a link (you may find this under paste special).

4 Ensure that the link option is selected and the object type (graph) is identified.

5 Save this new document and close it.

6 Change some of the data in the Monthly sales worksheet.

7 Save the spreadsheet.

8 Reopen the new document you created and check that the graph has changed to reflect the updated data in the spreadsheet.

Questions

18 Identify and give reasons for the most appropriate type of chart or graph to show the number of missed refuse collections shown in Table 8.17.

Year	Vesey	New Hall	Trinity
2010	2502	4571	3271
2011	2786	5728	3102
2012	1987	5645	2905
2013	2057	4972	2647

Table 8.17: Missed refuse collections.

19 Identify and give reasons for the most appropriate type of chart or graph to show the data shown in Table 8.18.

Student	Mark 1	Mark 2	Mark 3	Mark 4	Average
Name 1	98	40	36	84	65
Name 2	31	67	61	77	59
Name 3	62	58	29	38	47
Name 4	64	83	85	27	65
Name 5	87	45	64	42	60
Name 6	93	58	43	73	67
Name 7	99	29	55	92	69
Name 8	57	58	44	93	63
Name 9	45	43	98	55	60

Table 8.18: Student marks.

When producing graphs, it can often be useful to make the graph interactive by having buttons to select the required fields that are displayed.

To enable field selection buttons to be included within a graph, Developer Tools need to be enabled within Excel. If not already enabled, select the File tab from the toolbar at the top of the screen, then go to Options, then Customize Ribbon. Select the Developer check box in the Main Tabs section.

> **TIP**
>
> If using a Mac, go to the Excel menu, then select Preferences. Within Ribbon and Toolbar, click the Developer check box in the Main Tabs section.

PRACTICAL ACTIVITY 8.36

	A	B	C	D
1	**Names**	Test 1	Test 2	
2	David	48	56	
3	Amit	72	73	
4	Priya	73	70	
5	Jamal	61	66	
6	Louise	72	55	
7				

Figure 8.95: Test scores stored in a spreadsheet.

Open the spreadsheet **8.50_Chart-option-buttons. xlsx**, which contains the test scores for five students. The data is held in cells A1:C6 (see Figure 95).

The spreadsheet needs to include a graph, which can display the data selected using a button, rather than making two separate graphs.

To create two buttons, select the Option button from the Developer toolbar at the top of the screen and rename the buttons to 'Test 1' and 'Test 2' by highlighting the existing name, as shown in Figure 8.96.

Figure 8.96: Option buttons.

Right click the Option button, select the Control tab and then click in the Cell link box. Select an empty cell, such as F1 and press ok (see Figure 8.97). The contents of cell F1 will now show 1 if the first option button is pressed, or 2 if the second option button is pressed.

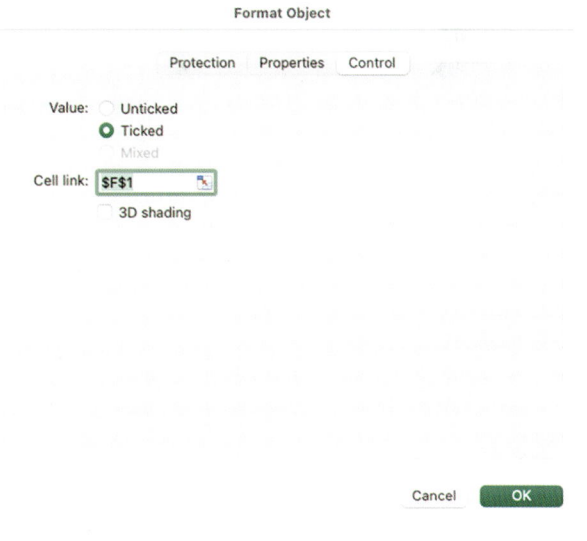

Figure 8.97: Linking a cell to the option buttons.

CONTINUED

Finally, the cells containing the data for the graph (G2:H6), which includes the data changed using the option buttons (H2:H6), can be selected and a chart inserted, such as a bar graph. If required the graph title can be changed and the option buttons included within the chart area (see Figures 8.98 and 8.99).

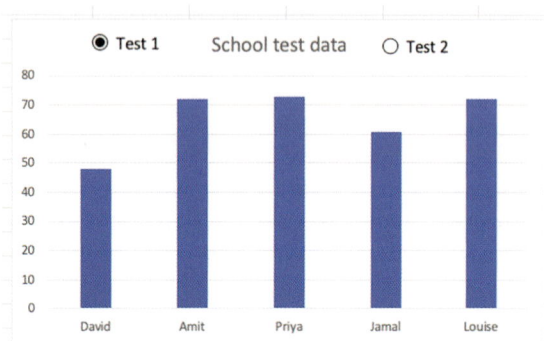

Figure 8.98: Chart showing Test 1 results.

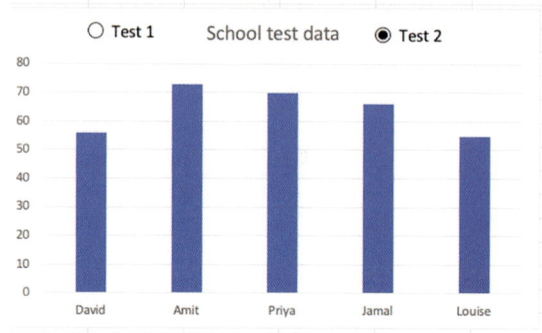

Figure 8.99: Chart showing Test 2 results.

REFLECTION

How might spreadsheets be used in other subjects you study at school? For example, are there projects you have completed where it would be useful to store data or use formulas to manipulate?

What features of a spreadsheet would have been useful for this project and how would you have used them?

PRACTICE QUESTIONS

The spreadsheet below shows cars that are owned by a driving school. It calculates the fuel type of each car, the cost per litre of each fuel type and the cost per gallon.

	A	B	C	D	E	F
1	**Registration**	**Make**	**Model**	**Fuel type**	**Cost per litre**	**Cost per gallon**
2	BX56JWL	Ford	Mondeo	Diesel	$ 1.25	$ 5.69
3	BX56JWM	Saab	Saab 9-3	Petrol	$ 1.17	$ 5.32
4	BX56JWN	Land Rover	Discovery	Diesel	$ 1.25	$ 5.69
5	BX56JWP	Smart	Smart Car	LPG	$ 0.85	$ 3.87
6	BX56JWR	Ford	Mondeo	Petrol	$ 1.17	$ 5.32
7	BX56JWS	Saab	Saab 9-3	Diesel	$ 1.25	$ 5.69
8						
9					**Fuel type**	**Cost per gallon**
10					Diesel	$ 5.69
11					Petrol	$ 5.32
12					LPG	$ 3.87

CONTINUED

Rows and columns are used in the spreadsheet.

1 a   Use an example from this spreadsheet to describe a row.   [2]

   b   Formulas and functions have been used in the spreadsheet. There are 4.55 litres in a gallon.

       i   Using an example, describe a formula.   [2]

       ii   Write the formula used in F2.   [1]

       iii Describe a function.   [2]

       iv   Identify the type of formula used in E2.   [1]

                                                                                          [Total 8]

2   The driving school would like to see all their petrol cars but not the other cars.

    a   Explain how the driving school could see all their petrol cars but not the other cars without
        losing any data.   [2]

    b   Explain how the fuel types could be identified quickly using a different colour for each
        without changing them all one by one.   [2]

                                                                                          [Total 4]

3   Absolute and relative cell referencing have been used within the spreadsheet.

    Using examples, explain how absolute and relative cell referencing have been used.   [4]

4   The spreadsheet model is going to be used to calculate the costs of using each car.

    a   Explain three advantages of using a spreadsheet to model the costs of using each car.   [3]

    b   Explain one disadvantage of using a spreadsheet to model the costs of using each car.   [1]

                                                                                          [Total 4]

SUMMARY CHECKLIST

☐   I can create and edit a spreadsheet structure to meet the requirements of an audience.

☐   I can create/edit spreadsheet structures.

☐   I can control data input using validation techniques.

☐   I can protect cells and their content.

☐   I can freeze panes and windows.

☐   I can create and use formulas within a spreadsheet.

☐   I can use absolute reference, relative reference, named cells and named ranges.

☐   I know and can understand why absolute and relative referencing are used.

☐   I can use functions within a spreadsheet.

☐   I can use appropriate input and error messages.

☐   I can format the content of cells and the emphasis of cells.

☐   I can appreciate the requirements, purpose and use of a spreadsheet.

☐   I can test a spreadsheet structure including formulas, functions and validation rules.

CONTINUED

- ☐ I can extract data from a spreadsheet using search facilities.
- ☐ I can sort data in a spreadsheet.
- ☐ I can summarise and display data using pivot tables and pivot charts.
- ☐ I can import and export data to and from a spreadsheet.
- ☐ I can create a graph or chart in a spreadsheet for a specific purpose.
- ☐ I can apply formatting to a graph or chart.

PROJECT

Figure 8.100: Rental car offices are often sited at transport hubs such as airports.

A vehicle rental business has recently invested in a new computer system. The business is in the process of setting up a spreadsheet to help them rent out their cars by calculating the correct rental price. The rental price is calculated based on a number of factors, such as the type of vehicle rented, how long the vehicle is rented for and the customer's previous driving convictions.

Open **8.51 Project.xlsx** and look at the **VehicleRates** worksheet.

The types of vehicle available are shown in A4:A11, which has a named range of 'VehicleTypes'.

The table in columns A to F shows the types of vehicles available, the minimum age of drivers for each vehicle, and the charge rates for each vehicle.

The table of points in cells G7:G9 refers to a set of ranges for the number of penalty points a driver may have on their driving licence. Penalty points are given to drivers when they have a driving conviction, such as if they are recorded driving too fast. Cells G6:G9 have been named Points.

Cell B13 refers to the number of drivers that will be hiring a vehicle. To setup the spreadsheet, complete the following tasks:

1   Merge cells C2:F2, give the merged cell a yellow shading and align the text centrally in the cell.

2   Resize columns A to F so that all the data is visible.

3   Name the range A4:E12 as **VehicleRates**.

4   Insert a new row between rows 5 and 6 for an 'Estate' vehicle that has a minimum age of 21 and charging rates of £34, £38 and £42.

The charge rate is determined by the number of driving conviction points that a driver has had in the last five years.

- 0 conviction points = Rate 1

- 1–3 conviction points = Rate 2

- 4–6 conviction points = Rate 3

For example, if a driver has three penalty points, they would be charged Rate 2. If there are any additional drivers, then whoever has the highest number of conviction points is used to determine the charge rate.

CONTINUED

Switch to the Quote worksheet.

The Quote worksheet is an input form used to calculate the cost of hiring a vehicle.

5   Create a validation rule in C16 that will only accept vehicles that exist in the named range VehicleRates. Use an appropriate error message if invalid data is input.

6   Create a drop-down box for the number of Conviction Points. The input range of the drop-down box should only contain the values from the named range Points and must be a form control, not a validation rule. The charge rate should be stored in F12.

7   Create option buttons for the number of additional drivers which can be 0, 1 or 2. The option buttons should be linked to cell B2 on the VehicleRates worksheet.

The quote reference is calculated by taking the initials of the driver and adding the year of the current date, followed by a hyphen, followed by the month of the current date, followed by another hyphen, followed by the day of the current date. For example, the reference for Caleb Andrews on 20 May 2022 would be CA2019-5-22.

8   Create a formula in F6 to calculate the quote reference.

The expiry date is calculated as seven days after the date of the quote. Assume the date of the quote is the current date.

9   Create a formula in F8 that calculates the expiry date of the quote.

The minimum driver age is calculated by looking up the type of vehicle in the VehicleRates table.

10   Create a function in F10 to find the minimum driver age.

11   Create a validation rule in C18 for the youngest driver age to be 18 years old. Use an appropriate error message if invalid data is input.

12   The hire rate per day is calculated by looking up the type of vehicle in the VehicleRates table and finding the correct column for the charge rate. Create a function in F14 to find the hire rate per day.

13   The number of days is calculated to be inclusive of both the date of hire and the date of return. Create a formula in F16 to show the number of days the vehicle will be hired for.

14   The hire rate is calculated by multiplying the number of days by the hire rate per day. Create a formula in F18 to calculate the hire rate. You should only use named cells within your formula.

If there is one additional driver, then there is a 15% additional cost. If there are two additional drivers, then there is a 22% additional cost.

15   Create a function in F20 to calculate the additional percentage based on the number of additional drivers selected. Format the cell to display this value as a percentage.

16   Create a formula in F22 to calculate the additional charge for additional drivers.

17   Create a formula in F24 to calculate the total cost of the quote including additional drivers.

18   Format any cells that contain currency to include a currency symbol and two decimal places.

CONTINUED

19 Test your spreadsheet works using the following test plan:

Test data input value	Type of test data	Expected result
Firstname: Merrick Surname: Woodward Date of Rental: 21/12/2023 Date of Return: 28/12/2023 Vehicle: Hatchback Youngest driver age: 22 Conviction Points: 5 Additional drivers: 1	Normal	Quote reference: MWyyyy-mm-dd (where yyyy is current year, mm is current month and dd is current year) Expiry date: (one week after current date) Minimum driver age: 18 Charge rate: 3 Rental rate per day: £38.00 Number of days: 8 Rental rate: £304.00 Additional drivers %: 15% Additional drivers amount: £45.60 Total quote: £349.60

20 Print a copy of the Quote worksheet in both normal view and showing formulas ensuring that no formulas or functions are truncated.

21 Protect the worksheet so that only input cells can be edited with all other cells being read-only.

22 Complete the test plan below for the input of Vehicle.

Test Number	Description	Type of Test	Input data value(s)	Expected output value(s)
1	Vehicle validation		Transit	
2	Vehicle		Sedan	'You must select a vehicle from the list'

23 Complete the test plan below for the input of Youngest driver age when booking a 9-seater vehicle.

Test number	Description	Type of test	Input data value(s)	Expected Output Value(s)
3	Youngest driver age validation	Normal		
4	Youngest driver age validation	Extreme		
5	Youngest driver age validation	Abnormal		

› Chapter 9

Chapter 9
Modelling

LEARNING INTENTIONS

By the end of this chapter, you will be able to:

- use what-if analysis
- describe the characteristics of modelling software
- explain the need for computer models
- evaluate the effectiveness of spreadsheet models
- explain how a model can be used to create and run simulations.

Introduction

A computer **model** is a representation of a real-world system or process. Computerised models are used to predict how a real-life system might behave. For example, a computer model can be used to show how traffic moves through a city or the effects of climate change on regions at sea level. A model is created through mathematical analysis of the real-world process. Details in a computer model can be changed to see what effects they have.

We use models because it is often cheaper and safer than experimenting on real-world processes. A **simulation** can be used to run the model. For example, testing the maximum speed of a new jet engine is cheaper in a simulation than building it and attaching it to an aeroplane.

KEY WORDS

model: a representation of a process

simulation: uses a computer model to predict real-life behaviour

9.1 What-if analysis

What-if analysis is the process of asking the question 'what would happen if…?'. The what-if analysis is used to work out answers to questions we may have about our model. For example, we may want to know what would happen if the temperature in the Arctic increases by $0.5\,°C$ (see Figure 9.1). Scientists can change the data in the computer model to give the answers. Scientists can then use the answers to predict what may happen.

KEY WORD

what-if analysis: experimenting with changing variables to see what would happen to the output if those variables changed

Figure 9.1: Scientists use what-if analysis to predict what may happen to the Arctic, its inhabitants and wildlife in the event of a rise in global temperatures.

Some examples of what-if questions for traffic modelling may be:

- What happens to traffic queues *if* we increase the number of lorries on the road by 20%?

- What happens to the air pollution level *if* we reduce the number of cars on the road by 15%?

- What happens to passenger journey times *if* we increase the number of buses on the road?

Part of what-if analysis includes the use of **goal seek**. This means setting a goal (what you want to find out) and then finding out what needs to be done to achieve that goal. Some examples of goal-seek questions might include:

- What price do we need to sell product X at in order to sell 5000 items per month?

- How many items do we need to sell to break even (zero profit and zero loss)?

ACTIVITY 9.01

Open the spreadsheet **9.01_bike hire.xlsx**, which is a model to calculate the profit that would be made for different numbers of bikes being hired.

1   a   What would happen to the profit if the number of short male mountain bikes booked was changed to 70 (see Figure 9.2)?

    b   What if there were no short male mountain bikes booked? Did any other data change when you changed the quantity booked?

2   What would happen to the profit if the junior hourly rate was increased to £12.50?

3   Experiment with changing other variables within the spreadsheet model. For each one, what happens to the outputs?

Figure 9.2: Mountain bikers.

WORKED EXAMPLE 9.01

9.01_bike hire.xlsx calculates the profits for a bike hire company. In Figure 9.3, the company wants to see how many bikes of a particular type they need to hire out to increase their profit to £2500.

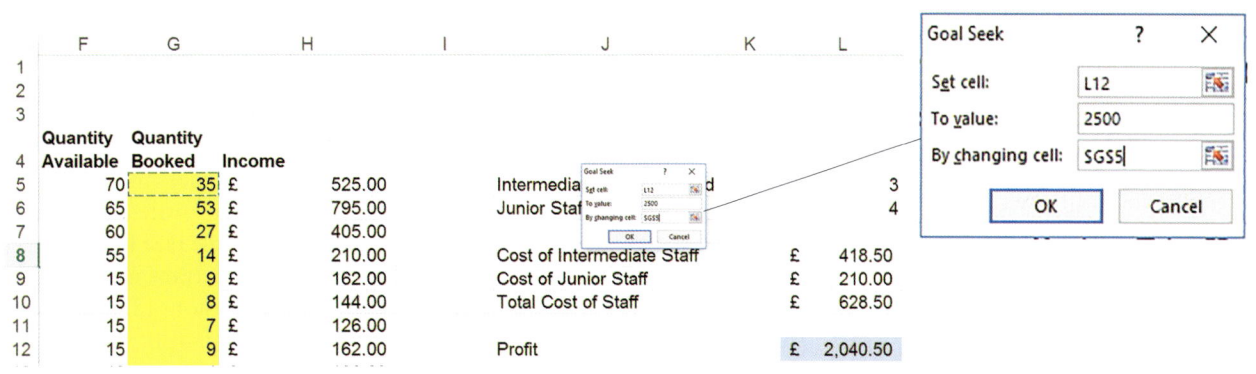

Figure 9.3: Goal-seek configuration.

CONTINUED

Figure 9.4 shows the result of the goal seek being 65.63333 bikes, which would of course need to be rounded up to 66 bikes.

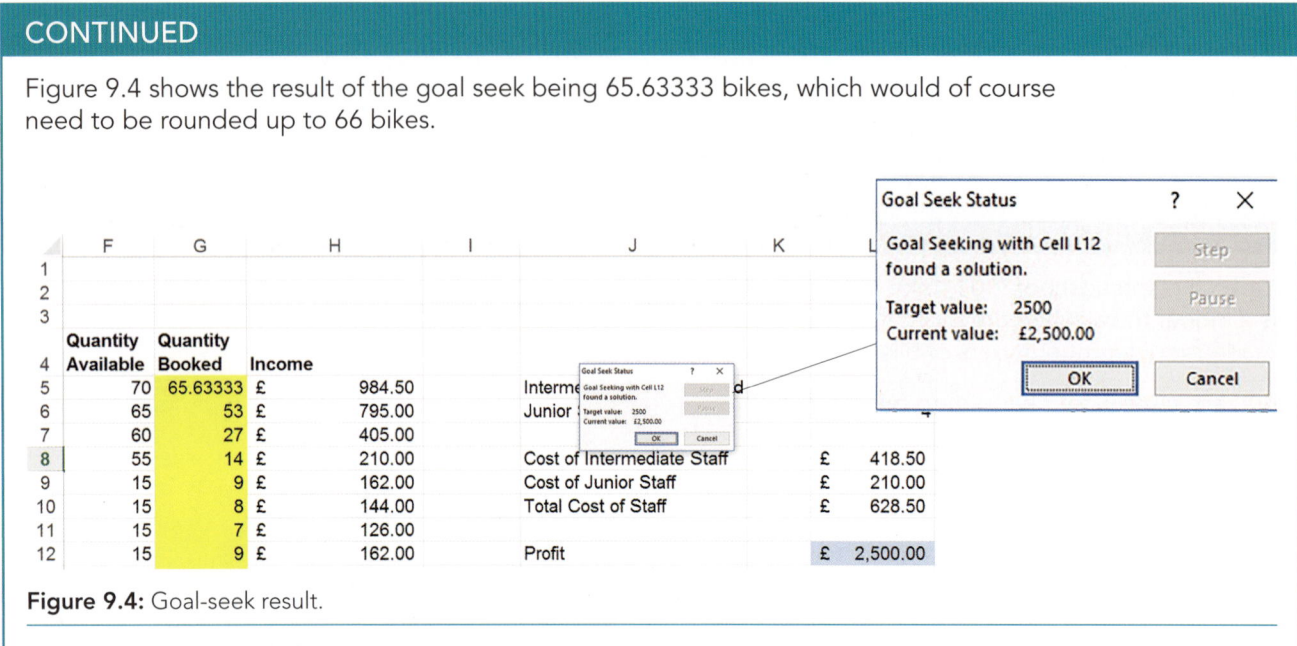

Figure 9.4: Goal-seek result.

ACTIVITY 9.02

Open spreadsheet **9.02_student marks.xlsx**, which shows exam and coursework marks for students in a class.

Use goal seek to answer these questions.

1 What coursework mark would John need to increase his total mark to 390?

2 John resits exam 3. What mark does he need to increase his total to 425?

3 Sameena resits her coursework. What mark does she need to get a total of 380?

4 Fathima hasn't taken exam 3 yet. What mark does she need to get a total of 250?

5 Experiment with setting your own goals.

9.2 Characteristics of modelling software

We can use specialist software to create models. We can also use simpler software like spreadsheets. Spreadsheets are often used to create simple models in finance or stock control.

More sophisticated software such as Cloonix can simulate a computer network. A computer network simulation produces a diagram of the devices connected to the computer network. It can identify the **Internet Protocol (IP) addresses** used on the network. The simulation allows wireless networks to be added and configured to see what the effects will be. You can simulate connecting devices to switches and data traffic can be analysed.

KEY WORD

Internet Protocol (IP) address: a unique address given to a device, normally by a router

Computer Aided Design (CAD) software is a type of simulation software. It enables designers to produce a model of a physical object. CAD software can simulate a kitchen, a building, a motor vehicle (see Figure 9.5) or an aeroplane. CAD software has features which allow you to view an object in two dimensions (2D) or three dimensions (3D). CAD software can also:

- change or adjust objects in the model
- add or remove objects
- view the model from different angles
- apply different effects such as colour and lighting
- focus on specific features such as the electrical wiring.

Figure 9.5: Engineers design car components using CAD software.

Figure 9.6: A rollercoaster will be modelled before it is erected to make sure it will be safe in operation.

Modelling software often includes the following features:

- the ability to change variables and data within the software to model different scenarios
- asking what-if questions or 'goal seek' to see what the result of changing variables might be
- formulas and functions to carry out calculations in the model
- automatic recalculation of formulas and functions
- rules that define how the model behaves
- the ability to view and analyse different parts of the model separately.

Modelling software can simulate a roller coaster to make sure it will be safe in operation.

- Variables: the height of each drop, the radius of loops, the starting speed of the carriage, length of each section and the weight of each carriage.
- Calculations: the amount of friction, how frictions slow the rollercoaster down, the effect of gravity on carriages, the g-force that will be experienced by passengers (see Figure 9.6).

What-if or goal-seek questions could be asked such as 'What would happen if we increased the starting speed by 2 km/h?' or 'What would happen if we increased the initial drop by 5 m?' Or for a goal seek, 'What is the minimum launch speed for the rollercoaster?'.

The effect of these changes in variables can then be modelled.

ACTIVITY 9.03

Experiment with a digital single-lens reflex (DSLR) camera simulator by changing the variables and seeing how this affects the end results (see Figure 9.7). You can find an example simulator on the CameraSim website.

1   What happens to the photo if you change the ISO from 200 to 800?

2   What happens to the photo if you slow the shutter speed?

3   What happens if you add flash to the photo?

Figure 9.7: You can change a range of variables such as shutter speed and aperture when using a digital single-lens reflex camera.

9.3 The need for computer models

Computer models allow us to run large and complex simulations. This makes it possible to test things in real life without individuals taking dangerous risks. Using a computer model also keeps costs down.

Training

Computer models can be used to train people to use equipment, for example airline pilots (see Figure 9.8) and nuclear power plant operators.

DID YOU KNOW?

Nearly 100 000 pilots a year were trained in 2020. Many pilots use simulators as part of their training.

Figure 9.8: Training on a flight simulator.

Models are used for training because there is less risk of injury to the trainees and instructors than learning in a real environment. Imagine if we train people to operate a nuclear power plant by using a real nuclear power plant. If the trainee makes a mistake, it could damage and injure. In the worst case, there could be an accident or explosion. This would have significant effects on the population and environment of a wide area. Models save cost because real equipment does not suffer wear and tear. Fuel or electricity is not required to operate machinery. The simulation can also work without the need for instructors. Once programmed, the simulation can be run again and again.

Computer models allow us to test unpredictable situations. For example, they can simulate turbulence for an aeroplane or failure in a nuclear reactor. This allows training on simple simulations first with more difficult scenarios added later.

Financial forecasting

Businesses and governments use financial modelling to predict what might happen to profits or the economy. It is too risky for a business to make sudden changes in the market place without testing them out with a model first. A variety of what-if questions can be asked using a model to determine how to make the most profit. A model can change the selling prices, adjust the quantity of products to supply, the times of year to sell and the effect of seasonal sales.

Buildings, kitchens, gardens and motor vehicles cost a lot of money to make. It is important to make sure that the measurements and designs are correct. Adjustments made later in the real world will cost a lot of money. Using a model allows a business to select the best and most cost-effective designs (see Figure 9.9).

Figure 9.9: Designing solar panels using CAD software.

Population growth

Models can be used to predict population growth. Governments want to know how a population may change so that they can plan for housing, transport and services. Scientists also model population growth in natural habitats for animals. They identify existing animal numbers and birth rates. They can then predict what future populations will be.

Experiment with the Wolfram population growth model. You can find the Wolfram model on the Wolfram Demonstrations Project website. Experiment with the model by changing the initial population, growth rate and carrying capacity (number of inhabitants that can survive on limited resources) variables.

What happens if:

1 you start with a low initial population and low growth rate, but inhabitants have a high carrying capacity?

2 you start with a high initial population and high growth rate, but inhabitants have low carrying capacity?

Design **two** what-if questions and ask a classmate to give you the answers to these questions using the simulation. Check whether their answers are correct.

Weather systems

Models can be used to forecast weather. A weather model uses patterns from the past and live data to predict the weather. Weather forecasts allow people to take precautions in bad weather, for example to protect homes and businesses from flooding during heavy rains or evacuate to a safe area in the event of a hurricane or cyclone. Farmers use weather forecasts to plan when to harvest crops, or when they need to be watered (see Figure 9.10).

Figure 9.10: Farmers can decide when to use mobile watering systems if dry weather is predicted by the weather model.

Weather system modelling can also compare historical data with current data. This can be useful to help understand how weather is changing over time.

Weather system modelling uses huge amounts of computer processing power. The models are very complex and make millions of calculations every second. They need to analyse and predict the impact of wind speed, temperature, moisture in the air, how air particles will react and many more variables. Weather forecasting now requires supercomputers.

The modelling system for weather in the United Kingdom was introduced in 1952. Since then, it has been developed and refined. This means that the weather model is now more than 70 years old!

Climate change

Climate change models consider the interactions between the atmosphere, oceans, land, ice and the sun. Climate change models are used for long-term predictions. It can be decades before we know if the model is accurate. Climate models include many rules such as the first law of thermodynamics, the Stefan–Boltzmann Law and the Clausius–Clapeyron equation. They will also include many things that cannot be predicted. This makes the models very complex. We can never know an exact solution to these problems. These complex models require the use of supercomputers. Climate change models are different from weather forecasting. Climate change models predict average weather conditions over a long period of time. Weather models predict over much shorter periods of time.

We can review weather models to see how accurate they were. We can test what was predicted against what really happened. We can use this comparison to see if the model was accurate and how it can be improved for the future.

Using an internet browser, go to the UK Met Office website. Navigate to the 'Learn About…' section.

Create a poster that shows how weather forecasts are made. Add information about your own country's weather forecasting models.

CONTINUED

Show your poster to a classmate and get one piece of feedback on how to improve your poster.

Make that improvement.

Queue management

Computer models can be used to help manage queues. It is useful for a business to predict the number of customers and calculate how long it takes to serve each customer. This helps to determine how many staff are needed to serve the customers. This allows the business to cut costs by not employing staff it may not need or only employing staff at certain times. The customer will also benefit from faster service from the business.

Queues can be simple or they can be complex. A queue in a supermarket is usually simple. However, a queue for a concert may be complex because different tickets may get access to the concert at different times. Some tickets may have priority.

Customer behaviour also forms part of a model. Some customers may choose to avoid a queue if it is too long. Some people may choose to switch between queues if one is getting smaller more quickly. Some customers may just give up and leave the queue. Variables in a queue include number of customers, number of servers, time to serve a customer and expected number of customers at different times of the day.

Traffic flow

Models can predict traffic flow. This helps with planning new roads, improving existing roads or seeing what might happen if a new shopping centre is built close to a residential area. Models will consider existing traffic movement and changes in the number of vehicles expected along a route. The model can be used to experiment with different traffic control measures such as traffic lights, traffic islands or speed limits. Transport planners can then see the effects of changing the roads without having to build the roads first. Variables within the model can include length of vehicles, vehicle speed, average acceleration of vehicles and congestion (see Figure 9.11). Different modelling techniques are used, such as the behaviour of single vehicles and the behaviour of a stream of vehicles. It can also simulate what happens if there is an accident and the road is blocked. Simulating an accident in real life is dangerous. A simulation means that we can predict this safely.

Figure 9.11: Simulating traffic before building roads can help prevent traffic jams at busy times.

ACTIVITY 9.06

Using an internet browser, go to the Onramp traffic simulation website and try out their model of road traffic flow.

Identify the variables that can be changed and what the effects are of changing these.

What questions could you ask of the model?

Construction modelling

Construction modelling can be used to design large buildings such as skyscrapers. The materials used can be modelled to make sure that they will support the weight of the building. Scenarios like earthquakes and strong winds can also be modelled to ensure that the building will not collapse (see Figure 9.12). It can also model the

Figure 9.12: Tall buildings will be modelled to make sure that they can withstand local weather challenges such as wind and storms as well as earthquakes.

number of people and how they may use lifts or walk around the building in order to make the design of each floor as efficient as possible.

A construction model can design something much smaller, like the layout of a new kitchen.

Variables such as lighting, worktops, cupboard doors, position of units, flooring and tiling can be changed to see what looks the best. Cupboards, drawers, dishwashers and cookers can be planned to use space efficiently. The model allows us to change the angle of view. The kitchen can be seen in a 3D environment. This allows us to see what the kitchen might look like from many different angles.

Questions

1 State three different ways in which models can be used.
2 Explain three advantages of modelling.
3 Explain two drawbacks of modelling.
4 Give a description and an example of what is meant by what-if analysis.
5 Describe the difference between a what-if scenario and a goal seek.

9.4 The effectiveness of spreadsheet models

There are a variety of tools within a spreadsheet to help with modelling:

- variables that can be changed to ask what-if questions
- formulas and functions which define the rules of the model
- graphs and charts which can show a graphical representation of the forecast
- instant, automatic recalculation of formulas and functions
- conditional formatting
- goal seek.

Table 9.1 outlines some of the benefits and limitations of spreadsheet models.

Benefits	Limitations
The ability to share the spreadsheet with colleagues easily.	They are only as accurate as the formulas, functions and rules they are programmed with.
Many people can experiment with the model once shared.	They may never simulate the real world precisely.
Many organisations own spreadsheet software.	The most accurate models need extremely complex rules.
	Complex rules require mathematical and computer expertise to create.
	It can take a very long time to create models that are very accurate.
	Spreadsheets can only be used to simulate numbers. They cannot simulate the effect on objects.

Table 9.1: The benefits and limitations of spreadsheet models.

Questions

6 Identify three characteristics of modelling software.
7 Describe, using examples, how a spreadsheet could be used to model the costs or savings to an organisation of moving premises.

9.5 Using models to create and run simulations

Remember that a simulation is the use of a computerised model to predict how a real-life system might behave. As with modelling, simulations can be used for training, forecasting and construction.

Table 9.2 summarises some of the advantages and disadvantages of using simulations and models.

Advantages	Disadvantages
We can experiment with different variations and answer what-if questions without needing to build a real-life example to test.	A simulation is only as accurate as the model it is based on.
Changes to a model can be made very quickly.	Simulation software and equipment can be very expensive to purchase.
The effects of changing variables and data in a model can be seen very quickly.	People need to be trained to use simulation equipment and software.
Alternative models and designs can be easily compared and used to see how they react differently.	Complex models take many years to develop, especially if they are designed to react like the real process.
Unusual, dangerous or frequent events (for example, earthquakes) can be tested without the need to wait for them to happen in real life.	It is impossible for a simulation to be a perfect representation of the real-world process.
There is no need to use actual equipment so equipment will not be damaged.	
Equipment failure can be simulated without putting people in danger.	
Simulations can be run faster than 'real time'. Simulations can predict months or years of data in a few hours.	

Table 9.2: Advantages and disadvantages of using simulations and models.

Natural disaster planning

Simulations can predict and show the effects of natural disasters.

It is impossible to do this in real life without the actual disaster happening. It is impossible to make them to happen or predict precisely when they may happen. If the planners wait for the natural disaster to happen, then it is too late to plan.

Simulations of earthquakes, volcanic eruptions, hurricanes/cyclones, bush fires and tsunamis can be used to see what the effects might be. Planners can experiment with different variables such as wind speed and direction to see how quickly a fire might spread, which will help them to plan evacuations and firefighting.

As with all simulations, these rely on the accuracy of the model. There are always things that a model cannot predict completely. This might include a sudden change in wind direction or wind speed. However, planners can experiment many what-if questions to plan for a large range of circumstances. This means that people can be better prepared when a natural disaster occurs.

Pilot training

It costs a lot of money to take off, fly and land large aircraft. Training pilots is very expensive. Flight simulators remove the fuel costs associated with taking off, flying and landing. They also remove the danger of trainee pilots making a mistake when flying.

Flight simulators use software and specialised equipment to simulate the inside of an aeroplane's cockpit. The equipment reacts in a similar way to a real aircraft. This means that the pilot can feel the physical effects of any movements that they make. This makes the simulation very realistic. The software includes the rules of the model. The rules define how the aircraft reacts in a variety of circumstances. Flight simulators cost hundreds of thousands of pounds because they are so complicated. However, it is still much cheaper than using real aircraft.

Another benefit of flight simulators is that pilots can practise landing and taking off at hundreds of different airports. A pilot would have to fly to each one using a plane in real life (see Figure 9.13). This would take a long time and cost a lot of money! Simulations give pilots

Figure 9.13: Flight simulators allow pilots to practise safely taking off and landing at the world's most technically difficult airports such as Toncontin Airport, Honduras.

Figure 9.14: Racing drivers may use simulators to learn track layouts in sports like Formula One.

the opportunity to respond to malfunctions such as an engine failure, cabin pressure failure or landing gear failure. These would be very dangerous to attempt in real life.

Learning to drive a car

Simulators help people to learn to drive a car. Many learner drivers start driving immediately on the road. They have no experience of a car's controls. Straightaway, they must deal with hazards such as other vehicles, pedestrians, cyclists, holes in the road and dangerous junctions. Learner drivers often drive more slowly. This means that they can cause an obstruction to other traffic. Other drivers may get frustrated if a learner makes a mistake.

Simulations allow a learner driver to become familiar with the controls of a car. They can also practise dealing with hazards before taking a car onto the road for the first time. A simulator is a safe environment to practise many different situations. The simulator can also be used when a learner driver needs to practise turning in the road or reversing around a corner for the first time. Experienced drivers can also use simulators to improve their driving skills such as on a motorway, in icy conditions or how to handle a car if it gets out of control, such as in a skid.

Simulations can be used for racing drivers. They can experiment with different car setups to find the optimum (best outcome) configuration for a racing circuit.

Racing drivers can use a simulator to drive the car to the maximum limits, knowing that crashing in the simulator will not be dangerous (see Figure 9.14). However, a simulation will never be the same as the actual car in a real-life situation. Remember that the rules of the model will never be perfect. Therefore, it is still necessary to practise using a real racing car.

Nuclear science research

Nuclear science can be very dangerous. A small accident could expose people to radiation. Radiation is very dangerous. It is therefore important to simulate new situations with nuclear reactions to try to avoid accidents. Simulations can predict nuclear reactions by adjusting the coolant temperature and changing the rate of reaction. What-if questions can be asked such as 'What happens if we use 30% more fuel in the reaction?'. The simulator will predict the outcome. It's also possible to speed up the simulation so that it is not necessary to wait hours, days or even years to see what the effects might be. The results can be seen very quickly.

It requires a lot of computing power to simulate nuclear reactions. Nuclear reactions involve millions of collisions. Even with supercomputers, nuclear scientists cannot represent all these collisions in a simulation.

UNPLUGGED ACTIVITY 9.07

You will debate whether a nuclear reactor should be built near to where you live. You will debate this with other classmates. Before you start:

1   Write down the advantages of building the nuclear reactor.

2   Write down the disadvantages of building the nuclear reactor.

3   Write down the advantages and disadvantages of simulating the building and running of a new nuclear reactor. Think about ideas such as:

Can the reactor be proven as safe, or not safe?

What things would the owner of the nuclear plant do to convince the local community that the nuclear reactor is safe?

What would the local community say to try to stop the nuclear plant from being built?

Think about whether you want to argue for or against the nuclear reactor. Use these ideas to argue either **for** or **against**.

4   Write down your argument regarding the nuclear reactor.

Debate your argument for or against with your classmates. As a group, decide whether or not you will build the nuclear reactor.

REFLECTION

Did you find the debate in Unplugged activity 9.07 helped you to consider the arguments on both sides, for and against? Were you in favour or against the building of the reactor? Would you be able to argue in opposition to your own viewpoint? What will you do to always make sure you consider a range of viewpoints, even if they are not your own?

Questions

8   Describe two advantages of using a simulator for pilot training.

9   Describe one disadvantage of using a simulator for learning to drive.

10 Evaluate the challenges of not being able to model a new traffic system, but instead having to build it and adjust it over a period of time.

11 Give three examples of situations a pilot needs to learn about that would be better learned on a flight simulator.

DISCUSSION POINT

Discuss what other models and simulations are used in real life.

PRACTICE QUESTIONS

	A	B	C	D	E	F
1	**Registration**	**Make**	**Model**	**Fuel type**	**Cost per litre**	**Cost per gallon**
2	BX56JWL	Ford	Mondeo	Diesel	$ 1.25	$ 5.69
3	BX56JWM	Saab	Saab 9-3	Petrol	$ 1.17	$ 5.32
4	BX56JWN	Land Rover	Discovery	Diesel	$ 1.25	$ 5.69
5	BX56JWP	Smart	Smart Car	LPG	$ 0.85	$ 3.87
6	BX56JWR	Ford	Mondeo	Petrol	$ 1.17	$ 5.32
7	BX56JWS	Saab	Saab 9-3	Diesel	$ 1.25	$ 5.69
8						
9					**Fuel type**	**Cost per gallon**
10					Diesel	$ 5.69
11					Petrol	$ 5.32
12					LPG	$ 3.87

The spreadsheet shows cars that are owned by a driving school. It calculates the fuel type of each car, the cost per litre of each fuel type and the cost per gallon.

1   The spreadsheet model is going to be used to calculate the costs of using each car.

   a   Explain three advantages of using a spreadsheet to model the costs of using each car.   **[3]**

   b   Explain one disadvantage of using a spreadsheet to model the costs of using each car.   **[1]**

                             [Total 4]

2   The driving school is considering purchasing a simulator to help students to learn to drive.

   a   Explain why a simulator would be used for this purpose.   **[4]**

   b   Explain the disadvantages of using a simulator for this purpose.   **[4]**

                             [Total 8]

3   Evaluate the use of simulators for nuclear science research.   **[8]**

SUMMARY CHECKLIST

- [ ] I can use what-if analysis.
- [ ] I can describe the characteristics of modelling software.
- [ ] I can explain the need for computer models.
- [ ] I can evaluate the effectiveness of spreadsheet models.
- [ ] I can explain how a model can be used to create and run simulations.

PROJECT

Figure 9.15: Ship's crew learn how to pilot a ship using a ship's bridge simulator.

You will design a poster to advertise a new simulator.

To design the poster, you will need to:

- Think of a new simulator that you think would be useful.

- Think about the data you will need for the simulator.

- What rules will you need?

- How close to 'real life' will your simulator be?

- What advantages and disadvantages are there to your simulator?

Design your poster and show it to a classmate.

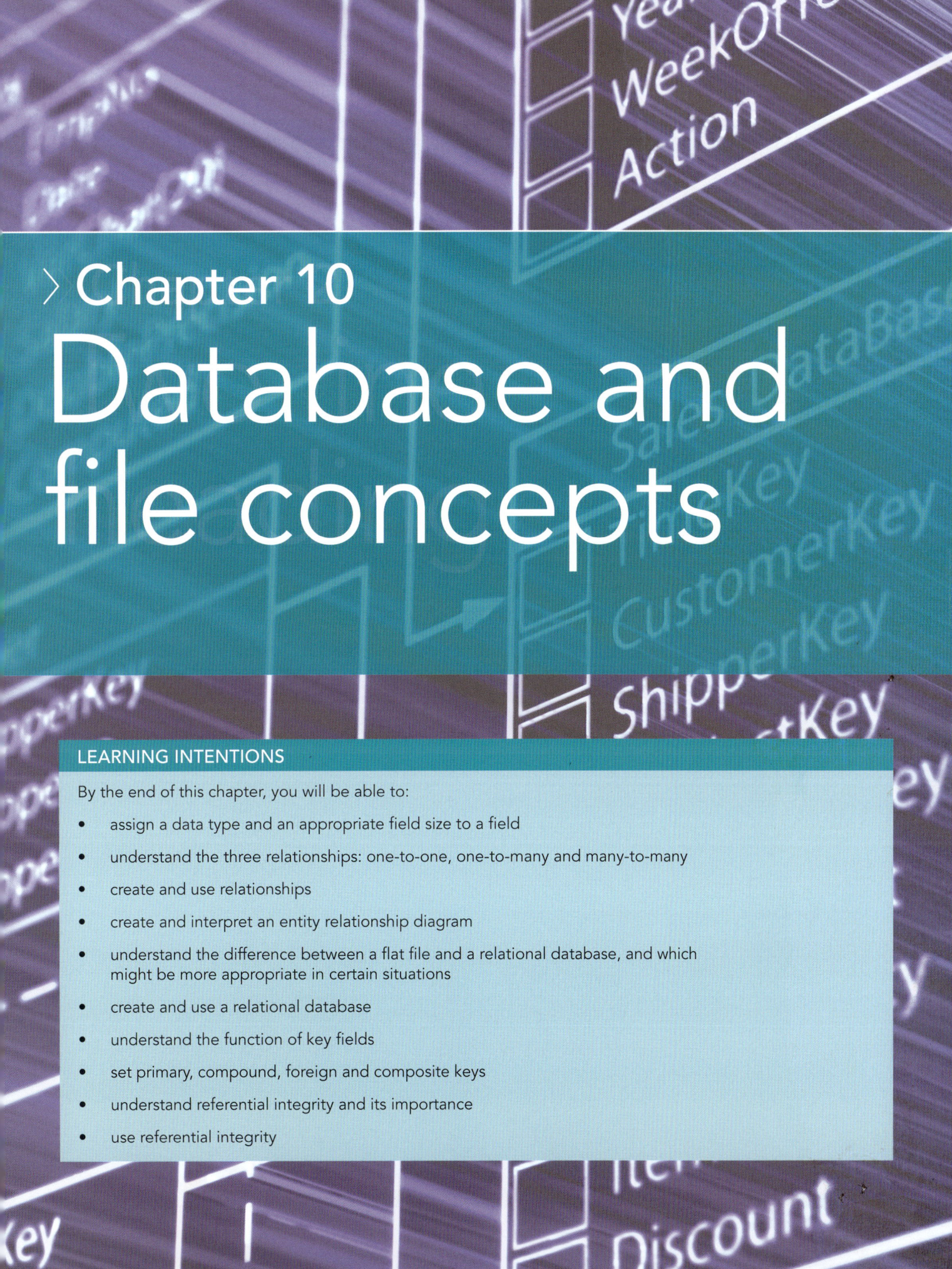

> Chapter 10
Database and file concepts

LEARNING INTENTIONS

By the end of this chapter, you will be able to:

- assign a data type and an appropriate field size to a field

- understand the three relationships: one-to-one, one-to-many and many-to-many

- create and use relationships

- create and interpret an entity relationship diagram

- understand the difference between a flat file and a relational database, and which might be more appropriate in certain situations

- create and use a relational database

- understand the function of key fields

- set primary, compound, foreign and composite keys

- understand referential integrity and its importance

- use referential integrity

CONTINUED

- validate and verify data entry

- perform searches on data

- select appropriate query types

- use arithmetic operations and logical functions to perform calculations within a database

- sort data

- design and create an appropriate data entry form

- design and create a switchboard/menu within a database

- import and export data

- design, create and edit a database report

- understand the characteristics of data in unnormalised form, and first, second and third normal forms

- discuss the advantages and disadvantages of normalisation

- normalise a database to first, second and third normal form

- understand the components of a data dictionary

- create a data dictionary and select appropriate data types for a given set of data and a given situation

- identify different data types

- understand static and dynamic parameters, and when they can be used in a query

- understand when simple, complex and nested queries should be used

- understand when summary queries, including cross-tab queries, should be used

- understand different file types and their uses

- understand what is meant by proprietary and open-source file formats and why open-source file formats are needed

- understand why generic file formats are needed

- understand the use of indexed sequential access

- understand the use of direct file access

- understand the use of a hierarchical database management system

- understand the features of a management information system (MIS)

- understand how an MIS can be used by organisations.

- discuss the advantages and disadvantages of different databases.

Introduction

A **database** is a collection of data stored in an organised way. Databases store data in tables. Each **table** contains similar data about something. For example, tables may store data on people, places, objects or events. We can search data using **queries**. We can also sort and **filter** data to organise it in different ways. We can use databases to help with tasks like stock tracking and payroll management. We can also use a database to store data for a mail merge (see Chapter 18 Mail merge).

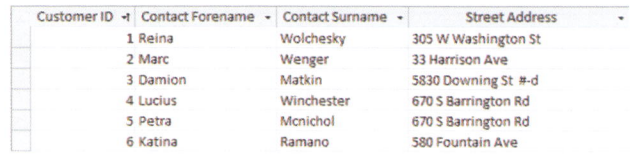

Figure 10.1: Customer table.

The columns in a database are called **attributes** or **fields**. In Figure 10.1, Customer ID, Contact Forename, Contact Surname and Street Address are all field/attribute names.

KEY WORDS

database: a structured method of storing data

table: a collection of related data, organised in rows and columns (for example, about people, places, objects or events)

query: a tool used to search for data in a database

filter: a tool to select certain data, and exclude other items of data

KEY WORDS

record: a common word for entity

entity: an object in the real world that we collect data on, for example a person, place, object or event; data about entities are stored in a table within a database

attribute: a category of information within an entity

field: a common word for attribute

10.1 Creating a database

Figure 10.1 contains data about customers (people). The data is displayed in a table. Tables contain rows and columns. Usually, the columns have headings. The headings tell us what data is stored in each column. For example, column 2 in Figure 10.1 contains the 'Contact Forename'. Rows store a complete collection of data about one thing. In Figure 10.1 the rows represent a collection of data about a person. Each row is called a **record**.

We use the term **entity** in database design. An entity is one single thing that exists, such as a person, place, object or event. We represent entities using a table. In Figure 10.1, the customer is the entity. The data about the entity is stored in the Customer Table. Each record stores a set of data about that entity.

UNPLUGGED ACTIVITY 10.01

Identify examples of fields and entities in the following databases:

Database 1: A music database.

Record_ID	Name	Artist	Year
1	Best hits of rock and roll	Brooks	1983
2	Pop and dance songs	Various	2020
3	Best classical music	Bach	2022

CONTINUED

Database 2: A fruit database.

Fruit	Colour	Country	Price
Apples	Green	UK	0.57
Coconuts	Brown/White	Malaysia	3.30
Bananas	Yellow	India	0.92

A database with a single table is called a **flat file** database.

We use a **primary key** on a database to identify each unique record. The primary key is a unique value that is linked to each record. A primary key can only exist once in a table. In Figure 10.1, Customer ID is the primary key. No other customer has the same Customer ID. If we look for Customer ID 4, we can see that it is the record for Lucius Winchester.

We use specific software to create and manage databases (see Figure 10.2). The software is called a **database management system** (DBMS). Sometimes, this is referred to as a relational database management system (RDBMS). This is because many databases include **relationships** between tables. Relationships link tables together. For example, we can link details about a car to a person who owns the car.

Figure 10.2: Spreadsheet software can be used to create a database, but there are many other software options.

DISCUSSION POINT

How do you think we can link two tables together using primary keys?

KEY WORDS

flat file: a database stored in a single table

primary key: a field that contains the unique identifier for a record

database management system: software used to manage a database

relationship: the way in which two entities in two different tables are connected

ACTIVITY 10.02

Open the database **10.01_Sales processing.mdb** and then open the table **Product**.

1   Identify four field names in the Product table.

2   Identify the primary key in the Product table.

3   How many records are in the Product table?

4   Identify two other tables within the database.

Data types

Each field in a table is assigned (given) a data type. The main data types are shown in Table 10.1. Only data of the type specified can be stored in the field.

data type	Example
Text	Only uses text/characters and symbols with no numbers. Example: This is text data
Alphanumeric	This is mix of text and numbers. Example: Text12343
Numeric (integer/decimal)	Uses numbers only. Example: 143.5342
Date/time	Specific format of numbers to make a date. Example: 2/5/2023
Boolean	Only has 2 values – usually TRUE or FALSE, or YES or NO. Example: FALSE

Table 10.1: Main data types assigned to fields in a table.

<table>
<tr><td style="background:#e8820a">KEY WORD</td></tr>
<tr><td>Boolean: a data type that can have two values, usually TRUE or FALSE</td></tr>
</table>

Autonumber is a special data type. It automatically assigns a number to a record. It starts at 1 and then 2, 3, 4 and so on. This is a quick way of creating a Primary Key. Autonumber does not use numbers again. If record 3 is deleted, the number 3 will never be given to another record.

Figure 10.3 shows a Product table. The fields in the table are assigned different data types:

- Product Name and Quantity Per Unit are alphanumeric (Short Text is the term used by Microsoft Access) which means they can include letters, numbers and symbols.

- Units in Stock is a Number (numeric) which has been set as an integer because it only contains whole numbers.

- Unit Price is Currency (numeric) which has been set as a decimal (real) because it can contain decimal values.

- Discontinued is Yes/No (Boolean) because it can only contain Yes or No values.

Field Name	Data Type
Product ID	AutoNumber
Product Name	Short Text
Supplier ID	Number
Category ID	Number
Quantity Per Unit	Short Text
Unit Price	Currency
Units In Stock	Number
Reorder Amount	Number
Units On Order	Number
Reorder Level	Number
Discontinued	Yes/No

Figure 10.3: Product data types.

Figure 10.4 shows an Order table. The fields in the table are assigned the following data types:

- Order Number is numeric but it is also set as an AutoNumber, which means a numeric value will be automatically assigned to it.

- Customer ID is numeric that has been set as an integer. It also matches the data type of the Customer ID in the Customer table that you can find within the database.

- Order Date is Date/Time and has been set as a date.

- Notes is alphanumeric but has been further defined as Long Text, which means that any amount of text can be assigned to it.

Field Name	Data Type
Order Number	AutoNumber
Customer ID	Number
Order Date	Date/Time
Notes	Long Text

Figure 10.4: Order data types.

Different database management systems use different names for data types. Microsoft Access uses 'text' to describe alphanumeric data, and 'number' is used for numeric data. Sometimes, database management software will also use formatted data as a data type. For example, 'currency' could be selected as a data type. Currency is a numeric and is also formatted with a currency symbol. For example, 445.00 is numeric, but £445.00 is a 'currency' data type.

Field size

Fixed length fields

We can set the size of a field. This limits the amount of data we can store in it. These are known as fixed length fields. Fixed length is normally used with text fields.

For text and alphanumeric we can set the maximum number of characters to store. For example, the Product Name in the Product Table is limited to 40 characters. Limiting the field size saves storage space in the database management system. Limiting the field sizes in the database can reduce the storage space needed for saving the database to a hard disk. This is less important for smaller databases. However, limiting field sizes in larger databases can have a major effect on reducing storage space.

Numbers can also have a field size. This could be defined as the number of digits or the maximum value that can be stored.

Dates are always stored in the same way. This means they always have the same storage size on a hard disk. However, we can display them differently when we view them. For example, we can view a date as 03/05/2022 or 10 December 2024. Database management systems often allow many ways of viewing dates.

> ### DID YOU KNOW?
>
> Some countries use day/month/year formats for dates. Other countries use month/day/year formats! It is always worth checking this when reading a date, or you might confuse 3 May with March 5.

Variable length fields

We can set text fields to variable length. Variable length allows a text field to store as little or as much data as possible. Variable length can also be called memo or long text data types. We use variable length data type for fields that contain notes or comments.

This data type is important because we may not know how much data will be stored in a field. If the field length is too long, then it wastes storage space. But we must ensure that the field length is long enough to store the longest required data item.

For example, we could limit a field length to ten to store a person's first name. This would store the name 'Alessandro' but would not store the name 'Bhuvaneswar'.

> ### ACTIVITY 10.03
>
> Open **10.01_Sales processing.mdb** and identify the data types and field sizes used within the tables.
>
> In a group, discuss whether these are the best data types to use. Would you change any? If so, why?

Questions

1 What are the columns in a database table called?
2 What are the rows in a database table called?
3 What is the name for a database with a single table?
4 What is the purpose of a primary key?
5 Give two data types in a database.

Linking tables with relationships

Relationships connect entities together. A **foreign key** is an attribute (field) in one entity that connects to a primary key in another entity. We often use the primary key from one table to link to another table. We can search for linked data when a table is linked to another table.

> ### KEY WORD
>
> **foreign key:** a field in a table that refers to the primary key in another table

In the Order table (see Figure 10.5a), the foreign key is Customer ID that connects to the primary key Customer ID in the customer table (see Figure 10.5b). For Order Number 4, the Customer ID 3 is looked up in the Customer table to find Damion Matkin.

a

Order Number	Customer ID	Order Date
1	2	28/05/2015
2	1	22/05/2015
3	5	06/05/2015
4	3	05/04/2015
5	7	06/05/2015

b

Customer ID	Contact Forename	Contact Surname
1	Reina	Wolchesky
2	Marc	Wanger
3	Damion	Matkin
4	Lucius	Winchester
5	Petra	Mcnichol
6	Katina	Ramano

Figure 10.5: Foreign key. **a** Order table. **b** Customer table.

One-to-one relationship

A one-to-one relationship is when each record in one table connects to only one record in another table. Each foreign key links to one primary key. Each primary key can only be linked to one foreign key value. The foreign key can exist on either side of the relationship.

In Figure 10.6a, The Sales Rep table stores details of the sales representatives within a business. This only contains basic information about their name, but their full employee details are stored in a separate table called Employee (see Figure 10.6b). Each sales representative only has one employee record and each employee record can only refer to one sales rep record.

a

Sales Rep ID	Last Name	First Name	Job Title	Title	Employee ID
1	Davolio	Nancy	Sales Representative	Ms	5
2	Fuller	Andrew	Vice President, Sales	Dr	6
3	Leverling	Janet	Sales Representative	Ms	1
4	Peacock	Margaret	Sales Representative	Mrs	2

b

Employee ID	Birth Date	Hire Date	Address
1	08-Dec-48	01-May-92	507 - 20th Ave. E.
2	19-Feb-52	14-Aug-92	908 W. Capital Way
3	30-Aug-63	01-Apr-92	722 Moss Bay Blvd.
4	19-Sep-37	03-May-93	4110 Old Redmond Rd.
5	04-Mar-55	17-Oct-93	14 Garrett Hill
6	02-Jul-63	17-Oct-93	Coventry House

Figure 10.6: One-to-one relationship. **a** Sales rep table. **b** Employee table.

One-to-many relationship

A one-to-many relationship is when each record in one table links to many (zero or more) records in another table. A foreign key exists within the table on the **many** side of the relationship and will connect to a primary key in the **one** side of the relationship. This is the most common type of relationship within relational databases.

In Figure 10.7a, the Category table stores data about the different categories of products being sold. Its primary key is Category ID. The Product table in Figure 10.7b stores data about the products. The Product table has a foreign key of Category ID. Each product can only have one category. Each category can have many products. There is one Category to many Products.

a

Product ID	Product Name	Category ID
1	Chai	1
2	Chang	1
3	Aniseed Syrup	2
4	Chef Anton's Cajun Seasoning	2
5	Chef Anton's Gumbo Mix	2
6	Grandma's Boysenberry Spread	2
7	Uncle Bob's Organic Dried Pears	7
8	Northwoods Cranberry Sauce	2
9	Mishi Kobe Niku	6
10	Ikura	8
11	Queso Cabrales	4
12	Queso Manchego La Pastora	4

b

Category ID	Category Name	Description
1	Beverages	Soft drinks, coffees, teas, beers, and ales
2	Condiments	Sweet and savory sauces, relishes, spreads, and seasoning
3	Confections	Desserts, candies, and sweet breads
4	Dairy Products	Cheeses
5	Grains/Cereals	Breads, crackers, pasta, and cereal
6	Meat/Poultry	Prepared meats
7	Produce	Dried fruit and bean curd
8	Seafood	Seaweed and fish

Figure 10.7: One-to-many relationship. **a** Product table. **b** Category table.

Many-to-many relationship

Many-to-many relationships are where many records links to many others in another table, and vice versa. Many records link to many records in both tables. They are generally not used in relational databases. If a many-to-many relationship exists, then it is converted to two sets of one-to-many relationships.

In Figure 10.8a, the Order table stores data about orders placed in a café. It includes data on what products are sold. It has a field called Product IDs that lists the products sold on each order. Each order can have many products. Each product can exist on many orders. There are many Orders to *many* Products.

a

Order Number	Customer ID	Order Date	Product IDs
1	2	28/05/2015	1, 8, 4, 3
2	1	22/05/2015	1, 7
3	5	06/05/2015	2, 5, 6
4	3	05/04/2015	4
5	7	06/05/2015	3, 8

b

Product ID	Product Name	Category ID
1	Chai	1
2	Chang	1
3	Aniseed Syrup	2
4	Chef Anton's Cajun Seasoning	2
5	Chef Anton's Gumbo Mix	2
6	Grandma's Boysenberry Spread	2
7	Uncle Bob's Organic Dried Pears	7
8	Northwoods Cranberry sauce	2
9	Mishi Kobe Niku	6
10	Ikura	8
11	Queso Cabrales	4
12	Queso Manchego La Pastora	4

Figure 10.8: Many-to-many relationship. **a** Order table. **b** Product table.

The drawback with many-to-many relationships is that single data items cannot be stored within the foreign key. In the Order and Product example (see Figure 10.8), the Product ID field contains more than one Product ID per Order. This causes problems and breaks the rules of first **normal form**. You will learn more about this later in this chapter.

> **KEY WORD**
>
> **normal form:** the extent to which a database has been normalised

> **ACTIVITY 10.04**
>
> Open **10.01_Sales processing.mdb** and examine the relationships. Identify the relationships that currently exist. For example, the relationship between Sales Rep and Employee is One Sales Rep to One Employee.

Creating and using relationships

One-to-many

When creating a one-to-many relationship, there are some rules to follow:

- The table on the **one** side must have a primary key.

- The table on the **many** side will have a foreign key.

- The data type and field size of the foreign key must match the primary key on the **one** side.

- Only data items that exist in the primary key on the **one** side can be used in the foreign key.

> **ACTIVITY 10.05**
>
> Open **10.01_Sales processing.mdb** and open the relationships.
>
> 1 Create a one-to-many relationship between Supplier and Product.
>
> 2 Create a one-to-many relationship between Order and the Sales Rep that dealt with the order. You will need a new foreign key in the Order table.

One-to-one

When creating a one-to-one relationship, there are also some rules to follow:

- At least one of the tables (table A) must have a primary key.

- The other table (table B) must either have a primary key that is also a foreign key and will link to the primary key in table A or a foreign key field with a unique **index** that will link to the primary key in table A.

- The data type and field size of the foreign key in table B and primary key in table A must match.

- Only data items that exist in the primary key in table A can be used in the foreign key in table B.

> **KEY WORD**
>
> **index:** a list of keys or KWs that identify a unique record and can be used to search and sort records more quickly

> **ACTIVITY 10.06**
>
> Open **10.01_Sales processing.mdb** and open the relationships.
>
> Create a one-to-one relationship between Sales Rep and Employee. Employee ID should be used as the foreign key in the Sales Rep table.

If you don't have a unique index or a primary key as the foreign key, then the database software is likely to assume you want to create a one-to-many relationship instead of a one-to-one relationship.

Entity relationship diagrams

An **entity relationship diagram (ERD)** shows the relationships (connections) between each entity.

> **KEY WORD**
>
> **entity relationship diagram (ERD):** a diagram that represents the relationships between entities

There are three types of ERD: conceptual data model, logical data model and physical data model. Each type of ERD shows more detail.

Conceptual ERD

The conceptual ERD shows how entities link to each other in the database system. Let's look again at the example of the café. A conceptual ERD would show that items are sold to customers. Many customers can buy one or more items. Many items can be bought by one or more customers. This gives the Conceptual ERD shown in Figure 10.9.

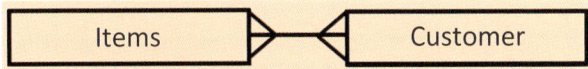

Figure 10.9: A conceptual ERD for a café.

However, a conceptual ERD does not show what fields and attributes exist in the database we want to create. It is more a plan of how the database is organised without the detail of how the data is stored.

Logical ERD

The logical model shows the attributes of each entity. It can also contain further entities to show how the data links together. In Figure 10.10, we can see the entity Order is created to show how Customer and Items link together.

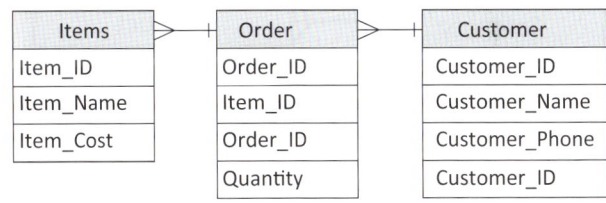

Figure 10.10: A logical ERD shows the attributes of each entity, and the relationship between each entity.

Physical ERD

The Physical ERD is the most detailed. The physical model includes details of whether fields are Primary or Foreign Keys. The Physical model also shows the data types for each field (see Figure 10.11).

In Figure 10.18:

- Each branch has many customers.

- But each customer can only be linked to one branch.

- Each customer can have many accounts.

- But each account can only belong to one customer.

- Each account can have many transactions taking place.

- But each transaction must be linked to one account.

- Each account can be of only one type but many types of account can exist.

Figure 10.19 shows the relationships that have been implemented in the Product table in the database **10.02_Sales processing 2.mdb**.

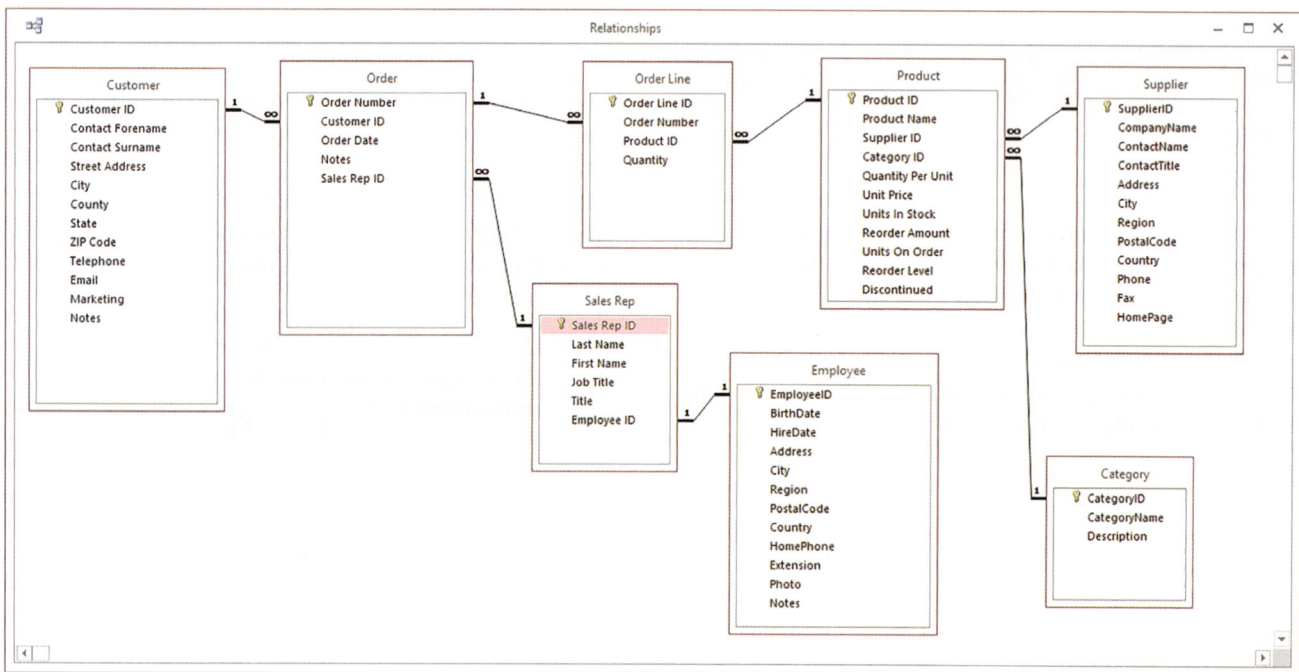

Figure 10.19: ERD implemented.

UNPLUGGED ACTIVITY 10.08

1 Draw ERDs to represent the following relationships:

    a One Airline Seat to one Customer.

    b One House to many Occupants.

    c Many Coaches to many Drivers.

2 Draw an ERD to represent a library model. Within the library, there are several books. There may be many copies of the same book, which are known as book copies. Customers can borrow a book copy, known as a 'loan'. A customer can have many loans but a loan will be for just one customer. Each loan will be for one book copy, but over a period of time each book copy can be loaned out many times (see Figure 10.20).

Figure 10.20: A library has many books that can be loaned to customers. The details of these are stored in a database.

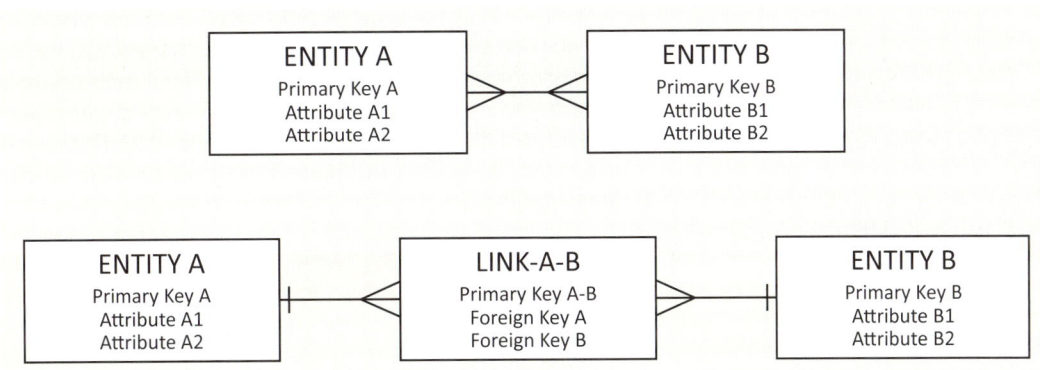

Figure 10.21: Entity A and Entity B can be turned from a many-to-many relationship into a one-many relationship through the use of a Link table.

Having many-to-many relationship exists is not ideal. We try to turn many-to-many relationships into two one-to-many relationships. We can do this by using a LINK table. The link table joins the two entities as shown in Figure 10.21.

A new primary key (Primary Key A-B) is created in the LINK table. The primary keys for each of the original entities are then used as foreign keys in the LINK table. In the example in Figure 10.22, each **kitchen unit** can include many **kitchen parts**. As each **kitchen part** can be used for many **kitchen units**, a LINK table is required (see Figure 10.23).

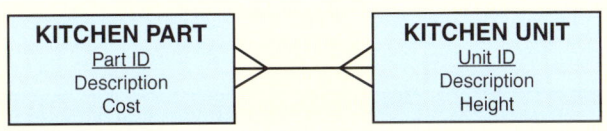

Figure 10.22: A kitchen contains many parts and units. This creates a many-to-many relationship.

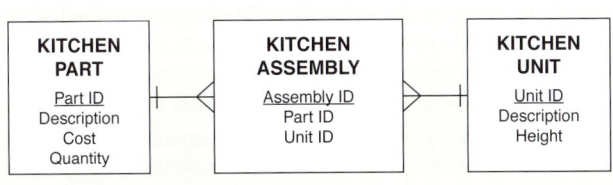

Figure 10.23: Using a link table called 'Kitchen Assembly' removes the issue of the many-to-many relationship.

The LINK table 'kitchen assembly' is for each combination of unit and part. It has its own primary key, but the primary keys from 'kitchen unit' and

'kitchen part' are also used as foreign keys. The quantity of each part needed for each unit is also stored. Figure 10.24 shows what some of the data might look like.

Kitchen unit

Unit ID	Description	Height (mm)
DR3-700	3-drawer unit	700
BU-700	Base unit	700
LR-2000	Larder unit	2000

Kitchen part

Part ID	Description	Cost ($)
HNG	Hinge	1.70
HND	Handle	5.99
SHL	Shelf	7.97

Kitchen assembly

Assembly ID	Unit ID	Part ID	Quantity
1	DR3-700	HND	3
2	BU-700	HND	1
2	BU-700	HNG	2
2	BU-700	SHL	2
3	LR-2000	HND	1
3	LR-2000	HNG	4

Figure 10.24: Database for kitchen units, parts and assembly.

The difference between a flat file and a relational database

A flat file database consists of a single table. A flat file database cannot have relationships as there is only one table. It is like looking at all the data in a single worksheet in a spreadsheet. It is called 'flat' because it only has two dimensions: fields and records.

Figure 10.25 shows an example of a simple flat file to store data about cars. The transmission column states whether the car is manual transmission (has a gear stick – M) or automatic transmission (A).

The flat file in Figure 10.26 stores data about driving lessons, the cars used and the learners taking the lessons.

The data about the car is repeated and the data about the learner driver taking lessons is also repeated. This causes problems if we want to change the details about the car. We must make sure that all the data about a car is changed. This means checking every row and editing it if needed. Repeating the same data many times is called **data redundancy**.

> **KEY WORD**
>
> **data redundancy:** having the same data repeated in many records

This example only contains a small amount of redundant data, but imagine if data about the distance each car had travelled, or the full address of the learner and their date of birth were stored.

ID	Registration	Reg Year	Transmission
1	BX03HMW	2013	M
2	BR54URS	2011	M
3	BA55WEP	2012	M
4	BC53PRS	2013	M
5	BD05ABC	2012	A
6	BE04RTJ	2011	M

Figure 10.25: Example of simple flat file used to store data about cars.

Lesson

Lesson ID	Lesson Date	Time Slot Start	Car Registration	Car Registration Year	Transmission	Forename	Surname	Mobile
1	25/08/2023	08:00	BR21URS	2021	A	Nadia	Afzal	07983 9xxxxx
2	28/08/2023	08:00	BD70ABC	2020	A	Roger	Drake	07612 5xxxxx
3	31/08/2023	11:00	BD73ABC	2023	A	Roger	Drake	07612 5xxxxx
4	01/09/2023	16:00	BD70ABC	2020	A	Nadia	Afzal	07983 9xxxxx
5	08/09/2023	16:00	BR21URS	2021	A	Nadia	Afzal	07983 9xxxxx
6	29/08/2023	19:00	BC67PRS	2018	M	Sally	Mastock	07421 1xxxxx

Figure 10.26: Flat file used to store driving lessons, the cars used and the learners taking the lessons.

Redundant data uses up additional memory. Data redundancy also causes problems because data can become inconsistent. For example, Roger Drake changes mobile phone number. Now we must go through the whole database and change the mobile number for Roger in every lesson that Roger has taken. If we forget to change a number, then the data becomes inconsistent. This affects the database. For example, a search may not produce accurate results because Roger has more than one phone number listed.

Another challenge of a flat file database is data entry. If we add a new driving lesson, then all the details of the car and the learner must be entered. This takes more time and can lead to mistakes. Having to enter more data than needed increases the risk of inconsistent data and errors.

There are benefits to flat file databases. Flat file databases are often simple to set up. Flat file databases do not have to have data types, field sizes or relationships. Flat file databases can be shared easily through email and across the internet. This is because the data is not dependent on specific file types or software. Flat file databases may be processed more quickly by a computer because there are no links to other tables or database systems.

Relational databases are useful when data must be kept accurate. Relational databases are also better at managing large stores of linked data. Relational databases reduce problems of inaccurate, inconsistent and redundant data by linking tables and using relationships.

For example, a relational database about a library includes separate tables for books, borrowers and loans.

Data from a relational database can be exported as a flat file database. This is because flat file databases can be processed more quickly. For example, we could export monthly salary payments from a relational database. The data can then be processed by a payments system.

The disadvantages of relational databases are based on cost and expert knowledge. Relational databases need expertise to plan to ensure that it is all set up correctly. The RDBMS also may cost more than the software for a simple flat file database system.

Processing a relational database takes longer, especially when it contains a lot of data. This means that you may need more powerful processors.

A relational database can be shared across a network or the internet. RDBMS allows security permissions to be set so that different types of user can access different tables. A flat file database cannot do this because the data is contained in one table.

Relational databases allow queries to search and sort data efficiently. Queries can select data from one or more tables when using a relational database. This means that it can combine data effectively to solve queries and analyse data or trends. A relational database can produce detailed and customised reports of the stored data. Relational databases are also flexible because additional fields and tables can be added without affecting the rest of the data.

UNPLUGGED ACTIVITY 10.09

Work with a classmate. Draw a table that lists the advantages and disadvantages of:

- flat file databases

- relational databases.

Compare your list with other classmates and share your ideas. Update your lists with any ideas that other classmates have that you do not.

DISCUSSION POINT

Use the list of advantages and disadvantages of flat files and relational databases that you created in Activity 10.09.

Discuss as a class:

1 Why both types of databases are needed.

2 What the biggest advantage of a relational database is.

3 What the biggest advantage of a flat file database is.

4 What the biggest disadvantage of a relational database is.

5 What the biggest disadvantage of a flat file database is.

The flat file used to store driving lessons, the cars used and the learners taking the lessons in Figure 10.26 could be stored in a relational database as a set of three tables, as shown in Figure 10.27.

Lesson

Lesson ID	Lesson Date	Time Slot Start	Registration	Learner ID
1	25/08/2023	08:00	BR21URS	10
2	28/08/2023	08:00	BD70ABC	11
3	31/08/2023	11:00	BD73ABC	11

Car

ID	Registration	Make	Model	Registration Year	Transmission
2	BR21URS	Vauxhall	Astra	2021	A
4	BC67PRS	Mini	Cooper	2018	M
5	BD70ABC	Nissan	Almera	2020	A

Learner

Learner ID	Forename	Surname	Address 1	Address 2	Post Code	Mobile	Licence Number
9	Sally	Mastock	15 Cloud Road	Kingston-Upon-Hull	KI8 6GU	07421 1xxxxx	MAST9999999SA9XX
10	Nadia	Afzal	23 Yandle Lane	Shrewsbury	KN3 7YY	07983 0xxxxx	AFZA9999999NI9XX
11	Roger	Drake	19 Spion Kop	Liverpool	L15 9PL	09612 5xxxxx	DRAK9999999RA9XX

Figure 10.27: Flat files stored as a set of three tables in a relational database.

Table 10.2 summarises the types of searches and queries that can be applied to flat files and those that can be applied to relational databases.

Flat file database	Relational database
A search or query has to load the entire database to find the data needed. For example, to find information about the car with registration BC53PRS, the database would need to search for every occurrence in the whole LESSON flat file.	A search or query only has to load the tables required. For example, to find the same information, only the CAR table would need to be loaded.
A search or query will find all the data required in one file. For example, to find all lessons taken by Roger Drake, a filter could be applied to the Forename and Surname columns.	A search or query would have to assimilate data from more than one table. For example, to find all the lessons taken by Roger Drake, their Learner ID would need to be looked up in the LEARNER table and then the Learner ID would need to be found in the LESSON table.
Running a query to find the number of vehicles with manual (gear stick) transmission would mean searching the whole file and then identifying unique occurrences of each car and counting only those that are manual transmission.	To run the same query would simply require filtering the CAR table to show only manual transmission and then a summary count of the number of records.

Table 10.2: Types of searches and queries that can be applied to flat file databases and relational databases.

Importing data

Data can be imported into a database from other files. This allows data that has been created in another system to be used within the database. The data files must be structured in such a way that the fields and records can be clearly separated. A common file type for this purpose is a comma separated values (csv) file. In a csv, the fields are separated by commas, records are separated by line breaks and speech marks are used to identify text. In a csv file, the field lengths are delimited. Delimited means that each field can be any length.

This is a csv file for books. The first row contains the field names.

"ID","Book title","Genre","Reading age","ISBN","Author"

1,"A Soldier's Tale","Thriller",12,"0-321-93561-1","B Rushmore"

2,"Hidden Gold","Mystery",10,"0-342-92763-X","J T King"

3,"Fearless","Action",14,"0-250-34751-9","K Lawrence"

There are other file types that allow data to be read into a database. Text files (txt) can also be used. Text files are usually formatted in the same way as a csv file. Text files can also use different characters to separate fields. Text files can be structured to have fixed length fields. A text file can use spaces to fill the gaps. For example, if a field was 15 characters long and the field size is 20, then five spaces could be added to the data to make sure it was 20 characters long.

This is a fixed length field text file for students:

1	Smith	Larry	9F
2	Nyakatawa	Paul	9B
3	Kalsi	Waheed	10R
4	Woolfenden	Howard	11M
5	Patel	Poonam	9N

ACTIVITY 10.10

Create a new database and import the following files:

- **10.03_Book.xlsx** (file includes row headings)
- **10.04_Student.xlsx**.

Creating a relational database

The first step in creating a database is to create the file that will be used. Once the data file has been created, we can then think about creating:

- tables
- relationships
- forms
- reports.

ACTIVITY 10.11

Create a new database called **10.13_My library**. The database will store data about books in a school library (see Figure 10.28).

1 Create a new database file.

2 Import the files:

    a **10.03_Book.xlsx**

    b **10.04_Student.xlsx**

    c **10.05_Copy.xlsx**

    d **10.06_Loan.xlsx**.

3 Check the data types for each field in each table and change if necessary.

4 Check the field lengths for each field in each table and change if necessary (do not leave them as 256 characters in length).

Save this file for use later in this chapter.

Figure 10.28: A school library can use the same database designs as a public library, as they all store data about books.

Function of key fields

Primary key

A primary key is a unique identifier for each record in a table. The field used for the primary key must contain unique values. A primary key cannot have any repeating values.

Examples of primary keys could include:

- registration plate for a car
- student number for a student
- product code for a product.

It is important that data used as a primary key never changes. This is because it can affect the relationship in the database. Some fields may appear to be suitable as a primary key, for example a registration plate on a car is unique to that car (see Figure 10.29). However, the registration plate may not be suitable in the long run. A registration plate for a car can be changed in some countries. For this reason, it is always best to use separate ID fields as primary keys.

Figure 10.29: Cars have unique registration plates, but registration plates may sometimes be changed by the new owner.

In Table 10.3, the ID fields should be used purely for the structure of the database. It is still possible to set another field to be unique, but the primary key should be used for relationships. If possible, the primary key should be set to increment automatically (e.g. AutoNumber).

Table Name	Primary Key
Car	CarID
Student	StudentID
Product	ProductID

Table 10.3: ID fields used to structure a database.

Compound key

Sometimes a database can use a **compound key**. A compound key uses two or more fields together and combines them to form a unique identity. These can be complex to use, especially within relationships.

KEY WORD

compound key: two or more fields that form the primary key; each field that comprises the compound key is itself a key from another table

Table 10.4 shows the products and quantities ordered for each order. If each order only includes each Product on one Order Line, then the combination of Order Number and Product ID is unique. This is an example of a compound key.

Order Number	Product ID	Quantity
1	1	1
1	2	2
2	3	1
2	3	1
3	4	1
4	5	1
4	6	1
5	5	1
5	6	2

Table 10.4: Order line.

Table 10.5 shows appointments for a doctor. If Doctor ID and Patient ID were selected as the compound key, then this would mean each patient could only see each doctor once and so this combination would not be suitable. If Doctor ID, Patient ID and Date were selected as the compound key then this would mean each patient could only see each doctor once each day. It may be acceptable to the doctor to see a patient only once per day, but if the doctor needs to see the same patient more than once on the same day, then a combination of all four fields including Time would be needed as the compound key.

A solution to this is to have an 'Appointments' table. This would have a unique ID 'Appointment ID'. This would mean that all appointments have a unique ID and the issues of compound keys are removed.

Doctor ID	Patient ID	Date	Time
1	1	5/11/23	12:00
1	2	2/9/23	13:00
2	3	18/9/23	13:00
1	1	12/11/23	12:00
2	3	18/9/23	17:30

Table 10.5: Appointments for a doctor.

ACTIVITY 10.12

1   Create a table of appointments as shown in Table 10.5.

2   Try to set the compound key to be a combination of Doctor ID and Patient ID. What went wrong and why did it happen?

3   a   Set the compound key to be a combination of Doctor ID, Patient ID and Date.

   b   Create a new appointment for Doctor ID 1 with Patient ID 2 on 12/2/23 at 14:00. Was the new appointment accepted?

   c   Create a new appointment for Doctor ID 1 with Patient ID 2 on 2/9/23 at 14:00. What went wrong and why did it happen?

Foreign key

A foreign key is a field in a table that links to the primary key in another table. A foreign key creates a relationship between two tables. The foreign key will always have the same data type and field size as the primary key. The foreign key must always be on the **many** side of the relationship. The foreign key will always link to a single primary key field.

In Figure 10.30, Customer ID in the Order table is a foreign key that links to the Customer ID in the Customer table.

Order

Order Number	Customer ID	Order Date
1	2	28/05/2015
2	1	22/05/2015
3	5	06/05/2015
4	3	05/04/2015
5	7	06/05/2015

Customer

Customer ID	Contact Forename	Contact Surname
1	Reina	Wolchesky
2	Marc	Wanger
3	Damion	Matkin
4	Lucius	Winchester
5	Petra	Mcnichol
6	Katina	Ramano
7	Leslie	Cackowski
8	Cristopher	Wiget

Figure 10.30: Customer ID is the foreign key.

ACTIVITY 10.13

1   Open the database **10.13_My library.mdb** that you created earlier.

   a   Assign primary keys to existing fields in each table.

      Each book has several copies. Each copy of the book can be loaned out several times. Each loan is for only one student and only one copy of a book. Each student can take out several loans.

   b   Create relationships between the tables.

CONTINUED

2   Open the database
     10.07_Driving school.mdb.

   a   Set the primary key for the
       Instructor table.

   b   Create a new primary key for the Car
       table (do not use Registration).

   c   Create a new primary key for the
       Learner table.

   d   Create a compound primary key for
       the Lesson table. You will need at least
       three fields for this.

   Each car can be used in several lessons.
   Each student can have several lessons. Each
   instructor can give several lessons. Each
   lesson will be for one student with one
   instructor in one car.

   e   Create relationships between the tables.

Setting key fields

It is important to consider which fields will be key fields.
The relationship between tables is created by linking
key fields. If a key field is changed later, it can cause
problems. Changing a key field can break links between
different tables and may stop the database from working
as it should.

It is very important to plan the key fields first for each
table, and to design the database thoroughly at the start.

Referential integrity

What would happen if we deleted the data in a linked
table? For example, what would happen if we deleted an
author from a database, but the author was linked to a
book using a primary key?

In this case, the field in the Book Table would still have
the primary key, but it would not link to any data in
the Author table. This means that the book now has no
author, which isn't right! We can use **referential integrity**
to stop this from happening. Referential integrity is a
tool in an RDBMS that stops linked data being deleted.
It ensures that foreign keys always link to data that
exists in a table.

KEY WORD

referential integrity: data in the foreign key of
the table on the 'many' side of a relationship
must exist in the primary key of the table on the
'one' side of a relationship

In Figure 10.31, Customer ID 5 does not exist in the
Customer table. This means that the Order table does
not contain referential integrity because the related
customer does not exist.

Order		
Order Number	**Customer ID**	**Order Date**
1	2	28/05/2015
2	1	22/05/2015
3	5	06/05/2015

Customer		
Customer ID	**Contact Forename**	**Contact Surname**
1	Reina	Wolchesky
2	Marc	Wanger

Figure 10.31: There is no referential integrity between
these tables.

Referential integrity is a type of lookup validation.
The RDBMS checks to see whether the record linked to
the foreign key exists before allowing the foreign key to
be used in a table. If the related record does not exist,
then the database will prevent the foreign key data from
being entered.

Referential integrity keeps data in a database accurate.
Many RDBMSs allow you to 'enforce' referential
integrity. This means that it will always check that
the references and tables linked by foreign keys exist.
Enforcing referential integrity will also stop you
deleting records which are linked to other tables
using a foreign key.

ACTIVITY 10.14

Open the database **10.08_Sales processing 3.mdb**

1 Open the **Order** table and add Sales Rep IDs 4, 5, 8, 11 and 15 to the records.

  a Which ones worked?

  b Which ones did not work?

  c Why didn't they work?

2 Try to create a relationship between Product and Category and enforce referential integrity.

  a What happens?

  b Why has this happened?

  c Correct any data that is causing this problem and try to create the relationship again.

Questions

6 State one type of relationship in a database.

7 Describe two advantages of a relational database when compared to a flat file database.

8 Explain the difference between a foreign key and a primary key.

9 What is the purpose of referential integrity?

Validate and verify data entry

Using validation rules

You studied validation in Chapter 1. Relational database management systems can apply validation rules to data. Data is accepted and stored in the database if it is allowed by the validation rules. If data does not meet the validation rules, then the data is rejected and an error message may be shown.

For example, in a database, the user is attempting to enter the location in the region where each Sales Rep is based. The user has four valid options: 'North', 'South', 'East' or 'West'. The user has accidentally entered 'Nor', which is not a valid option. An error message appears advising the user how to fix the problem (see Figure 10.32).

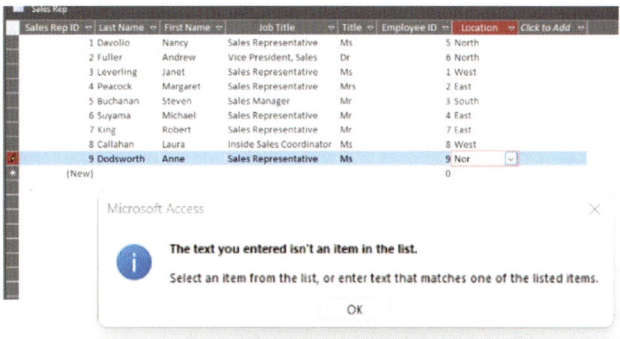

Figure 10.32: An error message appears if a value does not match the validation rule.

Figure 10.33 shows the rule that had been set up.

General Lookup	
Display Control	Combo Box
Row Source Type	Value List
Row Source	"North";"South";"East";"West"
Bound Column	1
Column Count	1
Column Heads	No
Column Widths	2.54cm
List Rows	16
List Width	2.54cm
Limit To List	Yes
Allow Value List Edits	No
List Items Edit Form	
Show Only Row Source V	No

Figure 10.33: Validation rule showing North, South, East and West must be used.

The rule ensures that the only data that can be entered must exist in the list that contains 'North', 'South', 'East' and 'West'.

ACTIVITY 10.15

Open the database **10.09_Sales processing validation.mdb** and open the table **Employee**.

1 Create a validation rule that will only allow the entry of 'UK' or 'USA' for the Country.

2 Create an appropriate error message.

There is a variety of validation rules that can be used within a database including:

- lookup in list (by looking up in a list entered within the rule)
- lookup in list (by using referential integrity)
- lookup in list (by using a lookup table)
- range
- data type
- format
- length
- presence.

Table 10.6 gives some examples of validation rules.

Type	Field	Rule
Lookup in list	Title	IN ("Mr", "Mrs", "Miss", "Dr")
Range	Date of Birth	>DATE() (must be after today's date)
Range	Date Joined	> 28/02/1995
Range	Reorder Amount	Between 1 and 2000
Range	Reorder Level	>0
Data Type	State	Like "<A-Z><A-Z>" (must be two text characters)
Format	Email Address	Like "*@*.*" (* means any character)
Length	Colour	Like "??" (must be two characters)
Presence	Forename	IS NOT NULL

Table 10.6: Examples of validation rules.

ACTIVITY 10.16

Open **10.09_Sales processing validation.mdb** and open the table **Customer**.

1 Create a validation rule to ensure the surname is present.

2 Create a validation rule to ensure that an email address includes the @ symbol and a full stop.

3 Create a validation rule to ensure the telephone number is 12 characters long.

Open the table **Product**.

4 Create a validation rule to ensure the Units in Stock is a positive number.

5 Create a validation rule to ensure the Reorder Amount is less than 1000.

6 Create a validation rule to ensure the Reorder Level is at least 0 and no more than 100.

Open the table **Employee**.

7 Create a validation rule to ensure the Hire Date is at least today.

8 Create a validation rule to ensure the region is two characters long and only contains letters.

9 Create a validation rule to ensure the extension is either three or four characters long and only contains numbers.

10 Create a validation rule to ensure the Hire Date is after the Birth Date.

Testing validation in a database

In Chapter 8, you looked at testing rules using valid, invalid and extreme data. You can do the same when testing validation in a database.

ACTIVITY 10.17

Open **10.09_Sales processing validation.mdb** and open the table **Customer**.

1   The State field has a validation rule applied to it.

   a   Try changing the state for Reina Wolchesky to NN. What happens? Why does this happen?

   b   Try changing the state for Reina Wolchesky to NM instead of MN. Why was this error allowed to happen?

   c   Identify five items of test data that could be used to test this validation rule.

2   The ZIP Code field has validation applied to it.

   a   Try different combinations of data to see whether you can work out what the validation rule is.

   b   Identify eight items of test data that could be used to test this validation rule. You should use valid, invalid and extreme.

Verifying data entry

In Chapter 1, you saw that validated data may not mean that the data is accurate. Verifying data is a method to ensure the data entered is accurate. You can verify data by comparing the data that has been entered into the database with the original data source.

ACTIVITY 10.18

Open **10.09_Sales processing validation.mdb** and open the table **Customer**.

1   Visually check that the data for Damion Matkin matches the original data that follows:

Contact Forename	Contact Surname	Street Address	City	County	State
Damion	Matkin	5830 Downing St	Denver	Denver	CO

ZIP Code	Telephone	Email	Marketing	Notes
80216	303-295-4797	damion@matkin. com	Yes	

2   Add the following data to the customer table and then visually check the data matches the source:

Contact Forename	Contact Surname	Street Address	City	County	State
Joel	Nardo	5150 Town Cir	Boca Raton	Palm Beach	FL

ZIP Code	Telephone	Email	Marketing	Notes
33486	561-395-2277	joel@nardo.com	Yes	

Performing searches

Sometimes we only want to view certain data in a database. To do this we can search for this data. We can search for data by identifying the criteria we are searching for. For example, we may want to search for all people in a school database who have brown hair. In this example, the search criteria will be 'brown' in the 'hair_colour' field.

We search for data in a database using a **query**. A query searches for data that matches the search criteria. When it finds all the data, it displays the records that match our search criteria. Queries can be used to search two or more tables at once.

> **KEY WORD**
>
> **query:** a question used to retrieve data from a database

Using queries to update data in tables

Queries can be used to update the data in a table. To make an update query, you follow the same steps to create a normal query. You will then need to edit the query type to 'Update' (see Figure 10.34).

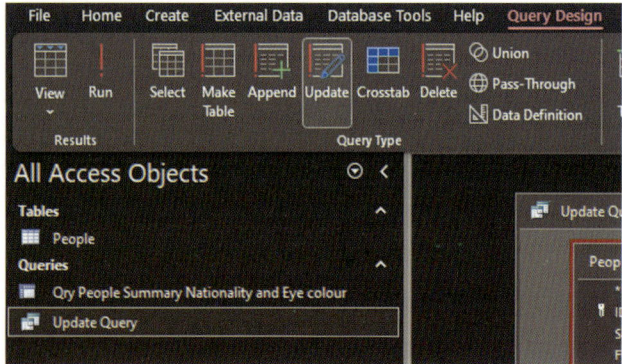

Figure 10.34: You can change a 'Select' query to an 'Update' query. This then allows you to update data in tables.

Once you have selected the 'Update' query, you can then select the fields you want to update and the criteria you want to use (see Figure 10.35).

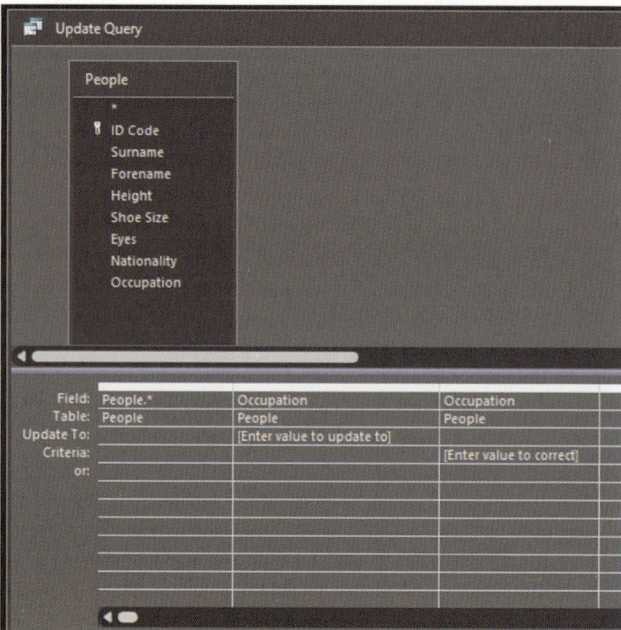

Figure 10.35: This 'Update' query will change a person's occupation based on the values entered when the query is run.

When run, the query confirms if you want to change the data in the table, as shown in Figure 10.36.

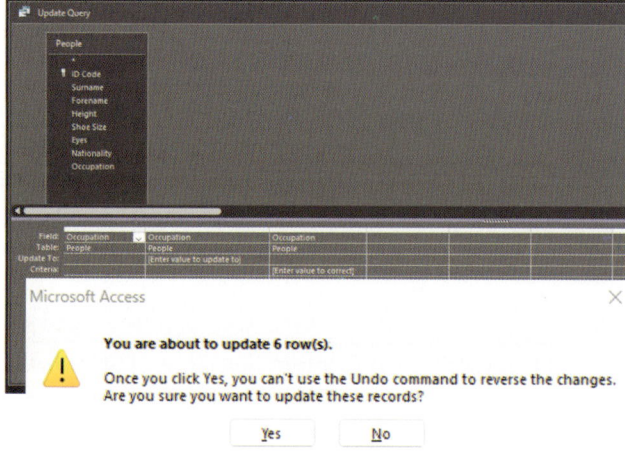

Figure 10.36: The query confirms that you wish to change the data.

Using queries to add or delete records

Queries can be used to add (append) and delete records in tables. The Append and Delete queries can be used to add new records or delete records from a database table.

ACTIVITY 10.19

In a pair, use the Microsoft Support library and other sources to write a guide on how to create an Append and a Delete query.

Use the database **10.10_People.mdb**. Create a copy of the database.

Use the copy of the database to:

- add three new people to the database

- delete the table of people.

Show your guide to other classmates. Get feedback on how easy your guide is to follow. Edit your guide to make it easier to use based on the feedback you have received.

Simple queries on a single criterion

A simple query has only one criterion (singular for criteria). A criterion is the rule that will be applied to the data.

Table 10.7 shows examples of when you would use a simple query for a particular outcome.

When creating a simple query, it is also possible to specify which fields will be listed.

Wildcards can be used to replace one or more characters in a search to mean any value. Table 10.7 shows two examples of how wildcards can be used. The * symbol replaces any number of characters. The ? symbol replaces one single character. For example, Like "?'*" would find anybody with an apostrophe as the second letter of their surname or Like "*-*" would find anybody who has a hyphen in their surname.

Field	Type	Criterion	Outcome
State	Text	="CA"	Lists all customers who live in CA (California).
Marketing	Boolean	True	Lists all customers who have agreed to receive marketing.
Mark	Numeric	100	Lists all students who achieved 100 marks.
Mark	<	<50	Lists all students who achieved less than 50 marks.
Price	<	>3.99	Lists all products with a price more than 3.99 (i.e. 4.00 or above).
Distance covered by car	>=	>=50000	Lists all cars with a distance travelled of at least 50 000 kilometres.
Width	<=	<=50	Lists all products with a width up to and including 50 mm.
Date of Joining	>	> 01/01/2010	Lists all employees who joined the company after 1 January 2010.
Appointment Time	>=	>= 12:00pm	Lists all appointments in the afternoon.
Surname	Wildcard	Like "A*"	Lists all customers with a surname starting with A.
Product Code	Wildcard	Like "??B??"	Lists all product codes where the third character is B.
Allergy	Boolean	NOT "Nut"	Lists all students who do not have a nut allergy.

Table 10.7: Query criterion and outcomes.

For example, Figure 10.37 shows a simple query that has been created to show all Sales Reps who have a Job Title of Sales Representative.

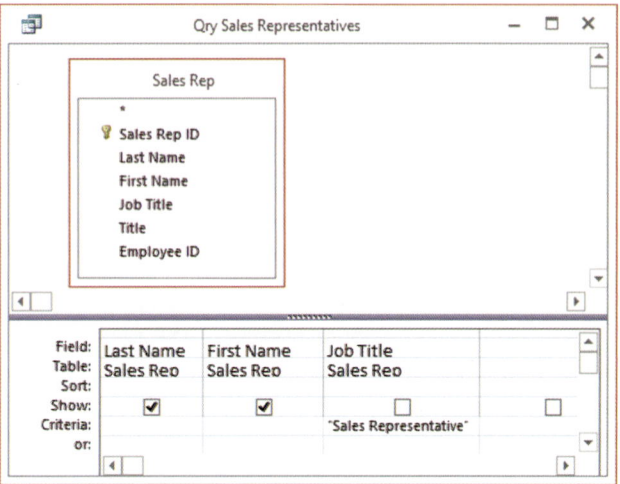

Figure 10.37: Sales rep query.

The criterion of Job Title = "Sales Representative" means that only sales reps with that job title will be listed. The only fields that will be listed are Last Name and First Name. Job Title will not be listed because the option to show it has been deselected. The result of the simple query is shown in Figure 10.38.

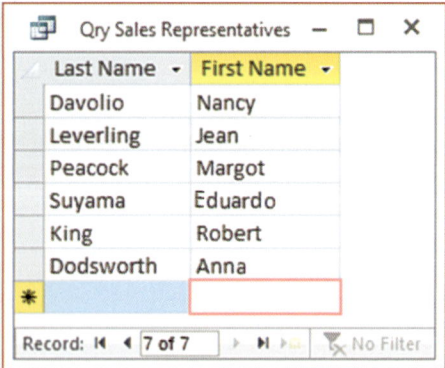

Figure 10.38: Sales rep query result.

It is also possible to include data from a related table. In Figure 10.39, a query has been created to show all Products over $75 including their categories. The CategoryName has been included from the Category Table, which is related to the Product Table through the Category ID.

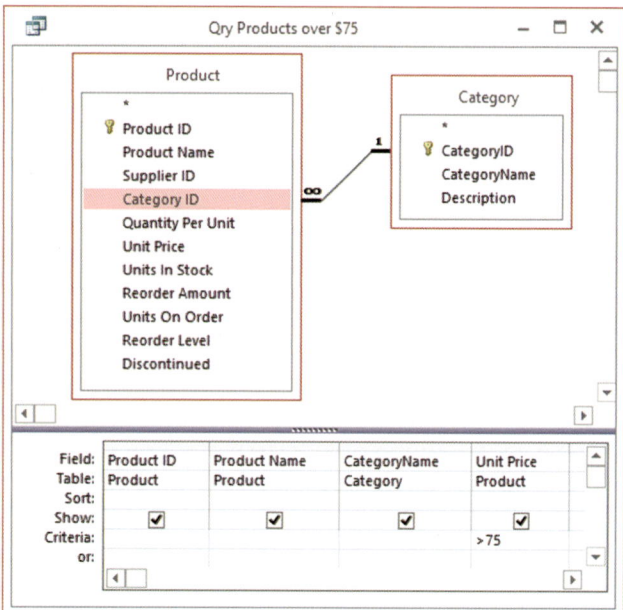

Figure 10.39: Product query.

ACTIVITY 10.20

Open **10.02_Sales processing 2.mdb**, identify which query is most suitable and then create queries for the following:

1. All UK employees.
2. All employees from Seattle.
3. All employees who were born on or after 1/1/1960.
4. All products that include the word 'bottles' in the quantity per unit.
5. All products with no units in stock.
6. The product name and supplier company name of all products that have been discontinued.
7. The names and categories of all products with at least 100 units in stock.
8. The names and price of products that are in the category 'Condiments'.
9. A list of all orders that were not placed on 6/5/15.
10. A list of all Sales Reps who do not have a job title of 'Sales Representative'.
11. A list of all products where the Units in Stock is less than or equal to the Reorder Level.

Complex queries using multiple criteria

Complex queries are queries that have two or more (multiple) search criteria. They use either the AND or OR Boolean operators. If all specified criteria need to be satisfied, then the AND operator is used. If any one of the specified criteria needs to be satisfied, then the OR operator is used.

For example, the table lists characteristics about some people.

Surname	Forename	Height	Shoe Size	Eyes	Nationality	Occupation
Greer	Wendy	1.85	7	Blue	British	Firefighter
Bernard	Charles	1.75	8	Blue	French	Welder
Pearce	Madison	1.85	8	Blue	American	Musician
Ivanova	Sofia	1.65	8	Brown	Russian	Road sweeper
Joo	Haeun	1.35	9	Brown	South Korean	Firefighter
Goswami	Lamar	1.75	9	Brown	Indian	Shop assistant
Kaya	Yusuf	1.95	10	Blue	Turkish	Teacher
Danshov	Aleksander	1.8	6	Hazel	Russian	Politician
Mallapati	Smriti	1.6	11	Hazel	Indian	Singer
Martinez	Maria	1.85	5	Green	Argentinian	Bus Driver

The complex query Eyes = Blue AND Shoe Size = 8 would return the following:

Surname	Forename	Height	Shoe Size	Eyes	Nationality	Occupation
Bernard	Charles	1.75	8	Blue	French	Welder
Pearce	Madison	1.85	8	Blue	American	Musician

As both parts of the query have to be satisfied, only people with both blue eyes and a shoe size of 8 will be listed.

The complex query Eyes = Hazel OR Eyes = Green would return the following:

Surname	Forename	Height	Shoe Size	Eyes	Nationality	Occupation
Danshov	Aleksander	1.8	6	Hazel	Russian	Politician
Mallapati	Smriti	1.6	11	Hazel	Indian	Singer
Martinez	Maria	1.85	5	Green	Argentinian	Bus Driver

As any one part of the query can be satisfied, all people with either hazel or green eyes are listed.

The complex query Eyes = Brown OR Nationality = Russia would return the following:

Surname	Forename	Height	Shoe Size	Eyes	Nationality	Occupation
Ivanova	Sofia	1.65	8	Brown	Russian	Road sweeper
Joo	Haeun	1.35	9	Brown	South Korean	Firefighter
Goswami	Lamar	1.75	9	Brown	Indian	Shop assistant
Danshov	Aleksander	1.8	6	Hazel	Russian	Politician

Aleksander Danshov does not have brown eyes, but he is Russian and so is included in the list. Similarly, Haeun Joo and Lamar Goswami are not Russian but because they have brown eyes they are included in the list.

The following nested query uses a combination of AND and OR and includes more than two criteria:

(Eyes = Blue OR Eyes = Brown) AND Height > 1.5

These are the results of the nested query:

Surname	Forename	Height	Shoe Size	Eyes	Nationality	Occupation
Greer	Wendy	1.85	7	Blue	British	Firefighter
Pearce	Madison	1.85	8	Blue	American	Musician
Ivanova	Sofia	1.65	8	Brown	Russian	Road sweeper

ACTIVITY 10.21

Open **10.02_Sales processing 2.mdb**, identify which query is most suitable and then create queries for the following:

1   All customers from Texas (TX) or Illinois (IL).

2   All customers who would like to receive marketing and live in Ohio (OH).

3   All products priced at least $50 with no units in stock, showing the Product Name and Supplier's Company Name.

4   All products over $30 supplied by companies in Germany.

5   All products under $30 supplied by companies in Denmark or Sweden.

6   A list of all products where the Units in Stock is less than or equal to the Reorder Level and the Units on Order is zero.

Nested queries

A query can also search an existing query. This can allow for very specific queries to be used on the data in the database. Using a query on a query is called a nested query.

In Figure 10.40, a query has been created to show all customers who live in California (CA). A nested query is then created on top of the California Query to find customers in the California Query who placed an order on 6/5/15.

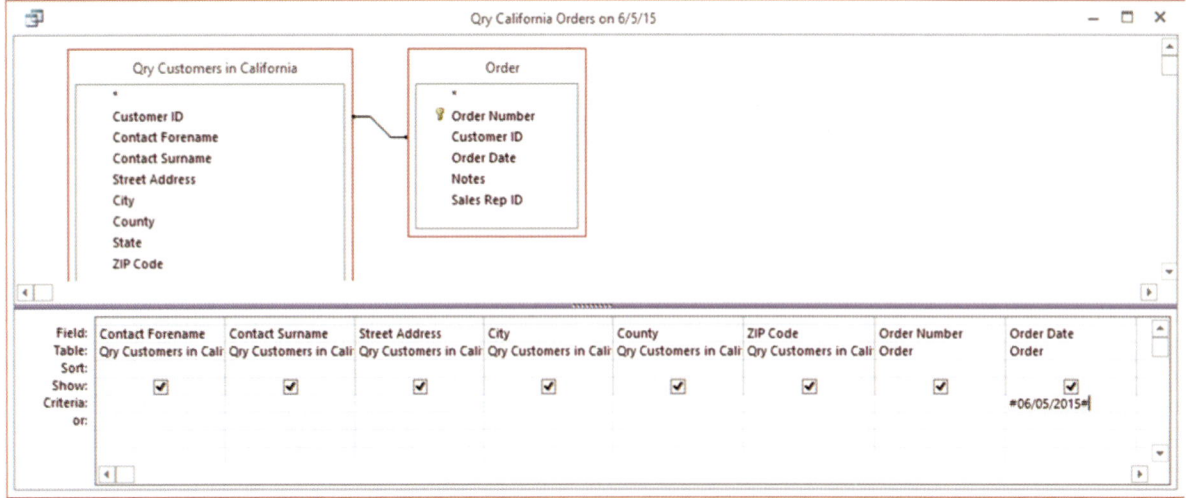

Figure 10.40: Nested query.

The new query is based on the California query and the Order table.

A nested query is the same as a query that has multiple criteria and uses the Boolean operator AND.

The benefit of using a nested query is that they are simpler to create. Building a complex query in one go can be confusing. Combining many search criteria in a query can make it hard to see whether the results are correct. Using nested queries with a single search criterion for each search is easier. It also means that each query can be used again for other purposes. Sometimes a nested query is necessary to create a cross-tab query that uses two or more tables.

> ### ACTIVITY 10.22
>
> Open **10.02_Sales processing 2.mdb**, identify which query is most suitable and then create a query based on the existing query 'Qry Products over $75' that will show those products in the Poultry category.

Using queries to find and remove duplicate records

Sometimes duplicate records are created within a table. They are often created accidentally. Duplicate records cause data redundancy and errors. A query can find duplicate records. Structured Query Language (SQL) can be used to create the query. Some RDBMS packages contain tools to automatically find duplicate records.

The table in Figure 10.41 contains duplicate entries for Marlene Atack and Wendy Greer.

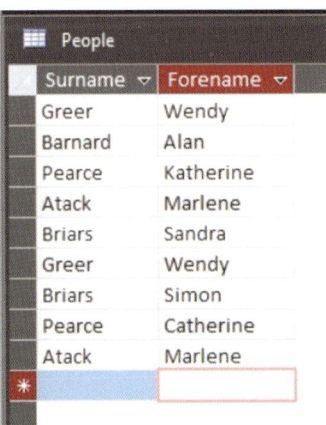

Figure 10.41: Duplicate records.

A Find duplicate queries wizard can be used to create a query to find the duplicate records (see Figure 10.42).

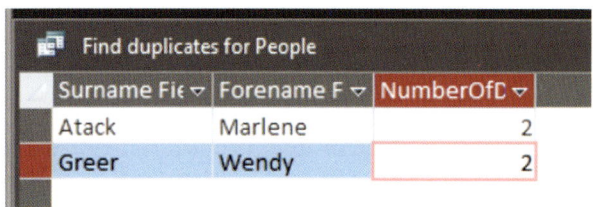

Figure 10.42: The query is called 'Find duplicates for People'.

We can find duplicate records and then delete them, as the data is repeated. SQL can also find and remove duplicates automatically.

Summarising data

A cross-tab query is used to summarise data. It can show information such as:

- the total number of records
- the sum of all values in a field
- averages
- other statistical data.

Figure 10.43 shows a cross-tab query that shows the total number of people in the database by nationality. It also breaks this down into how many people have which eye colour.

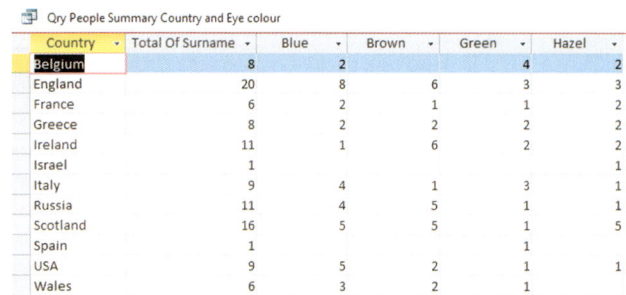

Figure 10.43: Cross-tab query.

This can also be seen in the configuration settings where the data is grouped by nationality and eyes as row and column headings and the surname is counted (see Figure 10.44).

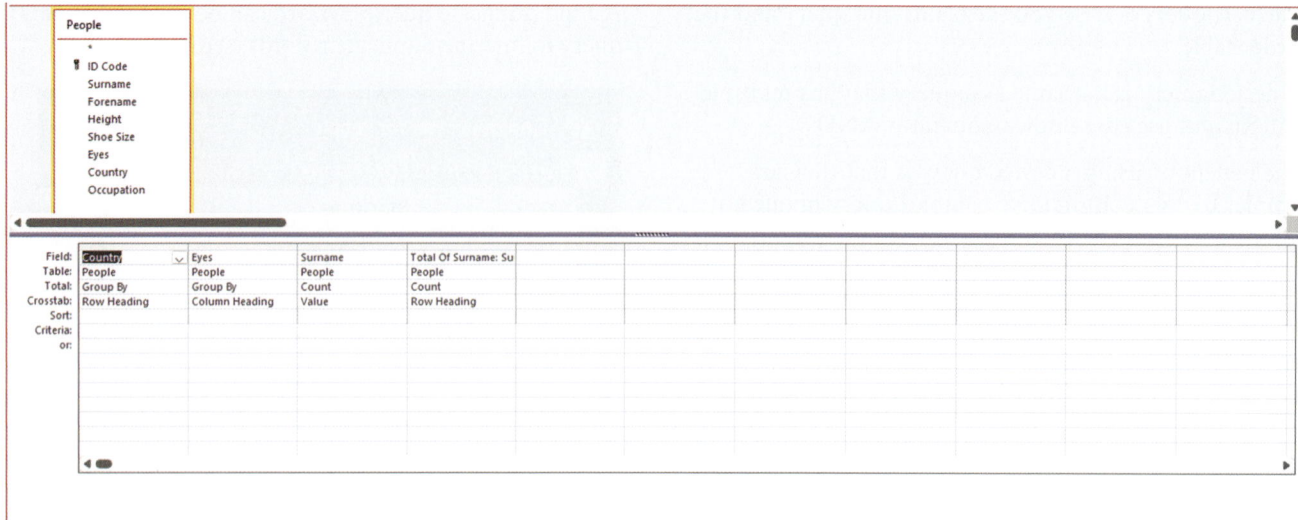

Figure 10.44: Cross-tab configuration.

You will notice that a new calculated field of 'Total of Surname' has been added that counts the total number of people. This is not essential unless the overall totals are required.

We can use nested queries to join tables and data together. This is called a cross-tab query. To create a cross-tab query we need to:

- create a query to join the tables together

- create a nested query to search the cross-tab query.

ACTIVITY 10.23

Open **10.10_People.mdb** and create cross-tab queries to show:

1   The number of people with eyes of each colour.

2   The number of people of each occupation (no need to have a column grouping).

3   The number of people of each occupation with each shoe size.

Open **10.02_Sales processing 2.mdb** and create cross-tab queries to show:

1   The number of suppliers in each country.

2   The number of customers in each state.

CONTINUED

3   The number of products in each category (the category names must be showing so you will need to join the Product and Category tables first).

4   The total price of each product in each category.

Selecting appropriate query types

When to use simple, complex, nested and summary queries

- Simple queries for a single search criterion.

- Complex queries when more than one search criterion is required.

- Nested queries in the following situations:

    - When an OR needs to be combined with an AND. This will avoid the problem of having to repeat the AND part of the query for each OR. It also avoids the problem of not getting the criteria in the correct order.

    - When there are lots of criteria. Nesting the queries makes it easier to understand.

- When we may want to reuse queries. Reusing a query saves the developer having to recreate some of the search criteria.

- Summary query in the following situations:

  - when we need multiple tables in a cross-tab query

  - when we summarise data from a cross-tab query.

- Cross-tab queries when data needs to be grouped by a field or type, for example to group a set of zoo keepers based on which animal species they are assigned to look after.

Pivot tables are used to summarise and present data. Pivot tables are usually interactive. This means that they have drop-down tabs that allow you to expand and shrink the data that you see. This allows to you see data at different levels of detail (see Chapter 8 to learn more about pivot tables).

When to use static and dynamic parameters

The queries seen so far use static **parameters**. Parameters are the values used within the search criteria. For example, we can program a query to search for people over 35 years old by using Age >= 35 as a criterion. Each time the query is run it will use Age >= 35 as the search parameter.

We use static parameters when we know that we will never need to change the search values, no matter how many times the query is used. For example, if you always search a membership table for 'Expired' in the membership details, then you could use a static parameter.

KEY WORD

parameter: data used within the criteria for a query

Dynamic parameters allow us to change the criteria we search for each time we run the query. This can be useful when the user needs to decide what those parameters might be. It also means we can reuse the query for different searches. For example, in Figure 10.45, a query has been created to show all customers in the (US) state that will be chosen by the user.

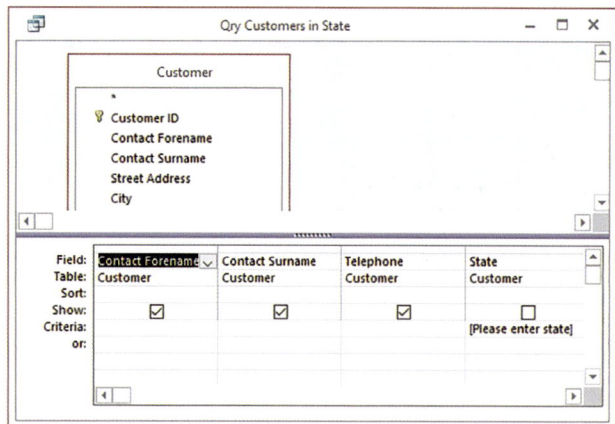

Figure 10.45: Dynamic query.

The criterion of <Please enter state> will be a prompt to the user to enter the state. Figure 10.46 shows what the prompt looks like when the query is run.

Figure 10.46: Parameter.

If the user enters AZ, then all the customers in Arizona will be listed (see Figure 10.47).

Contact Forename	Contact Surname	Telephone
Prince	Kauk	623-581-7435
Danny	Dales	602-225-9543
Lucas	Santellana	602-225-3469
Sabrina	Deppert	602-954-4343

Figure 10.47: Customers in Arizona.

The next time we run the query it will ask us for another state. If we enter TX then it will select the customers from Texas. We are using the same query but searching for different things!

Dynamic parameters can be used with ranges (<, >, <=, >=) and Boolean operators (NOT, AND, OR).

They can also be used alongside static parameters within a complex query.

ACTIVITY 10.24

Open **10.02_Sales processing 2.mdb** and create queries for the following (identifying whether to use static or dynamic parameters):

1   All sales reps with a title of the user's choosing.

2   All products with a price below the user's choosing.

3   All products with a reorder amount above the user's choosing.

4   All products with more than 100 units in stock that have a unit price below the user's choosing.

5   All products with a category of the user's choosing that are also above a price of the user's choosing.

Dynamic parameters are used when the search value changes each time the query is run. For example, if you wanted a query that would enable you to search for a specific product code. You may have many hundreds of item codes. You will search for different ones each time. The product code therefore is different each time. In this case, we use a dynamic query. We set the criterion to Product Code = <Please enter product code>.

Performing calculations with arithmetic operations and numeric/logical functions

Calculations can be performed on fields. Calculations can be created in forms, reports and queries. In a form, a text box is added to the form which includes the calculation (see Figure 10.48). The calculation must start with the equals (=) sign. This is the same as using a spreadsheet. Calculations use arithmetic and numerical/logical functions.

Figure 10.48: Databases can carry out calculations on data so the user will not need to do the calculations manually.

In the Order Form in Figure 10.49, the Total Price for each order line has been calculated by multiplying the Quantity by the Unit Price. The Order Total has been calculated by adding up all the Quantities multiplied by their corresponding Unit Prices.

The calculation for Total Price is = <Quantity> * <Unit Price>

The calculation for Order Total is = SUM (<Quantity> * <Unit Price>)

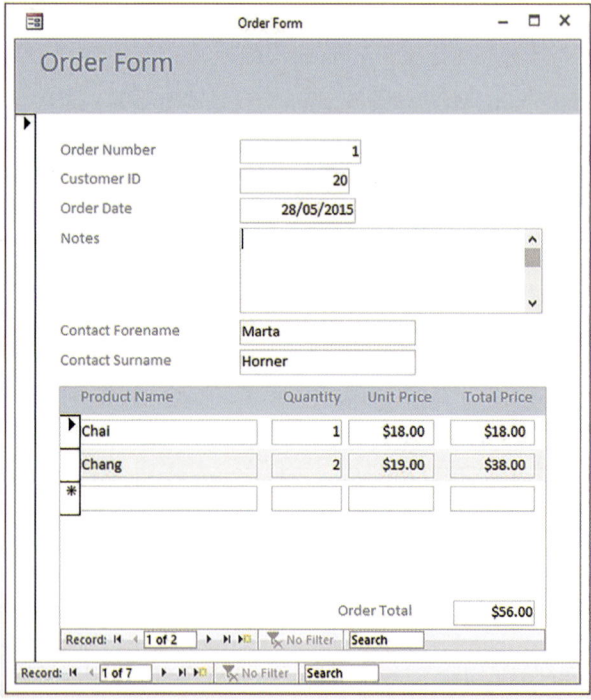

Figure 10.49: Order form.

Some database management systems (such as Microsoft Access) that calculate fields such as Total Price cannot be used in a SUM function. Therefore, the SUM has to use the full calculation rather than simply referring to =SUM(<Total Price>).

Calculations within reports are carried out in the same way as within forms. Within a query, the calculation needs to be defined by giving it a name and then identifying what the calculation will be.

In Figure 10.50, a query has been created to calculate how many products are left to sell before more need to be reordered.

The calculation subtracts the Units in Stock from the Reorder Level. To remove any products that are already below their Reorder Level, a criterion has been added that the total must be greater than zero. Here is an extract of the result of the query:

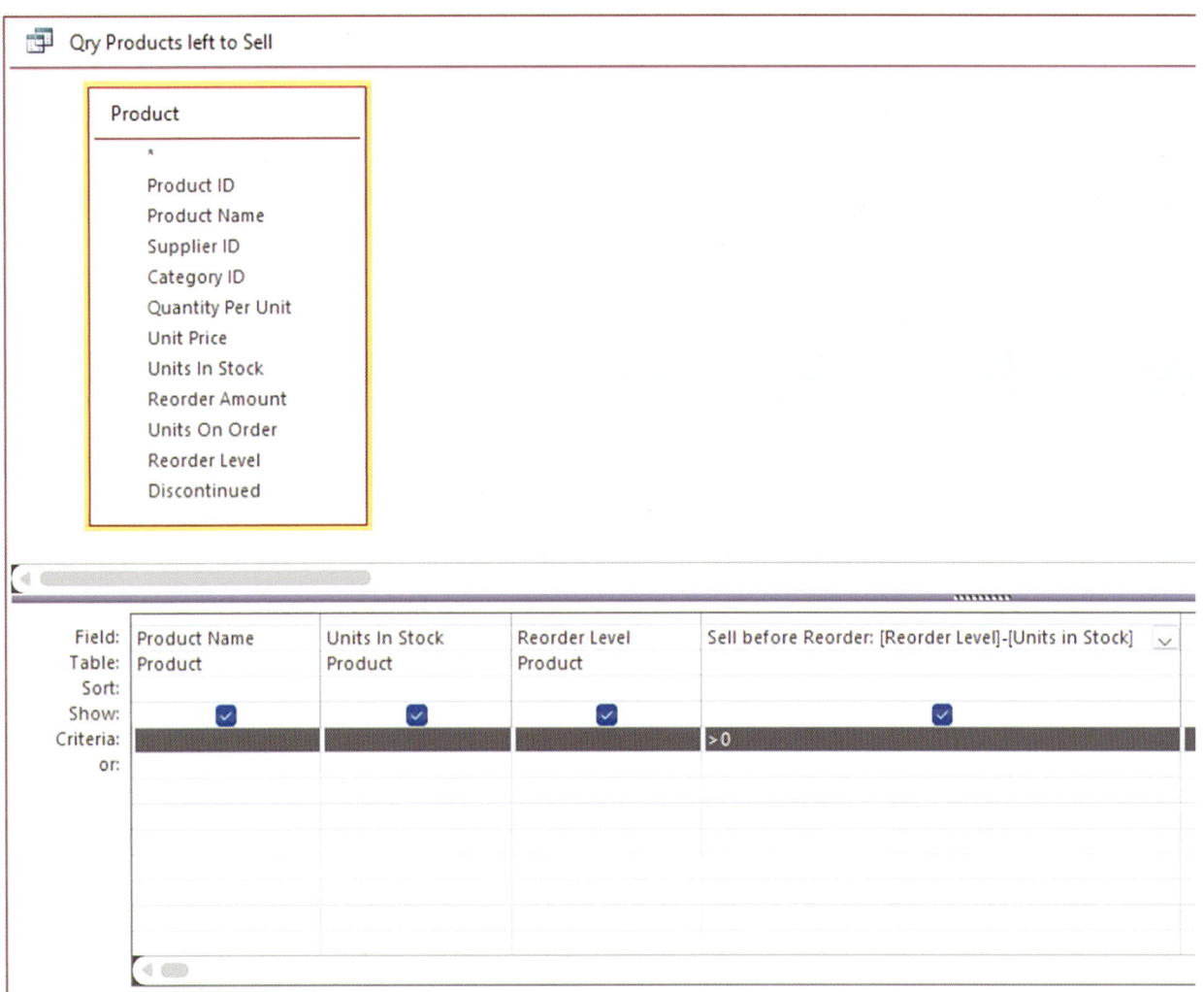

Figure 10.50: Query calculation.

Product Name	Units In Stock	Reorder Level	Sell before Reorder
Chang	17	25	8
Aniseed Syrup	13	25	12
Queso Cabrales	22	30	8
Sir Rodney's Scones	3	5	2

Surname	Forename	Eyes	Height
Saltings	Damien	Brown	1.85
Fontana	Giuseppe	Brown	1.95
Himura	Yuki	Green	1.75
Martinez	Maria	Green	1.85
Brown	Joseph	Green	1.9
Danshov	Aleksander	Hazel	1.8
Banton	Cedric	Hazel	1.85
Hammer	Daniel	Hazel	1.9

Table 10.8: Sorting data.

ACTIVITY 10.25

Open **10.02_Sales processing 2.mdb** and create a query to calculate the new Units In Stock when the Units On Order are added to the current Units In Stock.

Calculated controls and calculated fields

A calculated control and calculated field are both similar but are used in different places. A calculated control and calculated field both use a formula to create new data. They use the '=' symbol to show that a calculation is taking place. Both a calculated control and a calculated field use data in other locations to create this new data.

However, a calculated control is the name used when creating a Form or a Report in MS Access.

A calculated field is used when creating queries or tables.

Sorting data

Data can be sorted in ascending or descending order. We can sort data in a table, a query or a report. We can sort data using numbers, alphabetical characters, dates or times.

We can sort data using more than one field at a time. We often do this when sorting people's names. First, we sort by surname. However, many people may have the same surname. They may have different first names. So, we can set the forename as the second sort order.

The data in Table 10.8 is sorted in order of colour of eyes and then within each colour, it is sorted by height:

Surname	Forename	Eyes	Height
Bernard	Charles	Blue	1.75
Hughes	Carl	Blue	1.8
Greer	Wendy	Blue	1.85
Young	Rose	Blue	1.9
Cox	Arnold	Blue	1.9
Inan	Menekse	Blue	1.9
Hansen	Mathias	Blue	1.95
Xu	Huan	Brown	1.35
Li	Fen	Brown	1.64
Petrova	Alisa	Brown	1.7
Truong	Dinh	Brown	1.85

Designing and creating data entry forms

Data entry forms make entry of data into the database easier. Forms can also view existing data.

A data entry form must be designed carefully. You must consider who will use it and how to make sure it captures the data you need. It is important to make the form easy to use. The following techniques will help you to do this.

Font styles and sizes

Fonts should be plain and easy to read. A plain font is a Sans Serif font. Examples of Sans Serif are Arial and Calibri. It is important to use the same font for the whole form. This will make the form easier to read.

Font colour is also important. The colour of font should be dark where text/numbers appear on a light background, or light if they are on a dark background. Font size must be considered. Standard text should normally be between 10 and 12 point. Titles and subtitles can be in larger size. If you cannot fit all the text on a form, then you should try to reduce the amount of text instead of making the font size too small. Making the font size too small will make it very hard to read.

Spacing between fields

A well-spaced form helps the user to read and understand it. In Figure 10.51, the fields on the left are separated by space between each one. Each field has a box around it to separate it from other fields. The Inspections table is well spaced. Each field has enough space so that the user can read the data in each field.

Outlet Inspection Data Entry Screen

Outlet Code	01029
Outlet Name	Pizza Parlour
Floor	1
Location	B9
Telephone	0121392038
Opening Date	05/01/2011
Annual Fee	£140,000.00
Penalty Percentage	1.65
Penalty Fee	£2,310.00
Total Fee	£142,310.00

Renewal is due shortly – write to outlet

☐ Renewal Letter

Inspections

Inspection Name	Agency	Inspection Date	Pass	Penalty Incurred
▶ Health & Safety	H&S Executive	07/01/2011	☑	0
Health & Safety	H&S Executive	11/06/2011	☑	0
Food Hygiene	Trading Standards	28/02/2011	☐	35
Food Hygiene	Trading Standards	14/03/2011	☑	0
VAT	HM Revenue & Customs	19/08/2011	☐	20
*			▪	

Total Penalty Points: 55

Record: I◄ ◄ 1 of 5 ► ►I ►⊠ No Filter Search

Print Record | I◄ | ►I | Main Menu

Figure 10.51: Example of a well-spaced entry form.

Data flow

It is important to order each field in a sensible order. Figure 10.52 shows an example of a badly designed input form with poor data flows.

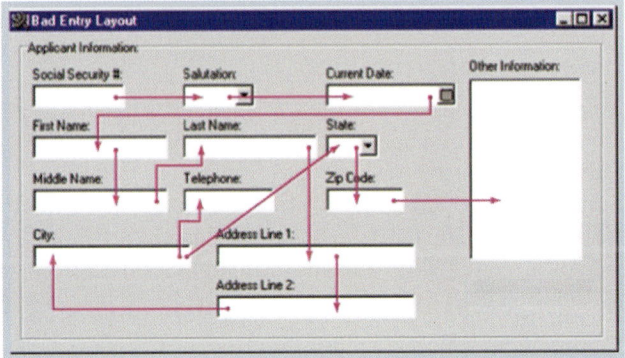

Figure 10.52: A poorly designed data capture form.

Spacing

There should be enough space between each character to enable the data to be viewed. Too much spacing means that the user will struggle to read the data because it is very spread out. Too little spacing means that the characters will overlap and it becomes hard to read. If single words have been used for field names (e.g. OutletCode), then the labels for the fields should include appropriate spacing (e.g. Outlet Code).

It is also important that any objects on the form are spaced appropriately. The width of the object and height of the object must allow the data to be entered and viewed clearly. For example, a box that contains 250 words must be wide enough to show all text that has been entered.

Objects and text must not overlap, otherwise it can be hard to read the form and understand what data is required to be entered in each box or space.

Use of white space

White space refers to the gaps on the form and the space between fields, labels and tables. A blank sheet of A4 has 100% white space as there is nothing on it! White space separates data and helps to make it easy to read and navigate. In Figure 10.51, you can see that there is white space used between the left- and right-hand sides, between field names and the data and between buttons.

> **TIP**
>
> Having white space between elements such as buttons may prevent the user from accidentally clicking on the wrong thing.

Form controls

Form controls allow users to enter, edit or display data when creating a Form. There are many different types of Form control.

- Navigation buttons allow the user to browse through records. Buttons allow a user to choose the next record, previous record, first record or last record in a table. Navigation buttons are shown in Figure 10.53.

Figure 10.53: Navigation buttons.

- Radio (option) buttons allow users to select a single option from a range of choices (see Figure 10.54). For example, when printing a document, print options may be available regarding how much of the document to print, such as all of the document, a range of pages or selected records (or pages). Only one of the radio (option) buttons can be chosen at a time.

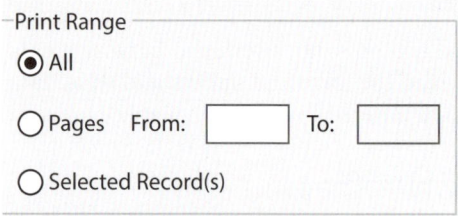

Figure 10.54: Radio buttons.

- Check (tick) boxes can be used to select multiple options. Check boxes can be true (ticked) or false (not ticked). Check boxes are used for Boolean data types. In Figure 10.51, a tick box has been used for whether a renewal letter has been sent. Check boxes are also used to identify whether inspections are passed or not.

- Drop-down menus allow users to select from a set of options. They are similar to Radio buttons. This is because both drop-down menus and radio buttons only allow one option to be selected. Drop-down menus take less space than radio buttons, but you cannot see all the options clearly. Radio buttons take more space because all the options can be seen. In Figure 10.53 you can see that each inspection can be selected from a drop-down menu. This means that the user is only able to select from the list. This also stops a user making spelling mistakes or entering inspections that do not exist. Both drop-down lists and radio buttons help maintain referential integrity.

Highlighting key fields

It may be helpful to highlight key fields. You could use a different colour for the background, or make the text bold. Figure 10.51 shows the Outlet Code in bold. There are no key fields displayed for the inspections or agencies.

Linked subforms

You can create a form inside a form. This is like nesting a query. A form inside a form is called a subform. Subforms are used to show data from related tables. Subforms are often used to show data from one-to-many relationships. The main form shows data from the **one** side of a relationship. The subform includes data from the **many** side of a relationship.

Figure 10.52 includes a subform showing the inspections that have taken place at each outlet.
There are many inspections to one outlet.

ACTIVITY 10.26

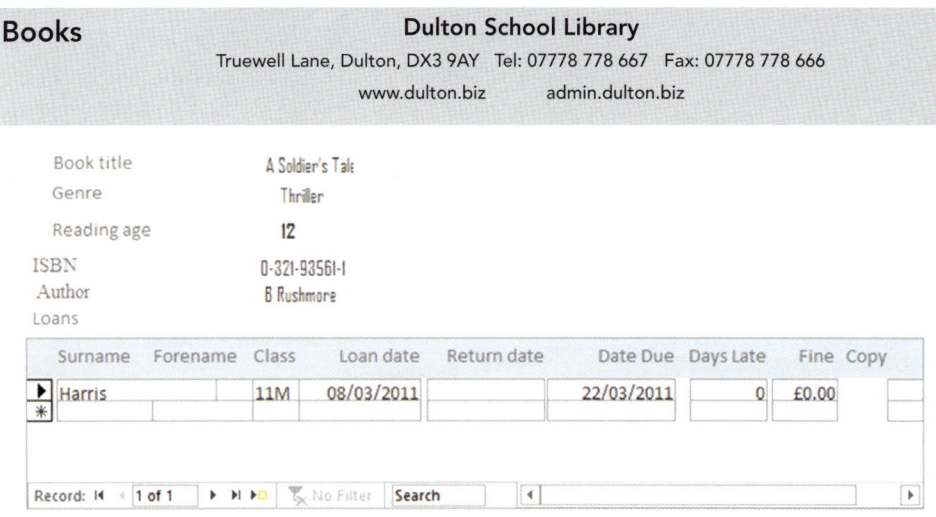

Figure 10.55: Data entry form.

1 a Evaluate the data entry form shown in Figure 10.55 from **10.12_Library.mdb**.

b Using the same database, create a data entry form for students.

c Using the same database, create a data entry form for books without the subform.

2 Using **10.11_Outlet monitoring.mdb**, recreate the data entry form named 'OutletInspectionDataEntryScreen'. You will need to use data from all three tables.

3 a Using **10.07_Driving School.mdb**, create a data entry form for lessons which shows all the details of each lesson. You should:

- use an appropriate title
- group information appropriately
- use drop-down menus to select the instructor, learner and car
- create navigation buttons.

b Create a data entry form for learners which includes a subform showing the date and time of any lessons they have. You should:

- use an appropriate title
- create navigation buttons
- use radio buttons to select a learner's gender.

c Extend the subform to show the name of the instructor and the make and model of the vehicle that will be used for each lesson.

4 Using **10.12_Library.mdb**, create a data entry form for students that includes a subform to show which books they have on loan. Your subform will need to include the tables Loan, Copy and Book. The Copy table shows each copy of each book as there are multiple copies of some of the books. You should:

- use an appropriate title for the form and subtitle for the subform
- use a drop-down menu to select the copy of the book that is on loan
- create navigation buttons on the main form
- ensure all the necessary data on the subform is showing and any unnecessary data is deleted.

Designing, creating and editing a database report

Reports show data from a table or query. Reports are structured to make data easy to read. Reports should include a title that describes the data it shows. Reports should also include the headings for each field.

Reports can sort data. A report can include summary data. For example, a report may include the total number of records, an average value and a total value. A report groups records together. For example, a report could group books by their genre. A query cannot group data in this way. A report can show summary data for each group as well as for the whole report.

Figure 10.56 shows a report listing all the instructors for a driving school.

The report has been grouped by Job Title so Instructors are shown first followed by Senior Instructors. The report has also been filtered to only show

instructors who are willing to work weekends. Within each group, the data is sorted by surname and the total number of instructors in each group is shown along with the average charge for the group. The total number of instructors willing to work weekends is also shown together with their average charge.

Instructors

Job Title	Instructor						
Surname	**Forename**	**InstructorID**	**Date of Birth**	**Transmission**	**Charge**	**Max Hours**	**Weekends**
Riaz	Serena	11	12/08/1980	A	£17.00	6	☑
Rogers	Sally	13	14/08/1982	A	£16.00	3	☑
Saxby	Wendy	10	11/08/1979	A	£16.00	1	☑
Smith	Jack	5	06/07/1974	M	£17.00	2	☑
Uxpern	Jean	2	03/04/1971	M	£16.00	4	☑
Walters	Peggy	8	09/08/1977	M	£15.00	3	☑

Total number of instructors in group:	6
Average charge for group:	£16.17

Job Title	Senior Instructor						
Surname	**Forename**	**InstructorID**	**Date of Birth**	**Transmission**	**Charge**	**Max Hours**	**Weekends**
Dean	Ben	17	02/07/1968	A	£19.00	3	☑
Kaur	Sameena	15	01/05/1969	A	£18.00	2	☑
Senior	Jon	16	18/05/1971	M	£17.00	8	☑

Total number of instructors in group:	3
Average charge for group:	£18.00
Total number of instructors	9
Average charge	£16.78

Figure 10.56: Report showing instructors at a driving school.

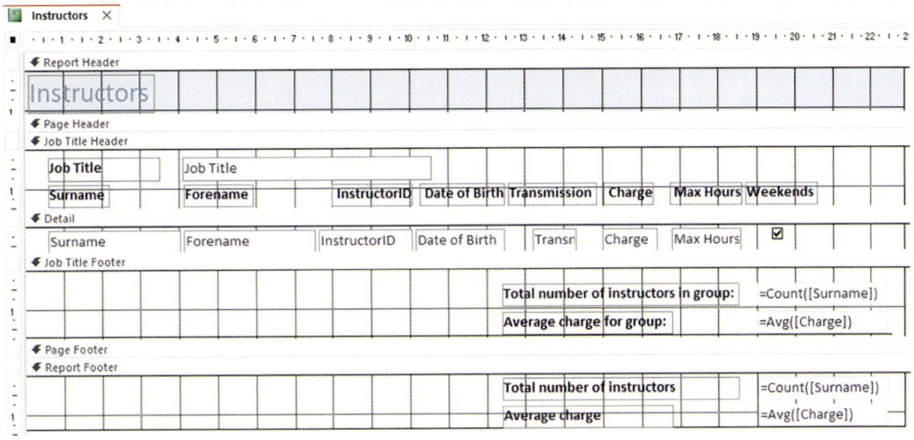

Figure 10.57: Report design.

Figure 10.57 shows how the report has been set up. The report header is the heading that appears at the top of the report. Page headers and footers can appear at the bottom of multi-page reports. The detail shows the data that will be listed. The Job Title header is the heading used for each group in this report. Data in the Job Title Footer appears at the bottom of each group in this report and shows the summary data. The report footer includes summary data for the whole report.

Reports output data to a screen or reports can be printed using a printer. Therefore, reports do not include form controls such as drop-down menus, navigation buttons, radio buttons or check boxes.

ACTIVITY 10.27

1   a   Using **10.10_People.mdb**, create a report to show all people in alphabetical order of surname.

    b   Create a query that shows all people from Italy. Create a report based on this query.

    c   Create a report to show all the people grouped by country. For each group, show the average height.

2   a   Using **10.12_Library.mdb**, create a report to show all the books grouped by Genre.

CONTINUED

    b   Create a report to show all the books that have been loaned grouped by each student. You will need to include the following fields from multiple tables:

    •   Student.Surname

    •   Student.Forename

    •   Student.Class

    •   Loan.Loan date

    •   Loan.Return date

    •   Copy.Copy

    •   Book.Booktitle

Designing and creating a switchboard/menu

Menus help users to navigate a database. Menus will help users select what they want to see or do. For example, a menu may allow a user to select what form to use or which report they want to view. A switchboard or menu should include a title, clear instructions and buttons for navigation and selection options.

Microsoft Access can create a menu automatically. This menu is called a switchboard. A switchboard manager creates the menu with links to forms, reports and macros. The switchboard also has an option to exit the RDBMS. The switchboard is a form. A table of actions is created. The Form lists the possible actions held in the table. It is possible to have multiple switchboards. This means that you can create sub-menus and organise your navigation efficiently.

Figure 10.58 shows a switchboard manager. The switchboard manager is used to add items to the menu. This example shows the 'Open Order Form' button being added to the switchboard.

The switchboard items are automatically stored in a table, as shown in Figure 10.59.

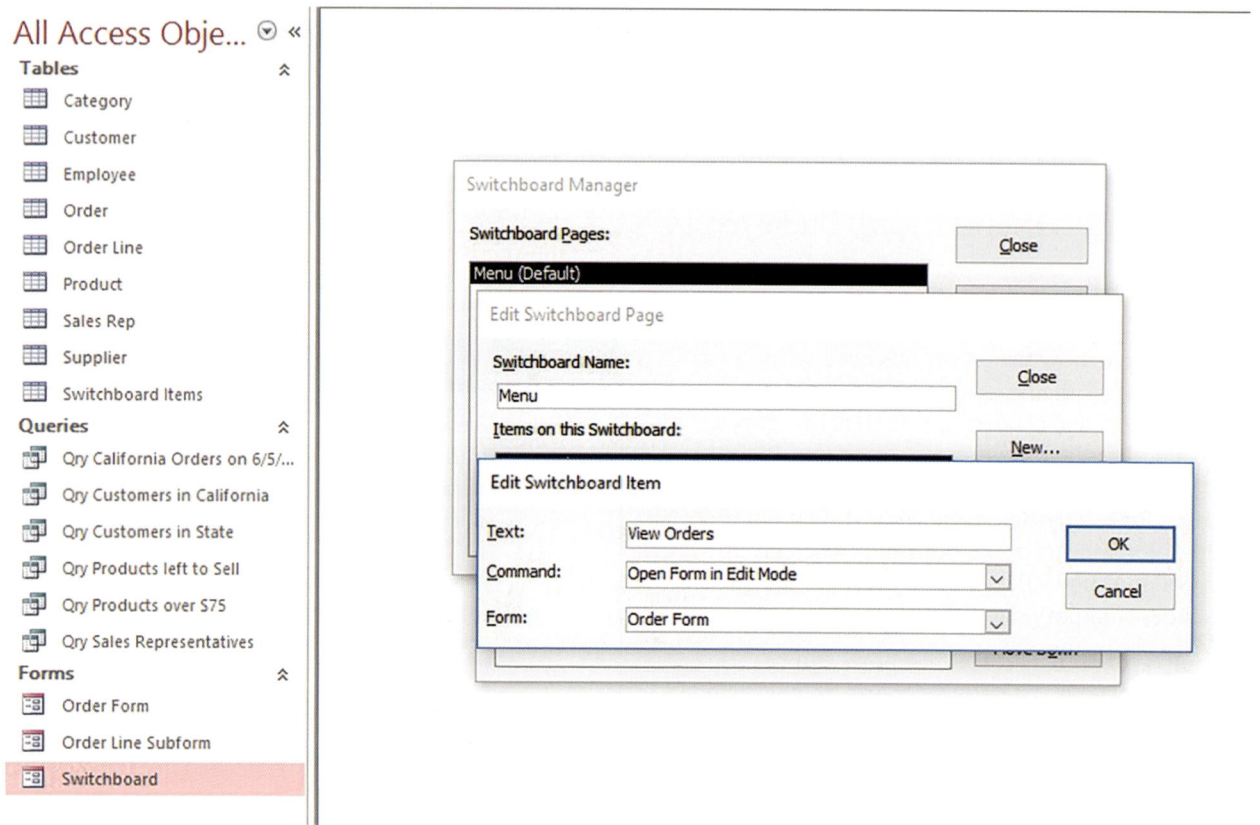

Figure 10.58: Switchboard manager.

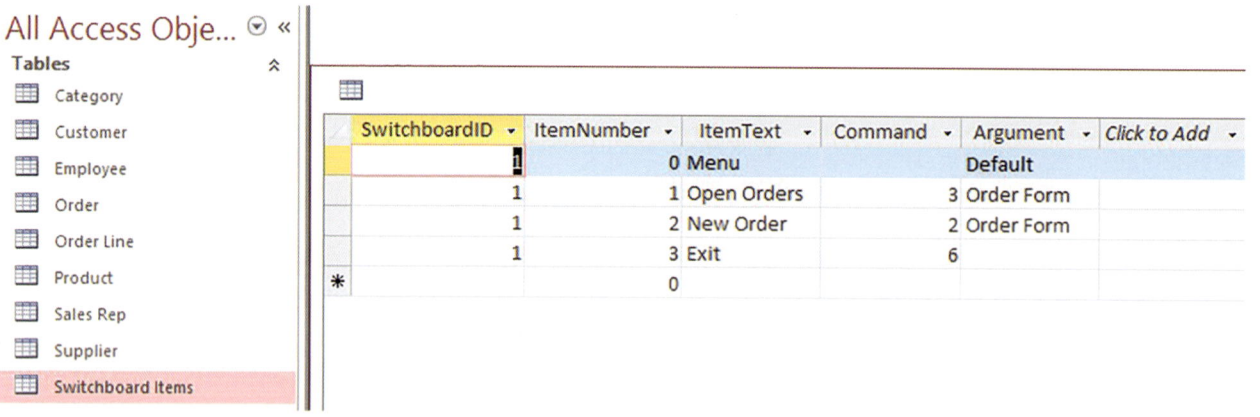

SwitchboardID	ItemNumber	ItemText	Command	Argument	Click to Add
1	0	Menu		Default	
1	1	Open Orders	3	Order Form	
1	2	New Order	2	Order Form	
1	3	Exit	6		
	0				

Figure 10.59: Switchboard table.

Figure 10.60 shows the switchboard form that is created automatically.

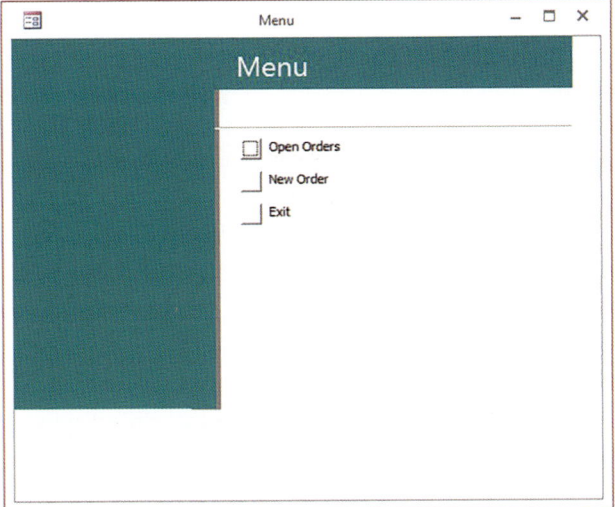

Figure 10.60: Switchboard form.

Exporting data

RDBMSs can export data to common formats and file types. This allows data to be shared. Sharing the data means that other users can read the data, even if they do not have **DBMS** software or do not know how to use it. Exporting data also allows it to be used in other programs. For example, an RDBMS can export data to a csv. Spreadsheet software can read the .csv file and display the data from the RDBMS.

Tables

Tables are exported as a delimited file in csv format. The data can contain things such as fixed length fields in text format. The rtf file format allows us to export entire tables. It is sensible to save the field names when saving to csv or text files.

Query

Data from queries can be exported in the same way as tables. Only the data that meets the criteria of the query will be exported.

Report

Reports include formatting, so the best method of export is to an rtf file, which will include all the original formatting. Data that is exported from a report to a text file will lose its formatting.

> **ACTIVITY 10.28**
>
> Open **10.01_Sales processing.mdb** and export the following:
>
> 1   The Customer table in csv format.
>
> 2   The UK Sales Reps query in fixed length fields text format.
>
> 3   The Categories of Products report in rtf format.

Questions

10   Describe the difference between a simple query and a complex query.

11   Give an example of when a dynamic parameter query might be used.

12   Identify the decisions involved in exporting data from a table.

13   What is the purpose of validation and verification?

14   Why is a nested query useful?

15   Explain why a dynamic parameter is useful to use in a query. Give one example of how this could be used.

16   Give three things you should consider when designing a form.

10.2 Normalisation to third normal form (3NF)

Normalisation is the process of structuring data within a database. The process starts with a flat file and finishes with a set of related tables. Normalisation ensures that each table is structured correctly and does not contain redundant data. Normalisation is completed in steps. Each step in the process is known as a normal form. Each normal form measures the extent to which the data has been normalised.

DID YOU KNOW?

There are six Normal Forms. However, many people stop normalisation after the 3rd Normal Form.

KEY WORD

normalisation (database): process of structuring data in a database

---

When describing tables, the following conventions will be used:

TABLENAME

Primary Key

Attribute 1

Attribute 2

TABLENAME (**Primary Key**, Attribute 1, Attribute 2)

Table names will be in capitals, primary keys will be underlined, and all attributes will be listed below the table name or within brackets.

Characteristics of data

Unnormalised form

Data in unnnormalized form (UNF) is a flat file. Unnormalised data contains **non-atomic data**, repeating groups of data and may include redundant data.

KEY WORD

non-atomic data: data items contain more than one item of data, for example 'Ushma Patel' is non-atomic as it contains the forename and surname

---

Unnormalised data contains repeating groups of data. A repeating group of data is when fields are repeated for each record or records have more than one set of data for a group of fields.

Redundant data exists when data is repeated unnecessarily. Table 10.9 contains non-atomic data.

Product ID	Description	Price
327BLF	Brown, Fabric	$35
327BPM	Brown, PVC	$25
327CLF	Cream, Fabric	$35

Table 10.9: Non-atomic data.

The colour and material separate items of data within the description. This causes a problem when trying to sort data by a specific characteristic, such as colour, or when trying to search by a specific characteristic.

First normal form

Data in first normal form (1NF) must satisfy the following criteria:

- all fields contain atomic data

- there are no repeating groups of data

- there must be a unique key.

Table 10.10 contains fields that are repeated for each record.

Surname	Forename	Subject 1	Subject 2	Subject 3	Subject 4
Gupta	Sharad	IT	English	History	
Rushton	Emily	Politics	Literature	Philosophy	Physics
Yeo	Steven	Maths	Physics	German	

Table 10.10: Repeated fields.

Surname	Forename	Book	Date Out	Date Due
Gupta	Sharad	Database Concepts	12/5/23	12/6/23
		The Secret History	12/5/23	12/6/23
Rushton	Emily	A Brief History of Time	14/5/23	14/6/23
Yeo	Steven	German Verbs	26/11/23	3/1/24
		The origins of Mathematics	5/1/24	5/2/24
		Astrophysics Explained	5/1/24	5/2/24

Table 10.11: Several sets of data per group of fields.

The Subject field has been repeated. This can be a problem when trying to search for all students studying the same subject or when a student only studies one subject (leaving several blank) or when a student needs to study a fifth subject.

Table 10.11 contains more than one set of data for a group of fields.

Some students have borrowed more than one book and so the fields Book, Date Out and Date Due contain more than one set of data per record. This could also be classed as non-atomic data as there is more than one data item per field.

In this example, Table 10.12 contains redundant data.

Order ID	Order Date	Product	Quantity	Price
3857	12/9/23	Marzipan	1	$5.72
		Flour	2	$1.38
2320	15/10/23	Marzipan	3	$5.72
		Sugar	1	$3.12
		Eggs	6	$0.20

Table 10.12: Redundant data.

The price is dependent upon the product and therefore it is being repeated unnecessarily. If we know the product, we know the price.

UNPLUGGED ACTIVITY 10.29

Describe the characteristics of data in UNF using examples from Table 10.13 of driving lessons.

Learner	Lesson Date	Instructor ID	Instructor	Price
Muhammad	30/5/23	4	Marcus Brown	$60
Hannah	6/6/23	4	Marcus Brown	$60
Kayode	31/5/23	3	Clare Joyce	$50
Sienna	1/6/23	4	Marcus Brown	$60

Table 10.13: Driving lessons.

In the following example, the ORDER table contains details of products ordered by customers:

ORDER

Order Date

Customer ID

Customer Name

Customer Address

    Product Code

    Description

    Quantity

    Price

Indented fields are a repeating group for each order.

To be in 1NF, this table needs:

- a unique key (**Order Number**)
- atomic data (Customer Name and Customer Address need breaking down)
- no repeating groups of data (products being ordered).

The ORDER table becomes:

ORDER (**Order Number**, Order Date, Customer ID, Customer Forename, Customer Surname, Customer Address 1, Customer Address 2, Customer Address 3, Customer ZIP Code)

A new table for the order of products needs to be added, but it needs to retain information about which order each order of products belongs to:

ORDERLINE (**Order Number**, **Product Code**, Description, Quantity, Price)

Order Number is retained in the ORDERLINE table as a foreign key. However, it is not unique and so cannot be used as the primary key. However, a combination of Order Number and Product Code are unique and so these become a compound key.

UNPLUGGED ACTIVITY 10.30

Normalise Table 10.14 of driving lessons to 1NF: LESSON (Learner, Lesson Date, Instructor ID, Instructor, Price)

Learner	Lesson Date	Instructor ID	Instructor	Price
Muhammad	30/5/23	4	Marcus Brown	$60
Hannah	6/6/23	4	Marcus Brown	$60
Kayode	31/5/23	3	Clare Joyce	$50
Sienna	1/6/23	4	Marcus Brown	$60

Table 10.14: Driving lessons.

Second normal form

Data in second normal form (2NF) has no partial key dependencies. This means that non-key fields cannot be dependent on part of a primary key. This can only apply to tables with compound keys.

When identifying partial key dependencies, some fields will only depend on a part of the compound key. We can solve this issue by making a new table. The part of the compound key becomes the primary key in that table.

The data that was dependent on the compound key is moved into the new table.

The orders database from the previous example now contains two tables:

ORDER (**Order Number**, Order Date, Customer ID, Customer Forename, Customer Surname, Customer Address 1, Customer Address 2, Customer Address 3, Customer ZIP Code)

ORDERLINE (**Order Number**, **Product Code**, Description, Quantity, Price)

Only the ORDERLINE table contains partial keys. Description and Price are dependent on Product Code, which is part of the compound primary key. Therefore, a new table needs to be created for products:

PRODUCT (**Product Code**, Description, Price)

The information stored in the ORDERLINE table that is not part of the PRODUCT table needs to be retained:

ORDERLINE (**Order Number**, **Product Code**, Quantity)

The Product Code field is retained in the ORDERLINE table as a foreign key because it is still necessary to know which products were ordered.

UNPLUGGED ACTIVITY 10.31

Normalise the table of ingredients below to 2NF:
RECIPE-INGREDIENT (**Recipe ID**, **Ingredient ID**, Ingredient Name, Measure, Quantity)

Recipe ID	Ingredient ID	Ingredient Name	Measure	Quantity
1	B	Flour	Gram	200
1	D	Eggs	Number	2
1	K	Water	Tablespoon	2
2	C	Milk	Millilitre	250
2	B	Flour	Gram	100

Third normal form

Data in third normal form (3NF) cannot contain non-key dependencies. This means all fields should be dependent on the primary key. Therefore, primary keys and compound primary keys can be ignored. All other fields should be examined to see whether they are dependent on any other non-key field.

The orders database from the previous example now contains three tables:

ORDER (**Order Number**, Order Date, Customer ID, Customer Forename, Customer Surname, Customer Address 1, Customer Address 2, Customer Address 3, Customer ZIP Code)

PRODUCT (**Product Code**, Description, Price)

ORDERLINE (**Order Number**, **Product Code**, Quantity)

In the ORDER table, all the customer data is dependent on the Customer ID, which is a non-key field. A new table needs to be created called CUSTOMER:

CUSTOMER (Customer ID, Forename, Surname, Address 1, Address 2, Address 3, ZIP Code)

The ORDER table now becomes:

ORDER (**Order Number**, Order Date, Customer ID)

Customer ID is retained in the ORDER table as a foreign key so it is still known which customer placed the order.

UNPLUGGED ACTIVITY 10.32

1 Normalise the table of students below to 3NF: STUDENT (**Student ID**, Forename, Surname, Year, Teacher Title, Teacher Surname).

Student ID	Forename	Surname	Year	Teacher Title	Teacher Surname
1	Hayley	Barrow	12	Dr	Suneal
2	Hajra	Hassan	10	Professor	Spicer
3	Otis	Lang	12	Dr	Suneal

2 This PROJECT table contains details of the employees working on projects for clients. It is currently in UNF. Normalise the data to 3NF.

PROJECT   End Date   Contact Name   Employee Hours
Description   Client ID   Employee ID
Start Date   Company   Employee Name

Here is an example of the data:

Description	Start Date	End Date	Client ID	Company	Contact Name	Employee ID	Employee Name	Employee Hours
Barton	28/2/23	31/12/24	512	Barton	Jerry	PK32	Tyrell Johnson	1052
Towers				Estates	Dean	JH45	Janice Spring	575
Haywoo	31/3/23	15/6/24	987	Haywood	Peter	JH45	Janice Spring	153
Manor				Estates	Gates	YR27	Amir Akhtar	372

Advantages and disadvantages of normalisation of data

The advantages and disadvantages of normalisation are shown in Table 10.15.

Advantages	Disadvantages
Normalisation removes duplicate data from a database. This reduces the size of the database.	Multi-table lookups and queries may take longer to execute using multiple-table databases.
Normalisation removes the potential for errors and inconsistencies.	It can be difficult to understand the data stored in tables. Foreign keys may mean very little to the user.
A normalised database is more efficient.	Nested queries are needed to look up data from linked tables. These queries can be quite complex and require expertise from the user.
Normalised databases allow searches using indexed fields.	Expertise is needed to build the database properly and to understand the process of normalisation.
Data can be linked across related tables.	

Advantages	Disadvantages
Maintenance tasks can be completed more quickly because tables do not contain redundant data.	
The database becomes more flexible. Adding new fields and tables becomes easier.	
Having smaller tables allows forms and reports to fit onto one screen or one page more easily.	
Security permissions can be applied to individual tables.	

Table 10.15: The advantages and disadvantages of normalisation.

Questions

17 Identify two characteristics of data in 1NF.

18 Describe one characteristic of data in 3NF.

19 Explain two advantages of normalisation.

> ### REFLECTION
>
> What did you do to learn the steps of normalisation? How easy is it to remember the different steps? How can you refine your learning to make it easier to remember each step?

10.3 Data dictionary

A **data dictionary** is a document or file that describes the structure of the data held within the database. It is known as metadata (information), which means 'data about data'. It is a tool that is used by database developers and administrators.

> ### KEY WORD
>
> **data dictionary:** metadata (information) about the database

Components of a data dictionary

A data dictionary consists of the following components or items:

- data about fields:
  - field names to identify each field
  - data types, such as text, integer, date/time
  - field size, such as the length of a text field or the maximum value of a numeric field
  - format of fields
  - default values which are values a field is set to be initially when a new record is created
  - primary keys, compound keys, composite keys and foreign keys
  - indexed fields that improve search times
  - validation rules that restrict data entry for that field.

- data about tables:
  - the primary key of the table
  - what sort order to use when displaying data
  - relationships to other tables
  - total number of records
  - validation rules that apply based on multiple fields within the table
  - permissions and security as to which users can access the table.

Table 10.16 is part of a data dictionary for fields in a product table and Table 10.17 shows a product table.

Attribute	Data Type	Field Size	Format
Product Code	Alphanumeric	6	XX99XX
Description	Alphanumeric	20	
Category Code	Integer	4	9999
Price	Decimal	3.2	$999.99

Table 10.16: Data dictionary.

Attribute	Validation Type	Rule	Error Message
Product Code	Format	Must be in the format of two letters, two numbers, two letters	Please enter a code that is two letters, two numbers, two letters
Description	Presence	Must be present	Please enter a description
Category Code	Look up in List	Must exist in Category Code in Category table	Please enter a category code that exists in the category list
Price	Range	Between 0.01 and 999.99	Please enter a price between 0.01 and 999.99

Table 10.17: Product table.

UNPLUGGED ACTIVITY 10.33

Use the knowledge you have on Data Types, Field Sizes and Formats to complete the table.

Attribute	Data Type	Field Size	Format
Employee ID			
Surname			
Forename			
Date of Birth			
Telephone			
Email			
Year Joined Company			
Pension Scheme?			

Discuss your answers with a classmate. Did you have similar answers? Discuss why you may have different answers. Now work together to create a table that you both agree is accurate.

Data types

It's important to know which data type to use so that we store the data correctly and process it efficiently. We looked at some data types when we learned how to create databases earlier in this chapter. There are some other data types too.

Text/alphanumeric

There are different data types used to refer to text data. The data type for text may be called alphanumeric. Text data type can contain any letter, number or symbol.

Numeric and percentage

Numbers are stored in two main formats. Data types for numbers are integer or real.

Integers are whole numbers. These can be negative or positive but cannot contain decimals.

Real numbers contain decimals. They can be positive or negative.

Numbers can be formatted as percentages or as currency. Currency values display a currency symbol. The currency symbol is not stored with the data but is shown when the data is displayed.

Percentage values are stored differently from other number values. A percentage is stored as a 'one hundredth' (1/100) of the value. For example, 25% is stored as 0.25 (25/100). However, it is displayed as 25%.

Table 10.18 shows examples of the different number formats.

Integer	Real	Currency	Percentage
9	9.05	$9.05	0.09 (9%)
−6	−6.2	−$6.20	−0.06 (6%)
232	232.0	$232.00	2.32 (232%)
−238	−238.00	−$238	2.38 (238%)

Table 10.18: Examples of number formats.

ACTIVITY 10.34

1   Use a spreadsheet to enter the following numbers:

5

60

0.32

0.2

Now format the cells as percentages. What has happened to the data and why?

2   Try typing this telephone number into a spreadsheet (without using spaces) and see what happens: 00442085555555

Telephone numbers should be stored as text. Telephone numbers cannot be stored as a number. There are two reasons for this:

- Computers do not store the first zeros in numbers. For example, 001122 would be stored as 1122 as a number in a computer. Many international dialling codes start with 00 and then use a number for each country. For example, 00 91 is the international dialling code for India and 00 51 is the international dialling code for Peru. Therefore, a computer would only store these as 91 and 51 if using a numerical data type.

- Some telephone numbers use formatting to help read the number more clearly. Some may use special characters such as '+' to show the international dialling code. For example, to call the UK from another country you need to dial '00 44'. This is often shown as '+44'. Notice that phone numbers also use spaces or dashes to show the number more clearly. For example, in the US, the '-' sign is used, for example 1-800-000-0000.

Therefore, to store telephone numbers we usually use Text fields.

Date/time

The date/time data type stores dates and times. The date/time data type will be able to work with days, months, years, hours, minutes and seconds. It will also enable dates and times to be sorted into a logical order.

Dates can be formatted in a variety of ways such as:

18/7/2023

18-07-23

18 July 2023

18th July 2023

July 18, 2023

However, they are always stored in the same way: day 18, month 7, year 2023. The symbols (such as th, / and -) are not stored, they are simply displayed.

Time can also be formatted in a variety of ways:

12:55 p.m.

03:05 hrs (five minutes past three in the morning)

Dates and times can also be combined to give a specific time on a specific date, for example:

12:55 18-07-23

Remember that days, months and years can be stored in a different order in different countries. It is important to specify this order when setting up a data type. For example, in the USA, the format is month, day, year (e.g. 7/18/2023), whereas in much of the rest of the world, the format is day, month, year (e.g. 18/7/2023). This can become a problem when the day part is 12 or less. What date is 5/10/2020? Is it 5 October or 10 May?

Boolean/logical

Boolean or logical data types only store two values. These two values are TRUE and FALSE. They are often shown as YES and NO. Microsoft Access refers to this data type as Yes/No.

Data can only be Boolean if the two possible answers are TRUE/FALSE or YES/NO. Just because there are two possible answers for the data does not mean that it is a Boolean.

Creating a data dictionary and selecting appropriate data types

You will need to select appropriate data types when creating spreadsheets and databases. Table 10.19 includes some guidelines to help you.

Rule	Data type
The data contains whole numbers only	Integer
The data contains a decimal number	Real
The data starts with a zero (e.g. telephone number)	Text
The data includes letters, symbols or spaces	Text
The data is a date, a time or both	Date/Time
The only values for the data are TRUE/FALSE or YES/NO	Boolean/Logical

Table 10.19: Data type rules.

A data dictionary is a table that shows all the fields in a database, and the data types and limits/validation that each field requires. It acts as a reference guide. This means that people can check the correct data type and limits are applied to each field as the database is created.

A data dictionary will help a company use consistent data types and limits for each field in a database.

For example, it may show that a field called 'Forename' is a text field that is 40 characters long.

Questions

20 Identify and describe three components of a data dictionary.

21 Select the most appropriate data type for the following information stored about flights:

Flight number (e.g. BA372)

Departure date

Departure time

Airport code (e.g. ACF)

Max number of passengers

Type (e.g. scheduled or charter)

Arrived?

22 Give reasons for the use of the text data type for storing a mobile phone number.

10.4 File and data management

File types

Data is saved in a file. Different software applications save data in different file formats. For example, music data may be stored in an .mp3 file, whereas graphics software may store data about pixels in a .jpg format.

Each file usually has:

- a header, which has metadata (data about the file)
- the main data
- an end-of-file marker.

File types are identified by their extension. For example, Students.txt has an extension of .txt which identifies it as a text file.

Table 10.20 gives some examples of file types.

Extension	File type	Purpose
.txt	Text	Stores plain text without any formatting. It is useful for transferring data between applications, but any formatting is lost.
.csv	Comma separated values	Stores structured data as plain text in rows with each column separated by commas. It is useful for transferring data between databases and spreadsheets or other applications that require data in a structured format.
.rtf	Rich text format	Stores text-based documents and includes the formatting (rich text). It is used to transfer data between different word processing or other text-based applications.
.docx	Microsoft Word XML	Stores Microsoft's word processing documents in open XML format by saving all objects separately within a compressed file.
.pdf	Portable Document Format	Used to share read-only documents in a common format that can be accessed by any PDF reader software. It is commonly used for storing documents on the web as its contents can be indexed by search engines.
.odt	OpenDocument Text	An open-source file type for word processor documents that is used by open-source word processors and is not tied to one manufacturer.
.ods	OpenDocument Spreadsheet	An open-source file type for spreadsheets that is used by open-source spreadsheet software and is not tied to one manufacturer.
.odp	OpenDocument Presentation	An open-source file type for presentations that is used by open-source presentation software and is not tied to one manufacturer.
.html	Hypertext Markup Language	Stores web pages that can be opened by any web browser.
.xml	Extensible Markup Language	A data file that uses markup language to define objects and their attributes. They are used to transfer data between applications and can be read by a simple text editor.
.avi	Audio Video Interleave (video file)	Microsoft's method of storing video files with very little compression. File sizes are very big but no data is lost.
.mp4	Moving Pictures Experts Group (MPEG) Layer-4 (video file)	Audio and video are compressed and videos can be shared across the internet.
.wav	Waveform Audio File Format	Stores audio files as waveform data and enables different sampling rates and bit rates. This is the standard format for audio CDs but does not include compression so files are large.
.mp3	MPEG Layer-3 audio compression	Stores audio files in a compressed format approximately 10% the size of .wav files. Enables audio files to be shared across the internet.
.bmp	Bitmap image	Stores images as uncompressed raster images, storing each pixel individually. They are large files but can be accessed by any software.
.jpg	Joint Photographic Experts Group (compressed image)	Stores images as compressed raster images. It is used by most digital cameras and is a common format for web graphics but its use of lossy compression can mean some quality is lost.
.png	Portable Network Graphic	Stores images as compressed raster images and can include background transparency making it useful when images are required on different colour backgrounds.

Extension	File type	Purpose
.svg	Scalable Vector Graphics	Stores images as two-dimensional (2D) vector graphics. It is a standard format for using vector graphics on the web.
.exe	Executable program file	Stores program object code which enables the program to be executed by the computer.

Table 10.20: Examples of file types.

File formats

Proprietary file formats

Proprietary (owned by someone) file formats are developed by software manufacturers for use with their software, for example .docx is the file format of Microsoft and is used for MS Word documents. Proprietary file formats allow software manufacturers to develop unique features in their software. Proprietary file types allow software to store data in the most suitable way for that program or feature. This allows the software developers to provide new features that otherwise would not be available to include. However, it is rare that proprietary file formats will open using other manufacturers' software. This means that you can only use the program you used to open them. This makes sharing files more difficult.

Table 10.21 gives some examples of proprietary file formats.

Extension	Software / file type	Manufacturer
.docx	Word processor	Microsoft Word
.wpd	Word processor	Corel Word Perfect
.msg	Email message	Microsoft Outlook
.ra	Audio/video streaming	Real Networks
.MOV	Movie	Apple
.psd	Graphics	Adobe Photoshop
.ai	Graphics	Adobe Illustrator
.accdb	Database	Microsoft Access

Table 10.21: Examples of proprietary file formats.

Open-source file formats

Open-source file formats are file types designed for use by any proprietary software or open-source software. Open-source file formats are free from copyright, patents and trademarks, and their structure is known publicly. Open-source file formats are maintained by an international standards organisation or a public interest group. The main advantage of open-source file formats is that the files can be shared between users of different software. However, open-source file formats can slow the development of new features in open-source software because new features will require the file format standard to be updated.

Table 10.22 gives some examples of open-source file formats.

File type	Type of data	Standards organisation
JPG	Compressed raster graphics	Developed by the Joint Photographic Experts Group (JPEG) and standardised by the International Organization for Standardization (ISO)
PNG	Compressed raster graphics with transparency support	ISO
ePub	E-book	International Digital Publishing Forum
XML	Extensible Markup Language	World Wide Web Consortium (W3C)
MPEG	Compressed video	Developed by the Moving Picture Experts Group (MPEG) and standardised by the ISO

Table 10.22: Examples of open-source formats.

Generic file formats

Some file formats enable data to be transferred between software. Data is exported from software into a generic file format and generic file formats can be imported into software. Generic file formats store essential data but do not include any formatting.

The two main generic file formats used with databases are csv and txt.

Using indexed sequential access

Sequential files store records in a database one after each other. The records are sorted into an order based on a field before they are stored. For example, data about customers might be sorted into surname order or customer ID order. This means that you can jump straight to surnames starting with 'S' if you are searching for a 'Saddiq'. Sequential files are particularly useful when batch processing data (see Figure 10.61). For example, when gas bills are being generated, the customer

file will be processed in order of customer ID. This then means the transaction files will also be processed in order of customer ID.

Figure 10.61: Magnetic tape drives use sequential file storage methods.

Table 10.23 shows an example of part of a master customer file showing the customers, the date the current meter reading was taken, the previous meter reading (amount of gas used) and the current meter reading.

Customer ID	Surname	Date of reading	Previous reading	Current reading
10	Black	12/1/23	32721	34872
11	Brown	15/12/22	02717	03281
12	White	8/1/23	47270	48572
13	Green	8/1/23	21827	23593

Table 10.23: Master customer file.

Table 10.24 is an example of part of a transaction file that will be processed to update the master customer file with new gas meter readings.

Customer ID	Date of reading	Meter reading
11	12/3/23	03692
13	12/3/23	23997

Table 10.24: Part of a transaction file.

Table 10.25 shows what the master customer file will look like once the transaction file has been processed.

Customer ID	Surname	Date of reading	Previous reading	Current reading
10	Black	12/1/23	32721	34872
11	Brown	12/3/23	03281	03692
12	White	8/1/23	47270	48572
13	Green	12/3/23	23593	23997

Table 10.25: The master customer file after the transaction file has been processed.

When reading sequential files, you must read the whole file step by step from the beginning because there is no way of knowing where each record is stored.

Indexed sequential files are similar to sequential files, but the file also has an index linked to the file. Each index is based on the field used to sort the file. A field with an index is known as a secondary key. The index file stores each secondary key value and an address location on the storage device (e.g. tape or disk). The index points to the first record in that sequence order.

To find a record the index is checked. Then the file can be read from the index until the record is found.

Indexed sequential file access reduces the amount of serial access when compared to simple sequential file access. However, it still works sequentially.

Both indexed sequential and sequential file access are slow. It is also a challenge to maintain files in sequential order when a new record is added, or a record is deleted.

In the example in Table 10.26, if Employee ID is the secondary key, then an index will exist with Employee ID as one column and the storage address as the other column. Rather than storing every single Employee ID, the index may store every tenth Employee ID, for example.

Employee ID	Storage address
0001	A8FB2DC3
0011	9AEB08E3
0021	8C4DDDF5

Table 10.26: Index storage.

Using direct file access

Direct file access stores records in a random order. There is no sequence. To store a file, a hashing algorithm (calculation) determines the address to store the record. The same hashing algorithm is used to locate the file later. The computer system can then directly access that record without having to read through other records. This is significantly quicker than using sequential access.

Using database management systems

Hierarchical database management systems

The hierarchical database model was created in the 1960s. Hierarchical database models are not used often in modern society. The hierarchical database model relies on a tree structure. In the tree structure each parent branch is the **one** side of a relationship and each child branch is the **many** side of a relationship. The tree structure only manages one-to-many relationships and only works in one direction. Hierarchical databases are only suitable for database models that have a strict hierarchy.

One such hierarchy is the file system used within computer systems. Figure 10.62 shows an example of a file system.

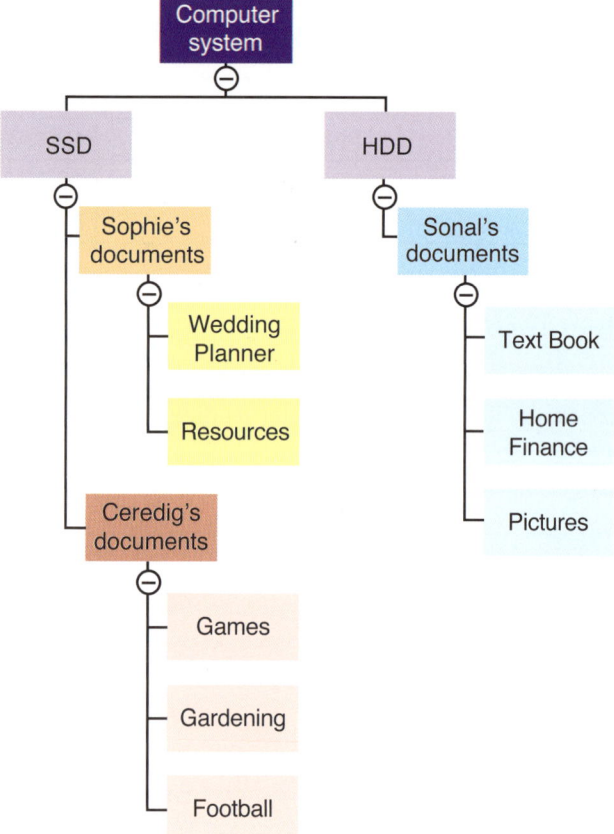

Figure 10.62: Folder structure.

Each disk contains folders. There may be further subfolders within each folder. Each subfolder has only one folder at the level above it. To find the data:

- the user browses through the system

- selects the disk the data is stored on

- then selects the folder

- then selects subfolders

- and then the file is found.

This same process is used when searching for data within a hierarchical database. This means that data at the top of the tree is very quick to access. Data deep down in the tree may take a long time to find.

For example, a bank could store data about customers and the accounts they hold, as shown in Figure 10.63.

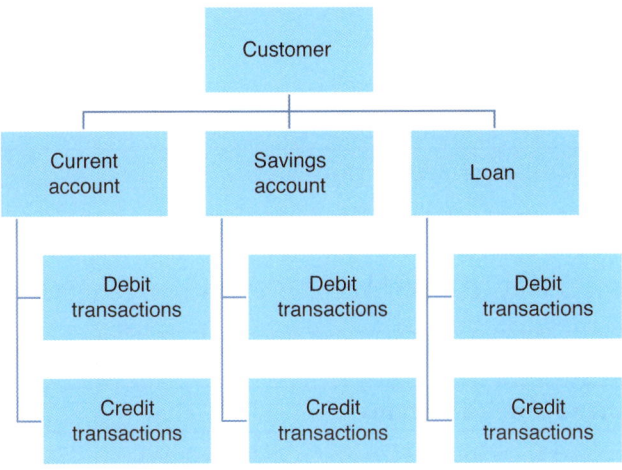

Figure 10.63: Hierarchical bank.

Network database management systems

A network database management system allows many-to-many relationships. This can help when a database needs to match a real-life model. The hierarchical model does not allow this. The network database model allows for entities to be owned by more than one 'parent' node. Because entities can be owned by more than one owner, the network database management system allows many different routes to access the same data. Figure 10.64 shows how a prescription may be owned by more than one parent node.

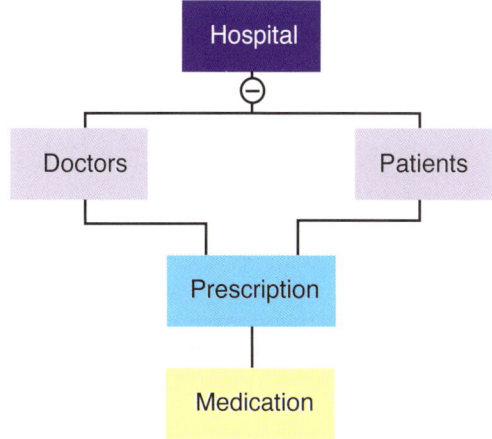

Figure 10.64: Both doctors and patients can be owners of prescriptions.

Object-oriented database management systems

Object-oriented database management systems (OODBMS) are built to match the ideas behind object-oriented programming.

Many high-level programming languages use the object-oriented programming (OOP) paradigm. This uses similar ideas as databases, such as entities. An entity is a real-life thing, or object in a database. An object in OOP is the same idea. An object is like an entity.

An OODBMS stores the data in the same way as an object in an OOP language. This means that a program that uses OOP can save the data to the database and then retrieve it afterwards. This solves the problem of the program losing any data once it is closed.

Therefore, an OODBMS is usually used alongside an OOP language or program. Common programming languages that may use an OODBMS are Java, C# and Swift.

Relational database management systems

A relational database management system (RDBMS) allows the creation and running of relational databases. It allows the user to create links between each record. These are called relationships. The RDBMS stops the need for many individually stored data structures. An RDBMS provides a standard framework for how data can be stored, represented and searched.

The key focus of the RDBMS is the use of tables and primary keys. This allows data to be stored in entities and then linked to other entities. An RDBMS is the best database model for managing and ensuring data consistency.

Advantages and disadvantages of database management systems

Table 10.27 lists the advantages and disadvantages of database management systems.

Advantages	Disadvantages
Hierarchical database management systems	
Simple storage diagrams/structure.	Limited to more simple data relationships.
Easier to follow than other styles of management system.	Not compatible with other database relationship models.
Stores data efficiently.	The structure is difficult to change after implementation.
A good model to use when large amounts of data are involved.	
Easy to understand and navigate.	
Network database management systems	
Allows the use of many-to-many relationships.	Designs can get very complicated.
All entities must have owners, which helps maintain data integrity.	The structure can be difficult to follow and understand.
Data is easily accessed.	Relies on the use of pointers to link records together.
There may be many different paths to access the data.	Does not have any database standards to follow.
Object-oriented database management systems	
Allows object-oriented programs to store data easily for later use once the program is closed.	Limited to being used with OOP languages.
Can manage complex data structures.	Need knowledge of OOP programming to design an OODBMS.
Can store complex data structures quickly.	Syntax can depend on the programming language being used. There is no consistency in how it is written.
Relational database management systems	
Maintains data consistency.	Administration of an RDBMS can be time consuming.
Uses a logical structure of entities and primary keys.	Can cost a lot of money to set up and run.
Can be used for a wide variety of applications, such as stock management, banking and online shopping.	Cost of RDBMS software is high.
Probably the most popular way of creating databases.	Not the fastest database model for accessing data.
Easy to maintain.	Has high requirements for computer memory.
Prevents data redundancy.	

Table 10.27: Advantages and disadvantages of database management systems.

Management information systems

A management information system (MIS) provides a business with summary information (see Figure 10.65). For example, it could summarise the total stock sold and the total stock ordered. An MIS could also show the total hours staff work, and compare this against the number of customers in the shop. The summary information is sent to managers. The summary information supports decision making. The MIS collates data from a database and presents it as reports and charts. These reports and charts can be produced by the RDMBs, MIS or an additional piece of software used to analyse the data.

Figure 10.65: Reports can be created to show different information.

Data from more than one database can be collected to produce reports. To create summary information, special software may collect data from multiple data sources and analyse all the data together. Software that takes data from more than one database is often referred to as an executive information system (EIS).

Features of a management information system

An MIS has the following essential features:

- data is collated from databases and other sources

- data is gathered from different sources

- data is analysed to provide the data that is required by management

- summary reports and charts are produced for managers to help with decision making.

Reports and charts are often reused. Reports and charts can take 'live' date and update automatically. This ensures the reports and charts are as accurate as possible.

How organisations may use management information systems

Information from an MIS helps managers to make decisions. Managers can look at the summary information and decide on suitable actions to take. Reports are normally provided at regular intervals. For example, a monthly sales report may be produced. Businesses also produce statements that summarise their finances at the end of every year. It is also possible for managers to request ad hoc (when needed) reports if they need additional information.

For example, managers within a large second-hand car business want to monitor sales. They want to identify trends in sales for different makes and models of car at different times of the year. They want to identify which cars are selling the most and which car sales make the most profit. They can then decide which second-hand cars they want to acquire to sell.

Marketing managers can analyse how effective a marketing campaign was by comparing sales figures during an advertising campaign with sales figures outside the advertising campaign. This will help them to decide whether to run similar campaigns in the future.

Questions

23   Explain why generic file types are needed.

24   Describe the steps involved to find a file using indexed sequential access.

25   Explain why direct access is used for databases in preference to indexed sequential access.

26   Describe two features of management information systems (MISs).

CONTINUED

- [ ] I can understand the characteristics of data in unnormalised form, first, second and third normal forms.
- [ ] I can discuss the advantages and disadvantages of normalisation.
- [ ] I can normalise a database to first, second and third normal form.
- [ ] I can understand the components of a data dictionary.
- [ ] I can create a data dictionary.
- [ ] I can select appropriate data types for a given set of data and a given situation.
- [ ] I can identify different data types.
- [ ] I understand and can use static and dynamic parameters in a query and understand their use.
- [ ] I can understand when simple, complex and nested queries should be used.
- [ ] I can understand when summary queries, including cross-tab queries should be used.
- [ ] I can understand different file types and their uses.
- [ ] I can understand what is meant by proprietary and open-source file formats.
- [ ] I can understand why open-source file formats are needed.
- [ ] I can understand why generic file formats are needed.
- [ ] I can understand the use of indexed sequential access.
- [ ] I can understand the use of direct file access.
- [ ] I can understand the use of a hierarchical database management system.
- [ ] I can understand the features of a management information system (MIS).
- [ ] I can understand how a MIS can be used by organisations.
- [ ] I can discuss the advantages and disadvantages of different databases.

PROJECT

OutletCode	00929
OutletName	Wimpy
Floor	3
Location	C4
Telephone	0121392075
AnnualFee	£85,000.00

InspectionName	Agency	InspectionDate	Pass	Penalty Points
Health & Safety	H&S Executive	08/01/2011	✓	50
VAT	HM Revenue & Customs	09/02/2011	☐	20
Food Hygiene	Trading Standards	23/02/2011	☐	35
Food Hygiene	Trading Standards	04/03/2011	✓	35
Franchise Quality Control	Franchise Partners	29/03/2011	☐	20
Health & Safety	H&S Executive	10/06/2011	✓	50

Figure 10.66: Outlet inspection card.

A shopping centre would like to monitor the inspections that are carried out at its food outlets. These inspections include Health & Safety, Food Hygiene, VAT and Franchise Quality Control. Figure 10.66 is an example of an Outlet Inspection Card that the organisation currently uses in a paper-based format.

1   Create a database that can be used by the shopping centre to monitor the inspections of its food court outlets (see Figure 10.67). Import the three files **10.14 outlet.txt**, **10.15 inspectionvisits.txt** and **10.16 inspectiontypes.txt**. Normalise the data to third normal form by removing redundant data and replacing it with appropriate foreign keys and adding any primary keys that might be needed.

Figure 10.67: Food court in a shopping centre.

2   Create relationships and enforce referential integrity for the database.

3   Penalty points are only applied if the inspection is failed. Using a query, create a calculated field that will show the 'Penalty Incurred' only if an inspection is failed.

4   a   Create a data entry screen that will look similar to Figure 10.66 and will allow the entry of data about outlets and their inspections. It should include a subform and only show the penalty if one was incurred.

   b   Create a drop-down menu that can be used to select the inspection type on the subform.

   c   Add a calculation to the form to calculate the total penalty due. The penalty is calculated as £100 multiplied by the total penalty points.

   d   Create a button that will print the Inspection Data Entry Screen for a single outlet.

CONTINUED

5 Create validation rules that will prevent invalid data being entered for the following scenarios:

a There are four floors (levels) in the Sheep Square Shopping Centre from 0 (ground) to 3.

b Inspection dates must always be after the opening date of an outlet.

6 a Produce a query to show the number of inspections passed between 1/2/2011 and 30/6/2011 for each type of inspection.

b Produce a query showing a list of the outlet codes for any outlets that have failed at least two inspections.

7 Create a graph that will show the Inspection Names on the x-axis and the Number of Passes on the y-axis using an appropriate title and clearly labelled axes.

8 Create a report that shows all failed inspections grouped by the type of inspection. The report should include the name of each outlet, the agency used for the inspection and the inspection date.

9 Create a menu that will open the following items and include an option to exit the application:

- Outlet Data Entry Screen

- Inspection Passes Graph

- Inspection Failure Report.

Video and audio editing

Introduction

Audio and video editing skills are increasingly needed by both individuals and businesses.

Some people make money through creating high-quality videos about anything from video games to makeup tutorials, including individuals who build a whole business around their video channels and rely on their video editing skills. There are also people who produce podcasts and rely on their audio editing skills (see Figure 11.1).

Many businesses also use the video and audio media to market their products or services, with large teams of people regularly used to ensure marketing material is high quality.

Figure 11.1: Making and editing videos has become common in daily life.

The ability to create high-quality video and audio is often dependent on an individual's creativity and accuracy. Creativity allows you to produce unique media that is attractive to the intended audience. Accuracy ensures that the video and audio meet any given brief for the media.

11.1 Editing a video clip

Video editing is the manipulation and organisation of short pieces of video, known as **clips**. Video editing software is used to do this. Before the development of video editing software, video was often edited by physically cutting and sticking together parts of the analogue tape that the video had been recorded on (see Figure 11.2).

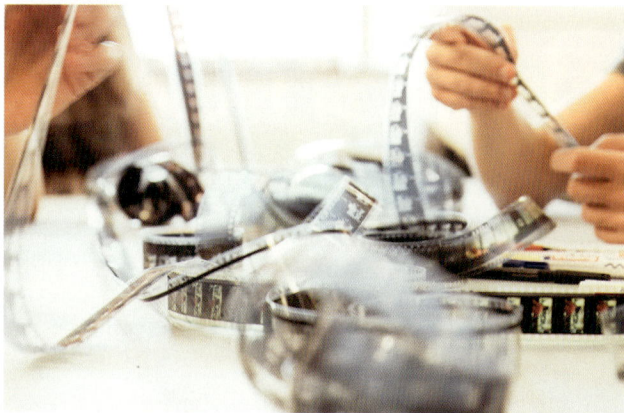

Figure 11.2: Cutting and sticking together (splicing) film.

Video often needs to be edited to remove any errors or mistakes during filming and to ensure the finished product is of a high quality. Videos also need to be edited to meet the requirements of the intended audience. For example, if a video is of a sporting event, key moments might need to be replayed, or if a video is produced for an educational training organisation, vocabulary related to the topic being studied could be displayed while someone is talking.

KEY WORD

clip: a short piece of a video or audio

There are many options available when editing video files using software. The software this chapter uses for video editing is Davinci Resolve. Other video editing software has similar features, although equivalent features may be located within other parts of the software, such as within a different menu.

Within Davinci Resolve, the 'Edit' mode will be used, unless otherwise stated. Edit mode can be selected by clicking on 'Edit' at the bottom of the screen.

Setting an aspect ratio and resolution

The **aspect ratio** of a video refers to the ratio of the width of an image in comparison to the height. The required aspect ratio will depend on the platform on which the video will be played. The two most common aspect ratios are 4:3 and 16:9.

The aspect ratio 4:3 is an older ratio for videos and is based on the shape of a **frame** on a traditional film strip (see Figure 11.3). It is the ratio used for most film and television programmes produced before the late 1990s.

KEY WORDS

aspect ratio: the proportion of a screen or video width to its height

frame: a single image in a video file

resolution: the number of pixels within a frame of video

Figure 11.3: Film strip frame.

The aspect ratio 16:9 is used for video recorded today, which is often referred to as widescreen.

Film, television and online video platforms typically use this ratio, so it is often the most suitable ratio to set when creating a video.

Figure 11.4 shows a comparison of the different ratios.

Figure 11.4: Comparison of aspect ratios.

The **resolution** can also be set for a video, which outlines how many pixels are used to represent the image by defining the number of pixels in width compared to the number of pixels in height. A resolution with a width of 1920 pixels and a height of 1080, which has an aspect ratio of 16:9, means that each frame of the video uses 2 073 600 pixels. Different platforms require different resolutions, depending how large the image will be when displayed and the quality required. 1920 × 1080 is the industry standard for high-definition (HD) video and is often referred to as 1080 p. The resolution for standard definition television is typically 640 × 480, which is often referred to as 480 p.

Questions

1   Find out what the resolution is for 4K.
2   Find out why black bars are sometimes added to the top or sides of a video.

The aspect ratio and resolution of a video can be defined when setting up the video for editing. It can also be set or changed when exporting a video file when the editing process has been completed.

To open the menu for the aspect ratio, click the small settings icon (cog) in the bottom right corner of the screen, then select one of the settings from the drop-down menu at the top. This will also provide a resolution for the video, which can also be manually changed if required.

To insert a video clip into your video, the video file needs to be imported into the software. To import a video file, select the 'File' option from the menu bar across the top of the screen. This will open a menu. Select 'Import File' from the menu, which will open a sub-menu. Select 'Import Media' from the sub-menu, locate and select the video file, then click 'Open'.

The video will appear in the file panel in the top left corner. To insert the clip into the video, click and drag the video clip to the timeline. The video's position on the timeline can be changed by clicking and dragging it to the required position.

Trimming a video clip to remove unwanted footage

Trimming a video clip enables unwanted content to be removed, such as unnecessary content at the start or finish. To trim a video clip, select the clip in the timeline and select the 'Trim' option in the menu bar. Select the option 'Trim Mode', which enables video clips to be trimmed within the software. Trim mode can also be

selected by clicking the second icon, named 'Trim edit mode' in the tool bar directly above the timeline (see Figure 11.5).

Figure 11.5: 'Trim edit mode' icon.

When in trim mode, move the cursor to the start or end of the video clip and it will change to show square brackets. Click and drag the video clip left or right to trim the content not required in the video clip.

It may be necessary to play the clip first to note the timings for the content that needs to be trimmed.

To change from trim mode to normal editing mode, select the option 'Normal Edit Mode' from the 'Trim' menu, or click the first icon, named 'Selection mode' in the tool bar above the timeline (see Figure 11.6).

Figure 11.6: 'Selection mode' icon.

Splicing/joining together video clips

When editing video clips, two clips may need to be joined together. This is useful as it means that if any effects are used, they will be applied to the whole clip.

To join two video clips together, both clips need to be selected. Select the first clip, press and hold shift, then select the next clip. Then, select the 'Timeline' option from the menu bar. From the timeline menu, select the option 'Join Clips'. This will join the clips together.

Adding titles, subtitles and captions

Titles

Titles are text-based slides that are used in videos. Text-based slides can be used at various points in a video to provide written information for the viewer. This text-based information can be used for various reasons, such as:

- to introduce the viewer to the video

- to clarify what the viewer will see, or has just seen, in a video

- to provide relevant facts and figures

- to provide information, such as an organisation's contact details.

To create a title slide, click the 'Effects' icon at the top of the screen. This will open menus in the bottom left corner. Select the 'Toolbox' option, then, from this menu, select the 'Titles' option. Locate the 'Text' option in the panel to the right. Click and hold this option and drag it right to the timeline.

Next, click the title slide in the timeline to edit it. This will open an editing panel for the slide on the right of the screen. Within this panel, there are options to change the appearance of the text, such as the font style, size, colour and alignment.

To change the timing for the title slide, right click on the title slide in the timeline and select 'Change Clip Duration' from the menu. A window will open to enter the required duration for the title slide.

Figure 11.7: Most of the plants we use for food need bees to help them pollinate.

Captions and subtitles

Captions and subtitles are text-based content that appear over the top of the video content as shown in Figure 11.8. Captions can be used to provide further information about what is being shown in the video clip. Subtitles can be used to provide a text-based version of any dialogue that is being spoken in the video. This is useful for many viewers, such as those with a hearing impairment, allowing them to read any speech that occurs in the video. Subtitles can also be used to display the spoken content in a different language, if required. Subtitles usually appear at the bottom of the video.

Captions and subtitles are created by adding a text layer over the video. To add text to a video clip, drag the 'Text' option above the video clip that the text is to appear on, which will create a new track on the timeline. Text can be edited by clicking on the clip.

The position of the text within the video clip can also be altered. The position can be changed by dragging the text when viewed in the preview pane, or specifying the x and y co-ordinates within the text editing windows.

Subtitles can also be added from within the 'Effects' library, under the 'Titles' section. To add subtitles, drag the 'Subtitle' track on the timeline, which will then display subtitles as text at the bottom of the video.

Figure 11.8: Adding a caption.

ACTIVITY 11.06

Add a caption to the BeeFly video that displays the text:

Bees are very important pollinators for fruits and vegetables. They help them grow!

Edit the text so that it appears on three lines, with a font style courier, font size 60 and the colour black.

Move the caption so that it appears in the top left corner of the video.

Adding appropriate credits

Credits normally appear at the end of a video and are used to display information about the creation of the video, such as who the producer and director are. Credits are also used to recognise the authors of any material that may have been used in the video, including for copyright reasons.

Using scrolling credits

The text for credits is normally set to scroll up the screen from bottom to top. To add credits, select 'Effects' from the top of the screen, then select 'Titles'. Drag the 'Scroll' option onto the timeline to add the credits, such as at the end of the video clips. Click on the text clip on the timeline, then text can be added in the 'Text' window.

To aid readability, each section of the credits typically starts with a heading, such as, 'Director', followed by the names of the relevant people. A blank line is then inserted before the next section begins.

ACTIVITY 11.07

Add appropriate credits to the end of your video.

Ensuring readability of text

Any text placed on screen must be readable by the viewer and therefore needs to be an appropriate colour, font and size. This is particularly important to ensure the video is accessible to as wide an audience as possible, such as people who may have vision loss.

White text is often used for text on screen and the colour chosen should not be distracting to the viewer. The font colour should also contrast with the background colour, so similar colour combinations, such as yellow text on a white background, or dark blue text on a black background, should be avoided. Where possible, the same colour text should be used throughout the video, although sections of the video containing a similar background colour to the text may need to have the text colour changed.

Fonts should be easy to read and large enough to be viewed on a small screen.

TIP

Sans serif fonts, which do not have extensions or additional strokes at the end of each letter, such as Arial, Helvetica and Roboto, are often considered simpler to read than more stylish, serif fonts.

ACTIVITY 11.08

Import the video file **11.02_BeeFlySlow .mov** into the software. Insert the video onto the timeline.

Add text to the BeeFlySlow video clip to display:

We need to take care of our bees.

Set a suitable format for the text.

Set the timing for three seconds.

Add further text to the BeeFlySlow video clip to display:

Without them we'll lose products such as honey, coffee and many fruits and vegetables.

Set a suitable format for the text.

Set the timing for seven seconds.

Create a smooth transition effect between the two text elements.

Add a text-based slide to the end of the video to display:

To find out more about bees visit the website <Insert a suitable website here>

Find a suitable website about the importance of bees to use in your video.

Format the text to be a contrasting colour to the background, which will enable it to be easily read.

Set the timing for five seconds.

Adding transitions and fading effects

Animations can be used to move from one video clip to the next, which is known as a **transition**. Transitions can improve the quality of a video. But if transitions are used incorrectly, the viewer may become frustrated, for example if the selected transition is distracting or takes place over an extended period of time.

KEY WORD

transition: the method with which one video clip merges into a second clip

A transition often added between video clips is a fading effect. A fading effect involves the first clip slowly disappearing (fading out) at the end and second next clip slowly appearing (fading in) at the start. Fading effects help create a higher quality video than if one video clip simply stops and the next clip immediately starts.

To add a fade effect between videos, move the mouse pointer to the top corner of a video clip, where a small white box will appear (see Figure 11.9). The white box can be dragged right at the start of a video clip for a fade in effect, or left at the end of a video clip for a fade out effect. While dragging the box, a timing box appears and the corner of the video becomes shaded, which shows the section of the video where the fade will take place.

Figure 11.9: Adding a fade effect.

Different animations between videos can be added using the effects library. Select 'Effects' from the top of the screen and select the option for 'Video Transitions'. Several different transitions will appear in the panel. To add a transition, click the transition and drag it onto the required video clip.

ACTIVITY 11.09

Import the video clip BeeFlower **11.03_ BeeFlower.mov** and insert it into your timeline, after the BeeFly video clip.

Fade out the BeeFly video clip for one second.

Fade in the BeeFlower video clip for one second.

Add a video transition of your choice to the beginning of the second BeeFlySlow video clip.

Resizing and cropping a still image to match a video's aspect ratio

The settings used when using still images within a video can be viewed by clicking the cog in the bottom right corner of the screen. Click 'Image scaling' on the left-hand side of the window, which displays the available options. By default, the 'Match timeline settings' box is ticked, which ensures the image size is automatically set to match the timeline settings. Alternative settings can be used, including deciding how the image is scaled.

Once a still has been inserted, the image can be cropped by selecting 'Inspector' at the top right of the screen, then adjusting the values within the 'Cropping' section of the window.

To resize the image, the 'Zoom' and 'Position' values within the 'Transform' section of the 'Inspector' window can be changed to ensure the image is displayed as required.

Adding audio to a video clip

Audio, such as music to play in the background of a video, can be imported by using the 'Import' option from the 'File' menu. The audio can be dragged onto the timeline at a suitable point and a new audio track will be created.

Editing audio within a video clip

Audio can be edited in a similar way to video clips, such as by trimming the start or the end of the clip.

To adjust the volume of an audio clip, the horizontal line located in the middle of the track's waveform can be dragged up to increase the volume, or dragged down to decrease the volume. For example, the volume of an audio clip containing background music might be decreased so it can be played quietly through the video.

To add a fade effect within an audio clip, move the mouse pointer to the top corner of an audio clip, where a small white box will appear. The white box can be dragged right at the start of an audio clip for a fade in effect, which will gradually increase the volume. The white box can also be left at the end of an audio clip for a fade out effect, which will gradually decrease the volume. While dragging the box, a timing box appears and the corner of the audio becomes shaded, which shows the section of the audio where the fade will take place.

Different audio transitions can be added using the effects library. Select 'Effects' from the top of the screen and select the option for 'Audio Transitions'. Several different transitions will appear in the panel. To add a transition, click the transition and drag it onto the required audio clip (see Figure 11.12).

Figure 11.12: Editing audio within a video clip.

Removing audio from a video clip

A video clip may contain audio that needs to be removed. For example, it may be that different audio is going to be played with a video clip, or that a certain part of the video is going to be silent.

To remove audio from a video clip, the audio track needs to be unlinked from the video track. To unlink the audio, click on the video clip to select it, then right click on the video clip and untick the 'Link Clips' option at the bottom of the menu. Next, ensure only the audio track is selected, then right click on the audio clip and select the option 'Delete Selected'. This will remove the audio from the video clip (see Figure 11.13).

Figure 11.13: Deleting an audio track.

ACTIVITY 11.12

Remove any audio from the video clips in your video.

Altering the speed of a video clip

When creating a video, clips can be altered to play faster or slower. For example, a video clip could be slowed down to make it easier to see what is happening at a certain point. Alternatively, a longer clip could be speeded up to show all the content in a shorter time.

Figure 11.14: Changing the speed of the video clip.

To alter the speed of a video clip, right click on the video clip in the timeline and select the option 'Change Clip Speed' from the menu (see Figure 11.14). Increasing the percentage within the 'Speed' box will speed up the clip, while decreasing the percentage will slow down the clip. Alternatively, the 'Frames per Second' box can be used to change the number of frames per second that are displayed. The higher the number of frames per second, the faster the clip will play.

ACTIVITY 11.13

Import another copy of the video clip **11.02_ BeeFlySlow .mov**

and insert it into your timeline after the BeeHoneycomb video clip.

Trim the clip so that it is five seconds long.

Alter the speed of the clip to 200%.

Using filters and colour correction

Filters can be used on both videos and images to change their appearance. For example, part of a video clip could be blurred to conceal part of the clip.

To add a filter, click 'Effects' at the top of the screen, then select 'Open FX', followed by 'Filters'. Select the filter and drag it to the video or image on the timeline that you want to filter.

ACTIVITY 11.14

Add the 'Box Blur' filter to the still image that you added to the end of your video.

Colour correction involves changing the colours used within a video clip to enhance their appearance or to add a certain colour effect. For example, orange and blue colours might be altered within a video clip to highlight the contrast between certain parts of the clip, such as a person's face and the background.

Within the 'Color' mode, a range of options are available to alter the colour within video clips and still images. For example, the 'RGB Mixer' can be selected from the toolbar in the middle of the screen and used to alter the appearance of red, green and blue colours.

Exporting a video clip in different file formats

Video editing software saves content using its own format, so, once editing has been completed, the video needs to be exported. The exported video needs to be in a suitable file format for the platforms on which it will mostly be played. When a video is exported, it combines all the elements in the video together into a single file.

To export a video, it first needs to be rendered. Rendering a video involves the computer processing all the data included in the video to create the exported video file. Rendering a video can take a long time, as it is a demanding task for the computer's processor to complete.

To render a video, select the 'Deliver' mode from the bottom of the screen. Click the 'Deliver' section at the bottom of the screen and a new panel will open. Ensure that 'Custom Export' is selected at the top of the screen and 'Video' and 'Export video' options are also selected. Enter a suitable file name and choose a location to save the file. The required file format can be selected from the 'Format' drop-down box.

The following file formats are often used to store video files:

- MOV, often referred to as QuickTime, which is commonly used on Apple devices
- WMV, which is often used for the Windows operating system
- AVI is widely supported, including by older devices
- MP4, which is also widely supported and often has small file sizes.

Once the required options have been selected, click 'Add to Render Queue' at the bottom of the screen. This adds the file to the queue of files to be rendered, which appears at the right side of the screen. The rendering process can be started by clicking 'Render All'. Once complete, the video file will be saved in the location specified.

Compressing a video to different resolutions

High-definition video typically uses a resolution of 1920 pixels across, by 1080 pixels down, which is often referred to as 1080 p. 1080 p provides excellent video quality on large screens, although such a large resolution is not required when viewing video on small screens, or when it is to be stored in certain formats. Reducing the resolution of the video reduces the file size, so video files can be transferred more quickly, such as when being streamed over the internet.

The resolutions often used for different media are shown in Table 11.1.

Media	Resolution
DVD	720 × 480 (NTSC) or 720 × 540 (PAL).
Internet, such as streaming video	Various. 640 × 480 or 1280 × 720 are often used, although 1920 × 1080 is becoming more common.
Smart phones	1920 × 1080 is typically used on modern devices.

Table 11.1: Resolutions for different media.

When rendering a video, the resolution can be selected from the 'Resolution' drop-down menu. Specific values can be entered by choosing the 'Custom' option from the menu.

Effects of different methods of compression on video

The file formats used to store video often compress video to reduce the size of the file. Apart from the RAW file format, which saves the raw data recorded by a video camera, each file format will compress the file using either a lossy or lossless **compression** method.

> **KEY WORD**
>
> **compression:** reducing the size of a file, such as an image or video file

Lossy compression will remove unnecessary data from the video file to make the file size smaller. Lossy will slightly affect the quality of the video file, but most of this will go unseen or unheard by most people. For example, a video containing a cloudy sky with many shades of white visible might have the quality reduced by only showing a few different shades of white, instead of the dozens within the original video.

Lossless compression will not remove any data in the compression process, which means the original quality of the video remains. Lossless compression can work in various ways. One method is for the compression software to identify repeating patterns in the file, such as large blocks of the same colour on a person's clothing, rather than storing the colour data for each pixel individually.

A range of file formats enable lossless and lossy compression to be used by selecting an appropriate codec, which can be chosen by using the 'Codec' drop-down menu when rendering a video. The type of file format and codec selected for a video file will depend on how important the quality of the video is, how large the file size can be for the platform and the type of platform it will be played on.

Questions

3 Find out which video file formats are suitable for the web.

4 Find out whether the file formats for the web use lossy or lossless compression.

ACTIVITY 11.15

Export your video in a file format that is lossless.

Export your video in a file format that is suitable for the web.

TIP

Always save a copy of the file in a generic file format as well as in the proprietary software format, which will enable the file to be edited using different software if required.

Advantages and disadvantages of export file formats

Table 11.2 lists the advantages and disadvantages of the different export file formats.

File format	Advantage	Disadvantage
AVI	Supported by a wide range of video editors and playback devices. File can contain several audio and video streams.	File sizes are large. Less efficient compression compared to other formats.
WMV	Good compression, leading to smaller file sizes. Digital right management (drm) can be used for copyrighted content.	Non-windows-based devices may not be compatible. Lower video quality when compared to other formats.
MOV	Supports several audio and video streams. Video and audio are high quality.	File sizes can be large when compared to other formats. Limited support on non-apple devices.
MP4	Good compression, leading to smaller file sizes. Large number of codec options available.	Format may not be supported by older devices. More advanced features may require additional codecs.

Table 11.2: Advantages and disadvantages of export file formats.

11.2 Audio editing

Audio editing involves the manipulation and organisation of audio (sound) clips. Before the development of audio editing software, the main method used to edit audio was to physically cut and stick together pieces of the analogue tape that the audio had been recorded on.

As with video editing, audio may also need to be edited to ensure it is of a high quality and any errors are removed, such as unexpected periods of silence. The audio may also need to be edited to meet the requirements of an application or audience. For example, a podcast might need editing to include a sponsor's advertisements, or an interview edited to ensure answers given can be heard clearly.

There are many options available when editing audio files using software. The software this chapter uses for audio editing is Audacity. The software is widely used, although other audio editing tools contain similar features.

Importing new tracks and adding a track to an existing audio clip

To have sound to edit, audio needs to be imported into the software. Multiple audio files are often imported into the software throughout an audio editing project. Each time audio is imported, it is added as a new **track**. A track represents a distinct sound recording within the software. If required, multiple tracks can be played at the same time.

To import an audio file, select the 'File' option in the menu bar, followed by selecting 'Import' then 'Audio'. Find the audio file to import and select 'Open'. The audio file will be imported into a track in the software and a visual representation of the sound is displayed, which is known as a **waveform**, as shown in Figure 11.15. The same method can be used to add tracks to an existing audio file within Audacity.

> **KEY WORDS**
>
> **track:** a specific recording, for example of one instrument or voice; the tracks can be edited separately and combined to play concurrently
>
> **waveform:** a visual representation of sound within audio editing software

Figure 11.15: Imported audio tracks.

> **ACTIVITY 11.16**
>
> Import the audio file **11.05_Piano_track-compressed.mp3**.

Normalising an audio clip

Sometimes when an audio recording is played back, it is quieter than expected. This can make it difficult to hear, particularly when played at the same time as other audio tracks. A method often used to increase the overall volume (also known as the amplitude) of an audio clip by a fixed amount is **normalisation**.

Normalisation analyses the audio recording to calculate the difference between the loudest peak in the audio's waveform and the maximum decibel limit, which is a unit for measuring the loudness of sound (often automatically set to 0 decibels). For example, if the loudest peak is –20 decibels, the difference will be 20 decibels. When the audio file is normalised, all the audio in the file will be increased by 20 decibels, which will result in it being made louder. However, using normalisation can lead to clipping, which is when audio gets so loud it becomes distorted.

> **KEY WORD**
>
> **normalisation (audio):** technique to edit an audio recording to increase the overall volume by a fixed amount

> **TIP**
>
> Use the technique of normalisation carefully to avoid distorted audio.

To normalise an audio clip, the section of the audio clip needs to be highlighted using the selection tool, which is in the centre of the toolbar at the top of the screen. The selection tool looks similar to an uppercase I. Once the selection tool has been chosen, move the cursor to the point in the sound clip that is to be removed. Click and hold the left mouse button, and drag the cursor along the sound clip to highlight the part of the clip to remove. Once selected, choose the 'Effects' option from the menu bar, then select the 'Normalize' option. This will open a window that will allow the maximum amplitude to be set. This shouldn't be set higher than 0.

Removing DC offset

A setting often combined with normalisation is DC offset. When sound is recorded, it is better for the waveform to be on the centre zero (0.0) point, which is represented by the horizontal line. However, recorded sound may be offset from the 0.0 horizontal line, which can occur when converting analogue sound to digital for use with the computer, such as when using poor quality or defective hardware. This can cause distortion and audible clicks in the sound, which become worse when recordings are made louder. Because of potential errors with subsequent editing processes, DC offset is often used before any other changes are made to an audio clip.

When normalising an audio clip, the window presented also includes the option to remove the DC offset. Selecting the setting to remove DC offset will bring the recording back to the 0.0 line and limit any distortion of the sound (see Figure 11.16).

Figure 11.16: Audio editing.

Trimming an audio clip

Trimming an audio clip allows unwanted sound within a clip to be removed, such as at the start or end of a clip. It may often be necessary to trim an audio clip to make it match the timing of a video.

To trim an audio clip of unwanted material, select the part of the clip to remove using the selection tool (see Figure 11.17). Click the cut tool, which looks like a pair of scissors on the tool bar, and the highlighted section of the audio clip will be removed.

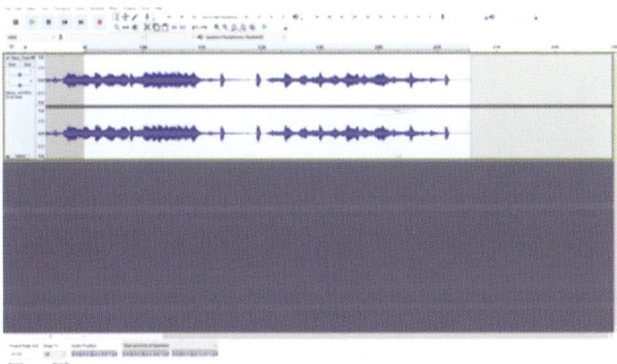

Figure 11.17: Selecting part of a track.

KEY WORD

trimming: removing part of an audio clip, such as to delete unwanted sound

Splicing/joining together two audio clips

Splicing an audio clip involves splitting it up into different parts so that only the required sound is available to use, then joining them back together. Splicing helps remove parts of an audio clip that are not needed, such as an unnecessary section in the middle. To splice a clip, the copy and paste tools can be used, along with trimming a clip if required.

For example, it may be that the sound at the start of an audio clip and a certain part in the middle are required for a project. The selection tool could be used to highlight the middle section required, which could then be copied. The appropriate position for the audio could be selected, then paste used to insert the sound. If required, the audio clip could also be trimmed to remove unwanted sound at the end.

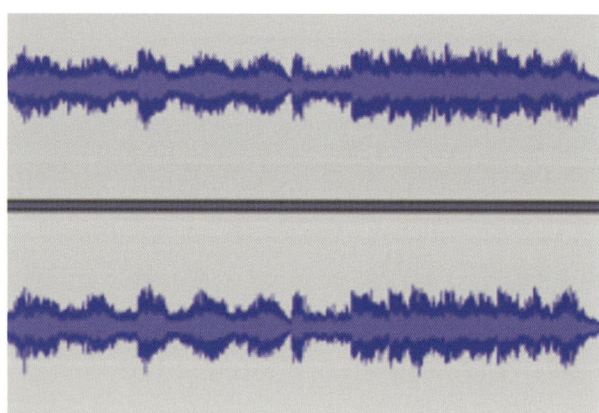

Fading in and fading out

If an audio clip suddenly starts or stops, it can appear abrupt or surprising to the listener. This may be the required effect, although a softer, more gentle entrance and exit for the audio may be needed. This can be achieved by fading in and fading out the audio clip.

To add a fade effect to the audio clip, highlight the part of the clip that needs to fade in or out. Select the 'Effect' option in the tool bar at the top of the screen, which will open a large menu. To fade the sound in, select the 'Fade In' option, or to fade the sound out, select the 'Fade Out' option, as shown in Figure 11.20.

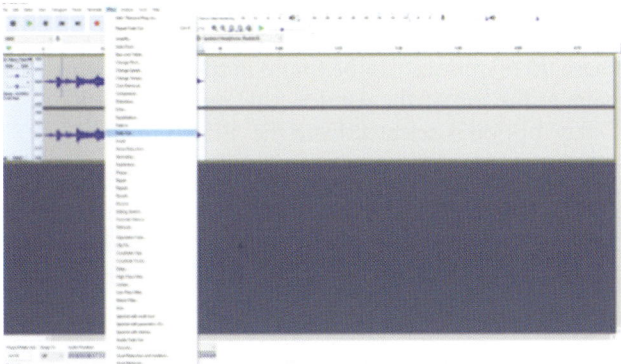

Figure 11.20: Fade out effect.

> **ACTIVITY 11.20**
>
> Add a fade out effect to the last five seconds of your sound clip.

Altering the clip speed

It is possible to slow down or speed up an audio clip. Speeding up an audio clip can often be entertaining, especially if it is done with voices, as it can make them sound squeaky. Audio clips can also be speeded up to create a different effect with the music, such as making it seem more upbeat. Slowing down a sound clip can also affect the feeling the sound creates, such as making it sound more relaxing. Musicians can often slow down an audio file when using it to practise a song. It can allow them to get used to playing the song before speeding it up to play at the correct speed.

To change the speed of your clip, highlight the sound clip and select the 'Effects' option from the menu bar, then select the option 'Change Speed'. Values can be

manually entered for the desired speed, or the blue sliding bar underneath the values used instead. Sliding the bar to the right makes the audio clip faster, while sliding the bar to the left makes the speed slower.

> **ACTIVITY 11.21**
>
> Import the sound clip **11.06_Bee_Voiceover.mp3**
>
> Experiment with speeding up the voiceover intro and listen to the effect it has on your voice.
>
> Remove this effect to return the intro to normal speed.

Changing the pitch

Pitch refers to how high or low a sound is. Sound is made by vibrations of particles forming a sound wave. Pitch is a measure of the sound frequency. The faster the particles vibrate, the higher the frequency of the sound and so the higher pitch of the sound. Figures 11.21 and 11.22 illustrate the difference between high-pitch and low-pitch sound waves.

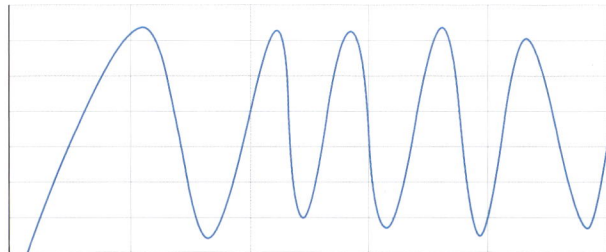

Figure 11.21: Example of high-pitch sound wave.

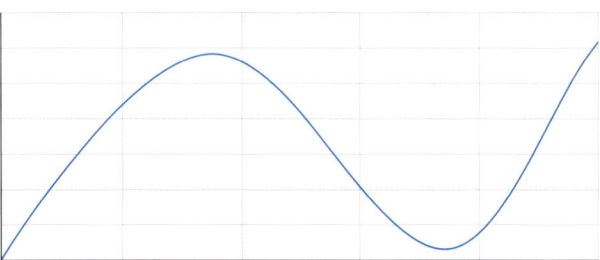

Figure 11.22: Example of low-pitch sound wave.

Certain sounds within an audio clip may be too high or too low. You can change the pitch of a sound clip by selecting the 'Effects' option in the menu bar. Select the option 'Change Pitch' from the menu. The pitch can be changed in two ways: by changing the key of the audio clip, or changing the frequency of the sound. Changing the key is useful if the music is played in a certain key and needs changing to a different key, such as if the music is recorded in the key of A major, but needs changing to the key of C major. Alternatively, the frequency values can be manually entered, or changed using the sliding bar underneath the frequency values. Sliding the bar to the right makes the pitch higher, while sliding the bar to the left makes the pitch lower.

ACTIVITY 11.22

Move the Bee_Voiceover audio clip to be played at the end, so that it finishes at the same time as the piano music.

Lower the pitch of the voiceover by 5%.

TIP

You can use the 'Time Shift Tool' in the tool bar to move a section of sound.

TIP

If a person's voice is being recorded to enable a character to speak in an animation, such as a cartoon, the pitch can be altered to make the recording more appropriate to the character. For example, if a voice recording has been made for a young character, a higher pitch might be used to make the voice sound more realistic.

Adding or adjusting delay/echo

An echo is a repetition of sound, which is caused by sound waves being reflected off obstructions, such as walls. Adding an echo effect to an audio clip can make it

sound more distinctive. The echo effect may be useful if a sound needs to be emphasised within an audio clip.

To add an echo to an audio clip, highlight the section of the audio clip and select the 'Effects' option from the menu bar. Select the option 'Echo'. There are two values to consider when an adding an echo. The first, delay value, represents how long it will take to echo the sound, and the second, delay factor, represents how loud the initial echo will be and how it will fade.

An echo effect can also be created using a different option in the 'Effects' menu. This is the 'Delay' option (see Figure 11.23). This option can be used to create multiple echoes of the sound and change how the sound is echoed. There are three different delay options: regular, bouncing ball and reverse bouncing ball. These three options can be found in the drop-down menu at the top of the window that opens when the 'Delay' option is selected from the 'Effects' menu.

A regular delay will set a fixed time between each delay, a bouncing ball delay will make the echoes increasingly closer together and the reverse bouncing ball will make the echoes increasingly further apart. The number of times for the sound to echo can also be set.

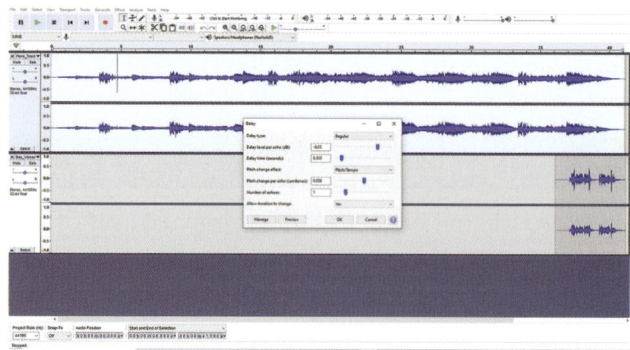

Figure 11.23: Adding a delay.

ACTIVITY 11.23

Add an echo to the voiceover intro. Set the delay to 0.5 seconds and the decay to 0.5.

Adding or adjusting reverberation

Reverberation is an effect used to make it appear that sound is being played in a larger room. If sound is played in a larger room, the acoustics of the room often cause the original sound to be repeated, creating a slight echo effect. A reverberation effect is therefore often used to create a fuller and softer feel to sound.

To add reverberation to an audio clip, highlight the clip and select the 'Effects' option from the menu bar. Select the option 'Reverb'. There are several values that can be used to change the reverberation, although the simplest to change is the 'Reverberance' value. Increase it to add reverberance and decrease it to remove reverberance.

ACTIVITY 11.24

Increase the reverberance by 10% for the Bee_Voiceover audio clip.

Changing an audio clip from stereo to mono

The piano audio clip in the imported audio file has two different tracks. This is because it has been recorded in stereo, which means two separate tracks are used for the recording. These two tracks can be just a duplicate of each other, as they are in the piano audio clip, or they can contain different content. The different tracks can be set to play through different channels with a sound system. For example, when using speakers in a sound system, the left channel track plays through the left speaker and the right channel track through the right speaker.

An audio clip can also be mono. The clip has a single track. When played through multiple speakers, they will all play the same track.

DID YOU KNOW?

Surround sound systems are often used to create 3D effect in films, as different sound effects can be heard from different speakers, such as those placed behind the viewer. This can make it seem like the sound is coming from different places. 5.1 surround sound systems use six channels for audio, with five speakers placed around the room (centre, left front, left back, right front, right back), plus a dedicated low frequency effects (LFE) channel used for bass, which is connected to a special type of speaker, known as a subwoofer.

To change an audio clip from stereo (see Figure 11.24) to mono (see Figure 11.25), highlight the sound clip and select 'Tracks' from the menu bar. Select the 'Mix' option, then 'Mix Stereo Down to Mono'.

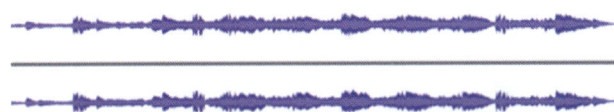

Figure 11.24: Stereo.

Figure 11.25: The same audio clip in mono.

ACTIVITY 11.25

Change the Piano_Track audio clip from stereo to mono.

When compressing audio, the concepts of **sample rate** and **sample resolution** affect the size of the audio file and the quality of the sound recording.

> **KEY WORDS**
>
> **sample rate:** the number of times sound is sampled in a second
>
> **sample resolution:** the number of bits that are used to represent each sound sample

Sample rate

During the digital recording of audio, samples of the analogue sound are taken at set intervals. This is called sampling. The number of samples taken in a period of time is called the sample rate, which is measured in hertz (Hz). If one sample is taken per second, this would be a sample rate of 1 Hz. Most music recordings, including sound stored on audio CDs, are taken at a sample rate of 44.1 kHz. This means the sound is sampled 44 100 times in a second.

The effect of the sample rate can be seen by looking at an example of a sound wave representing analogue sound in Figure 11.29.

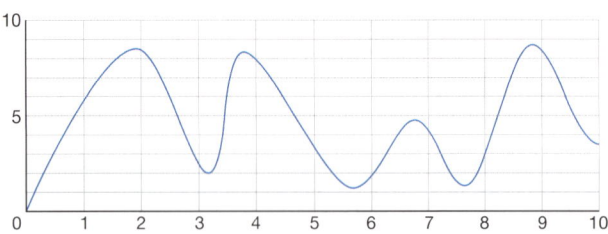

Figure 11.29: Analogue sound wave.

Table 11.2 shows the sample of sound that is recorded at each time interval.

Sample value	6	8.5	2.5	8	3.5	2	4.5	3	8.5	3.5
Time sample	1	2	3	4	5	6	7	8	9	10

Table 11.3: Sample of sound recorded at each time interval.

If these sample values are then plotted on the same graph, this shows the difference in the initial sound, to the sound sampled (see Figure 11.30).

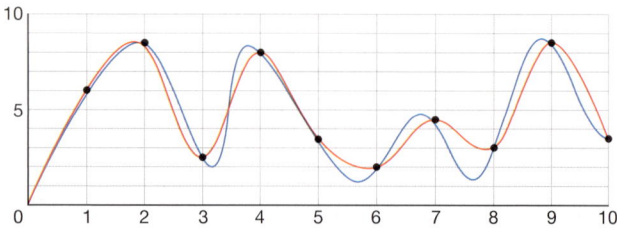

Figure 11.30: Analogue sound wave with sampled sound wave.

Figure 11.30 shows that the sound wave differs significantly in places. This is because a sound sample wasn't taken at that certain point, so the detail in that part of the analogue sound is missed.

If the sample rate was doubled in the given example, the resulting sound wave after sampling would be a closer representation of the initial analogue sound wave. This means that the quality of the digital recording of the sound would be a truer representation of the original analogue.

It also means that the file would need to store twice as many samples, so this will increase the size of the file.

> **ACTIVITY 11.28**
>
> Draw your own sound wave example like the wave shown in Figure 11.30. Record the sample value at each time sample. Draw the resulting sound wave that is recorded and compare this to your original sound wave.
>
> Double the amount of time samples are taken of the original sound wave. Draw the resulting sound wave that will now be recorded. Is this closer to the original than the first?

Sample resolution

When sound is sampled, the volume of the sound wave is recorded. The number of bits used to store the volume is known as the sample resolution. Sample resolution is important when recording the different volumes of sound. A low sample resolution, for example 4 bits, would limit the level of volume that could be recorded, as only 16 different values can be stored. A high sample resolution, for example 32 bits (4 294 967 296 different values), would allow for an extremely accurate recording, but the size of the file created would be large, so streaming could be affected by buffering and downloading could take a long time. The usual sampling resolution used for audio recorded digitally is 16 bits (65 356 different values), which is used for CDs.

The size of an audio file is dependent on the sample rate and sample resolution. The approximate size of a sound file can be calculated using:

Sample rate × sample resolution × length of sound file

Question

5   a   Calculate the size of a file in megabytes (MB) that is two minutes in length, has a sample rate of 44.1 kHz and a sample resolution of 16 bits.

b   Compare the file size if the sample resolution is increased to 32 bits.

Exporting an audio clip in different file formats

Audio needs to be exported to a suitable file format for the media on which it will be played. Selecting a universal file format allows the sound file to be played on many devices, using different software platforms, although a specific format may be required for certain technologies. A device may also have restrictions on the file size required or the amount of storage available, which can impact on file size.

To export audio, select 'File' from the menu bar and select the option 'Export'. Several file formats are available for the audio file, including:

- MP3, commonly used file format supported by many devices

- MP4a, newer format providing better audio quality than MP3 files of the same size

- WAV, uncompressed file format providing high-quality audio

- AAC, high-quality audio with efficient compression; often used within an MP4 container, as outlined next.

Select an appropriate format and give the file a suitable filename, along with choosing a suitable storage location.

Effects of different methods of compression on audio

As size is an important factor when streaming or downloading music, sound files are often compressed.

As with compressing video, each audio file format will compress the file using either a lossy or lossless compression method.

Lossy compression will remove unnecessary data from the audio file to make the file size smaller, such as sound that may not be audible to the human ear. Lossy compression will slightly affect the quality of the sound file, although this may not always be noticeable. MP3, MP4a and AAC are popular audio lossy file formats. A lossy format is used when the accuracy and quality of the audio is not essential, but the file size needs to be smaller. Lossy compression is often used when streaming music, so that less bandwidth is required to stream the sound file. This makes the ability to stream the music accessible to more people, especially those that only have access to low bandwidth connections. It would also mean that users streaming via a mobile connection would not use as much of their data allowance.

Lossless compression will not remove any data in the compression process, which means the original quality and accuracy of the recording will be retained. Lossless compression can work in various ways, such as by identifying repeated patterns in the audio file and storing them more efficiently. WAV is a popular lossless file format for storing audio, although WAV is uncompressed. Lossless compression is often used for recordings of live music, such as classical music played by an orchestra. This allows the listener to have the most accurate experience of the sound created.

Some audio file formats, such as MP4a and WAV, are stored in a structure called a container. Metadata related to the audio recording is stored within the container alongside the audio, which enables information about the recording to be included, such as the name of the artist or the date of recording. The container also contains data related to how the audio is stored and compressed, which enables it to be played on a device. Audio file formats simply containing the raw audio stream do not use a container. AAC can be saved as a file without any container structure, although it is often stored within a container format, such as MP4.

ACTIVITY 11.29

Export your audio file in a file format that is lossy.

Export your video in a file format that is lossless.

The export file format used needs to be carefully considered, as there are a number of advantages and disadvantages to each method, as shown in Table 11.3.

Export file format	Advantages	Disadvantages
MP3	Supported by a wide range of devices and media software. Small file size.	Lossy compression can lead to poor audio quality.
MP4a	Container format that can hold a variety of audio file types. Well supported by mobile devices.	Not as widely supported as MP3.
WAV	Lossless format, leading to excellent audio quality.	Lack of compression means the file size is large.
AAC	Higher quality sound than MP3s. Small file size.	Not as well supported as MP3.

Table 11.4: Advantages and disadvantages of export file formats.

ACTIVITY 11.30

Now, import your audio file into the video editing software and add it to your video file. Import the file in the same way that you imported video clips. You can simply drag the file from the media section to the timeline, when imported, to add it to your video.

Export your BeeProject video with the audio and be proud of your audio and video editing skills!

DISCUSSION POINT

1   Who do you think the audience is for the video that you have created?

2   What do you think the intended purpose is of the video that you have created?

REFLECTION

What similarities and differences were there between editing audio and editing video?

Which media did you find easier to edit? Why was it easier to edit?

PRACTICE QUESTIONS

1   Define what is meant by the aspect ratio of a video.   [1]
2   State why a trimming tool would be used on a video clip.   [1]
3   Explain two advantages of using captions on a video clip.   [2]
4   Explain two advantages of using a lossy compression method on a video file.   [2]
5   Explain one disadvantage of using a lossless compression method on an audio file.   [1]
6   Explain what is meant by the sample rate of an audio file and how it affects the file size.   [2]

SUMMARY CHECKLIST

- [ ] I can edit a video clip to meet the requirements of its intended audience and purpose.
- [ ] I can edit an audio clip to meet the requirements of its intended audience and purpose.
- [ ] I know and can understand the different compression methods and file formats that can be used for audio and video.
- [ ] I know how to use typical editing features in audio and video editing software and know why they are used.
- [ ] I know how the size of an audio file is affected by the sample rate and sample resolution.

PROJECT

Figure 11.31: Editing a video.

In a pair, create a video, using video editing software on a computer, to advertise your school to potential students. Within your video, you could include:

- images from the school, such as photographs of the buildings, facilities and student work and activities – remember to make sure that you have permission before taking any photos

- interviews with staff and students, such as the Headteacher, a captain of a sports team or a leader of an activity

- additional audio related to school activities, such as from a music lesson or drama performance.

Your video should use a variety of video and audio editing techniques, such as:

- titles, subtitles and captions

- transitions and pan / zoom effects

- end credits

- fading in / out of audio.

Before starting your video, carefully think about the audio and video clips required, along with the setup of your video, such as the resolution and aspect ratio required.

Chapter 12

IT in society

LEARNING INTENTIONS

By the end of this chapter, you will be able to:

*   understand what is meant by digital currencies, including different types, characteristics and uses

*   understand the use of blockchains as distributed ledgers for cryptocurrencies

*   discuss the impacts and risks of digital currencies on individuals, businesses, governments and the global economy

*   discuss the advantages and disadvantages of different types of digital currency

*   understand what is meant by data mining, including the process, stages and how and why data mining is used

*   discuss the advantages and disadvantages of data mining to individuals and organisations

*   understand what is meant by social networking services/platforms, including types, uses and impact on individuals, businesses, organisaitons and governments

*   discuss the advantages and disadvantages of different types of social networking services/platforms

*   understand the impact of IT on society, including monitoring and surveillance

*   understand technology-enhanced learning, the methods of delivery and impact

*   discuss the advantages and disadvantages of different methods of delivery of technology-enhanced learning.

Introduction

IT has become an integral part of our society. It is difficult to imagine a society without any form of digital technology in it. IT affects many aspects of our lives. It affects how we spend our money, how our data is stored and mined and how we communicate and learn. Almost every part of life uses some form of IT (see Figure 12.1).

Figure 12.1: IT is everywhere in our lives.

12.1 Digital/ Electronic currency

Digital currency is money that only exists in a digital format. The terms digital currency and electronic currency are often used to mean the same thing.

Digital currency is different from normal currency. Normal currency can exist in both digital and physical form. For example, the Indian Rupee exists as notes and coins. The Rupee is also stored digitally in bank accounts. A digital currency does not have notes or coins.

Types, characteristics and uses of digital currencies

There are several types of digital currency:

- cryptocurrency

- central bank digital currency

- stored-value cards.

> ### KEY WORD
>
> **digital currency:** money that only exists in digital format

Cryptocurrency

Cryptocurrencies are digital currency. All cryptocurrencies are based online. The use of cryptocurrencies is growing. Currently, cryptocurrencies are used mainly for investment: people buy, store and

Figure 12.2: A private investor buying and selling cryptocurrencies.

- Debit cards: banks use debit cards to allow customers to withdraw money from their account and pay for goods or services online. The transactions are processed by the bank. All the transactions are recorded.

- Electronic point of sale (EPOS): EPOS systems record all the transactions that a business makes (see Figure 12.4). It then communicates with the banks to ensure that the money a customer spends is transferred to the shop's or business's bank account. A single company will operate EPOS for many different shops or businesses. They record and process all of these transactions in a central location.

- Centralised systems will communicate with a single system, such as a bank account. The bank account is controlled by a single bank. The bank follows agreed rules to manage and look after the money.

Figure 12.4: An EPOS records the transactions a shop makes when a customer buys their goods.

Decentralised systems

Decentralised systems are the opposite of centralised systems. Decentralised systems do not have a single place where currency is monitored or stored. The currency may not be looked after by a single entity or person. Decentralised systems rely on a trust-based system to look after the money. People use decentralised systems to avoid paying fees to banks for money transfers. Special software is needed to record and process all of the transactions.

Examples of systems that use a decentralised approach include:

- Cryptocurrencies such as Bitcoin and Litecoin: the updating of transactions and processes are managed by many different computers, rather than a single computer.

- Peer-to-peer electronic monetary systems: this allows people to make transfers from their bank account to another bank account. Some social media networks also allow this, for example the 'WeChat' wallet.

- Mobile electronic (digital) wallets: this is often done with online technology or mobile phones using systems such as Google Pay or Apple Pay. These store the details of an individual's bank cards and allow them to make purchases without having the physical bank card with them.

- Decentralised currency systems are often known as **virtual currency**.

> **KEY WORD**
>
> **virtual currency:** digital currency that is decentralised

> **DISCUSSION POINT**
>
> Imagine a world where physical currency does not exist. All payment transactions are digital. How would the world change?

Opinions are divided over the use of decentralised currencies. Some people support their use. Decentralised currency allows people and businesses to avoid paying the financial transaction charges of banks in a centralised system. Other people believe that decentralised systems allow people to make payments that are very hard to trace. This can help criminals hide their money and payments.

Use of blockchains as distributed ledgers for cryptocurrencies

Blockchain is a new technology. Its original function was to record transactions that took place when trading cryptocurrencies. Blockchain is now also being used for other purposes. For example, blockchain can be used to track company assets, or patents (the legal right to make, use or sell inventions).

How does blockchain work? Blockchain links all the transactions that take place. Each transaction is linked to the previous transaction. Each transaction is known as a 'block'. This is why it is known as blockchain. All the blocks are linked together – creating a chain (see Figure 12.5).

Figure 12.5: Each transaction or 'block' is linked to the next block. This forms a long chain of linked blocks.

Once a transaction has been recorded, it can never be changed. If a mistake is made in recording a transaction, then a new transaction must be completed to correct the mistake. As the chain of blocks grows it becomes more and more secure. Blockchain is viewed as being 'tamper proof'. This means that it is nearly impossible to edit or change details in a blockchain without being noticed.

The record of all blocks in a blockchain is known as a ledger (see Figure 12.6). A ledger is stored once only. There are no duplicate records made of the ledger. The ledger is stored (distributed) across many different systems or computers. This makes the ledger a distributed ledger. The updates to the ledger rely on people's computers to process the changes. This is because no one person 'owns' the distributed ledger.

Blockchain is a **peer-to-peer** monetary system. This is because the databases may be stored across both public and private networks.

Figure 12.6: A ledger was originally a large book used in accounting to record a company's financial transactions.

KEY WORDS

blockchain: a database that stores records of transactions across many different computers and systems

peer-to-peer: a type of network in which each computer on the network has the same level of importance: peer-to-peer networks have no central server

ACTIVITY 12.02

Use the internet to research what blockchain is and how it is used to monitor payment transactions. Draw a diagram to show how blockchain works.

Impacts and risks of digital currencies

Individuals

Many individuals are able to access and use digital currencies. This is because they can use the technology needed to use digital currencies. However, some people may not be able to use the technology. This means that they may be disadvantaged. They may not have access to the internet to use digital currencies, or may not be technologically aware.

Digital currencies can also change value very quickly. For example, when Bitcoin was first used, it was worth

$0.003. At its highest value, Bitcoin was worth $68 000. That is almost 1500 times difference. Imagine having the money in your bank account increasing by 1500 times! However, Bitcoin has also gone down in value. In one year, Bitcoin dropped by nearly $10 000 per coin.

People who invest in digital currencies can make a lot of money, but there is also a high risk that they could lose a lot of money as well.

Businesses

Businesses can use digital currency to avoid paying the fees and charges that banks often request. This means that they can make more money when using digital currency. Blockchain is viewed as being very secure and therefore low risk. However, in 2024, not may people use digital currency. Therefore businesses must still use more recognised forms of currency like cash, or current banking systems.

If the value of digital currency varies greatly, then businesses are also affected by this. They could find that their profits are suddenly reduced if the value of digital currency falls rapidly. This can put their businesses at risk.

Governments

Governments control inflation and the national currency. This helps governments to keep the economy stable. If people use digital currency, the government loses the ability to control this as closely. This could lead to challenges within a country's economy. Many countries limit the amount of national currency that is produced. Cryptocurrencies avoid these limits.

Being able to trace money helps to stop crime. Criminals often try to move large amounts of money through banking systems. The banks have ways to detect this, and can raise concerns with the local police force or crime agencies. Digital currencies reduce the risk of criminal activity being detected. Hackers and cyber criminals often use cryptocurrency for making payments and receiving money as it is much harder to trace.

Global economy

The global economy is based on the ecominies of all the countries in the world. If one country's economy is struggling, it can affect the global economy negatively.

However, because digital currency is universal, it does not belong to one country. This makes it easier to pay for goods and services across the world as there is no need to exchange one currency into another.

The number of people using cryptocurrencies across the world is currently very small and the risk is limited. But as the number of people and businesses using cryptocurrencies grows, so will the risk to economic growth and the global economy.

Advantages and disadvantages of different types of digital currency

Table 12.1 sets out the advantages and disadvantages of different types of digital currencies.

Digital currency	Advantages	Disadvantages
Cryptocurrencies	The usual charges that can apply to bank transactions are not present for cryptocurrency. People can invest in Bitcoin and may make money if they sell it for a higher rate. It is very difficult to create counterfeit currency for a cryptocurrency, because of all the security it involves.	The decentralised systems allows a level of anonymity that some believe encourages criminal activity and allows it to go untraced. There have been several examples where businesses have been hacked and Bitcoin has been stolen. As the system is decentralised, there is no bank to help resolve this kind of theft.
Stored-value cards	Open-loop cards are flexible allowing the individual to top up the monetary amount when they wish or can afford to do so.	The use of stored-value cards prevents a person from getting into debt, as they can only spend the set amount that is stored on the card.

Digital currency	Advantages	Disadvantages
Central bank digital currency (CBDC)	As no physical currency will need to be exchanged between banks, the cost of transactions will be reduced. The banks' ability to speed up the exchange of money will be greatly improved. Some believe that if physical currency became obsolete, in favour of cbdc, criminal acts such as money laundering and tax evasion would decrease, as these often rely on the use of physical currency. It costs money to produce physical currency, therefore if it ceased to exist, then these costs would be saved and could be invested into the security of a CBDC.	Some people like the privacy of the anonymity that they can have with using physical currency. If a person pays with cash, there is no record of their details attached to that payment at the bank.
Debit cards Credit cards Electronic point of sale (EPOS)	A person doesn't need to carry physical money around, which could be easily lost. If a card or mobile device is lost, the user can contact their bank to stop any monetary transactions from the card or device. All transactions are completed using encrypted methods, so data is sent securely. The use of contactless payments can speed up payment for products and services. If a user is in a different country, they don't need to have the physical currency of that country available in their wallet. They can use a digital method and the banks involved will electronically change the transaction from one currency to the other.	As data is sent electronically, there is always the risk that the transactions could be hacked. Small traders such as street vendors or small shops often rely on cash because digital payments attract a small transaction fee from banks. Some people are anxious about the thought of contactless payments. Scammers can use fake payment machines to deduct money from people's accounts. Some may think that people can lose track of their spending as they are not handing over physical money for the transaction. If a card or device is lost, it is possible for another person to use it for contactless payments, before the user has chance to cancel it.
Peer-to-peer electronic monetary systems	These speed up the process of transferring money between people. These systems reduce the fees and charges a person may need to pay.	These have fewer controls and therefore can be more risky.
Mobile electronic wallets	Many bank cards can be stored in a wallet. An electronic wallet reduces the risk of theft of cards. Devices that use digital wallets (such as mobile phones) often have lots of security, such as fingerprint recognition, to stop fraudulent use.	If a wallet is hacked, a person will gain access to all of the card details. Payments can be made via 'contactless' methods: these are easier to intercept.

Table 12.1: Advantages and disadvantages of digital currencies.

Questions

4 Describe the difference between a centralised and decentralised system.

5 Give one advantage and one disadvantage of a CBDC.

12.2 Data mining

Data mining is a form of data analysis. The process of data mining involves searching through and analysing large sets of data to identify patterns and trends. For example:

- Businesses may use data mining techniques to help identify future trends and customer behaviour. They will use the information to better guide decision making.

- Educational institutions may use data mining to learn more about their student populations to help them improve the learning environment.

- Financial institutions can use data mining to detect fraud.

- Healthcare providers may use data mining to improve patient care.

- The large sets of data used are stored in data warehouses. A data warehouse is a central collection of data. It may include past data and current live data. All of this data is stored in one system so that it can be analysed all together.

Artificial intelligence (AI) uses data mining to help predict actions and outcomes. Having all of the data in one place allows the AI program to search through and learn about the patterns of data. This helps it to predict and make conclusions with much more accuracy.

KEY WORD

data mining: the process of collecting large sets of data and analysing them to identify patterns and trends

We need powerful computers to mine data effectively. We need powerful computers because the amount of data to process and analyse is massive. For example, we would need a very powerful computer to analyse data in a stock market. Hundreds of megabytes of data are generated each day. The prices of the stocks and shares, the quantity bought and sold, the amount of shares each transaction processed, the bids and offers for shares etc. are all stored. All of this data must be analysed to try to predict what will happen. This needs to be done very quickly so that stock traders can make decisions in seconds.

ACTIVITY 12.03

Data mining is very important to many businesses. It is also used in stock markets to try to predict trends in share prices. Research the advantages and disadvantages of needing very powerful computers to carry out effective data mining. What effects are there? Can these be avoided? Jot down some notes. In a group, share and discuss your findings.

The process and stages of data mining

The process of data mining involves several different stages.

Stage 1: Business understanding

First, the business needs to set its business objectives. Understanding objectives will allow the business to identify the data needed for data mining. An in-depth analysis takes place to discover the exact objectives. The business can then develop a project plan and determine the criteria for success.

Other important factors are then taken into account once the business objectives are identified. The project plan will include:

- the resources available

- the constraints

- a data mining plan

- objectives.

The data mining plan involves developing the right questions to interrogate the data.

Stage 2: Data understanding

The data understanding stage involves initial data collection. Data is gathered from available sources. The integrity, accuracy and the properties of the data must be checked. This ensures that the data is suitable and appropriate.

Next the data is interrogated using queries developed in the business understanding stage. This helps the business understand whether enough data has been collected. It shows the business if the objectives can be met.

Stage 3: Data preparation

Data preparation is the largest and most time-consuming stage in the project. The following actions are carried out on the data:

- Selection: the correct data will be identified and extracted so that the data mining process takes place on the data linked to the objectives.

- Cleansing: the data is checked for inconsistencies or errors before it is used. Duplicate data or data with missing values may be removed.

- Construction and formatting: the data is then checked and put into the correct format and layout for the data mining to take place.

These actions make sure that the data is in the form required for the business. This process allows patterns and trends to be established.

Stage 4: Data modelling

Test scenarios are created to model the data. This allows the business to understand if the models are suitable for its business needs. For example, think about a car manufacturer. They want to know whether to build a new car, or whether to modernise a current car. They will create models which could include the change in population or a change in the financial state of the customers. They may set new colours, prices or features for the car. The data can then be mined to predict the outcomes of these scenarios. For example, the data mining may find that the colour blue is decreasing in popularity and therefore to avoid using this as a colour for the new car.

Stage 5: Evaluation

The evaluation stage reviews the results generated by the models. The outcome of this review may produce new business needs. This depends on the patterns and trends identified.

Stage 6: Deployment

Reports and other materials are used to present the findings of the data mining process to the stakeholders (all those with an interest in the business such as the owners, shareholders, employees) of a business. This information is used by the stakeholders to decide what actions the business will take next.

The actions which are taken by the business are known as the 'deployment' of the findings. The deployment is a list of actions that the business will take, based on the results of the data mining.

The data mining process can be repeated using different models and data if the results do not meet the requirements. Or more data modelling is completed to refine the information gathered from the first data mining process.

Use of data mining

Many different types of organisation use data mining to help them plan and make better decisions.

National security and surveillance

National governments use data mining to analyse intelligence data. The results of data mining on intelligence data help to safeguard national security and may reduce the risk of a terrorist attack or other dangerous activity in a country.

Using data mining to analyse **surveillance** is controversial (something that causes disagreement). Many people argue that data mining should not be used. Many people argue that it should. For example, we can data mine CCTV footage and telephone calls to predict criminal activity. However, this may breach a person's right to privacy if it is done in secret, and the person is innocent. Also, data mining can onl predict what *may* happen, not what *will* happen.

> **KEY WORD**
>
> **surveillance:** the act of watching a person or place: this can be done in secret

Data mining is used for corporate surveillance. Corporate surveillance is when a company monitors a person's or group of people's behaviours and actions. Companies will mine people's data and use it for marketing purposes or sell the results of the data mining to other companies. This can be controversial if companies do not ask for permission, or if they use data from other sources by accident. For example, a marketing company may mine shopping data about people using online stores. They can then sell this data to online retailers.

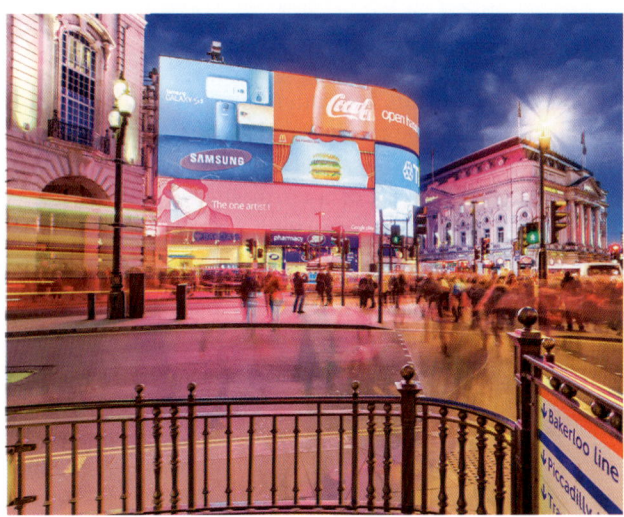

Figure 12.7: Companies use data mining to determine what adverts to display on advertising boards.

A business can use corporate surveillance to make their products more attractive to customers or create personal advertising to individuals (see Figure 12.7). This is also known as data profiling.

Business

Businesses use data mining for many reasons. Data mining can help businesses to:

- predict customer spending trends

- predict product trends

- hire suitable staff.

Data mining is valuable to a business. If a business can predict what products customers will buy before their competitors, then they can gain an advantage. Data mining may help increase sales revenue and profits for the business.

Businesses also use data mining to help customer relationship management (CRM). CRM aims to improve customer loyalty focus on customer needs. Data mining allows a business to understand customer needs more clearly. The business can then use strategies to meet these customer needs. For example, data mining may identify that customers are buying more recyclable products. The business can then aim to make its products recyclable.

Question

6   How could a business make use of data mining when hiring staff?

Research

Research helps industries such as pharmaceuticals, space exploration, engineering and technology. Data mining is often used in research. Research companies can analyse the research data of several companies by using data mining. Data mining speeds up research and development for industry, universities and companies.

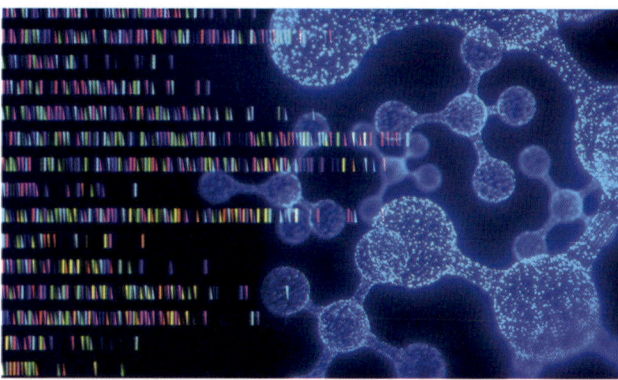

Figure 12.8: Data mining genetic data can help to identify possible cures and treatments for diseases.

Data mining is used in bio-informatics. Data mining analyses biological data to extract medical patterns and trends. This can be used in gene finding and disease research and diagnosis (see Figure 12.8).

Healthcare

Data mining is increasingly used to improve healthcare (see Figure 12.9). It is used to identify best practice in healthcare and to reduce costs. Data mining can be used to predict the number of patients that visit healthcare facilities. This allows hospitals to provide the right number of staff to care for patients.

Figure 12.9: Data mining may help to improve healthcare.

The analysis of social and economic trends

Data mining is used to analyse social and economic data and predict future trends. Many companies and governments use data mining to predict changes in the global economic market. This allows governments to prepare for possible future crises.

For example, a government can collect data about the COVID-19 pandemic in their country. They can then use the data to model what may happen in a future pandemic. This may include how people acted, how effective treatments were and how healthcare facilities were affected. They can then use this to develop a better way to respond to future pandemics, which could save people's lives and reduce the impact on the economy.

Advantages and disadvantages of data mining to individuals and organisations

Many individuals and organisations have concerns about the ethical and privacy implications of data mining.

One concern is how online advertising is targeted at individual users. Many companies use tracking cookies in their websites. A 'cookie' is a term for a small piece of code in a website that sends data back to the owner of the website. Tracking cookies on websites gives companies data about what you search for on the internet. Tracking cookies can also tell companies what things you buy online, which websites you visit and how often you buy things. This data is mined. The analysis will tell a company what things you may be likely to buy in the future, and where you may buy it from. The company can then target you with adverts for this product or service. This may encourage individuals to buy things they do not really want or cannot afford.

Imagine you research the symptoms of a medical condition on behalf of a friend who has asked you to find information. This data is then mined by a company. They then target you with adverts for proprietary medicines. They also send you details of local healthcare clinics who can help you. This advertising is not suitable for you, as you were searching for a friend. But the company believes that it is, because the cookies will send the data from your searches back to the company.

Many people are concerned about privacy. People feel that it is unethical for companies to collect data to share it with other companies. Many countries have laws that stop companies collecting data without permission.

There is also a big advantage of having important data from a range of sources in one place. This makes it more efficient to mine and therefore faster and more effective for companies. With data in one place, companies can respond more quickly to new developments and mine new data more quickly. However, there is a risk of having data all in one place. This data could be stolen, destroyed or damaged. Therefore a company could lose a lot of valuable data all at once. The company would then have to spend time and money to gather all the data again, and re-mine it.

Stealing the data could mean companies are held to ransom by hackers – and may choose to pay sums of money to get their data back.

Table 12.2 shows the advantages and disadvantages of data mining to individuals and organisations.

Advantages	Disadvantages
It allows organisations to make strategic decisions that can help maintain or increase their revenue.	The process of data mining, the software tools and the skilled staff required are very expensive.
It allows organisations to understand their customers and create the products they need.	Many people see the practice of data mining as both unethical and an invasion of their privacy.
It allows individuals to see targeted product advertising based on the things they already like. This means online adverts could be more meaningful to them. It could also help them see products they would like but do not currently know about.	Storage costs for data are very expensive, therefore this can also increase the cost of the process of data mining.
It allows governments to predict future crises that they can then plan strategies and solutions for to help handle or avoid them.	The masses of data stored prove a great security issue, as hackers will want to gain access to the data because it has a high value.
It allows businesses to save costs either by understanding how to streamline what they already do, or by not investing in a future product that they can now be aware may not be desirable.	The outcomes produced by data mining are only predictions based on patterns and trends in past data. They are not an accurate science and it is very possible for them to be incorrect.

Table 12.2: Advantages and disadvantages of data mining.

Example case study of data mining

A very high-profile case involving data mining was the Facebook and Cambridge Analytica scandal. The case involved the way companies collect, use and share people's data. The case involved ethical issues about how they collected people's data. Laws were in place to protect people's data. However, the companies Facebook and Cambridge Analytica were accused of using **loopholes** in the law to unethically collect and mine data.

> **KEY WORD**
>
> **loophole:** a mistake or omission in a law that allows people to avoid obeying the law as it was designed to be followed

Cambridge Analytica was a political consultancy firm that mined data. It collected personal data from millions of Facebook profiles. They did this without the permission of the Facebook users. This data was then mined and used for political advertising purposes. The results of the data mining were used to influence public opinion. In December 2022, Meta (the owner of Facebook), without admitting wrongdoing, agreed to pay US$725 million to settle legal action over the use of the mined data.

In 2018, a new European Union (EU) law was implemented to help control the practice of data mining for EU residents. This made it a legal requirement to seek permission from EU citizens to use their data. The law gave clear requirements and definitions on how data can be collected and used. The new law forced companies to consider questions such as 'Why am I collecting this data?', 'What do I intend to do with this data?' and 'Do I have the users, consent to use this data?'.

Question

7 Describe different ways that data mining could be used in a school to support students.

12.3 Social networking

Social networking is an important part of many people's lives. Many people rely on social networking for entertainment, communication and as a source of news. People use social networks to share information about their daily lives. Many people post personal data to social networks. People can post personal data on topics such as:

- how they feel
- what makes them happy

- what annoys them
- what they are eating
- where they go on holiday
- personal beliefs (see Figure 12.10).

Figure 12.10: Personal information such as a person's emotions can provide data miners with useful information on a person.

> **KEY WORD**
>
> **social networking:** the use of websites and apps that allow users to communicate and interact

Types and uses of social networking services/platforms

There are many different social networks, for example chat rooms, instant messaging, forums, email, blogs and video apps. These are all forms of communication technologies called **social media**. Users normally use these technologies on a personal computer or smart phone. Many social media platforms are accessed via a website or an app.

> **KEY WORD**
>
> **social media:** a range of software programs that allow users to interact and share information with other people via the internet

Chat rooms

A chat room is an online service that allows a user to send messages to many other users. It is similar to talking to many people in a room.

Chat rooms may be based on a specific topic or issue. For example, chat rooms can be used to discuss climate change, sport fixtures and politics. To use a chat room you normally have a username and password. This identifies you and helps you identify other people.

> **DID YOU KNOW?**
>
> A username is also known as a handle.

When a user logs in to a chat room they can see other users who are online. The user can also type messages and send them to the chat room or directly to other users. Messages are displayed as a dialogue onscreen. Chat rooms are interactive. They run in 'real time' and allow multiple users to communicate and discuss topics.

Chat rooms are mainly used by individuals. However, businesses and organisations can also use chat rooms, for example to advertise products and services. A business that wants to know whether they should create a new product could use a chat room as a method of gaining feedback from customers. A chat room could be set up to discuss the product and a selection of users could be sent the login details. When the users enter the chat room, the business could ask questions or make comments about the product. The users can then have a conversation with the business about the product (see Figure 12.11).

Figure 12.11: Businesses may communicate with their customers through chat rooms.

scale. Microblogs have become a popular source of news for people around the world. News platforms post headlines on a microblog platform. They then include a web address to the full article on the website.

Blogs and articles are often used in education, finance and heathcare. Many industries like these have experts who write about the latest ideas or research in this area. For example, a doctor may blog about new surgery techniques or drugs that are available to treat diseases. Education experts may blog about teaching techniques, or the latest developments in their subjects.

Figure 12.13: A vlogger records a video for their followers.

News broadcasters like the BBC, CNN, China News Service or Asian News International will often use a range of social media platforms to make news stories available for people to read. Sometimes this may be directly, by publishing an article on a website, or platform. Sometimes this may be as an advert on other social media platforms.

Impact of social networking services/platforms

Social networking affects individuals, businesses, organisations and governments.

Impact on individuals

Social networking can have a positive impact on our lives.

- It allows us to communicate with people on a global scale. Family and friends that live far from us or in different countries can share stories and videos about their lives. This helps people feel more connected and less socially isolated. Being connected to family and friends can contribute to people's sense of well-being.

- It allows us to connect with new people and exchange information with others who share similar thoughts and beliefs through common interest groups. Broadening our knowledge helps to avoid intellectual isolation and is positive for people's physical and mental health.

However, social networking can also negatively affect a person's life and well-being across all age groups. Some critics of social networking point out the following concerns:

- Social media encourages constant comparison of our lives with others. Social media influencers often post pictures of expensive cars, jewellery, holidays and houses. This may cause some people to feel dissatisfied believing that everyone else has a better life than them.

- Views expressed in social media may influence people to think in certain political or stereotypical ways and may lead to ideological polarisation. Ideological polarisation is where a person is influenced to believe in very extreme viewpoints. This means that they ignore or do not accept that other viewpoints exist, and that their view is the only correct one.

- Social networking can allow people to hide behind an anonymous online profile. People can create fake accounts with fake emails. Creating fake accounts allows people to post controversial and harmful content. This content can be used in cyberbullying or can promote dangerous actions or ideas. Cyberbullying can cause serious physical and mental health issues for those affected. Spreading harmful content can lead people to have beliefs about different societies and cultures that are untrue.

Instant access to content may affect some people more than others and could become addictive.

ACTIVITY 12.06

1   Do you think that social media is having a positive or a negative influence on our lives?

   What are the benefits of social media? Are there any issues with the way we currently use social networking? Create a list of benefits and drawbacks. Share your list with a partner. Add any extra benefits/drawbacks to your list.

2   Write a short news article on your feelings about the impact of social media.

Questions

8   Describe how blogging can be used to spread information.

9   Give two benefits and two drawbacks of social media use in today's society.

Impact on businesses

Social networking platforms are used by many businesses as a marketing tool. An active online social networking presence may mean the difference between a customer choosing to buy the business's brand and products over those of its competitors.

Social networking platforms often allow businesses to post adverts. There is often an advert during and between videos. Most adverts allow you to close the advert after a short time (for example, 5 seconds). Because many users of social networking see so many adverts they are likely to close the advert as quickly as possible. Closing the advert means that the advert has little effect. However, social networking allows businesses to reach audiences on a global scale. Being able to reach people across the world helps businesses increase their sales and income.

Businesses will often use social media and cookies to help target people with product information. This could be specific types of product, or promoting how products are created. For example, a business could learn from an individual's use of social media that they like to use recycled products. The business could use this information to promote their products made from recycled materials.

Product information can also include safety information. Blogs and social media posts can promote how to use a business's products safely, or promote safety features. For example, car adverts on social media often promote the safety features of the car.

Social media is often used to get customer feedback. It allows customers to respond quickly to prompts, or reply with smiley faces or similar 'emoticons' to give feedback to businesses.

Forums are often used to gather feedback as the comments can be reviewed by the business. The business can then respond to customers and provide feedback directly to them.

DISCUSSION POINT

What is the most effective way that you have seen a business use social networking?

UNPLUGGED ACTIVITY 12.07

Imagine you have launched a new business. You want to promote your business. What forms of social media would you use? Write a plan of how you would use social media to promote your business.

Impact on organisations

Many organisations such as social enterprises, charities and weather forecasting services have a presence on social networking platforms. Their websites often ask users to follow them on social media platforms such as Facebook, Twitter/X, YouTube, TikTok, Instagram and LinkedIn. This allows followers to learn about the work of the organisation and receive news updates. Organisations use their social media presence to share and promote information about environmental issues, health matters and weather warnings for extreme weather. International charities may use their social media presence to alert followers to natural disasters around the world and request donations to support their work.

Impact on governments

Governments use social media to communicate policies to their citizens and to distribute useful information on a large scale. For example, they can promote healthcare advice and safety guidance. Many governments use social media to alert people to national safety issues. If there is a health emergency or a natural disaster within a country, the government, police and health authorities can use social networking to distribute vital information about how people can keep themselves safe (see Figure 12.14). Social networking can be used to give citizens early warning of disasters like a cyclone or an earthquake. This can help save people's lives.

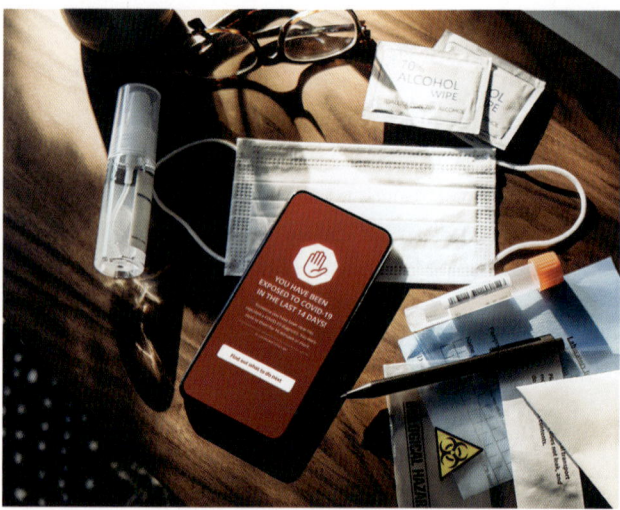

Figure 12.14: Governments use social media to inform citizens about important information such as health alerts.

Social networking also allows governments to gain feedback from their citizens through a discussion of current issues and government news. It also allows citizens easier access to government.

Governments need to ensure that any information they distribute through social networking platforms is accurate. Where a situation is changing rapidly, governments have to ensure information is up to date and does not give a false or distorted view of events. Negative feedback about the government's actions or policies needs to be handled carefully. Some governments may fear negative criticism and unrest and may censor information about current issues. This may lead to people gaining a false impression of what is occurring in their country, or not being told the whole truth.

DID YOU KNOW?

In 2022, the US government spent around $66 billion on advertising on social media.

In 2021, Transport Canada spent $6060 on Google ads for a drone safety advertising campaign (see Figure 12.15).

Figure 12.15: Operating a drone safely.

Advantages and disadvantages of different types of social networking services/platforms

Table 12.3 gives a summary of the advantages and disadvantages of social networking services/platforms.

Advantages	Disadvantages
It allows communication to occur on a global scale between individuals, businesses and organisations.	Users can feel overloaded by the huge quantities of information and communication available.
It allows users to feel included as they can share thoughts and ideas with those who share similar ideas, beliefs and opinions.	Some users can feel excluded and believe that everyone else appears to have a better life than them.

Advantages	Disadvantages
It allows organisations, including governments, to distribute important information to people that could be lifesaving in critical situations.	Some organisations, including governments, could falsely represent certain situations and influence opinions of people that are built on censored information.
It allows some individuals to make a living writing an online blog or vlog that others enjoy reading.	Social networking influencers can sometimes lead followers to think or do things that may be harmful, such as over exercise or spend on items they cannot afford.
It allows users to seek advice or support on various issues, including technical support and healthcare. This can result in an improved level of customer service and care.	Contributions to platforms, such as forums, can often be made by people who may not be qualified to give advice or support. This might lead to a person acting on incorrect advice and possibly causing harm.
It aprovides a stream of news and entertainment for users.	May cause social media dependency.
It can expose people to news stories that they otherwise may not be aware of.	News stories can be sensationalised (made shocking or exciting) and falsely reported.
It keeps people's information secure and private, which protects them from cybercrime.	It allows a level of anonymity that can encourage users to participate in bad or sometimes criminal behaviour.

Table 12.3: Advantages and disadvantages of different types of social networking services/platforms.

DISCUSSION POINT

Do you think social media is beneficial or not for society?

12.4 The impact of IT

The use of IT has changed many areas of society.

The impact of IT on society

IT in sport

In sport, IT is used to help referees make more informed decisions during matches. These decisions could change the outcome of a game. In rugby union, the referee can use video replay to see if the ball is out of play or if a try is scored. Football and cricket also use IT in this way. Cricket and tennis use automated ball tracking to check if the umpire's decision was correct. In cricket, special software tracks the motion of the ball and shows whether it would hit the stumps. In tennis, a system called HawkEye allows players to challenge the decisions of the umpires judging the match.

Some people welcome the use of video technology in this way. They believe that video replays make the play fairer and ensure correct decisions are made in games. However, other people feel that it delays the play and takes away from the responsibility that the referee has to make the correct decision on the first occasion.

ACTIVITY 12.08

Research how IT has affected your favourite sport. For example it could be 'HawkEye' in tennis, or the 'television match official' (TMO) in rugby. IT can be found in many other sports like swimming, sailing, cricket and baseball.

Create a poster about how IT has affected the sport. Add to this whether you think this has made the sport better or less fun to watch or take part in.

IT in manufacturing

Manufacturing uses robotics on assembly lines for products such as cars. (You learned about control technologies in Chapter 3.)

Robotics allow heavy items in the car making process to be moved to areas where humans need them to fit to the car. This means that humans avoid working on dangerous elements of manufacturing. Robotics in manufacturing also create a more consistent and accurate product. This is because the robot will work to the same standard consistently. A human is more likely to make mistakes. This could be because they are tired, or they are distracted by things happening around them. Robotic systems work for much longer periods of time without a break. With the correct level of maintenance, robotic manufacturing could be set to run for 24 hours a day (see Figure 12.16).

Robotics in manufacturing can result in people losing their jobs. This is because robots can do the jobs that humans can do. This leads to people not liking the use of robotics, even though robots have many advantages for the company. Robotics are very expensive. If a business cannot afford robotic equipment, this can put them at a competitive disadvantage against those businesses in their industry that can.

Figure 12.16: IT in manufacturing.

ACTIVITY 12.09

In a pair, produce an information leaflet explaining how computer aided design (CAD) and 3D printing are used in manufacturing. Use the internet to do your research. Include images in your leaflet.

IT in healthcare

IT systems allow patients to be constantly monitored with great accuracy. IT systems can measure their heart rate, analyse blood samples and even train doctors and nurses in how to perform certain procedures through simulations. Robotics are now able to carry out simple surgery, or assist surgeons during an operation.

IT has enabled many advancements in healthcare. Amputees can be given artificial limbs which are

controlled through the use of technology. This area of healthcare is called bionics. The use of bionics means that people can be provided with opportunities to walk or use their hands again. This allows them to live a fuller life and either gain, or regain, the same abilities as most other humans have. Bionics are often used on soldiers who have been wounded in battle. Bionics provide them with the ability to use their wounded limbs again. Or the whole limb could be replaced.

Nanotechnology provides great advancements, especially in the use of drugs to treat disease. Nanotechnology is when technology is used to manipulate individual atoms and molecules. Nanotechnology can be used to target the delivery of drugs in a very precise way. Particles can be engineered to locate cells in the body. For example, nanotechnology can target cancer cells and deliver drugs directly to these cells. This can help to reduce any damage or unnecessary treatment being delivered to healthy cells.

Smart devices can be designed to be implanted into different parts of the body. We often use devices like this in the brain or heart. These smart devices can monitor the body and detect health issues. For example, in the future a brain monitor may be able to detect the very early signs of Parkinson's disease before they fully develop. This allows treatment to start much sooner. Pacemakers monitor and control the electrical signals in the heart. Pacemakers prevent people from having heart attacks.

IT in education

The use of IT in education is a growing trend. Technology, such as interactive whiteboards, can be used in the classroom to make lessons more visual and appealing. This may enhance the learning process for students.

Educational technology aids online learning (see section 12.5 Technology-enhanced learning).

ACTIVITY 12.10

Discuss with your teacher whether your school has any plans to introduce new IT into your school in the future. If this isn't possible, discuss what IT you think would benefit your learning.

Work to create a presentation for your school board about what IT you want to see introduced in your school, and why you think it would be useful to have.

IT in banking

You have already studied how IT is used in the development and management of digital currencies (see 12.1 Digital currencies). Banks rely heavily on the use of IT. Banks need IT to manage huge databases of financial transactions made daily.

IT allows people to access physical currency using Automated Teller Machines (ATMs).

> **DID YOU KNOW?**
>
> A teller is a person who is responsible for dealing with customers' cash in a bank.

ATMs use IT to check whether a person has enough money in their account.

The introduction of IT for this purpose means that people no longer need to queue in the bank to withdraw their money. It also allows people to access their money 24 hours a day.

Many banks now provide access to bank accounts using a mobile app. Customers download the app onto their mobile device. Customers can then set up access to their account by entering their personal details. The customer uses specific login details to access their online account using the app.

Mobile banking apps can carry out most banking services online. These services include:

- checking their bank balance
- viewing bank statements
- setting up direct debits
- applying for loans and overdrafts
- paying bills
- transferring money between accounts.

The development of banking apps means that people do not need to travel to a branch of their bank. This is very useful if the person lives many miles from a branch. Online banking also gives people more choice over which bank they have an account with. Before mobile banking, people often had to use the closest bank, rather than a bank of their choice.

There are many advantages of online banking. These include:

- needing to visit a branch less often as many services are available online
- avoiding queues in bank branches
- the ability to use banking services 24 hours a day, 7 days a week
- using banking services without leaving home
- viewing transactions online without needing to wait for paper statements to be delivered.

Some banks offer better deals and interest rates to customers using online apps. Banks have lower costs if people bank online. This means that the customer can benefit from these savings.

IT in e-business and finance

E-business

Online retail is now very common and often seen as an easy way of buying and selling goods and services. Goods and services are often cheaper online. This is because businesses do not need physical premises to sell their goods. This means that businesses do not need to pay rent or utility bills.

One of the main advantages of online shopping for the customer is the ability to compare prices of goods or services without the need to visit a physical shop (see Figure 12.17).

Figure 12.17: Online shopping means you can browse through many items quickly without having to spend time visiting a shop.

Online shopping has become increasingly popular with the rise of smart devices. Smart devices allow you to order anything online regardless of where you are (if you have an internet connection!). When a customer arrives at a store only to find it does not stock a particular item, for example, they can use their device to order the item from the online store instead.

Online shopping can be better for the environment because stock and items can be stored in warehouses instead of lots of individual stores or shops. Shops use resources such as air-conditioning, heating, lights, water and electricity. Online shopping allows customers simply to see an image without the need for a shop display. A disadvantage of shopping online is that it is difficult for customers to see the quality of products online or check the size of an item. This can mean that many products may be returned.

Finance

People can use mobile apps to request loans and mortgages and buy insurance. IT allows customers to compare the different offers available to them without leaving home. People can also set up online investment portfolios online and use IT to check them regularly.

There are now special websites that compare all the deals on specific products (like car insurance) on the internet. The websites show customers which deals would be best for their needs. These websites are called aggregate websites.

IT in entertainment and media

Social networking services offer users a continuous source of entertainment and media. This allows users to access news stories around the world. Social networking has made people more aware of world events. The use of IT has also allowed people to be amateur journalists themselves. Many people record events as they happen and use social media platforms to broadcast this to a wider audience. This has had both a positive and a negative impact. Self-broadcasting allows people to see what has happened very quickly. Sometimes this can be before the traditional news media arrive. This can give viewers a truer impression of what is happening. But self-broadcasting may not be accurate. Bystanders may broadcast inaccurate reports or spread false information.

DID YOU KNOW?

In the 1800s, news often took many weeks to be reported. The Battle of Trafalgar between British, Spanish and French ships took over two weeks to be reported in London. News about another famous battle in America, the battle of Alamo (Texas), took more than two months to reach the newspapers in London, England.

There are many news aggregator apps, such as Flipboard and Google News, that collect news stories from many different media sources. Aggregator apps allow people to read articles from a range of sources. This means that people can compare what one story says against another. Aggregator apps allow users to set their news interests and then the software will search for stories that it thinks will interest the user.

IT in the family and home

Smart devices such as Amazon Alexa and Google Home systems can be used to control many different services in the home. Householders can control lighting, heating, climate control, security, entertainment and household appliances from remote locations. This facility can help to save money and can also be better for the environment. For example, a smart device may sense when no one is at home and change the thermostat/climate control accordingly.

Today, high-speed internet connections allow individuals in a household to stream entertainment, play games, use social media and browse the internet at the same time.

IT in government and politics

Social networking platforms may be used to raise awareness of different political policies, causes and issues. Online petitions encourage people to promote the changes they want to see in society. The use of IT in politics in this way can allow government to see what issues people are worried about. This allows a government to prioritise what actions they take, or what laws they design. IT helps people have a voice and may get government to discuss issues that they believe need solving.

IT also allows governments to provide services online. For example, people may be able to pay their taxes online, or apply for official documents such as a passport or a driving licence. IT makes accessing these services much easier for people, and also saves money for the government because they need fewer staff than if they run face-to-face services.

The impact of IT on monitoring and surveillance in society

The use of IT in monitoring and surveillance has become very important. Many police authorities use IT to monitor criminal activity and to locate criminals when crimes have been committed. IT has allowed facial recognition, number plate recognition and CCTV (closed-circuit television) to be used to help prevent crime (see Figure 12.18).

Figure 12.18: IT systems allow CCTV cameras to stream video to security services to keep people safe on the streets.

Law enforcement agencies often combine the use of facial recognition software with CCTV images. Railway stations, shopping centres and airports use CCTV. A law enforcement agency can scan the CCTV images using facial recognition software. They can do this to trace suspects or criminals. This may tell them if a suspect has passed through a train station or walked along a town centre street. This type of analysis can save a lot of time. Without IT, law enforcement agents would have to watch hours of CCTV recordings to see if they could spot the criminal. Facial recognition and CCTV could also be useful in finding a missing person, for example if a child becomes separated from their carer in a large shopping centre.

Many people install technology to protect their home and property:

- Simple CCTV systems can be set up to monitor the area around a house or inside the home. If motion is detected, the system sends an alert to the householder's mobile phone. The householder can view real-time footage of their home using the CCTV cameras.

- Smart doorbells contain a speaker, microphone and camera linked to the householder's phone. When someone presses the doorbell, the householder is able to see who is at the front door and speak to that person. Smart doorbells allow householders to 'answer' the front door even if they are not at home (see Figure 12.19).

Figure 12.19: A smart doorbell helps to keep people safe by allowing someone to see who is at the door, before opening it.

Dashcams (dashboard cameras) are cameras that record the journey of the car when the car is moving. If the car is involved in an accident, the driver of the car will have video footage of the accident for their insurance company. This can help show what happened, and who was at fault. Dashcam footage can also help police authorities. If a crime has taken place, police may ask if any drivers who were nearby have dashcam footage of the area. The police can analyse the dashcam footage to see if they can find evidence of the crime, such as a getaway car, or people running away from the scene of the crime.

It is argued that using IT for monitoring and surveillance does not have any regulation or control. It takes time to create laws and regulations to monitor the use of technology. Often, the development of the technology moves faster than laws can be passed to monitor it.

Many people feel that the ability to record video in public without limit is an invasion of their privacy, and that there needs to be a greater level of laws and regulation governing their use in this way.

12.5 Technology-enhanced learning

Teaching and learning has been improved by technology. The development in technology has allowed the introduction of online learning and online courses. Many tutorials are available on websites such as YouTube. There are many educational websites such as Lynda.com and edx.org. The growth of digital learning allows people to access knowledge, information and education. Access to many websites and courses are free. Digital courses and learning also allow people to learn at their own pace and in their own time. For example, some people learn from websites late at night. This may be because they work during the day and could not attend a school or university (see Figure 12.20).

Figure 12.20: Online learning helped many students keep up to date with school work during the COVID-19 pandemic.

The quality of the resources on educational sites can differ greatly. Many sites, like YouTube, are not regulated. This means that the level and quality of education or training in videos may be poor. Using amateur videos to learn from could mean that the tutorial provides incorrect advice.

For example, many people post videos on how to fix cars or technology like mobile phones and fridges. However, the person who posts this video may not be a qualified engineer. The person may show you how to fix the problem, but they may not show you how to fix it safely. Amateur videos showing cyclists how to fit lithium batteries to turn their pedal bicycles into electric bicycles have led to some bicycles catching fire.

DID YOU KNOW?

YouTube stores more than 800 million videos. Users watch more than 1 billion videos a day!

Methods of delivery of technology-enhanced learning

Computer-based training

Businesses and organisations use technology to create training courses for employees. These courses are accessed using computers. This is called computer-based training. Computer-based training provides training resources but does not normally have a tutor to teach the course. The person using the course will use the resources to study on their own, or with other people studying the course. The resources used in a computer-based learning course can be a mix of text, sound, video and images. Different uses of text, audio, video and images allow the course to present training information in an effective way. Computer-based training is designed to deliver training to users in a step-by step process. Computer-based training normally allows a user to learn at their own pace. Computer-based training often includes automatically marked tests to show how much the user has learned.

Many businesses use computer-based training to allow employees to develop their skills and knowledge. This benefits the company because employees may become better at their job and can work more quickly or accurately. Computer-based training benefits staff because they develop more skills and may be eligible for a promotion or a pay rise.

Online tutorials

Online tutorials present guides on how to complete short tasks. For example, there are tutorials on how to build a computer, how to complete video games or how to install software. There are also tutorials on hobbies such as sports refereeing, cycling, swimming or knitting.

YouTube is often used to store videos for tutorials. Online tutorials allow a user to learn at their own pace and in their own time. Online tutorials allow a person to view the tutorial repeatedly. A person can keep watching the video until they have learned how to do the task.

Networked courses

Networked courses are a form of online learning. They help learners to connect with other learners as well as their tutors. This is known as **collaborative** learning.

> **KEY WORD**
>
> **collaborative:** working together to achieve a goal

Networked courses can make the learning process more enjoyable because you can talk to users. Talking to other users means that you can share feedback and take part in discussions.

Networked courses encourage learners to support each other throughout the course. The learning process is led by a tutor. The tutor encourages participation from each learner. Learners are often asked to share thoughts, opinions and resources from their work or educational practices. Other learners are then asked to comment on each other's contributions. Learners can then offer advice on how to improve their skills and knowledge.

Massive open online courses

Massive open online courses (MOOCs) are a popular online learning method. MOOCs can be accessed by many people at once. MOOCs are usually free but sometimes you need to pay for access. MOOCs often include recordings of lectures, have video, text and pictures and use forums. A forum allows people using the MOOC to interact with other learners and the tutors. MOOCs can be created on any topic. MOOCs allow people to learn at their own speed. People can use MOOCs to develop additional career skills or explore new interests. A user's progress can be assessed using **peer review**, written assignments or automatically

marked online tests. MOOCs allow a person to demonstrate learning and understanding of new skills, which may be of interest to an employer.

> **KEY WORD**
>
> **peer review:** assessment by other people who have a similar skill level

Video conferencing

Figure 12.21: Video conferencing allows people to see and speak to each other from across the world.

Video conferencing uses a video camera and software on digital devices (see Figure 12.21). Many digital devices have video cameras built in. Examples include smart phones, tablets and laptops. External video cameras for computers are often called web cams. Video conferencing needs an internet connection. Video conferencing software often allows a user to share the content on their screen with other users that are part of the conference. GoogleMeets and Microsoft Teams are examples of video conferencing software.

Teaching and learning can use video conferencing. A teacher can teach lessons using video conferencing software. The software allows them to speak to their students and show a video of the teacher. The teacher can also share resources to support the learning process. Using a video or web cam gives learners a more personal learning experience. This is because the student will be able to both see and speak to their teacher. Video conferencing also allows learners to ask questions in real time and check on any learning that they may be unsure about.

Method of delivery	Advantages	Disadvantages
Video conferencing	As learners can ask questions in real time, this may improve their level of learning and understanding. As learners can see and hear their educator, this may feel like a more personal learning experience and may create an increased level of motivation for the learner as they may find it more engaging. The educator can often share what is displayed on their screen with other learners, which could be useful if a demonstration needs to be given.	Video conferencing software can require high broadband speeds that may not be available in some areas. If internet quality is poor, video and sound may break up. The quality of the lesson depends on how well the teacher can communicate over video conferencing. Only a small number of learners will be able to be part of the videoconference, and this will be limited by the capabilities of the software and the internet connection. This may leave some people waiting a long time for a place on a course.

Table 12.4: Advantages and disadvantages of different types of technology-enhanced learning.

Questions

10 Give three different areas that IT has had an impact on.

11 Explain why using IT to enhance surveillance and monitoring of people can be considered to be controversial.

REFLECTION

Were there any concepts in this chapter that you found difficult to understand?

If so, what could you do to gain a better understanding of them?

PRACTICE QUESTIONS

1 Explain what is meant by a cryptocurrency. [3]

2 Explain two advantages and two disadvantages of the use of digital currency. [4]

3 Explain the difference between a chat room and a forum. [4]

4 Describe the process of data mining. [8]

5 Explain two ways that data mining can be used. [4]

6 Explain two advantages and one disadvantage of learners using a MOOC to improve their work-based skill set. [6]

7 Discuss the impact of central banks moving to a digital based currency only. [6]

8 Discuss the impact of the use of IT in banking and finance. [6]

SUMMARY CHECKLIST

- [ ] I can recognise a range of different digital currencies, how they are used and the advantages and disadvantages of each.

- [ ] I can describe how blockchain is used in digital currencies.

- [ ] I can describe the processes involved in data mining, how it is used and the advantages and disadvantages.

- [ ] I can recognise a range of different types of social networking services/platforms, how they are used and the impact they have.

- [ ] I can understand the impact IT has on a range of different areas of society.

- [ ] I can recognise the different methods that can be used to deliver technology-enhanced learning, including the advantages and disadvantages of each method.

PROJECT

Figure 12.22: A local food store uses robotics to help serve the customers who shop in the store.

You are creating a news report on how IT has affected society in your local area.

Use the internet to research how IT has been used in your local area. For example:

- automated services

- CCTV and monitoring

- electronic banking

- digital devices at home, in school or in businesses.

See whether you can find local news stories about IT developments in your area.

Research both advantages and disadvantages of these technologies in your local area.

Use your research to prepare a five-minute news story about different examples you have found.

At the end of your news story, discuss the advantages and disadvantages, and reach a conclusion as to whether you feel IT has had a positive impact, or a negative one in your local area.

Chapter 13

New and emerging technologies

LEARNING OUTCOMES

By the end of this chapter, you will be able to:

- understand a range of new and emerging technologies

- identify and understand the impacts of new and emerging technologies on a range of areas in society.

- discuss the advantages and disadvantages of new and emerging technologies.

Introduction

The world of technology is constantly changing. Scientific research and development is the source of new and **emerging technologies**. Many new and emerging technologies have a positive impact on our society. They help improve many areas of life. For example, they can benefit individuals, organisations, medicine and healthcare, scientific research and the environment.

KEY WORD

emerging technologies: technologies that are still in development and their full potential has not yet been reached

An emerging technology may be either a new technology or an existing technology that is being developed. It is important to remember that emerging technology is technology that has not yet reached its full potential.

13.1 Types of new and emerging technologies

Artificial intelligence

Artificial intelligence, also known as AI, is a type of technology that enables computers to behave as a human would. AI can react to input and can make decisions (see Figure 13.1).

AI can learn, plan, recognise speech and solve problems. AI is a rapidly developing technology.

DID YOU KNOW?

One of the earliest pioneers of AI was Alan Turing. Alan Turing was a British computer scientist. He is famous for heading up a top-secret group of code-breakers during the Second World War. Turing became fascinated by the possibility of intelligent machines that could make decisions in a human-like way.

AI systems are based on sets of rules. AI systems use rules to make decisions. The decisions depend on the input the system receives. The AI system can then adapt the decisions it makes as it learns and then develops its own learning. The algorithms that allow an AI system to develop knowledge are called machine learning algorithms.

DISCUSSION POINT

How would you feel about an artificial intelligence system taking over the role of your classroom teacher?

Figure 13.1: The robot picker uses AI to determine whether the tomato is ready to be picked.

Machine learning allows AI machines to identify and create patterns in input. This allows the system to analyse and learn. This then influences the decisions it makes later. AI systems need access to a knowledge base. An AI system will mine the data (see Chapter 12). This knowledge base allows the AI system to learn what is usually the 'correct' response and what may be a 'wrong' response. It develops patterns and relationships between the knowledge base it trains on. Machine learning is a core part of AI.

Table 13.1 summarises some of the advantages and disadvantages of AI.

Advantages	Disadvantages
Increased level of precision and accuracy; likely to have a lower error rate than a human.	Requires a high level of skills to program so can be very expensive to create.
Can replace the need for humans in tedious, repetitive or dangerous tasks.	The storage requirements for the program and knowledge base can be large, which is costly.
Machines do not require rest, so can be used 24/7.	There may be ethical and moral issues creating intelligent computers.
Can make logical decisions without emotion and so provides a more rational outcome.	They are not fully capable of human emotions such as sympathy and empathy.
Can analyse large sets of data much more efficiently and quickly than a human.	As AI is based on rules, this can affect its ability to be creative.

Table 13.1: Advantages and disadvantages of AI.

DISCUSSION POINT

Well-known writers/authors are complaining that their work has been data mined by AI and that AI is therefore plagiarising their work! What do you think about this?

Questions

1   Describe how AI works.
2   Give two benefits of AI.
3   Give one drawback of AI.

Autonomous transport systems

An autonomous transport system can operate on its own. The autonomous transport system is not directly controlled by humans. Both self-driving cars and driverless trains are being developed as part of the next generation of transport systems.

Self-driving cars

An autonomous or self-driving car does not require a human driver. It relies on AI systems to operate the car, navigate using GPS and park the car at its destination. A self-driving car must be able to process and recognise what happens around it. If the car does this correctly, then it is able to avoid collisions with other vehicles, objects or people (see Figure 13.2).

Figure 13.2: Autonomous cars use sensors to detect and avoid humans. For example, it must be able to spot people crossing the road at a crossing.

Some people view self-driving cars as a positive thing. They reduce the chance that people will drive when tired. It removes the emotional reactions of drivers.

Both emotions and tiredness often cause accidents. Those in favour of self-driving cars believe that removing tiredness and emotions from driving will reduce accidents.

Some people view self-driving cars as a negative thing. They believe that self-driving cars cannot make moral and ethical decisions. The safety of self-driving cars also depends on the quality of the algorithms the car uses to drive. The quality of the algorithms affects the AI's ability to make effective decisions in critical situations.

DISCUSSION POINT

What if two self-driving cars have an accident? Who is at fault and should pay for the damage?

Autonomous trains

Trains can also be autonomous. Some cities have autonomous trains.

Autonomous trains are easier to program than self-driving cars.

DISCUSSION POINT

Why do you think autonomous trains may be easier to program than autonomous cars? Think about the inputs, outputs and learning/processing that takes place.

Autonomous trains mean that there is no need for drivers. This saves the train companies money. Trains use sensors and data input to work out speed, location and distances. Sensors on the doors allow them to be opened and closed without a human. Drivers can get tired and make mistakes. Drivers can also only work for several hours before they need a break. Automation removes these challenges.

However, there are drawbacks to autonomous trains. What if a door didn't close properly? A driver could get out and check to see what the problem was. An automated train could not do this. Human drivers can also talk to passengers in an emergency. An autonomous train may rely on automated announcements. Humans also tend to have more trust in other humans to do things than automated machines.

DISCUSSION POINT

Would you trust a fully autonomous aeroplane that had no human pilots?

Augmented reality

Augmented reality (AR) mixes computer-generated images with a person's view of the real world. Augmented means 'to add to'. AR creates an interactive experience. It enhances the view of the real world with extra elements such as text, audio, animations and video.

Figure 13.3: Augmented reality apps can help people see what furniture would look like in their home.

AR was developed in the 1960s. As technology has advanced, AR has continued to develop. AR is a great example of an emerging technology. The potential of AR grows as the technology we have access to grows as well.

AR often uses a digital camera and sensors to read data from the surrounding environment. It then uses a display to merge the real world and the AR.

AR can be used with smart phones. Many companies use AR to allow you to see their products in 'real life'. For example, you can use AR to show what a sofa or chair may look like in your living room (see Figure 13.3). AR could show you how clothes may look on you. You can change the colours and style of the clothes without being in the shop.

Each storage crystal is about the size of a grain of sugar. A storage crystal can store roughly one terabyte (1 TB) of data. Imagine how much data could be stored on a single disk as a result!

Large amounts of data are stored each day. The size of the hardware to store data is very important when storing lots of data. Small reductions in the size of the storage devices can have major effects on the cost and size of the storage facilities needed.

Holographic data storage takes up very small amounts of space. For example, the CERN data centre, a large particle physics laboratory in Switzerland, generates 30 petabytes of data a year. Traditional storage devices could take up hundreds of metres of physical space (see Figure 13.12). However, holographic data storage would be very much smaller and so take up much less space. This will reduce the cost of storage too.

Figure 13.12: Data storage facility.

Holographic data storage is very new technology. This means that many of the world's computers will not be able to use it. Because holographic storage is very new, it uses expensive technology. This makes it very costly to produce. A holographic storage device could cost tens of thousands of pounds.

Holograms can only store a limited amount of data. Currently, that's around 300 gigabytes of data. Most modern hard discs can store 1 terabyte of data as standard. Therefore, it has limitations in terms of the cost per megabyte to store data.

Additionally, holographic storage has not yet been tested fully, or for long periods of time, so it is not known how robust this method of storage is.

Table 13.5 lists some of the advantages and disadvantages of holographic data storage.

Advantages	Disadvantages
Large amounts of data can be stored on a very small medium.	It is not compatible with current methods of data storage. This would make reading the data very difficult.
It will make the storage of large amounts of data much more portable.	The technology required to use holographic data storage is currently very complex and expensive.
It is capable of storage millions of bits of data at a time, making transfer rates much faster than current methods.	

Table 13.5: Advantages and disadvantages of holographic data storage.

ACTIVITY 13.06

Research 4th generational optical storage and prepare a short presentation explaining it and what its probable effect will be.

3D printing

3D printing uses a special printer to create a 3D model of something designed on a computer. The printer can use many different materials. For example, it can print in plastic or metal (see Figure 13.13). Some 3D printers use concrete and can print a house!

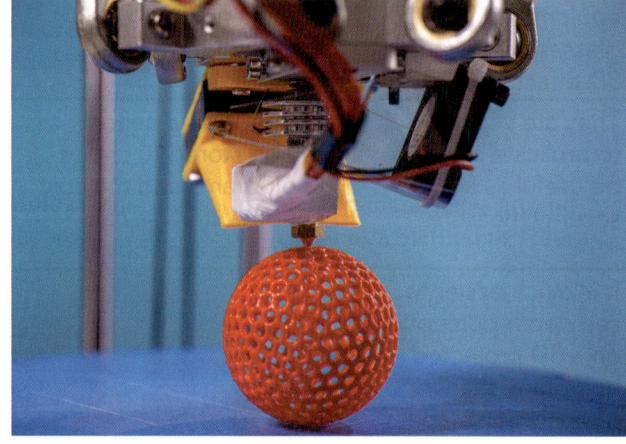

Figure 13.13: A simple 3D printer prints a ball using plastic.

3D printing has existed since the 1980s. However, the methods used for printing and what we use 3D printing for are still evolving. The cost of 3D printers is getting cheaper. Eventually, many households may be able to afford the technology.

A 3D printer requires a 3D software-based model. The software model is created using computer aided design (CAD). The data about the model is sent to a 3D printer. The 3D printer then prints a physical model of the software model. The 3D printer prints many very thin layers of material on top of each other.

3D printing is used by manufacturing businesses in many different industries, including:

- Dentistry – for example, to print teeth and crowns (upper part of a tooth).
- Prosthetics – for example, new limbs and body parts such as hip joints.
- Medical tools and equipment – for example, surgical instruments.
- Houses – 3D printers use concrete to print houses quickly and at low cost.
- Replacement parts – for example, parts for cars, boats and machinery can be made using a 3D printer.
- Jewellery – bracelets and rings can be 3D printed in metal.

Bio-printing

3D printing has revolutionised many areas of the medical industry, as described before.

We can also use 3D printers to print human cells. This is called bio-printing. A special 3D printer uses biomaterials to create tissue-like structures. This technique can also be used to print organs and artificial blood vessels. Bio-printing can also be used to aid other medical research like drug manufacturing.

Bio-printing reduces the need to use real organs for medical research. Biomedical printing techniques may soon allow us to create artificial organs that can replace human organs. This will mean that people will not wait as long for transplants.

Printing in space

3D printing has become an increasingly valuable practice in space. If something breaks on a space station, the crew may wait for a long time for another rocket to arrive with a replacement part. However, a 3D printer could print the new part quickly. This means that repairing a breakdown could take hours, rather than months.

DISCUSSION POINT

How would you feel about having a 3D printed artificial organ inserted into your body?

Table 13.6 lists some of the advantages and disadvantages of 3D printing.

Advantages	Disadvantages
The speed at which certain objects can be made is greatly increased using 3D printing.	It has become much easier to build dangerous and counterfeit items, which causes greater security and fraud issues.
A 3D printer will create the exact same product from a model.	At present, 3D printers are only capable of creating relatively small items. Developments are progressing to increase the size of the objects that a 3D printer can create.
Much more flexible when creating complex models, especially those with difficult or complex designs.	3D printing reduces the number of manufacturing jobs, as it can replace the need for humans to create the products.
The cost of creating each product with a 3D printer will often be much cheaper.	3D printing requires a relatively high level of power consumption. This can be harmful to the environment as it increases emissions.
The level of consistency when making many of the same item is much greater than when created by a human.	The waste plastic from 3D printing is usually thrown away and has a negative effect on the environment.

Table 13.6: Advantages and disadvantages of 3D printing.

Questions

8   Why is 3D printing an important emerging technology?

9   What are the risks of 3D printing?

Vision enhancement

Vision enhancement is used to enhance our ability to see in extreme conditions. For example, vision enhancement can help people to see in the dark. Two types of vision enhancement are night vision and thermal vision. Night vision, such as night vision goggles, collects all available light and amplifies it to create a visible image. An image that uses night vision is often green in appearance.

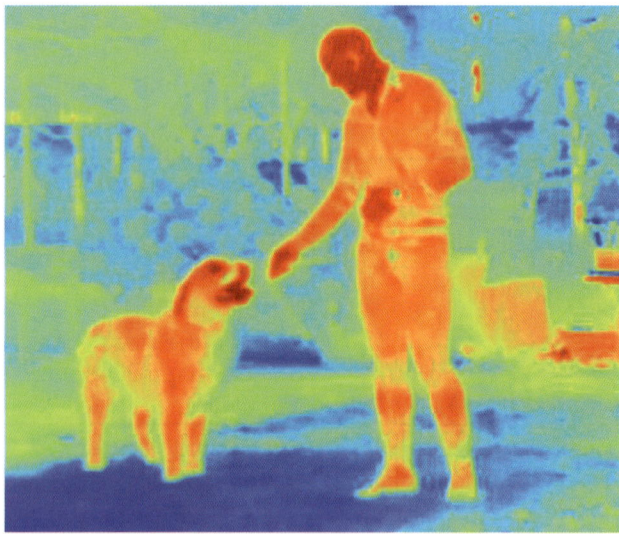

Figure 13.14: Thermal imaging allows us to see different spectra of light. Here we can see the difference between heat and cold.

Thermal vision captures the infrared light emitted as heat by objects such as humans and animals (see Figure 13.14). It will also detect the heat from fires.

Thermal imaging is often used to find people in the countryside or the dark. The heat from the body can be clearly seen against the cold ground. Thermal imaging is also used when searching in emergency situations like a collapsed building.

Table 13.7 shows some advantages and disadvantages of vision enhancement.

Advantages	Disadvantages
Allows us to see in extreme conditions.	Technology is very expensive.
Can help with search and rescue.	Not easily repairable at home and needs to be sent to special manufacturers for repair.
Can aid safety when climbing mountains or exploring caves.	

Table 13.7: Advantages and disadvantages of vision enhancement.

Wearable computing

Wearable computing is worn on the body (see Figure 13.15). Most often, wearable computing is worn on the wrist such as a smart watch or fitness tracker. Fitness trackers can be used to monitor a person's heart rate while they are exercising. They can also be used to record blood pressure and the number of steps as part of a person's daily lifestyle. Wearable computing also refers to clothing or accessories that have some form of computer-based components embedded into them. This could include glasses, headsets, t-shirts and trainers. Some wearable computing devices have a specific purpose. For example, sports people may wear GPS trackers to measure sporting performance.

Exercise brings rewards

Organisations are now providing employees with health trackers. The employees earn rewards based on the amount of exercise they record. They may be provided with points for the number of steps that they record each day. These points can be spent on rewards. Rewards may be gift vouchers or holidays.

Figure 13.15: Wearable technology.

Patient care and monitoring

Health trackers can be used to monitor serious health issues. A person could have their heart rate constantly monitored if they have heart issues. If a problem occurs, then the device can send an alert to a medical professional or family member. This can happen instantly. This could save a person's life.

Table 13.8 lists some of the advantages and disadvantages of wearable computing.

Advantages	Disadvantages
It allows greater access to important statistics regarding our daily health. This can improve our ability to monitor our health.	Users can become obsessed with their health statistics, which can lead to damaging thoughts.
Users can sync their fitness devices together and can encourage each other and set each other challenges, improving people's motivation to exercise.	There can be compatibility issues between devices, such as fitness trackers and mobile phones, that may mean data cannot be shared between them.
It can aid communication by allowing a user to see alerts for any text messages or emails that they have received on their wearable device. Some can even be used to make telephone calls. This removes the need for the user to take their mobile out of their pocket or bag.	The accuracy of some health trackers can be poor, as they are designed to monitor the 'average' person and not the bespoke health of each person.
	Some people are concerned about the security of their data that is gathered by their wearable device. It is also possible for companies to use the data that is collected for marketing purposes, which users may not be aware of.

Table 13.8: Advantages and disadvantages of wearable computing.

ACTIVITY 13.07

Research how wearable technologies are being developed to monitor health issues.

Pick one technology and create a poster that shows how it monitors health issues.
For example, you may choose the latest monitors that help people with diabetes.

DISCUSSION POINT

How do you think our world will continue to change through the development of emerging technologies?

Blockchain

We looked at the use of blockchain in Chapter 12 as distributed ledgers for cryptocurrencies. Blockchain is an emerging technology. Blockchain allows transactions to be stored securely. Each block stores a transaction and an image of the block before it. Each block is therefore linked to the previous block. These blocks make a long chain. This is why it is called blockchain.

Blockchain makes it very hard to change an individual block, because each block has an image of the block before it. This means that we can check that an earlier block is valid. This is because we have the hashed image of the block.

Cryptocurrency transactions are usually stored in blockchain because of the security of blockchain (see Chapter 12 for more information on cryptocurrencies). Many countries are now using blockchain in their currency transactions. Blockchain can also be used in sales and payment transactions.

Blockchain offers a secure method of storage but there is one major disadvantage of the use of blockchain. People set up computers to process the blockchain transactions. These computers are very powerful. All blockchain transactions are linked and stored in the cloud or on other computers. This requires a vast amount of energy to process and store all the transactions.

PRACTICE QUESTIONS

1 Identify one advantage and one disadvantage to the user of wearable technology such as a health tracker. **[2]**
2 Explain three ways that 3D printing can be used in medical circumstances. **[3]**
3 Explain two advantages to a surgeon of using augmented reality technology when performing surgery. **[3]**
4 Explain two disadvantages that emerging technologies have on the environment. **[4]**
5 Discuss the impact on employees of the use of AI in manufacturing. **[8]**
6 Evaluate the potential impact on an organisation of using holographic data storage to archive data. **[6]**

SUMMARY CHECKLIST

- [ ] I can understand what is meant by a new and emerging technology.
- [ ] I can recognise a range of new and emerging technologies and understand how they are used.
- [ ] I can understand the impact of a range of new and emerging technologies on areas of society such as individuals, organisations, medicine and healthcare, scientific research and the environment.
- [ ] I can discuss the advantages and disadvantages of new and emerging technologies.

PROJECT

Create a presentation about new and emerging technology (see Figure 13.20).

Your presentation should look at one area in your life. It could be focused on your personal life, school or your local town or village.

Research ideas about how emerging technology can benefit the area that you have chosen. Identify emerging technology that you would want to use. Describe what the technology is, and how you would use it to make things better. You can use the internet to do deeper research into areas you may not know about.

Present your presentation to your classmates and discuss your ideas with them.

Figure 13.20: In the future, robot couriers may deliver your packages.

> Chapter 14
Communications technology

LEARNING INTENTIONS

By the end of this chapter, you will be able to:

- understand different types of network, their characteristics and uses, and their advantages and disadvantages

- understand the role and operation of different components in a network

- understand the different types of network server, their role and operations in a network, and advantages and disadvantages of each type of server

- understand the characteristics, uses, and advantages and disadvantages of cloud computing for individuals and organisations

- understand about speed of data transmission across networks, including bandwidth and bit rate, and data streaming

- understand properties, features, characteristics and applications of transmission methods, including the effect on bandwidth, and advantages and disadvantages of data transmission methods

- understand different methods of sending data over a network, including packet switching, circuit switching and message switching, and the purpose and use of network addressing systems

CONTINUED

- understand the definition of a network protocol and the purpose and use of protocols in the preparation, addressing, sending and receiving of data across a network, including the internet

- understand about the management of network traffic, static and dynamic routing, the function of routing protocols, and the use of layers in protocols and firewalls

- understand the methods, uses and operation, security issues, and advantages and disadvantages of different methods of wireless data transmission

- understand about mobile communication systems, including cellular networks and how satellite communication systems are used for transferring data

- understand a range of network security threats to stored data and files, the impact of network security threats on individuals and organisations, and a range of prevention methods of network security issues, including the advantages and disadvantages of each method

- understand how threats and risks are identified in disaster recovery management, how to control threats, and the strategies to minimise risks.

BEFORE YOU START

- Do you have a basic understanding of a LAN, a WAN and a range of network topologies?

- Do you have a basic understanding of a range of network components including hubs, switches, routers and bridges?

- Do you have a basic understanding of security methods that can be used in a network?

Introduction

Before the 1990s, most computers were not connected to other computers (see Figure 14.1). Since then, it has become very common for computers to be connected to **networks**. Now, nearly every computer is connected to at least one network.

KEY WORD

network: two or more computers or devices connected together so they can communicate and share data and resources

Figure 14.1: An office worker using a computer in the early 1980s. This computer is not connected to any other devices, including the internet.

When computers are connected, a network is created. The simplest form of network is two computers connected, but most networks are much larger and more complex than this. Two laptops sharing the same Wi-Fi are a network, but every computer connected to the internet is also part of a network (see Figure 14.2).

Figure 14.2: The tablet and laptop in this picture are connected to the same Wi-Fi network. Therefore, this is a network.

The primary reason we create networks is to share data and resources, and to communicate with other people. Computers connected to the internet, for example, can access most of the same online data, and can communicate with other computers connected to the internet.

14.1 Networks

Characteristics of networks

Each network has its own characteristics (traits) that make it unique or bespoke. These can be broken down into its **topologies**, its **architecture** and its **protocols**.

KEY WORDS

network topology: the arrangement or pattern in which all devices on a network are connected

network architecture: the layout of a network, both logical and physical

network protocols: a set of rules that determine how computers on a network communicate with each other

Topologies (physical and logical)

Any device connected to a network is known as a node. A network's topology is the arrangement of nodes within a network. There are two categories of topology to be aware of: physical and logical. Every network has a physical and a logical topology.

Physical

The physical topology is how the nodes are physically connected to each other. There are four common types of physical topology, as shown in Table 14.1 and Figures 14.3 to 14.6.

Type	Description	Image
Bus	In a bus, all of the nodes are connected directly to a central cable that runs through the network. Data is sent up and down the central cable until it reaches the correct node. The cable is known as the backbone.	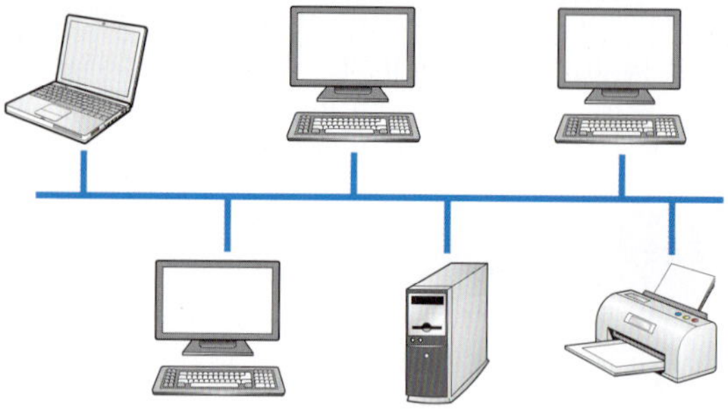 **Figure 14.3:** Bus topology.
Star	A star topology connects all nodes indirectly through switches (devices for connecting computers, which you'll learn more about in section 14.2). All communications are passed through the switch or switches in the topology.	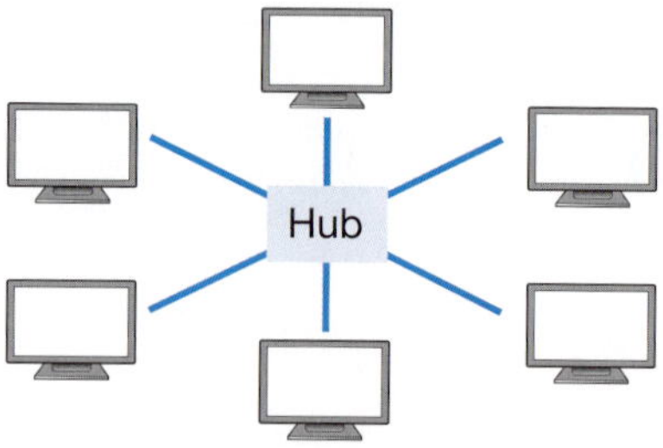 **Figure 14.4:** Star topology.
Ring	Ring topologies are comprised of nodes that can only connect to the two nodes on either side of it. This set-up creates a single pathway for data to travel, and the topology resembles a circle.	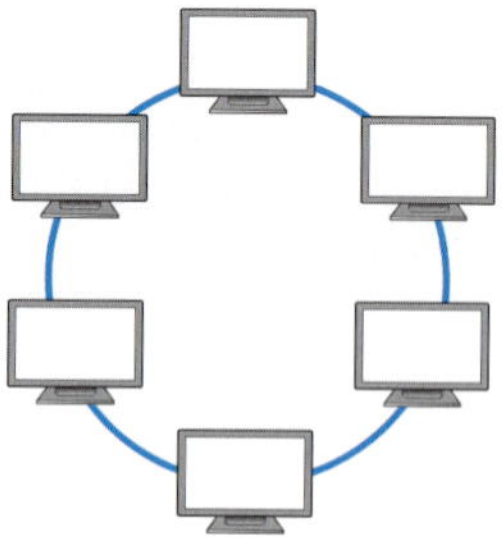 **Figure 14.5:** Ring topology.
Mesh	Mesh topologies are popular because they are efficient. In a full mesh topology, every node is connected to every other node, meaning data can be sent across many different routes.	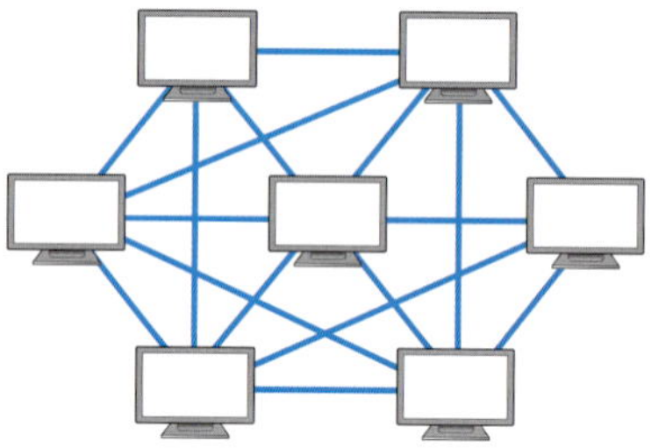 **Figure 14.6:** Mesh topology.

Table 14.1: Types of physical topology.

Logical

Logical topology is how data flows through a network. It is bound to a network protocol that determines how nodes communicate with each other.

The logical topology refers to the different roles the nodes in the network play, determined by the protocols and the architecture of the network. This means that two networks could share the same physical topology but have different logical topologies. Depending on how you set up a network, a node could be a client or a server, which you will learn more about later.

Think of topology like a house. The house always remains the same: the rooms are the same size, the staircases are always in the same place, and the house is fully connected, but you could have your bedroom upstairs or downstairs, or move it to any room. The room would not change, but the function of the room changes (see Figure 14.7).

Figure 14.7: Any of the rooms in this house could be swapped, just like any nodes can be swapped to play a different role in a network.

Protocols

Protocols are instructions for how different computers in a network communicate with each other. For example, all computers communicating via the internet use the Internet Protocol (IP). You will learn more about protocols in section 14.6.

Architecture

Network architecture refers to the physical and the logical layout of a network, including transmission equipment, infrastructure (such as wired or wireless), software and communication protocols, and the transmission of data between nodes. In summary, network architecture is the complete layout of the network, whereas the protocols and topologies are part of the architecture.

Each type of network you will look at in this chapter has its own architecture.

Types and uses of network

There are several different types of network:

- local area network (LAN)
- wide area network (WAN)
- client–server
- peer-to-peer
- virtual private network (VPN)
- mobile networks.

Local area network/wide area network

A **local area network (LAN)** is a network of computers and other devices that are connected within a small geographic area, such as a home, school or small business. A LAN could be as simple as two computers connected within a home. It could also be as extensive as 100 computers, several peripheral devices such as printers, and other network components, such as switches and servers, connected in a small business. Individuals and organisations create LAN networks to allow them to efficiently share data and resources, such as peripherals.

> **KEY WORDS**
>
> **local area network (LAN):** a relatively small network that is located within a single building or site

Table 14.2 lists the differences in the characteristics of LAN and WAN networks.

Characteristic	LAN	WAN
Data transfer rate	Capable of higher transfer speeds up to 1 Gb per second.	Often restricted to lower transfer speeds, normally less than 200 Mb.
Data transmission errors	Fewer errors are likely to occur because data is transferred over a shorter distance.	Greater chance of errors occurring as data is transferred over longer distances.
Method of connection	Normally connected using copper wire, fibre optic cables or radio waves. It could be a mixture of all three.	Connections could include copper wire, fibre optic cables, radio waves, microwaves, public telephone systems, leased lines, transmission towers and satellites.
Security	Can normally be kept more secure as a smaller number of devices need securing. Most of the security required is the responsibility of the network owners.	More vulnerable to security issues as a larger number of devices need securing. The organisation will normally need to rely on the security measures of others for part of the network, so they will not be able to control security in these areas.
Ownership	Most of the network components and devices are owned by the individual or organisation, so they can control and maintain them.	Parts of the network are often owned by a third party, so they have to rely on the control and maintenance of others.

Table 14.2: Characteristics of LAN and WAN networks.

A **wide area network (WAN)** is a network of computers and other devices that are connected over a large geographical area. The largest example of a WAN is the internet. Businesses and organisations, such as banks and the police force, use WAN networks because they have multiple branches or offices over a large geographical area that need to be connected to share data and resources. A WAN in these examples is normally a LAN network in each location that is connected together to create a WAN.

KEY WORD

wide area network (WAN): a relatively large network that is normally two or more LANs that are linked

LAN and WAN networks are set up to share data, storage and peripheral devices. We can identify the differences between LAN and WAN networks by comparing their characteristics (see Table 14.2).

UNPLUGGED ACTIVITY 14.02

Using the characteristics of LAN and WAN outlined in Table 14.2, create a list of advantages and disadvantages of LAN and WAN.
Think about the different scenarios each one would be useful for when making your list.

Client–server

A client–server network is one that contains two types of computers, a **client** and a **server**. The server or servers in a client–server network are a central point of control and provide a dedicated function such as print server for the network. All other computers in the network are called clients. The client computers in the network are all connected to the server to allow it to perform its dedicated function. Most downloadable content (such as videos, games or software) comes from a client–server network.

KEY WORDS

client: a computer in a network that is not a central point of control

server: a computer in a network that is a point of control

UNPLUGGED ACTIVITY 14.03

Draw a diagram to represent a client–server network. The network must contain eight computers, two printers, a print server and a file server.

What kind of physical topology is this?

Peer-to-peer

A peer-to-peer network contains computers known as **peers**. A peer-to-peer network can be as simple as two computers connected in a household. A peer-to-peer network can also contain hundreds of peer computers connected using the internet. The main reason that peer-to-peer networks are created is to share data. A peer-to-peer network has a decentralised structure, which means that it does not have any central point of control , for example Skype (see Figure 14.8). Therefore, each peer in the network has the same level of responsibility and capability.

KEY WORD

peer: a computer of equal importance in a peer-to-peer network

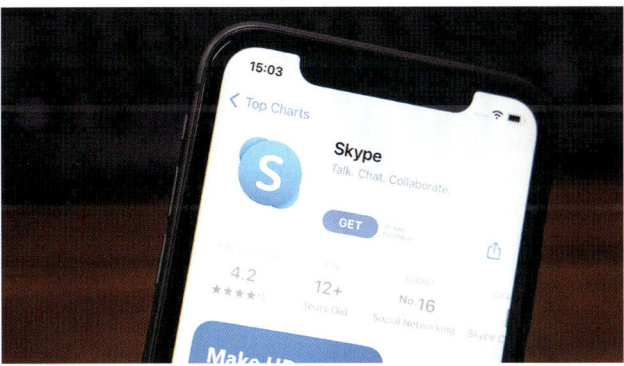

Figure 14.8: Skype uses a peer-to-peer network through the Skype application.

Each user in the peer-to-peer network stores data on their computer. The user can choose to keep this data private, which means other peers in the network are not able to view it. They can also choose to make the data public, which means that other peers in the network are able to view the data too. If a peer computer in the network has a peripheral, such as a printer attached to

it, the user can make the printer public so that other peer computers can use it too.

Peer-to-peer networks can be used to share large files such as audio, software and videos. Audio and video files are accessed by users using a dedicated peer-to-peer software. The software links people who have the files with people who want the files, so that the data can be exchanged. This method of file sharing has proved controversial because of its use in the piracy of music and movies. However, the use of a peer-to-peer network does not necessarily mean the content is pirated: some companies use peer-to-peer to distribute their software, which users often pay for.

BitTorrent is a communications protocol that is often used in peer-to-peer file sharing. It allows the transfer of large files such as videos. BitTorrent does this through distributing the load of downloading the file across several sources on the network. Several sources (known as hosts) are collated to create a swarm. Each host will be given pieces of the file. The BitTorrent protocol allows the user to join the swarm and download parts of the file from the available hosts. The protocol will download the file in pieces, simultaneously, from various hosts in the swarm. The protocol can then rearrange the pieces to create the completed file.

As a basic example, ten hosts may have 10% of a movie file each. The BitTorrent protocol would download all ten parts of the file simultaneously and put the ten pieces back to form the full movie (see Figure 14.9).

Each piece of the file is protected to stop it being modified by any users. Each user trying to download the file is called a peer and each user that is providing an upload of the file, as part of the swarm, is called a seed.

Figure 14.9: The pieces of the file fit back together, a bit like a jigsaw, to ensure the file is complete and in the correct order.

Hubs and switches

If only two computers are connected in a network, a simple ethernet connection between the two can be made (see Figure 14.12). If several computers need to be connected, a component needs to be used to connect the devices and manage the traffic. There are two devices that can be used for this purpose. They are a **hub** and a **switch**.

Figure 14.12: An ethernet cable being plugged into a device.

KEY WORDS

hub: a network component that joins computers together and forwards units of data (data packets) to all connected devices

switch: a device used to connect computers and other networked devices together, which can receive and forward data

A hub is a component in a network to which each device is connected using a wired connection (see Figure 14.13). If one device wants to send data to another device in the network, the data will go via the hub. The hub receives the data from the sender and then forwards the data on to every other device connected to the hub. The other devices connected to the hub will ignore the data sent to them if they are not the intended destination. The computer that is the intended destination will receive the data.

A hub may be an active or passive hub. A passive hub will just send the data to the other devices as described. An active hub will amplify (boost) and regenerate the signal used to send the data to make the signal stronger. Because the hub forwards the data to all connected devices, there is a lot of unwanted traffic in the network.

This can often cause an issue called data collisions. The data sent only needs to be received by the intended destination device. To overcome the problem of data collisions, another network component called the switch was developed.

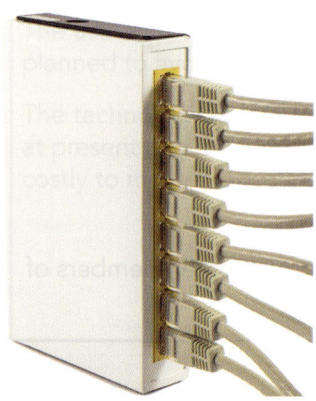

Figure 14.13: Hub.

A switch is used in the same way as a hub, to connect devices together (see Figure 14.14). The difference between a hub and a switch is the way they each forward the data received to its destination. A switch can examine each data packet it receives and forward the data packet only to the intended destination. Switches know which device to send the data to because, when the devices are connected to the switch, the switch creates a MAC address source table. When it receives a data packet, it looks at which MAC address is the intended destination of the packet and then forwards it to that device. This reduces the amount of traffic on the network because data is only sent to the destination device, and not to every device it is connected to on the network. This also reduces the number of data collisions.

Figure 14.14: Switch.

Repeaters

Signals sent by devices may deteriorate (get weaker) as they travel around a network. Signals may deteriorate as a result of interference in the transmission media (the cables that are used to transmit data around a network). To try to maintain the original quality of the signal as it travels around a network, a component called a **repeater** can be used. A repeater can be used at various points in a network to boost the signal as it passes through the repeater. A repeater can be used to boost a wired signal, or a wireless signal, and they are capable of retransmitting both analogue and digital signals.

KEY WORD

repeater: a network component that is used to boost a signal in data transmission

---

Wireless access points

The network component required for devices to connect to a network using a wireless connection is a **wireless access point**. A wireless access point allows a wireless device to connect to a wired network. It receives wireless data signals and then uses the wired network to transmit them to their destination, often via a switch. Switches support the connection of multiple wireless devices to the same wireless access point, effectively creating a wireless LAN. Although a wireless access point will support the connection of multiple devices, it often has a limit of 15 to 20 devices. For this reason, larger organisations will have multiple wireless access points distributed throughout the building. The signal strength for connection to a wireless access point also deteriorates with distance.

Bridges

Some businesses and organisations may be based in different buildings on the same site. This will mean that their LAN is split up and spread across different buildings. This can result in parts of the LAN being too far apart to operate effectively. The signal can deteriorate too much, travelling from one device to another. The different parts of the LAN can be connected more effectively using a network component called a **bridge**.

A bridge uses MAC addresses to forward data to the correct destination, like a switch. However, a bridge works slightly differently from a switch. It examines the

data packets it receives, checking them against the MAC address source table. If the bridge finds that the data packet's destination is in another part of the network, for example another building on the site, it will forward the packet 'across the bridge' to that part of the LAN. If the bridge finds that the packet's destination is within the same part of the network, for example within the same building, it will just ignore the packet and allow it to continue to its destination.

KEY WORDS

wireless access point: a network component that receives and transmits radio signals to allow wireless (Wi-Fi) connection to a network

bridge: a network component that connects segregated parts of a LAN

Gateways and routers

Some businesses such as banks have different branches or locations, sometimes within the same city. Each branch of the bank will have its own LAN network. The branches may want to share data about their customers, so they need to connect their LANs together. LANs can be connected using a component called a **gateway**. A common gateway component that is used to connect LANs is called a **router**.

One of the primary roles of a router is to assign each device that is connected to it with an **IP address**. An IP address is an address that is unique to the device and can be used to identify its location in the network.

KEY WORDS

gateway: a network component that joins different LANs together

router: a network component used to connect LANs together, and to connect LANs to WANs

Internet Protocol (IP) address: a unique address for each node/device on a network

---

ACTIVITY 14.07

To find out what your IP address is in Windows:

1 Select Start.

2 Go to Settings.

3 Select Network & internet, and then Wi-Fi.

4 Select the Wi-Fi network you are currently connected to

5 Under Properties, you will find your IP address listed next to IPv4 address.

If you are on an Apple Mac:

1 Select the Apple menu and click System Settings.

2 Go to Network and then select Wi-Fi.

3 Next to the network you are connected to, select Details.

4 Scroll down to see your Mac's local IP address.

A router is used to connect LANs and also to connect LANs to WANs (see Figure 14.15). A router acts in a similar way to a switch, but with two main differences. The first is that a switch will only forward data packets to their destination within a single network. However, a router is used to forward data packets outside the current LAN to other networks. The second is that a switch examines data packets and looks for the MAC

address to check the packet's destination. A router looks for the IP address of the destination device and uses this to send the data packet there.

Figure 14.15: A router.

Questions

6 What is the purpose of a hub?

7 Why could a hub be considered inefficient?

8 Why would you use a switch?

9 Describe the function of a bridge.

10 Explain what a MAC address is.

14.3 Network servers

There are several types of server that could be included in a client–server network. Table 14.4 lists the servers and the dedicated function that each performs.

Server type	Function
File server	Stores and manages data files so there is no need for client computers to have a lot of storage space.
	Allows users to use any client computer in the network and be able to access their files and any publicly shared files.
	Able to do a central back-up of all data.
Web server	Stores, processes and transmits web pages.
Mail server	Sends and receives emails.
	Stores incoming emails for the user that can be downloaded when requested.
	Forwards outgoing messages to the correct destination.
	Often has security checking software that will scan emails for issues such as known viruses and malware. Mail servers can also be set to check for inappropriate content and spam.

Server type	Function
Applications server	Installs and runs software applications.
	Provides a platform to run both desktop and web applications.
Print server	Receives print jobs from client computers and sends them to the correct printer, which allows many client computers in a network to use the range of printers available.
	Can be set to print to a specific printer.
	Can be set to find the next available printer, or the closest printer to the client. If many jobs are sent to the print server at a time, it will queue the jobs until it can deliver them to a printer.
File transfer protocol (FTP) server	Manages the transfer of data that uses the ftp (see 14.6 Network protocols).
	Keeps a log of all activity involving FTP.
	Often used in the transfer of files over the internet.
Proxy server	Acts as an intermediary (go-between) between clients and other servers by receiving client requests and forwarding them to the relevant server.
Virtual server	Shares the hardware of another server.
	Created using virtualisation software on another server; multiple virtual servers could be created on one physical server.
	Can act as any of the above servers. For example, businesses sometimes use third-party virtual servers as a web server for the business to host its website. This allows the hosting company the ability to host several businesses' websites on the hardware of a single physical server.

Table 14.4: Types of network server.

The role and function of servers in a network

Servers can be grouped together to provide functionality that would not be possible with a single computer. As a group, the servers have a huge amount of processing power. Servers that are grouped in this way are called a **server farm** and they can be used to execute (carry out) very large tasks, as all servers can be used to execute one or more parts of the task at the same time. There are often thousands of servers in a server farm (see Figure 14.16).

KEY WORD

server farm: a group of servers in the same location that have a huge amount of processing power

DID YOU KNOW?

One of the largest server farms is owned and maintained by Google. It has more than 10 000 servers.

Figure 14.16: A server farm has huge processing power.

The operations of servers in a network

Most client–server networks operate using a request and response method of communication between servers and clients. A typical operation in this method is a client sends a request to a server to ask the server to perform a task and the server responds by performing the task. You could think of this as being similar to a server in a restaurant: if you ask them for something, they will serve it to you (see Figure 14.17).

Figure 14.17: A client asks a server for something, and the server provides it. This is a bit like a restaurant server.

Advantages and disadvantages of servers

Table 14.5 sets out the advantages and disadvantages of servers.

Server type	Advantages	Disadvantages
File server	Convenient for file sharing.	Requires an IT specialist to set up.
	Useful for collaborating without creating numerous versions of the same file.	If the server fails, files are inaccessible until the issue is resolved.
	Easy organisation of a large quantity of files.	File servers can be expensive.
	Minimal training required to use them.	
Web server	Relatively easy to configure.	Web server hosting can be expensive.
	Supported and maintained by its host.	Security risks are relatively high.
	Can support a large amount of data.	Requires regular maintenance by its host.
		Can be slow if there is a lot of traffic or if configured poorly.
Mail server	Typically means mail reaches the user faster.	Sometimes spam emails are miscategorised and delivered to the user, or non-spam emails are classified as spam.
	Provides virus and spam protection.	
	Often no user charges.	Complex to set up and run.
	Email streams can be customised.	

Server type	Advantages	Disadvantages
Applications server	Usually a firewall present between web servers and applications servers. Enhances performance of applications. Easy to generate back-ups.	Usually requires other supporting components. Network delay is relatively likely. Coding and maintenance require skill and time.
Print server	Using powerful, dedicated hardware means printing is fast and efficient. Use of a print server centralises management of printing, meaning IT staff at a company can control printing from a singular node. Easy to add new devices to the network. Can queue print jobs to avoid network overload. Generally very reliable.	Print servers take up space and require expertise for upkeep. They are not cheap. Large print jobs can create a heavy burden on the network. Single point of failure: if the server fails, you cannot print.
FTP server	Allows high levels of control. Strong data recovery opportunities. Allows large files and folders to be transferred between computers.	Requires large amounts of memory. Data is not always encrypted. Weak passwords can be guessed for access. Not always user-friendly.
Proxy server	Provides an added level of security in a network, protecting clients directly accessing resources on another server. For this reason, proxy servers can also be set to act as firewalls. Hides a user's IP address.	Lacks data encryption. Proxy may not always be compatible with a local network. Blocked websites can be accessed through a proxy server, which could expose people to problematic content.
Virtual server	Can greatly reduce costs to an organisation. Many operations can be automated, saving time and resources. Easy recovery after a disaster because nearly all virtual servers have features to aid with this.	High upfront cost. More difficult to find a root cause when there is an error. Can require a lot of training to use.

Table 14.5: Advantages and disadvantages of servers

14.4 Cloud computing

Cloud computing offers individuals and organisations a range of internet services such as storage of data and software, and access to resources such as servers. Examples of providers include Dropbox and Google Drive. Some cloud computing services are free to users; others may be subscription or usage based.

> **KEY WORD**
>
> **cloud computing:** using a network of servers hosted on the internet to store and manage data

There are different levels of services offered by cloud computing providers:

- Infrastructure as a service (IaaS): the provider hosts some of the network resources that are used by businesses, such as servers. Businesses can gain access to these resources using the internet.

- Software as a service (SaaS): the provider allows users access to the provider's software applications.

- Platform as a service (PaaS): the provider hosts platform resources that can be used to build software applications. Users can gain access to these resources using the internet.

Uses of cloud computing

One of the most common uses of cloud computing by the individual is to store data. Many applications now offer the service of storing data linked to the application, and other personal data, on cloud resources. These are normally a collection of servers in a remote location. Cloud computing can also be used in organisations so that several people working on the same project can access the same data, which makes version control and co-working much easier. Cloud computing is especially useful for new or small businesses who may not have the capital (money) to invest in hardware and want to use free or cheap software.

Advantages and disadvantages of cloud computing

Table 14.6 sets out the advantages and disadvantages of cloud computing.

Advantages	Disadvantages
Individuals and organisations do not need to purchase additional hardware to store data and software.	Individuals and organisations are reliant on a third party to keep their data secure. They have little control over the security measures that are put in place by the cloud provider.
Individuals and organisations do not need to host their own development platforms to develop applications software.	If the resources provided by the cloud provider fail, for example a server fails, then the data or software stored on that server will become unavailable.
Organisations do not need to employ technical staff to maintain the hardware used to store data and software that is provided by the cloud provider.	Cloud computing resources can only be updated or refreshed (e.g. changes to a Google Doc) when connected to the internet, so if an internet connection is unavailable, the resources cannot be updated.
Individuals and organisations do not need to create a back-up of their data, because this is automatically carried out by the cloud provider.	
Individuals and organisations can access their data and software applications from anywhere in the world, as long as they have an internet connection.	
Individuals and organisations do not need to worry about updating software applications that are accessed using the cloud, because this will be carried out by the cloud provider.	
Organisations can quickly boost the performance of their network by employing more resources from the cloud. For example, if an organisation is expecting more data traffic to their server from an online sale, they could increase the capacity of the web server to allow it to handle the temporary increase in traffic. They could then reduce it again after the sale to save costs.	

Table 14.6: Advantages and disadvantages of cloud computing.

14.5 Data transmission across networks

Speed of transmission

One very important factor that affects the performance of a network is **bandwidth**. The bandwidth of a network is the measure of the frequencies available on the channels of communication in the network. Bandwidth is also used to describe the maximum amount of data that can be transferred across a network within a given time, which is usually one second. Therefore, the more bandwidth a connection has, the more data it can transfer at a single time.

The **bit rate** is a similar measure to bandwidth. The bit rate is a measure of how many bits of data are transferred in a given period of time. It is different from the bandwidth in that bandwidth is a term used to describe the performance ability of a network, whereas bit rate is used to describe the rate at which a particular file, such as a video file, is transferred. The bit rate of a transfer will not exceed the bandwidth, because the bandwidth will be the maximum possible bit rate. For example, a network could have a bandwidth of 100 mega bits per second (Mbps) but a video file that is transferred from one computer to another over the network may be transferred at a bit rate of 75 Mbps.

Data streaming

Bandwidth and bit rate are important when streaming audio and video files. When a file is streamed, either live (real time) or on demand (not live), it removes the need to download and store the whole file before it is played. Data is streamed as a series of bits to the receiving device. The receiving device will have a temporary storage area called a buffer. Data will be stored in the buffer as it is downloaded, before it is needed as the video or audio is played. Data is removed from the buffer to be played and at the same time added to be ready to play when required.

Properties, features and characteristics of different transmission methods

To connect devices together in a network, a wired or wireless connection will be necessary.

There are three main types of cable that can be used to create a wired connection between devices. The cables are fibre optic, copper cable (coaxial and twisted pair) and lasers, as shown in Table 14.7.

Transmission method		Advantages	Disadvantages	Applications
Fibre optic	A type of cable that is made up of lots of very fine threads of glass. These are covered with an outer layer. The use of fibre optic cables is becoming more common in networks because they can transmit data quickly.	Has the highest level of bandwidth available out of the cabled methods, but nowhere near as much as lasers. Can carry signals for a much longer distance without deterioration.	Has the highest cost for manufacture and purchase. Can be difficult to install due to how fragile the glass tubes can be.	Used in modern internet connections and in high performance networks where large amounts of data are transmitted.
Copper cable – coaxial	A type of copper cable that has a central wire surrounded by an insulating layer. Coaxial cables also have an outer layer that acts like a jacket. Coaxial cables are used to carry radio frequency signals.	Cheap to manufacture and purchase. Lower error rate because the central wire is within a faraday shield (a shield used to block electromagnetic interference).	Has the lowest level of bandwidth of the three cable types. The way in which a coaxial cable is insulated can make it difficult to install and maintain.	Used in applications such as TV and Cable TV connections as well as some internet connections.
Copper cable – twisted pair	A type of copper cable that has two separate insulated wires that are twisted around each other. Twisted pair cables are then covered by an outer layer that acts like a jacket. Twisted pair cables transmit electric current.	Crosstalk (a signal transmitted from one channel to another) is minimised. Is the lowest cost to manufacture and purchase. Has a higher level of bandwidth than coaxial.	May be affected by electromagnetic interference. Has the shortest distance that a signal can be carried before it will begin to deteriorate.	Used for telephone communications and normally as part of an ethernet network.
Lasers	Lasers use high-power beams to transmit light signals. The beams travel directly through the air.	Has exceptionally high bandwidth. Quick to set up compared to laying cables.	Lasers require a line of sight to work, meaning they can be impacted by weather or physical objects, which makes them quite impractical for use in volatile environments or cities.	Lasers are useful for disaster communications. Often used as back-up if cables fail. Used for outdoor events requiring high speed data feeds.

Table 14.7: Different data transmission methods and their characteristics.

UNPLUGGED ACTIVITY 14.10

1   Write the names of the four types of transmission methods on separate small pieces of paper or card.

2   Write each advantage and disadvantage for all three cable types on separate pieces of paper or card. Make sure every advantage and disadvantage is on a separate piece, and that none of the cable types are identifiable through the description of their advantages and disadvantages alone. For example:

> **Disadvantage**
>
> Costs the most to manufacturer.

3   Shuffle each of the advantages and disadvantages.

4   Match up the advantages and disadvantages with the cable types. Do this untimed at first, and then try to see if you can do it in under a minute.

Did you match everything up correctly? Were there any you matched incorrectly more than once? If so, how will you remember these advantages and disadvantages in the future?

Effect of the medium on the available bandwidth

Different means of transmitting data have different bandwidths: fibre optic has significantly more bandwidth than copper cables, but lasers have an incomprehensibly high bandwidth. Per second, lasers can transmit well in excess of the amount of data travelling across the internet in the same second. Therefore, how fast you can transmit data is dependent on the method of transmission. You could send large photo files very quickly via a laser, but this could take minutes or hours with copper cables.

The bandwidth available will limit the quality of the audio or video file that can be streamed. For example, if a user has a connection with a bandwidth of 2 Mbps, it is unlikely they will be able to stream an ultra-high definition (HD) (4K) movie from an online streaming service (see Figure 14.18). The data required to produce each frame in the video would be too much to transmit using the bandwidth available. A bandwidth of 32 Mbps is generally required to stream an ultra HD movie.

Figure 14.18: The amount of bandwidth available will affect the quality of a video or movie. Have you ever given up watching a movie online because it is too slow?

Questions

11   Define the term bandwidth.

12   Describe the relationship between bandwidth and bit rate.

13   What do you think would happen if a buffer were not used when streaming data?

14   Outline two advantages and two disadvantages of fibre optic cables.

14.6 Network protocols

Protocols are instructions for how different computers in a network communicate with each other. Protocols are essential to ensure data is transferred efficiently and securely across a network.

Purposes and uses of protocols

Protocols are a set of rules that govern how data is formatted and processed, and allow computers to communicate with each other regardless of the software and hardware differences they may have.

Table 14.8 summarises the main network protocols.

Protocol	Function
Transmission control protocol (TCP)	TCP allows two computers to establish a connection.
Internet protocol (IP)	A protocol which sets out rules for communicating over the internet. You will often see TCP/IP mentioned together, as they were designed to complement each other. The Internet protocol (IP) sets the rules for the transmission of data, but cannot error check the packets. TCP provides reliable, ordered and error-checked delivery of the packets.
Internet control message protocol (ICMP)	An error reporting protocol that is used to generate error messages to transmit to the sender when network problems cause delivery problems with data packets.
Address resolution protocol (ARP) and inverse address	The ARP protocol is responsible for translation of an IP address into a MAC address for a device. ARP is necessary for use between the network layer and the data link layer of the OSI model (the use of protocol layering and the Open systems interconnection model is covered later in this chapter).
Inverse address resolution protocol (InARP)	Performs the opposite role to the ARP. InARP translates a MAC address into an IP address.
Dynamic host configuration protocol (DHCP)	A network management protocol that is used to assign IP addresses to devices on a network. DHCP manages the assignment of the addresses so that a network administrator does not need to manually carry out this task.
User datagram protocol (UDP)	A protocol often used for time-sensitive communication across the internet such as video playback. UDP does not formally establish a connection before data is sent, meaning data packets are sent directly to its target without checking the order of the packets or whether they have arrived safely. It is therefore considered quite unreliable.
Hypertext transfer protocols (HTTP and HTTPS)	HTTP is the protocol that is used for transferring the content of web pages across the internet, from a web server to a browser. HTTPS is the secure version of HTTP that incorporates the use of the SSL protocol (see below).
File transfer protocol (FTP)	Responsible for the transfer of files between a client and a server in a network.
Tunnelling protocol, e.g. L2TP	Mainly designed to increase the privacy and security of data. Tunnelling is a communications protocol that allows for the secure transmission of data from one network to another. Tunnelling allows private data packets to be sent across a public network through a method called encapsulation. Encapsulation is when private data packets are made to look like public data packets, so that they can be sent across a public network. Tunnelling is an important protocol used in VPNs.
Simple mail transfer protocol (SMTP)	Used to send email from a computer to a mail server, and between different mail servers.
Post office protocol (POP), e.g. POP3	Used to retrieve emails from a mail server. When the user checks their mailbox, the email is sent from the server to their device. The protocol then deletes the email from the server.

Protocol	Function
Internet message access protocol (IMAP)	Used to retrieve email from a mail server. IMAP has one main difference from POP, which is that the email is not deleted from the server by the protocol. The only time the email is deleted is when the user chooses to delete it.
Telnet	Allows a user to connect remotely to another computer, using the internet, via a command-line interpreter, which process commands and outputs results.
Secure shell (SSH)	Provides a secure way to access a computer over an unsecure network. SSH does this using strong authentication and encryption methods for communication.
Internet protocol security (IPSec)	Mainly designed to increase the privacy and security of data. IPSec is designed to encrypt and authenticate data packets that are sent across the internet. IPSec is also part of the tunnelling process for a VPN.
Secure sockets layer (SSL)	Mainly designed to increase the privacy and security of data. SSL is designed to ensure connections made between web clients, such as user devices, and web/mail servers are secure. SSL uses both public and private keys to encrypt data that is transmitted over the secure connection. SSL is still used in some applications, but it has now mostly been replaced by the use of TLS.
Transport layer security (TLS)	Mainly designed to increase the privacy and security of data. TLS is the updated version of SSL. TLS uses updated and more secure encryption algorithms than SSL.

Table 14.8: Network protocols.

Methods of sending data over a network

The term used for transmitting data packets across a network is **switching**. There are three main types of switching: packet switching, circuit switching and message switching.

Packet switching

The main function of a network is to transmit data from one device to another. To understand how this occurs and how networks are structured, it is also important to understand how the data is packaged to be transmitted across the network. Instead of being sent bit by bit, data is normally transmitted across networks in small bundles, or packets.

The structure of packets

What these packets contain varies depending on the type of network. For example, if a packet is sent over the internet, it will contain more elements to allow it to be directed to the right place. While the contents of a packet differ, most packets contain at least a header, a payload and a trailer.

You could think of packets of data as separate envelopes, containing letters (see Figure 14.19). Each envelope always has a stamp, an address and a letter inside. In different countries, the requirements may be different: the address might be formatted differently or a different stamp is needed. This is similar to how different networks require different contents in the packets.

Figure 14.19: Data packets can be compared to mail.

The header could include:

- The **IP address** of the sender. This is called the source IP address.

- the IP address of the receiving device. This is called the destination IP address.

- the sequence number of the packet. This is so the receiving device can reorder the packets to obtain the original data.

- the **MAC address** of the sender and the receiver. If the packet passes through a router, these will be removed as they are no longer necessary, as they are only used by a switch.

- any protocols used.

The payload will include:

- the actual data from the file that is being transmitted.

The trailer could include:

- a flag that tells a device it has reached the end of the packet.

- any error checking methods that are used.

The data sent in the header and trailer are all designed to make sure that payload data arrives at its intended destination without any errors.

The modes of connection

In packet switching, the data packets sent across the network can take any available path. There is no set pathway and each data packet could be sent along a different pathway. For example, packets sent from Computer A could be sent via any of the several switch components in the network. The packets will be collated and reordered when they reach Computer B. Packet switching is normally used when packets are sent across the internet. In this case, they will be sent via routers.

There are two main modes of transmission in packet switching. These are connection mode (also known as virtual circuit switching) and connectionless mode (also known as datagram switching). Frame relay and transmission control protocol (TCP) are two types of connection packet switching. Ethernet, internet protocol (IP) and user datagram protocol (UDP) are types of connectionless packet switching. In connection packet switching, a session is created before any data is transferred. The session becomes a fixed channel for the data to travel. In connectionless packet switching, there does not need to be any prior arrangement set up between devices to transmit the data. Connected and connectionless modes are described in Table 14.9.

Mode	Function
Connection	
Frame relay	In frame relay, data is separated into units called frames. Any methods of error correction that are used are carried out by the devices at the end points of transmission, which is one advantage of frame relay, as it helps speed up transmission.
	If an error is detected in a frame, that frame is dropped. The devices at the endpoints will then detect the dropped frames and retransmit them. This makes frame rate most suitable for sending data where the error rate is likely to be low.
	There are two main methods of connection in frame relay. The first is permanent virtual circuits (PVC), which are connections intended to exist for long periods of time, even if data is not currently being exchanged. The second is switched virtual circuits (SVC), which are temporary connections designed to exist for a single session.
Transmission control protocol (TCP)	In the TCP protocol, a connection is created and maintained until the application software at each endpoint has finished exchanging data.
	The TCP protocol determines how the data is broken down into packets, which it gives to and receives from the network layer in the TCP/IP model. It is responsible for providing error free data transmission and managing the flow of the data.

Mode	Function
Connectionless	
Ethernet	Ethernet is a traditional protocol used to connect devices, via a wired connection, to form a network. Ethernet makes sure that network devices format and transmit data in a way that other devices on the network will understand. Most networks that are set up within a home or school are likely to use ethernet.
Internet protocol (IP)	IP is the protocol that is used when data is sent across the internet. It is the protocol that is responsible for delivering the packets of data to the receiving device.
User datagram protocol (UDP)	UDP is an alternative protocol to the TCP. There are two main differences between this protocol and the TCP. The first is that this protocol sends the data in units called datagrams. The second difference is that this protocol does not control the flow of data or carry out error checking. For this reason, the exchange of data using UDP is often faster than using TCP.

Table 14.9: Connected and connectionless modes of packet switching.

Questions

15   List two things that might be contained in the header of a data packet.

16   Briefly explain what a network protocol is.

17   List three network protocols and state their purpose.

18   What is post office protocol (POP) used for?

19   Which protocol is responsible for the transfer of files from a server to a client?

Circuit switching

In circuit switching, a direct path is created between the sending and the receiving device. These pathways transmit the data packets from one device to another across the network. The data is transmitted each time using this dedicated path, as shown in Figure 14.20.

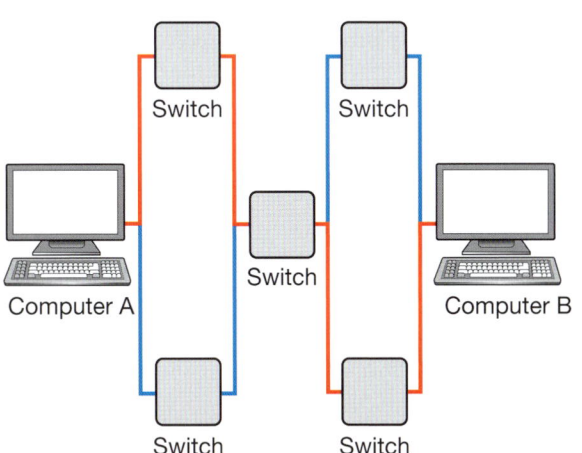

Figure 14.20: Circuit switching.

While data is being transmitted from Computer A to Computer B, no other computers in the network can use the same pathway. When the data transmission is completed, the path is then released for use by other data transmission across the network.

Message switching

Message switching is like an intermediate method between circuit switching and packet switching. Message switching is like circuit switching in that all the data packets are sent along the same path, and it is like packet switching in that any path from Computer A to Computer B can be taken. The data packets are sent from Computer A to the first switch device. The device holds the data packets until all of them have arrived. The switch then sends the data packets onto the next switch, which holds onto the data packets until all of them have arrived. The data packets are sent from switch to switch in this way, until they reach Computer B. This is known as the store and forward method of sending messages across networks.

> **UNPLUGGED ACTIVITY 14.11**
>
> Draw a diagram to represent the method of message switching.
>
> Compare your diagram with a partner's. Do they look the same? If not, examine why and what could be corrected in either.

The purpose and use of network addressing systems

IP addresses are unique identifiers given to a device on a network. As discussed earlier, IP addresses allow devices to be identified as unique when connected to a network.

There are two versions of IP address: IP4 and IP6. IP4 was the original version. IP4 is a 32-bit numerical address. As more devices connected to the internet, we started to run out of possible combinations for IP addresses, so IP6 was developed. IP6 is a 128-bit address that allows for many more possible combinations of IP address.

An IP address can be either static or dynamic. A static IP address means that the device will always have the same IP address. A dynamic IP address means that the IP address could change for each internet session. Most devices operate with a dynamic IP address set-up. A user will normally need to request a static IP address from the internet provider if they want one.

A media access control (MAC) address is also a unique number assigned to each network interface controller (NIC), which is a circuit board inside a computer that enables it to be connected to a network. The MAC address allows a network to identify any device. Although a device's dynamic IP address changes depending on the network currently being used, a MAC address is specific and unique to the device.

Static and dynamic routing

Routers use routing tables to work out the most efficient path for network traffic to take to reach its destination.

A routing table is stored on the router and lists all the available routers to particular network destinations. Routers need to use routing protocols to specify how they communicate with each other. Routing protocols help select the route that data travels from one device in a network to another.

Routing can be static or dynamic:

- Static routing is used when there is a single or preferred route for network traffic to reach its destination. The route is preconfigured (arranged in a set way). Static routing uses small routing tables.

- Dynamic routing uses algorithms to compute multiple different routes for network traffic and decide the best one.

There are advantages and disadvantages to both static and dynamic routing methods, as shown in Table 14.10.

Routing	Advantage	Disadvantage
Static	Easy to implement in a small network. Very secure. Predictable, because the same route is always used. No update mechanisms are required, as it is done manually. Requires less time to compute than a dynamic route.	Only useful for simple networks. Manually updating the route can be difficult and time-consuming if the network changes. If the link fails, manual intervention is needed. No alternative routes are available.
Dynamic	Useful in larger, more complex networks. Automatically adapts if the network changes or a link fails.	Can be difficult to implement initially. Requires more bandwidth, CPU and memory for update mechanisms.

Table 14.10: Advantages and disadvantages of static and dynamic routing.

Functions of routing protocols

There are three main types of routing protocol:

- Interior gateway protocols are used to specify how routers communicate with each other within a network, such as a LAN.

- Exterior gateway protocols are used to specify how routers communicate with each other between different networks.

- Border gateway protocols are a specific kind of exterior gateway protocol that manage the process of exchanging packets of data across the largest network, the internet.

Use of protocol layering

There are two main network models that many networks are built on. The models are the transmission control protocol/internet protocol (TCP/IP) suite and the open systems interconnection (OSI) model. Both models outline rules and standards about how communications should take place over a network. Each is split into several layers. This is so that each layer can operate independently of another, which allows the functions that take place at each layer to be easily adapted, if necessary.

The OSI model has seven different layers. Table 14.11 summarises the functions of each layer in the OSI model.

Layer	Function
Application	The application is the top layer of the model which directly interacts with data from the user. Software applications, such as web applications and email clients, rely on the applications layer to communicate. However, user applications, such as word processing packages, are not included in this function. The applications layer is responsible for managing the protocols that allow meaningful data to be presented to the user. It manages protocols such as hypertext transfer protocol (HTTP) and simple mail transfer protocol (SMTP).
Presentation	The primary function of the presentation layer is to prepare data ready for use in the applications layer. Presentation could involve the translation, encryption and compression of data. The presentation layer makes sure that the data is translated into a form that will be understood by the receiving device. If the devices are communicating over a secure connection, the data will be encrypted. The presentation layer will also decrypt any data that is received, and will also compress data to increase the speed of transmission.
Session	The time that passes between a communication link being opened and closed again is called a session. The session layer makes sure that the session is open for long enough to allow all the data to be transmitted and then closes it immediately as soon as the transmission is completed.
Transport	The transport layer is responsible for breaking down the data from the session layer into segments. The data segments are then given to the network layer. The transport layer is responsible for reassembling the segments at the receiving device. The transport layer is also responsible for flow control (the best speed for transmission) and error checking. It checks that all the data has been received and will request a retransmission if it is not complete.
Network	The network layer breaks down the data segments from the transport layer into smaller units, known as data packets. The network layer is then responsible for reassembling the packets after transmission. The network layer is also responsible for routing, which is the process of finding the best path across the network. The network layer performs these tasks when data is transmitted from network to network. A router is one of the key network components in this layer.
Data link	The data link layer performs a very similar role to the network layer, but rather than transmitting data from network to network, it is responsible for transmitting data from node to node within a network. The data link takes the packets created at the network layer and converts them into frames. A switch is one of the key components in this layer.
Physical	The physical layer involves the physical equipment that is used to transmit the data, such as the cables. In the physical layer, data is broken down into bits to be transmitted as binary. The physical layer is also responsible for reassembling the bits into frames after transmission.

Table 14.11: Layers in OSI model.

Layer	Function
Application	The application layer condenses the roles of the application, presentation and session layers from the OSI model. The application layer uses several protocols to provide a standardised exchange of data. The protocols it uses include HTTP, SMTP, post office protocol (POP) and file transfer protocol (FTP).
Transport	The transport layer in the TCP/IP suite is comparable to the transport layer in the OSI model. The transport layer is responsible for maintaining end-to-end communications between devices. There are two main protocols that are used at this level. The first is the transmission control protocol (TCP) and the second is the user datagram protocol (UDP).
Network	The network layer is also known as the internet layer and it is comparable to the network layer in the OSI model. The network layer breaks data down into packets and transmits the data network to network. There are two main protocols that are used at the network level. The first is the internet protocol (IP) and the second is the internet control message protocol (ICMP).
Link	The link layer is also known as the physical layer and it merges the roles of the data link layer and physical layer from the OSI model. A protocol used at this level is the address resolution protocol (ARP).

Table 14.12: Layers in TCP/IP suite.

The OSI model is a logical model that can be applied when creating a network. An alternative set-up is the TCP/IP suite. The TCP/IP suite is a condensed version of the OSI model. It has four layers, rather than the seven outlined in the OSI model. The TCP/IP suite was developed by the US Department of Defense and is intended to be a more advanced version of the OSI model.

The four layers of the TCP/IP protocol are shown in Table 14.12.

Questions

20 What is the purpose of an IP address?

21 List the four layers of the TCP/IP protocol.

22 Explain the difference between static and dynamic routing.

23 List two advantages and two disadvantages of static routing.

REFLECTION

How will you remember all the network protocols? Are there any that you struggle to understand and may need to revisit?

14.7 Wireless technology

Telecommunications

Telecommunications, often shortened to telecoms, is the transmission of information instantly over long distances. Telecoms includes phones, cellphones/mobile phones, satellites, radio and the internet. However, post or mail is not telecommunications, because the information is not received instantly.

KEY WORD

telecommunications: the transmission of information instantly over long distances, such as a phone call

Data is transferred via telecommunications circuits. A single circuit comprises two stations. Each station has a receiver (which receives data) and a transmitter (which transmits, or sends, data). The signals can be transmitted via wire, cables, optical fibre, or wirelessly through electromagnetic fields or light.

Mobile communication methods all enable us to practise telecommunications.

Methods of wireless transmission data

There are several types of wireless methods that can be used to connect devices in a network. These include Wi-Fi, Bluetooth, infrared, microwaves, radio and near field communication.

Wi-Fi

Wi-Fi uses radio signals and is the most commonly used wireless communication method (see Figure 14.21). Each device that wants to make a wireless connection will broadcast a radio signal. A router or a WAP will receive these wireless signals and process them. The router or WAP will also broadcast radio signals that will be received and processed by each device when it is receiving data that has been transmitted. Wi-Fi currently transmits data at frequencies of 2.4 GHz and 5 GHz. These frequencies are much higher than those used by mobile networks. These are considered high frequencies, which are required to send larger amounts of data. The current limit for Wi-Fi data transmission is approximately 450 Mbps.

Figure 14.21: Wireless communication.

Bluetooth

Bluetooth also uses radio signals to create a wireless connection between two devices. It uses the radio frequency 2.45 GHz. To establish a connection, devices need to be within 10 m of each other. There is currently a limit of eight devices that can be connected at any given time using Bluetooth.

The two devices requesting a wireless connection using Bluetooth must have matching profiles. Bluetooth profiles are a set of rules that allow devices to complete a specific task. For example, if a mobile device wants to connect to a headset to allow sound to be transmitted, a specific profile is used (see Figure 14.22). Devices must share the same profile in order to pair devices. Mobiles and headsets share the same profile, so they can be paired. The profile system stops pointless Bluetooth connections being made. For example, connecting a wireless mouse to a digital camera – the mouse cannot be used to control the camera as it is not designed for this function. A mouse and a camera do not have the same profiles and cannot be paired.

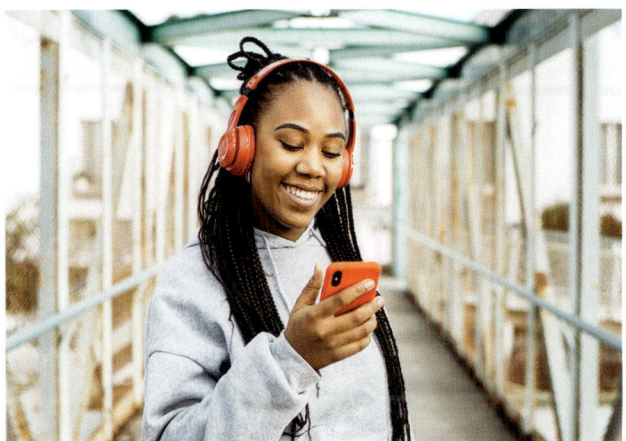

Figure 14.22: Wireless headphones have the same profile as a mobile phone.

To create a connection, the Bluetooth transmitter is turned on in a device. The device will then begin to transmit the radio signals. Any device that has a matching profile, within range, will pick up the radio signals and will then identify with the sender as a possible device to connect to. The required device for connection can then be chosen. The devices will then be paired together. Sometimes, pairing requires entering a pin code for added security.

For example, you can send photos on your phone using Bluetooth. Once selected from the Bluetooth menu, your phone will transmit a radio signal to pick up a receiving phone which also has Bluetooth switched on.

When your phone identifies potential receivers, you can select the correct device from the menu. Once selected, the recipient receives a notification asking if they wish to accept the photo.

Figure 14.23: Apple Airdrop, which allows Apple mobile users to share pictures easily, uses Bluetooth, but it also requires a Wi-Fi connection.

Infrared

Infrared connections use infrared radiation as their method of connection. Two different types of infrared connection can be made, which are line-of-sight mode and scatter mode. In line-of-sight mode, there must be a direct line of sight between the sending device and the receiving device. This means that there can be no obstacles in the way. In scatter mode, a device broadcasts infrared into a certain area and any device may receive it directly or through reflection of an obstacle. The sending device will need the ability to produce an infrared signal and the receiving device needs an infrared sensor to capture the infrared signal.

Infrared lasers can also be used to transmit data from one device to another in a network. Laser data transmission works in a similar way to fibre optic, in that it uses the properties of light to transmit the data. Rather than travelling through physical transmission media like fibre optic transmission, laser transmission relies on data travelling through free space.

Microwaves and radio waves

In data transmission, the terms 'microwaves' and 'radio waves' are often used interchangeably. This is because microwaves and radio waves are both types of electromagnetic radiation that can be used to transmit data and power. Microwaves have shorter wavelengths

and are therefore generally used for short-distance communications. Radio waves have longer wavelengths and are therefore generally used for long-distance communications. Considering this, the waves used in both Wi-Fi and Bluetooth are technically microwaves. However, historically, the term 'radio waves' has been applied to the technology used in wireless data transmission.

Near field communication (NFC)

Near field communication (NFC) allows devices near each other to communicate without the need for an internet connection (see Figure 14.24). An NFC chip is one part of a wireless link. Once activated by another chip, small packets of data between the two devices can be shared or transferred when held no more than a few centimetres from each other. There is no pairing code or internet connection required, because NFCs use chips that run on small amounts of power.

Figure 14.24: An example of NFC would be using contactless payment through your phone or watch.

Internet of Things

The **Internet of Things (IoT)** is a system of connected devices, such as smart phones, smart watches and smart technology, e.g. smart heaters in our homes, via the internet, enabling them to collect and exchange data.

KEY WORD

Internet of Things: connects devices over the internet, allowing them to share data; the IoT gives us the ability to connect objects that have historically not been connected, such as weather stations and phones, or mail boxes and watches

The devices connected via the Internet of Things often rely on wireless transmission methods like Wi-Fi. For example, via Wi-Fi, you can use your phone to control your thermostat at home. Access to wireless transmission methods has meant that the Internet of Things has gained traction as a concept in recent years.

Advantages and disadvantages of wireless transmission methods

Table 14.13 lists the advantages and disadvantages of wireless transmission methods.

Wireless method	Advantages	Disadvantages
Wi-Fi	Several wireless capable devices can connect to a single router or WAP. The high level of frequency used means that large amounts of data can be transmitted at a time. More recent Wi-Fi standards are backward compatible with previous ones. Has quite a large range of approximately 100 m. Doesn't require a line of sight, so it can work through obstacles.	The speed at which data can be transferred decreases as more devices connect to a wireless network. Less secure than a wired connection. Radio signals can be subject to interference.
Bluetooth	It requires a low level of power consumption. It doesn't require a line of sight, so it can work through obstacles. Can be made more secure by requiring a PIN code for connection. There will be less interference as other wireless connections transmit on different frequencies.	Has a limit of 10 m for a connection. A limit of eight devices can be connected at a time. Has a lower level of bandwidth available than Wi-Fi.
Infrared	It is the most secure form of connection. Low cost to manufacture and purchase. It requires a low level of power consumption. It does not get any interference from radio frequencies.	Cannot be transmitted through obstacles. If it uses line-of-sight mode, there must be a direct line of sight between the two devices. It can only be used to connect two devices. It has a short range with a limit of approximately 1 m. May be subject to interference from bright sources.

Wireless method	Advantages	Disadvantages
Near field communication (NFC)	Efficient and less power intensive than other wireless communication types. Quick and easy to use. Using NFC to make payments is generally more secure.	Very low data transfer rates. Expensive for companies to adopt. Only useful for very short distances of 10–20 cm.

Table 14.13: Advantages and disadvantages of methods of wireless data transfer.

Security issues

There can be security issues associated with the use of wireless data transmission. This is because wireless connections do not have the same level of protection as a wired connection. Wired networks are normally limited to a building or single site, and there are often locks and other security methods in place to stop an unauthorised person entering the area and gaining access to the network.

As a result, there are two main protocols designed to improve the level of security of a wireless network. They are:

- Wired equivalent privacy (WEP). WEP is designed to provide a wireless network with a similar level of security to a wired LAN. WEP does this by encrypting data transmissions sent using a wireless connection.

- Wi-Fi protected access (WPA). WPA is a standard required of devices equipped with a wireless internet connection. WPA is designed to provide a more sophisticated encryption method than WEP.

- Firewalls can be configured to control access to networks, too, by setting rules about which stations on a network can send or receive packets, or by limiting which devices can join a network. Other preventative security methods, detailed in Chapter 5, such as strong passwords and good practice, are all applicable to wireless connections, too.

UNPLUGGED ACTIVITY 14.13

Work in a group of five.

Take it in turns to go round the group. Each person needs to state one advantage or disadvantage of a form of wireless data transmission. Try to go round the group four times. Write down every point covered and compare your group's answers to Table 14.13. Fill in any gaps and discuss with your group how you might remember the ones you missed going forward.

Questions

24 Define telecommunications.
25 Briefly outline how Bluetooth pairing works.
26 Identify two examples where an infrared wireless connection could be used.
27 Give one example of where NFC could be used.
28 What is the Internet of Things?

14.8 Mobile communications systems

Cellular networks

Mobile networks are broken down into small areas called cells. At the centre of each cell is a radio base station that transmits and receives messages. The base stations connect to public telecommunications services allowing access to the internet.

Cells vary in size:

- picocells cover an area of less than 200 metres

- microcells cover an area up to 2 kilometres

- macrocells cover larger regions.

This is where the term 'cellphone' in American English comes from!

There have been several generations of mobile networks, each providing faster access speeds and greater reliability:

- 1G networks: the first generation of mobile networks. They use analogue signals. 1G networks are largely limited to voice and text message communications.

- 2G networks: the second generation of mobile networks. They switched from analogue to digital transmission, improving signal quality. 2G networks were able to connect with each other, allowing a phone to use other networks.

- 3G networks: the third generation of mobile networks. 3G networks increased data transmission speeds up to 2 Mbps, allowing internet access, video transmission and online gaming.

- 4G networks: the fourth generation of mobile networks. In theory, 4G networks allow data transmission speeds of up to 1 Gbps, allowing greater use of video streaming facilities.

- 5G networks: the fifth and most recent generation of mobile networks. 5G networks offer the fastest and most reliable connections available. When they are fully established, the average download speed should be approximately 1 Gbps. They have tested speeds up to 1.5 Gbps at present, but could prove to be capable of even faster speeds.

How satellite communication systems are used for transferring data

A communications satellite is a machine that has been transported into space and set to orbit the Earth (see Figure 14.25). These satellites are used to transmit radio waves from one place on Earth to another.

The radio waves that are transmitted can carry most things radio waves on Earth are used for, including telephone calls, internet data and television broadcasts.

Satellites are complex machinery. Their main components are a solar powered battery, a transponder and various antennas.

Figure 14.25: Satellite dishes on Earth receive and transmit information from/to orbiting communications satellites.

Preparing communications data for sending and receiving

Any data that is intended to be sent using satellite communications needs to be converted to radio waves. The data is transmitted in the form of radio waves from a ground station on Earth. The transmission process is called the uplink. The radio waves travel through the layers of the atmosphere up to the intended satellite (either a chosen satellite or the nearest in orbit). The antennas on the satellite are the component that initially receive the radio waves. The transponder processes the data, which can often involve boosting the signal. The antenna then transmits the radio waves back to the destination ground station on Earth. This process is called the downlink (see Figure 14.26).

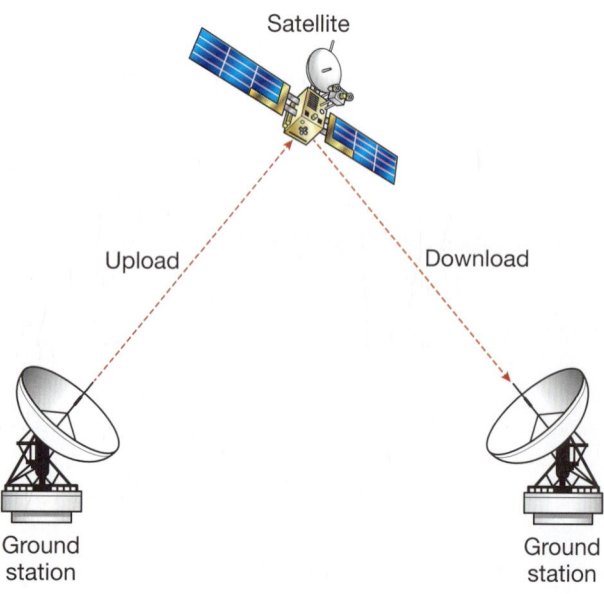

Figure 14.26: Uplink and downlink to a satellite.

ACTIVITY 14.14

Use the internet to research further information about what a ground station looks like and how they are used. See if you can find out where there are satellite ground stations in your country.

Global positioning systems

Satellites are also used in navigation systems such as global positioning systems (GPS). A GPS uses satellites to work out a user's current location.

DID YOU KNOW?

One of the most well-known satellite navigation systems is the Navstar GPS. Navstar GPS currently has 24 satellites in orbit. At any time on Earth, a user will usually be in the line of sight for at least ten of these satellites. However, only three or four are actually needed to work out a user's location.

A process called **triangulation** is used to find the location of a user. The user's device, such as a mobile telephone, receives radio signals. Each navigation satellite constantly beams radio waves that are sent towards Earth. The user's device will receive these radio waves.

A device must pick up radio waves from at least three satellites and the GPS will then be able to pinpoint their location (see Figure 14.27).

KEY WORD

triangulation: the process of pinpointing the location of a device, using radio signals from a satellite

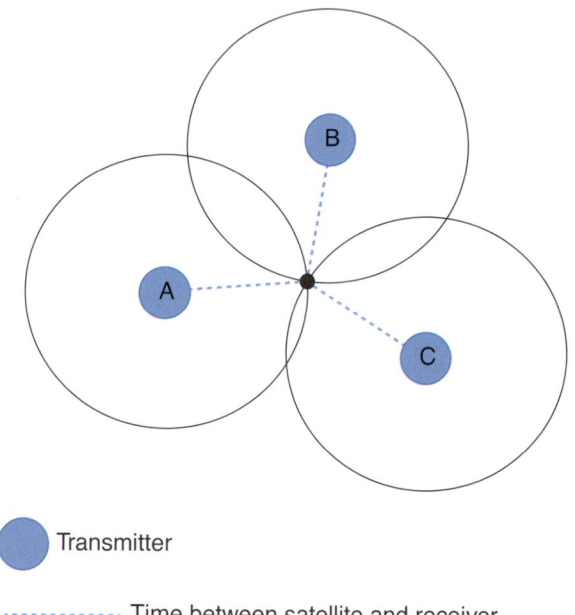

⬤ Transmitter

----------- Time between satellite and receiver

● Receiver

Figure 14.27: Triangulation by three GPS satellites.

If the user's device receives a signal from satellite A, this means they must be somewhere in the area currently covered by satellite A. If it also receives a signal from satellite B and satellite C, the user must be at the point where the area covered by all three of the satellites meets.

Global mapping systems

Web mapping platforms (or global mapping systems) offer satellite imagery, street maps, aerial photography, and sometimes even street views, of the entire planet. They can be used for route planning, including information on when and where you can catch a bus or train. An example of this is Google Maps. Google Maps maps the Earth by superimposing satellite images and aerial photography onto a 3D globe, allowing users to see a birds-eye view of locations (see Figure 14.28).

The satellite images are collected by imaging satellites which are purpose built. The resolutions of these satellites vary but the images are often supplemented with aerial photography, which is higher resolution but more expensive per square metre.

Figure 14.28: a: A satellite image of Zakarpattia Oblast, Ukraine. **b:** A mock-up of an imaging satellite in orbit.

DISCUSSION POINT

What do you think the positives and negatives of a global mapping system like Google Maps are?

Surveillance

Many devices are equipped with GPS devices, including mobile telephones and cars. As well as giving the user the ability to find out their location, this technology can also be used by others for surveillance purposes. It is possible to use a GPS to find out where another person is by tracking their device. These devices often keep a log of all GPS activity, so it is possible for a person to gain access to that log and see exactly where the device (and therefore possibly the user) has been.

Ultra-high-definition television

Satellites are used in broadcasting ultra-high-definition TV (UHD TV). UHD TV requires a lot of bandwidth to sustain the quality. Satellites, with their large bandwidth availability and wide coverage, allow viewers to receive consistent quality no matter where they are, as long as they are within the satellite coverage.

This works by the UHD TV signal being caught and reflected back to the satellite dish. Then, the signal is connected with coaxial cables that feed the UHD TV receiver.

14.9 Network security

Network security threats

Data is an organisation's or individual's most important asset. This makes data vulnerable to theft and misuse. There are a range of network security threats.

Brute force

Individuals may try to break into a computer system to gain unauthorised access. This may involve stealing a user's login details and then guessing their password using many different possible combinations, or the attacker may build software that can work out the user's password. Obtaining unauthorised access in this way is known as a **brute force attack**.

Users or organisations with poor network policies are often most at risk of brute force attack. Using strong passwords generated by a password manager can help reduce the risk of a brute force attack.

KEY WORD

brute force attack: a hacking method that involves guessing passwords and obtaining manual access

Denial of service

A **distributed denial of service (DDoS)** is a type of cyber attack that overwhelms a website with traffic, usually across many devices, which intends to take the website offline. This can be a form of protest against an organisation. A website going offline, even temporarily, can affect sales by blocking access of legitimate customers, damage reputation and damage the distribution of a message or campaign.

> **KEY WORD**
>
> **DDoS:** a cyber attack that overwhelms websites with traffic to take them offline

Malware

Malware refers to any software that is designed to disrupt or damage a computer system or gain unauthorised access. Malware includes worms, spyware and ransomware. (To refresh your understanding of malware, look back at Chapter 5.2.)

A user will normally unknowingly download the malware onto their computer. The malware is often disguised in a file download or a link that the user is enticed into clicking.

Botnets

An attack may come from a single third party and computer, or it could be distributed across many computers. Botnets are a group of computers controlled by software to perform harmful acts. Any user's computer could be made part of a botnet, often by the user downloading malware. Malware is downloaded onto the computer and will often stay dormant until the third party wants to use the computer in an attack. Each computer that is infected with this type of malware is called a bot. When the user wants to carry out an attack, they 'wake up' the malware in the bots and use them to form a botnet. A botnet can be used to carry out attacks such as a distributed denial of service (DDoS) attack.

Malicious actors

There are people that steal data to use it for criminal activity, such as identity theft, or to cause damage to data, and therefore cause damage to the company. These people are called **malicious actors (perpetrators)**. The use of networks has made accessing data through malicious means a greater risk.

> **KEY WORD**
>
> **malicious actor (perpetrator):** a group or entity whose mission is to affect or cause harm in the digital world; they perform malicious (deliberately hurtful) acts against individuals or organisations, usually with a personal agenda

Structured query language injection

Structured query language (SQL) is a programming language used to maintain databases.

An **SQL injection** is a technique used to destroy, modify or retrieve data. By inserting SQL code as data, an attacker can execute commands that retrieve data from the database. SQL injections usually happen over the internet. The result can be the destructionof important data, or other problematic behaviours. In its most extreme form, an SQL injection can give an attacker complete control of a device.

> **KEY WORD**
>
> **SQL injection:** an attack used to destroy, modify or retrieve data

Poor network policies

Poor network policies may increase the likelihood of an attack on a network. As well as using a password manager, individuals and organisations can put a range of other preventative methods in place to help protect their data. We will look at methods of preventing network security issues later.

Impact of network security threats

Individuals and organisations need to carefully consider the impact of security threats. There are two main reasons why unauthorised users carry out security attacks: either to obtain personal data or as an act of sabotage or revenge.

Individuals need to be cautious of any of their personal data being accessed and stolen. This could lead to criminal acts such as fraud and theft of their identity, which in turn can lead to financial or personal consequences.

Organisations need to be equally cautious of their stored data being accessed and stolen or manipulated/modified and destroyed. Data is a very important asset to organisations, as it is used in the day-to-day functioning of the organisation. Without it, they are unlikely to be able to function at all. Not being in operation could lead to a loss of business and profits. If the data is stolen because the organisation's security has been breached, this could also damage the organisation's reputation.

Questions

29   Describe a DDoS attack.

30   Define the term malicious actor.

31   List two impacts of a cyber attack.

Methods of preventing network security issues

Use of physical methods

The simplest way to protect data is to use physical methods. Organisations can install a digital door lock or entry system at the entrance to their office or building so that only employees who know the code or have a door pass can enter. Other physical methods that could

Figure 14.29: Security guards can monitor who enters sensitive areas.

be used are CCTV, security guard and alarm systems. CCTV will allow an organisation to see who is trying to gain unauthorised access. Security guards should allow only authorised users to gain access to a place where the data is stored, for example a server room (see Figure 14.29). Secure areas could also be protected with an alarm system that will alert the organisation if an unauthorised person tries to gain access.

UNPLUGGED ACTIVITY 14.15

There are advantages and disadvantages to physical methods for securing data. Copy and complete the table to outline what some of those advantages and disadvantages could be.

Physical method	Advantages	Disadvantages
Barrier		
Lock requiring a key or PIN code		
Security guard		
CCTV		
Alarm system		

How software methods can prevent unauthorised access

Data can also be protected using software methods.

Biometric methods

An employee may be required to provide biometric data, such as their fingerprint, iris or facial features to access data. A biometric device will scan their biometric data and check to see if it matches data stored in a database. If it does, the employee will be allowed to gain access. Biometric devices are useful because biological data is unique to the user and very difficult to fake. Biometric devices could also be used to secure individual devices in a similar way. Modern mobile telephones have biometric devices installed that require a user to provide their fingerprint, for example, to gain access to the device (see Figure 14.30).

Figure 14.30: A door which has been set up with fingerprint access, a form of biometric data.

Anti-malware, anti-virus and anti-spyware

Anti-malware, anti-virus and anti-spyware software can be used to protect data, files and systems. The software is designed to scan a computer system for malware. If it finds any malicious files, it quarantines the malware (puts it in a designated safe area) and allows the user to delete it. Anti-malware software can sometimes monitor the data that is downloaded in real time. It can scan each download and, if it finds malware present, can alert the user before the file is downloaded. The quicker this kind of software finds malware, the less damage the malware can carry out.

Firewall

A firewall can be used to prevent unauthorised access or damage to data. A firewall can be hardware based or software based. A firewall examines incoming and outgoing traffic to a computer or a network. The firewall can be configured (set) to recognise malicious traffic by providing it with rules and criteria to check the traffic. If traffic is detected that does not meet the rules or criteria, then it can be rejected.

Encryption

Encryption will not stop the data from being stolen, but it will mean that if the data is stolen, it will be meaningless to the third party, unless they are able to get the key to decrypt it.

Access rights

An organisation can protect data by only allowing access to those that directly need the data. This is called access rights. The username that an employee is given in an organisation is often what indicates their access rights. The permission to access the data that the employee requires can be attached to their username, so they are not able to see any data that needs to remain confidential. This can prevent data being damaged.

UNPLUGGED ACTIVITY 14.16

Copy and complete the table to outline what some of the advantages and disadvantages of different software-based methods could be.

Software-based method	Advantages	Disadvantages
Biometrics		
Anti-malware		
Firewall		
Access rights		
Encryption		

ACTIVITY 14.17

A company has asked you to give a presentation to its leadership team about how they can improve their data safety practices. They want five recommendations of how to implement better practice. Work in a small group to create this presentation. Make sure you:

- Describe and explain the threats of poor practice.

- Explain the benefits and the disadvantages of the methods you recommend.

14.10 Disaster recovery management

In an organisation, a disaster is anything that may put the operations of the organisation at risk through data loss and business disruption. Disaster recovery is a planning process that allows an organisation to plan for disaster and put in place measures that will minimise the risks. To be able to plan for protection against a disaster, the possible disaster first needs to be identified. Disasters include:

- cybercrime or malware infection, which can block access to a computer and data

- equipment or power failure, which can result in the loss of work/data

- natural disasters, which may result in the loss of equipment or data (see Figure 14.31)

- criminal activity, such as theft

- accidental events that disrupt standard practice, such as dropping equipment or spilling a drink over a keyboard or tower (see Figure 14.32).

DISCUSSION POINT

Can you think of a disaster that has happened somewhere in the world in recent years that has put an organisation at risk?

Figure 14.32: Spilling a drink over a computer can lead to data loss if the computer breaks and data is not backed up.

Figure 14.31a and 31b: Natural disasters like flooding or earthquakes can have a negative effect on organisations.

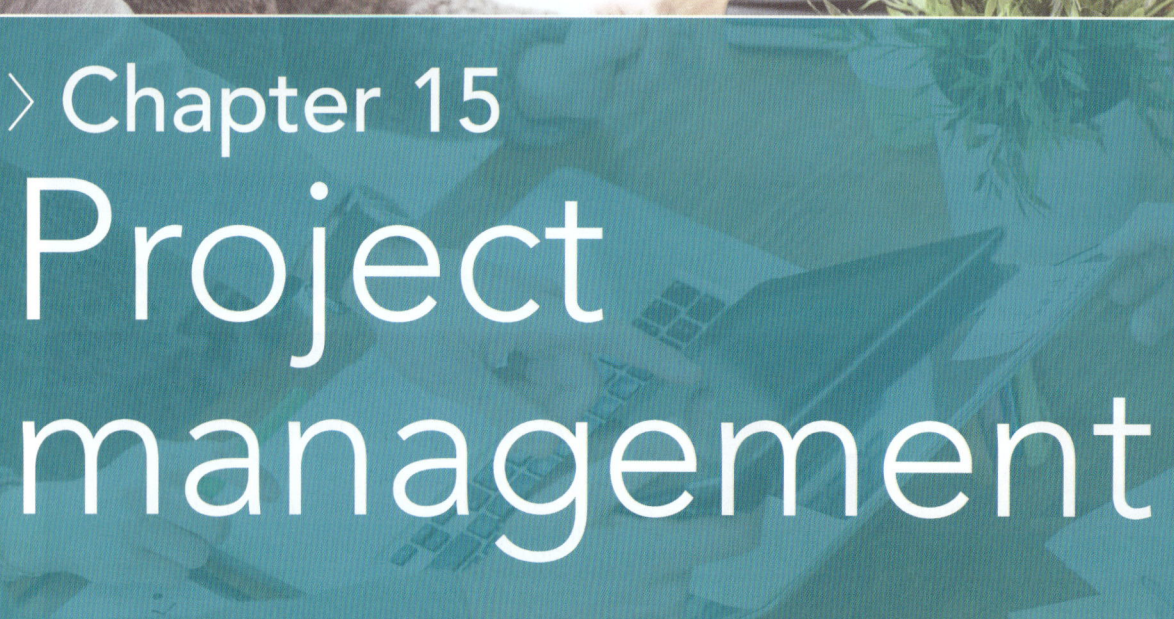

> # Chapter 15
> # Project
> # management

LEARNING INTENTIONS

By the end of this chapter, you will be able to:

* describe the stages of the project life cycle

* describe how project management software supports managing projects

* discuss the strengths and weaknesses of project management software for supporting projects

* use and describe tools and techniques for project management

* describe advantages and disadvantages of project management tools.

Introduction

Organisations use project management to help projects stay within budget and on schedule. Organisations want to ensure that all the tasks required to complete a project are carried out in the most efficient and cost-effective way. Projects can be large, such as installing new ICT systems across the organisation, or small, such as redecorating an office. The organisation's project management team may use a range of project management tools to assist them with project planning. An example of a project management tool is a Gantt chart (see Figure 15.1).

Figure 15.1: Project planning uses a range of tools, including Gantt charts.

15.1 Stages of the project life cycle

A well-managed project ensures deadlines are met, **resources** are available, and that each person knows the job that they are meant to do.

The project management process is usually carried out in four main stages: project initiation, planning, execution and monitoring, and project close, as shown in Figure 15.2.

KEY WORD

resources: people, equipment, facilities or funding required to complete a project

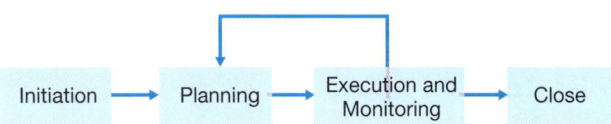

Figure 15.2: Project life cycle stages.

Project initiation

The project **initiation** stage sets the goals of the project. This defines what the project will do, and why there is a need for the project. A number of aspects need to be determined during the project initiation stage.

KEY WORD

initiation: start of a project

Objectives

The project initiation stage identifies objectives. Each project will have set objectives. For example, a project may be to install a new IT system for a business. Each large objective may be split into smaller objectives. Installing an IT system could be divided into:

1   purchase the equipment
2   prepare the building (cabling and power sources)
3   install the new machines

4   check that the machines work

5   ensure users are satisfied.

Each of these objectives could then be subdivided into even smaller objectives. It is important to list all the objectives at the start of the project.

All projects will have a person who is called the owner of the project. This is usually the person who wants the project to be completed. The owner could be an external customer, or an internal member of staff. The owner of the project will usually agree to the objectives at the start. This means that they agree that all the objectives they want to achieve have been listed.

Resources

The initiation stage identifies the resources required for the project. Resources may be items like new computers or cables. Resources can also be people such as IT technicians or electricians. Time is also a resource. Resources usually cost money. Projects can run over time and money if all resources are not identified at the start. This is because more resources need to be bought later.

Success criteria

Success criteria are essential elements of the project that must be completed. These are not the same as goals. For example, the success criteria for installing an IT system could include 'Must have enough machines for 150 people', 'Must use Windows OS' or 'Must have 2 monitors per machine'.

Stakeholders and their needs

Stakeholders are anyone who has an interest in the project (see Figure 15.3). For example, a stakeholder could be the user of the new IT system. Stakeholders are important as they comment on the success criteria and say what they want from the project. They can impact the goals and the success criteria.

Project scope and high-level schedules

Project scope defines how 'large' the project is. In big projects, some tasks may need to be outsourced to other businesses. For example, connecting a new electricity supply to a building for the IT system needs to be completed by the local electricity company. Connecting the electricity is called 'out of scope' as this is not something to include in the project.

Figure 15.3: Stakeholders may include the end-users who will be using the new IT system.

A high-level project schedule sets out a rough plan of the tasks involved and how long they will take. This will be based on the resources, goals and success criteria.

Project planning

> **DID YOU KNOW?**
>
> There is a common phrase: 'failing to prepare is preparing to fail'. This means that if you do not plan something fully, then it is most likely to fail.

Projects are planned so that all stakeholders know what to do during all stages of the project. Budgets and schedules are created for the project. Milestones will be set. Milestones are dates by each part of the project must be completed. Tasks for one milestone are done first, before the tasks of milestones that come later. A **Gantt chart** is produced to show the order in which tasks should be completed.

> **KEY WORD**
>
> **Gantt chart:** a chart used for planning a project

Resources are allocated to tasks. Resources need to be available at the time they are needed. For example, an electrician will be allocated to the project at the time when the electrical work needs to be completed. The most important part of planning ensures that appropriate time is allocated to each task, and resources for each task are organised so that tasks can be completed on time.

It is also wasteful to have resources not being used during the project. For example, you would not hire an electrician to install the software for the IT system. You may also group the tasks for the electrician into one milestone. This means that you can hire the electrician once, and complete all the tasks. For example, they could connect the new power supply, and fit all of the new wiring that may be needed. Hiring an electrician many times for short periods of time is inefficient and may cost more money.

Project execution and monitoring

Implementing the plan

Once the project plans are completed, a start date to begin to implement the plans is set. The project starts on the start date. The **execution** of a project is the 'doing' part. This is when the milestones are completed.

Implementation of the project plan completes the stages and goals listed in the project plan.

> **KEY WORD**
>
> **execution:** the development stage of a project

Monitoring progress against time

As each task is completed it is monitored. Monitoring checks that each part of the project is going to be completed on schedule (on time). It is important that the plan is followed closely. This helps to make sure that resources are used at the appropriate times. Delays to tasks will mean that tasks that are scheduled to occur later will also be delayed.

Each project will have a project manager. The project manager informs each member of the project team about their role, their responsibilities and the milestone dates by which they are expected to have completed their tasks. The project manager is responsible for keeping the project to schedule (see Figure 15.4).

Projects are not always completed on time. This is often because smaller tasks may take longer to complete and milestones may not be met. Each delay affects the next section of the project, and so the delays increase

as the project moves forward. However, good project monitoring can identify where delays may occur. This allows a project manager to re-plan small sections of the project to help ensure the whole project remains on schedule.

The project manager also monitors the performance of the project team to ensure they carry out their roles effectively. The project manager monitors expenditure and compares it against the budget. This helps to ensure that the project does not spend more than its allocated budget. The project manager also ensures the scope of the project does not grow beyond the agreed boundaries.

Cost and quality

A project manager will check that the costs of the project stay within the budget that was set. Sometimes this may not be possible. For example, during the COVID-19 pandemic, there was a shortage of processors and as a result the cost of processors rose quickly, so installing an IT system became more expensive. It is important that increases in costs are discussed with the stakeholders. If the project becomes too expensive, it may need to be cancelled.

Alternatively, costs may go down. For example, a different electrician may be able to complete the jobs required for less money.

A project will also be monitored for quality. Each task will be checked to ensure it is completed well. For example, the work of the electrician will be checked to ensure that there are enough cables and the cabling is installed correctly. It is important to monitor the quality of the tasks completed because it will often cost more money and delay the project if mistakes are only noticed later in the project life cycle.

Figure 15.4: All aspects of the project will be monitored to ensure work is completed on time.

Reporting to stakeholders

The stakeholders in a project will want to know how the project is progressing in terms of:

- time
- delays
- cost
- quality.

During the project execution stage, the project manager will prepare reports to give to the stakeholders. (see Figure 15.5) This allows them to monitor the progress of the project and provide input if needed.

Figure 15.5: A project manager will monitor the project as it progresses.

Project close

A handover happens between the project team and the client when the project is complete. The client reviews the project with the project manager. If the client is happy that everything is finished as expected then the client signs off the project as completed. When the client signs the project off it means that there is no further work to carry out. When it is signed off then any contracts will be closed with the workers. Any resources will also be released. This means that they are no longer needed and other people or projects can use them.

At the end of the project monitoring and execution stage, a review takes place. The review will look at what went wrong and what went well. The review will cover questions such as:

- Was the project schedule maintained?
- Was the project completed within budget?
- Were all resources available when required?
- Has the project met the original requirements?

The review of the project will be stored. Reviews are used to help plan future projects. The reviews will help projects avoid the same mistakes that may have happened in other projects.

Questions

1 Identify three things that project initiation will find.
2 State the connection between resources and tasks.
3 What does a Gantt chart show?
4 Explain why monitoring progress is needed in a project.
5 Explain why the project manager may need to re-plan parts of the project.
6 State the risk of not monitoring the quality of completed tasks.
7 Give two examples of review questions.

15.2 Project management software

Types of project management software

There are many different types of project management software. Many examples of project management software can be used on different devices.

Examples of project management software include Jira, Wrike, Miro and Monday. Microsoft also produces project management software called Microsoft Project.

Project management software is often run on a desktop computer or laptop. However, some projects may need project management software to run on mobile devices such as smart phones or tablets.

Some project management software is web-based. This allows management of projects across the globe. Web-based project management software means that people from different countries can log in and update projects.

DISCUSSION POINT

What projects would benefit from:

- mobile project management software?
- web-based project management software?

Project management software often has different **licensing** options. Personal licences allow you to use the software on a home computer. You cannot use the software for work purposes for a business or organisation. This could be useful if you have a project at home, such as building a shed in the garden.

Single-user licences can be used within an organisation or business. However, they only allow one person to use the software at once. Collaborative project management software allows many people to log in to the software at the same time. This will allow many people to use the project management software at the same time. This is useful if you have large projects with many project managers and stakeholders.

> **KEY WORD**
>
> **licensing:** the rules on how you can use something, for example software

Uses of project management software for supporting projects

Planning

Project management software can be used to schedule project-based tasks to meet milestones and to allocate resources to each task. Project management software can link documents relating to the project such as budgets, goals, requirements and resources to specific tasks. Users will then have access to the data and information that they require to complete each task on schedule and within budget.

Project management software provides users with templates for the planning stage. Templates can be used to set up initial project plans and budgets. Templates from previous successful projects may be repurposed for the current project. Using project templates allows all projects in an organisation to have common, collaborative and recognisable structures.

Scheduling of tasks

Tasks are jobs that are completed as part of the project. Project management software can be used to schedule and track the progress of tasks. Within project management software, a Gantt chart can be used to show an overview of the tasks required to complete a project. The Gantt chart shows this on a timeline. Gantt charts allow a project manager to assign numbers of hours or days to each task. Each task can also be given a deadline for completion. Gantt charts often sort or group tasks automatically.

The project manager can use the project management software to identify which tasks are dependent on other tasks. Dependent means that a task cannot start until another task has been completed. Tasks can be delegated to different members of the project team. Tasks are given a priority and can be sorted from most important to least important. A priority list helps identify which task should be completed first.

Project management software also allows:

- a project manager or team member to record how many hours are spent on each task
- each task to be marked as complete
- milestones to be created for crucial points of the project
- highlighting of key project parts
- a calendar to be produced of events, milestones and progress achieved.

Allocation of resources

Resources are the equipment, property or people needed to complete a task. Resources must be defined in the project management software. The availability of resources must also be identified. This allows the project manager to know when each resource can be used. Each resource is given a cost. A cost can be assigned to any resource. Giving a resource a cost allows the project manager to see how resource use affects the budget. Resources can be assigned to tasks. Each resource is given a number of hours or days it will be used for. This helps the project manager to know what resources are used when. This is very important when people are resources. If you allocate too many tasks to one person at the same time, they will not be able to compete these tasks. This leads to a person becoming stressed. They may rush tasks. This means that the task may not be completed to a good standard.

Costings

Resources often have costs assigned to them. This allows the project manager to calculate the total cost of each task. The cost of a task is based on how many hours each resource is used for and how much each resource costs to use per hour. The project management software also records any extra expenses incurred by team members. The project management software will add these to the overall cost. The project management software can track how much is being spent over different time periods. For example, it could show graphs of the daily, weekly and monthly spending (see Figure 15.6).

Figure 15.6: Project management software tracks spending and displays it over set periods.

Project management software can report the total costs for individual resources or a set of resources. It can also export data about the project. It can export to common file types such as .xlsx or .csv. This means that other software (such as spreadsheet software) can then analyse the data.

Communication and collaborative working

Project management software has communication and collaborative working tools which help team members to **collaborate** during the project:

- Calendars: each team member has a calendar. The calendar shows what tasks the team member should be currently working on. Calendars can be synchronised with other third-party calendars, such as Google, iCal or Outlook. This allows team members to use mobile devices to check calendars rather than having to be at a desktop. This helps to ensure that each member's availability is up to date. Shared calendars enable meetings to be scheduled with each team member. Documents can be attached to these meetings so that all members of the meeting can review the documents before the meeting.

- Instant messaging/video chat/video conferencing: these tools enable team members to communicate

in real time. They can use these tools to share ideas and discuss progress. Real-time communication is also useful if team members work in different countries.

- Shared documents: projects often use cloud storage for documents. This acts as a central store and allows team members to access the documents from wherever they may be. Documents can be assigned to tasks, resources or milestones. Changes to the documents can be tracked. Tracking changes allows each team member to see editing and changes to the document. Many documents also allow different versions to be saved or restored. Some storage management software emails team members to inform them when changes to documents have been made. Some project management software sends direct messages to a person's email when documents are changed or updated.

- Discussions/forums: these can be set up for tasks, documents or milestones. It allows team members to discuss tasks, documents or ideas. Forums are very useful when team members are not in the same time zone. Team members can see comments made by other team members and reply. Forums can email notifications to team members when comments are made. They can also send alerts to project dashboards.

- Progress: the software informs team members and project managers of progress made on each task. Team members update tasks to show how close they are to finishing the task. The progress is fed into the project plan. When changes are made to the project timeline, automated email notifications are sent to all affected team members.

> **KEY WORD**
>
> **collaborate:** work together

Decisions

Communication and decisions in project management software are usually recorded. This means that decisions can be tracked. Each decision can be linked to the person who made the decision and why that decision was made.

Project management software can also highlight potential issues. The project management software can suggest what changes need to be made. For example, it may suggest changing the timeline or allocating additional resources. These issues can be monitored to check if the issue has been resolved.

Project management software can compare differences between the project plan and current progress. The project management software can show how much time was spent on a task compared to how much time was planned for that task. This means that lessons can be learned for future tasks that are similar in nature.

The project management software identifies a **critical path**. A critical path shows all tasks that must be completed if the project is to meet its deadline. Critical paths are monitored closely. It is important to identify potential delays in advance. Resources are diverted to critical tasks if they fall behind. This can help the project to meet its deadlines and recover any lost time.

KEY WORD

critical path: the tasks that must be completed on time for a project to complete on time

Advantages and disadvantages of project management software

Table 15.1 sets out the advantages and disadvantages of project management software.

Advantages	Disadvantages
Can manage very large projects efficiently.	May be expensive to buy. If there are many users, several licences will be required – this will add to the cost.
Can produce a range of outputs for users to see how the project develops.	The business may not be able to afford to buy the software most appropriate for their requirements.
Can automatically update areas of the project if changes are made to another part.	Special training is often needed to use the software effectively. Additional training may be needed for different users.
Can send out automated reminders and updates to people.	Can be difficult to set up. This could lead to inaccurate results later.

Advantages	Disadvantages
Can be used to make calculations very quickly.	Team members may rely too much on software, and not realise that something is wrong if the software does not raise an alert.
Can analyse and make suggestions to projects to help save money and time.	Backups of the data need to be made in case of computer failure.
Can reduce the number of people required to manage the project. This can make communication between people and control of the project more effective.	Access and security levels will need to be set up properly to enable users to get access to the information they need.
Stakeholders can use the software for a summary of what stage the project has reach and any potential issues.	

Table 15.1: Advantages and disadvantages of project management software.

Questions

8 Explain how project management software can be used for allocating resources to tasks.

9 State the purpose of project management software.

10 Give two things that project management software can control or monitor.

11 Give two reasons why a company may choose not to use project management software.

ACTIVITY 15.01

Use the internet to research the following:
- What percentage of projects are successful?
- What percentage of projects run over budget?
- What percentage of projects in a company are likely to fail?
- What percentage of projects meet all their goals?

WORKED EXAMPLE 15.02

Task	Days	Dependencies
A	3	
B	2	A
C	6	A
D	1	B
E	3	C
F	5	D
G	4	E, F
H	3	G
I	2	G
J	3	G

First, add any tasks to the diagram that have no dependents (see Figure 15.9).

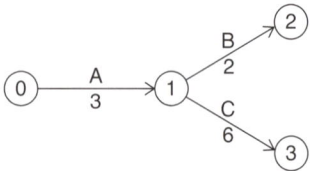

Figure 15.9: Network activity diagram part 1.

Then add on any tasks that are dependent on task A (see Figure 15.10).

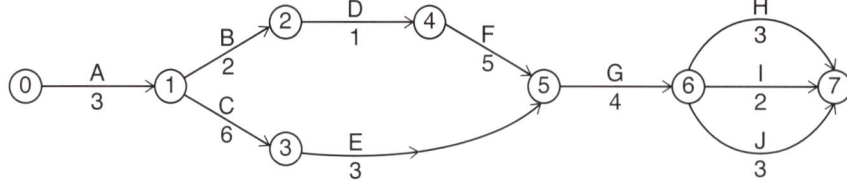

Figure 15.10: Network activity diagram part 2.

Continue task by task until there is a completed diagram (see Figure 15.11).

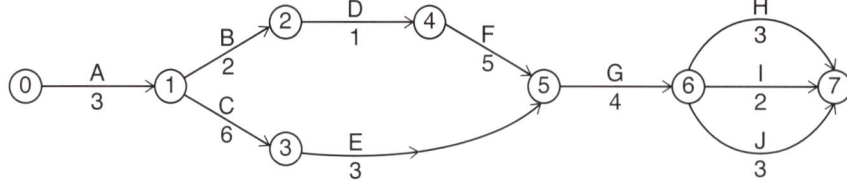

Figure 15.11: Network activity diagram part 3.

UNPLUGGED ACTIVITY 15.03

Complete a network activity diagram for the following scenario:

Task	Days	Dependencies
A	3	
B	5	
C	4	
D	18	A
E	16	B
F	12	C
G	7	E, F
H	11	D, G
I	2	H

Network activity diagrams can be extended to include the earliest start time (ES) and earliest finish time (EF) of a task. The ES of the first task is 0 and the EF of the first task is the length of that task. The ES of all other tasks is the latest EF of its dependents.

ES of task = latest EF of dependents

The EF of any task is calculated as:

EF = ES + length of task

The float time can also be added to each task. The float time is calculated by subtracting the EF of a task from the ES of the next task:

Float time = EF of task − ES of next task

WORKED EXAMPLE 15.03

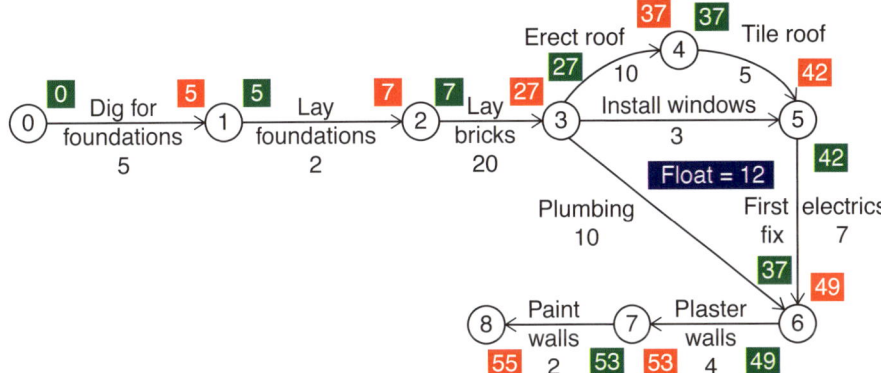

Figure 15.12: Extended network activity diagram.

The network activity diagram in Figure 15.8 has been extended (see Figure 15.12). The extended diagram shows the ES in green, the EF in red and float time in blue.

The ES for dig for foundations is day 0 because it is the first task. The EF for dig for foundations is day 5 because the task will take five days. This means that the ES of the next task (lay foundations) is also day 5 because it can only start when the foundations have been dug.

EF for lay foundations = ES for lay foundations
+ length of lay foundations
EF for lay foundations = 5 + 2 = 7

When it comes to parallel tasks, the ES of a task is the latest EF of its dependents. The EF for installing windows is day 30, but the EF for tiling the roof is day 42. As these are both dependents for first fix electrics, the ES for first fix electrics must be day 42.

The ES for first fix electrics is day 42 but the EF for installing the windows is day 30 meaning there are 12 days of float time.

Note that when working in days, the EF and ES are the beginning of the day. For example, if the EF of task 2 is day 4 then task 2 should be finished by the beginning of day 4, or the end of day 3. This will then enable task 3 to start at the beginning of day 4.

> **UNPLUGGED ACTIVITY 15.04**
>
> Extend the CPM from Unplugged Activity 15.02 to include the ES, EF and float time for each task.

Using a network activity diagram helps to allocate the right resources to a task. For example, additional resources can be allocated to a task that needs to be completed earlier than planned. This is known as 'crashing'. Additional resources can be moved from tasks with high float times. This is because it's not critical that those tasks finish at their earliest possible finish time. If resources cannot be taken from float tasks, then additional resources will incur additional costs. For example, in Figure 15.12, we need to complete the laying of bricks five days early. However, there are no float tasks available to take resources from. Therefore, we would need to buy additional resource, which increases the project budget. By contrast, if we need to build the roof earlier than planned, then resources could be taken from the plumbing task. This is because the plumbing task has a float of 12 days.

Advantages and disadvantages of critical path method

Table 15.2 shows the advantages and disadvantages of the critical path method.

Advantages	Disadvantages
Creates critical paths of shortest and longest options.	Must have all times for task completion.
Lists resources needed.	Must know all dependent activities.
Gives total times.	
Can show float times.	
Shows dependent activities.	

Table 15.2: Shows the advantages and disadvantages of the critical path method.

Performance evaluation and review technique (PERT)

Performance evaluation and review technique **(PERT)** is used to plan, schedule and manage project tasks or activities. PERT can also identify a critical path. PERT is more suitable for research and development projects or non-repetitive projects. This is because PERT uses estimates of time for tasks/activities not actual times.

> **KEY WORD**
>
> **PERT:** performance evaluation and review technique

PERT uses symbols to represent tasks/activities. Tasks/activities are represented by arrows. Milestones are usually represented by circles. These are also called nodes. PERT and network activity diagrams use similar symbols and can look very similar.

> **TIP**
>
> Remember, PERT uses estimated time for tasks; CPM uses actual time for tasks.

PERT uses the following to estimate the time for a task/activity:

- The most optimistic time: this assumes that everything will go right and no problems will occur.

- The most likely time: this is a prediction based on what may or may not go wrong, and the chances of that happening.

- The most pessimistic time: this assumes that anything that can go wrong will go wrong.

$$\text{estimated time} = \frac{4 \times \text{most likely time} + \text{optimistic time} + \text{pessimistic time}}{6}$$

Advantages and disadvantages of PERT

PERT uses the following to estimate the time for a task/activity:

Advantages	Disadvantages
Creates critical paths.	Uses average times.
Not all timings need to be as precise or known.	Must know all dependent activities.
PERT uses estimated times.	
Gives a range of times for completion (optimistic, likely, pessimistic).	

Table 15.3: Shows the advantages and disadvantages of PERT.

Gantt charts

A Gantt chart shows the start and finish dates of each task. A Gantt chart also shows the dependents of each task, the progress of each task and the current position within the project. Each bar within a Gantt chart represents a task. Each bar can be shaded in to show the percentage of the task that has been completed. Arrows are used to show which tasks are dependent on other tasks. A line or other indicator can be used to show the current position (time) within the project. It is also possible to identify the resources required.

To create a Gantt chart, you need the following information:

- the list of tasks
- how long each task will take
- which tasks are dependent upon dependents
- start date of the first task
- resources that are allocated to each task.

Some programs that create Gantt charts (such as Gantt Project) only work in days/months. This means that you may need to convert time in hours to time in days, for example a task that takes 6 hours converts to 0.25 days.

WORKED EXAMPLE 15.04

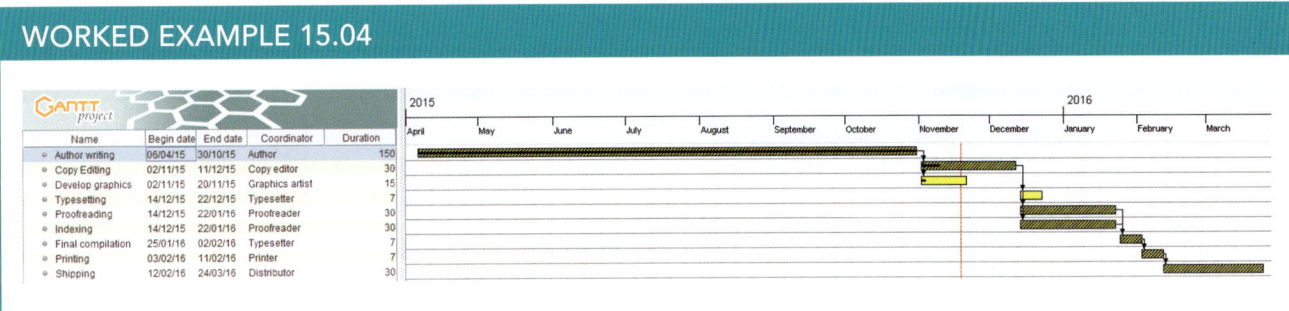

Figure 15.13: Gantt chart.

Figure 15.13 shows a Gantt chart for producing a book.

On the left-hand side is the task list. The task list has start dates and times, coordinators and the duration. The yellow bars represent the time that each task takes. This makes it easier to see the float time available. Dependencies are shown by the arrows from the end of a dependent task to the start of another task. The black lines represent how much of each task has currently been completed and the red line represents the current time. Therefore, assuming that the progress is correct, the project is running slightly behind schedule. The diagonal lines on the yellow bars represent the critical path.

ACTIVITY 15.05

This was created using GanttProject, which can be used to open the files.
You can download the GanttProject software for free.

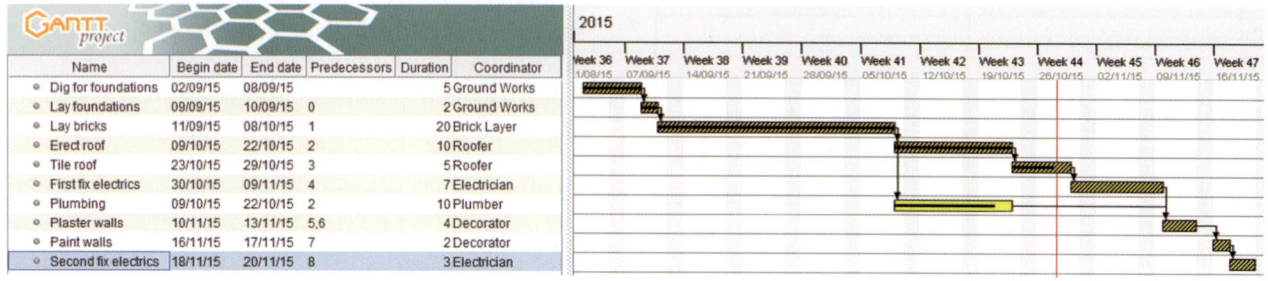

Figure 15.14: Gantt chart for house extension.

Interpret the Gantt chart for building a house extension in Figure 15.14. Open the Gantt chart **15.01_House extension.gan**. This was created using GanttProject, which can be used to open the files.

1 Which task has float time?

2 Which tasks are currently in progress (started but not finished)?

3 The plumbing appears to be behind schedule. Will this affect the whole project finish date? Why?

4 Which tasks are the dependents for plastering the walls?

UNPLUGGED ACTIVITY 15.06

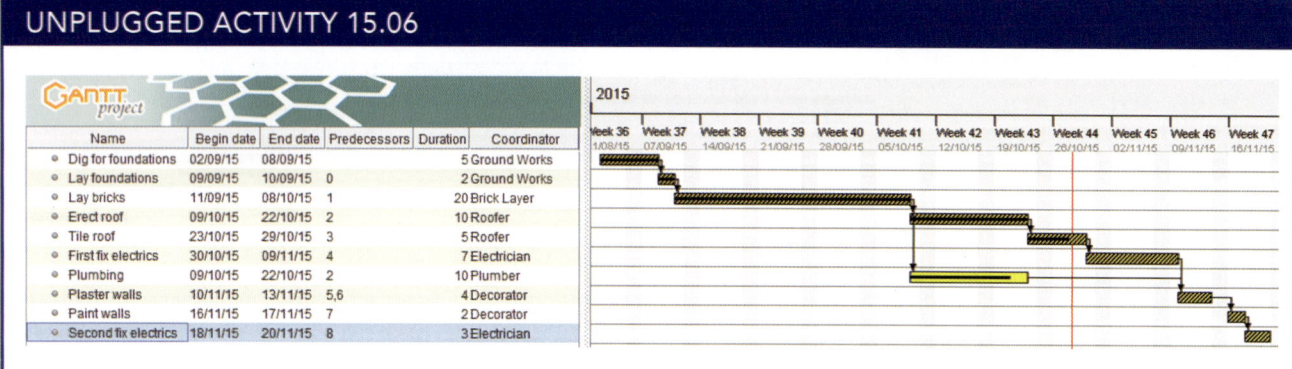

Figure 15.15: Resource chart for house extension.

Figure 15.15 is the resources chart for the house extension project. Look at when each resource will be being used. What do you notice about the weekends?

WORKED EXAMPLE 15.05

Task A starts on 1 January 2023.

Task	Days	Dependencies	Resources
A	3		R1
B	2	A	R1
C	6	A	R2
D	1	B	R1
E	3	C	R2
F	5	D	R3
G	4	E, F	R3
H	3	G	R5
I	2	G	R2
J	3	G	R6

First, create a list of tasks, the duration and the resources required and identify the start and finish dates of the first task (see Figure 15.16).

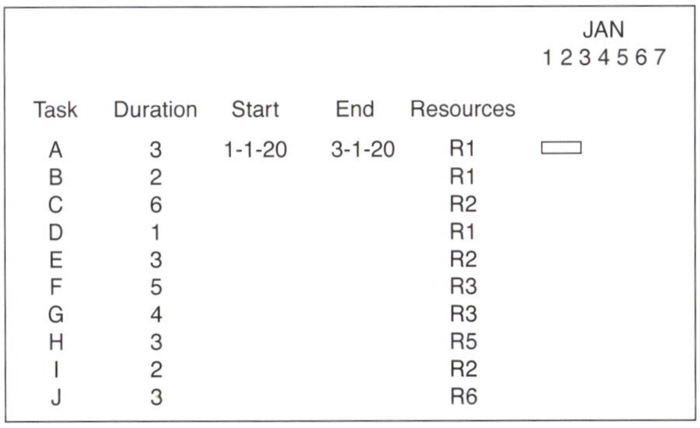

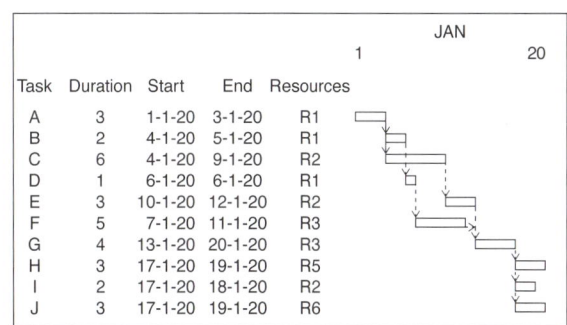

Figure 15.16: Gantt chart part 1.

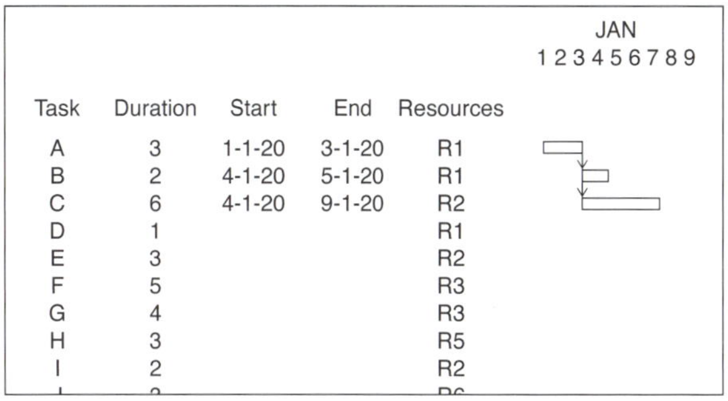

Then add on any tasks that are dependent on task A, to start the day after task A finishes (see Figure 15.17).

Figure 15.17: Gantt chart part 2.

Continue task by task until there is a completed Gantt chart, as shown in Figure 15.18.

Figure 15.18: Gantt chart part 3.

ACTIVITY 15.07

Complete a Gantt chart for the following scenario commencing on 1 April 2023.

Task	Days	Dependencies
A	3	
B	5	
C	4	
D	18	A
E	16	B

Task	Days	Dependencies
F	12	C
G	7	E, F
H	11	D, G
I	2	H

Advantages and disadvantages of Gantt charts

Table 15.4 sets out the advantages and disadvantages of Gantt charts.

Advantages	Disadvantages
Shows dependencies.	Must know the following information: • how long each task will take • which tasks have dependents • start date of the first task • resources that are allocated to each task.
Each row is a task, which helps to track the tasks more easily.	May need to convert time into hours or minutes, which can be confusing and make it harder to read.
Progress can be clearly tracked with how complete each task is.	

Table 15.4: Advantages and disadvantages of Gantt charts.

Work breakdown structure (WBS)

All the tools so far have broken the project down into manageable tasks/activities. However, very large projects may contain hundreds of tasks/activities all at once. This can be very difficult to interpret. Hundreds of smaller tasks/activities may also create anxiety for individual team members who may be concerned about the number of tasks to be completed.

To help manage those tasks, a hierarchical decomposition of the project can be created as a work breakdown structure (WBS). A WBS forms a hierarchical diagram with tasks allocated to sub-tasks or project phases.

In a software development project, the project might be broken down into stages of a development life cycle as shown in Figure 15.19.

A project manager would then be responsible for each stage. For example, a project manager might be responsible for the testing stage of a software development project. Each stage would be broken down further to show the phases involved in each stage (see Figure 15.20).

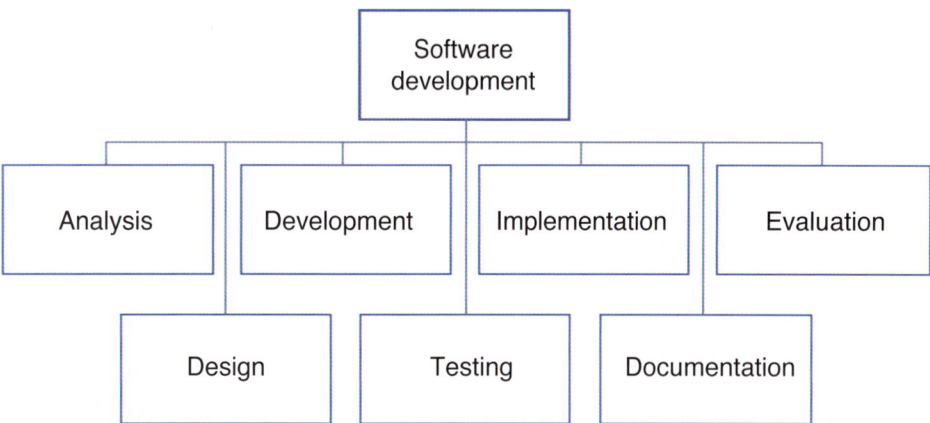

Figure 15.19: Work breakdown structure for software development.

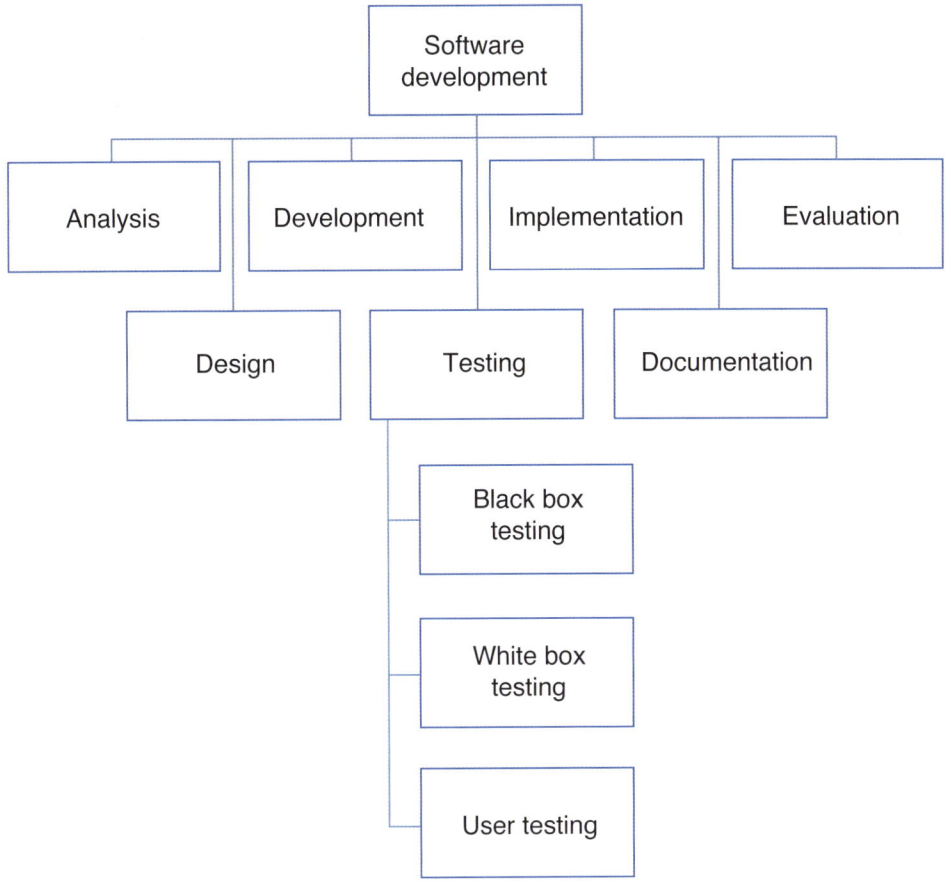

Figure 15.20: WBS for software development with testing expanded.

Question

12 Give one advantage for each of the following
project management tools: Critical path method,
PERT and Gantt charts.

REFLECTION

What was the hardest thing to remember about
project management? What methods did you use
to remember the stages of project management?
What can you think of to help you remember the
stages of project management in the future?

> # Chapter 16
System life cycle

LEARNING INTENTIONS

By the end of this chapter, you will be able to:

- define different types of system

- describe the stages in the system life cycle

- describe methods of research and their advantages and disadvantages for a given situation

- understand the content and purpose of specifications

- construct diagrams to represent system processing and the flow of data through a system

- design data storage, input forms and output reports

- create a test plan and understand its purpose

- select appropriate test data

- describe the differences between alpha and beta testing

- describe the differences between white box and black box testing

- explain the advantages and disadvantages of different types of testing

- describe different methods of implementing a system

- explain the advantages and disadvantages of each implementation method for a given situation

- describe types of documentation and explain why each is needed

- describe the contents of documentation

- explain the advantages and disadvantages of different types of documentation

- explain methods of evaluating a new system

- describe different types of maintenance and explain why each is needed

- explain how each type of maintenance is carried out

- explain the advantages and disadvantages of different types of maintenance

- explain different types of prototyping and explain why each is needed

- explain the advantages and disadvantages of each type of prototyping

- describe the stages and processes of different software development methodologies

- explain the advantages and disadvantages of different software development methodologies.

BEFORE YOU START

- Do you understand what a project is?

- Do you understand the structure of a database?

- Do you know what validation means?

- Are you able to draw a flowchart?

Introduction

A computer **system** is a combination of systems that function together. The hardware system consists of different physical components, such as the CPU, keyboard and storage devices, which work together. The software system combines different programs, which could share data to perform a range of tasks. Computer systems will often use both hardware and software, such as through using software to analyse readings recorded by a hardware input device. For example, the software within a fire alarm system could regularly check the data from temperature monitors and smoke sensors, then perform a number of actions should a fire be detected, such as sounding an alarm and informing the fire service.

When a business or organisation sets up a computer system or upgrades an existing system, a lot of work goes into planning, designing, testing, implementing, evaluating and then maintaining the system. These processes are all part of the system's life cycle.

A computer system must meet the needs of everyone who will be using the system, known as the end users. End users may include managers, employees and customers.

KEY WORD

system: a collection of components to form a whole system

16.1 Stages in the system life cycle

The life cycle of a computer system usually consists of five main stages, as shown in Figure 16.2. Each stage includes a range of tasks. Following the final stage, the system life cycle may repeat, with changes or additions being made to the system, such as taking in feedback from the end users.

1   **Analysis**. During the analysis stage, the current situation is researched and the requirements of the new system determined.

2   **Design**. Information from the analysis stage is used to examine the processing required and how data flows through the system. Inputs, outputs and data storage are also examined during the design stage.

3   **Development and testing**. Once the system has been designed, the required hardware may be purchased and/or the required software developed. Testing of the system takes place, with changes made to the system where required.

4   **Implementation**. In the implementation stage, the system begins to be used. This will include the development of user documentation. The system is also evaluated to ensure it is suitable for the intended use.

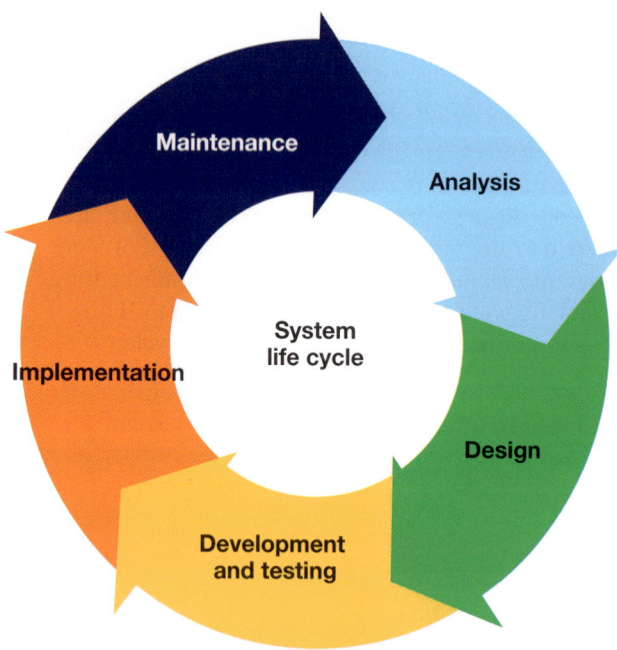

Figure 16.1: System life cycle.

5   **Maintenance**. Maintenance takes place to ensure the system continues to work as expected.

Stage 1: Analysis

Before a computer system can be set up or upgraded, the business or organisation first needs to carry out some research to understand the given situation, including how current systems and processes work, and determine what the requirements are for the new system. This will involve **analysis**.

KEY WORD

analysis: the process of researching a given situation and finding out the requirements

---

Methods of researching a given situation

The organisation can use a variety of methods to research a given situation.

Questionnaires

Questionnaires are used when information is required from a large number of users but it would be impractical to interview them all. A large number of users also means there is a large sample size for the results of the questionnaire to be analysed. Questionnaires may not be suitable when there are only a small number of users involved because there is not a large enough sample size to gauge opinion, and it would be quicker to conduct interviews. However, questionnaires could be used as an alternative to interviews if it is impossible to arrange an appointment time with a user or users. A disadvantage of questionnaires is that they do not allow the opportunity to ask the user to explain their choice of answers without contacting the user again.

Questions need to be asked in a way in which the required information can be obtained from users but also so that the responses can be easily analysed. This often means providing multiple-choice responses so that each response can be counted (see Figure 16.2). It is also important to ensure that the questionnaire does not take too long for users to complete, as users may not wish to complete the questionnaire, or answer all the questions, if it is too long.

WORKED EXAMPLE 16.01

During the analysis for a new school reports system, it is decided to find out from students, teachers and parents what information should be included in the report. One question that could be asked would be:

Please rate from 1 to 5 the importance of having the following information on the school report (1 is not important, 5 is very important):

- Attendance total half days
- Percentage score for each end of year exam
- Attendance percentage
- Average score for all exams
- Number of negative behavioural events
- Comment from subject teacher
- Number of positive praise events
- Targets from subject teacher
- Academic grade for each subject
- Comment from personal tutor
- Position/rank in class for each subject
- Target grade.

This question will allow the school to consider the importance given to each piece of information by students, teachers and parents. This will help to decide what information should be included in the report.

Another way to ask this question would be:

Please list any information you would like to be included in the school report.

This question would make it difficult to quantify the responses and analyse the findings as each respondent may give very different answers. By providing a list, respondents are given a starting point.

A combination of multiple-choice questions, opinion ratings and open questions can be used within a questionnaire. A range of question types can provide a balance of quantitative analysis of closed questions (expecting yes/no answers) and a qualitative analysis of open questions, where users are able to suggest alternative ideas to those presented by the questionnaire. Questions should also be written in a way which does not threaten users and the way they currently do their work. Users should be given the opportunity to return their questionnaires anonymously, as more honest answers are likely to be given if it is not clear who has given the response.

Figure 16.2: Completing a paper questionnaire.

Questionnaires can be completed online, which enables the results to be immediately stored and readily available for detailed analysis in the form of graphs and tables. Filters can be applied to the results and responses can be compared based on the answers given to another question. For example, a filter could be applied to compare the responses of all people who work part-time, compared with people who work full-time.

Interviews

Interviews involve a direct conversation between the person undertaking the analysis and the organisation (the client). Where there is a single end user or small group of end users, interviews are often used because questions can be asked of the users allowing a conversation to take place. This gives opportunities for follow-up questions. Even in large organisations, interviews may be used with key stakeholders or specific groups.

Questions for interviews should be selected to obtain the required information from the client or end users. The questions might vary depending on who is being interviewed. For example, if management are being interviewed, then the questions could focus on the requirements of the organisation as a whole and the information that is required for decision making. If end users are being interviewed, then the questions could be aimed at finding out what the users need to make their jobs more efficient (see Figure 16.3). Interviews can also take place with groups of users or focus groups that represent user groups or customers.

Figure 16.3: End users discuss ways to make their jobs more efficient.

It can sometimes be difficult to find a time when client or end users are available, or to get everyone together in a focus group. Interviews can be a time-consuming process, particularly when there are many interviews to complete.

Honesty is important during interviews so that the interviewer can get an accurate picture of how tasks are completed. This can sometimes be difficult to achieve because end users may not want to admit to taking shortcuts in their tasks, or to not carrying out tasks to the best of their ability. In these situations, anonymous questionnaires can get more honest responses.

Observation

Observation involves the person that is doing the analysis watching the processes that take place within an organisation to find out how tasks are completed. This can involve sitting with users to understand the tasks they have to complete, with an opportunity to ask questions of the users to find out further information, which could form part of a **user requirements specification**. This can give a good understanding of the current input data, processing methods and output information. Other options can include visiting different parts of an office or other business locations throughout the day to see how tasks are undertaken.

KEY WORD

user requirements specification: what a user needs a new system to do

One disadvantage of observations is that when users are being observed, they may do things differently from normal, or they may try to be more efficient, which does not give the observer a true picture of what is happening. The observer needs to be able to identify how long tasks genuinely take and any inefficiencies that could be reduced. By observing users directly, the person that is doing the analysis can get first-hand experience of any inefficiencies and can plan to overcome these. During observations, some users may not like being watched and this may lead to additional stress. The user may therefore not perform as they would do in normal work conditions. Although observations can take up a lot of time, it is often a good way to find out how an organisation works.

Document analysis

Documents used by an organisation can be analysed to understand how information within an organisation is currently being used.

UNPLUGGED ACTIVITY 16.01

Figure 16.4: Shop till receipt.

Examine the receipt in Figure 16.4.

1 Identify the output information that is included on the receipt.

2 Identify any calculations that are likely to have taken place on the receipt.

3 Identify which information is likely to be the same for all receipts and which information is likely to be different for each receipt.

It is important to look at examples of any documents that show data from an existing process, such as information output following a task, or to understand what data is being collected for input to a system. Sometimes it may be possible to identify processes that take place by looking at documents. It is also possible to estimate the amount of data that is likely to be required if the volume of documents is known.

Document analysis should not be used on its own, but must be used with other analysis methods, because it is difficult to identify the processes just by looking at documents. Examination of the documents also only shows data that is currently used. It does not give an opportunity to find out what additional data an organisation might need, or what data the organisation does not need. This information could be found out by following up document analysis with interviews.

Advantages and disadvantages of research methods

Table 16.1 sets out the advantages and disadvantages of different research methods.

Method	Advantages	Disadvantages
Questionnaires	Efficient data collection from a large number of users. Users can submit responses anonymously.	Questionnaires can be time consuming to develop. Information provided can be limited.
Interviews	Enable a detailed analysis of users' views. Further questions can be asked to clarify responses.	Time consuming to undertake. Limited number of responses collected.
Observation	Enables tasks undertaken to be seen in person. Links between different processes can be identified.	Takes a long time to perform research. Users can behave differently when being watched.

Method	Advantages	Disadvantages
Document analysis	Existing data and forms can be studied in detail. Requires limited involvement from users.	May not be clear how documents are used within the organisation. Other data required may not be identified.

Table 16.1: Advantages and disadvantages of the different methods of researching a given situation.

Content and purpose of specifications

Following research and analysis of the given situation, three types of specification are usually produced to understand and document the requirements of the system to be developed. They include user requirements specification, design specification and system specification. These documents help ensure the system meets the needs of the end users and other stakeholders.

User requirements specification

A user requirements specification sets out (specifies) what the organisation or client needs the system to do. The specification is written in consultation with the client, who will approve it (see Figure 16.5).

A user requirements specification should include:

- the purpose of the system
- the main objectives of the system
- data that must be output from the system (for example, invoices, sales reports)
- data that needs to be input to the system to generate the outputs, including any screens or data collection forms
- validation and verification that is needed for input data
- processes that need to take place to convert inputs into outputs or to store data
- data that needs to be stored
- functional requirements, such as performance measures
- deadlines for each milestone within the project (see Chapter 15 for more information on project milestones).

Figure 16.5: The user requirements specification is written in close consultation with the client.

WORKED EXAMPLE 16.02

Here is an extract from a user requirements specification for a new local government website. The extract shows specific data that is required on the home page, in addition to what has been specified to be included on each page:

- Quick links
- Show list of links editable by content manager
- Initially to be:
    - How can I get involved? (go to Get involved)
    - How can I stand for council? (go to Elections)
    - When is the next steering group meeting? (go to Meetings)
    - When is the next information evening? (go to Key dates)
    - How do I report a problem? (go to Reporting)
    - When are the next elections? (go to Elections arrangements)
- News list:
    - Picture, news title, date (taken from list of news)
    - Button: view all news
    - To show latest four news articles

CONTINUED

- What's on list:
    - Picture, event title with hyperlink, date and time (taken from List of events, Key dates and Meetings)
    - Button: view all events
    - Button: view all key dates
    - To show next four events.

System specification

A **system specification** lists all the software and hardware that are needed for the new system. The software is often identified first, as the hardware is often dependent on what software is needed. Only software that is needed to run the system should be specified. There may be different software identified for different types of user and process.

Once the software is known, the minimum hardware required to run that software can be identified. In addition to this, the amount of storage space required for the data being used by the system needs to be considered.

The system specification may plan for higher than minimum specifications, so that the system functions at a reasonable speed. These hardware specifications will include the processing power and the amount of memory required. External hardware components that are needed should also be specified and these should be based on the requirements of the user.

Design specification

The **design specification** is an illustration of how the system will look, what the data structures will be and how the system will function. It is intended to give the client an idea of what the system will look like, including the user interface, before it is developed, so that the client's feedback can be incorporated into the final designs.

KEY WORDS

system specification: the hardware and software needed to run the system

design specification: illustration of how the system will look, what the data structures will be and how the system will work

You will look at the following parts of a design specification in more detail later in this chapter:

- flowcharts
- data flow diagrams
- data collection forms
- screen layouts
- validation routines
- data dictionary.

In addition to this, a design specification could include:

- house style (logos, colours, fonts, styles, sizes)
- screen sizes
- connectivity diagram to show links between screens
- purpose of calculations.

Questions

1 Identify five stages in the system life cycle.
2 Explain why interviews are more often used than questionnaires for smaller groups of users.
3 State the purpose of the system specification.

Stage 2: Design

During the **design** stage, the overall structure of the system and details of the system components are designed. Diagrams can be used during the analysis stage to describe how a current system or process works, or diagrams can be used during the design stage to demonstrate how a new system will work. The required data storage is defined, including any databases or files used. Input forms and output forms are also designed during this stage.

> **KEY WORD**
>
> **design:** the stage in the life cycle when the design specification is produced

System processing and flow of data through a system

Within a system, data is processed, for example organised or changed. Data is then passed, or flows, from one part of a system to another. It is important to document the flow and processing of data using diagrams.

Data flow diagrams

A **data flow diagram (DFD)** shows how data flows throughout a system. A DFD does not show the order of processes. The diagram uses different symbols to show the different elements as the data moves around the system (see Table 16.2).

> **KEY WORD**
>
> **data flow diagram (DFD):** data flow diagram that shows how data moves around a system

element	Purpose	Symbol
Data flow	This shows the data flowing from one part of the system to another.	→
Process	This is an action that uses or manipulates data.	
Data store	This is a place where data is stored. For example, this could be a hard disk, cloud storage or a paper file.	
Data source or destination (inputs and outputs)	This is an external entity where the data originates or is intended to go. For example, this could be a customer or supplier.	
Duplication data source or destination	This is where the system has more than one source where data originates or is intended to go to avoid crossing data flow.	

Table 16.2: DFD elements and their symbols.

Element	Purpose	Symbol
Input	Shows an input for the system, such as data entered using a keyboard.	
Output	Shows an output for the system, such as results displayed on a screen.	
Flow line	Shows the direction of flow.	
Process	An activity within the system, such as searching a database for certain data.	
Single document output	A single printed document.	
Multiple document output	Multiple printed documents.	
Magnetic disk file	Data stored in a file on a magnetic disk.	
Magnetic tape file	Data stored in a file on a magnetic tape.	
Display	Output on a visual display.	

Table 16.3: Flow chart elements and their symbols.

WORKED EXAMPLE 16.05

Figure 16.10 is a system flowchart for taking a hotel booking online.

Hotel bookings are input manually using a keyboard. While editing the booking, the data that has been input is displayed on the screen. Data for the guest who will be staying at the hotel is retrieved from the guests file. When the data has been input, it is validated and a process then saves the booking and prints a booking confirmation document that can be sent to the guest.

Each morning, guest arrival sheets, which include information about each guest and the room they will be staying in, are printed. Also in the morning, a checkout list is printed that shows which rooms are due to be vacated that morning and therefore need to be cleaned.

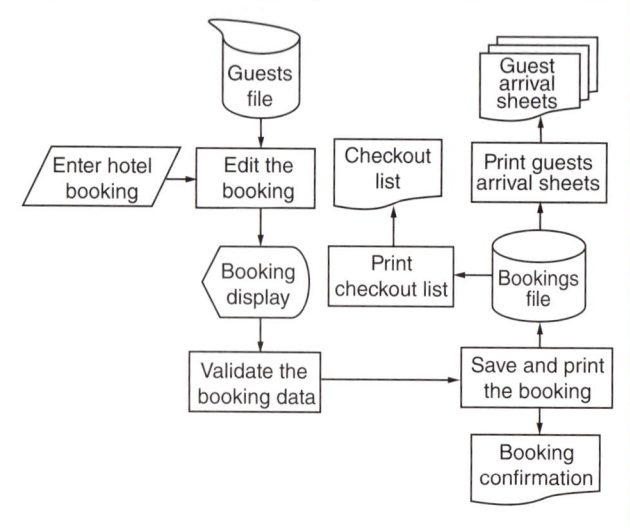

Figure 16.10: Online hotel booking flowchart.

UNPLUGGED ACTIVITY 16.04

Create a system flowchart for the following scenario.

A pizza delivery company accepts orders for pizzas by phone. The customer is asked for their address and the system checks the address is in the delivery file. The customer is asked for their order and the telephone operator inputs the order into the system. The order is added to the orders file. Payment details are then taken from the customer, which are saved to the payments file. A receipt is printed for the customer and an order sheet is printed for the chefs (see Figure 16.11).

Figure 16.11: Pizza boxes.

WORKED EXAMPLE 16.06

This is an example of a data dictionary for a table about students.

Attribute	Data type	Length	Format	Validation rule	Default value	Sample data	Primary key	Foreign key
Student ID	Integer	6	999999	Autonumber		459283	Yes	
Forename	Text	20	Xxxxx	Required		Sofia		
Surname	Text	20	Xxxxx	Required		Perez		
Tutor group	Text	3	99X			12A		TUTOR GROUP – TgId
Date of birth	Date	8	DD/MM/YYYY	<= 10 years before today		12/04/2012		
Date joined	Date	8	DD/MM/YYYY	>= 10 years after date of birth		01/09/2023		
Date left	Date	8	DD/MM/YYYY	> [Date Joined]				
Disability	Boolean	1		Required	False	True		

To create a system flowchart, identify the processes that take place within the system. Then identify the different files that will be used. Use flow lines to connect process to data files with the arrow pointing towards the data file if data is being stored, or the arrow pointing towards the process if data is being retrieved.

If user input is required, then add the input symbol at the appropriate place with the arrow pointing towards the process. Identify any documents that are produced by the system and link each one with a process with the arrow pointing from the process to the document.

Data storage

Databases

A data dictionary should be created to describe how data will be stored in tables within a database. The fieldnames should be identified along with their data type, field size and format. Primary keys and foreign keys should be identified, including the names of tables which the foreign keys link to. Any input masks, validation rules or default values should be identified for each field, along with an example of what typical data might look like. (You can find information about databases, including primary and foreign keys, in Chapter 10.)

UNPLUGGED ACTIVITY 16.05

Complete the following data dictionary for a table of vehicles. You may find it helpful first to review your understanding of data types, field sizes, primary and foreign keys and validation (see Chapter 10).

An entity relationship diagram should be created to show the relationships between the tables that will be used. (There is more detailed information about entity relationships in Chapter 10.)

Attribute	Data type	Length	Format	Validation rule	Default value	Sample data	Primary key	Foreign key
Vehicle registration								
Make								
Model								
Engine size (cc)								
Transmission								
Number of doors								
Imported?								

Files (input and output)

Any files that will be used to import data should be designed, including the intended format of data within the file. Similarly, any files generated by the system should be designed, including the format in which the data will be exported. For example, data might be stored in a file as comma separated or tab delimited. The data stored within the file should also be specified, including the expected data type, length and format of each column.

Input forms

Features and elements of forms

Data collection forms are documents that are used to collect data without the use of a computer (see Figure 16.12). These could include membership application forms, questionnaires, job applications or reply slips. It is important to design the form in such a way that the required data can be collected.

Data collection forms typically contain several features and elements, such as:

- use a black font and any images should be in black and white, as the document may not be printed in colour and may not be visible to people completing the survey

- include instructions about how to complete the form

- give clear instructions about where the form should be returned

- identify which questions must be answered and which are optional

- provide enough space for each answer

- use tick boxes for multiple-choice lists

- make it clear how many options are allowed to be chosen from a multiple-choice list

- ensure all fonts are consistently used

- avoid cluttering the form with too much information or too many questions

- ensure the font style and size are legible

- if the respondent needs to complete a scale (e.g. 1–10), then explain what the scale represents (e.g. 1 = very dissatisfied, 5 = neither satisfied or dissatisfied, 10 = very satisfied).

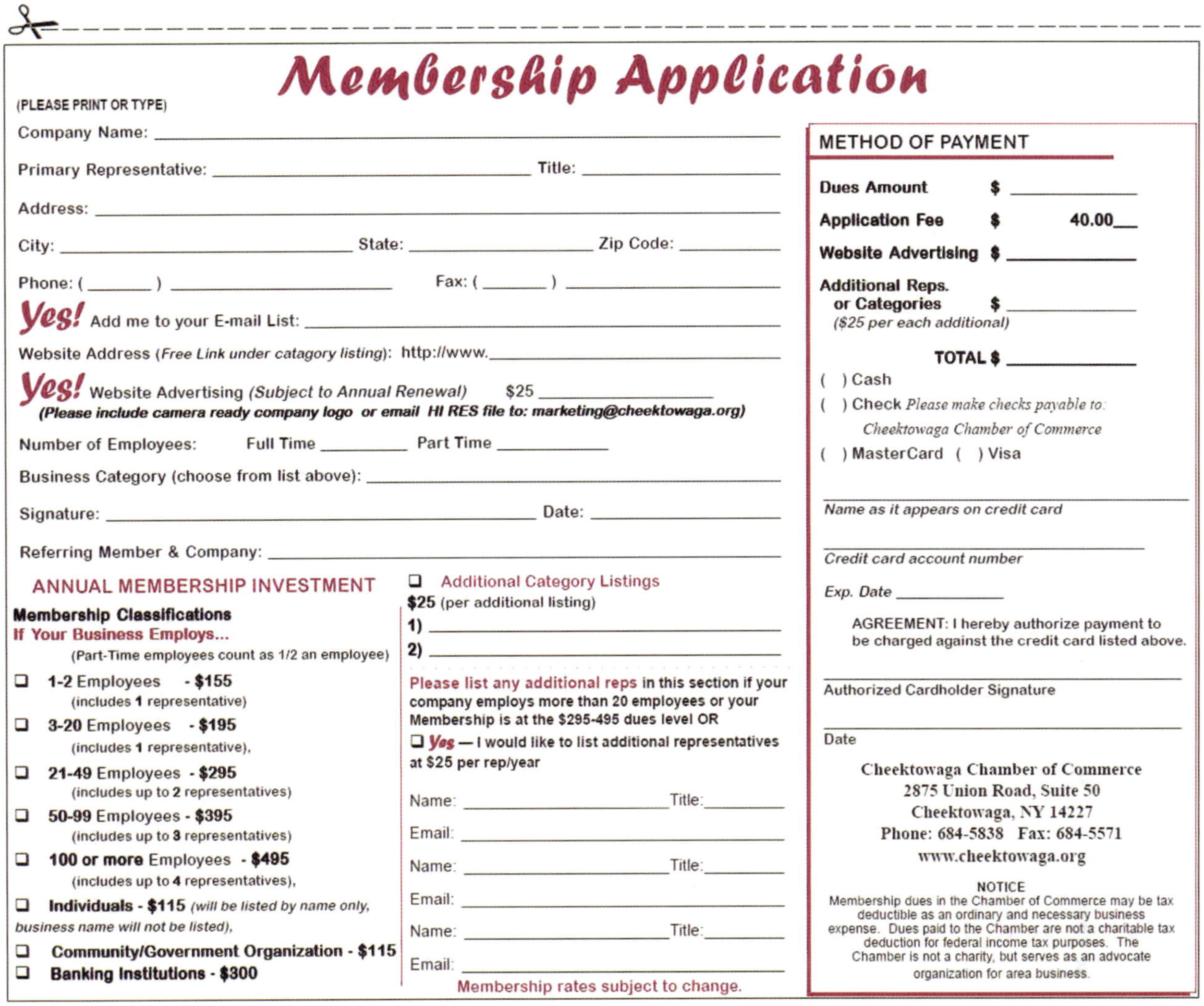

Membership Application

(PLEASE PRINT OR TYPE)

Company Name: ____________________

Primary Representative: ____________________ Title: ____________

Address: ____________________

City: ____________ State: ____________ Zip Code: ____________

Phone: (______) ____________ Fax: (______) ____________

Yes! Add me to your E-mail List: ____________________

Website Address (*Free Link under catagory listing*): http://www.____________________

Yes! Website Advertising (*Subject to Annual Renewal*) $25 ____________

(Please include camera ready company logo or email HI RES file to: marketing@cheektowaga.org)

Number of Employees: Full Time ________ Part Time ________

Business Category (choose from list above): ____________________

Signature: ____________________ Date: ____________

Referring Member & Company: ____________________

ANNUAL MEMBERSHIP INVESTMENT

Membership Classifications

If Your Business Employs...

(Part-Time employees count as 1/2 an employee)

- ❑ **1-2** Employees - **$155** (includes **1** representative)
- ❑ **3-20** Employees - **$195** (includes **1** representative),
- ❑ **21-49** Employees - **$295** (includes up to **2** representatives)
- ❑ **50-99** Employees - **$395** (includes up to **3** representatives)
- ❑ **100 or more** Employees - **$495** (includes up to **4** representatives),
- ❑ **Individuals - $115** (*will be listed by name only, business name will not be listed*),
- ❑ **Community/Government Organization - $115**
- ❑ **Banking Institutions - $300**

❑ Additional Category Listings

$25 (per additional listing)

1) ____________________

2) ____________________

Please list any additional reps in this section if your company employs more than 20 employees or your Membership is at the $295-495 dues level OR

❑ *Yes* — I would like to list additional representatives at $25 per rep/year

Name: ____________ Title: ________

Email: ____________________

Name: ____________ Title: ________

Email: ____________________

Name: ____________ Title: ________

Email: ____________________

Membership rates subject to change.

METHOD OF PAYMENT

Dues Amount **$** ________

Application Fee **$** **40.00**

Website Advertising **$** ________

Additional Reps. or Categories **$** ________

($25 per each additional)

TOTAL $ ________

( ) Cash

( ) Check *Please make checks payable to: Cheektowaga Chamber of Commerce*

( ) MasterCard ( ) Visa

____

Name as it appears on credit card

____

Credit card account number

Exp. Date ________

AGREEMENT: I hereby authorize payment to be charged against the credit card listed above.

____

Authorized Cardholder Signature

____

Date

Cheektowaga Chamber of Commerce
2875 Union Road, Suite 50
Cheektowaga, NY 14227
Phone: 684-5838 Fax: 684-5571
www.cheektowaga.org

NOTICE

Membership dues in the Chamber of Commerce may be tax deductible as an ordinary and necessary business expense. Dues paid to the Chamber are not a charitable tax deduction for federal income tax purposes. The Chamber is not a charity, but serves as an advocate organization for area business.

Figure 16.12: Example of a data collection form.

Appropriate use of forms for data collection

Paper-based forms are typically used when data collection can take place in a variety of locations, without the use of technology. Paper-based forms are usually quicker to create than electronic forms, as detailed technical knowledge is not usually required to create the form. However, care needs to be taken to ensure the paper-based form can accurately record the required data to input into the system. It can also be time consuming to enter the data into the system, such as by a person manually typing the data on the form.

Electronic forms can enable data to be entered directly into the system, with the data viewed and analysed while being collected. Electronic forms can be programmed to ask the user specific answers based on previous responses, along with ensuring data entered is valid before being submitted. The use of electronic forms relies on the availability of technology and internet connectivity. This may be an issue for individuals that do not have access to modern technology (see Chapter 6 The digital divide).

UNPLUGGED ACTIVITY 16.06

Explain how the application form in Figure 16.13 could be improved.

Membership Application Form

Name_____

Address_____

Gender_____

Age_____

Do you have any disabilities? Y/N

Which of the following types of movie do you watch? ☐ Horror ☐ Action
☐ Drama ☐ Comedy ☐ Other

Figure 16.13: Poorly designed data collection form.

Validation and checking of data collected by forms

Validation rules should be used wherever possible and be appropriate to reduce the number of possible input errors. Where possible, drop-down boxes should be used instead of lookup validation checks. For example, if a category needs to be selected, then a drop-down box should be used to select that category, rather than requiring the user to type in the category.

When designing a validation rule, identify:

- the input data that is to be validated

- the type of validation rule to be used

- the rule that will be used

- the error message that should appear if the data input is invalid.

Error messages should clearly guide the user as to what to do to correct the error. Table 16.4 gives examples of validation rules for a range of input data.

Input data	Validation type	Validation rule	Error message
Surname	Presence	Surname must be entered.	Please enter a surname.
Date of birth	Range	Date of birth must be at least 18 years earlier than today.	Applicant must be at least 18 years old.
Application number	Type	Must be a whole number.	The application number must contain only numbers.
Telephone	Length	Must be between 3 and 15 digits.	Telephone number must be between 3 and 15 digits.
Product code	Format	XX999XX9	The product code must be in the format XX999XX9 where X is a letter from A to Z and 9 is a number from 0 to 9.

Table 16.4: Examples of validation rules.

In addition to validation rules, any intended methods for verifying data input, such as visual checking, double data entry or hash control, should be specified. (You can find more detailed information about these verification methods in Chapter 1.)

Input screen layouts

A screen can be used to ask the user to input data and to output information to the user, or a mixture of both. For example, Figure 16.14 shows information about a property that is for sale. It also allows the user to enter details about an existing property or add details about a new property.

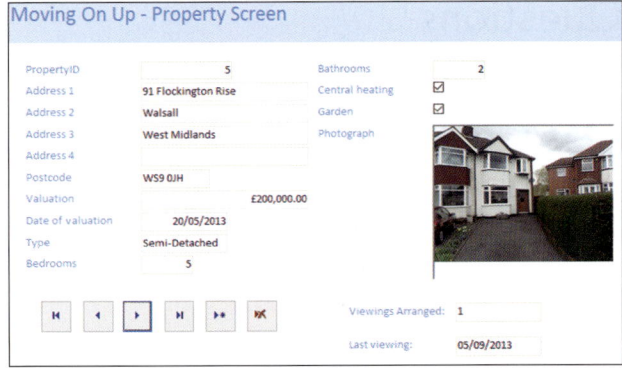

Figure 16.14: Example of an input screen.

When designing an input screen:

- Use colour carefully and appropriately. Different colours could be used for questions and responses or for different types of data. Colours that the user expects should be used, for example the colour red to display a warning.

- Ensure all fonts are used consistently.

- Avoid cluttering the screen with too many elements, such as multiple text boxes, although it is helpful to fit all elements on a single screen if possible.

- Ensure the font style and size are legible.

- Include instructions about how to complete the form.

- Identify which questions must be answered and which are optional.

- Provide enough space for each answer.

- Use tick boxes for multiple-choice lists that can have more than one response.

- Use drop-down boxes (combo boxes) or option buttons (radio buttons) for multiple-choice lists that can only have one response.

(You can find more detailed information about the types of form controls that can be used on input forms in Chapter 2.)

When designing an input screen layout, it is only necessary to indicate where questions and responses will go, the types of response options and the styles to use. The layout of any information should also be indicated.

Figure 16.15 shows an example of a screen design. The way the input screen will be displayed is part of the next stage of the system life cycle.

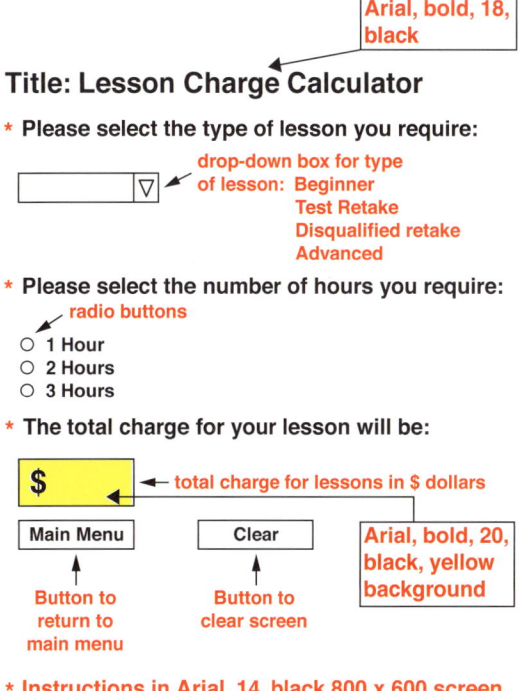

Figure 16.15: Example of a screen design.

Output reports

Output screen layouts

The design of output screen layouts is similar to input screens, except that there is no need for input elements, such as text boxes. However, controls may be required for the user to navigate information output, such as when viewing multiple results output from the system. For example, a scroll bar may be needed to move up and down large sections of text, or clickable buttons could be used to move between different screens.

Printed copy layouts

When designing a printed copy layout, as well as following the same principles for output screens, you need to consider the size of paper that will be used, the width of margins and the intended audience. Printed copies can often include tabular data.

WORKED EXAMPLE 16.07

Products			
Description	Category	Supplier	1
Description	Category	Supplier	1
Description	Category	Supplier	1
Description	Category	Supplier	1
Page n of nn 2		Total products: ## 3	

Key:

- ■ field from the database
- ■ field titles (should appear at top of every page)
- ■ data that should appear at the bottom of the whole report only
- ☐ data labels

Figure 16.16: Example of report listing for products.

Figure 16.16 shows a report for listing all the products available.

1   The description, category and supplier data will be repeated for each record in the PRODUCTS table.

2   n = page number, nn = total number of pages.

3   ## = total number of products in PRODUCTS table.

In addition to these points, the size of paper, size of margins, font styles and sizes, colours and any gridlines should also be specified.

UNPLUGGED ACTIVITY 16.07

Design the layout of a report that will show a list of all the students in your class, including their dates of birth and contact details.

Questions

4   Identify the purpose of a data flow diagram (DFD).

5   Identify one rule for data flows within a level 1 DFD.

6   Describe the difference in usage between a tick box and an option button.

Stage 3: Development and testing

The **development** and testing stage involves producing each part of the system and ensuring it functions as expected. **Software developers** (see Figure 16.17) may use different methods of software development and these are discussed later in the chapter.

KEY WORDS

development: the stage in the system life cycle when different parts of the system are produced

software developer: someone who designs and creates computer programs

Figure 16.17: A software developer designs and creates computer programs.

Test plans

Testing is necessary because software may contain **bugs** that cause the system not to function as expected. Bugs need to be found and fixed. It is important to ensure that the system is bug free, so that the users can use the system knowing that it will work reliably and behave as expected. Although it is challenging to ensure a system is free of bugs, a **test plan** can help to minimise the number of bugs by ensuring that all pathways through a system and examples of data input have been tested.

A test plan will identify the tests needed for each element of a system, such as when data is input or buttons are clicked. The test plan will include different types of test data, including valid, invalid and extreme, as outlined next and in further detail in Chapter 8, so that inputs are thoroughly tested. Without a test plan, important parts of testing could be missed and bugs left undiscovered. A test plan will also cover the user's requirements and ensure that they are tested.

A good test plan will include all features and functionality to ensure the whole system is tested. The test plan will be continually updated to reflect any new areas to test as the software is developed.

As outlined in Worked example 16.8, a test plan identifies what is being tested, the type of test, the input data that should be used to test it, the expected result of the test and space to record the actual result. Each test should be numbered.

WORKED EXAMPLE 16.08

The extract below, from a test plan tests the input of data where the date must be between 1/1/23 and 31/12/23 inclusive, and in the format dd/mm/yy.

The reason the test for 31/12/23 failed to be accepted may be because <31/12/23 was used in the validation rule rather than <=31/12/23. Similarly, the reason 31/12/23 failed to generate an error message may be because >= 31/12/23 was used in the validation rule rather than >31/12/23.

Number	Description	Type of test	Input data	Expected result	Pass/Fail
1a	Test the input of join date.	Valid	12/5/23	Accepted	Pass
1b		Extreme	1/1/23	Accepted	Pass
1c		Extreme	31/12/23	Accepted	Fail – error message displayed
1d		Invalid	15/7/22	Error message: the join date must be in 2023	Pass
1e		Invalid	4/6/19		Pass
1f		Extreme	31/12/23		Fail – accepted
1g		Extreme	1/1/23		Pass

Table 16.5: Extract from a test plan.

A parcel delivery company uses a number of codes to identify different types of parcel (see Figure 16.18). The code must start with an upper case letter between D and P (inclusive). Create a test plan to test the input of data for an upper case character to be input, which must be between the letters D and P (inclusive) in the English alphabet.

Figure 16.18: Parcel delivery.

In addition to testing input data, it is important to test that all calculations work as expected. Each input for a calculation will need to be identified and an expected result determined. Table 16.6 shows an example of how testing of calculations might be planned and executed.

Any links or buttons also need testing. Table 16.7 shows how a navigation button (main menu) and an action button (clear) would be tested.

Number	Description	Type of test	Input data	Expected result	Pass/Fail
2	Discount formula works for 2 hours	Calculation	Charge per hour = $26 on quote worksheet	Test retake = $50 in 2 hours column	Pass
3	Function for lesson charge	Calculation	Lesson type = advanced Number of hours = 2 on quote worksheet	Total charge = $38	Fail = $3.80

Table 16.6: Examples of test plan for calculations.

Number	Description	Type of test	Input data	Expected result	Pass/Fail
4	Main menu button	Button	Click on main menu button on quote worksheet.	The main menu worksheet opens.	Pass
5	Clear button	Button	Lesson type = advanced, number of hours = 2 Click on the clear button on quote worksheet.	Lesson type = (blank) Number of hours = (blank).	Fail – number of hours remained as 2

Table 16.7: Example of a test plan for buttons.

Test data

As part of testing a system, a simulation of 'live data' has to be created for the purposes of testing. This is known as **test data**. Sufficient test data needs to be generated to ensure that the system will perform adequately when a large amount of data is entered. There will also need to be specific types of data to test different scenarios within the software, including validation rules and queries.

KEY WORD

test data: data that will be used for testing a system

When testing the input of data that is to be validated, Table 16.8 shows the types of data that should be included as test data.

Type of test data	Description
Valid (also called normal data)	Data that will be accepted by the validation rule.
Invalid (also called abnormal or erroneous data)	Data that will not be accepted by the validation rule.
Extreme (also called extreme data)	Data that will be accepted by the validation rule, but it is at the limit of acceptability.

Table 16.8: Types of test data.

UNPLUGGED ACTIVITY 16.09

Select test data to test the input of numbers in the range 2500 to 5000.

Test data is also needed to test queries. Records will need to be created where there is data that meets the criteria of the query, does not meet the criteria of the query, only just meets the criteria of the query and only just fails to meet the criteria of the query. Where there is more than a single criterion, data should also be selected that only meets part of the criteria in case both parts have not been set up correctly.

WORKED EXAMPLE 16.09

The following data for records could be used to test the query for people in the job role 'engineer' and aged 50 or over.

Record number	Job role	Age	Reason
1	Engineer	65	Both criteria met.
2	Designer	25	Both criteria not met.
3	Engineer	25	Job role part met, age part not met.
4	Tester	65	Job role part not met, age part met.
5	Engineer	50	Job role part met, age part only just met.
6	Engineer	49	Job role part met, age part only just not met.

The more criteria that are used, the more records that will be required to test the query fully.

UNPLUGGED ACTIVITY 16.10

Data is stored about cars, including their make, model, registration number, transmission (automatic or manual), colour, distance travelled and year of registration. In a table, select test data that could be used to test the query to find all automatic transmission cars that were registered before 2016 (see Figure 16.19).

Figure 16.19: A database could be used to identify all cars of the same model in this car park.

Parallel running

Parallel running is when a new system and an old system are run at the same time. On an agreed date, the new system will become live, but the old system will continue to run at the same time. Data will need to be duplicated from the old system to the new system, then any new data will be input into both systems, with output also produced from both systems. Parallel running will continue until the organisation is confident that the new system is working satisfactorily.

Direct changeover

Direct changeover is when a date is chosen for the old system to stop running and the new system to start running. The systems do not run at the same time and there is a clear break from the old system to the new system. Data will need to be transferred from the old system to the new system before the new system can be used.

Phased implementation

With phased implementation, parts of the new system will be introduced at different times. Phased implementation often takes place when there is a large system with functionality that can be easily separated into sections. The old system will run until a date that has been agreed, at which point part of the old system will be stopped and part of the new system will start. After a period of time, another part of the old system will be stopped and another part of the new system will start. Phased implementation will continue until all the new system is in place.

Pilot implementation

Pilot implementation takes place when part of an organisation starts to use the new system, while the rest of the organisation continues to use the old system. If the new system works successfully for the pilot implementation group, the system can then be implemented in other parts of the organisation. The pilot group may also be able to deliver training, or provide support, to the rest of the organisation when the system goes fully live.

Advantages and disadvantages of each implementation method

The most suitable changeover method will depend upon the circumstances surrounding a new system. Factors that will need to be considered include:

- how critical the system is to the running of the organisation
- cost of implementation
- number of users in the organisation
- the size and complexity of the new system.

The advantages and disadvantages of each method, and their suitability for a given situation, are shown in Table 16.11.

Implementation method	Advantages	Disadvantages	Suitable when...
Parallel running	If the new system fails, this is the least risky because the organisation can continue to run using the old system. The accuracy of the new system can be tested against the old system and any bugs fixed.	Duplication of data input means additional costs. There may need to be additional hardware installed, as the old hardware is still being used, which will require physical space. Data may be input differently into the two systems, meaning that the data is not the same in both systems.	A system is critical to the operations of the organisation and any issues could have serious consequences. The performance of the old and new systems need to be compared. The old system and new system can be easily integrated.

Implementation method	Advantages	Disadvantages	Suitable when...
Direct changeover	This is cost-effective to implement, as there is no duplication of systems or input data. The data being used will be consistent because it is only being used in one system at a time. There is no need for the new system to be compatible with the old system.	This is a risky method because a bug or bugs could lead to the system crashing (failing) with no backup. All the training will need to be done in advance of changeover and, if there are a lot of users, this could result in some forgetting what they have learned by the time they start to use the new system.	The old system is unreliable or does not meet the organisation's needs. A quick changeover is possible from the old system to the new system. Training and support are available to help users move to the new system immediately.
Phased implementation	Bugs can be identified and fixed within the part of the system that has changed, rather than the whole system. End users can be trained how to use each part of the new system and spend time using the new part, before being trained in the next phase.	Delays can occur waiting for each phase to be running successfully before the next phase can start. Users will be using both new and old systems, which could lead to confusion about how to complete a task and data being updated in the wrong system. Both the old and new systems need to be compatible for data to be used across both systems.	The new system is large or complex, so it would be challenging to implement at once. The organisation wants to minimise the likelihood of any issues with the implementation. Users need time to learn about how different parts of the new system function.

Implementation method	Advantages	Disadvantages	Suitable when...
Pilot implementation	Bugs found during implementation will only affect the pilot group that is using the system.

Bugs found by the pilot group can be fixed before the system is installed for all users.

The pilot group can train other users on how to use the system, as they will already be familiar with its operation. | This is a slower method of changeover because the rest of the organisation has to wait until the pilot has been completed satisfactorily.

Users in the pilot group might be anxious about using the new system, as it may still have bugs, while users outside the pilot group may be disappointed that they have not been offered the opportunity to try the new software first.

Both the old and new systems need to be compatible with each other for data to be shared between the pilot group and the users still using the old system. | The new system includes a number of new features, or is very different from the old system.

The system needs further testing before being implemented fully.

The new system requires a large amount of training. |

Table 16.11: Advantages and disadvantages of implementation methods and their suitability in a given situation.

REFLECTION

How will you remember the different types of implementation methods and their suitability for different situations? Would you create a resource such as a mind map? Or is there another method you would use?

Questions

11 Identify four methods of implementation.

12 Describe one situation when direct changeover would be more appropriate than parallel running.

13 Describe one situation when pilot implementation would be more appropriate than phased implementation.

ACTIVITY 16.11

A number of computer systems have failed during implementation. Research some examples of major system failures, such as those relating to air traffic control systems (see Figure 16.20). Produce a list of what lessons could be learned from these failures.

Figure 16.20: Air traffic controllers use complex computer systems.

Documentation

As part of the implementation stage, documentation will be produced to provide further information about the system, for example a description of the hardware needed to run the system and how to operate certain features. Much of the content within the documentation can be reused from documents previously produced, such as flowcharts and business requirements. However, some of the documentation, such as instructions for users and marketing teams, will involve writing new content.

Requirements documentation

The **requirements documentation** provides a reference point for both the system developers and users to ensure the system meets the intended purpose.

The requirements documentation outlines the functionality of the new system (how it will work) and includes:

- functional requirements describing the system's behaviour, including inputs and outputs

- non-functional requirements covering other aspects of the system, such as reliability, security and performance

- business requirements identifying the business goals and objectives the system needs to address

- system requirements outlining the hardware, software and infrastructure needs.

Design documentation

Design documentation provides an overview of the construction of the system. The design documentation includes an outline of the system architecture (the different parts of the system and how they fit together). It provides:

- an overview of the main system components, along with data flows

- designs for data storage, such as the structure of the system's database, and for the user interface, which defines the layout and design of the user interface and any forms used

- details of the software design, such as the algorithms used and the network design, which describes the network infrastructure elements.

Design documentation helps developers ensure the system's technical requirements are understood and guides the implementation of the system. The documentation may be referred to as a reference point by developers and users as the system is implemented and helps to support the maintenance of the system.

> **KEY WORDS**
>
> **requirements documentation:** provides an overview of the functionality and needs of the new system
>
> **design documentation:** gives a summary of how the system will be constructed

Technical documentation

Technical documentation is an overview of the structure of the system, how it was put together and how it works. It includes:

- a data dictionary to show how data has been structured within the system

- any programming code will be annotated to explain their purpose, along with a list of variables, including their datatypes and purpose

- all validation rules, with the criteria used for successful input and the error messages that they generate

- the purpose of calculations within the system and an explanation given of how each calculation works

- a list of all buttons and links, including where they are located and what their function is

- all files used by the system and their purpose

- flowcharts to show how different parts of the system work and other diagrams that may have been used during design and development, such as entity relationship diagrams and screen connectivity diagrams.

> **KEY WORD**
>
> **technical documentation:** an overview of the structure of the system, how it was put together and how it works

The technical documentation will also include:

- an installation guide for teams installing the system, both initially and in the future

- all the results of testing, including any known bugs

- backup routines to show where files are stored, how the routines were configured and how to restore them from a backup

- security settings documented to show which groups have access to each part of the system and the permissions they have been granted

- list of software and hardware requirements.

Technical documentation is also needed so that anybody carrying out future maintenance on the system will be able to understand how the system was developed and how it is configured. It may be that the person carrying out future maintenance was not part of the original development team and so will not be familiar with the system without the technical documentation. Even if it is the same person or team carrying out the maintenance, they will need the documentation to remember the structure of the system.

User documentation

User documentation is a guide giving instructions to the user. It can be in electronic or printed format. A contents page should be included with page numbers and an electronic version would include hyperlinks to those pages. An introduction to the purpose of the user guide should be included. All the software and hardware requirements will be listed within the guide if applicable to the user.

The main part of the user guide will be the instructions on how to use the system. This should include written instructions, together with screenshots of the software and/or photographs of hardware. Screenshots and photographs can be annotated with labels. Bullets or numbering should be used to break down instructions into manageable tasks.

A glossary will show an alphabetical list of any technical terms that have been used within the user guide, along with a definition of each of those terms. There should be a troubleshooting section that includes a table of common problems and error messages, together with a description of what might have caused the problem and possible solutions for overcoming the problem. An index will be included at the end of the user guide with page numbers for each common term.

WORKED EXAMPLE 16.10

This is an example of a troubleshooting guide for a printer.

Problem	Cause	Solution
Orange light displayed on printer.	No paper in feeder tray.	Add paper to the feeder tray.
Red light displayed on printer.	Paper is jammed in the printer.	Open the paper feeder tray and check there is no paper stuck. Open the back door and check there is no paper stuck. Open the toner door, remove the toner and check there is no paper stuck. If any paper is found, gently pull any paper out and remove it.
Error message on computer says 'Printer Offline'.	Printer is turned off. Printer is not connected to the computer.	Turn on printer. Ensure the USB cable is connected between the computer and the printer.

CONTINUED

Below is an example of a troubleshooting guide for an order processing system.

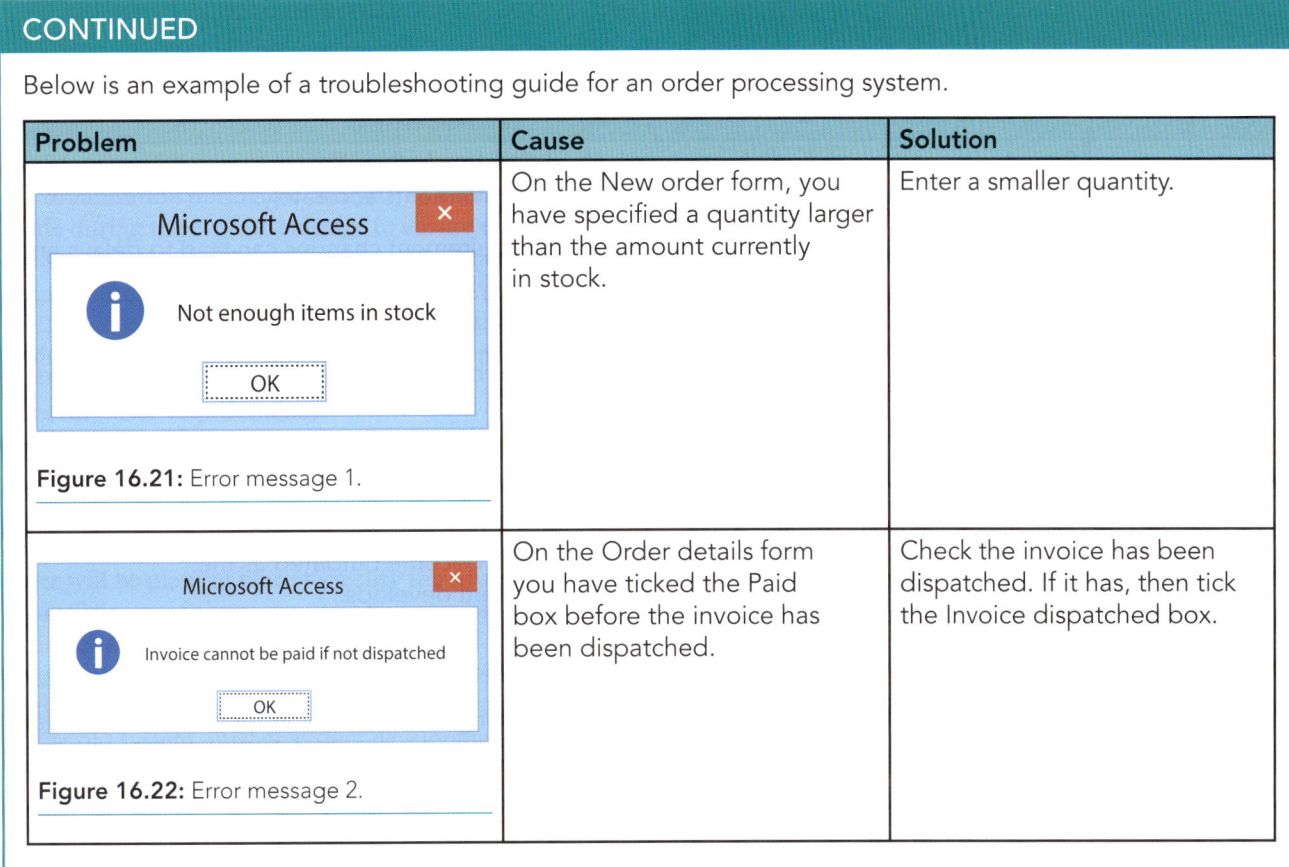

Problem	Cause	Solution
Microsoft Access ✕ ℹ Not enough items in stock OK **Figure 16.21:** Error message 1.	On the New order form, you have specified a quantity larger than the amount currently in stock.	Enter a smaller quantity.
Microsoft Access ✕ ℹ Invoice cannot be paid if not dispatched OK **Figure 16.22:** Error message 2.	On the Order details form you have ticked the Paid box before the invoice has been dispatched.	Check the invoice has been dispatched. If it has, then tick the Invoice dispatched box.

User documentation is needed so that the user can learn how to use the new system, or look up how certain features are supposed to work. The troubleshooting section will be important for the user to understand what has caused an error to occur and what they need to do to fix the problem and/or prevent the error from occurring again.

UNPLUGGED ACTIVITY 16.12

Find a user manual for an electronic device or appliance at home. Identify the different sections that are used and compare them with those listed in Worked example 16.10.

Marketing documentation

Marketing documentation refers to the materials created to promote the system to potential users. Marketing documentation outlines the key features and functions of the system through providing an overview of the system's capabilities. Marketing documentation may include product brochures or presentations, along with case studies outlining real-world examples of how the system has been used successfully. Content from other documentation or resources, such as screenshots and support materials, might also be provided to help understand the system.

KEY WORD

marketing documentation: materials to promote the benefits and functionality of a system

Marketing documentation enables the benefits and features of the system to be described. Marketing documentation should highlight the main advantages of the system and the problems it solves. It may contribute to the success of the system by creating a positive image of the system for users.

maintenance was used to make the changes to the system and to ensure the company complied with the government's requirements.

Preventative maintenance

Preventative maintenance involves taking practical measures to stop problems arising within a system. Preventative maintenance is needed for both hardware and software to identify and address issues before they arise, which includes ensuring the system is kept secure. During preventative maintenance, systems might be updated, such as through using the latest drivers and ensure antivirus software is up to date. Hardware is cleaned and storage devices examined to check for errors and optimise disk space. Backup and recovery plans also form part of preventative maintenance, along with educating users on using the system appropriately, such as how to shut down the system correctly at the end of the working day.

For example, during preventative maintenance, an organisation's hardware is regularly cleaned to stop dust from blocking any fans, with regular scans of storage media carried out to ensure they are working properly. Data is also regularly checked for consistency and integrity, with the performance of the system monitored to ensure that the processor, memory and storage are all working efficiently.

Figure 16.23: Like cars, software needs to be regularly maintained to ensure good performance.

Corrective maintenance

Corrective maintenance ensures errors, bugs, or even system failures, are resolved so the system functions as intended. These errors need to be corrected quickly so there is limited impact on an organisation and users can continue to use the system. In particular, issues relating to system performance can be frustrating to users and have a negative impact on their use of the system (see Figure 16.23).

For example, a graphics application would intermittently stop responding for several seconds. Corrective maintenance was undertaken to identify the bug causing the application to stop responding, which was then fixed and users were able to use the software without interruption.

Advantages and disadvantages of types of maintenance

Table 16.13 lists the advantages and disadvantages of different types of maintenance.

Types of maintenance	Advantages	Disadvantages
Perfective	System functionality improves as new features are implemented and performance improves. Users' feedback can be used to make changes to the system.	Can require significant development effort, which can take a long period of time. Modifying existing code could introduce bugs or alter system performance.
Adaptive	Enables the system to remain compatible with technology and business requirements. Helps ensure the technology remains up to date and can be used in the future.	Integrating new technologies can be technically challenging. Changes might introduce compatibility issues, so thorough testing is needed.
Preventative	Helps prevent system failures and downtime. Avoids large costs associated with emergency repairs.	Ongoing costs are needed to carry out preventative tasks. Careful planning is needed to ensure tasks do not impact usage of the system.

Types of maintenance	Advantages	Disadvantages
Corrective	Addresses issues preventing the system working as intended. Issues are addressed immediately to minimise the impact on users.	Corrective maintenance needs to be reactive, which can be challenging and costly to implement. Users cannot use parts of the system while corrective maintenance is being completed.

Table 16.13: Advantages and disadvantages of different types of maintenance

16.2 Methods of software development

A number of different methods of working can be used to produce software during the development stage. The most common methods of software development include agile, iterative, incremental, rapid application development and waterfall.

Agile

The agile approach to software development involves breaking down the project into small stages and continuously delivering working software within a short period of time. The agile approach is iterative. This means that each stage in the development process is repeated until the system is complete.

Agile can respond to the client's changing requirements, even late in the development life cycle. It is expected that the client's requirements will evolve (change) as the project develops. Agile enables change to be managed and the software developed for the benefit of the client.

Agile values collaboration between developers and users more highly than design processes and tools. Similarly, it is more important that working software is developed rather than having comprehensive supporting documentation. While planning is necessary, flexibility is more important in the agile approach and so responding to change is essential.

Unlike the waterfall model outlined later, which has separate phases throughout the system life cycle, the agile approach uses iterations. An iteration is a timebox (a set period of time). During an iteration the planning, design, development and testing of part of the software takes place. At the end of an iteration, a working solution for that part of the software is ready for

demonstration. Several iterations are usually required before a product is ready to be released or updated.

As an iteration includes designers, developers and testers, they are expected to work closely together. This ensures a collaborative approach to each iteration. Each team will also include a customer representative, sometimes referred to as a product owner, who represents the client and must be available to developers throughout an iteration. Working closely together means that feedback is instantaneous and enables a flexible approach to be taken to the design and development. Agile is both iterative and incremental. It's incremental because each iteration can be planned to be improved upon in future iterations. It's important not to get the words iteration and iterative confused. Each iteration increments the existing functionality and each iteration is iterative in nature.

Iterative

Iterative development is about planned rework throughout a project. It allows for feedback to be given by the customer and improvements to be made based on that feedback. It usually involves building a part of each section of the system before seeking feedback and then revisiting the whole solution to make improvements.

> **KEY WORD**
>
> **iterative:** creating a system or adding new functionality in a repetitive cycle

Within iterative development, each part of the system is divided into different parts, with a small amount of development undertaken on each part at a time. Iterative development delivers a working version of the software each time, although it may not be complete. Iterative development usually has less regular involvement from

Question

18 Describe the differences between incremental and iterative methods of development.

16.3 Prototyping

A **prototype** is an early version of a software solution with limited functionality. It is used to demonstrate how a system will look and function (see Figure 16.25). A prototype is usually focused on the user interface, rather than any data structures. It is used so that the client can get a feel for the new system before it is developed and can provide feedback that can then be acted upon. The client is also able to compare the prototype against the requirements specification. The development team's interpretation of the requirements specification may lead to changes in the specification.

Figure 16.25: A robot prototype, like a software prototype, shows designers at an early stage of development how the robot will look and function.

KEY WORD

prototype: an early version of a software solution with limited functionality

Types of prototyping and why each is needed

Evolutionary prototyping

Evolutionary prototyping is iterative in nature, with the initial (first) prototype including the core functionality and features of the system. The initial prototype is presented to the client. The client's feedback is recorded and areas for improvement identified. Following this discussion, the developer will continue improving the prototype focusing on the requirements of the client. Another prototype will be produced and feedback will again be obtained from the client. This process will continue as the product evolves from a goal to a useable piece of software.

Incremental prototyping

Incremental prototyping also involves an iterative approach. When using incremental prototyping, requirements are specified and an initial prototype is developed containing certain functions. The prototype is then reviewed, with the requirements re-examined and clarified, and the prototype is improved based on feedback.

Each prototype will build on the previous one and include more functionality until a final product is built. At each stage, only clearly understood requirements are developed. Each prototype can be functional and, if required, can be used by the client until the next iteration of the prototype is ready. This means that the end users may request enhanced or new features that they discover they require as the prototypes are being developed, which were not identified at the initial requirements specification stage.

Throwaway prototyping

With throwaway prototyping, the prototype developed will never become part of the final delivered software and will be discarded (thrown away). Throwaway prototypes are developed to quickly explore and develop ideas, with the prototype used to make decisions about how the new system should be produced. As throwaway prototypes do not form part of the new system, they may simply simulate certain functionality, rather than being fully implemented or integrating with the whole system.

Throwaway prototyping enables the requirements to be fine-tuned early in the system life cycle, which can be more cost-effective than trying to make changes later when a lot of work has been carried out.

Rapid prototyping

Rapid prototyping focuses on quickly producing working prototypes which are similar to the new system. The prototypes are used to gather feedback from users and to validate requirements. Unlike throwaway prototyping, the rapid protype will be incorporated into the final system.

Rapid prototypes typically require more development than throwaway prototypes, as key features may be implemented, or the prototype integrated with other parts of the system.

Advantages and disadvantages of each type of prototyping

Table 16.15 lists the advantages and disadvantages of each type of prototyping.

Type of prototyping	Advantage	Disadvantage
Evolutionary	Allows for the system to be refined over time. Users are closely involved.	User involvement can lead to additional requirements being specified. Frequent changes to the prototype need to be carefully managed.
Incremental	Functioning parts of the system are available from an early stage of development. Changes can be made based on user feedback.	Careful planning is needed to ensure prototypes can integrate with the whole system. Key features for each increment need to be identified.
Throwaway	Ideas can be quickly explored and discussed. User requirements can be clearly determined.	Prototypes cannot be used within the new system. Effort may be wasted if the ideas in a prototype are not incorporated into the system.
Rapid	Feedback can be gained quickly from the user. Prototypes form part of the new system.	Prototypes may have limited functionality due to the rapid speed of development. Can be challenging to integrate prototypes into the system.

Table 16.15: Advantages and disadvantages of each type of prototyping.

Question

19 Compare and contrast evolutionary and throwaway prototyping.

DISCUSSION POINT

The original developers of a system are often not involved with maintenance of the system. To what extent do you feel they should be involved with this process? What might be the advantages and disadvantages of having them involved?

PRACTICE QUESTIONS

Thornhill Estates runs several hotels. It would like a new software solution to manage room bookings, dinner reservations and purchases across all its hotels. It has asked a software developer to produce the software for them. The software developer will follow the system life cycle.

1 a State one purpose of analysis in the system life cycle. [1]

 b Suggest four reasons why questionnaires would be appropriate for researching how bookings are currently managed at the hotel. [4]

 c State three other methods that could be used to research the current booking system. [3]

[Total 8]

2 The analyst will interview a group of users to create a requirements specification.

 State the purpose of a requirements specification. [1]

3 The designer will create a design specification based on the requirements specification.

 a Identify three factors that should be considered when designing a screen layout. [3]

 b Using an example, show how a validation rule could be designed for the hotel booking system. [3]

 c Apart from keyboards, mice and monitors, describe three external hardware components that will be needed by the hotel system. [3]

[Total 9]

4 An evolutionary prototype approach will be used during the design and development of the software.

 a Define the term 'prototype'. [1]

 b Justify the manager's choice of an evolutionary approach. [4]

[Total 5]

5 Once the system has been developed, it will need to be tested.

 a Describe two differences between white box and black box testing. [4]

 b Explain one reason why beta testing might not be appropriate for the hotel system. [2]

 c Explain why invalid test data is used. [2]

[Total 8]

CONTINUED

6 The system will be installed in a pilot approach and user documentation will be provided to the hotel staff.

    a Justify the choice of the pilot implementation for the hotel system. [4]

    b Explain why the user documentation should include troubleshooting and glossary sections. [4]

    c Suggest four reasons why the hotel system may require maintenance in the future. [4]

[Total 12]

SUMMARY CHECKLIST

- [ ] I can define different types of system.
- [ ] I can describe the stages in the system life cycle.
- [ ] I can describe methods of research for a given situation.
- [ ] I can understand the content and purpose of specifications.
- [ ] I can construct diagrams to represent system processing and the flow of data through a system.
- [ ] I can design data storage, input forms and output reports.
- [ ] I can create a test plan and understand its purpose.
- [ ] I can select appropriate test data.
- [ ] I can describe the differences between alpha and beta testing.
- [ ] I can describe the differences between white box and black box testing.
- [ ] I can explain the advantages and disadvantages of different types of testing.
- [ ] I can describe different methods of implementing a system.
- [ ] I can explain the advantages and disadvantages of each implementation method for a given situation.
- [ ] I can describe types of documentation and explain why each is needed.
- [ ] I can describe the contents of documentation.
- [ ] I can explain the advantages and disadvantages of different types of documentation.
- [ ] I can explain methods of evaluating a new system.
- [ ] I can describe different types of maintenance and explain why each is needed.
- [ ] I can explain how each type of maintenance is carried out.
- [ ] I can explain different types of prototyping and explain why each is needed.
- [ ] I can explain the advantages and disadvantages of each type of prototyping.
- [ ] I can describe the stages and processes of different software development methodologies.
- [ ] I can explain the advantages and disadvantages of different software development methodologies.

PROJECT

Figure 16.26: Learning to drive with a professional driving instructor.

A driving instructor currently uses their mobile phone to take bookings from people learning to drive. The driving instructor checks their calendar to see if they are available and suggests some other times if they are unavailable. The driving instructor then adds the booking to the calendar.

The driving instructor is finding that taking bookings is time consuming and they are unable to answer the phone during lessons. They would therefore like to move to an online booking system and have asked for your help.

Working in a group, produce a presentation explaining to the driving instructor how a new booking system could be developed. Within your presentation, you should include:

- An overview of the system life cycle.

- At what points during the system life cycle the driving instructor will need to be involved in the production of the system, for example the driving instructor will need to be involved during the analysis stage.

- How the system will be maintained once it has been developed.

- Use presentation software to make your presentation. Examples of content from documents or diagrams used within the system life cycle, such as test plans or user interface designs, should be included from other systems to help develop the driving instructor's understanding.

Chapter 17

Data analysis and visualisation

LEARNING OUTCOMES

By the end of this chapter you will be able to:

- transform and clean data to extract meaningful information
- get data from different sources, including:
    - comparing and consolidating data from two data sources
    - splitting data into discrete fields
- merge and combine data into required fields
- display data to communicate information, including:
    - pivot table reports
    - pivot charts.

BEFORE YOU START

- Do you know how to input and import data into a spreadsheet program and create formulas and use functions?

- Can you display the data using graphs and charts?

- Can you investigate a situation and identify which fields are needed to store and manipulate the data?

- Can you display the same information to different audiences so that they understand the information?

Introduction

The purpose of a spreadsheet and a database is to store and analyse data. Spreadsheets and databases provide **information** and answer questions such as:

- How much profit did a business make over the year?

- Which salesperson has made the most sales?

- Which member of a football team scored the most goals in the least amount of playing time?

Once the answers have been found, they must be communicated in a form that can be easily understood by different groups. This is called **data visualisation** and includes formats such as summative tables, charts and graphs (see Figure 17.1).

Figure 17.1: Businesses rely on high-quality data to make decisions.

First, data is analysed and then it is visualised. In Chapters 8, 9 and 10, you have covered analysing data using spreadsheets and databases.

KEY WORDS

information: data that has been given context by being processed, organised or structured in a meaningful and useful way, so that it conveys meaning and knowledge

data visualisation: the graphical representation of information and data

17.1 Transforming and cleaning data

If the answers provided by processing the data are to be relied on, then the data on which they are based must be accurate and in a format that can be analysed. There is a saying that if you put garbage in, then you will get garbage out (see Figure 17.2).

Figure 17.2: Garbage in, garbage out! Data must be accurate and correctly formatted if it is to provide meaningful information.

A visual inspection of the data can highlight obvious problems such as missing data, dates that are formatted incorrectly, numbers formatted as text or a percentage given as a number rather than being formatted as a percentage.

Figure 17.3 shows a spreadsheet where the data has inconsistencies. The inconsistencies must be corrected before meaningful information can be extracted.

	Employee ID	Full Name	Department	Age	Hire Date	Annual Salar	Bonus %	Country
1								
2	E02002	Kai Le	Engineering	47	05/02/2022	$92,368	0	United Kingdom
3	E02003	Robert Patel	Sales	58	10/23/2013	$45,703	0	United Kingdom
4	E02004	Cameron Lo	IT	34	24/03/2019	$83,576	0	China
5	E02005	Harper Castillo	IT	39	07/04/2018	$98,062	0	Brazil
6	E02006	Harper Dominguez	Engineering	42	18/06/2005	$175,391	24	United Kingdom
7	E02007	Ezra Vu	IT	62	22/04/2004	$66,227	0	United Kingdom
8	E02008	Jade Hu	Accounting	58	27/06/2009	$89,744	0	China
9	E02009	Miles Chang	Finance	62	02/19/1999	$69,674	0	China
10	E02010	Gianna Holmes	IT	38	09/03/2011	$97,630	10	United Kingdom
11	E02011	Jameson Thomas	Finance	52	05/02/2015	$105,879	10	United Kingdom
12	E02012	Jameson Pena	IT	49	12/10/2003	$40,499	0	Brazil
13	E02013	Bella Wu	Finance	63	03/08/2014	$71,418	0	United Kingdom
14	E02014	Jose Wong	IT	45	15/11/2017	$150,558	23	China
15	E02015	Lucas Richardson	Marketing	36	22/07/2018	$118,912	8	United Kingdom
16	E02016	Jacob Moore	Marketing	42	24/03/2021	$131,422	15	United Kingdom
17	E02017	Luna Lu	IT	62	07/26/1997	$64,208	0	United Kingdom
18	E02018	Bella Tran	Engineering	45	05/08/2010	$254,486	33	China
19	E02019	Ivy Chau	Sales	61	03/03/2019	$54,811	0	China
20	E02020	Jordan Kumar	IT	29	11/11/2017	$95,729	5	Brazil
21	E02021	Sophia Gutierrez	Accounting	63	08/02/2009	$102,649	6	United Kingdom
22	E02022	Eli Dang	Accounting	45	11/16/2015	$122,875	12	United Kingdom
23	E02020	Jordan Kumar	IT	29	11/11/2017	$95,729	5	Brazil
24	E02023	Lillian Lewis	IT	43	14/08/2013	$83,323	0	United Kingdom
25	E02024	Serenity Cao	Sales	31	21/10/2018	$66,721	5	China
26	E02025	Parker Lai	Accounting	48	29/11/2006	$246,400	36	China
27	E02026	Charles Simmons	Sales	55	27/10/1997	$113,525	6	Brazil
28	E02027	Jayden Luu	Accounting	64	13/05/2004	$184,342	22	China
29	E02028	Brooks Richardson	Marketing	58	24/11/2020	$151,341	22	United Kingdom
30	E02030	Peyton Wright	Marketing	41	05/13/2017	$153,370	10	United Kingdom
31	E02031	Wyatt. Dinh	IT	50	15/03/2002	$72,860	0	China
32	E02032	Ruby Alexander	Finance	59	13/08/2001	$255,610	36	United Kingdom
33	E02033	Axel Oh	Sales	26	24/10/2020	$84,962	0	China
34	E02034	Axel Ramirez	Human Resources	55	04/12/2017	$103,795	7	Brazil
35	E02035	Liliana Chang	IT	32	11/01/2018	$97,509	0	China
36	E02031	Wyatt Dinh	IT	50	15/03/2002	$72,860	0	China
37	E02036	Leonardo Carter	Human Resources	50	07/09/2022	$54,931	0	United Kingdom
38	E02037	Landon Gonzales	Engineering	54	30/08/2009	$88,689	0	United Kingdom
39	E02038	Amelia Dominguez	Accounting	31	9/23/2015	$158,184	15	Brazil
40	E02039	Silas Ross	Marketing	47	10/02/2016	$48,523	0	United Kingdom
41	E02040	Jeremiah Cheng	Marketing	26	05/02/2022	$70,946	0	China
42	E02041	Chloe Chin	Finance	62	13/11/2021	$134,487	10	United Kingdom
43	E02042	Ella Martinez	Finance	35	06/04/2012	$76,111	0	United Kingdom
44	E02039	Silas Ross	Marketing	47	10/02/2016	$48,523	0	United Kingdom

Figure 17.3: Spreadsheet data with inconsistencies.

The following inconsistencies can be seen by examining the spreadsheet.

- There are extra spaces before, in the middle of and after the employee names.

- There are inconsistencies in the Hire Date column with most in dd/mm/yyyy format and some in mm/dd/yyyy format.

- The Annual Salary column is formatted as text and so could not be used in calculations.

- The bonus percentage is given as a number rather than a percentage.

- There are duplicates in the data.

Correcting these inconsistencies so that the data can be analysed and displayed, is called **cleaning** the data.

KEY WORD

cleaning data: part of the data transforming process; it involves identifying and resolving issues such as missing values, duplicates, errors, inconsistencies and formatting problems

ACTIVITY 17.01

Open **17.01_EmployeeData.csv** in a spreadsheet and find and correct the inconsistences listed above.

REFLECTION

Were you able to find and correct all the consistencies just by looking at the spreadsheet? Finding duplicates and reformatting data can be difficult. Can you suggest any ways that you could search through the data more carefully?

Spreadsheet functions and tools to transform and clean data

There are functions and tools in a spreadsheet that can help to **transform** and clean the data. You can use these functions and tools to:

- delete extra spaces
- convert all dates to the same format
- format numbers as a currency or percentage
- remove duplicates.

KEY WORD

transform data: the process of converting data from one format or structure to another, to make it more suitable for analysis or processing

Deleting extra spaces

In Activity 17.01, you should have removed the extra spaces before, in the middle of and after the employee names (see column B in Figure 17.3).

Instead of going into each one and removing the extra spaces, there is a function called TRIM() that will do the same task for you. It cannot be done in the Full Name column itself because a function is needed to do this. You will need to add the function which uses data from the Full Name column to an empty column.

PRACTICAL ACTIVITY 17.02

Open **17.01_EmployeeData.csv**.

In cell J2, enter the formula =TRIM(B2)

This will remove the extra spaces in this person's name in cell B2 and copy it into cell J2, as shown in Figure 17.4.

The TRIM() function removes the extra spaces from all names in column B and writes them in column J.

Paste back the corrected names in column J into column B by copying them and pasting them as values using Paste Special. (You can refresh your memory of Paste Special in Chapter 8.)

Delete the names in column J.

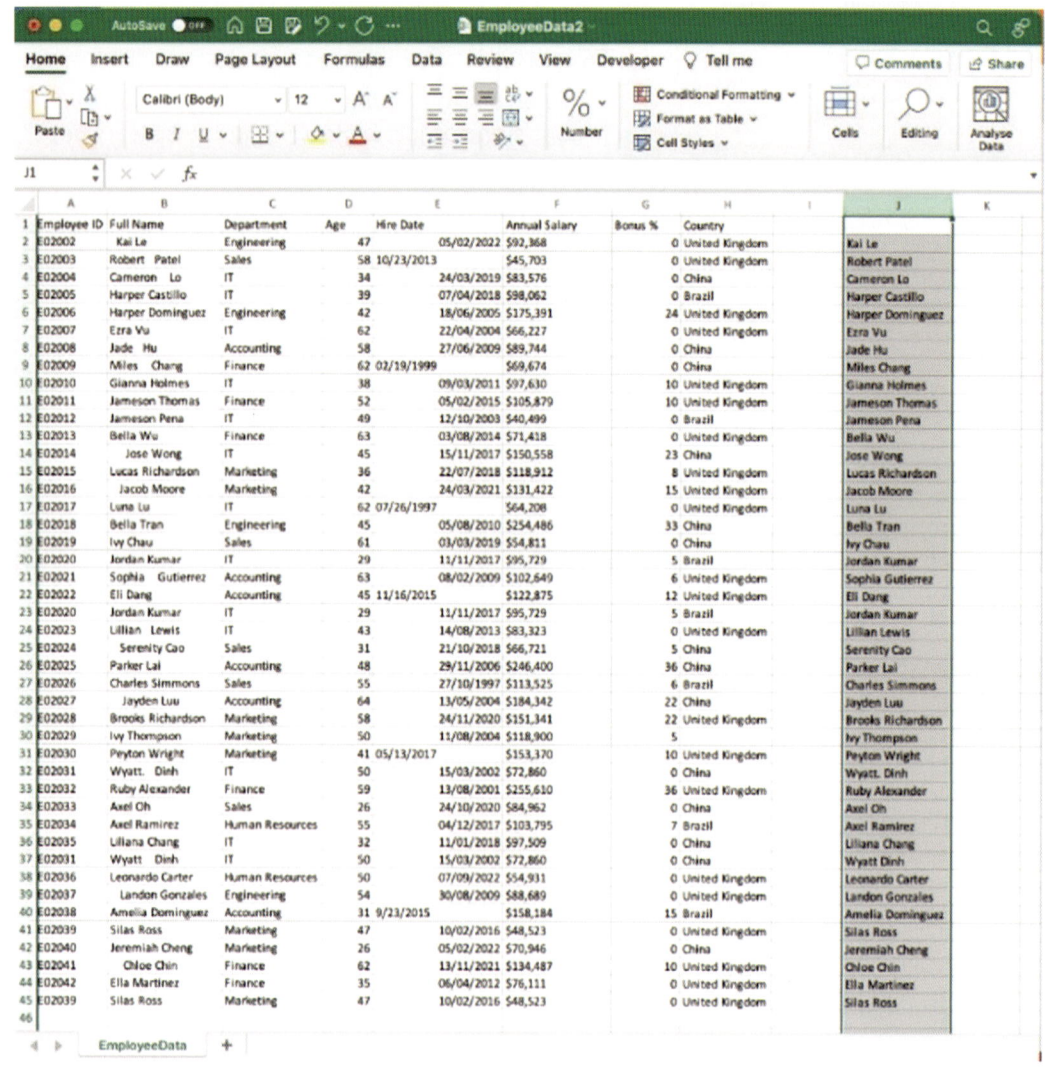

Figure 17.4: The TRIM() function copied to the end of the column.

Converting all dates to the same format

In the spreadsheet in Figure 17.3, most of the dates are in the UK format of dd/mm/yyyy but some of the dates are in the US format of mm/dd/yyyy. These dates appear as text and are aligned to the left. They need to be changed to the UK format.

PRACTICAL ACTIVITY 17.03

Open **17.01_EmployeeData.csv**.

Sort the data according to Hire Date in descending order. This will separate the US format dates from the UK formatted dates so that they can be reformatted (see Figure 17.5).

	A	B	C	D	E	F	G	H
	Employee ID	Full Name	Department	Age	Hire Date	Annual Salary	Bonus %	Country
2	E02038	Amelia Dominguez	Accounting	31	9/23/2015	$158,184	15	Brazil
3	E02022	Eli Dang	Accounting	45	11/16/2015	$122,875	12	United Kingdom
4	E02003	Robert Patel	Sales	58	10/23/2013	$45,703	0	United Kingdom
5	E02017	Luna Lu	IT	62	07/26/1997	$64,208	0	United Kingdom
6	E02030	Peyton Wright	Marketing	41	05/13/2017	$153,370	10	United Kingdom
7	E02009	Miles Chang	Finance	62	02/19/1999	$69,674	0	China
8	E02036	Leonardo Carter	Human Resources	50	07/09/2022	$54,931	0	United Kingdom
9	E02002	Kai Le	Engineering	47	05/02/2022	$92,368	0	United Kingdom
10	E02040	Jeremiah Cheng	Marketing	26	05/02/2022	$70,946	0	China
11	E02041	Chloe Chin	Finance	62	13/11/2021	$134,487	10	United Kingdom
12	E02016	Jacob Moore	Marketing	42	24/03/2021	$131,422	15	United Kingdom
13	E02028	Brooks Richardson	Marketing	58	24/11/2020	$151,341	22	United Kingdom
14	E02033	Axel Oh	Sales	26	24/10/2020	$84,962	0	China
15	E02004	Cameron Lo	IT	34	24/03/2019	$83,576	0	China
16	E02019	Ivy Chau	Sales	61	03/03/2019	$54,811	0	China
17	E02024	Serenity Cao	Sales	31	21/10/2018	$66,721	5	China
18	E02015	Lucas Richardson	Marketing	36	22/07/2018	$118,912	8	United Kingdom
19	E02005	Harper Castillo	IT	39	07/04/2018	$98,062	0	Brazil
20	E02035	Liliana Chang	IT	32	11/01/2018	$97,509	0	China
21	E02034	Axel Ramirez	Human Resources	55	04/12/2017	$103,795	7	Brazil
22	E02014	Jose Wong	IT	45	15/11/2017	$150,558	23	China
23	E02020	Jordan Kumar	IT	29	11/11/2017	$95,729	5	Brazil
24	E02020	Jordan Kumar	IT	29	11/11/2017	$95,729	5	Brazil
25	E02039	Silas Ross	Marketing	47	10/02/2016	$48,523	0	United Kingdom
26	E02039	Silas Ross	Marketing	47	10/02/2016	$48,523	0	United Kingdom
27	E02011	Jameson Thomas	Finance	52	05/02/2015	$105,879	10	United Kingdom
28	E02013	Bella Wu	Finance	63	03/08/2014	$71,418	0	United Kingdom
29	E02023	Lillian Lewis	IT	43	14/08/2013	$83,323	0	United Kingdom
30	E02042	Ella Martinez	Finance	35	06/04/2012	$76,111	0	United Kingdom
31	E02010	Gianna Holmes	IT	38	09/03/2011	$97,630	10	United Kingdom
32	E02018	Bella Tran	Engineering	45	05/08/2010	$254,486	33	China
33	E02037	Landon Gonzales	Engineering	54	30/08/2009	$88,689	0	United Kingdom
34	E02008	Jade Hu	Accounting	58	27/06/2009	$89,744	0	China
35	E02021	Sophia Gutierrez	Accounting	63	08/02/2009	$102,649	6	United Kingdom
36	E02025	Parker Lai	Accounting	48	29/11/2006	$246,400	36	China
37	E02006	Harper Dominguez	Engineering	42	18/06/2005	$175,391	24	United Kingdom
38	E02029	Ivy Thompson	Marketing	50	11/08/2004	$118,900	5	
39	E02027	Jayden Luu	Accounting	64	13/05/2004	$184,342	22	China
40	E02007	Ezra Vu	IT	62	22/04/2004	$66,227	0	United Kingdom
41	E02012	Jameson Pena	IT	49	12/10/2003	$40,499	0	Brazil
42	E02031	Wyatt. Dinh	IT	50	15/03/2002	$72,860	0	China
43	E02031	Wyatt Dinh	IT	50	15/03/2002	$72,860	0	China
44	E02032	Ruby Alexander	Finance	59	13/08/2001	$255,610	36	United Kingdom
45	E02026	Charles Simmons	Sales	55	27/10/1997	$113,525	6	Brazil

Figure 17.5: All of the dates in a different format are at the top of the column and are formatted as text.

CONTINUED

To change the US formatted dates to the UK format, highlight them and select `Text to Columns` in the `Data` ribbon.

Select `Delimited` and all the delimiters should be deselected (see Figure 17.6).

Then click `Next`.

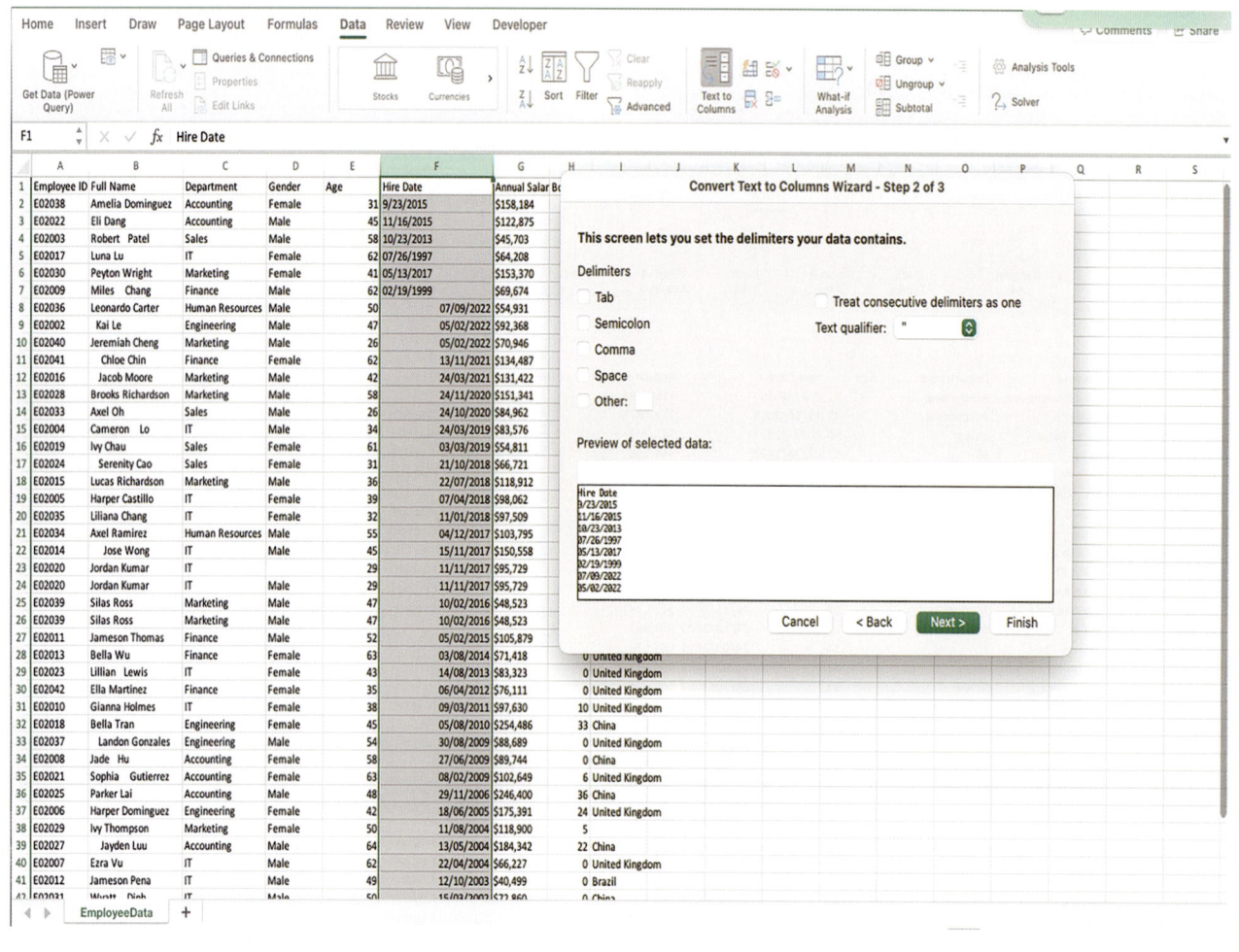

Figure 17.6: Text to Columns with all of delimiters unselected.

CONTINUED

In the next window, select `MDY` as the date format of the dates to be reformatted to the UK format (see Figure 17.7).

Click `Finish` and the dates will be converted to the correct format.

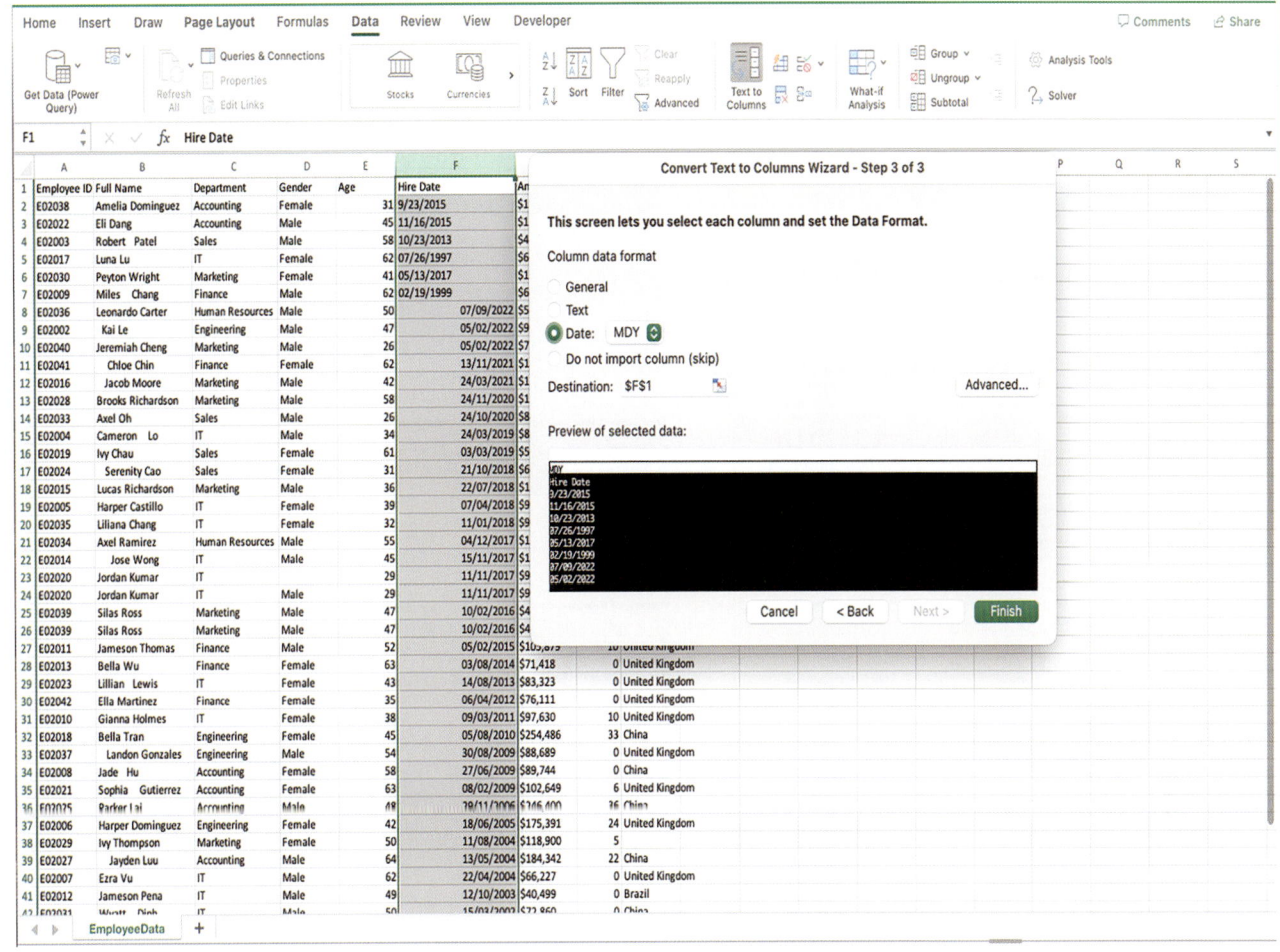

Figure 17.7: MDY selected as the date format.

Formatting the Annual Salary column as currency

The Annual Salary column is formatted as text even though it has the $ sign and so cannot be used in calculations (see Figure 17.8). The Annual Salary column can be reformatted as currency using `Text to Column`.

PRACTICAL ACTIVITY 17.04

Highlight all of column F, but not the Annual Salary column heading, and select `Text to Column` and then select `Fixed Width`.

Select `Next` and move the delimiter line so that it is just after the $ sign, as shown in Figure 17.8. This is where the text will be split.

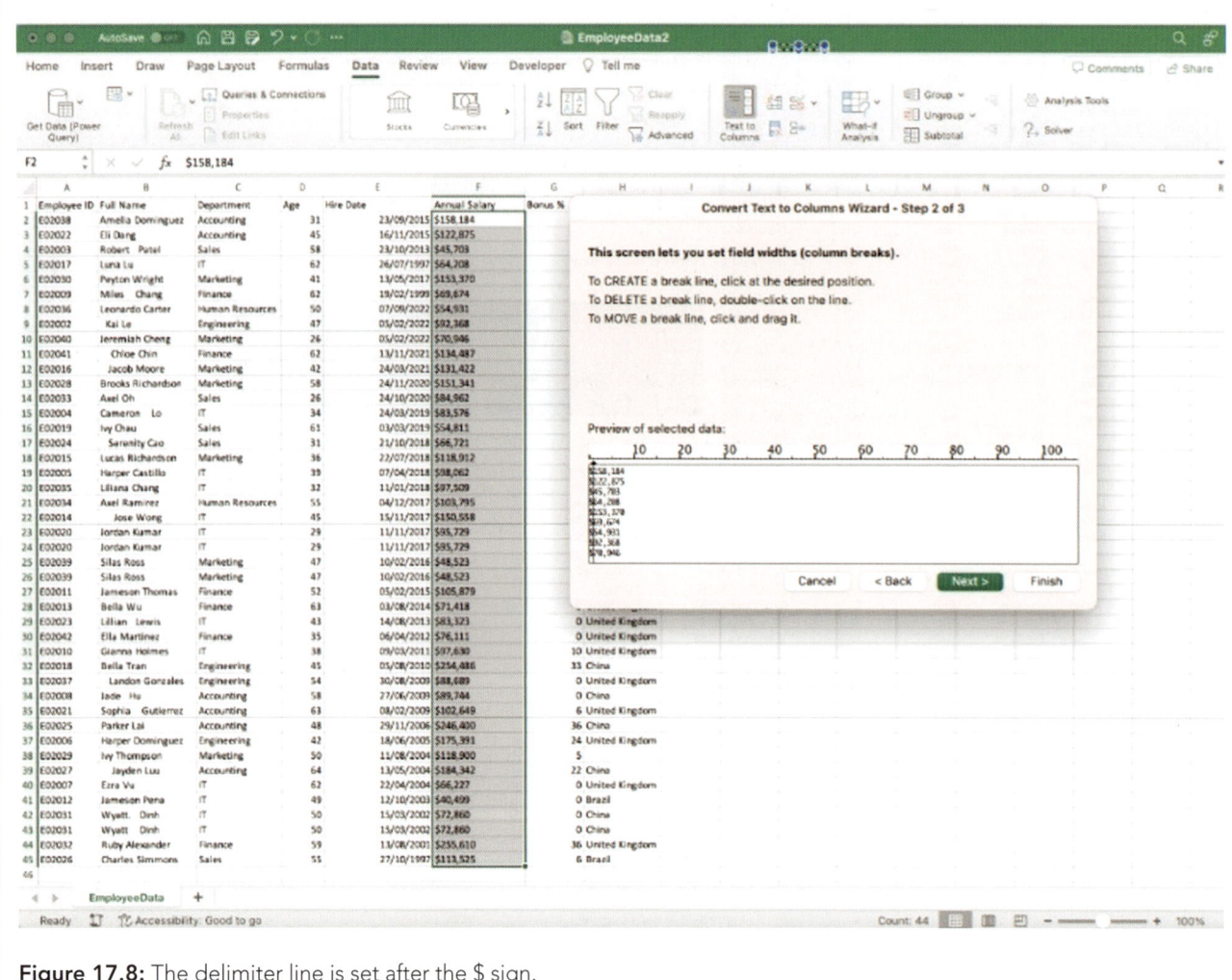

Figure 17.8: The delimiter line is set after the $ sign.

CONTINUED

In the next window, set the destination to J2 as shown in Figure 17.9.

Select **Finish** and column J will contain the $ signs and column K, the numbers.

Format the numbers in column K as currency and then copy and paste back into column F, overwriting the data.

Delete the data in columns J and K.

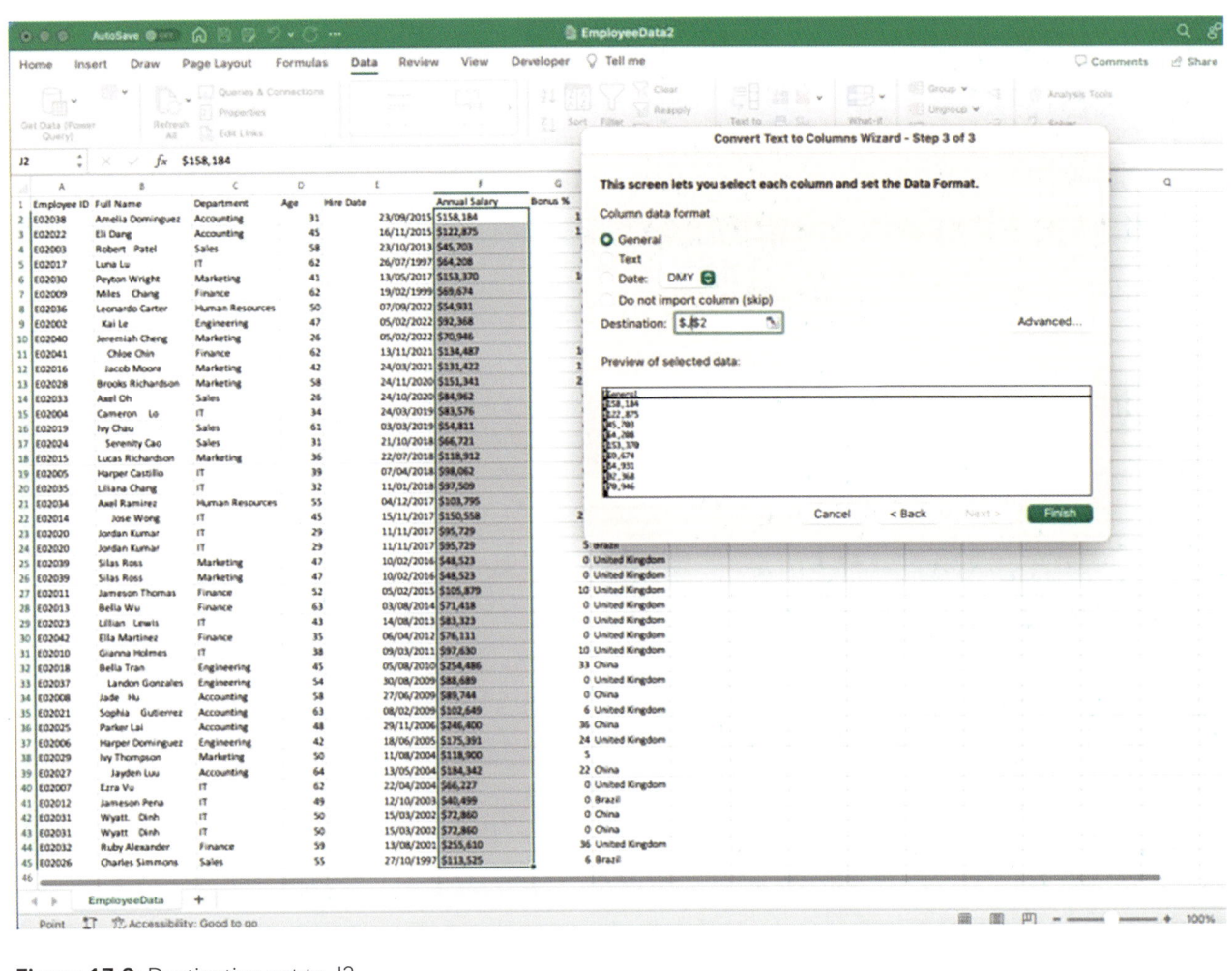

Figure 17.9: Destination set to J2.

Formatting the Bonus column as percentage

The data in column G is formatted as numbers rather than percentages and will give inaccurate results when trying to work out how much bonus an employee has earned.

The Bonus column can be reformatted as percentages.

PRACTICAL ACTIVITY 17.05

Open **17.01_EmployeeData.csv**.

Enter 1% into any free cell and copy this cell.

Highlight the data in column G and select `Paste Special`.

Select multiply as the operation and click `OK` (see Figure 17.10).

The numbers in column G will now be formatted as percentages.

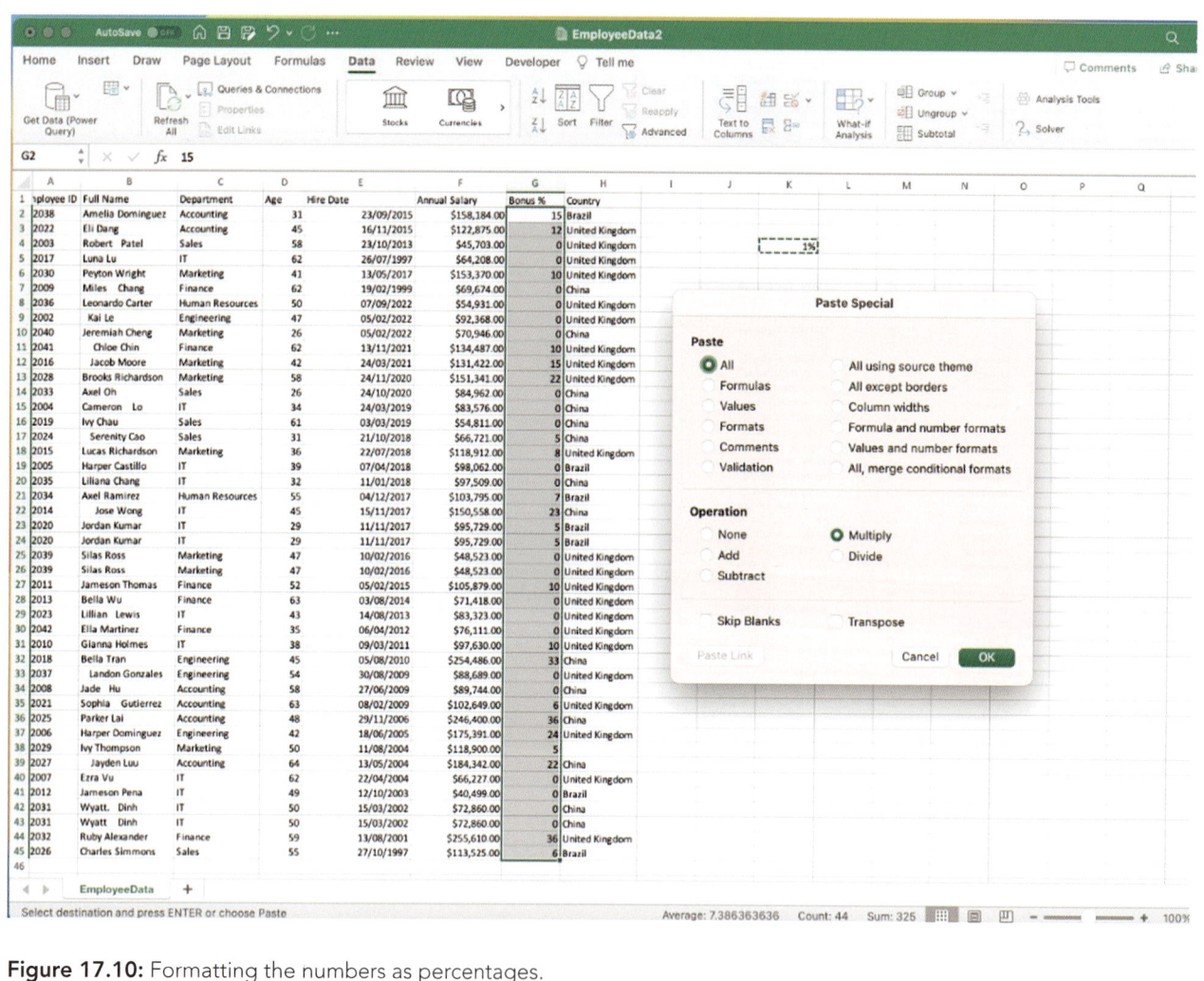

Figure 17.10: Formatting the numbers as percentages.

Removing duplicates

There are only 44 records in the spreadsheet we have been using, but there could be thousands of records and it would be impossible to locate duplicates by just looking through the data.

The Employee ID column is the only one that should contain unique data, identifying a particular employee. This is the column to check to see whether an employee has been included more than once.

PRACTICAL ACTIVITY 17.06

Open **17.01_EmployeeData.csv**.

Highlight all the data in the spreadsheet, select `Remove Duplicates` in the `Data` ribbon and select

`Employee ID` as the column to check (see Figure 17.11).

Select `OK`. You will be advised that three duplicates have been removed and 41 unique values remain.

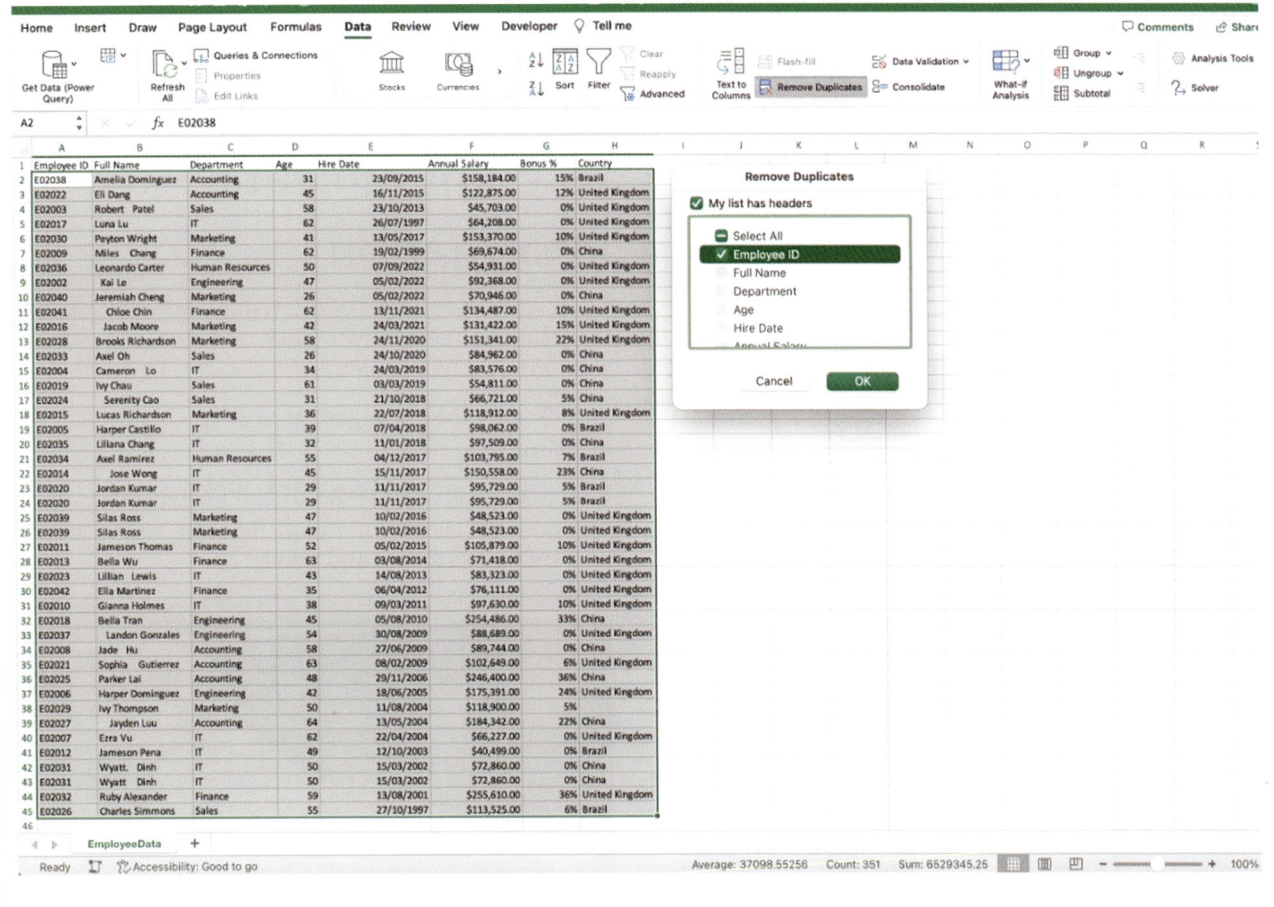

Figure 17.11: Selecting Employee ID as the column to check for duplicates.

UNPLUGGED ACTIVITY 17.07

To reinforce the methods you have just used to transform and clean data, with a partner and without looking at the spreadsheet or the coursebook, describe what you would do remove extra spaces, change date formats, remove duplicates, change numbers to percentages and text to numbers. You could each do one in turn.

Figure 17.12: The gym.

ACTIVITY 17.08

- Open **17.02_Gym.csv** in a spreadsheet program and adjust the column widths so that all the data can be viewed.

- Check all the data and correct any errors so that all currency and date data are formatted correctly and there are no duplicates.

- Save the spreadsheet as **17.02_Gym.xlxs**.

Once data has been transformed and cleaned, it is ready for analysis and visualisation.

17.2 Displaying data to communicate information

There are various ways of analysing data and displaying the results including pivot tables and pivot charts that you looked at in Chapter 8.

Specific data may be highlighted using conditional formatting.

Functions such as COUNTIF and COUNTIFS can also be used to create summaries of the data, which can then be displayed as charts and graphs.

ACTIVITY 17.09

Open **17.03_CleanEmployeeData.xlxs** and analyse and visualise the data in the following ways.

1 Add conditional formatting so that the data of Brazil will be highlighted when the name is written into cell J2. Ensure that the whole row is highlighted and not just the country cells. Make a screenshot showing the results.

2 In case users misspell a country name, add a list box where they can select a country name.

3 Create a worksheet named **Information** to analyse and visualise the data using the COUNTIFS function and pivot tables and charts, as shown in Figure 17.13.

These should be displayed on a new worksheet named **Information**. The tables and charts should show:

- the salary ranges of employees of different ages

- the employees from different countries working in the different departments of the company.

Figure 17.13: Displaying the data.

Questions

1   Explain what is meant by the following terms:
    a   Transforming data
    b   Cleaning data
    c   Visualising data.

2   Explain the difference between an absolute and a relative cell reference when using spreadsheet software.

3   When creating a database, explain what is meant by the data being in:
    a   First normal form.
    b   Second normal form.
    c   Third normal form.

17.3 Getting data from different sources

Often, the data to be analysed and displayed may come from different sources and may need to be organised before it can be used. For example, the data may need to be split into fields so that the data can be imported and merged.

If the data is being imported into a database, then you will need to consider the fields and tables required so that the database can be normalised to third normal form (3NF).

Data held in a csv or spreadsheet file does not have to follow the rules imposed on databases and there may be repeating and redundant data.

The database will require key fields and suitable ones may need to be added.

ACTIVITY 17.10

Figure 17.14 shows the data held by a cat rescue centre about the cats they have and the people who adopt them.

The rescue centre has used this spreadsheet to store its data but now wants to use a database because data is being repeated in the spreadsheet when the same person adopts several cats. Also, a cat may be returned to the centre if the adoption is not successful and so could be adopted several times. All cats are checked to see whether they have a microchip and, if not, one is inserted. Each microchip has a unique identification number.

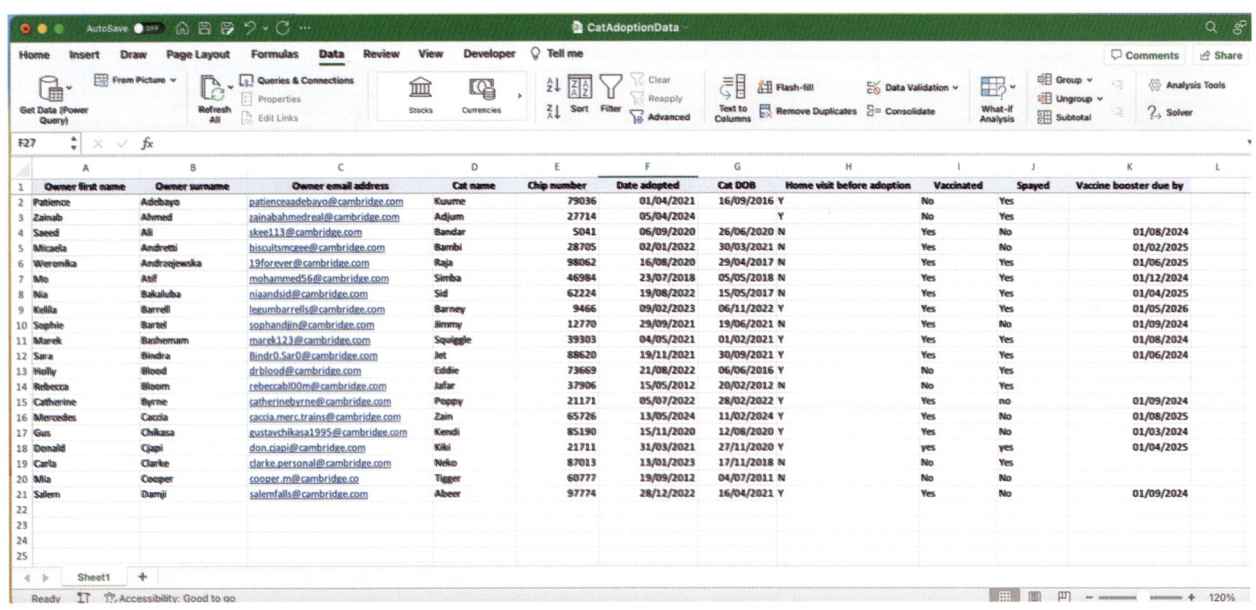

Figure 17.14: Data held by the rescue centre.

CONTINUED

The database should allow data about new cats and owners to be entered as well as being able to import this existing data. To make it relational, extra fields may be needed.

Open **17.04_CatAdoptionData.xlxs** and examine the data.

1   Using the data, create the fields and tables required for a relational database normalised to third normal form (3NF).

2   Import the data from the spreadsheet into the appropriate tables.

3   Create forms to display the data about the cats, the customers and the adoptions and allow new data to be entered.

4   These forms should be accessed from a main switchboard form, as shown in Figure 17.15.

5   The other forms should be opened by clicking command buttons. They should be pop-up forms, as shown in Figures 17.16 and 17.17.

Figure 17.15: Main switchboard form.

Figure 17.16: Cat form.

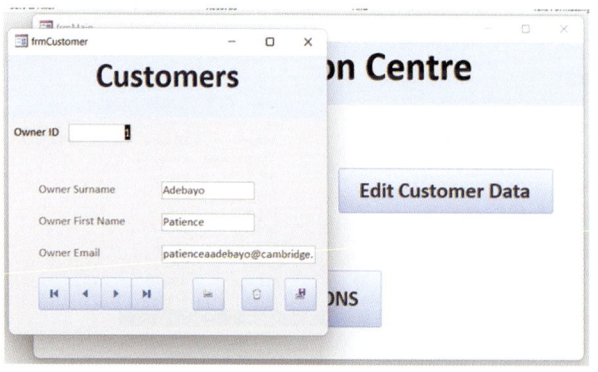

Figure 17.17: Customer form.

CONTINUED

6 The adoptions form should have the cats and customers forms as sub-forms but they must be protected so that they cannot be edited when they are sub-forms (see Figure 17.18).

7 When a new adoption record is being created, the user should be able to select the customer and cat from drop-down lists, as shown in Figures 17.19 and 17.20.

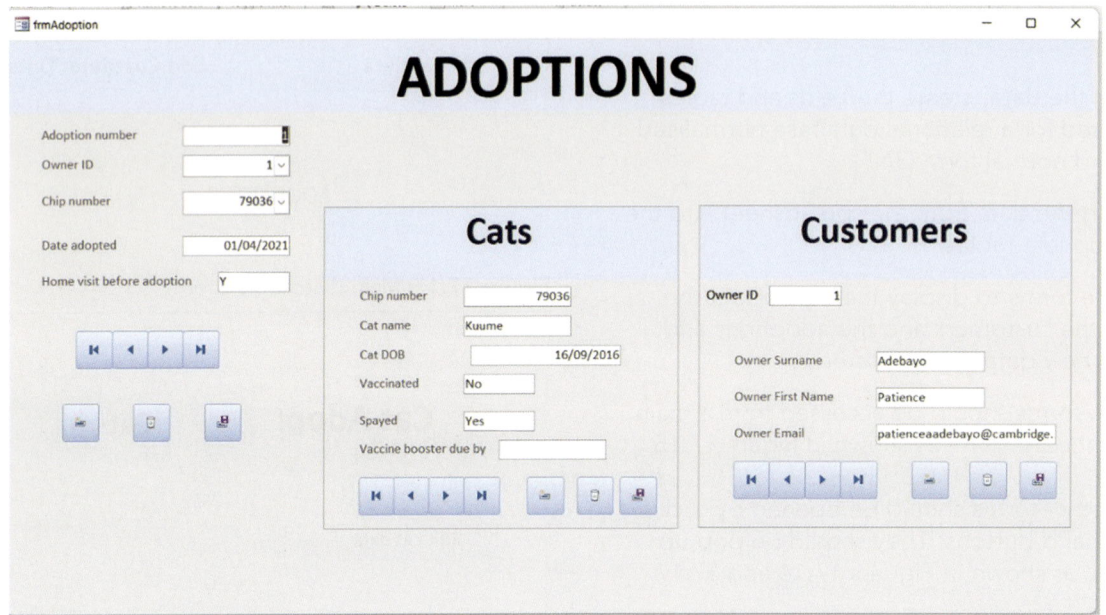

Figure 17.18: Adoptions form with sub-forms.

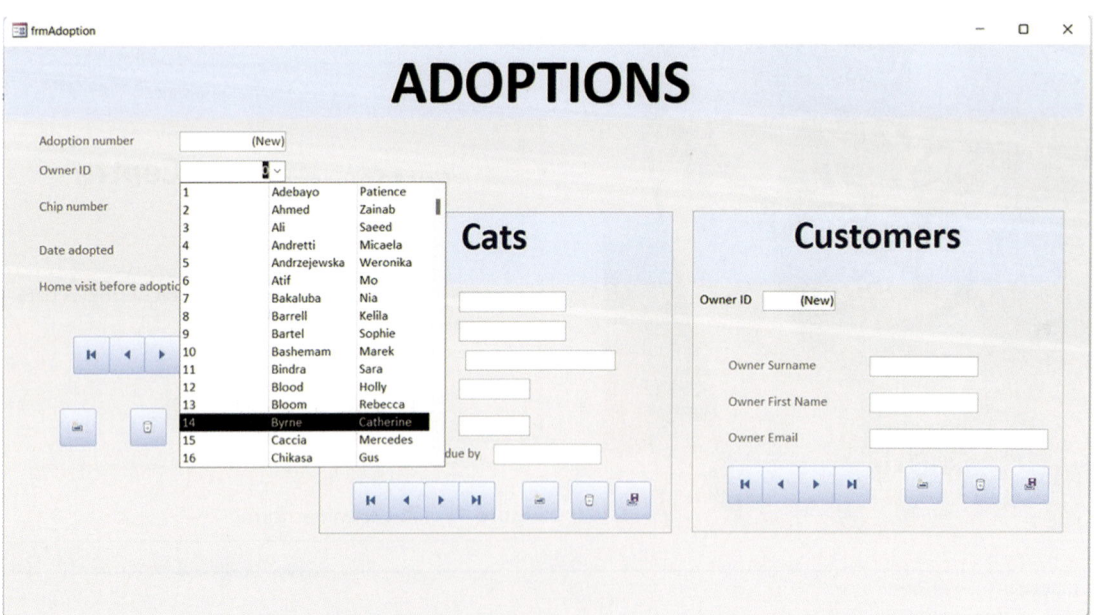

Figure 17.19: Selecting the customer for a new record.

CONTINUED

Figure 17.20: Selecting the cat for a new record.

REFLECTION

- How did you decide which tables and fields were required to store the data in a relational database?

- Did you have problems importing the data? Did you keep on trying until you succeeded or did you look for help online or from a teacher?

PRACTICE QUESTIONS

Open the spreadsheet **17.05_ExamQuestion1.xlxs**.

The worksheet labelled Employee Data contains information about employees and the countries where they are located. Column A shows the Employee IDs. In each ID there is a three-letter country code indicating their location.

The worksheet labelled Countries and Codes contains information about the different countries and their codes.

1   Using an inbuilt feature of the software or functions, extract the country codes from the Employee ID column and place them in the corresponding cells in Column H.

Create a document named **Exam Question 1 Evidence** followed by your name and explain how you extracted the codes to column H.   [7]

2   Extract a list of unique country codes from column H and display the data in cells J3 and below.

In your document explain how you did this. You may use screen shots.   [7]

CONTINUED

3 In the Countries and Codes worksheet the codes and the countries associated with them are shown.

Using a function, display the countries next to the codes in column K in the **EmployeeData** worksheet. [2]

4 Use a function to display the total salary paid to the employees from each country in cells L3 and below. [2]

5 Use conditional formatting to highlight the cells in range J2:L9 where the total salary is $1 000 000 or above. [2]

6 In your document, explain how you did this. You may use screen shots. [5]

SUMMARY CHECKLIST

- [ ] I can clean data to ensure there are no errors or discrepancies in the data.
- [ ] I can transform the data so that it is more suitable for processing.
- [ ] I can decide on suitable fields for storing the data.
- [ ] I can import and merge data.
- [ ] I can use pivot tables and pivot charts to display the information.

PROJECT

Figure 17.21: Data visualisation of world population.

Collect data of your own that you can transform, clean, analyse and visualise using both a spreadsheet and a database.

For example, you could collect data about members of your group, using a questionnaire, or research different countries using the internet. You could collect data on population size, growth rate, gross domestic product, health data and so on (see Figure 17.21).

You should:

- create the spreadsheet and database structure that will allow you to store the data

- enter the data and ensure that the data is consistent and accurate

- analyse and visualise the data using charts, pivot tables, reports and so on.

> # Chapter 18
Mail merge

LEARNING INTENTIONS

By the end of this chapter, you will be able to:

* explain when and why mail merge is used

* discuss the need for data sources and master documents

* use, create and edit source data using appropriate software

* create a master document structure

* link a master document to a source file

* insert fields and properties

* specify rules for selecting and excluding recipients and for managing document content

* set up manual completion, automatic completion calculations and calculated fields.

BEFORE YOU START

- Do you know how to create documents using a word processor?

- Do you know how to create data sources using a database or spreadsheet?

Introduction

Businesses often market new products or services to their customers. They will often have a list of customers in a database. Businesses can use their database of customers to create a **mail merge**. Mail merge allows businesses and organisations to produce a single letter and then combine the letter with the name and address of each recipient from a database. This is a cost-effective way of communicating the same information to large numbers of recipients.

Mail merge can also be used to insert names and addresses on envelopes and labels.

KEY WORD

mail merge: the automatic insertion of data, such as names and addresses, from a source file into a master document, such as a letter or email

18.1 The need for data sources and master documents

A mail merge automatically inserts data from a **source file** (database) into a **master document** such as a letter (see Figure 18.1).

KEY WORDS

source file: the file containing the data that will be merged into the master document

master document: the template that will be used for all records

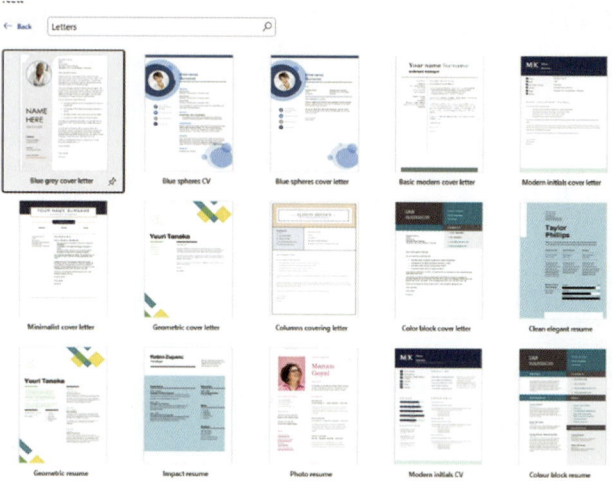

Figure 18.1: Master documents create a template to send similar documents to many different people. These are some of the many 'Letters' templates provided by Microsoft Word.

Mail merge may be used to send similar documents to many different people. For example, a hospital may want to send letters to all patients who have appointments at a weekly clinic. The master document will provide the same information to all patients such as the address of the hospital, directions to the clinic and whether the patient needs to bring any medication with them. The additional information that needs to be included in the letter is the patient's address and appointment time. This information will come from a source file.

By creating a master document and merging each patient's information from the source file, the hospital needs to produce only one letter rather than many individual letters. Mail merge greatly reduces the amount of time the hospital spends on administration as the process of Mail merge takes only a few seconds.

Figure 18.2 shows how a data source is merged with a master document to produce individual documents.

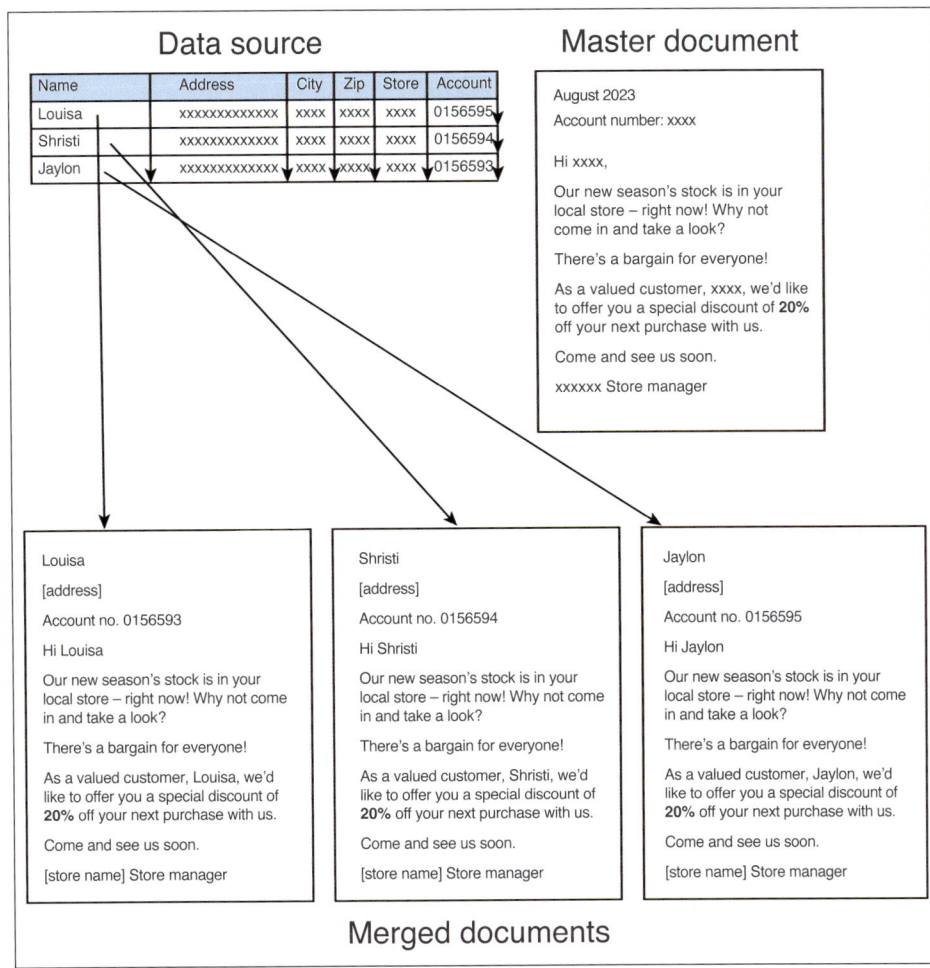

Figure 18.2: Mail merge documents.

Questions

1 State two things needed to create a mail merge document

2 Give one advantage of using a mail merge document.

18.2 Creating, editing and using source data

Creating source data

A source data file is a file that stores all the data you want to use in a mail merge. Source data is often kept in a database or a spreadsheet (see Figure 18.3).

	A	B	C	D
1	**Animal Name**	**Animal Type**	**Age**	**Colour**
2	Thunder	Bear	3	Black
3	Storm	Eagle	2	Brown/White
4	Breeze	Budgie	5	Blue
5	Lightning	Cheetah	3	Yellow
6				
7				
8				

Figure 18.3: An example of a data source using a spreadsheet.

The simplest way to create a data source is to use a spreadsheet. Each column contains headings for the data being stored. Each row contains a record of each thing/item being stored. For example, Figure 18.3 shows a data store of animals in a zoo. Each column stores an item of data about each animal. Each row stores all the data for one animal.

Data stores can store data on many different things. Common data stores include:

- names, addresses and other information about people

- details of things that people may buy at a shop

- information about vehicles.

Figure 18.4: A driving instructor may create a data source of the learners they are teaching how to drive.

Source files may be in a variety of formats including:

- database table

- database query

- spreadsheet

- word-processed table

- variable length text file (for example, comma-separated values)

- fixed length text file

- email contacts (see Figure 18.4).

KEY WORD

field: a category of information from the data source

Editing the source data

To change the data in the master document, you will need to edit the data source file. A master document often 'locks' the data source when the master document is open. 'Locking' the data source file means that you cannot open and edit the data source file. You must close the master document before editing the source file. Changes to the source file are automatically seen in the master document.

Sometimes word-processing software allows you to edit the source data directly from within the word processor.

WORKED EXAMPLE 18.01

The file **18.06_Learner letter with fields.docx** has been used to edit the data source and change Patricia Thomas' surname to Donaldson (see Figure 18.5).

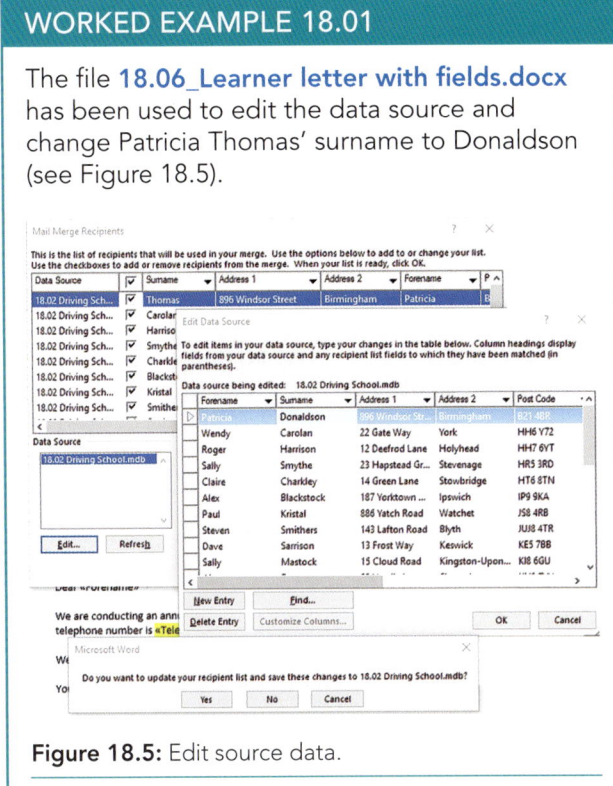

Figure 18.5: Edit source data.

TIP

Typing in the parenthesis { } will not work and they can be manually added by typing Ctrl/F9.

TIP

Be careful when you edit the data source because other users may be using it and so any changes you make would affect other users.

18.3 Link a master document to a source file

The master document needs to know the source location of the data. You therefore need to link the master document to the data source.

A master document must ensure that:

- the correct field names are selected

- appropriate charts and tables are embedded.

It is possible to change the data in a source table. This can also include changing the field names. If you change a field name in the source data, it will break the link to the master document. The master document will not know where the data is now stored. If you open a master document and it cannot find the correct fields, it will usually ask you to locate the correct field from the data source.

It is possible to embed charts and tables into a master document. When you embed something, you create a link to the original chart or table. This means that if the chart or table changes, then the master document table/chart will also change.

WORKED EXAMPLE 18.02

The master document **18.07_Learner letter. docx** has been linked to the Learner table in the data source **18.09_Driving school.mdb** (see Figure 18.6).

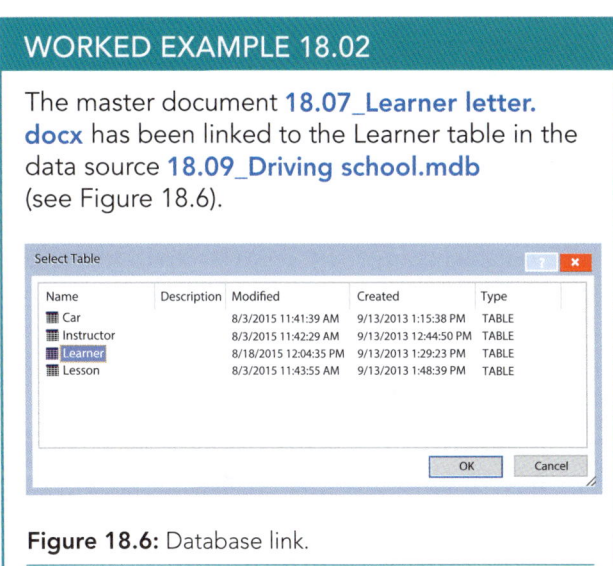

Figure 18.6: Database link.

The records from the data source are identified in the master document in the recipient list (see Figure 18.7).

CONTINUED

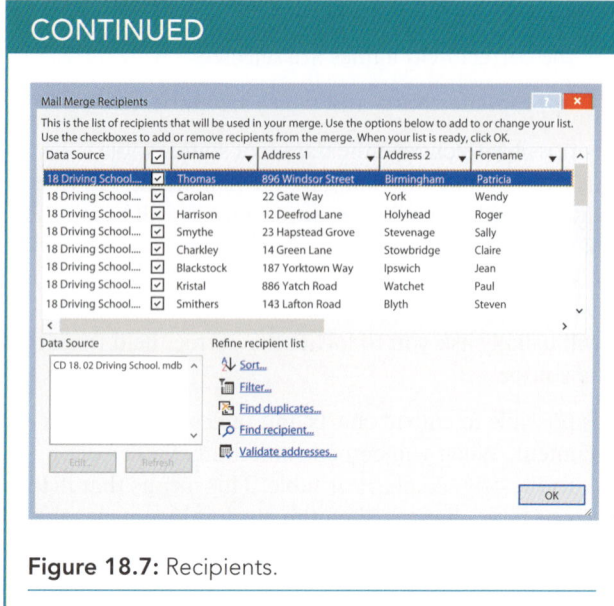

Figure 18.7: Recipients.

Question

3   State the purpose of the master document.

ACTIVITY 18.02

1   Open the master document **18.10_New class.docx** and link it to each of the following data sources one at a time. Finish by linking it to the query from the database.

   a   **18.01_Student.csv**

   b   **18.02_Student.rtf**

   c   **18.03_Student.txt**

   d   **18.04_Student.xlsx**

   e   **18.05_Student.mdb** (link to the Student table)

   f   **18.05_Student.mdb** (link to the query)

2   Create a new word-processing document and set it up to contain labels. Link the document to the data source **18.05_Student.mdb** using the query Qry Student Teacher. Using merge fields, create a set of labels that shows each student's name, their class and their teacher.

ACTIVITY 18.02

3   Open the letter that you wrote for IT Distribution Inc. Use it as a master document and link it to the table **Customer** in **18.11_Sales processing.mdb**.

4   Create a new word-processing document that is linked to the **Sales Rep table** from **18.11_Sales processing.mdb**. Use the mail merge labels feature to create a business card for each sales representative. You can create business cards instead of labels by selecting a business card page layout from the label options.

Identifying and using correct field names

Linking the master document to the source file tells the master document which file to use. A master document needs to know which fields to put into the document, and where to place them.

WORKED EXAMPLE 18.03

18.06_Learner letter with fields.docx includes the merge fields from the Learner table in **18.09_Driving school.mdb**. In Figure 18.8, the merge fields are highlighted in yellow and have been inserted in place of the placeholder names that appeared in Figure 18.6.

CONTINUED

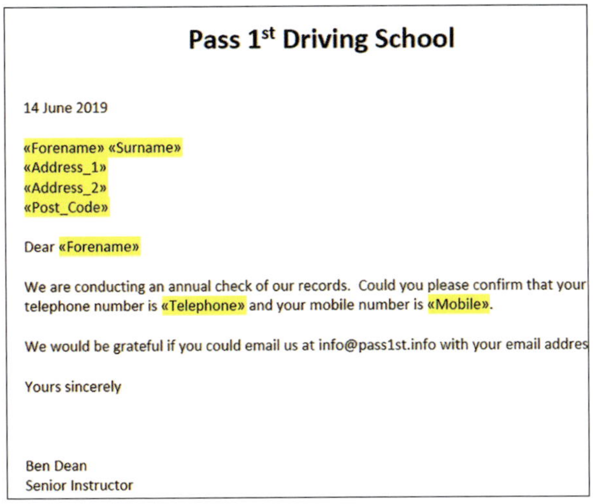

Pass 1st Driving School

14 June 2019

«Forename» «Surname»
«Address_1»
«Address_2»
«Post_Code»

Dear «Forename»

We are conducting an annual check of our records. Could you please confirm that your telephone number is «Telephone» and your mobile number is «Mobile».

We would be grateful if you could email us at info@pass1st.info with your email address

Yours sincerely

Ben Dean
Senior Instructor

Figure 18.8: Merge fields.

When you eventually run the merge, the fields will be replaced with data from the Learner table.

ACTIVITY 18.03

1 Use the master document **18.10_New class. docx** that you linked to the query in the database **18.05_Student.mdb**. Insert merge fields for forename, surname and class.

2 Open the letter that you wrote for IT Distribution Inc. and linked to **18.11_Sales processing.mdb**. Insert merge fields in the appropriate places.

Embedding a chart or table

Embedding leaves the data in the original source document but also shows the data in a word-processed document. Any changes you make to the source

KEY WORD

embedding: importing data from a data source so that any changes to the data source are shown in the new document

document will be automatically updated in the word-processed document. The data is refreshed from the source file every time you open the document.

Embedding tables

You can embed data in tabular format within a document. Any changes you make to the data in the data source will be updated in the document.

WORKED EXAMPLE 18.04

The master document **18.12_Attendance Report.docx** is a report that has been written to summarise the attendance of students in a school. The attendance data has been embedded from the spreadsheet **18.13_School attendance.xlsx** (see Figure 18.9).

Any changes you make to the selected data in **18.13_School attendance.xlsx** will be updated automatically in **18.12_Attendance Report.docx** the next time it is opened.

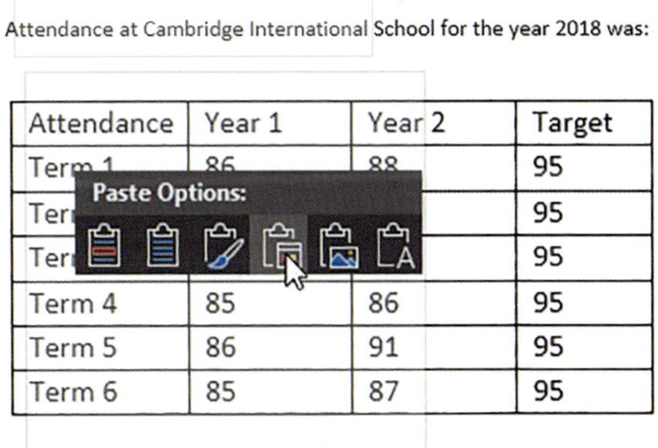

Attendance at Cambridge International School for the year 2018 was:

Attendance	Year 1	Year 2	Target
Term 1	86	88	95
Ter			95
Ter			95
Term 4	85	86	95
Term 5	86	91	95
Term 6	85	87	95

Paste Options:

Figure 18.9: Paste and link.

Note that paste link options may vary depending on the version of Office and that newer versions will have the Paste special dialog.

CONTINUED

You can also update the data while the main document is open by clicking Update Link (see Figure 18.10).

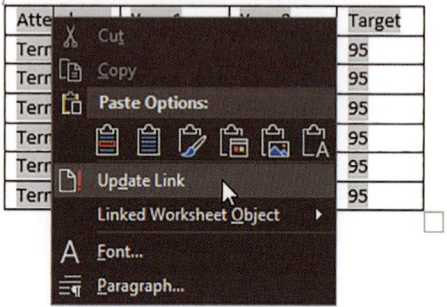

Figure 18.10: Updating embedded data.

Embedding charts

Similarly, you can embed data into a document from a graph or chart. Any changes to the original graph or chart will be updated automatically in the document.

WORKED EXAMPLE 18.05

18.12_Attendance Report.docx is a report that has been written to summarise the attendance of students in a school. The chart showing attendance data has been embedded from the spreadsheet **18.13_School attendance.xlsx**. The chart is shown in Figure 18.11. You will need to re-link the document **18.13_School attendance. xlsx** to **18.12_Attendance Report.docx**.

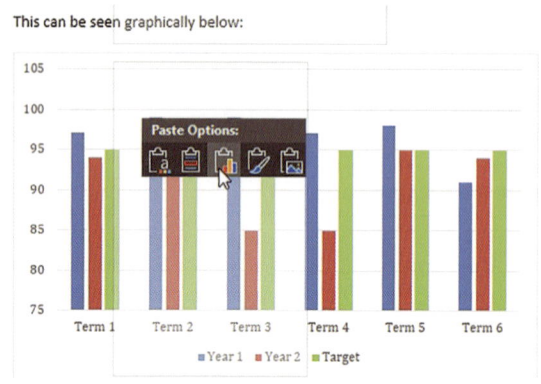

Figure 18.11: Embedding a chart from a spreadsheet.

CONTINUED

Any changes you make to the chart in **18.13_School attendance.xlsx** will be updated automatically in **18.12_Attendance Report.docx**.

Question

4   State the purpose of linking a chart.

ACTIVITY 18.04

1   Create a new word-processing document. Write a brief report summarising the results of the votes for head prefect at your school. The report should include embedded data from the table in **18.14_Graphs and charts.xlsx** and an embedded pie chart from the same data source.

2   Save and close your report.

3   Open **18.14_Graphs and charts.xlsx** and change the number of votes for Adrian Smith from 4 to 40.

4   Save and close the spreadsheet.

5   Reopen your report and check that the data and chart have updated automatically to show 40 votes for Adrian Smith.

Perform mail merge using the master document and data sources

The mail merge is ready to complete once the fields have been added. The software carries out the merge process. The final step is to tell the software to complete the mail merge. We can preview the results of a mail merge before we print the merged letters. The mail merge output can:

- print letters directly to a printer

- save letters into a document: the document will contain all the merged letters

- attach each letter to an email address.

18.06_Learner letter with fields.docx can be previewed. The data from the first record of the data source **18.09_Driving school.mdb** is highlighted in yellow (see Figure 18.12).

Pass 1ˢᵗ Driving School

18 August 2015

==Patricia Thomas==
==896 Windsor Street==
==Birmingham==
==B21 4BR==

Dear Patricia

We are conducting an annual check of our records. Could you please confirm that your telephone number is ==0555 555 555== and your mobile number is ==0777 777 726.==

We would be grateful if you could email us at info@pass1st.info with your email addres

Yours sincerely

Ben Dean

Figure 18.12: Merge preview.

1. Open **18.06_Learner letter with fields. docx** and merge to a new document. Notice how all the records have been included so that there is one letter for every learner.

2. As you have added merge fields, use the master document **18.10_New class.docx** to merge to a new document.

3. Open the letter that you wrote for IT Distribution Inc. Merge the letters to send as emails to the email address field in the Customer table.

Questions

5. What is the difference between a source file and a master document

6. Why might a data source be locked?

7. What might happen if a link from a master document to a data source is broken?

8. Name two things that you can embed into a mail merge.

18.4 Creating a master document

Creating a master document for letters

A master document is the template for the merge. All recipients from the data source will receive the same text, but with their merge data being unique for each letter. We can create a master document for letters, emails, memos and faxes.

The file **18.07_Learner letter.docx** is a master document. It is a letter written to learner drivers in a driving school (see Figure 18.13). The words in italics are the data that needs to be inserted about each learner driver and will be obtained from the data source.

Notice how a standard letter includes the letterhead of the organisation sending the letter, the date of the letter and the full name and address of the recipient of the letter. When you produce a letter on a computer, it should always have all the text (except the letterhead) aligned to the left.

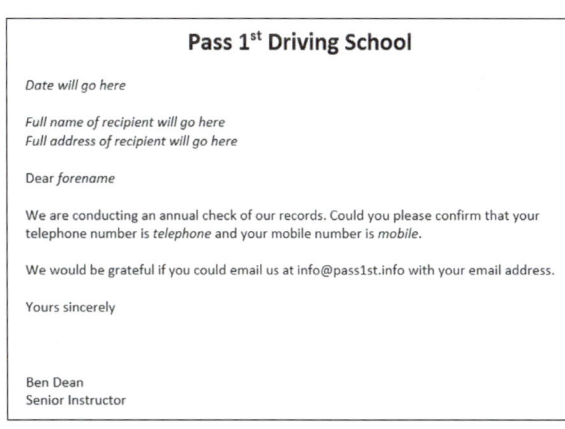

Figure 18.13: Master document.

ACTIVITY 18.06

Create a master document that you will use to write to customers of the company IT Distribution Inc. You should create the letter in a standard letter format, including space for the recipient's name and address. Your letter should invite the customer to participate in a survey with the opportunity to win one of ten prizes each worth $250. Tell customers that the survey is available online and is available for two months from the date of the letter.

Creating a master document for labels

Mail merge can be used to print address labels. To make a mail merge for labels you will need to set up the master document as a table. Each cell in the table represents a label. Each cell contains all the needed merge fields from one record from the data source.

Word-processing software often has templates for labels. These are usually for common label sizes. However, sometimes you may need to create a custom label. This may be because it is an uncommon size or shape. For example, bar code printers or large shipping labels may need to be created as a custom label master document (see Figure 18.14).

Figure 18.14: Custom labels are needed for unique things like barcode labels or shipping labels.

DISCUSSION POINT

What are the main differences between a mail merge for a letter and a mail merge for labels?

WORKED EXAMPLE 18.08

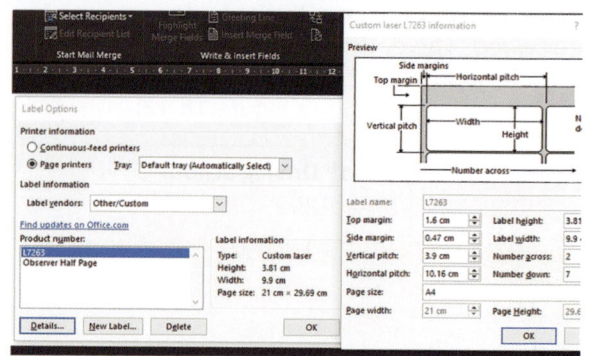

Figure 18.15: Setting up the labels.

The file **18.08_Instructor Labels.docx** has been set up to use labels. It is set up to use the labels named L7263, which defines the measurements of the label (see Figure 18.15).

The label layout has been merged with the Learners table from the data source **18.09_ Driving School.mdb**. A table is created for each label and a <<Next Record>> field is added to each of the cells in the table except the first one. The <<Next Record>> field means that the next record from the data source will be displayed so that each cell contains data about a separate record from the data source (see Figure 18.16). You will need to set the 'Show text boundaries' option to see the document as labels.

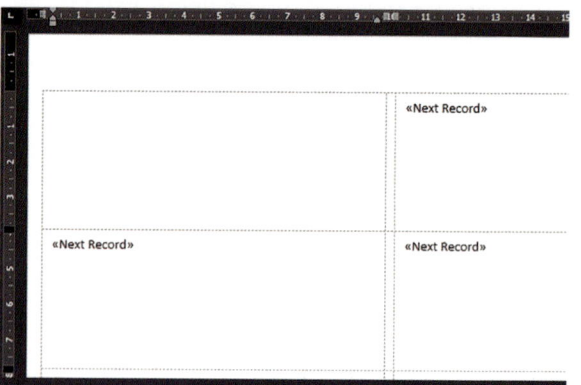

Figure 18.16: Initial label merge structure.

CONTINUED

Merge fields can now be added to the first label (see Figure 18.17).

You can update the rest of the labels to include the same merge fields as the first label.
A preview of the labels shows the merged content (see Figure 18.18).

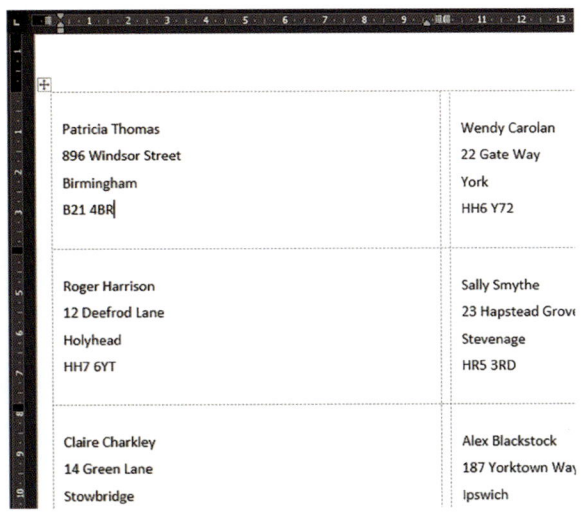

Patricia Thomas	Wendy Carolan
896 Windsor Street	22 Gate Way
Birmingham	York
B21 4BR	HH6 Y72
Roger Harrison	Sally Smythe
12 Deefrod Lane	23 Hapstead Grove
Holyhead	Stevenage
HH7 6YT	HR5 3RD
Claire Charkley	Alex Blackstock
14 Green Lane	187 Yorktown Way
Stowbridge	Ipswich

Figure 18.18: Preview of merged labels.

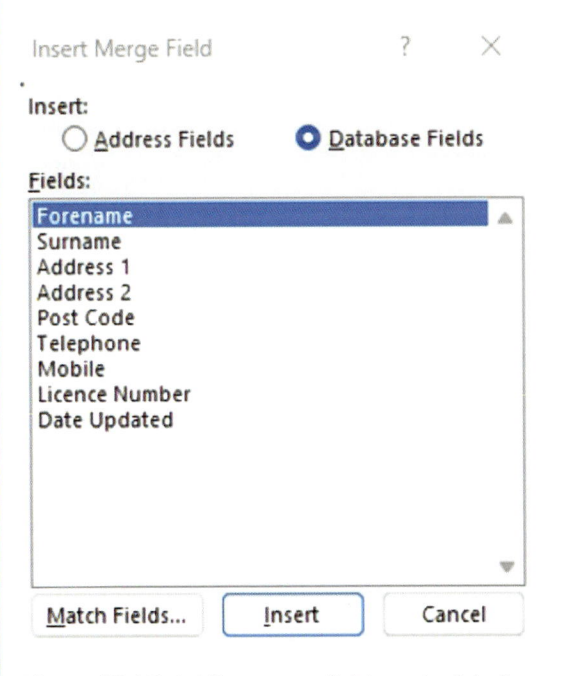

Figure 18.17: Adding merge fields to the labels.

Creating a master document for a directory

A mail merge for a directory is like a mail merge for labels. A mail merge for a directory is made using a table. The first row of the table contains the headings for the data. Each row contains the fields of the data.

To set up a directory in Microsoft Word:

1   Use the Mailings Menu, Click the Start Mail Merge tool and then select the Directory option.

2   Select the recipients in the Learner table in the same way you did earlier.

3   Create the document header. For example:

Header

Forename	Surname	Address 1	Address 2	Post Code

4   Create the main body of the document. For example:

Main body of document

<<Forename>>	<<Surname>>	<<Address 1>>	<<Address 2>>	<<Post Code>>

5   Preview the mail merge.

ACTIVITY 18.07

Use the data source **18.09_Driving School.mdb** to create a directory of all driving instructions. Include the fields:

1   Forename

2   Surname

3   Address 1

4   Address 2

5   Post Code

Compare your directory with another classmate. Did you get the same results?

18.5 Inserting fields and properties

Inserting specified merge fields

A source file contains the data that is to be merged. We can add the fields we want to merge into the master document. To do this, first link the data source to the master document. Then use the 'Mailings' toolbar to 'Insert Merge Field' (see Figure 18.19).

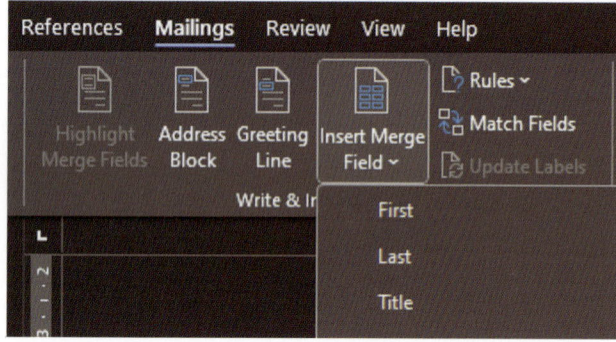

Figure 18.19: Using the 'Insert Merge Field' button allows us to select the fields we want to include in a master document.

Inserting document properties

Properties of the document can be included automatically including:

- filename
- author
- document title
- creation date
- number of pages.

ACTIVITY 18.08

Open a word-processing file that you have created and that includes more than one page. Experiment by adding the document properties into your document.

Inserting document fields

Document fields display content automatically within the document. Examples include page numbers or automatic data/times.

The 'Insert' menu in Microsoft Word allows you to insert 'Quick parts' (see Figure 18.20).

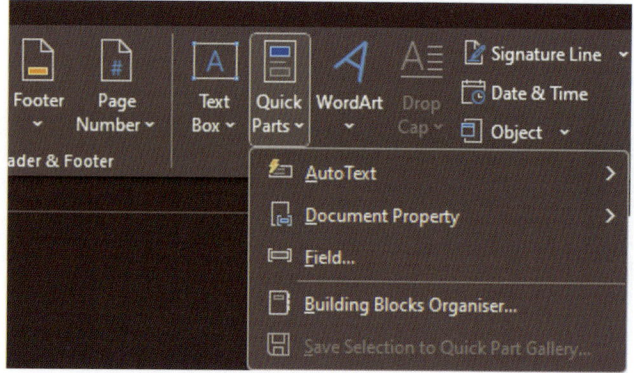

Figure 18.20: The Quick parts menu in Microsoft Word.

There are also document field options in the 'Mailing' toolbar as well.

Inserting date/time fields

You can include the current date or time in a document. Each time you open the document the date/time field is refreshed. This updates the field to the current date or time.

WORKED EXAMPLE 18.09

You can choose a variety of date and time formats. Ticking the **Update automatically** option will ensure the date or time is automatically updated (see Figure 18.21).

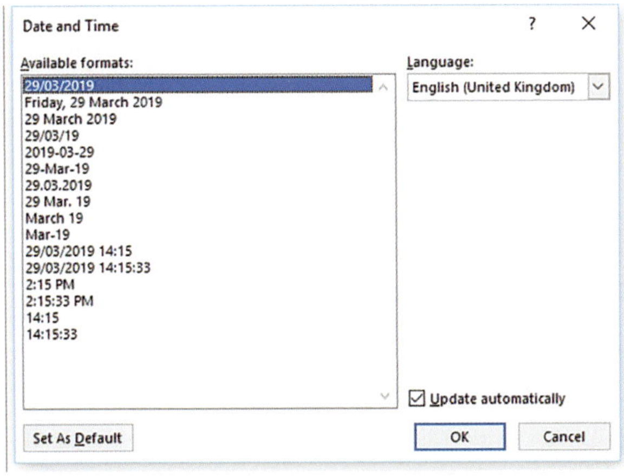

Figure 18.21: Inserting a date field.

ACTIVITY 18.09

1   Open the file **18.15_Vehicle Data Sheet.docx**, which has been merged with the Car table from **18.09_Driving School.mdb**.

2   Add a sentence that states the date and time the document was printed, for example 'This document was printed on <<date>> at <<time>>'. The date and time should automatically update.

3   Open the letter that you wrote for IT Distribution Inc. Add the current date to the beginning of the letter so that it updates automatically.

18.6 Setting up fields for manual completion

Manual completion of fields gives the opportunity to include data that is not stored in the data source.

We can use a **prompt** to allow the user to add data manually to a mail merge. A prompt is a question that asks the user to enter the data that they want to add manually.

KEY WORD

prompt: a question asked to the user, which requires a response

Creating appropriate prompts for a user

It is important to use clear prompts when asking a user to add data manually. For example, an empty box will not tell a user what data should be entered (see Figure 18.22).

Figure 18.22: Software that allows manual data entry will ask you to insert the text for a Prompt. This text describes what data the user should enter.

Using Fill-in and Ask fields

WORKED EXAMPLE 18.10

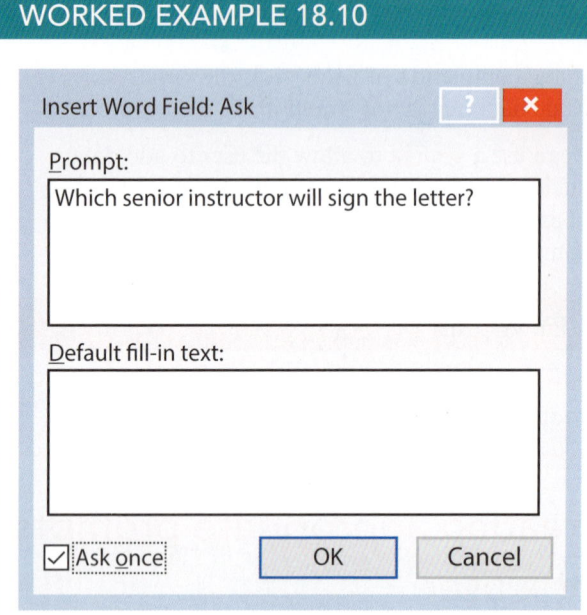

Figure 18.23: The Prompt text is clear, and describes what data the user needs to enter.

18.16_Learner letter with fill-in prompt.docx asks the user to enter the name of the senior instructor who will sign the letter (see Figure 18.23).

The Fill-In prompt rule can be viewed as a merge field code (see Figure 18.24).

> We would be grateful if you could email us at info@pass1st.info with your email address.
>
> Yours sincerely
>
>
> { FILLIN "Which senior instructor will sign the letter?" \o }
> Senior Instructor

Figure 18.24: Fill-in code.

CONTINUED

When you process the mail merge, the user is prompted for the name of the senior instructor, as shown in Figure 18.25.

Microsoft Word	?	✕

Which senior instructor will sign the letter?

Ben Dean

> OK   Cancel

Figure 18.25: Prompt.

Microsoft Word uses rules to control the mail merge. Fill-In is a rule. It is often used to ask for one item of data that is the same for every letter. By deselecting 'Ask once', you can have a different response for every recipient. Note that the Ask and fill-in fields are only activated during the merge.

DID YOU KNOW?

Many different types of word-processing applications allow you to make mail merges. However, each software program may use different commands or key words to describe the same functions.

ACTIVITY 18.10

1   Open the master document **18.10_New class.docx** to which you have added merge fields. Add a Fill-In prompt for the name of the Head of Year.

2   Open the letter that you wrote for IT Distribution Inc. before you completed the mail merge process. Add a Fill-In prompt for the date when the survey will close.

Sometimes the same data is repeated in a document. To allow this, an Ask prompt can be used instead of a Fill-In prompt. The Ask prompt stores the response in a bookmark. The bookmark can be placed many locations in a document.

WORKED EXAMPLE 18.11

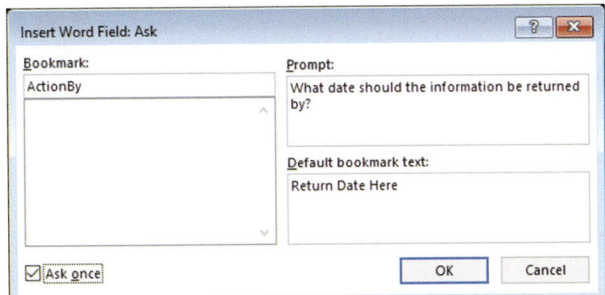

Figure 18.26: Ask.

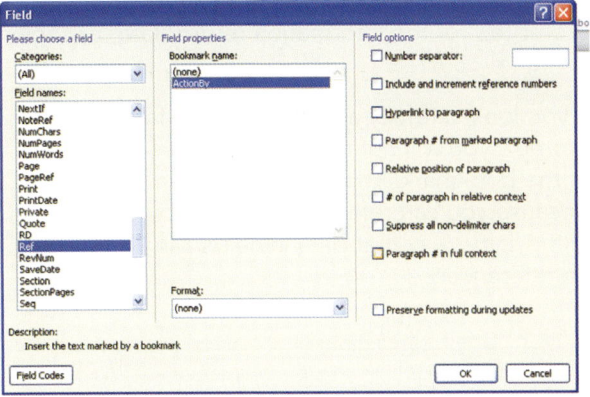

Figure 18.28: Reference point.

18.17_Learner letter with ask prompt.docx
prompt asks the user to enter the date by which the information should be returned. You will notice that the difference from the Fill-In prompt is that the Ask prompt needs a bookmark to be defined (see Figure 18.26). This has been defined as 'ActionBy'. You will also notice that the default text has been completed. This is necessary to be able to reference the bookmark.

You can view the Ask prompt rule as a merge field code, but its location is not important because the bookmark will be referenced in the required locations (see Figure 18.27).

> Yours sincerely
>
> { FILLIN "Which senior instructor will sign the letter?" \o }
> Senior Instructor
> { ASK ActionBy "What date should the information be returned by?" \d "Return Date Here" \0 }

Figure 18.27: Ask code.

You now need to reference the bookmark in the document. You can do this by inserting a reference point (see Figure 18.28).

In Figure 18.29, you can see two reference points highlighted in yellow that have been inserted.

You can also view these as merge codes (see Figure 18.30).

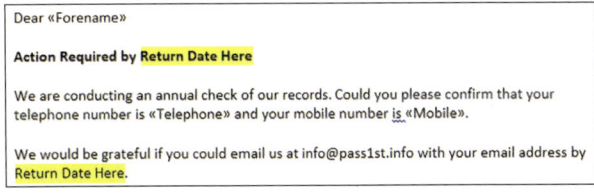

Figure 18.29: Reference point text.

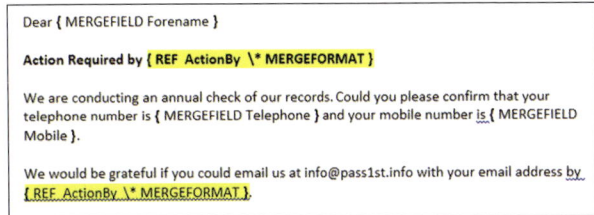

Figure 18.30: Reference code.

CONTINUED

When you process the mail merge, you are prompted for the information return date, as shown in Figure 18.31.

If you look carefully at the field code for the Ask prompt, you will notice that it includes the name of the bookmark. This can be useful in other ways because you can reference the data by other rules in the same way that data in fields can be referenced.

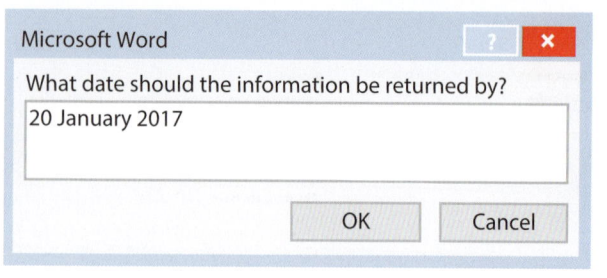

Figure 18.31: Prompt.

ACTIVITY 18.11

Open the master document **18.10_New class. docx**. You will already have added merge fields to this. Instead of a Fill-In prompt, add an Ask prompt for the name of the Head of Year and assign a bookmark. Insert references to the bookmark at the end of the document where the Head of Year will sign and a new sentence that will inform the parents who the Head of Year will be.

Setting up fields for automatic completion calculations

Merged data can have calculations performed on it. For example, we could create a calculation that gives a discount on the total bill. A calculation can be performed on a merge field. When a calculation is performed, it is known as a **calculated field**.

KEY WORD

calculated field: an arithmetic calculation on a field from the data source

WORKED EXAMPLE 18.12

The file **18.18_Instructor letter with calculation. docx** has been merged with the Instructors table from **18.11_Sales processing.mdb** (see Figure 18.32).

«Forename» «Surname»

Statement of Tax

Your hourly charge is £«Charge»

The amount of tax we collect from this is

Figure 18.32: Instructor letter.

The formula option has been selected and a formula added to multiply the charge by 0.2. The number format has been set to currency with two decimal places, as shown in Figure 18.33.

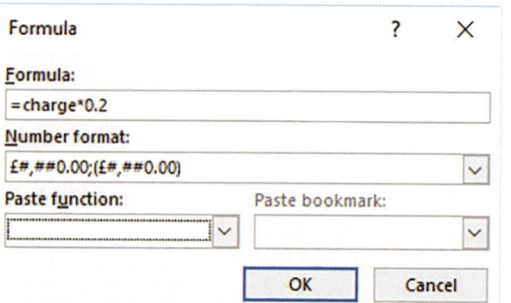

Figure 18.33: Setting up a calculated field.

CONTINUED

> **Statement of Tax**
>
> Your hourly charge is £«Charge»
>
> The amount of tax we collect from this is !**Undefined Bookmark, CHARGE**

Figure 18.34: Bookmark error.

This initially gives an error because 'charge' doesn't mean anything (see Figure 18.34).

The field codes can be edited using Alt+F9 and the Charge merge field can be inserted in place of 'charge' within the calculation (see Figure 18.35).

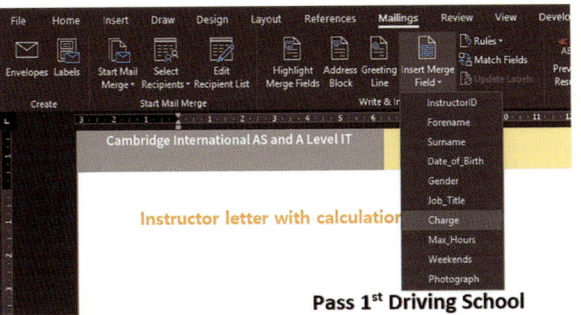

Figure 18.35: Including a merge field in a calculation.

> **Statement of Tax**
>
> Your hourly charge is £{ MERGEFIELD Charge }
>
> The amount of tax we collect from this is { ={ MERGEFIELD Charge }*0.2 \# "£#,##0.00;(£#,##0.00)" }

Figure 18.36: Calculated field with merge field.

The merge field is now included within the calculation (see Figure 18.36).

The merge codes can be hidden (ALT+F9) to view the result of the calculation (see Figure 18.37).

> Danny Sampson
>
> **Statement of Tax**
>
> Your hourly charge is £15
>
> The amount of tax we collect from this is £ 3.00

Figure 18.37: Preview of calculation.

ACTIVITY 18.12

1   Open the file **18.15_Vehicle Data Sheet.docx**, which has been merged with the Car table from **18.09_Driving School.mdb**. You will need to re-link this document to the **18.09_Driving School.mdb**.

2   Add a calculated field that states when the MOT (vehicle safety test) is due. The MOT is due three years after the vehicle was registered.

3   Open the file **18.18_Instructor letter with calculation.docx**. You will need to re-link this document to the **18.11_Sales processing.mdb**. which has been merged with **18.11_Sales processing.mdb**.

4   Add a sentence and a calculated field that tells the driving instructor their maximum number of hours available during weekdays (multiply the Max Hours by five).

5   Challenge: add a sentence and a calculated field that tells the driving instructor their maximum number of hours available during the week. This should include weekends for those who have opted to work weekends (if Weekends field set to TRUE).

Questions

9   Why are manual completion fields useful?

10   What is a calculated field?

18.7 Specifying rules

Sometimes a letter or email may need to be sent to specific recipients within the data file. For example, a reminder to pay an annual membership fee by a certain date may need to be sent to selected recipients only. The sort needs to be set up so that only the records of the members who need to pay the membership fee are selected. Similarly, records in the data file may need to be excluded from the mail merge. For example, members who have already paid their membership fee will not need to receive a reminder. The sort will need to exclude their records from the data file so they are not sent a reminder.

A rule is a merge field code that controls which records are selected and which records are excluded.

Rules for selecting recipients

Editing

You can select recipients from the list. This means you do not have to use the whole list of recipients when you complete the mail merge. Using Rules allows you to filter or select specific records for the mail merge (see Figure 18.38). For example, you can select all customers whose Surname starts with the letter 'M'.

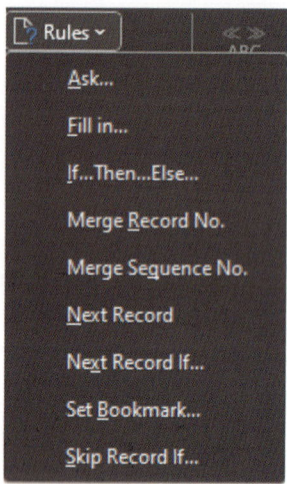

Figure 18.38: You can use rules to select and edit the mail merge list that you merge from.

Sorting

Data sources may not be sorted in the order required for the mail merge. The user may want a specific order for each mail merge. A sort can be made in the word-processing software to allow the order of the data in the source file to be changed. The sort is a temporary sort for the mail merge. It does not make a permanent change to the order of the data in the source file.

Filtering

Data sources may contain thousands of records. Rules may be set to select only the records required in the mail merge. A **filter** may be used to select the record.

KEY WORD

filter: selecting records from the source file based on certain rules

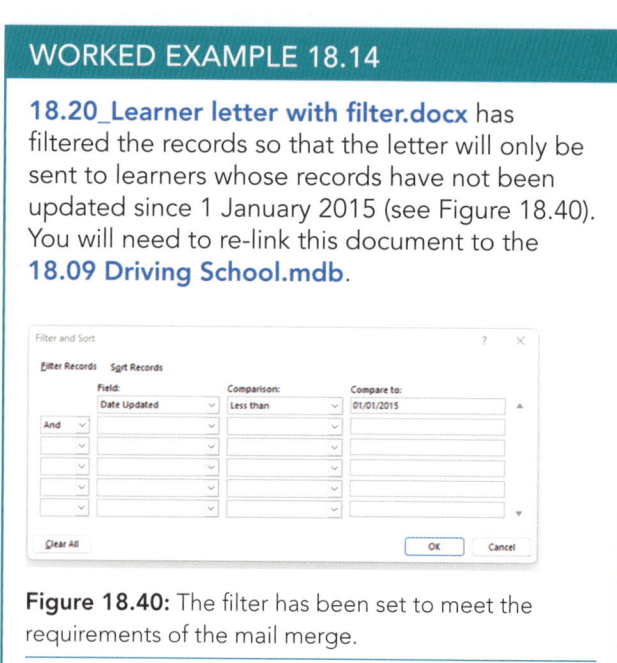

CONTINUED

The recipient list now only includes the filtered records, so the letter will be sent only to those recipients.

ACTIVITY 18.13

1   Open the master document **18.10_New class.docx** to which you have previously added merge fields. Set the filter so that the letter is only sent to students in class 9F.

2   Change the filter so that the letter is sent to students in classes 9F or 9B.

3   Change the order of merged letters so they are sent to students in surname order. If any students have the same surname, then they should be sorted by forename.

4   Open the letter that you wrote for IT Distribution Inc. Set the filter so that the merged email is only sent to customers who have agreed to receive marketing and live in the state of California (CA).

5   Change the order of the merged email so they are sorted by postcode or ZIP code.

Excluding recipients by inserting conditional fields

IF THEN ELSE

Data sources are often fixed and cannot be changed. Instead, specific data can be selected using the master document. The IF THEN ELSE rule can be used to insert text using specific **conditional fields**. Only the data that meets the requirements of the IF THEN ELSE rule will be merged.

KEY WORD

conditional fields: select records to use in a mail merge from a data source by using Boolean logic

WORKED EXAMPLE 18.15

18.21_Learner letter with condition.docx is to have a new sentence that asks users to confirm their driving lesson type (manual or automatic) has been stored correctly. It uses an IF THEN ELSE to confirm the lesson type the user has.

1   IF the Lesson Type is M

2   THEN it inserts the text Manual

3   ELSE it inserts the text Automatic.

Figure 18.41 shows how the IF statement was set up.

This can be seen in field code view, as shown in Figure 18.42.

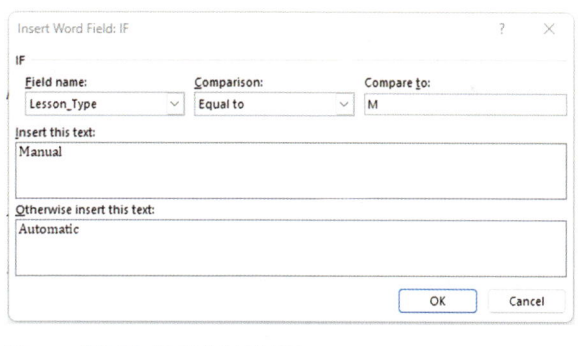

Figure 18.41: IF THEN ELSE statement.

{ IF M = "M" "Manual" "Automatic" }

Figure 18.42: IF THEN ELSE field code.

This will work for situations where there are only two alternatives. When more than two alternatives are required, you will need to use a different method. One option is to use a series of IF THEN ELSE rules to cover every situation.

WORKED EXAMPLE 18.16

Some records may not have the lesson type recorded. In this situation, the letter should state 'that they have an 'UNKNOWN' lesson type. There are now three options: A, M or <blank> in **18.22_Learner letter with conditions.docx** (see Figure 18.43). ELSE cannot be used because it would apply the second outcome to both of options two and three. Here, three separate IF THEN ELSE rules have been used without defining the ELSE part.

Our records show that you want an { IF = "" "UNKNOWN"}{ IF = "A" "Automatic"} { IF = "M" "Manual"} car.

Figure 18.43: Separate IFs.

The other option is a nested IF THEN ELSE rule. This involves using another IF THEN ELSE rule as the ELSE part of the original IF THEN ELSE rule. You can only manipulate this in field code view.

TIP

Note that the nested IF THEN ELSE rule does not work in LibreOffice.

ACTIVITY 18.14

1 Open the file **18.15_Vehicle Data Sheet.docx**, which has been merged with the Car table from **18.09_Driving School.mdb**.

2 Change the field for the Transmission so that it automatically displays 'Manual' instead of 'M' and 'Automatic' instead of 'A'.

3 Open the letter that you wrote for IT Distribution Inc. Add a sentence that tells customers who live in California (CA) that they have a special discount. If they live in California then the sentence should read 'As you live in California, you are entitled to a special 10% discount until the end of this month'.

Skip Record If

The rule Skip Record If does not use a record for the mail merge if the conditions are met. The mail merge will skip over (exclude) a record and go to the next record.

WORKED EXAMPLE 18.17

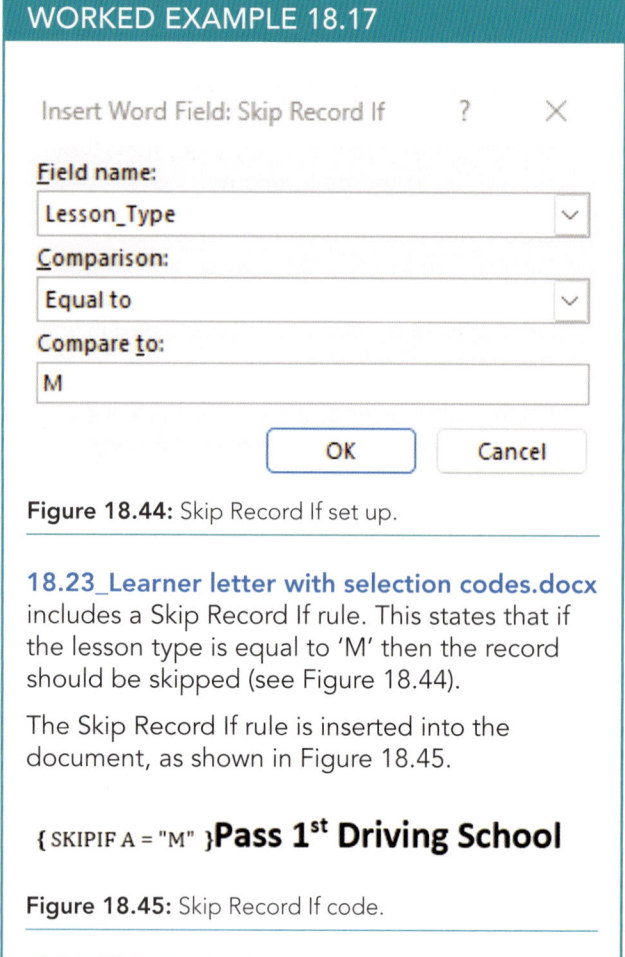

Figure 18.44: Skip Record If set up.

18.23_Learner letter with selection codes.docx includes a Skip Record If rule. This states that if the lesson type is equal to 'M' then the record should be skipped (see Figure 18.44).

The Skip Record If rule is inserted into the document, as shown in Figure 18.45.

{ SKIPIF A = "M" }**Pass 1ˢᵗ Driving School**

Figure 18.45: Skip Record If code.

Rules must be inserted at the beginning of a master document. When using Microsoft Word, you will need to complete the merge to see which records have been skipped. All the fields still show when previewing the merge.

Next Record If

Using the rule Next Record If allows data to be grouped on to pages.

WORKED EXAMPLE 18.18

The driving school wants to list all automatic lessons on one page and manual lessons on another page.

Next Record If will allow the driving school to choose the Comparison of 'Automatic'.
The driving school will also need to sort the data in the data source or in the mail merge first.

The steps for Next Record If are:

1. Place the cursor where the data from the next record is to appear.

2. Go to Mailings > Rules > Next Record If.

3. In the Field name list, choose the merge field name, in this example 'Lesson_Type'.

4. In the Comparison box, choose how the data is to be compared, in this example 'Equal to'.

5. In the Compare to box, enter the value that is to be used, in this example 'Automatic'.

ACTIVITY 18.15

1. Open the master document **18.10_New class.docx**.

   a. Add a rule to skip records for class 9B.

   b. Add a second rule to also skip records for class 9F.

2. Open the letter that you wrote for IT Distribution Inc. and remove any filters that you have applied.

   a. Add a rule to skip records for customers who have chosen not to receive marketing (this is a Boolean field that can be TRUE or FALSE).

   b. Add additional rules to skip records for customers who are based in New York (NY), California (CA) or Texas (TX).

REFLECTION

How well did you remember the stages of creating a mail merge? Did you clearly understand the differences in filtering, sorting and selecting data from a data source?

What other ways do you think you could use to remember the different ways to create a mail merge?

Questions

11. Why would you use an IF THEN ELSE statement?

12. What two things do applying rules to a mail merge allow?

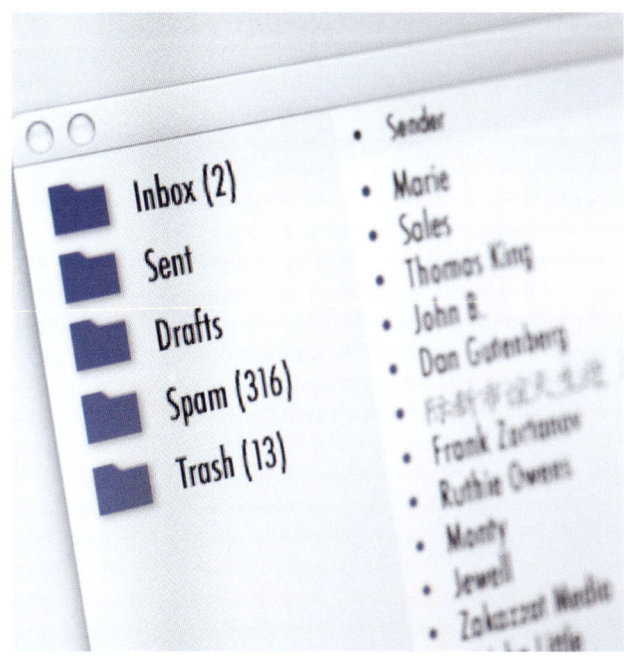

PRACTICE QUESTIONS

1 Service to You is a company that carries out car servicing at the customer's home address. They store details in a database of the services they have carried out and when the next service is due. When a customer's car is due a service, Service to You uses mail merge to write a letter to the customer to let them know.

    a Describe the term mail merge. [2]

    b Describe the steps involved in creating a set of mail merged letters. [6]

                    [Total 8]

2 Service to You sends out letters once a month.

    Explain how Service to You can use mail merge facilities to only send letters to customers whose cars are due a service in the next month. [4]

3 Explain the difference between IF THEN ELSE and Skip Record. [4]

4 Sharene has written a report to her manager to show the sales figures for members of her team. She has embedded a graph in her report. Describe the term embedding. [2]

SUMMARY CHECKLIST

- ☐ I can use, create and edit source data using appropriate software.
- ☐ I can create a master document.
- ☐ I can link a master document to a source file.
- ☐ I can specify rules for:
  - ☐ selecting recipients
  - ☐ excluding recipients.
- ☐ I can set up fields for:
  - ☐ manual completion
  - ☐ automatic completion.
- ☐ I can use calculated fields.

PROJECT

Figure 18.46: Every product should have a product ID, product name, unit price and so on.

1   Create a new word-processing document and link it to the Product table in **18.11_Sales processing.mdb**.

2   Create a product information sheet using mail merge fields from the Product table. The product information sheet should include the Product ID, Product Name, Quantity Per Unit, Unit Price, Units in Stock, Reorder Amount, Units on Order and Reorder Level.

3   Sort the data so that it will be merged in order of Product Name.

4   The product information sheets should only be printed for stock that has NOT been discontinued.

5   At the top of the product information sheet should be the date the sheet is printed. This should automatically be the current date.

6   At the bottom of the document should be the name of the person who printed the document. This should be populated using the word field FILL IN.

7   Use the conditional field Skip Record If to skip any products that are in Category ID 3.

8   If the Unit Price is above $60 then the phrase 'HIGH VALUE ITEM' should be displayed.

9   The Sale Price should be displayed. The Sale Price is 30% on top of the Unit Price.

10 The total value of stock for each product should be displayed.

11 Merge the product information sheets to a new document.

> # Chapter 19
Graphics creation

CONTINUED

- export an image in different file formats
- change solid and gradient fills
- use vector images
- create a vector image that meets the requirements of its intended application and audience
- use vector drawing tools
- use selection tools to select parts of a vector image
- use fill tools to colour elements
- use Node and Path editing
- convert bitmap images into editable vector shapes
- use bitmap images
- use selection tools to select parts of a bitmap image
- work with colour
- use brush, pencil and pen tools
- use tools/filters to alter parts of an image
- resize an image/canvas
- know and understand the effects of different methods of compression on images
- manipulate text
- select font style
- fit text to path or shapes
- set text in a shape
- convert text to curves.

BEFORE YOU START

- Do you know the differences between bitmap and vector graphics?
- Have you created and changed images using software such as Microsoft Paint or Adobe Photoshop?

Introduction

In this chapter, you will learn about the tools to edit and create both vector and bitmap graphics. You will use Adobe Photoshop.

Vector and bitmap graphics

Vector graphics are created using shapes and coordinates (see Figure 19.1). Mathematical formulas and calculations are used to draw the image and fill areas with colour. If the size of an object changes, the computer recalculates the object's properties, such as the length of a curve, and accurately redraws the object. Vector graphics are often used for diagrams, logos and technical drawings.

KEY WORD

vector: an image that uses geometric points and shapes; calculations are used to draw the image

Figure 19.1: A vector image.

Figure 19.2: A bitmap image.

Bitmap graphics are made up of small squares called **pixels**. Each pixel can have one colour, with images typically containing thousands of pixels. If the size of a bitmap graphic is increased, the pixels are enlarged, which can make the pixels more noticeable and it goes blurry. Bitmap graphics are typically used for photographs and scanned documents (see Figure 19.2).

KEY WORDS

bitmap: an image made up of small squares, called pixels; each individual pixel can only be one colour

pixel: a small square of one colour, which can be combined to create a bitmap image

---

Questions

1   Describe bitmap graphics.

2   Describe vector graphics.

19.1 Common graphic skills

A range of software tools are used to create and edit digital graphics.

Graphics tools

The graphics skills described next can be used when working with both vector and bitmap graphics.

Add, remove, select and order layers

Layers contain parts of an image, or an effect, that can be put on top of each other to create the final image. By using layers, parts of an image can be moved or edited independently, without affecting other parts of the image.

KEY WORD

layer: a 'surface' onto which an image or object is placed; each object is placed on a separate layer and they are stacked on top of each other

---

On the right-hand side of the screen is the Layers menu, as shown in Figure 19.3.

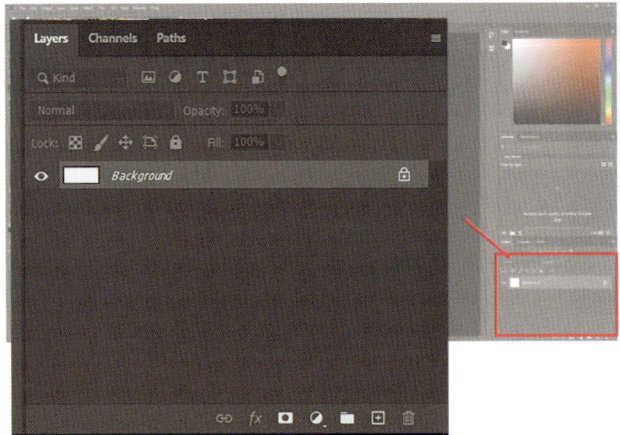

Figure 19.3: Layers menu.

To create a new layer, click the new layer symbol, then double click the layer name to change it (see Figure 19.4).

Figure 19.4: New layer symbol.

To delete a layer, drag the layer, using the left mouse button, to the bin in the bottom right-hand corner of the screen (see Figure 19.5).

Figure 19.5: Bin symbol.

The layer that is listed at the top of the Layers menu is in the front of the image. In Figure 19.6, the blue ellipse is in front of the rectangle, because the layer is higher up. To select the active layer, click on its name in the Layers menu.

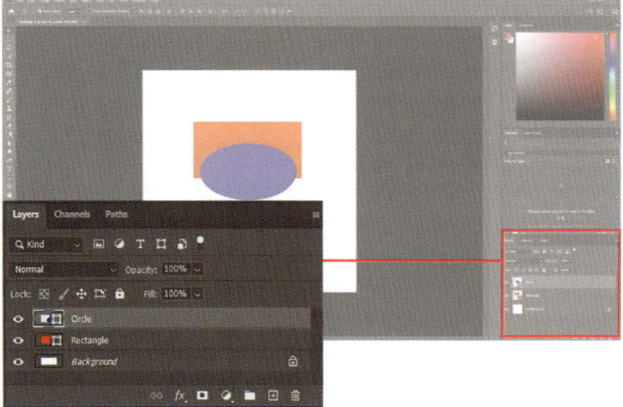

Figure 19.6: Ranking of layers.

To change the order of the layers, such as to make the red rectangle come to the front of the image, drag the rectangle layer above the circle layer, as shown in Figure 19.7.

Figure 19.7: Changing the order of layers.

To raise a layer, drag it one position up within the layers list, or, to lower a layer, drag it one position down.

To bring a layer to front, drag the layer to the top of the layers list, or, to send a layer to the back, drag the layer to the bottom. Alternatively, layers can be arranged by selecting the `Layer` menu, then `Arrange`. In this menu, there are options for layers to bring forward (raise), send backward (lower), bring to front (place on the top) and send to back (place on the bottom).

Questions

3   When might the order of layers need to be changed?

4   When rearranging layers, in what different ways can layers be raised or lowered?

UNPLUGGED ACTIVITY 19.01

Layers are often compared to drawing parts of an image on different pieces of paper, which can be placed on top of each other. Working with a partner, draw and cut out four unique shapes, such as a square, circle, rectangle and triangle. Place the shapes on top of each other and discuss if all shapes can be seen, plus what parts of each can be seen. Ask your partner to change the order of the shapes by using appropriate language, such as 'send to back', then discuss whether the same shapes or parts of shapes can be seen. Repeat the process with the shapes in different orders and share your findings with the rest of the class.

ACTIVITY 19.02

1   Create two layers and draw an image in each layer, such as by using the Paintbrush or Rectangle Tool. Move the layers to change the order.

2   Open a background image, such as **19.01_ Background.jpg**. Add new objects, for example more trees, buildings and people, in new layers. Position the layers so that the new objects are in front of the background.

Toggle visibility of layers

The visibility of layers can be changed, or toggled on or off, so that only certain layers can be seen. Toggling the visibility of layers enables a layer to be more easily seen, particularly when working on a detailed image.

The visibility of layers can be altered by clicking on the eye symbol next to the name of the layers, within the Layers section (see Figure 19.8).

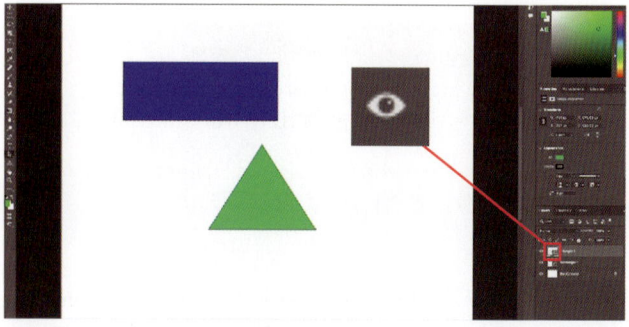

Figure 19.8: Toggle visibility of layers.

Lock/unlock layers

Locking a layer stops changes being made to the layer while an image is being edited. For example, when a layer is locked, it cannot be edited, deleted or have paint tools used.

To lock a layer, click on the name of the layer in the Layers section, then click the padlock icon. The layer can be unlocked if required by clicking the padlock icon again (see Figure 19.9).

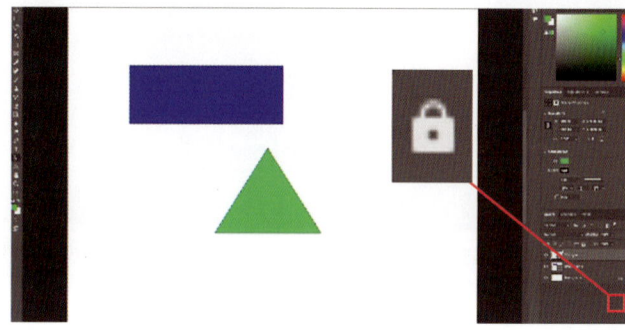

Figure 19.9: Locking and unlocking layers.

Change opacity/transparency

Opacity describes a lack of **transparency**. Opacity is defined for each graphical object as a percentage, which represents how transparent an image is. For example, 20% opacity means that the image is 80% transparent. Opacity can be changed to mask, or hide, an image or part of an image.

opacity: the lack of transparency of an image; at 0% opacity the image is fully transparent

transparency: to what extent an object can be seen through

To change the transparency (opacity) of a layer, select the layer in the layer menu. Use the drop-down menu next to Opacity and the slider to adjust the value (see Figure 19.10).

Figure 19.10: Opacity option.

WORKED EXAMPLE 19.01

Change the opacity of the magenta rectangle, so that the green rectangle can be seen through it.

First click on the layer for the magenta rectangle (see Figure 19.11).

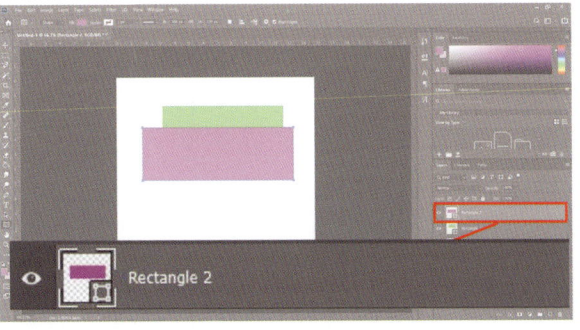

Figure 19.11: Layer option for magenta rectangle.

CONTINUED

Click on the opacity button and drag the arrow to the left. Watch the magenta rectangle as you move it to get the transparency you need (see Figure 19.12).

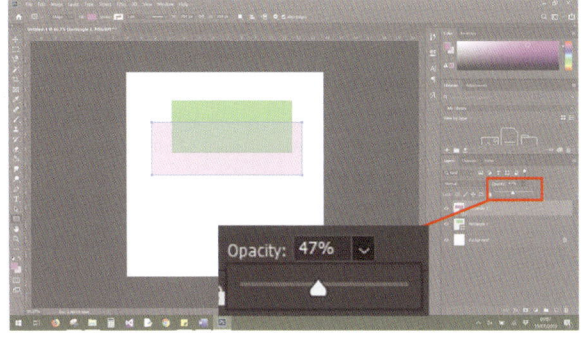

Figure 19.12: Opacity slider for a layer.

Blend/flatten/merge layers

Blend mode enables colours from one layer to be mixed with colours from the layer beneath, which gives the effect of the colours blending in. Blending is often used when a layer of textures is added to an image.

A number of different blend modes are available within Adobe Photoshop, such as Dissolve or Colour burn. The blend mode can be selected from Layers section in the drop-down menu next to the Opacity slider (see Figure 19.13).

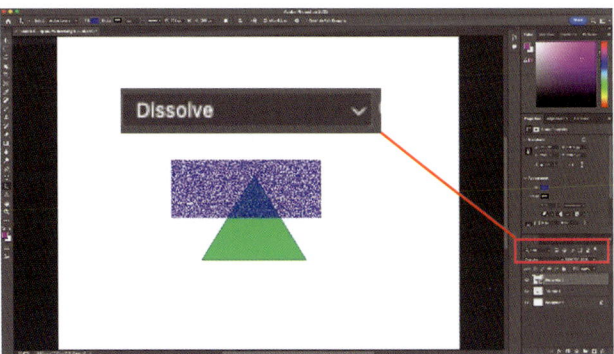

Figure 19.13: Selecting the blend mode.

Figure 19.14: Skewed rectangle.

Flatten combines all layers in an image into one layer. To flatten an image, right click one of the layers in the Layers section and choose `Flatten Image`. Alternatively, merge enables specific layers to be combined. Select the required layers from the Layers menu by clicking on the layers while holding down the `Ctrl` key (Windows) or `Cmd` key (Mac), then clicking the right mouse button on a selected layer and choose `Merge Layers`.

Questions

5   What is meant by flattening an image?

6   How can multiple layers be selected within an image?

Transform tools

Transform tools are used to modify the appearance of an object, such as through changing the object's size or rotating it.

To transform an object, the object's layer should first be selected, followed by the part of the object to change. Various selection tools are available for vector and bitmap graphics, as described next.

Resize

The resize tool changes the size of an object to make it larger or smaller. When an image is resized, the dimensions (the width and height) can be changed independently.

To resize an object, select the object, then drag the small white squares that will appear on the object to resize the object to the required dimensions.

Skew

Skew enables a tilt or a slant to be applied to part of an object. For example, in Figure 19.14, the rectangle has had both of its edges skewed.

To skew an object, click the `Edit` menu, then `Transform Path`, then `Skew`. Once selected, move the squares on the object to skew the object.

Reflect

Flip, or reflect, creates a mirror image of the shape either horizontally or vertically.

To reflect an object, select the `Edit` menu, then `Transform Path`. Select `Flip Horizontal` and `Flip Vertical` as required.

Rotate

Rotate enables a shape to be turned. Click the `Edit` menu, then `Transform Path` and select the required angle of rotation. Alternatively, placing the cursor close to the corner of an object changes the cursor to an arc shape, which enables the left mouse button to be used to drag the shape to the required rotation.

Move

The Move tool can be used to change the location of a shape. Click the `Move` tool from the toolbar, then click and drag the shape to the new location.

Scale

Objects within Adobe Photoshop can also be scaled to a particular size, which maintains the ratio between an object's width and height, and therefore prevents distortion. To scale an object, select the `Edit` menu, then `Transform Path`, followed by `Scale`.

Shear

The Shear tool enables specific points along a curve to be pulled in different directions. Select the `Filter` menu, then `Shear`. To define the points for the curve, click on the vertical line, then drag a new curve point in the required direction. Within the `Undefined Areas` options, `Wrap Around` fills newly created space in the image using the opposite side's content. `Repeat Edge`

`Pixels` uses the colours of pixels on the edge of the object being manipulated to complete the image.

Apply envelope and perspective

Envelopes are used to reshape or distort objects, which is often known as a warp. A mesh grid is typically used as an envelope, with various points of the mesh dragged to warp the object. To warp an object, select the `Edit` menu, then `Transform Path`, followed by `Warp`.

An object's perspective can sometimes be altered, for example if certain camera angles are used when taking a photograph. To change the perspective, select the `Edit` menu, then `Perspective Warp`. The area to manipulate can then be defined and the image dragged to change the perspective as required.

Questions

7   What is the difference between the functionality of the Scale and Shear tools?

8   What does the Skew tool do?

Grouping or merging tools

When creating an image, it may contain multiple items or objects. Objects can all be changed and moved individually, although it can be useful to work with a number of objects in the same way. Grouping or merging objects combines them into one object. The combined object can then be moved or changed together.

Group and ungroup

To select multiple objects, click on the objects in the Layers section while holding `Ctrl` key (Windows) or `Cmd` key (Mac). Clicking on a single layer while not holding the `Ctrl` key (Windows) or `Cmd` key (Mac) will enable a single layer to be selected again.

Layers can be put into groups to help keep different parts of an image organised. To put layers into groups, click the `Create a new group` icon at the bottom of the Layers section, then drag the required layers into the folder. To ungroup the layers, right click on the group name and selected `Ungroup Layers`.

Combine/join, add/subtract and intersect object

When layers are in a group, the layers can be joined or linked, which enables the layers to be moved or modified together. To link layers together within a group, select the required layers and click the `Link Layers` icon at the bottom of the Layers section.

Shapes can also be added to by combining them into a single layer. To combine shapes, draw the first shape required, then select `Path Operations` from the top menu and select `Combine Shapes`. Additional shapes can then be drawn, which will be combined with the existing shape (see Figure 19.15).

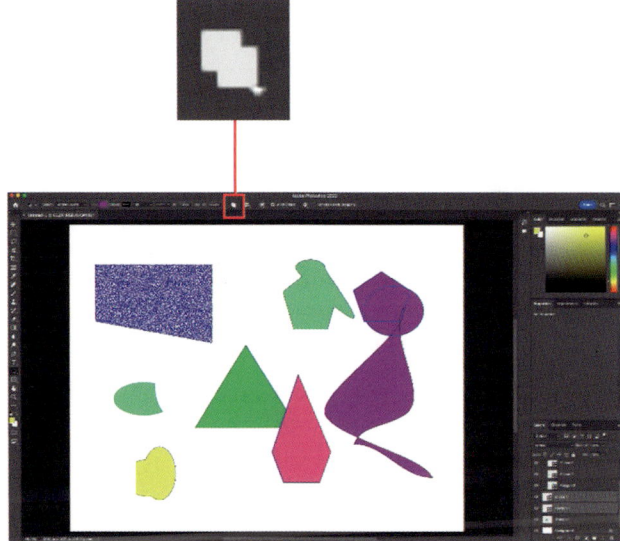

Figure 19.15: Combining shapes.

Objects can also be combined in different ways. The Subtract front shape option enables the front shape to cut into the existing shape and the Intersect shape areas option only shows the area that intersects. Finally, the Exclude overlapping shapes area keeps every part of the shapes apart from the intersecting area.

Once individual objects have been combined and edited, a single object can be created by clicking on `Path Operations` and selecting `Merge Shape Components`.

ACTIVITY 19.04

1 Using the image you manipulated in Activity 19.03, select all the objects you added for part of an image, such as your drawing of a tree. Group the items then link them. The items should now move as one rather than as separate components.

2 Rotate one of the items you have added in a layer in Activity 19.03, such as a tree. Move it to a new location.

3 Insert the bench from **19.02_Bench.jpg** into the background on **19.01_Background.jpg**. Resize the bench and move it into a suitable position.

Alignment and distribution tools

Align left, right, top, bottom and centre

The **Align** tool enables two or more objects to be lined up along a set point, such as their top edges.

To align objects, first select the required layers, then choose the `Layer` menu, followed by `Align` and then the required option (see Figure 19.16).

KEY WORD

align: make objects line up along a set point

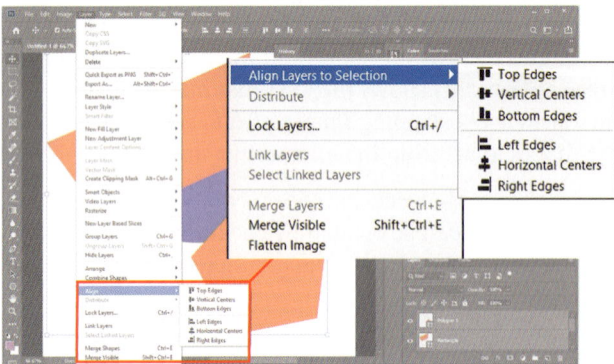

Figure 19.16: Align menu options.

Vertical and horizontal distribution

Distribute enables layers to have consistent spacing between them. The Distribute tool evenly spaces out the layers selected, based on horizontal or vertical distances.

KEY WORD

distribute: make the space between objects the same

To use Distribute, highlight at least three layers. Select the `Layer` menu, then `Distribute` and choose whether the distribution should be performed horizontally or vertically (see Figure 19.17).

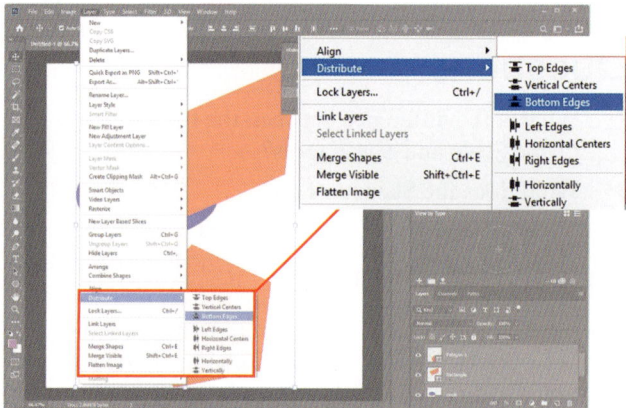

Figure 19.17: Distribute menu options.

Order, raise and lower objects, and bring to front and send to back

Ordering, raising and lowering layers, along with bringing layers to the front or sending them to the back, can be found in the Add, remove, select and order layers section previously.

Layout tools

Rulers

Rules are visible on the horizontal and vertical axes of the screen. Rulers enable the size of an object to be viewed, along with the distance between objects.

To turn Rulers on and off, select the `View` menu and then click `Rulers`. The tick indicates that rulers are visible (see Figure 19.18).

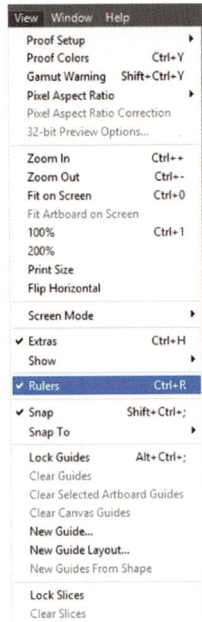

Figure 19.18: Rulers on/off options.

Rulers can be displayed in centimetres (cm), inches or pixels. To change the unit of measurement, double click on one of the rulers and then choose the required units (see Figure 19.19).

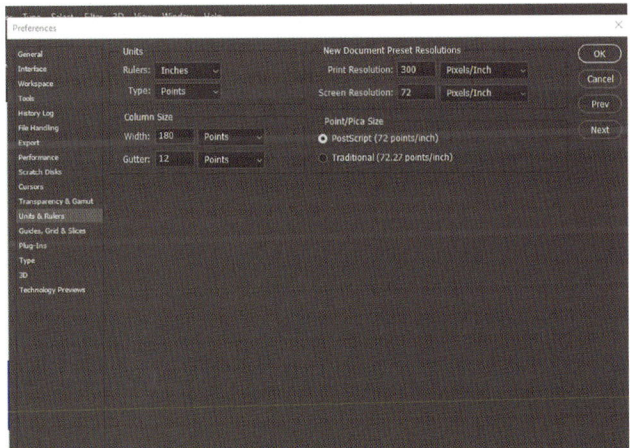

Figure 19.19: Ruler measurement unit options.

Grids

A grid can be displayed on the background of the image to help position and align objects. The grid is used as a guide and does not appear when printing or exporting images.

To enable or disable the grid (turn the grid on or off), select the View menu, then Show and then Grid (see Figures 19.20 and 19.21).

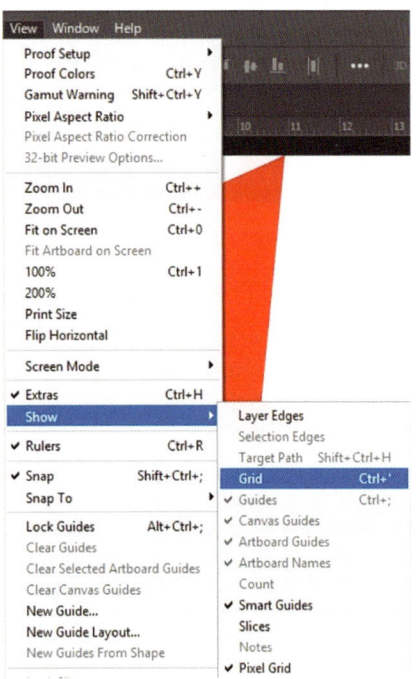

Figure 19.20: Grid option.

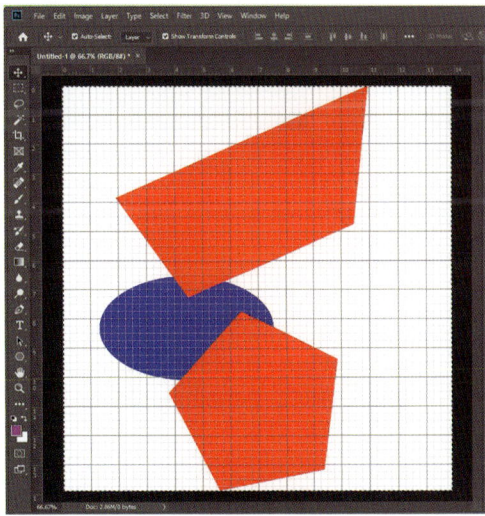

Figure 19.21: Image with the grid displayed.

Question

9   How can grids and rules be shown or removed when editing an image?

Guidelines

Horizontal or vertical lines, known as guidelines, can be placed at specific points on an image. For example, a vertical guideline could be positioned at 3.5 inches across the image. The guidelines can then be used to align objects and make sure objects are drawn to the correct size.

> ### WORKED EXAMPLE 19.02
>
> Create a new vertical guideline.
>
> First click the `View` menu and then `New Guide`.
>
> Then select `Vertical` from the new menu. Enter the position where you want the guideline to appear, in this case at 3.5 inches. Then click `OK` (see Figure 19.22). 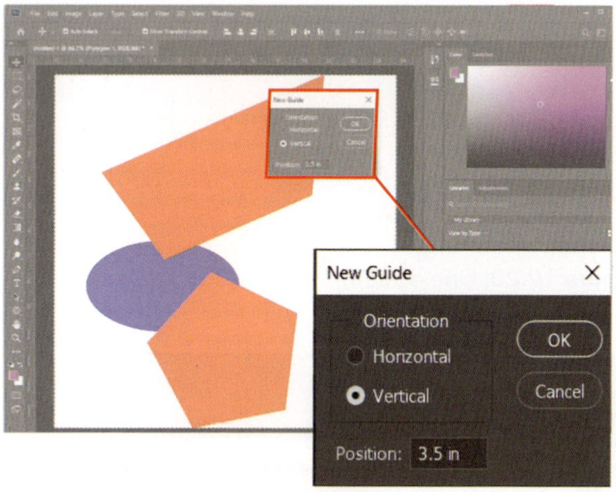
>
>
> **Figure 19.22:** Vertical guideline option.

Snapping

Snapping helps create accurate images by only allowing objects to be placed on gridlines. If more freedom is required to edit or draw objects, snapping needs to be turned off.

> ### WORKED EXAMPLE 19.03
>
> Set the shapes to snap to meet the guidelines.
>
> First click `View` and then if `Snap` is not ticked, click it.
>
> When you want more freedom, click on the `Snap` button again to untick it (see Figure 19.23). 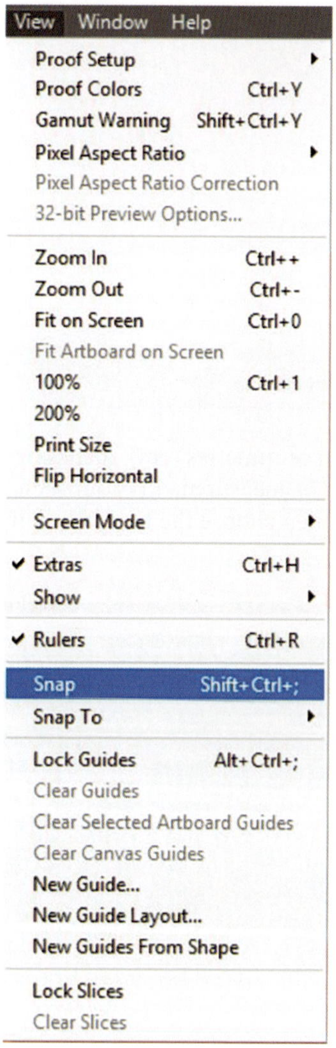
>
>
> **Figure 19.23:** Snap options.

Colour picker tools

A colour can be selected using the colour palette within the Colour section on the right of the screen (see Figure 19.24).

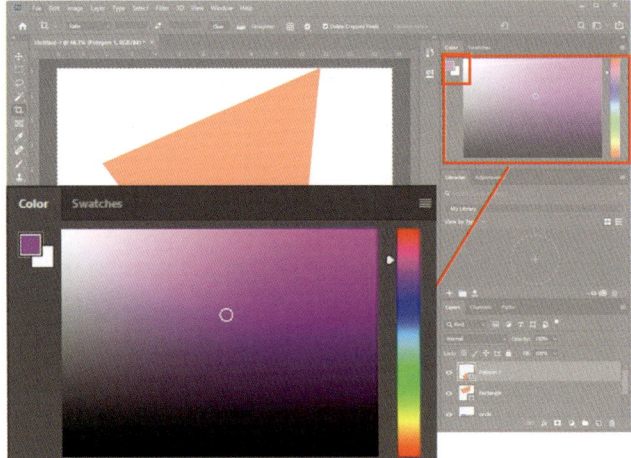

Figure 19.24: Colour options.

To use colours from an existing image, the eyedropper tool can be used to select a colour.

Click the `eyedropper` tool from the menu, then click on the colour required in the image. The colour will then appear in the colour palette (see Figure 19.25).

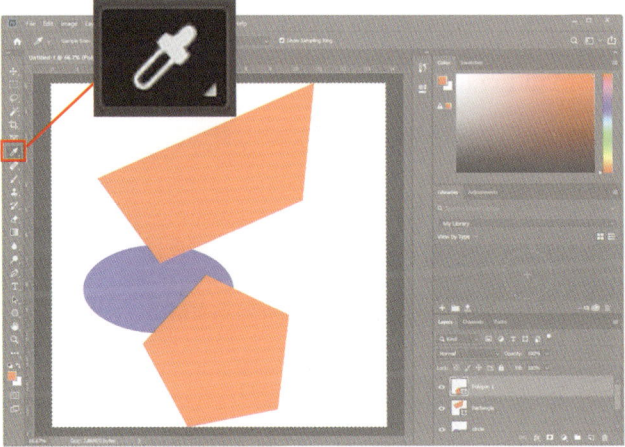

Figure 19.25: Eyedropper tool colour selector.

Crop tools, including crop/clip to objects

Cropping enables part of an image to be removed. To crop an object, select the crop tool from the left-hand side of the screen and then drag the corners of the image in to show the area you want to keep. Once the area has been selected, press the `Enter` key to complete the crop.

WORKED EXAMPLE 19.04

Crop the image so only a square from the centre of the image is produced.

First click on the `Crop` button on the left-hand menu. Adjust the size of the box by clicking on the edges or corners (see Figure 19.26). When you have a square in the centre of the screen, click `Enter` to complete the crop.

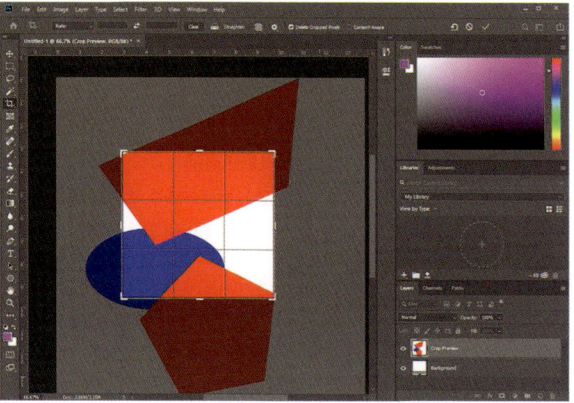

Figure 19.26: Cropping.

ACTIVITY 19.05

Using **19.01_Background.jpg**, crop the bottom layer of soil from the image and the top of the sky above the clouds. Make sure you have the correct layer selected before you begin, otherwise you will crop the wrong image.

Question

10 What different methods can be used to select colours to use in an image?

Colour systems

Many different colour systems are used to produce colours when creating graphics.

RGB

RGB is an acronym for Red/Green/Blue. RGB produces colours by combining different amounts of red, green and blue. RGB is typically used when producing digital images, such as those viewed online. In Adobe Photoshop, the amount of each colour is represented by a two-digit hexadecimal value. Hexadecimal values can be from 0 to F, with the letters A to F representing the number 10 to 15, which enables 16 distinct values to be stored. Having two hexadecimal values enables 256 (16 × 16) different values to be represented for each colour. The higher the hexadecimal value, the more of that colour is present.

RGB colour codes are written in the form RRGGBB, which is the amount of red, then green, then blue. For example, the colour code FF0000 shows red (RR) with the value FF (the highest value), with no green (GG) or blue (BB), which displays a strong, bright red colour.

KEY WORD

RGB: red/green/blue colour system; all colours are a combination of quantities of red, green and blue

HSL

HSL is an acronym for Hue/Saturation/Lightness. HSL is an alternative to RGB.

The Hue represents the base colour, such as red, green or blue, and is based on a colour's position on a colour wheel between 0 and 360 degrees. On a colour wheel, red is at 0 degrees, green is at 120 degrees and blue is at 240 degrees (see Figure 19.27).

Figure 19.27: Colour wheel spectrum.

The saturation is the percentage of that colour being used, with 100% being the most amount of colour. Lightness is a percentage from black (0%) to white (100%).

KEY WORD

HSL: hue/saturation/lightness colour system; all colours are a combination of the hue saturation and lightness selected

For example, the colour in Figure 19.28 has a hue of 100, with 50% saturation and 50% lightness.

Figure 19.28: Hue 100, with 50% saturation and 50% lightness.

Increasing the saturation to 100% produces the colour shown in Figure 19.29.

Figure 19.29: Hue 100, with 100% saturation and 50% lightness.

Increasing the lightness to 95% (100% would make it white and invisible) is shown in Figure 19.30.

Figure 19.30: Hue 100, with 100% saturation and 95% lightness.

Questions

11 What do the letters RGB stand for?

12 What colour will FF0000 create?

13 What colour will 00FF00 create?

14 What colour will 0000FF create

15 What colour will 000000 create?

16 What colour will FFFFFF create?

ACTIVITY 19.06

Find a colour generator online and try experimenting with HSL.

Enter values for the hue, saturation and lightness and guess what colour will appear.

Work as a pair and test each other by giving your partner the numbers for a colour and ask them what colour they think it will produce.

CMYK

CMYK is an acronym for Cyan, Magenta, Yellow, Black. CMYK is a colour system typically used within printers. Different colours can be made by mixing these four colours.

KEY WORD

CMYK: cyan/magenta/yellow/black colour system; all colours are a combination of these four colours

Each colour is given a number as a percentage from 0 to 100, which represents how much of the colour is included.

CMS

CMS, or the Colour Matching System, enables graphics software to reproduce colours already present within an image. For example, if an image of a car contains a certain shade of red, CMS can be used to find out RGB, HSL and CMYK values, which can then be used elsewhere within the image.

The need for different image resolutions

An image's **resolution** describes the amount of detail that is within an image. Resolution is measured in the number of pixels per inch (PPI). The more pixels that are used within an image, the more detail an image can have. However, the more pixels that are used within an image, the more data needs to be stored, so the file size is larger.

KEY WORD

resolution: the amount of detail within an image; the higher the resolution, the more detail can be stored in an image

Images are typically viewed on screen or in print. However, screens and printers have their own maximum resolutions. Even if a high-resolution image is developed using graphics software, the resulting image can be limited by the hardware being used to display or view it, regardless of how much detail is in the image. Having a low-resolution image on screen or in print can lead to a loss of quality, such as pixelation, where the pixels become visible, or blurriness.

To change the resolution in Adobe Photoshop, the size of the image needs to be changed. Click `Image` on the top menu bar and then `Image Size`.

The width and height of the image can be changed, along with the resolution (see Figure 19.31).

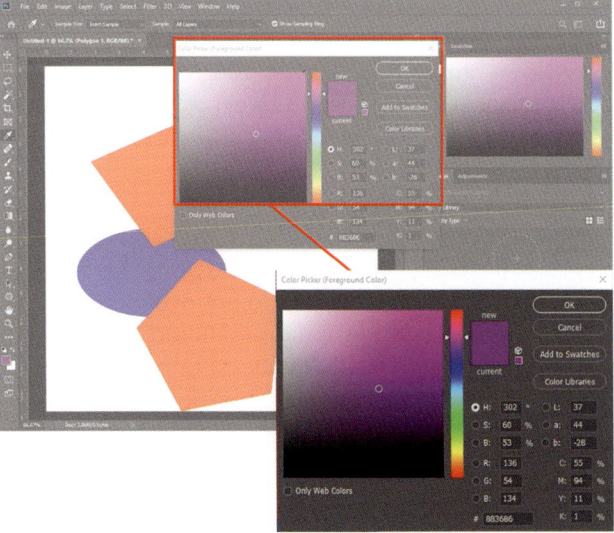

Figure 19.31: Width, height and resolution options.

Different bitmap and vector file formats

File format	Image type	Description
bmp	Bitmap	**Bitmap:** Provides a range of colour options, including black and white, four-bit (16 colours) and eight-bit (256 colours). The smaller the number of colours, the smaller the file size, although the quality also decreases. bmp provides high-quality images without using compression, which can lead to large file sizes. Bitmap images are often used for photographs, or images with a large amount of detail.
gif	Bitmap	**Graphics Interchange Format:** A compressed format that can reduce the file size and is commonly used for online images. The gif file format allows for transparent backgrounds and is restricted to 256 colours. gif is often used for simple animations.
jpg or jpeg	Bitmap	**Joint Photographic Experts Group:** A common format, which is widely supported and often used for sharing photographs. The image is compressed when saved and decompressed when opened. The level of compression can often be altered to gain a balance between file size versus quality. jpg images do not allow for transparency.
png	Bitmap	**Portable Network Graphics:** The PNG format uses lossless compression to reduce the file size and is often used for web-based graphics. It has a range of colour options and images can have transparent backgrounds, although images tend to have larger file sizes than jpg.
tif or tiff	Bitmap	**Tagged Image File** Format: tif is often used when high-quality images are required, such as in publishing, as the file format supports a large number of colours and large file sizes.
svg	Vector	**Scalable Vector Graphic:** Ideal for graphics that might need to be resized, without losing quality. It is often used to design logos for use on the web.
pdf	Vector and bitmap (exported as a document)	**Portable Document Format:** Used to distribute documents that required their layout to remain the same, which can include both bitmap and vector graphics.

Table 19.1: File formats.

There are a range of file formats used to save images. The file format can be selected by choosing an option when saving or exporting the image. Some of these are shown in Table 19.1.

> **TIP**
>
> When choosing a file type, do not overwrite the original file. If the compression reduces the quality, you may be unable to retrieve the original file.

Exporting an image in different file formats

Within Adobe Photoshop, there are two methods to change the file format. The first is to use 'Save As' and select a different file type. The second method is to Export the image. Click `File` then `Export As` and select the required file format.

ACTIVITY 19.07

Open an image you have already created. Save or export the image in each of the available file types. Compare the images and look at the differences between them.

Changing solid and gradient fills

The fill colour used for objects within an image can be altered, including changing from a solid to gradient fill. The required steps are included in the 'Fill tools to colour elements' section for vector graphics and in the 'Working with colour' section for bitmap graphics.

Questions

17 Name three bitmap image formats.

18 What bitmap image format might be used when editing photographs for inclusion on a website?

19 Name one vector image format.

19.2 Vector graphics

There are a range of software tools that can be used to create and edit vector graphics. When creating vector graphics, the intended audience needs to be carefully considered and appropriate objects chosen to meet their requirements. For example, if producing a technical diagram, specific symbols may be needed to ensure it meets the requirements of the audience. Alternatively, if producing a logo for an organisation, it may be necessary to include certain colours within the graphics produced.

Vector drawing tools

Freehand drawing

Freehand drawing tools can be selected from the Pen tool menu. Hold the left mouse button down on the menu to see the available options (see Figure 19.32).

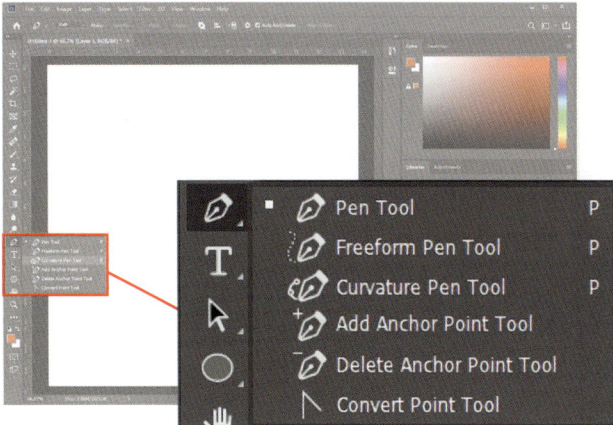

Figure 19.32: Pen Tool menu.

The Pen Tool can be used, along with a colour from the right-hand menu, to draw on the **canvas**.

> **KEY WORD**
>
> **canvas:** the area in graphics software where graphics can be created and edited

The Pen tool creates shapes by placing nodes, known as anchor points, on the canvas, which are joined to make a shape. Further information is outlined in the Node and Path editing section later.

Bézier curves

Bézier curves provide a method of drawing arcs within graphics software, which can be easily scaled.

> **KEY WORD**
>
> **Bézier curves:** smooth curves made of paths that can be scaled indefinitely

A curve can be created using the Curvature Pen tool to first draw a straight line.

Once the straight line has been drawn, select a midpoint on the line and drag it to create a curve (see Figure 19.33).

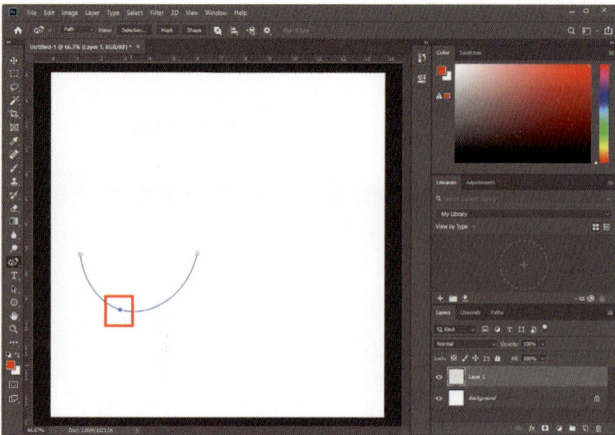

Figure 19.33: Curve 'mid' point.

Straight lines

To draw a straight line in Adobe Photoshop, hold the left mouse button down on the Rectangle Tool to view the available shapes and select `Line Tool` (see Figure 19.34).

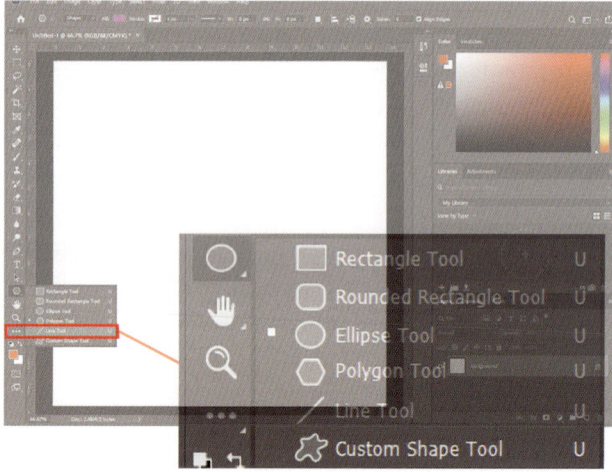

Figure 19.34: Line tool.

Shape tools

The Shape menu has inbuilt shapes to allow rectangles, ellipses and polygons to be drawn. Many other shapes can be created by modifying the properties of these basic shapes.

To create a circle, hold down the Shift key while dragging an ellipse.

To draw a star, create a polygon with the number of edges needed for the star. The number of edges can be specified in the options at the top of the screen. Then, within the Properties section on the right-hand side of the screen, click on `Set star ratio` to alter the appearance of the shape (see Figure 19.35).

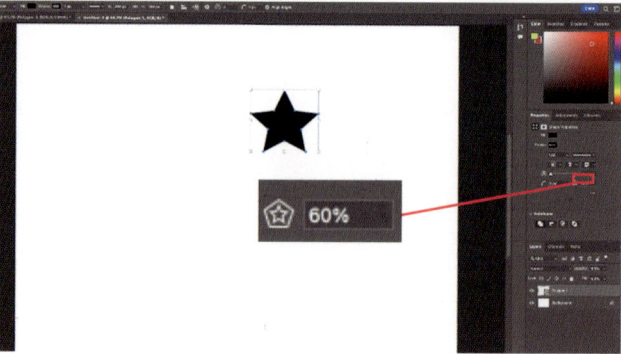

Figure 19.35: Drawing a star.

To draw a spiral in Photoshop, create a new image with the same width and height, such as 500 × 500 pixels, as explained in Section 19.1. Use the shape menu to create a coloured rectangle and drag the shape to cover exactly half of the image. Select the Filter meu, then Distort, then Twirl. The angle of the swirl can be altered by moving the slider up and down.

Application of envelopes and perspectives

How to use envelopes and/or alter perspective is explained in Transform tools in Section 19.1.

Selection tools to select and manipulate parts of a vector graphic

Convert to curves

The Curvature Pen tool can also be used to curve straight lines on existing objects. Select the shape using the Path Selection tool, then choose the `Curvature Pen Tool`. Click and drag from any position on a straight line to produce a curve.

Replication

Parts of an object can be copied, or replicated, using copy and paste. To replicate part of an object, select the required part using a selection tool, such as the Elliptical Marquee tool, then choose `Copy` from the Edit menu. Deselect the selection, by clicking `Deselect`, then go to Paste in the Edit menu. The copied part of the image will be pasted as a new layer.

Transformation tools

Details of the available transformation tools are described in Transform tools in Section 19.1.

Fill tools to colour elements

A Fill Tool allows a colour to be used to fill a selected area. For example, when using Adobe Photoshop, if the colour red is selected, followed by the Fill Tool, an object can be filled with the colour red by clicking inside it.

To fill an image, select the Paint Bucket tool, choose your colour and then click the image you want to change (see Figure 19.36).

Figure 19.36: Fill tool options.

A gradient fill enables two colours to be selected, with Adobe Photoshop gradually altering the colour from the first to the second. To use gradient fill, first select the area to fill using a selection tool, such as the Rectangular Marquee selection tool.

Select the first colour, followed by the second (see Figure 19.37).

Figure 19.37: Colour gradient options.

There are a range of pre-set gradient fills that be selected, which appear once the Gradient Fill tool has been selected at the top of the screen (see Figure 19.38).

Figure 19.38: Pre-set gradient fills.

ACTIVITY 19.08

Use a Fill tool to change the colour of the sky, trees and mountains in **19.01_Background.jpg**. Make sure you have the correct layer selected first. Change the fill colour of the bench in **19.02_Bench.jpg** by use a fill pattern or gradient.

Node and path editing

Adding, moving and deleting nodes to simplify paths

A path refers to a number of connected points, known as nodes, or anchor points, which are used to make up a shape or a selection. For example, for a triangle, an anchor point is located in each corner, with a path between them.

When anchor points are added to the canvas using the Pen tool, paths are created between the anchor points to produce a shape.

The Pen tool can also be used to add anchor points to the paths of existing shapes by selecting the edge of the required shape. Alternatively, right click on the path and select `Add Anchor Point` (see Figure 19.39).

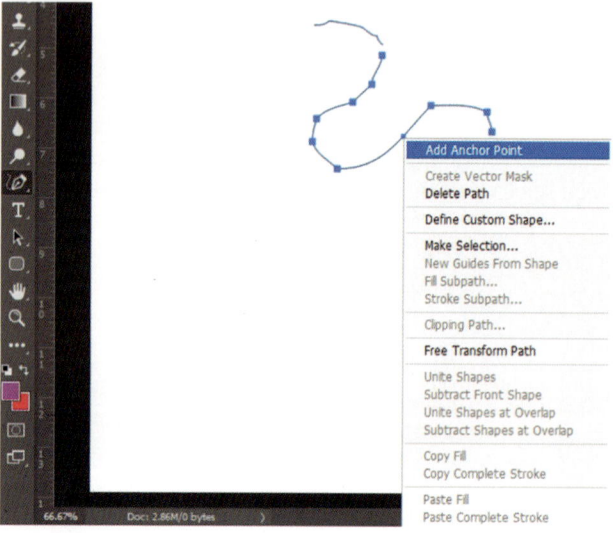

Figure 19.39: Adding an anchor point.

Anchor points can then be moved to modify the path by left clicking on the new anchor point, then dragging the mouse.

Existing anchor points can be deleted to change and simplify a path. To delete an anchor point, click on an existing anchor point when using the Pen tool. Alternatively, right click on the anchor point and select `Delete Anchor Point` (see Figure 19.40).

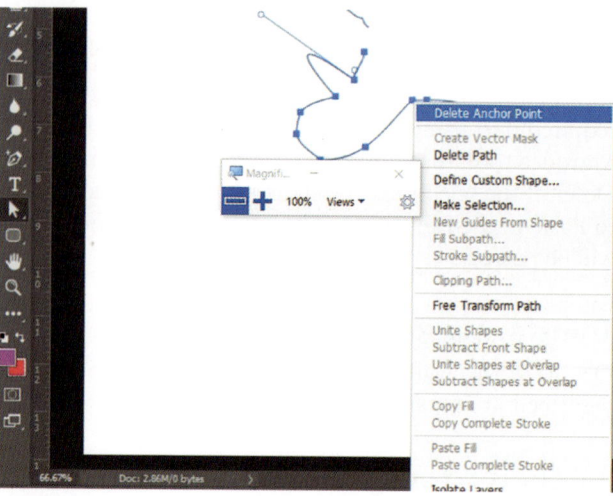

Figure 19.40: Menu option for deleting an anchor point.

ACTIVITY 19.09

Select the nodes on one of the mountains on **19.01_Background.jpg**. Manipulate the shape of the mountain. Make it higher and change the angles of each side. Repeat this with the copy of a tree you have made and change the shape of the trunk.

Using Bézier handles

A Bézier handle allows the curve of a path to be altered. To use Bézier handles, choose the `Direct Selection Tool` from the left-hand menu and click on an anchor point (see Figure 19.41).

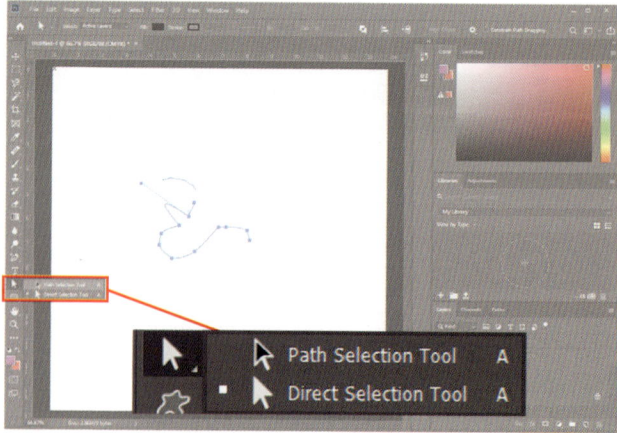

Figure 19.41: Direct Selection tool.

A direction line will appear from the anchor point, which has a small circle on the end, known as a Bézier handle. The Bézier handle can be clicked and dragged to change the curve.

Working with symmetrical, asymmetrical, cusp and smooth nodes

Symmetrical and asymmetrical nodes cannot be created using the Pen tool. Transform tools, such as reflect and move, as explained in Section 19.1, can be used to create symmetrical and asymmetrical designs.

Smooth curves can be adjusted using a Bézier handle, as explained in the previous section.

Cusp anchor points occur when two curves meet at a point, such as when drawing an image of a heart. When using the Pen tool, hold `Alt` (Windows) or `Option` (Mac) to select the Bézier handle. The direction line connected to the Bézier handle will now move independently of the other line and can be moved to create the required point.

Align and distribute nodes

Multiple anchor points can be aligned by using the Path Selection tool from the left-hand menu. Hold down Shift to select two or more anchor points, then choose `Path alignment` from the toolbar at the top of the screen. Various alignment options are available, such as to align to the left edge. Distribute options are also available within the Path alignment menu, which enables different paths to be equally distributed (see Figure 19.42).

Figure 19.42: Alignment and distribution options.

Convert bitmap images into editable vector shapes

Bitmap images created in Adobe Photoshop can be converted into editable vector shapes. This can be useful if an image is going to be used within graphic design or digital arts, such as a logo or icon, as the graphics can be easily resized for use in a variety of contexts.

To convert a bitmap image into a vector shape, first highlight the area to export using a selection tool, such as the Magnetic Lasso tool.

Open the Paths menu by selecting `Window` from the top menu, then `Paths`. From the Paths menu, choose `Make Work Path` (see Figure 19.43).

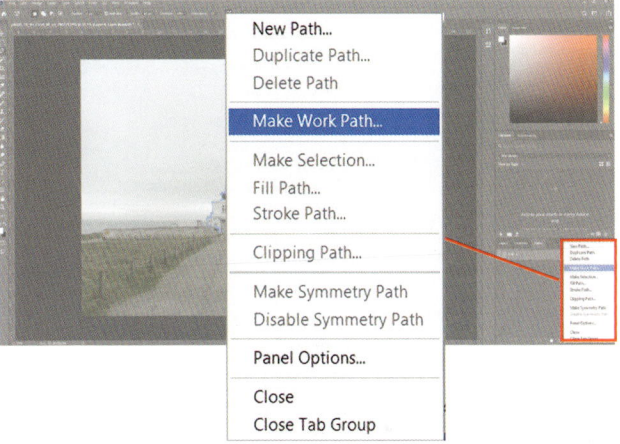

Figure 19.43: Make Work Path menu.

Set the Tolerance value: the lower the number, the more precise the shapes are (see Figure 19.44).

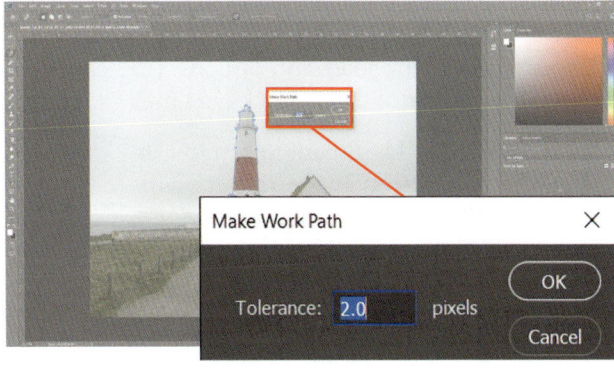

Figure 19.44: Setting Tolerance.

Once a path has been selected, the selection can be exported as a vector. To do this, click `File`, `Export` and then `Paths to Illustrator` (see Figure 19.45 This creates an illustrator vector file containing the editable shape.

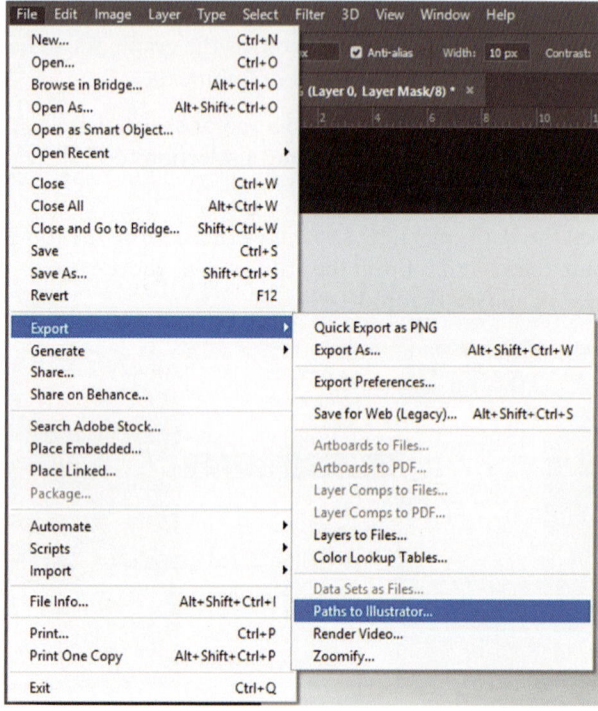

Figure 19.45: Export menu.

Not all images can be converted into exact vector graphics. For example, the edge of certain parts of an image might be difficult to define, or the edge could be challenging to trace.

ACTIVITY 19.10

Choose **one** of the following options. (You can complete more options if you have time).

1   J.B. Garden Landscaping would like you to create an image to put on its website. The image should be a brown arrow pointing to the right, on top of a green rectangle. Create the image for J.B. Garden Landscaping.

2   Haven's Creations would like you to create a logo of a series of clouds of different shades of grey overlapping each other. Create the image for Haven's Creations.

CONTINUED

Figure 19.46: Drinks bottles.

3   Robson's Refreshments would like you to create an image of bottles of soda of different sizes on a table (see Figure 19.46). Create the image for Robson's refreshments.

4   Bhavin's Buildings would like you to create a logo of a high-rise building. The building needs to be at least ten storeys with an image of a cloud behind the top of the building. The building should be an appropriate colour to stand out against a pale blue background. Create the image for Bhavin's Buildings.

Advantages and disadvantages of converting a bitmap image into an editable vector shape

Converting a bitmap image into an editable vector shape means it can be scaled without loss of quality. The mathematical equations used to create a vector image mean the edges and lines appear well defined, which results in a high-quality image. Each part of the image can also be easily edited, such as adjusting the shape of certain sections. The file sizes of vector images are typically smaller than those produced when using a bitmap image.

However, converting bitmap images to vector images can result in a loss of detail and realism; particularly if reproducing photographs which use a range of complex colour palettes and shapes. Converting bitmap images can be complex and time consuming, including the need to manually trace certain areas, which requires precision and skill. In addition, there can be compatibility issues with graphics software if vector files aren't fully supported.

Questions

20   What are two advantages of converting a bitmap image into a vector shape?

21   What are two disadvantages of converting a bitmap image into a vector shape?

19.3 Bitmap images

Bitmap graphics can be created and edited using a range of software tools. As with vector graphics, the requirements of the audience and application need to be carefully considered when producing bitmap images. For example, when editing a photograph for a website, you may need to crop the image to a particular size and improve the contrast, or when producing an image for an advertisement, you may wish to combine eye-catching filters with bright colours to create a striking image.

Selection tools to select, remove or hide parts of a bitmap image

A selection tool enables parts of an image to be edited and manipulated. A range of tools are available within graphics software to select parts of a bitmap image.

Rectangular and elliptical shaped areas, including circles, can be selected by using the Rectangular Marquee tool or the Elliptical Marquee tool on the left-hand side of the screen. Once the tool has been selected, click and drag on the image to select the required area.

Lasso

The Lasso tool enables freehand drawing around the area of an image to be selected. Once the tool has been clicked, hold the left mouse button down to select the area (see Figure 19.47).

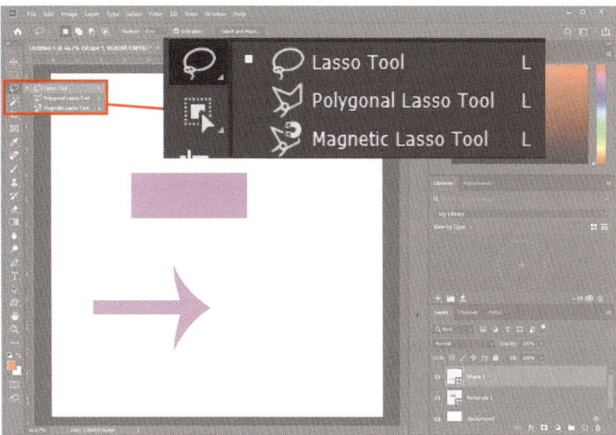

Figure 19.47: Lasso tool.

Alternatively, the Magnetic Lasso tool will stick to an edge within an image, such as a line or a specific colour, and can therefore be easier to use than the standalone Lasso tool (see Figure 19.48).

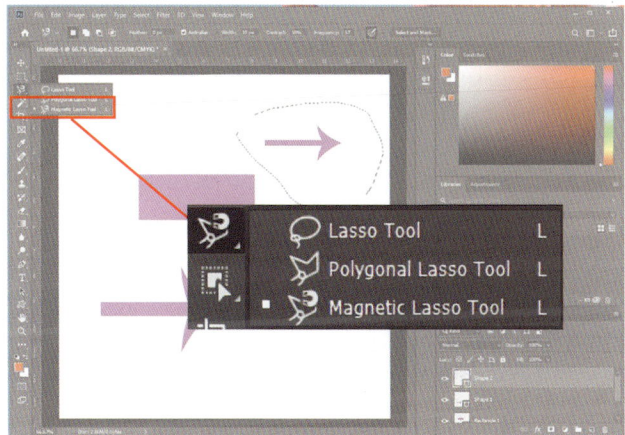

Figure 19.48: Magnetic Lasso selection tool.

TIP

When using a selection tool, ensure the correct layer is chosen. If a different layer is chosen, then an incorrect part of the image will be selected.

Magic Wand

The Magic Wand tool enables pixels to be selected based on their colour. Hold the left mouse button down on the magic wand to select the `Magic Wand tool` (see Figure 19.49).

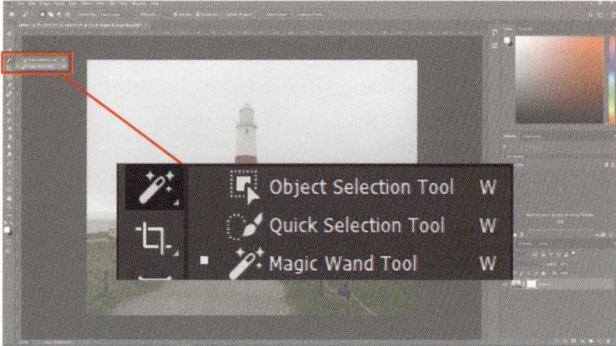

Figure 19.49: Magic Wand tool.

Click and drag the area to select. The Tolerance, which can be viewed at the top of the screen, can be altered to determine how wide a range of colours is included within the selection.

The higher the value of the Tolerance, the wider range of colours the Magic Wand tool will select. The lower the value of Tolerance number, the more precise the colour needs to be.

Questions

22 What does the Lasso tool do?

23 What does the Magic Wand tool do?

Colour select

Information on selecting a colour can be found in the Colour Picker tools part of Section 19.1.

Cut out

To cut out part of an image's background, click on the Background layer in the Layers section, then select the required part of an image to cut out using a selection tool. Use the `Select` menu, then `Inverse`, which will select the other parts of the image, then click `Add Layer Mask` from the bottom of the Layers section (see Figure 19.50).

Figure 19.50: Cutting out part of an image.

The selected part of the image will be cut out and replaced with other graphics if required.

Crop

Information on how to crop an image can be found in the Crop tools part in Section 19.1.

Masking tools

The Add Layer Mask tool described within the Cut out section previously can also be used to cut out parts of a layer, which will then reveal the layers underneath. Click on the required layer in the Layers section, then select the required part of an image to cut out using a selection tool. Use the Select menu, then Inverse, which will select the other parts of the image, then click `Add Layer Mask` from the bottom of the Layers section. The selected part of the layer will be cut out to show the layers underneath.

ACTIVITY 9.12

1 Open **19.03_New York.jpg**. Add a new layer and add the image from **19.04_Helicopter.jpg**.

2 Move the helicopter to an appropriate position in the sky and rotate it so it fits into the skyline.

3 Open **19.03_New York.jpg** and **19.04_Helicopter.jpg**. Add further copies of the helicopter onto the New York image in the same layer. Select all these layers (you may need to use the Shift or Ctrl button to select more than one), then group or merge the layers into one layer. You should now be able to move them together.

4 Use a selection tool (for example, the Magnetic Lasso tool) to highlight one of the buildings in **19.03_New York.jpg**. Copy this image and paste it into a new layer. Move the building so it looks as if it belongs in the city. Repeat this with other buildings to create your own version of New York.

5 Open **19.05_Frog.jpg**. Crop the image so only the face and eyes of the frog are visible.

Working with colour

Solid and gradient fills

Information on solid and gradient fills can be found in 'Fill tools to colour elements' in Section 19.2.

Convert to black and white, and greyscale

An entire image, or just part of one, can be converted from colour into black and white, or greyscale.

Greyscale mode can be chosen by selecting the `Image menu`, then `Mode` and `Grayscale` (see Figure 19.51).

> **TIP**
>
> Grayscale is the US spelling of greyscale.

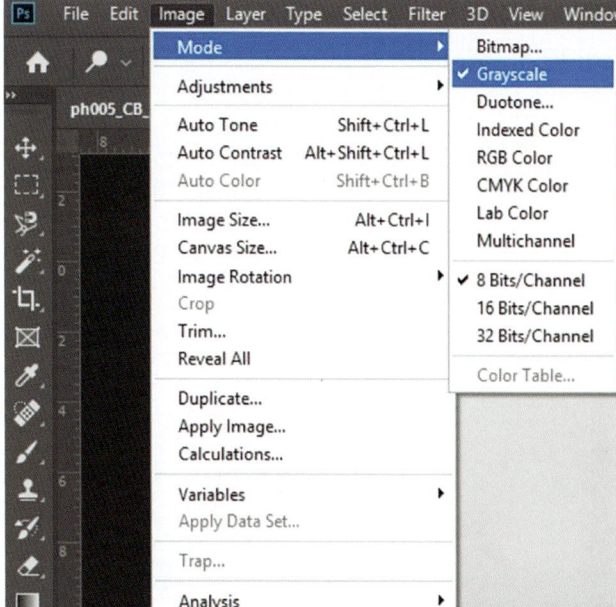

Figure 19.51: Selecting Greyscale mode.

To change a specific part of an image to be in greyscale, select the area required using one of the selection tools. From the Image menu, choose `Adjustments` and then `Desaturate` (see Figure 19.52). Only the area selected will become greyscale.

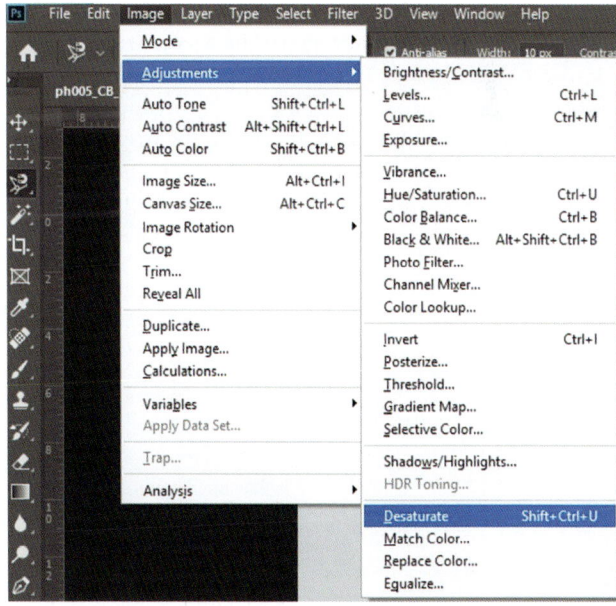

Figure 19.52: Selecting Desaturate in adjustments menu.

The adjustments menu has options to adjust the colours in other ways, including to Black and White.

Adjust brightness, contrast, colour balance, shadows and highlights

Adjusting the brightness allows the overall lightness or darkness of an image, or part of an image, to be changed. Adjusting the contrast changes the difference between the various colours in the image. Both the brightness and contrast can be changed from the Image menu, then select `Adjustments` and then `Brightness/Contrast` (see Figure 19.53).

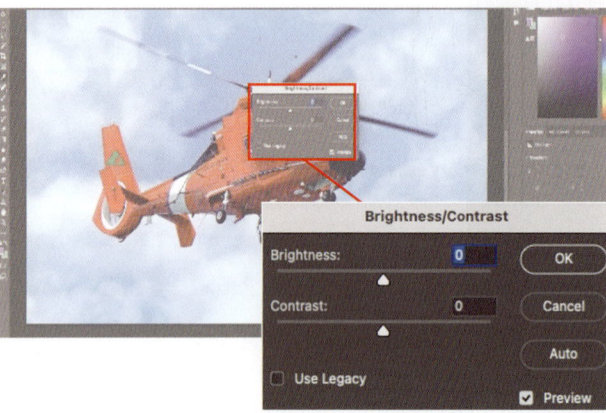

Figure 19.53: Brightness and contrast sliders.

Changing the colour balance allows adjustments to be made to the overall mixture of colours in an image, or by correcting imperfections within the colours used. To alter the colour balance, go to the `Image menu`, `Adjustments`, then `Color Balance` (see Figure 19.54). The existing brightness of each pixel is considered by Adobe Photoshop to help maintain the original brightness when the Preserve luminosity box is ticked, which prevents the image being either too bright or too dark.

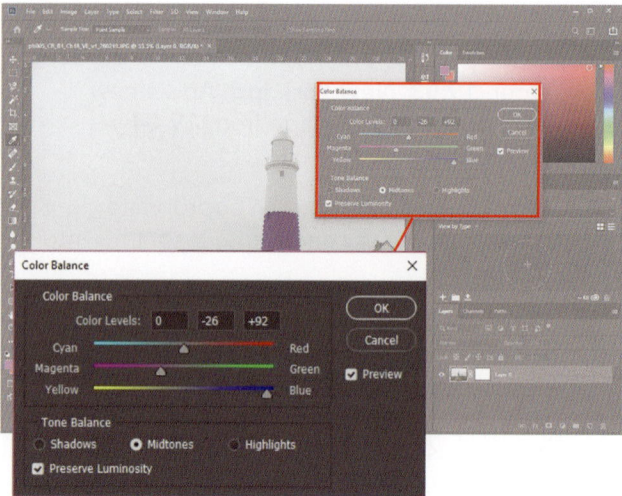

Figure 19.54: Colour balance sliders.

Shadows and highlights within an image can also be changed, which can be used to adjust parts of an image that may be too dark or too bright, such as when backlighting causes silhouettes within a photograph. Shadows and highlights can be adjusted in the `Image menu`, then select `Adjustments` and `Shadows/Highlights`.

ACTIVITY 19.13

1   Open **19.06_Village.jpg**. Change the colour to black and white, duotone and a range of other colours. Compare turning an image to black and white then to duotone, rather than straight to duotone.

2   Take a photograph and open it in Adobe Photoshop. Change the image so only the main focus of the photograph is in colour; the rest should be in black and white.

Brush, pencil and pen tools

The brush and pencil tools enable freehand drawing to take place using the mouse.

The colour of the brush or pencil can be selected from the Colour section, with various options for customising how the tool draws available from the top of the screen (see Figure 19.55).

The Pen tool was explained in Section 19.2, Vector images.

Figure 19.55: Brush tool menu option.

Tools to alter parts of an image

There are a range of other tools available that can be used to alter parts of images.

Distort

The Distort tool enables an image to be stretched in a specific direction. A similar effect can also be achieved with the Warp tool, which can be used to change the shape of an item. For example, an image of a high-rise building could be altered to make the building appear more curved (see Figure 19.56).

Figure 19.56: Warped images.

The Distort and Warp tools can be accessed from the Edit menu, then selecting Transform, followed by Distort or Warp. Dragging the boxes on the edges of the grid that appears can be used to modify the image (see Figure 19.57).

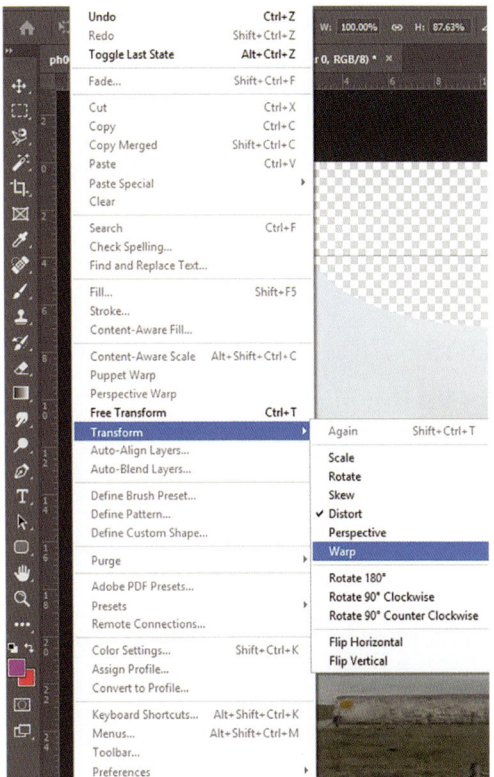

Figure 19.57: Selecting Warp menu option.

Clone

Clone creates an identical copy of part of an image. For example, if an image contains a tree, which could be duplicated to be included within another part of the image, the Clone tool can be used to 'paint' a copy of the tree in a different place, without having to trace the outline and copy it.

To use the clone stamp, select the Clone Stamp button (see Figure 19.58).

Figure 19.58: Clone Stamp button.

Hold `Alt` (Windows) or `Option` (Mac) and click the area of the image to clone. Move the cursor to where the clone should be created, then click and hold the left mouse button down to draw the image.

Erase

To erase part of an image, select the required section, then go to the Edit menu, then Clear.

Questions

24 What does the Distort tool do?

25 When might you use the Clone tool?

Filters to alter parts of an image

Along with the tools to alter parts of images, various effects can be applied to images using filters.

Blur

There are numerous filter tools available, including the Blur tool, the Sharpen tool and the Smudge tool, which can be accessed from the left-hand toolbar (see Figure 19.59).

Figure 19.59: Blur, Sharpen and Smudge tools.

The Blur tool reduces the focus on part of an image. The amount an image is blurred can be altered using the top toolbar. Drag the Blur tool repeatedly over the area of the image to blur; the more times the Blur tool is used over an area, the more blurred it will become (see Figure 19.60).

Figure 19.60: Percentage of blur.

Smudge

The Smudge tool produces an effect similar to running a finger through wet paint, by enabling a colour to be pushed through part of an image. The Smudge tool can be used to enable different parts of an image to be blended together.

Sharpen

The Sharpen tool increases the contrast between two parts of an image. For example, an edge between a light and dark area can be sharpened to make it more defined.

Red eye removal

The Red Eye tool will automatically remove a red eye effect within a photograph, which is caused by a camera flash. Click the Red Eye tool and draw a box across, or click, the red pupil. The Red Eye tool uses the other colours from the eye to fill in the pupil's colour (see Figure 19.61).

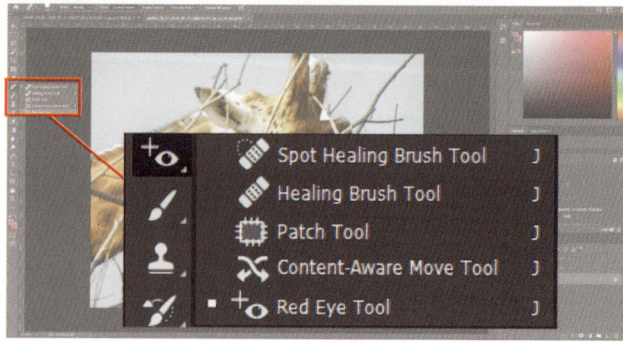

Figure 19.61: Red Eye tool.

Question

26 What copyright issues need to be considered when copying and modifying images, such as those downloaded from the internet?

ACTIVITY 19.14

Select **one** of the following activities.

1   Choose a photograph of yourself, a pet, or of your friends. Make sure you have their permission before using an image of someone else. Use the Smudge, Red Eye Remover and Clone tools to edit the image and either make it better or worse.

2   Create a 'spot the difference' puzzle. Take an image and create a copy of it. Make several subtle changes to this image and challenge someone to spot the differences between the two images.

3   Open **19.07_Fruit bowl.jpg**. Use the Sharpen, Distort and Blur tools to alter the image. For example, you could make the fruit the focus by increasing the contrast and blurring other elements. You could also use other tools mentioned, for example the Clone tool, to add more fruit to the image.

Resizing the image/canvas

An image can be resized, although bitmap images may pixelate and become blurry if they are increased too much in size. The image size can be changed in the Image menu, then Image Size.

The canvas size can also be changed, rather than just the image, which can be used to increase or decrease the space available to create graphics. The canvas size can be changed by selecting `Image` and then `Canvas Size` (see Figure 19.62).

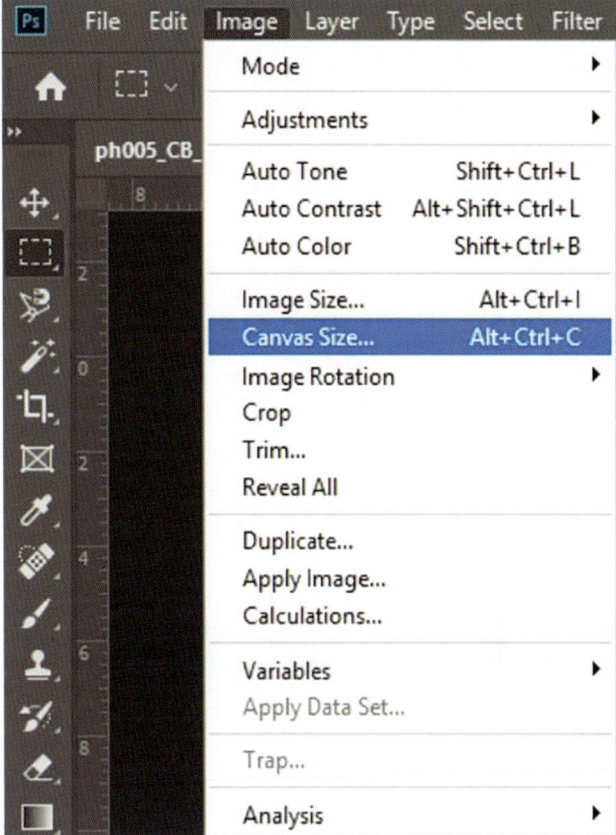

Figure 19.62: Selecting Canvas Size menu.

The new size of the canvas can be entered in pixels, centimetres (cm) or inches (see Figure 19.63).

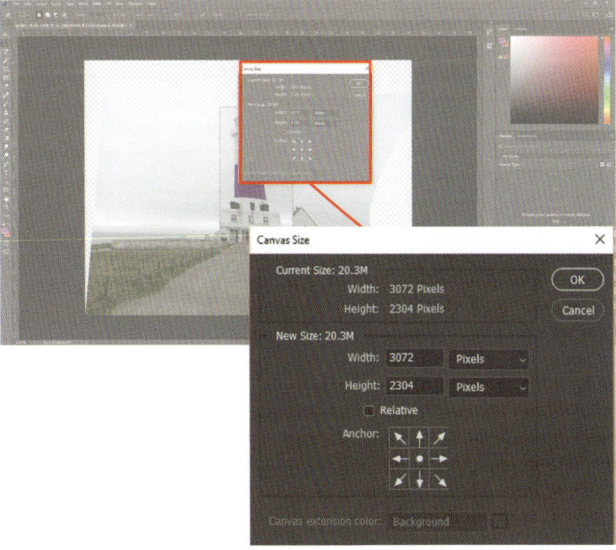

Figure 19.63: Canvas size measurement options.

When increasing the canvas size, the additional background around the image may appear as a checkerboard in grey and white, which means it is transparent. To change the background from transparent, the background can be filled with a colour, or colour gradient, or the image size increase to fill the new space.

Changing colour depth

The **colour depth** of an image is the number of different colours that can be included within the image. The higher the colour depth, the more colours can be used in the image, although the file size will increase.

The colour depth represents the number of bits allocated to each pixel. If 1 bit is used per pixel, then there are two possibilities; 0 or 1, so, 1 bit can only represent two colours.

If the bit depth is increased to 8 bits, there are $2^8 = 256$ different unique colours available, with 16-bit colour enabling $2^{16} = 65\ 536$ different colours.

Therefore, to store an uncompressed image containing 100 pixels using 1 bit colour, which has two unique colours, $100 \times 1 = 100$ bits are required. However, if the same size image uses 8-bit colour, which has 256 unique colours, then the file size is 100×8 bits = 800 bits (or 100 bytes).

To change the colour depth, select `Image` and then `Mode` (see Figure 19.64). 8-bit, 16-bit and 32-bit colour can all be selected.

> **KEY WORD**
>
> **colour depth:** the number of colours that can be represented in the image

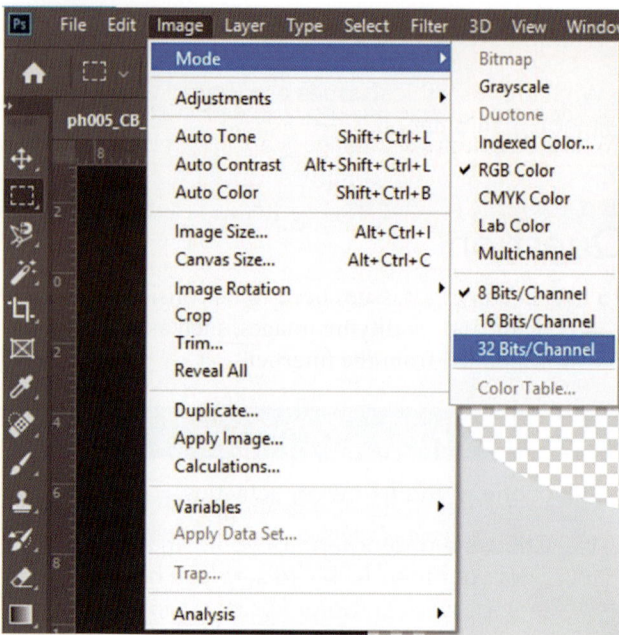

Figure 19.64: Image/Mode menu.

Changing resolution

Changing the resolution is described in the section on The need for different image resolutions in Section 19.1.

Questions

27 How many different colours can be stored if an image has a colour depth of 4 bits?

28 How many bits per pixel are required to store an image with only two colours?

19.4 Compression

Compression is a mechanism to reduce the size of a file. An image might need to be compressed because the file size is too large, for example where an image needs to be sent via email, or if the amount of storage available on a device is limited. Images transferred using the internet, such as those viewed on websites or social media, may be compressed so that they do not take as long to download.

There are two methods of compression: lossless and lossy.

Lossless compression

Lossless compression reduces the size of the image file but does not change the appearance of the image. When the compressed image is opened, it is identical to the original. Lossless compression can work in various ways. A method often used by graphics software is to identify repeating patterns within an image, such as large blocks of the same colour within the background, rather than storing the colour data for each pixel individually.

Lossy compression

Lossy compression also reduces the size of the image file. Unlike lossless compression, some of the data is removed. When an image compressed using lossy compression is opened, it is not identical to the original. For example, the image may have fewer colours. As data is removed when lossy compression is used, the file size of a lossy compressed image will typically be smaller than a lossless compressed image. Depending on the lossy compression method used and the amount the file is compressed, the changes to the image may or may not be visible.

KEY WORDS

lossless compression: a method of compression where the decompressed image is identical to the original

lossy compression: a method of compression where the decompressed image is not identical to the original

---

REFLECTION

How will you remember the difference between lossless and lossy compression? Are there any examples of images you have seen, or particular features of images, that could help you remember?

19.5 Text

Text can be added to an image by selecting the Text tool. Text can be added horizontally or vertically. Click the `Text Tool`, then click in the location to add the text, followed by typing the text (see Figure 19.65).

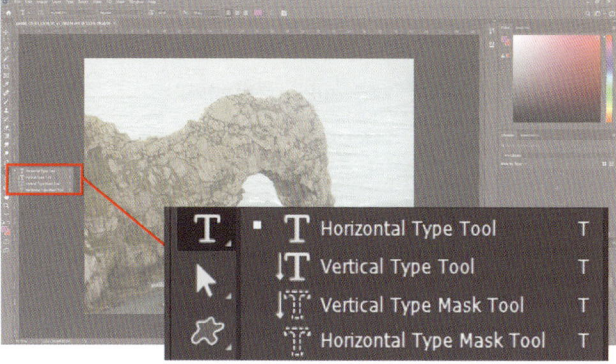

Figure 19.65: Text tool options.

Selecting font style

Font face and size

By clicking on text entered using the keyboard, the font face and size of the text can be changed. The font face and size options are displayed at the top of the screen (see Figure 19.66).

Figure 19.66: Inserted text and Text tool options.

Adobe Photoshop has a Character window with additional text options. Select `Window` and then `Character` if the Character window is not already open (see Figure 19.67).

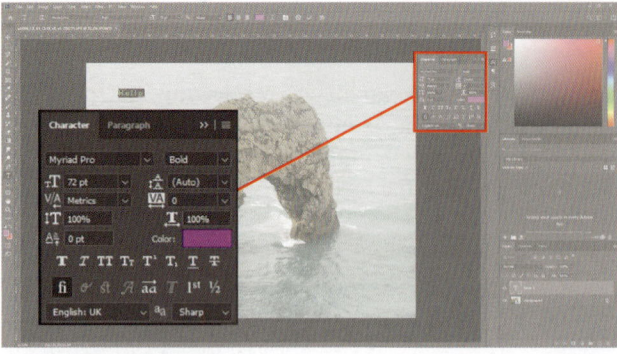

Figure 19.67: Inserted text and Character options.

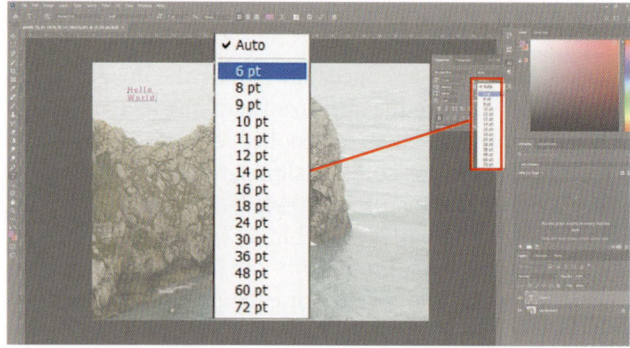

Figure 19.69: Inserted text and line spacing options.

Kerning, letter spacing and line spacing

The spacing between letters within a word can be altered within the Character window. Adobe Photoshop also enables **kerning** to be modified, which is the spacing applied to specific pairs of letters to make text more visually appealing and to improve readability (see Figure 19.68).

> **KEY WORD**
>
> **kerning:** changing the spacing between pairs of letters to improve the readability of text

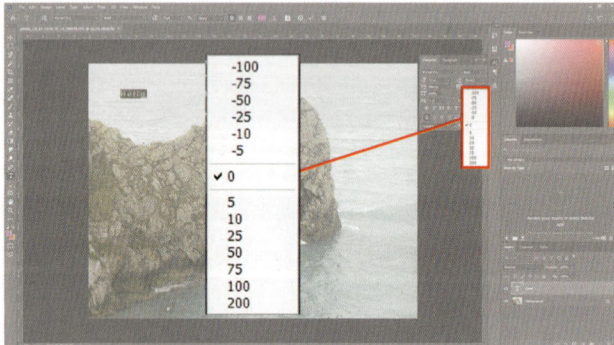

Figure 19.68: Inserted text and kerning options.

Changing the amount of space between lines is also available within the Character window (see Figure 19.69).

Fitting text to path or shape

Once text has been written, the text can be warped, such as by displaying the text in an arc. Choose the Create Warped Text option from the top menu and then choose the required shape from the Style menu, such as an Arc or a Flag. Change the settings to adjust the appearance of the shape (see Figure 19.70).

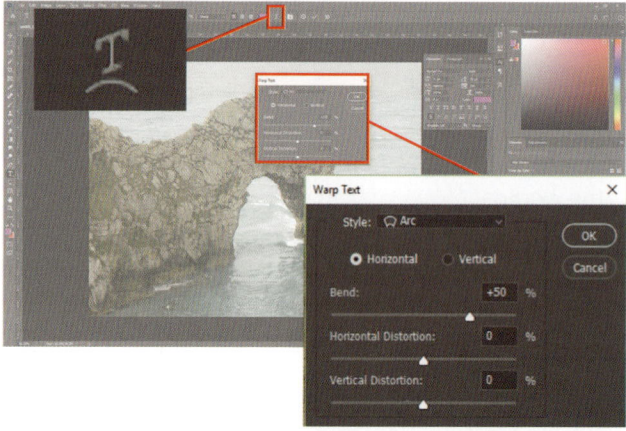

Figure 19.70: Warp text options.

Text can also be aligned to match a shape or along a line. Select an edge of a shape, or a line drawn using the Pen tool, then select the Horizontal Type tool. When moving the mouse to the shape edge or line, the cursor will change to a wavy line. Click the left mouse button and edit the default text displayed.

Setting text in a shape

To add text within a shape, the shape first needs to be drawn, such as by using the custom shape tool. Click the `Text Tool` and then click inside the shape, and the text typed will be located within the shape (see Figure 19.71).

Figure 19.71: Inserting text in a shape.

Converting text to curves

Text can be converted into an outline shape, such as a curve, which can then be manually manipulated. Select the text to convert, then from the top menu choose `Type` and then `Convert To Shape`. The text can now be modified in the same way as a shape (see Figure 19.72).

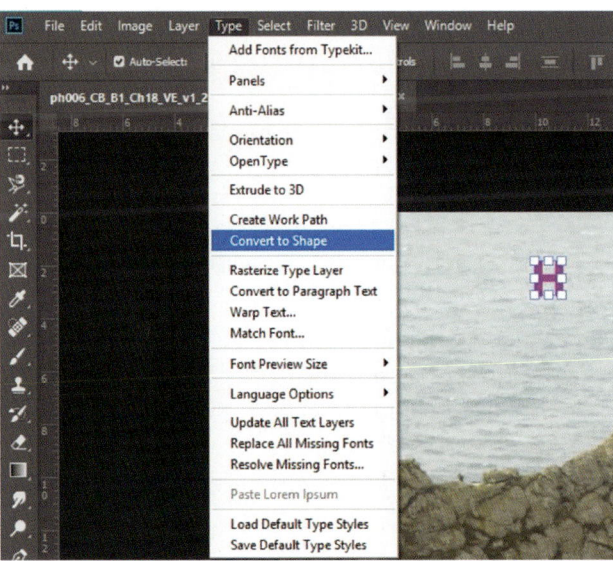

Figure 19.72: Converting text to shape option.

Use of text and its manipulation within graphics software

Text is often used within graphics software to add titles and labels to parts of an image. The tools available to manipulate text within graphics software enable the appearance and positioning of text to be altered in ways not possible with other software, such as word processors. In particular, as text can be converted into shapes, the range of tools available within the graphics software can also be used to manipulate text.

WORKED EXAMPLE 19.05

Figure 19.73: Finished logo.

Create the logo for Sunshine Holidays shown in Figure 19.73.

Select the colour yellow from the palette and draw an ellipse (see Figure 19.74).

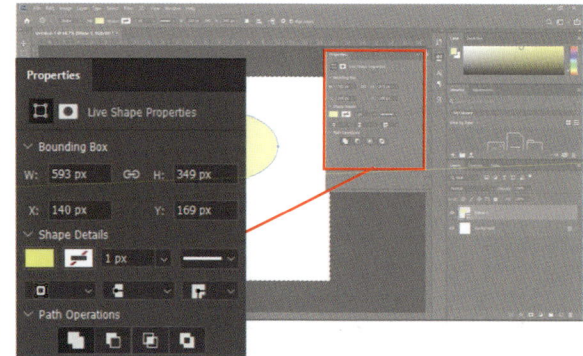

Figure 19.74: Selecting logo shape and colour.

CONTINUED

Enter the text Sunshine Holidays in black, select the Arc shape and then change the Bend value until it is how you want it to appear (see Figure 19.75).

Adjust the shapes until they are in the correct position.

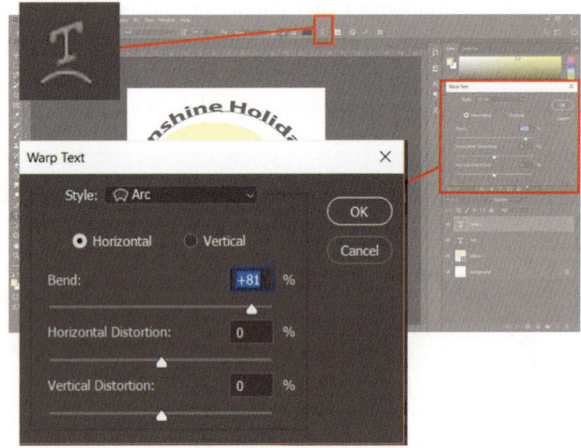

Figure 19.75: Inserting text with distortion sliders.

ACTIVITY 19.15

Draw a curved line, similar to that in Figure 19.76, above the trees in **19.01_ Background.jpg**. Give the image a title. Adjust the text properties so the title is in keeping with the rest of the image. For example, similar colours to those found elsewhere in the image could be used for the text, text size and colour, so it fits in with the scene.

Figure 19.76: Curved line.

ACTIVITY 19.16

Continue with the option you chose in Activity 19.10.

1   J.B. Garden Landscaping needs a bitmap image to be the faded background of their website. It should be made up of different plants including trees and flowers that have been combined from a range of images. Create the image and then fade it to 30% opacity.

2   Haven's Creations sells cakes and would like an image of a single cake to add to their logo. Extract an image of a cake and position it in an appropriate place on their logo.

3   Robson's Refreshments has launched a new juice drink, Robson's Berry Crush. The size of the juice drink label should be 20 cm wide by 6 cm high. There must be images of a range of berries and the name of the drink in an appropriate place.

4   Bhavin's Buildings would like a border for the bottom of their website that has a range of buildings that appear as a skyline. Create the skyline border.

PRACTICAL ACTIVITY 19.17

Plant Horizons is an online company that sells houseplants. They want the logo in Figure 19.77 to be created.

Figure 19.77: Finished logo.

1   First click on the arrow next to the Shape symbol. Select `Nature` from the options (see Figure 19.78).

2   Select a shade of green from the palette (see Figure 19.79).

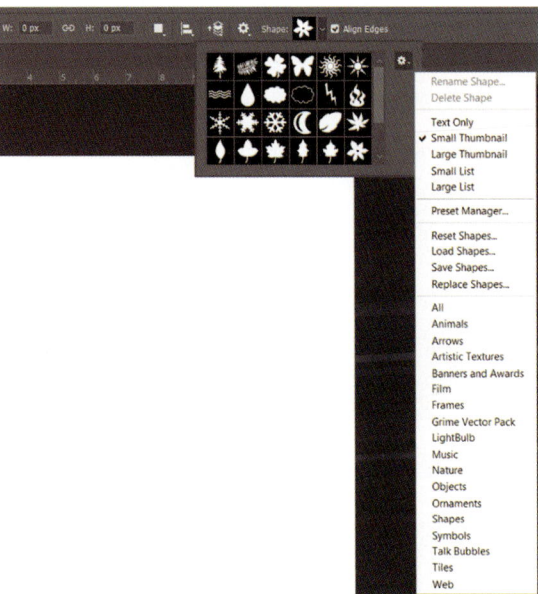

Figure 19.78: Selecting 'nature' shapes.

Figure 19.79: Selecting green shade.

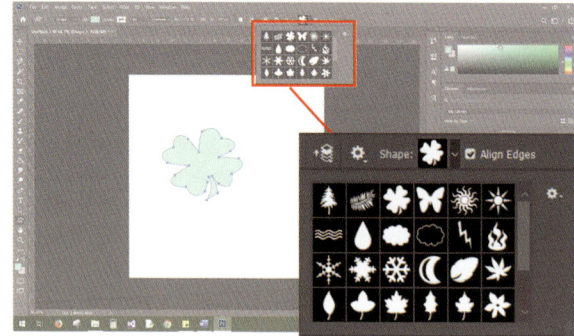

Figure 19.80: Selecting leaf shape.

3   Click on the Text tool to add the company name. Choose your font style and size from the top menu. Choose the colour black, and centre-align the text (see Figure 19.80).

4   Select the leaf and draw it on the screen (see Figure 19.81).

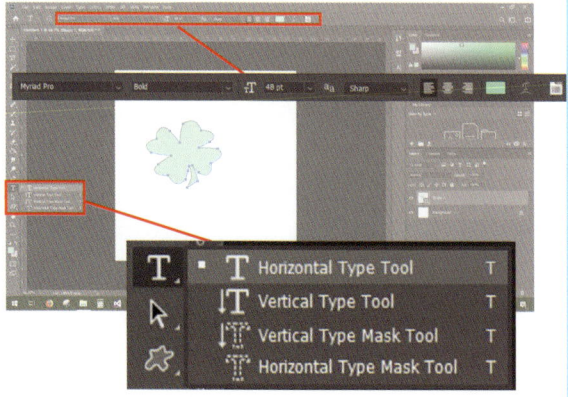

Figure 19.81: Selecting text options.

Figure 19.82: Flower images.

5   Type the company name, Plant Horizons.

Plant Horizons would also like the background image similar to Figure 19.82 creating for their website.

6   First, find three images with three different types of flower in. Make sure they are all different colours; that the images have the flower unobstructed (blocked) by another object; and that the flower is facing forward (towards you).

Figures 19.83a and 19.83b: These images would work well because the flowers are not obstructed by anything else and are facing forward.

Figure 19.84: The flowers in this image wouldn't be very useful because they are all overlapping and not facing forward.

7   Save the three images as jpegs.

8   Open your first flower image and select the Magnetic Lasso tool (see Figure 19.85).

9   Drag the tool around the image, click the left mouse button if it won't lock exactly where you want it to (see Figure 19.86).

Figure 19.85: Image of a pink flower.

Figure 19.86: Flower selected with the Magnetic Lasso tool.

CONTINUED

10   Copy the image and paste it into a new file that is 1000 pixels by 1000 pixels. Change the size of the image so it fits (see Figure 19.87).

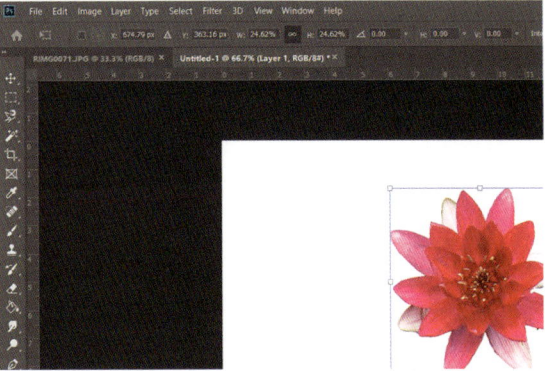

Figure 19.87: Selected flower image pasted into a new file.

Figure 19.88: Second flower added.

11   Open the image of your second flower and repeat the process. Change the opacity of both flowers to between 60 and 70% (see Figure 19.88).

12   Open the image of your third flower and repeat the process (see Figure 19.89).

Figure 19.89: Third flower added.

Figure 19.90: Exporting image.

13   Export the image as a gif (see Figure 19.90).

Challenge yourself

Make a logo for the business you set up in the Project at the end of Chapter 14 using the skills you have learnt in this chapter.

REFLECTION

Did this chapter contain any new terminology that you found difficult to understand or remember? What strategies could you use to help you? For example, you could focus on vector graphic terms first, or perhaps examine tools linked to certain image effects. Share your approach with a partner. Change your approach if you need to.

PRACTICE QUESTIONS

1   Titania's Televisions needs a new logo.

The company has asked for there to be a rectangular television with a gradient fill from top to bottom and a small triangular stand similar to this image:

The outline should be in dark blue, and no more than 4 pt thick.

The word Titania should be inside the television, in a sans-serif font, in an arc. The font colour should be green.

a   Create Titania's logo and save it as a vector graphic. It should be no more than 250 by 250 pixels.   [13]

b   Explain why a vector graphic is more appropriate for a logo than a bitmap image.   [4]

c   Explain how lossy compression can reduce the file size of an image.   [6]

[Total 23]

2   Kim's theme park needs an image for the homepage of her website.

a   Draw a rollercoaster using a rectangle and distort the top. Add six evenly spaced circles for wheels, and a black line to act as a track and as a rectangle. Inside this rectangle should be the word Rollercoaster in a green sans-serif font, set across an arc to follow the rollercoaster shape.   [15]

b   Suggest an appropriate file type to save the image. Justify your choice.   [3]

c   Explain the difference between the RGB and CMYK colour schemes.   [4]

[Total 22]

SUMMARY CHECKLIST

- [ ] I can work with layers to raise, lower, bring to front and order layers.
- [ ] I can use Transform tools to resize, skew, flip, rotate, move, scale and shear images.
- [ ] I can use grouping or merging tools to group, ungroup and flatten images.
- [ ] I can use alignment and distribution tools such as left, right, top and bottom alignment, and vertical and horizontal distributions.
- [ ] I can use layout tools such as rulers, grids, guidelines, snapping.
- [ ] I can use colour picker tools.
- [ ] I can use crop tools.
- [ ] I know and understand the properties of different colour systems (RGB, HSL, CMYK, CMS).
- [ ] I know and understand the need for different image resolutions (impact of too high/low resolution on an image on screen/in print).
- [ ] I know and understand how to select different bitmap and vector file formats (svg, bmp, jpg, png, gif, tif, pdf).
- [ ] I know and understand how to change the opacity of all or part of an image.
- [ ] I can create a vector image using vector drawing tools such as:.
  - [ ] freehand drawing, Bézier curves and straight lines
  - [ ] shape tools: rectangles, ellipses, circles, arcs, stars, polygons and spirals.
- [ ] I can create a vector image using selection tools to select parts of a vector image.
- [ ] I can create a vector image using fill tools to colour elements (including gradient fills).
- [ ] I can create a vector image using Node and Path editing such as:
  - [ ] adding and moving nodes
  - [ ] deleting nodes to simplify paths
  - [ ] using Bézier handles
  - [ ] align and distribute nodes.
- [ ] I can convert bitmap images into editable vector shapes.
- [ ] I know and understand the advantages and disadvantages of converting a bitmap image into an editable vector shape.
- [ ] I can create a bitmap image using selection tools to select parts of a bitmap image such as Lasso, Magic Wand, Colour Select tools.
- [ ] I can adjust colour levels in a bitmap image such as brightness, contrast, colour balance, shadows, highlights, convert to greyscale.
- [ ] I can use tools/filters to alter parts of a bitmap image, such as distort, clone, blue, sharpen and red eye removal.
- [ ] I can resize an image/canvas.
- [ ] I know and understand lossy and lossless compression.

CONTINUED

☐ I know how to change the colour depth and resolution of an image.

☐ I know and understand the effects of different methods of compression on images.

☐ I can select font style (face, size, kerning, letter spacing and line spacing).

☐ I can fit text to path or shape (aligning text along a line or around a shape).

☐ I can set text in a shape.

☐ I can convert text to curves (convert fonts into editable vector shapes).

PROJECT

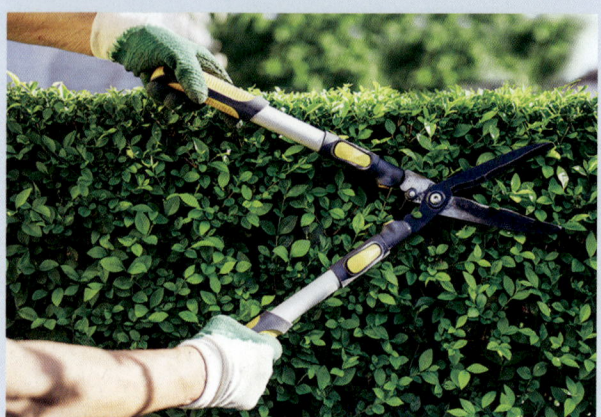

Figure 19.91: Trimming a hedge.

A local gardening company has asked for a new logo to be created. The logo should be based on an image of a leaf, with the company's name, 'Greenfingers', around the edge of the image.

The company would like vector graphics to be used, which will mean they can have separate image files produced to use the logo on their website and company vehicles.

1   Working in pairs, find a suitable photograph of a leaf, then trace the bitmap to create a vector graphic.

2   Once the leaf vector graphic has been created, make the image more visually appealing, such as by adding other garden related graphics, such as trees, plants or gardening tools. The text tools should be used to add the company name around the leaf shape.

3   Once the image has been completed, export the image into a file format suitable for use on the company's website, followed by a larger, high-quality image to use on the company vehicles.

> **Chapter 20**

Animation

LEARNING INTENTIONS

By the end of this chapter, you will be able to:

- create an animation (stop motion and key frame that meets the requirements of its intended application and audience
- configure the stage/frame/canvas for an animation
- import and create vector objects
- control object properties
- use inbetweening ('tweening') tools
- set paths
- use layers
- apply masks
- control animation
- understand the basic principles of animation
- understand the different animation types and methods
- understand the components of an animation
- understand the use of animation variables
- understand the advantages and disadvantages of different animation types.

Introduction

In this chapter, you will learn about **animation** and how to use the animation software Adobe Animate. You will learn about different types of animation and the components of an animation.

KEY WORD

animation: a series of images that are played one after another to simulate movement

Frames and key frames

An animation is made up of many individual images, known as frames. Small changes are made between each **frame** within an animation, which are then played very quickly, one after another, so that the subject looks like it is moving. Figure 20.1 shows a series of frames for a puffin landing.

Figure 20.1: A series of frames showing a puffin landing.

A **key frame** identifies the start or end point for an action within an animation. For example, when animating a person tripping over, a key frame might

be the person running upright, with the next key frame being the person laying on the ground.

KEY WORDS

frame: one screen, or page, where an image is drawn; a series of these frames are played quickly, one after the other, to create the animation

key frame: a frame identifying the start or end point for an action within an animation

Question

1   What is the difference between a frame and a key frame?

20.1 Different animation types and methods

There are many forms of animation. It can often be difficult to determine the animation method used. All animations use the basic principle of rapidly showing a number of frames, one after the other.

Cel animation

Cel (celluloid) animation was the first type to be developed. This involves individually drawn frames, which are usually drawn by hand. Each object within the

KEY WORD

cel animation: (also called cell animation) individual images are drawn on separate sheets, then layered on top of one another. The images are photographed, one frame at a time

animation, such as a character, is drawn on a separate medium, such as a transparent celluloid sheet, which is filled in with colour. Each sheet is then layered on top of each other, with a photograph taken to create a frame. The images appear as an animation when viewed quickly in succession. Cel animation can contain thousands, or even millions, of individual frames.

Stop motion

Stop motion animation is where objects are made of physical materials and have photographs taken of them in different positions. By making small changes to the positions of the objects and taking a photograph each time, the images can then be viewed as an animation. Films and TV programmes are often made using this technique (see Figure 20.2).

> **KEY WORD**
>
> **stop motion animation:** photographs are taken of physical objects; the objects are moved slightly each time and the photographs combined to create the animation

Figure 20.2: Stop motion animation.

ACTIVITY 20.01

Find a physical object that can have its appearance easily changed, such as a character made out of modelling clay or plastic building blocks. Take a photo of the object and keep the camera in the same position. Make a small change to the character's appearance, such as moving an arm a small amount upwards, then take another photo from exactly the same location. Repeat this process and aim to take 10–20 photos in total. The photos will later be combined to make a stop frame animation.

Time lapse

Time lapse is a form of photography, where a camera is set up and automatically takes a photograph at set-time intervals, such as once every minute. The photographs are then shown in sequence to create an animation of what has happened. It is often used for events that take place over a long time, such as a plant growing (see Figure 20.3).

> **KEY WORD**
>
> **time lapse:** a camera automatically takes a photograph every set period, such as once a minute, and these are combined to create an animation

Figure 20.3: Time-lapse photography.

Flip book

A **flip book animation** is similar to a cel animation in that each frame is drawn individually and usually by hand. In a flip book, the images are drawn with each frame on a new page. The pages are then turned by hand very quickly, so that the images appear to move (see Figure 20.4).

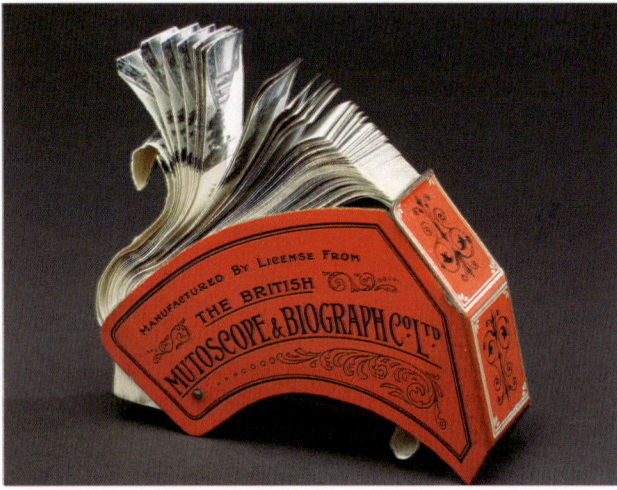

Figure 20.4: Flip book animation.

UNPLUGGED ACTIVITY 20.02

Create a ten-frame flip book animation for a simple character, such as a stick person. For example, the stick person could start with their legs together, then be drawn to make it look like they are walking across the page (see Figure 20.5).

Figure 20.5: Stick person.

CGI, 2D and 3D

CGI stands for computer-generated imagery. This refers to any images, whether still or moving, that are created using a computer (see Figure 20.6). These could be **2D (two dimensional)**, with the images drawn using a computer on the x and y axes without any depth. CGI 2D animations are often cartoons. CGI can also be **3D (three dimensional)**, with objects developed and manipulated (having their appearance changed) using a computer. When people say, or hear, CGI, they often automatically think about 3D animations, such as those seen in feature length animated films.

KEY WORDS

flip book animation: each page of a book that has a different image drawn on; when flicked through, they create an animation

CGI: an abbreviation of computer-generated imagery; any image (still or moving) that is created using a computer

2D (two dimensional): only on the x and y axes, for example a traditional cartoon

3D (three dimensional): has x, y and z axes, with objects having depth

Figure 20.6: Computer-generated imagery (CGI).

Advantages and disadvantages of different animation types

Method	Advantage	Disadvantage
Cel animation	Complete control over each component of the animation. Layers can be quickly moved and changed. Can be created without using a computer.	Time consuming to draw objects by hand. Errors within drawings or movement can be difficult to correct. More limited ranged of movement and effects compared with CGI.
Stop motion	Can be inexpensive to produce. Range of objects can be easily manipulated, such as modelling clay or toy figures.	Small movements of models can be challenging. Mistakes within the animation can be difficult to change.
Time lapse	Taking of photographs can be automated. Can be used to capture natural phenomena, such as a flower blooming.	Equipment needs to be reliable. May need to take place over a long time for changes to be noticeable.
Flip book	Only requires a pencil and book/paper to produce. Convenient to take from one location to another.	Time consuming to draw each frame individually. Additional frames cannot be easily inserted. Usually lasts for a short period of time.
CGI (2D/3D)	Can automate movement of objects. Greater range of effects can be used compared with other methods, such as gradually changing from one image into another (morphing). Changes can easily be made, including correcting mistakes and experimenting with different tools and techniques.	May require expensive equipment. Software can be time consuming and challenging to learn. Objects can be complex to develop before they can be animated, particularly in 3D.

Table 20.1: Advantages and disadvantages of different animation types.

You will need to carefully consider which type of animation to use, as there are a number of advantages and disadvantages to each method, as shown in Table 20.1.

Questions

2   Describe cel animations.

3   What is a time-lapse animation?

4   How do you create a stop frame animation?

5   Name the animation that involves drawing an image in a book and then changing the image.

6   What does CGI stand for?

20.2 Software tools for creation and editing of animations

Software tools can be used to create animations for a range of applications, or purposes, and audiences. An animation's purpose and audience should be carefully considered to ensure their requirements and needs are met. For example, an animation to show safety information to adults before an aeroplane flight should clearly display all information without distraction and the viewer should be made aware of what they need to do in an emergency. For an animation to advertise a children's television programme, the characters within

ratios depending on what the animation is used for. For example, if producing a film for widescreen televisions, an appropriate aspect ratio needs to be selected so the animation does not appear incorrectly. It is important to consider where your animation is most likely to be viewed when setting up the stage, which will enable you to decide on a suitable aspect ratio. When starting a project in Adobe Animate some common options are displayed to choose from (see Figure 20.10).

Common aspect ratios are shown in Table 20.2.

Ratio	Description
4:3	This is the aspect ratio used in older televisions, so is rarely used now. It is 4 units wide to 3 units high. The stage could be 2000 pixels wide by 1500 pixels high.
16:9	This is the ratio that is currently most widely used for TV. It is also commonly used in computer monitors and laptops. It is 16 units wide to 9 units high. The stage could be 1600 pixels wide by 900 pixels high.
2.35:1	This is widescreen and used for films. It is 2.35 units wide to 1 unit high.
16:10	This is commonly used for smart phone displays. It is 16 units wide to 10 units high.

Table 20.2: Common aspect ratios.

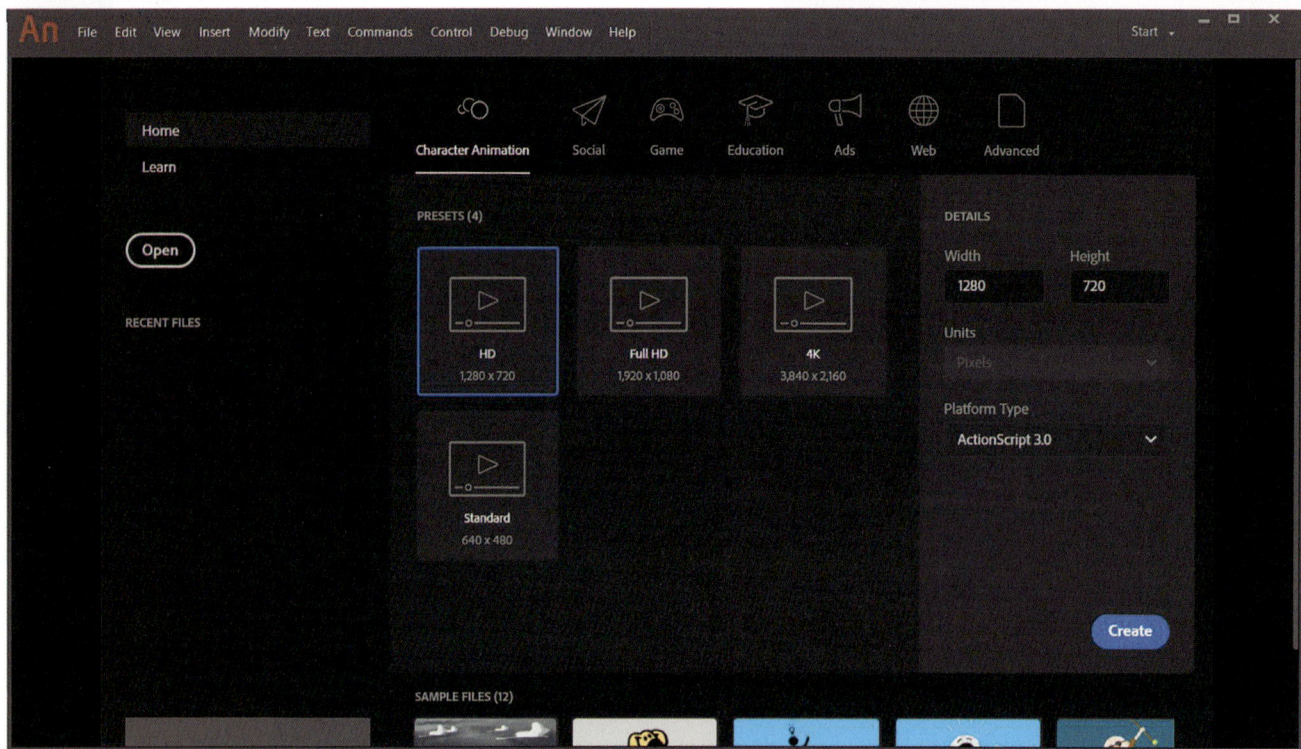

Figure 20.10: Common aspect ratio options when starting a project.

Using rulers, guides, grid settings and snapping options

The stage has several features that can help lay out animations.

Rulers enable the size and position of items to be viewed. Rulers can be turned on and off by clicking `View` from the top menu, then clicking `Rulers`.

The **grid** option displays a grid on the background of the stage. This can help align objects to the same gridline. To turn the grid on or off, click `View` from the top menu, then `Grid` and then `Show Grid`. The grid can be altered, such as by changing the size of the grid's squares or how it is displayed, by selecting `Edit Grid`, which brings up a menu. In Figure 20.11, there is 1 grid line for every 10 pixels, although this can be increased or decreased.

KEY WORDS

ruler: a tool that lets the position of items be viewed on the screen and helps draw them to the correct size

grid: a tool that displays a grid on the background of the screen to help with alignment

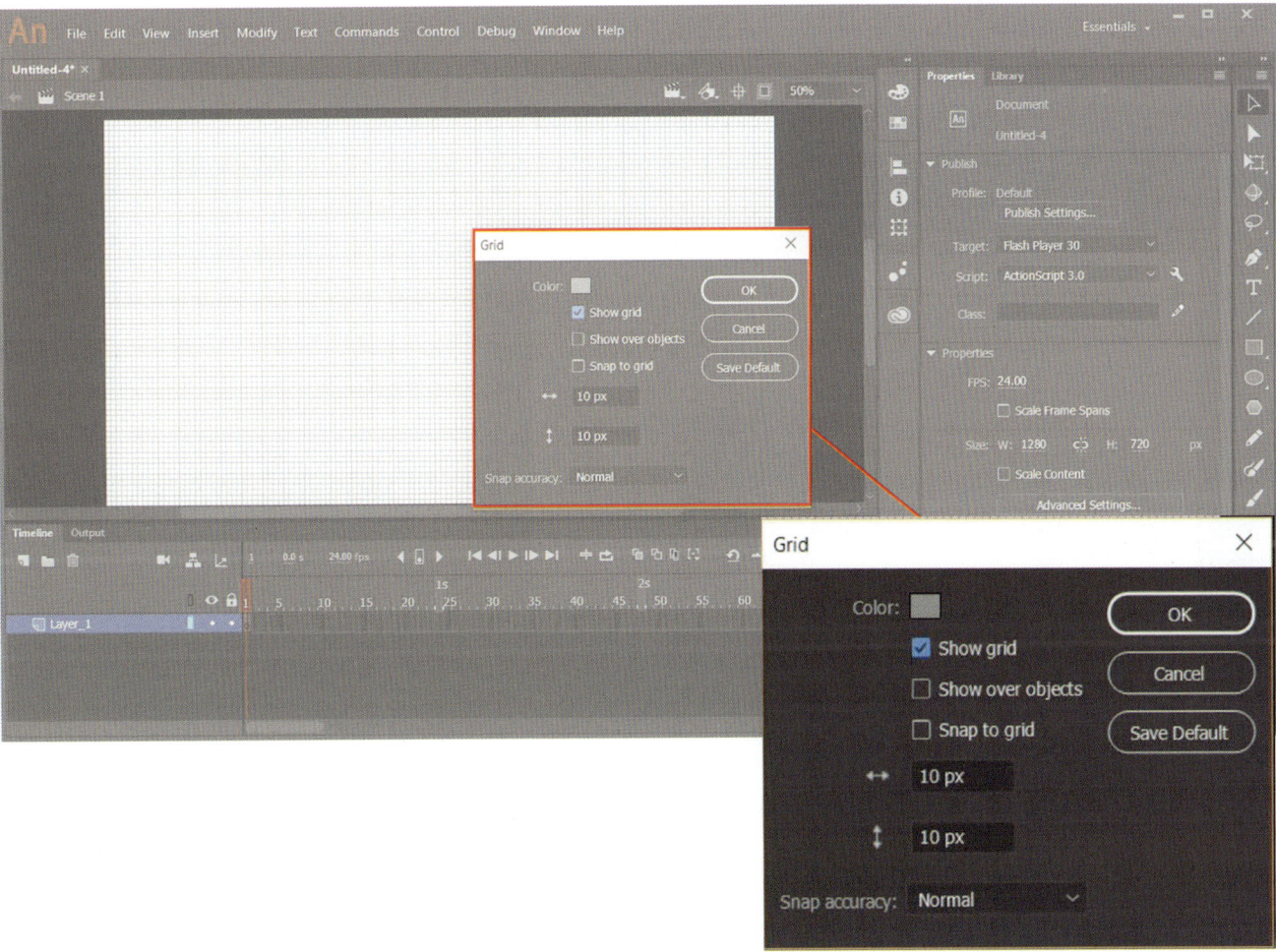

Figure 20.11: Grid options.

The **snapping** option, `Snap to grid`, makes sure all objects align to one of the grid lines by slightly adjusting their position if required.

Other snapping options can be accessed from the `View` menu. These allow Adobe Animate to align objects automatically to:

- display lines from the object to let you line it up with other elements, using the option `Snap Align`

- other objects, using `Snap to Objects`

- specific pixels or lines of pixels, using `Snap to Pixels`.

Guides can also be added to the stage. Guides are lines that can be positioned to help you line up your objects. Turn on guides by selecting `View` from the top menu, then select `Guides` and then `Show Guides`.

The lines are then dragged down from the top of the screen, as shown by the green arrows in Figure 20.12. The red lines are the guides that then appear. You can change the colour of the guide lines by choosing `Edit Guides` from the `Guides` menu.

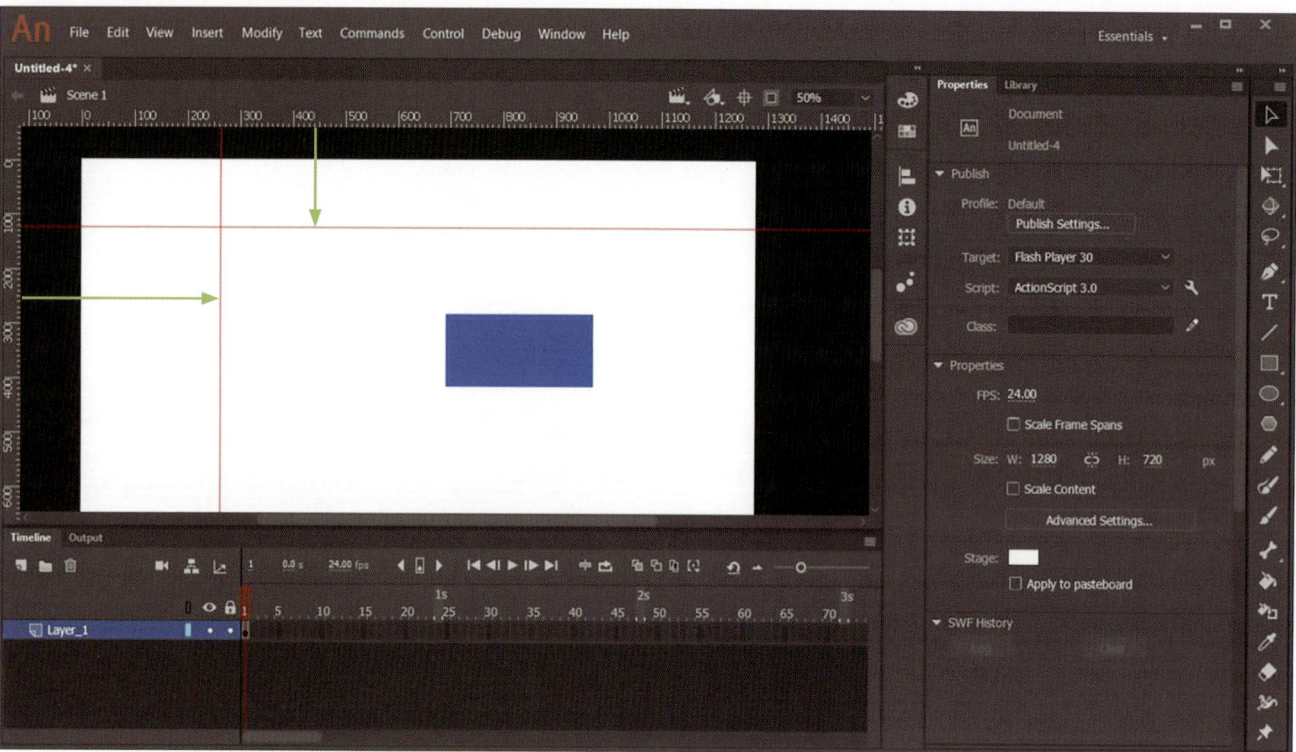

Figure 20.12: Positioning guides.

Questions

7 What is a frame in animation?

8 Describe what a ratio of 4:3 means and when is it used.

9 Name two other common ratios and when they are used.

10 Explain the purpose of rulers, grids and guides.

11 Explain the advantage(s) of using snapping.

Importing and creating vector objects

To move and manipulate objects within an animation, each object is named, which is known as a **symbol**. Figure 20.13 shows how to name a symbol. If required, multiple objects can be grouped together into one symbol. To convert a selection to a symbol, use the selection tool, then right click the item. Choose `Convert to Symbol`, then give the symbol a suitable name.

All symbols appear in the **library**, which is a record of all the symbols in the animation. New instances of a symbol can be created by dragging its name onto the stage. Up to 20 instances of the same symbol can be created and animated separately, although if one symbol is altered, the rest will also change.

Vector graphics are based on mathematical equations to determine the image's points, lines and curves, rather than using individual pixels, which means they can be resized without pixelating or reducing the quality of the image. There is more information about vector graphics in Chapter 19, Graphics creation.

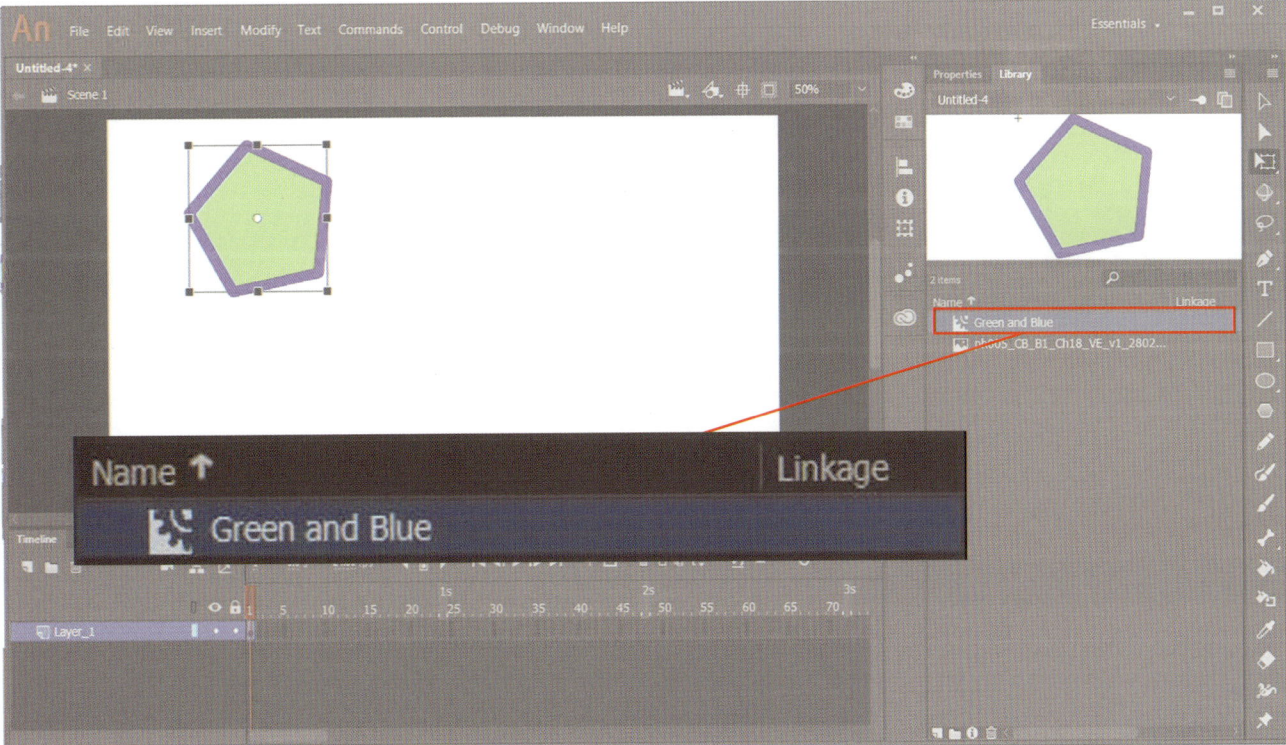

Figure 20.13: Naming a symbol.

Tracing bitmaps

Existing images, such as a photograph, can be imported into the library, or onto the stage. To import an image, click `File` from the top menu bar, then `Import` and either `Import to Stage` or `Import to Library`. Find the image and click `Open` to import it.

Bitmaps cannot be animated like vector graphics, as they are not made of coordinates and calculations. They might also pixelate when enlarged. To try to prevent this, bitmap images can be converted into a vector graphic. This is called **tracing bitmaps**.

A disadvantage of exporting to a vector graphic is that some of the detail is lost. For example, if the image is a photograph, then it might not appear exactly as the original. It will also not be possible to edit the image in the same way, such as by using the bitmap image manipulation tools.

To trace a bitmap, first drag the bitmap image from the library onto the stage, as shown in Figure 20.14.

With the object selected, select `Modify` from the top menu, and then `Bitmap`, then `Trace Bitmap`.

Within the options shown on screen, as shown in Figure 20.15, the lower the colour threshold, the more accurate it will be. Adobe Animate will usually give the most appropriate threshold automatically. Click `OK` and then the bitmap will be turned into a vector. Sections of the image can be selected and manipulated independently.

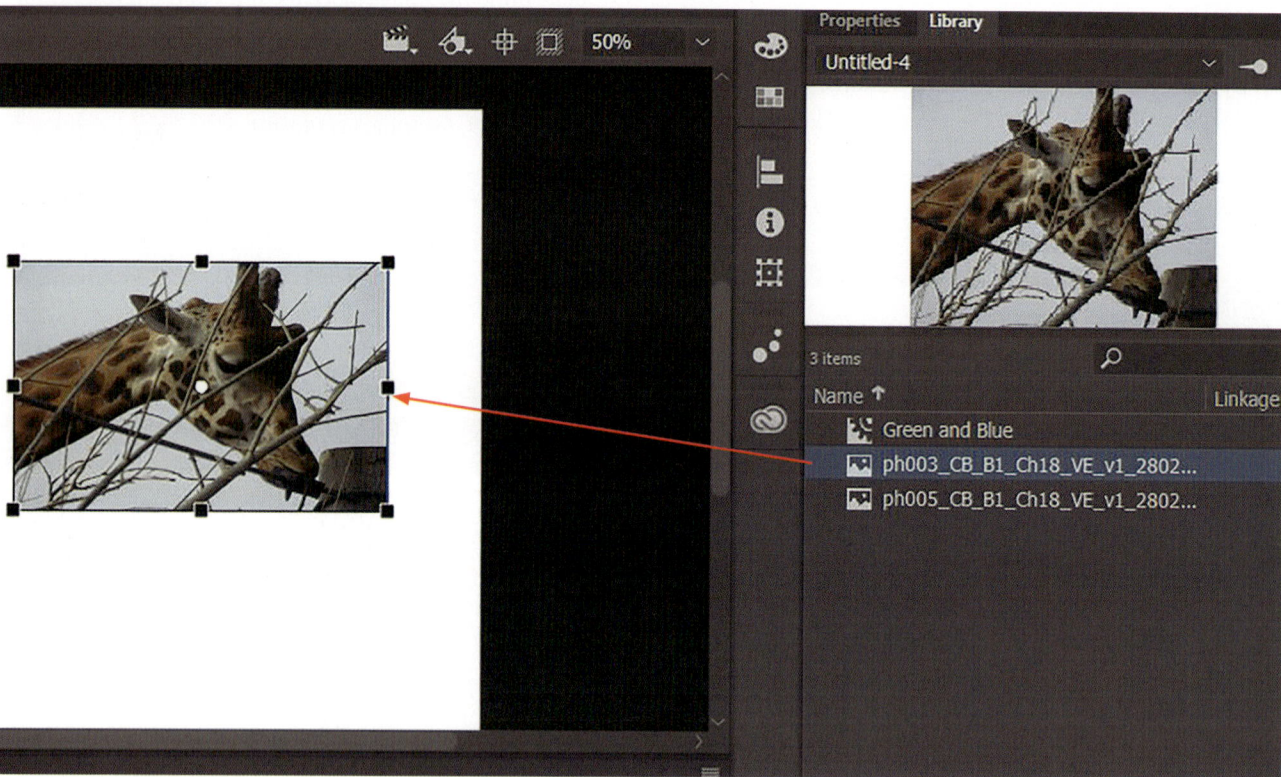

Figure 20.14: Getting an image from the library.

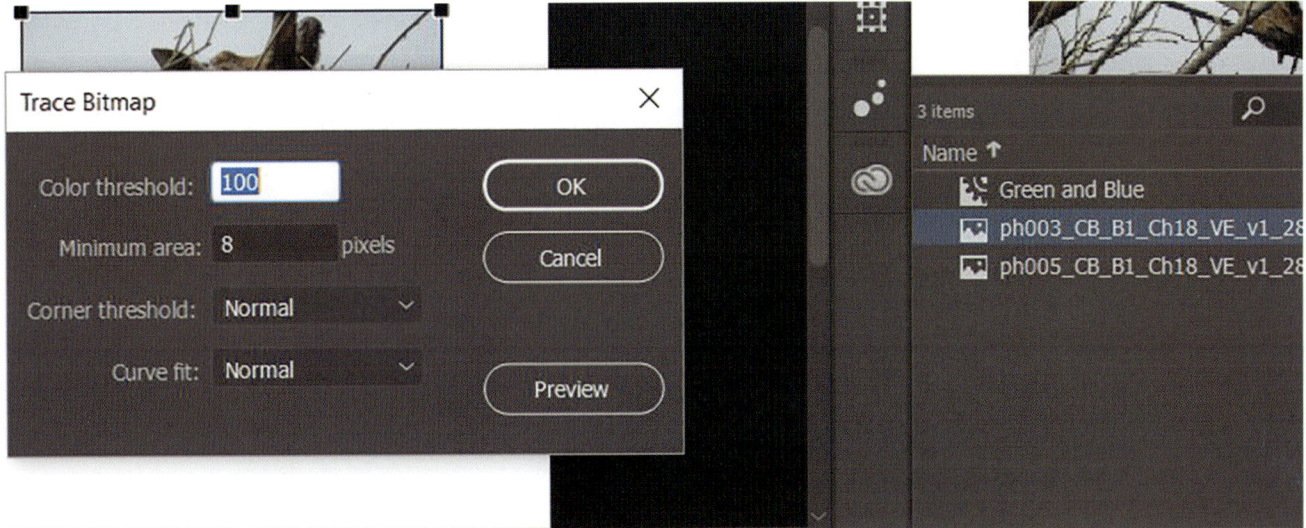

Figure 20.15: Bitmap manipulation options.

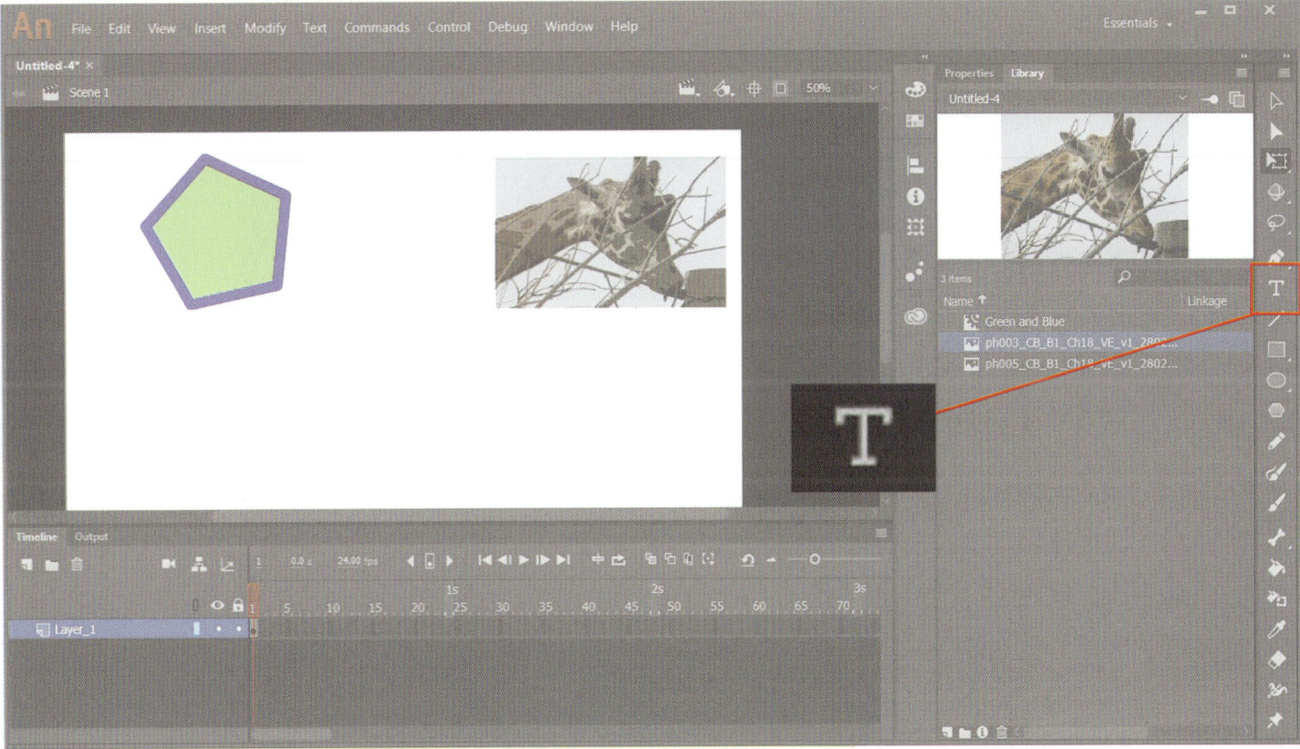

Figure 20.16: Text tool button.

Adding text

Text can be added to the stage using the text tool, which lets you edit the style, size and colour. Text is treated in the same way as objects, so you can change the opacity (lack of transparency) and manipulate the object in the same way as vector images.

To add text, click the T on the toolbar (see Figure 20.16), then click on the stage where you want the text to appear.

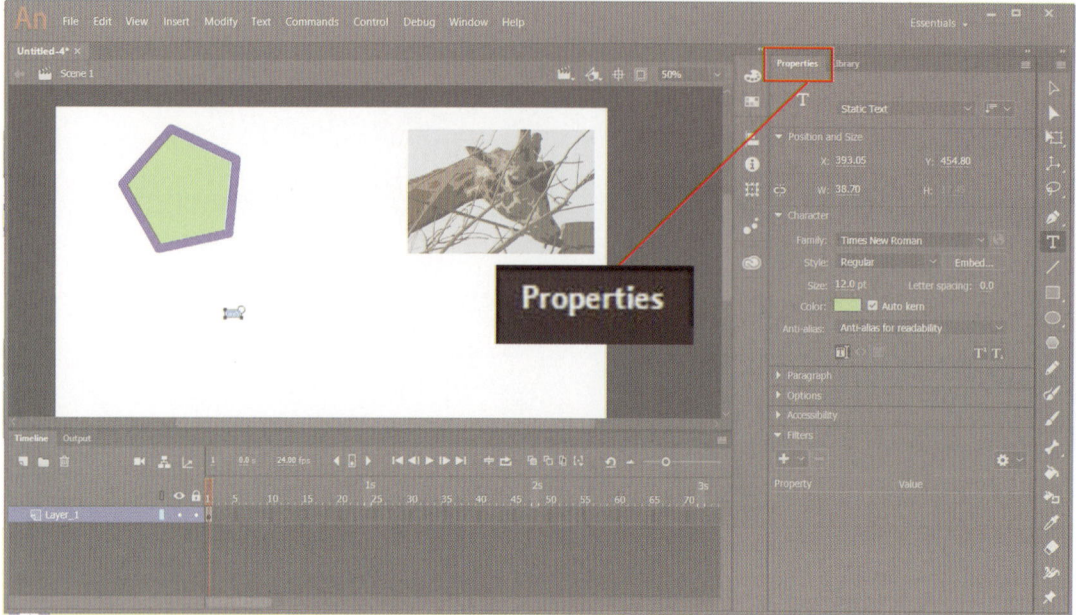

Figure 20.17: Text properties options.

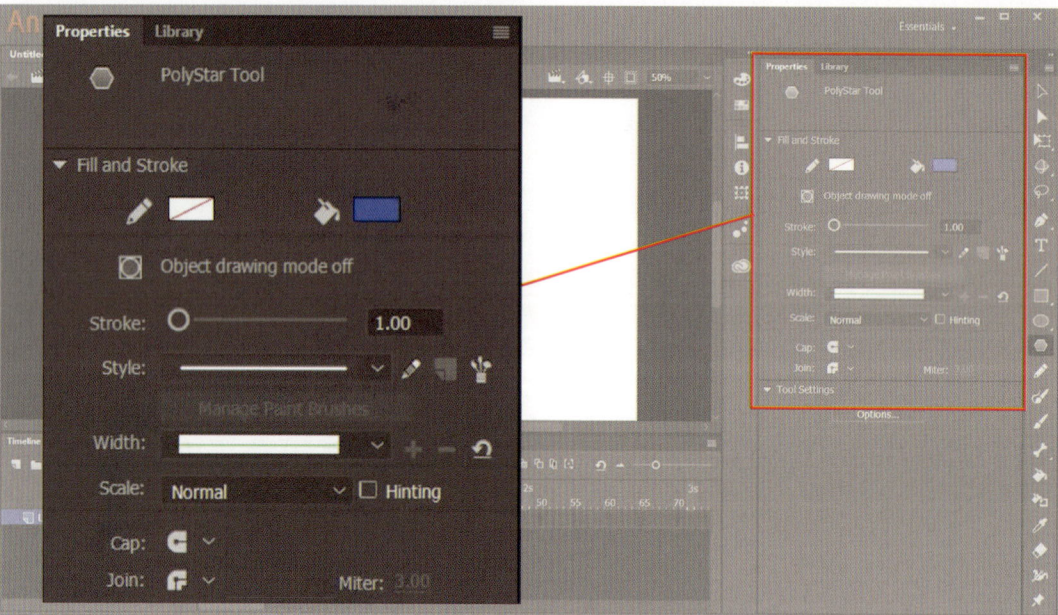

Figure 20.18: Properties options.

Click Properties to change properties, such as the font name, size and colour (see Figure 20.17).

Controlling object properties

The side toolbar has a range of shapes you can use to create vector graphics. Clicking one of the shapes brings up its Properties menu, where you can select various options, such as fill colours, line colours, size and style, before drawing the shape or line on screen (see Figure 20.18).

Fill and stroke settings

The `Line` and `Fill` options are accessed by clicking on them independently (see Figure 20.19).

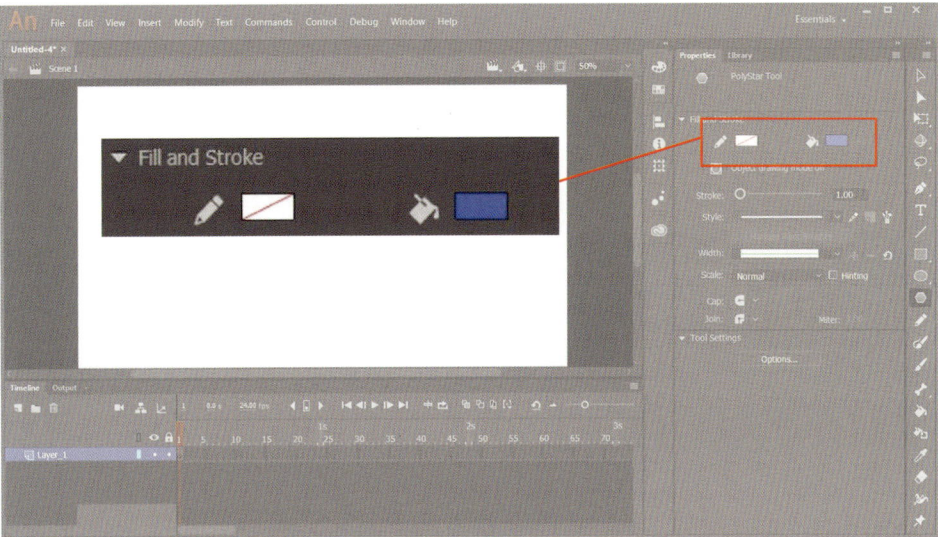

Figure 20.19: Line and fill options.

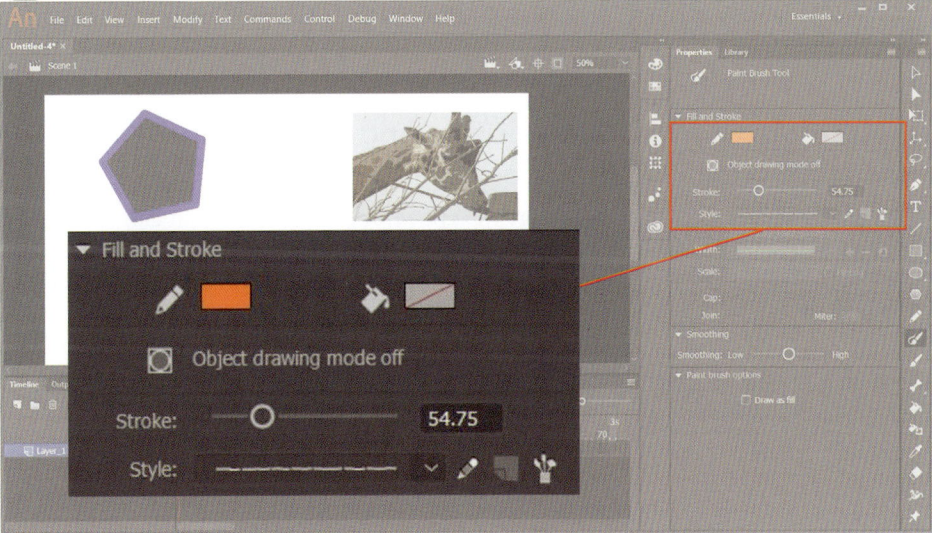

Figure 20.20: Fill and stroke options.

The menu to choose the colour will then appear. Select the colour from the block.

When an image is selected using a drawing tool, there are additional properties to choose from.

For example, for the paint brush tool, the `Stroke` option is the size of the line you will draw and there are a range of styles that produce different patterns (see Figure 20.20). There is only a line colour option as the paint brush tool only draws lines; it does not draw shapes to fill.

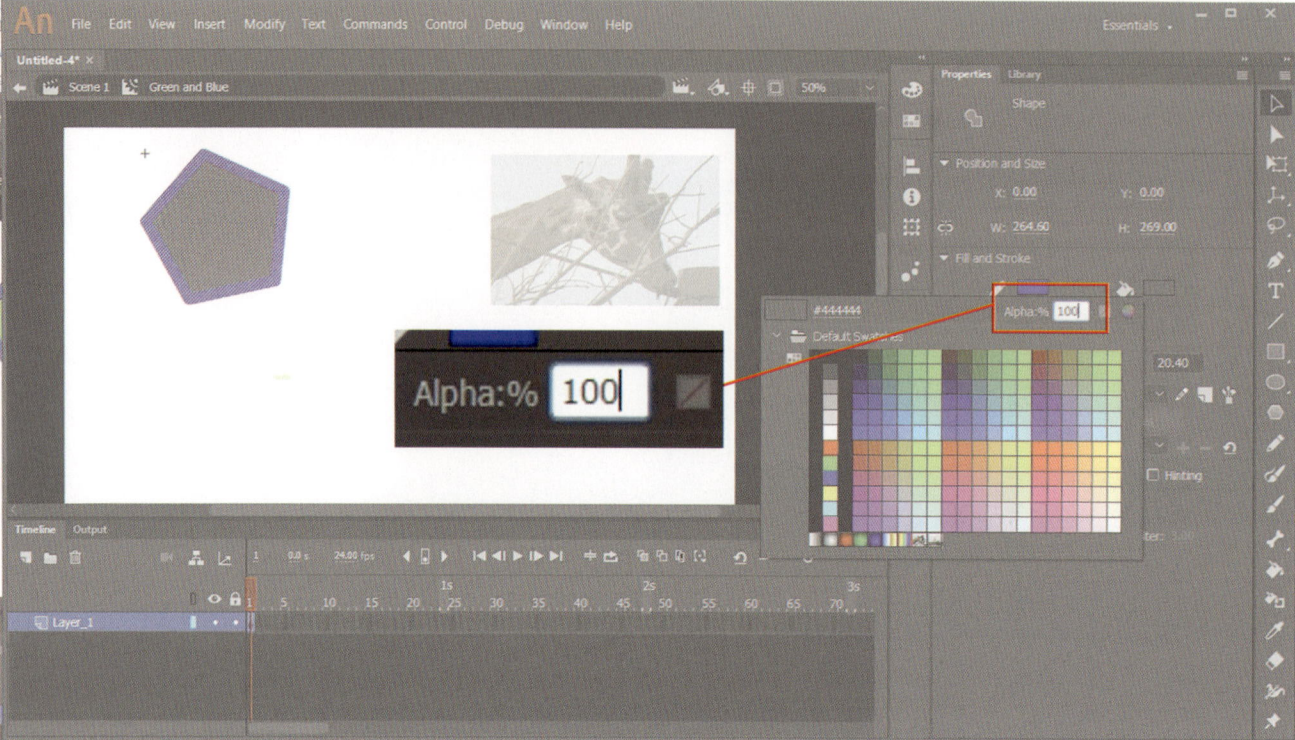

Figure 20.21: Opacity (Alpha %).

Transparency

The transparency of an object or a piece of text can be changed. In graphics software, this may be referred to as the opacity or the alpha channel. This is measured as a percentage: 0% opacity will lead to a fully transparent, invisible image, while at 100%, the image is fully visible with no transparency.

The visibility of an object can be set when it is created. It can also be manipulated during an animation to make objects appear and disappear. To change the opacity of an image, select its `Properties` and go into `Fill` options, as shown in Figure 20.21.

Size position and orientation (transforming)

To change the appearance of an image, it can be **transformed**. Transform allows the size of the object to be changed, rotated, or have its centre point changed (so it can rotate from a different place on the object). Use the selection tool to select the object to change (hold down `Shift` and click to select more than one object). Right click on the item, select `Transform` and then `Free Transform`. These options can also be accessed independently from the `Transform` menu, as shown in Figure 20.22.

KEY WORD

transform: changing the dimensions, rotation, colour fill, opacity, etc. of an object over a certain number of frames between two key frames

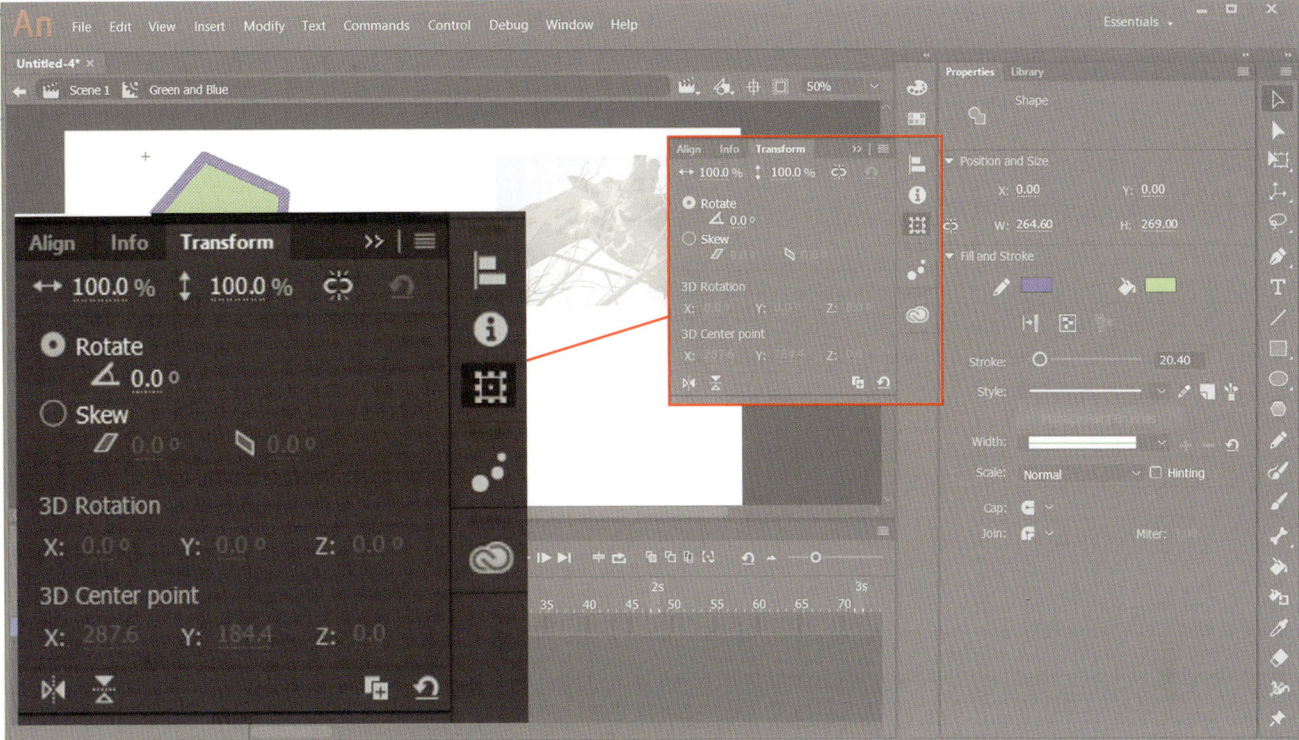

Figure 20.22: Transform options.

Questions

12   Describe how vector graphics are made.

13   What is the difference between line and fill colours?

14   Which option do you select to rotate a shape or object?

Setting paths

The route a symbol takes when moving around the stage is known as a **path**. Defining a path enables frames to be automatically generated between start and end points, which is discussed in more detail when examining inbetweening ('tweening') tools next.

Using layers

An animation is made up of **layers**. Each layer has its own set of frames that can be animated independently. Without layers, the entire image would need to be manipulated within each frame, rather than separate parts.

For example, if a stick person is to be animated to look like they are walking, the elements that need to be separate might be:

- left arm
- right arm
- left leg
- right leg
- head
- body

These elements might need to be separated further. Depending on the level of detail required, 'left arm' may need to be 'upper left arm' and 'lower left arm'.

Each layer is shown on the **timeline** and needs to be given an appropriate name to describe its function.

> **KEY WORDS**
>
> **path:** route a symbol takes when moving around the stage
>
> **layer:** an object or image within an animation containing its own frames, which can be manipulated independently
>
> **timeline:** the place that controls the order the frames are run, along with timings and the positioning of the layers

To create a new layer, click `Insert` and then `Timeline`, then `Layer`. To change its name, double click the layer name beside the timeline and change the text.

Folders can also be created for layers. Complex animations may have hundreds of layers, so related layers can be grouped together. For example, consider the stick person walking animation. A folder called 'stick_person' could be created, with all the layers for that person in the folder. A separate folder could then be created for other layers, such as those for the background.

To create a folder, click `Insert`, then `Timeline`, select `Layer Folder`. Layers can be dragged into the folder and double clicked to rename.

The timeline is made up of frames in chronological order from left to right, as shown in Figure 20.23. Each small rectangle represents a frame, with a filled grey rectangle showing how many frames where the symbol will be displayed.

If there is no rectangle for a layer in a specific frame (for example, frame 30), then the items in that frame do not exist when that frame is displayed. In Figure 20.24, 'blue_oval' does not have a frame beyond frame 10, whereas 'green_rectangle' has frames up to frame 15. This means on the current frame selected (frame 15 as shown by the red rectangle on the number 15), only the 'green_rectangle' is visible.

It is important to also order symbols using layers. The symbol in the highest layer in the timeline is in front of all the others.

In Figure 20.25, the layer 'blue_oval' is at the top, and on the stage it appears in front of the green rectangle.

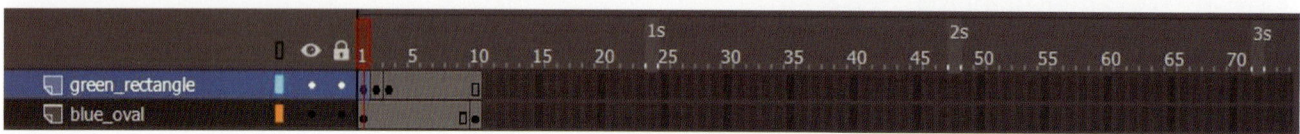

Figure 20.23: Timelines.

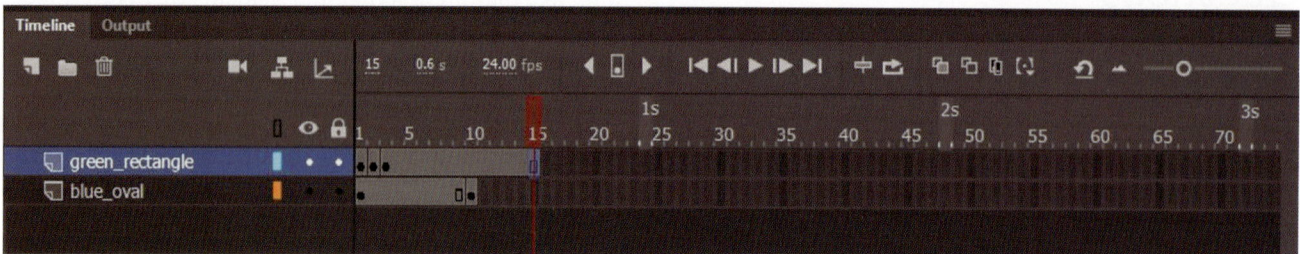

Figure 20.24: Green rectangle timeline.

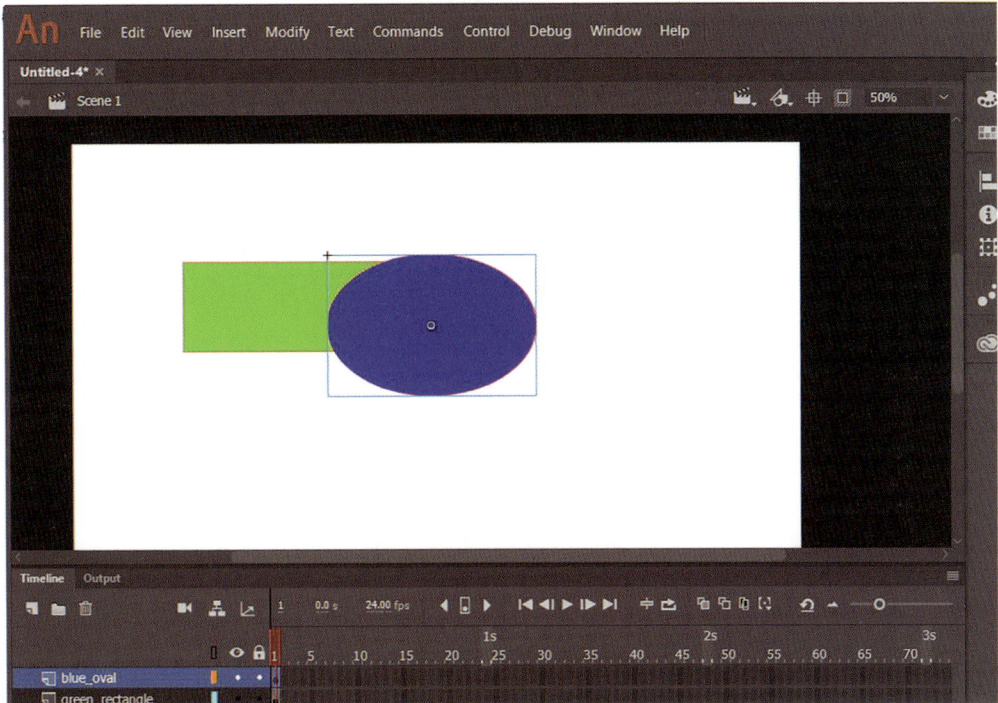

Figure 20.25: Blue oval in own layer overlapping the rectangle.

If the layers are swapped in the timeline, their order will be reversed on the stage. The green rectangle is now in front, as shown in Figure 20.26.

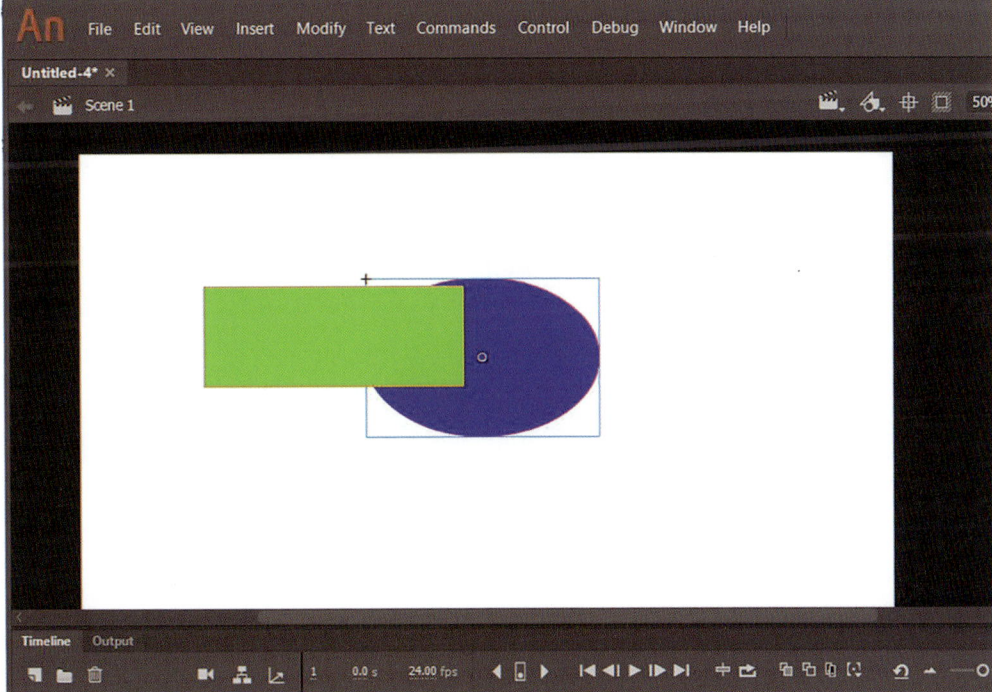

Figure 20.26: Order of layers swapped so that there is no deletion of part of the rectangle.

Questions

15 What is a layer?

16 Why are layers used in animation?

Inbetweening ('tweening')

An animation created solely with frames and key frames can be quite robotic unless very small changes are made between each key frame. Making changes like this can be time consuming. By inserting an 'inbetween' animation (also referred to as simply a tween), the computer can generate the animation automatically by filling in the spaces in between key frames. For example, if moving a drawing of a fish across the screen, the start location (A) and end location (B) can be set as key frames, with the computer determining the required movement to get the fish from A to B.

Key frames are represented by a dot in the frame on the timeline, as shown in Figure 20.27.

For example, 'green_rectangle' is in one position in frame 1. It then changes in frame 2, and frame 3; it then does not change again. 'blue_oval' is created in frame 1; it does not change then until frame 10.

To add frames and key frames, right click the frame to add a frame or key frame, then choose `Insert Frame` (or `Insert Keyframe`) from the menu.

When applying a tween to a layer, it will affect every item in that layer, so it is important to make sure that each individual item has its own layer.

There are two types of tween: motion and shape (including size and colour).

Motion tween

A motion tween only deals with the movement of an object, such as moving from one place to another, and its rotation.

To create a motion tween in Adobe Animate, the item you tween needs to be set as a symbol before starting to move it. Create the first key frame with the symbol in its starting position and add frames up to the point where the tween should end (see Figure 20.28).

Figure 20.27: Key frame dots.

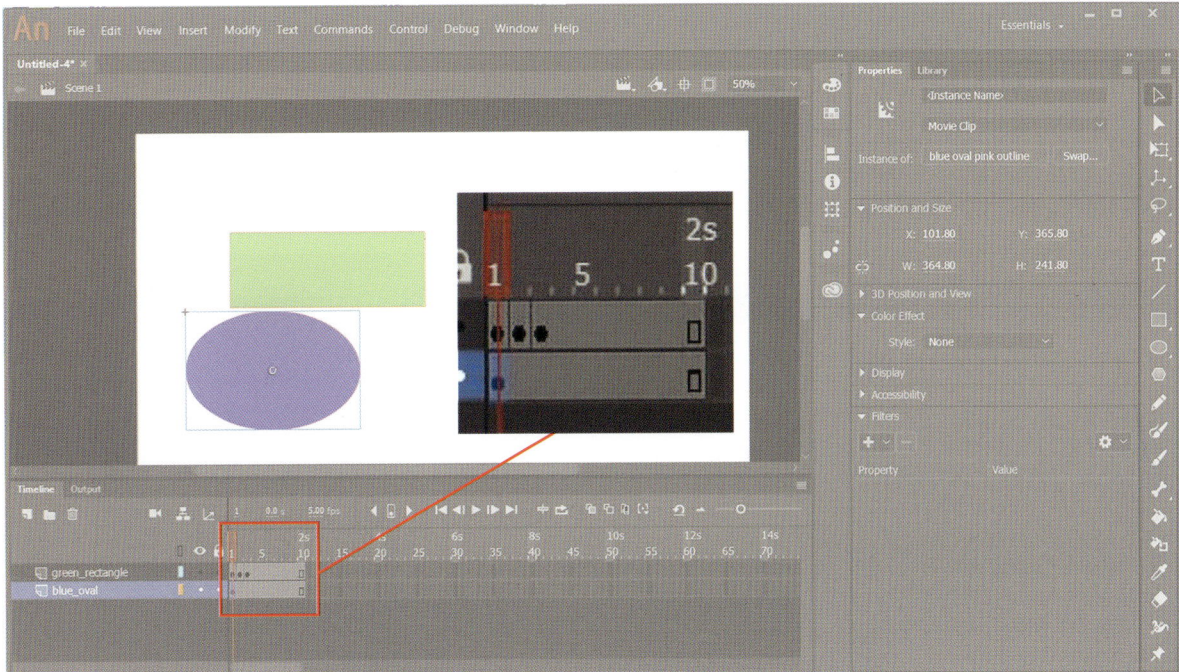

Figure 20.28: Starting a motion tween.

Then, right click the added frames and select `Create Motion Tween`.

Insert a key frame in the frame where the animation should end and then, with this frame selected, move the object to the end position (see Figure 20.29). The object can also be rotated if required.

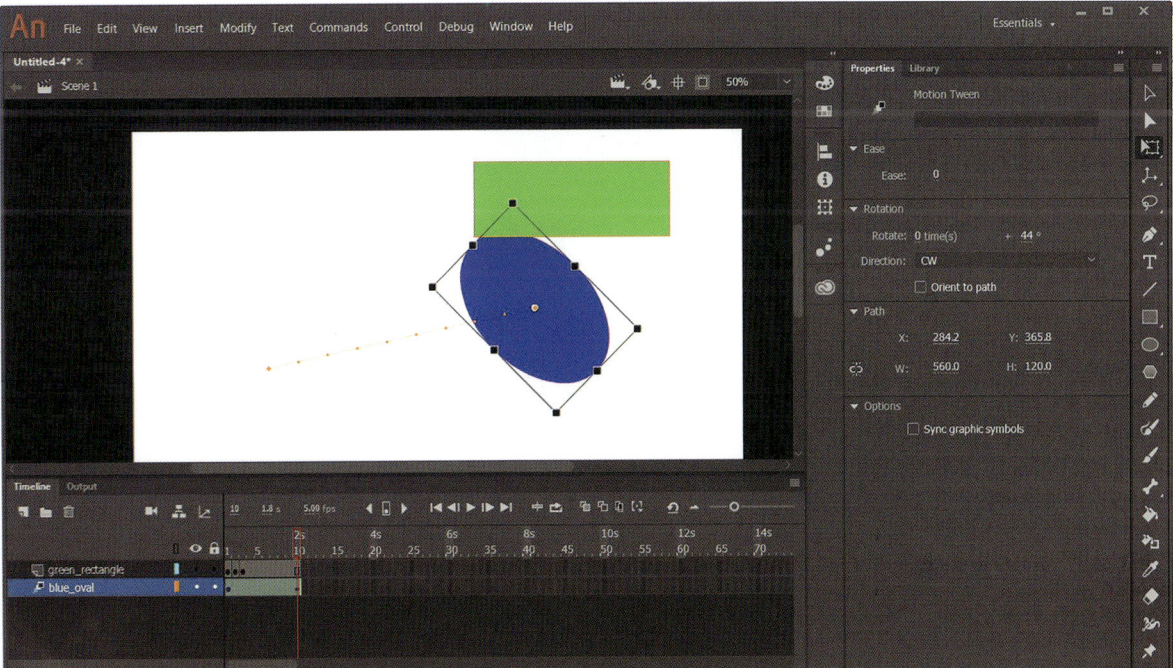

Figure 20.29: End of motion tween.

WORKED EXAMPLE 20.01

In this example, we will create an animation where a red circle moves to each corner of the screen using inbetweening.

Rename the layer 'redcircle', choose the line colour red and fill colour red, then draw the circle, as shown in Figure 20.30.

Figure 20.30: Rename the layer.

CONTINUED

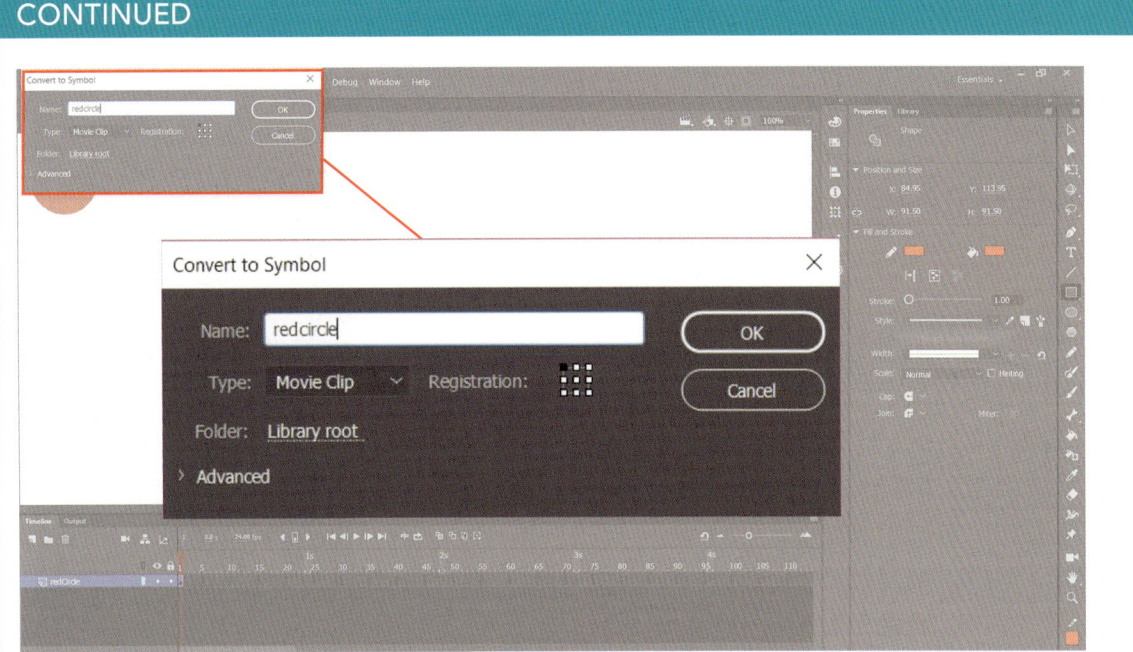

Figure 20.31: Convert the red circle to a symbol.

Convert the red circle to a symbol with a sensible name (see Figure 20.31).

Add frames to frame 15, and then `Create Motion Tween` (see Figure 20.32).

Figure 20.32: Add frames.

CONTINUED

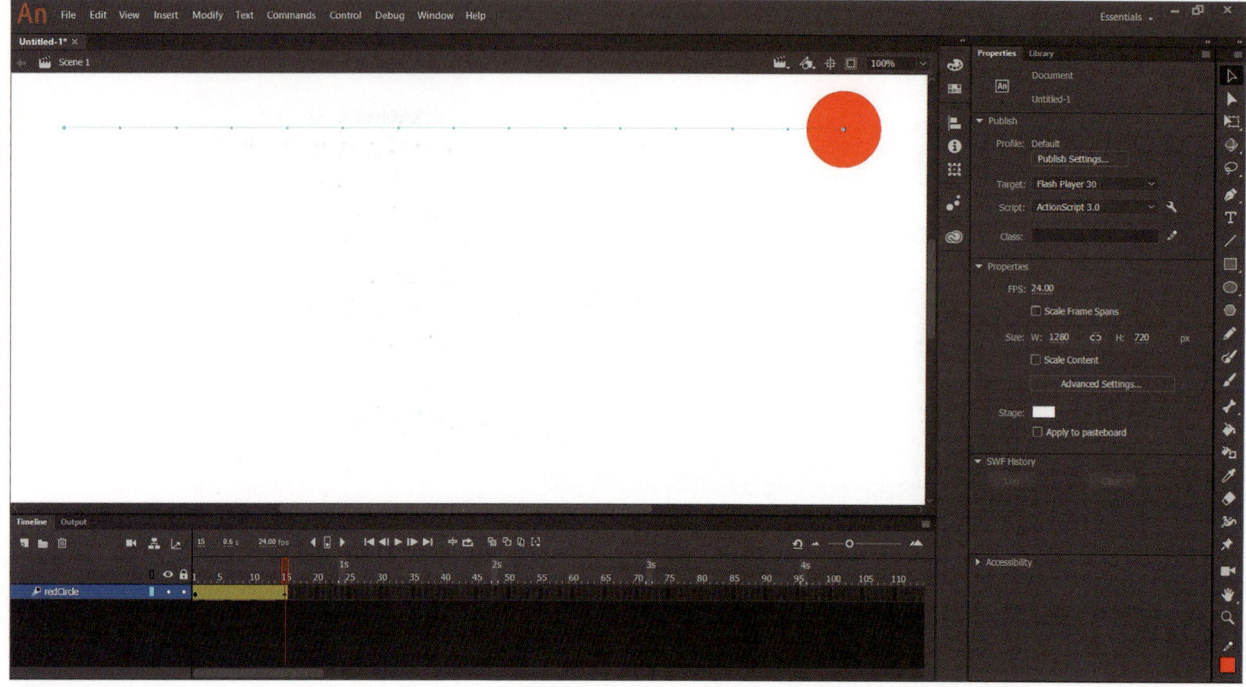

Figure 20.33: Add a key frame.

Add a key frame on frame 15 and move the circle to the top right corner of the screen, as shown in Figure 20.33.

Repeat to make the ball move to all four corners of the stage.

ACTIVITY 20.04

1 Create a ball and make it move around the screen.

2 Create a car animation where the car appears on screen and drives around a track that is drawn on the background using a motion tween. Save the file as **carAnimation.**

3 Reopen the file **myName.** Use a motion tween to create an animation of each letter of your name flying onto the screen one by one, eventually displaying your full name.

4 Add fish to the file **underwaterScene** that you created earlier. Make each one move using a motion tween. Add a bubble for each fish and use a motion tween to make the bubbles float to the surface.

5 Reopen the file **stickPerson**. Create an animation with your stick person. Make them walk across the screen. Challenge yourself and make them perform other actions such as jumping, running and dancing. You could introduce a second person by copying your folder of layers and animating them separately.

A path can be drawn for a symbol to follow, with a motion tween set to follow this path.

Within Adobe Animate, first add the key frame where the path should start and another where it should end.

Right click and select `Create Classic Tween`. This will turn the frames blue, along with having an arrow added to the timeline.

Right click the layer and select `Add Classic Motion Guide`, then use the drawing tools to draw the path, as shown in Figure 20.34.

Select the first key frame and drag the object so its centre (the circle that appears) locks onto the start of the path. Then, select the last key frame and drag the object so its centre locks onto the end of the path. That will create the motion path tween (see Figure 20.35).

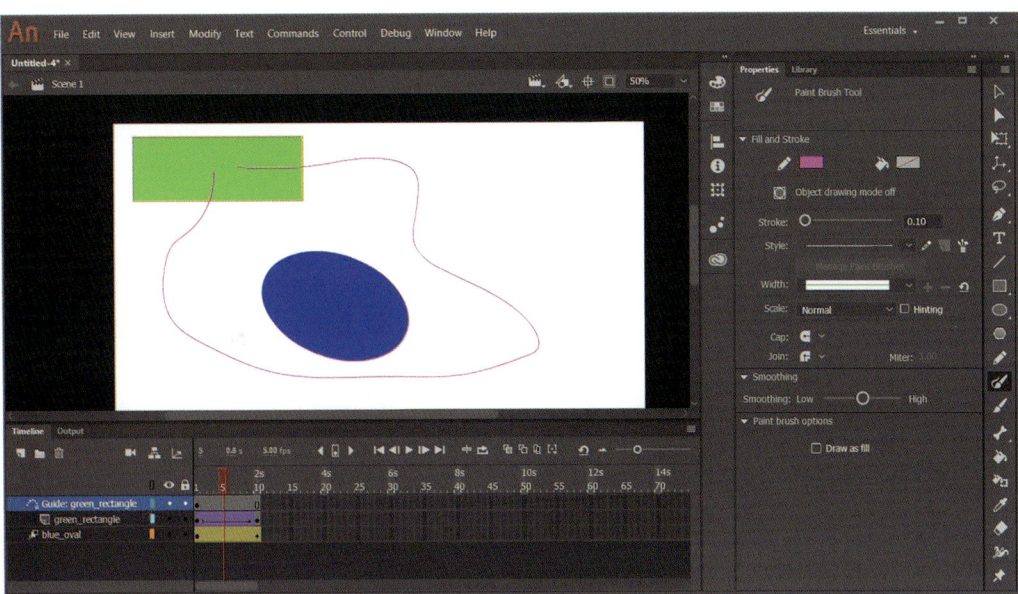

Figure 20.34: Drawing a path.

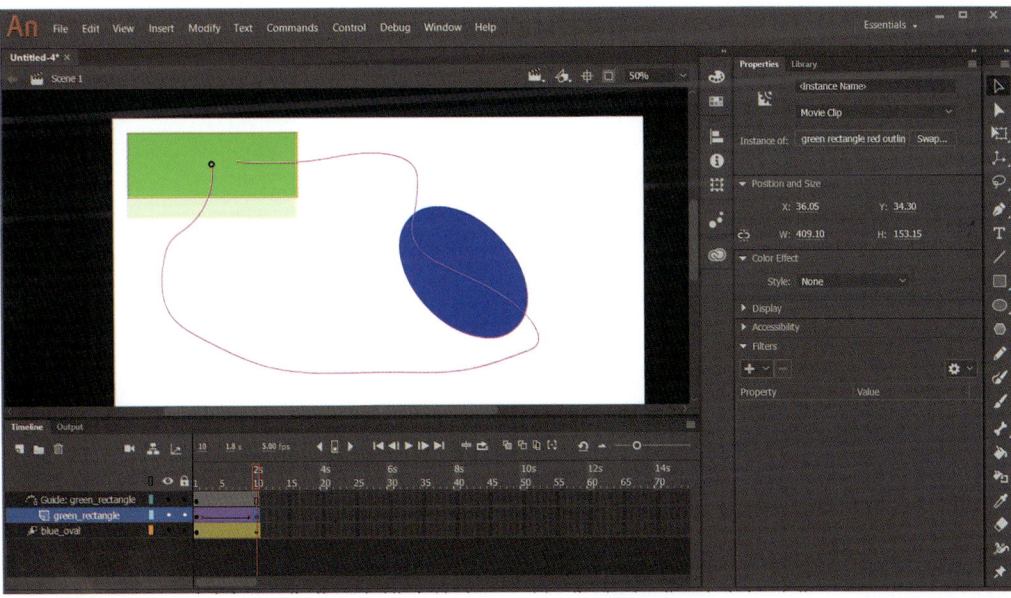

Figure 20.35: Creating a motion path.

ACTIVITY 20.05

1 Create a red ball. Draw a path for the red ball to follow and animate it so it follows the path.

2 Add a second ball with a new path and animate it to follow that path.

3 Reopen the file **carAnimation** created earlier. Make the road include a number of bends. Draw a path to make the car move around the track.

4 Reopen the file **underwaterScene** created earlier. Add an octopus to the underwater scene. Draw a path for the octopus to follow and animate it.

Shape tween, including size and colour

A shape tween enables a shape to be changed into a new shape, along with altering the size and colour. For example, a small red square could be turned into a large blue circle, with the computer generating each step of the transformation. A shape tween can also include movement, so the shape will change while it moves.

In Adobe Animate, a shape tween cannot take place on a symbol, as the symbol is in the library and cannot be changed in this way. To create a shape tween, draw an object using the drawing tools, such as a shape or line, but do not convert it to a symbol. Add the object in the key frame where the shape tween should start. Next, add frames to where the shape tween should end, in the same way as a motion tween, as described in the previous section. Right click on the frames on the timeline and select `Create Shape Tween`.

Next, right click in the frame where the tween should finish and then select `Insert key frame`.

With the new key frame selected, either change the colour, shape or size of the image. Alternatively, delete the contents of the frame, and draw a new image.

Questions

17 What is the difference between a motion tween and a shape tween?

18 Explain why inbetweening produces smoother animations than frame-by-frame animations.

Applying masks

A **mask** can make it so that only certain parts of an image are visible. In Adobe Animate, masks are added in their own layers.

KEY WORD

mask: a layer that involves shapes, or other components, that restrict what can be seen of the other layers

To add a mask, right click the layer you want to become a mask and select `Mask`. The layer beneath automatically becomes a sub-layer of the mask.

Draw the shape for the mask in the first layer (see Figure 20.36).

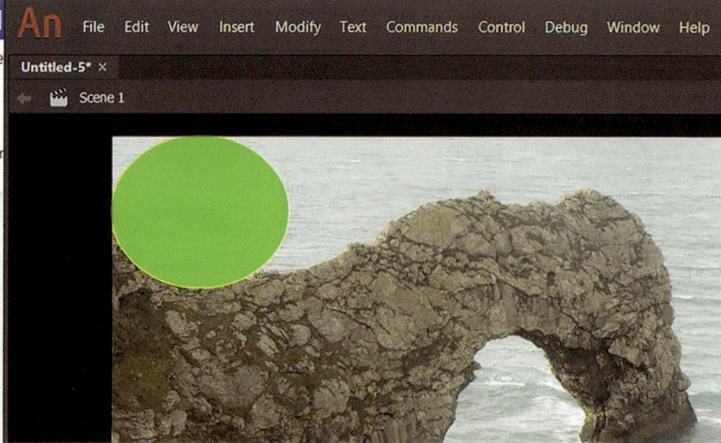

Figure 20.36: Mask shape.

Click the `padlock` on the timeline to lock this layer. The image can then be viewed through the masked area.

Rather than a mask revealing part of an image, it is also possible to add a concealing mask to hide parts of an image. To use a concealing mask, select the required part of the image, then hold Alt (Windows) or Option (Mac) and click Add Layer Mask from the bottom of the Layers section.

A mask can be adjusted by double clicking on the mask in the Channels panel, then changing the opacity and the edges.

Masks can be animated in the same way as an ordinary symbol by removing the padlock to unlock the layer, and then adding the required movement.

Question

19   Describe the purpose of a mask and give an example of how it can be used.

Controlling animations

Adjusting frame rates

An animation's **frame rate** relates to the number of consecutive (following one after the other) frames that are shown each second, which is measured in frames per second (fps). For example, 10 fps means that ten frames will be displayed for each second of the animation, so a 200-frame animation would be 20 seconds in length (200 frames/10 fps = 20 seconds). The higher the frame rate, the quicker the frames change and the smoother the animation appears, although more frames need to be produced.

The frame rate can be changed by entering a different number of frames above the timeline.

KEY WORD

frame rate: the number of consecutive frames shown each second, measured in frames per second (fps)

DID YOU KNOW?

Traditional cel animations are often shown at 24 fps, which gives the impression of objects moving smoothly to the viewer. In video games, developers often try to animate objects at 60 fps to make the movement within the game as realistic as possible (see Figure 20.37).

Figure 20.37: Video gamer.

Question

20   What effect will increasing the frame rate have on an animation?

Looping or stopping animations

To test-run an animation, click `Enter` on the keyboard, or click the play symbol above the timeline, as shown on Figure 20.38. The stepping tool within the animation play controls moves through the animation one frame at a time.

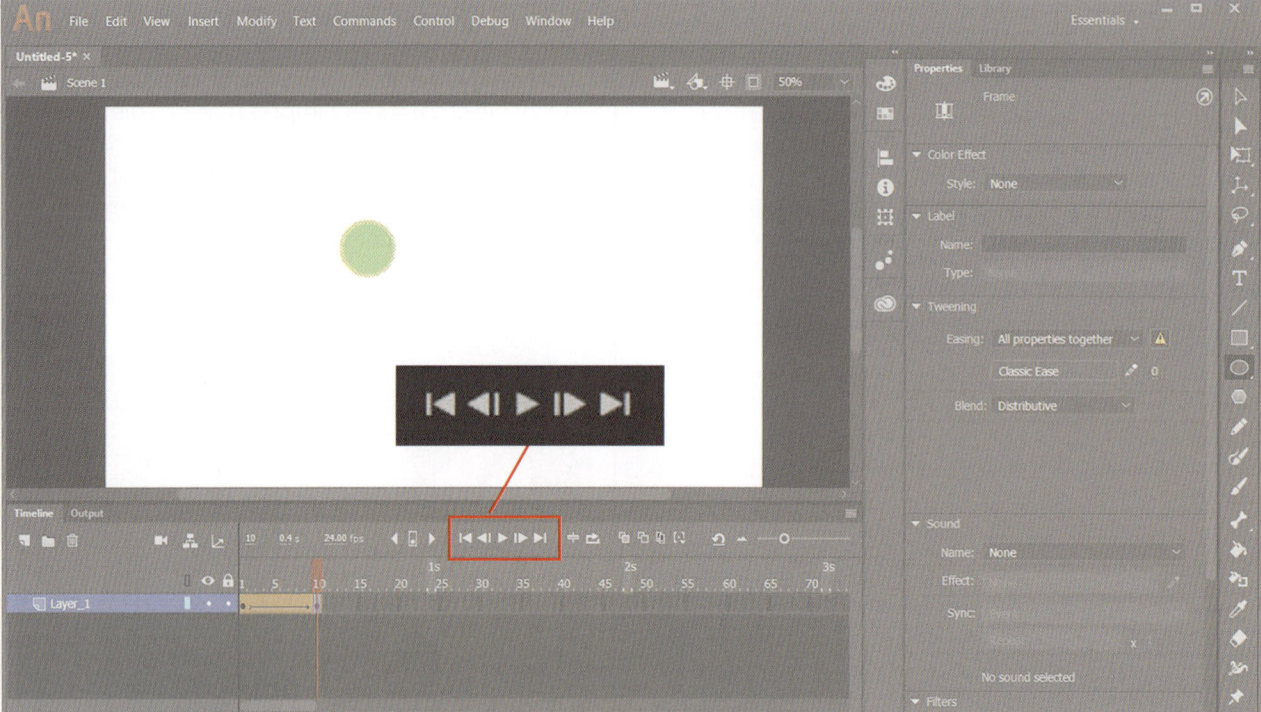

Figure 20.38: Animation play symbols.

To watch the video on loop, select the `Loop` option above the timeline, as shown in Figure 20.39.

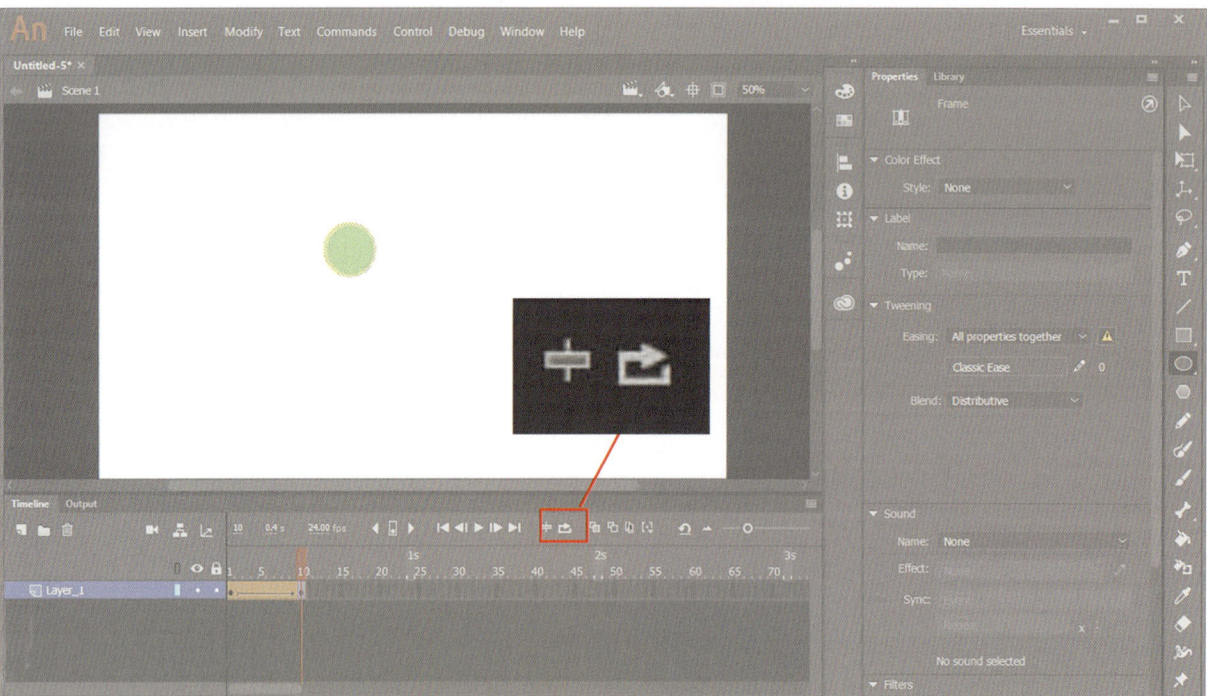

Figure 20.39: Animation loop option.

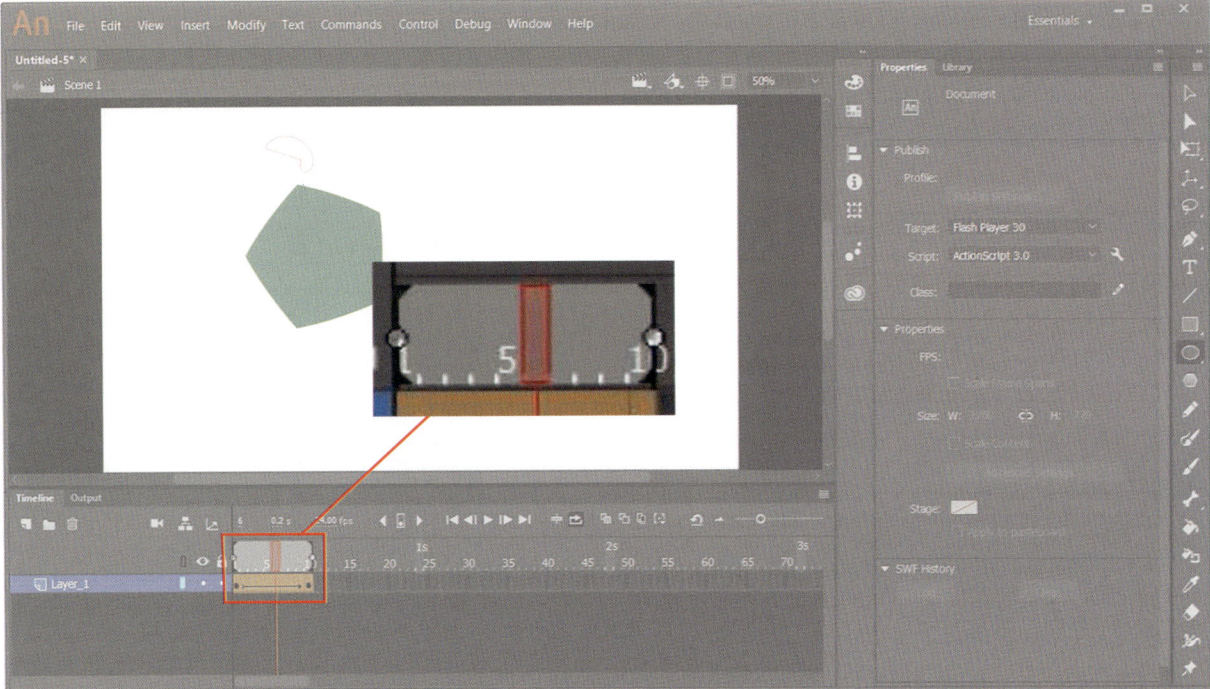

Figure 20.40: Selection of frames to be looped.

Specific frames can be looped by dragging the grey box over the frames (see Figure 20.40).

To stop the animation when it is playing, click the `Play` button. While the animation is playing, the button changes to the pause symbol.

To view the animation looping continually in a separate window, hold down `Control` and press `Enter`.

20.3 Basic principles of animation

Frames and key frames

An animation is made up of many individual images, known as frames. Key frames identify the start and end point for an action at different points within an animation. Look back at the Introduction to recap your understanding of frames and key frames.

Property key frames

Property key frames allow the speed of movement to be consistent within a tween. For example, if copying a tween, the key frames may not be evenly spaced and this will make the symbol move at different speeds. In Adobe Animate, enable roving key frames to deal with this issue.

For example, in the tween in Figure 20.41, the orange dots show the key frame changes and are not evenly spaced.

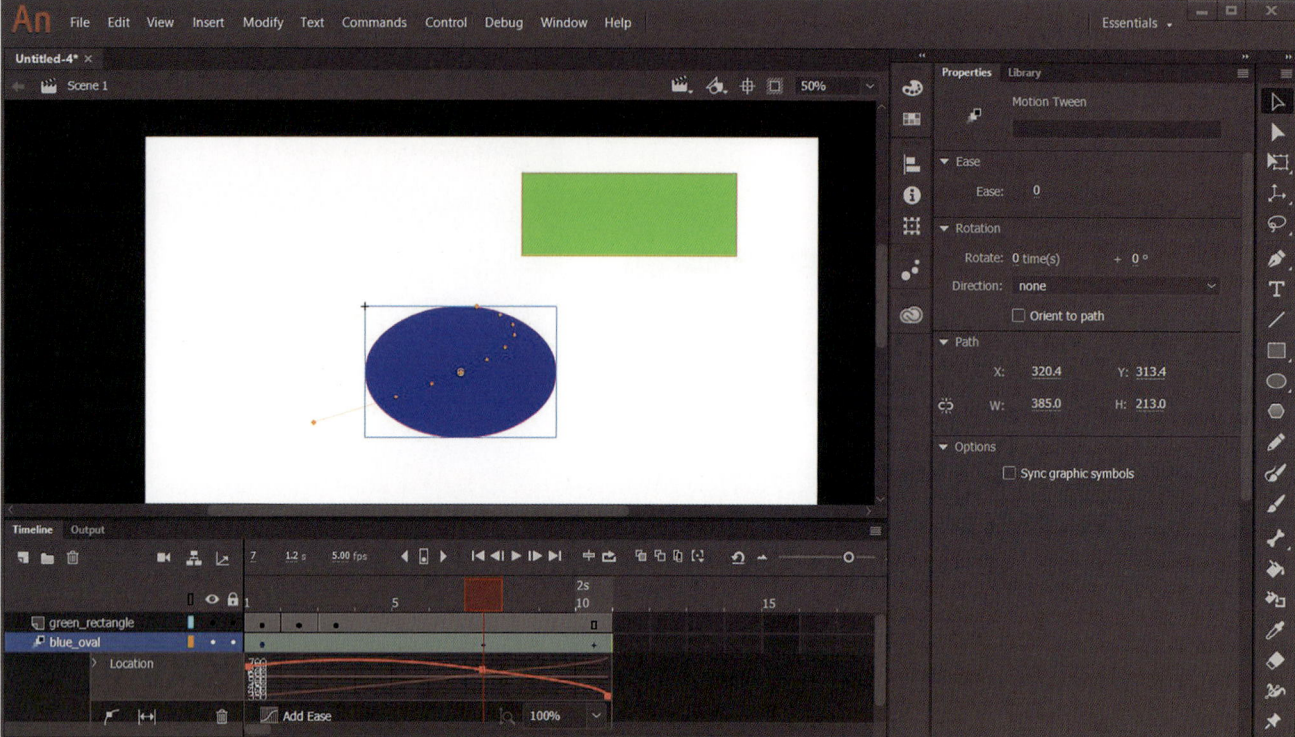

Figure 20.41: Key frames uneven spacing.

To change the spacing of the key frames, right click the tween in the timeline, select `Motion Path` and then `Switch key frames to roving`. This will even out the spacings.

Timings and coordinates

Timing and coordinates were discussed in the previous section. Timing, including the number of timelines, is examined when discussing layers. Coordinates are examined when configuring the stage.

Inbetweening ('tweening') tools

The use of tweening tools to change motion, shape, size and colour were described in the previous section.

Morphing and its effects

Morphing involves an object smoothly changing into another object, such as when using shape tweening. However, morphing is not limited to shapes and could also involve more complex objects, such as smoothly transforming one person's face into another. Morphing is often seen in feature films and can be used in both 2D and 3D animations, along with being used as a live action special effect.

> **KEY WORD**
>
> **morphing:** an object smoothly changing into another object

WORKED EXAMPLE 20.02

Figure 20.42: Line drawn on stage.

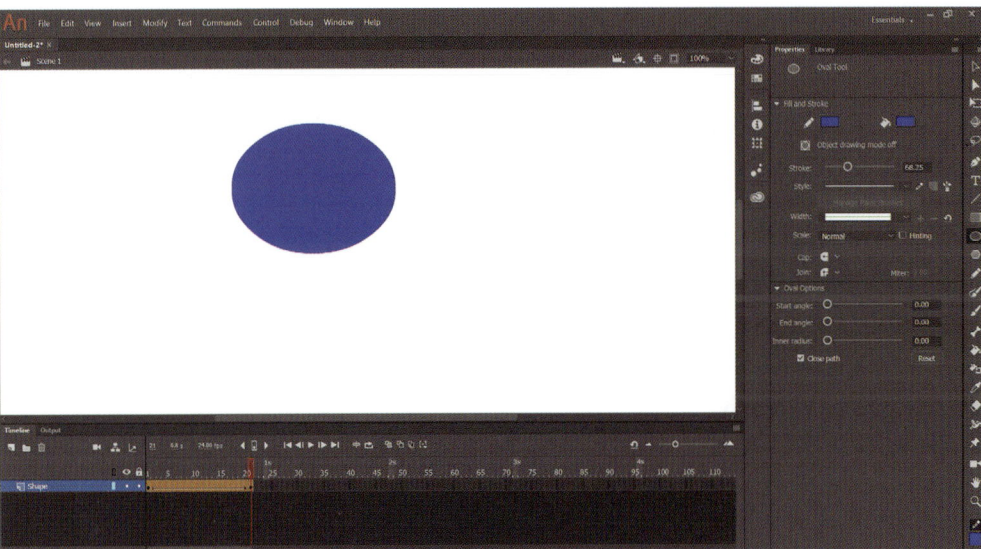

Figure 20.43: Blue circle in the last key frame.

In this example, we will create an animation where a black line turns into a blue circle, then a red rectangle, then back to a line.

First create a new file and add a layer with the name **shape**. Draw the line on the stage, as shown in Figure 20.42.

Add frames, then right click and select Create Shape Tween. Right click on the last frame and create a key frame.

Delete the line in this key frame and draw a blue circle (see Figure 20.43).

CONTINUED

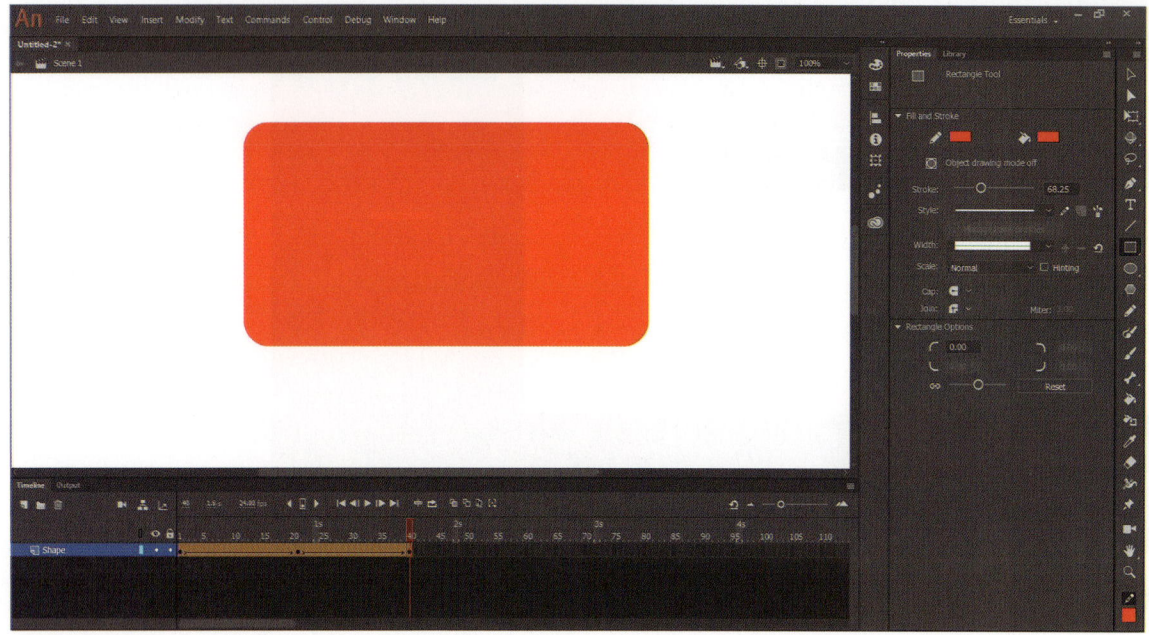

Figure 20.44: Red rectangle in the last key frame.

Repeat the process this time drawing a red rectangle (see Figure 20.44).

Finally, to make the red rectangle change back into a black line, repeat the steps again, but this time copy the line from frame 1 and paste it into the new key frame.

ACTIVITY 20.06

1. Create a shape tween that changes a red circle into a blue square.

2. Create a shape tween that changes a rain cloud into a sun.

3. Create an animation that shows seasonal changes during a year. For example, a river and forest showing:

   a. lush, green, sunny days

   b. leaves changing to red and orange and falling

   c. a frozen river with barren trees

   d. new growth emerging.

4. Open the file **underwaterScene**. Make the bubbles change shape, for example get smaller as they move to the surface.

5. Open the file **myName**. Make each letter of your name morph into the next letter.

ACTIVITY 20.07

Choose from **one** of the four options below:

1 Create an animated introduction to a TV show or film. Make sure you include images of the main characters and text introducing the title. Make use of opacity and tweens.

2 Extend your underwater scene to include a range of sea life. Animate the background and plants to create a continuous, repeating scene.

3 Create an animated cartoon that shows a day in the life of the cartoon's central character. Use a range of techniques, including some key frame animation and tweens.

4 Create a new show-intro to your favourite TV show, using a range of animation techniques.

REFLECTION

Reflect on how you completed the task in Activity 20.07. How did you approach the task? What difficulties did you encounter when completing the task? What would you do differently when completing a similar task in the future?

DISCUSSION POINT

Morphing enables animation effects to be used that produce movement that is impossible in the real world, such as smoothly changing from one face into another. Should viewers be made aware that these techniques are used when viewing an animation?

Exporting to an appropriate file format

Once you have created your animation you will need to export it to a file format for use in other formats.

Click `File` from the top menu, then `Export`.

There are several export options to choose from, as shown in Table 20.3.

Export option	Description
Image	This creates one image file for every frame in your animation.
Movie	You can create an .swf file, which is a Flash file commonly used in websites, although this is being phased out of use.
Video	You can create a video through Adobe Media Encoder, or convert to a .mov file.
Animated GIF	This will create an animated .gif file that you can integrate into a website.

Table 20.3: Animation export options.

ACTIVITY 20.08

Export your finished animations into an appropriate format. When you have developed your web development skill, use them to create a website to display your animations.

20.4 Components of an animation

The different parts of an animation are often referred to as components.

- **Primary components** are the focus of the animation, such as the leading characters or significant objects.

- **Secondary components**, such as sound and background images, enhance the animation and can help accentuate (emphasise) movement.

Other components relate to the setup of the animation, such as the frame rate or aspect ratio.

KEY WORDS

primary component: the focus of the animation, such as the main characters

secondary component: components that enhance the animation, such as backgrounds and sound

20.5 Use of animation variables when creating animations

Variables store data about different components in an animation and can be changed during the animation. For example, variables are used to store the width of the line produced by a drawing tool, or to store the coordinates of an object on the stage.

Variables can also be used to control, or manipulate, parts of an animated object. For example, in 3D animations, wireframe models are created on the computer of the objects being animated. An example of a wireframe model is shown in Figure 20.45.

Figure 20.45: Wireframe.

Within these wireframe models, an animation variable, known as a hinge or **avar**, is used to control the position of part of the animated object to be manipulated. For example, each part of a finger could be manipulated individually to make it move realistically.

KEY WORD

avar: a hinge on a wire-model object that lets you manipulate its position

DID YOU KNOW?

Within the 1995 animated film *Toy Story*, the character Woody uses over 700 avars, including over 200 in his face.

DISCUSSION POINT

1   Which type of animation do you think was the most important to be developed and why?

2   Animations are often included within online content, such as on web pages and within apps. Do you feel animations enhance online content, or are they a distraction?

PRACTICE QUESTIONS

1   Saif owns a small independent comic shop named Saif's Comics.
  a   Saif wants a short animation that will appear as a banner across the top of his website.
      Create an animation to meet the following requirements.
      •   The aspect ratio must be 2.35:1.
      •   The background must remain black throughout.
      •   The name 'Saif's' should appear at the start of the animation, then each letter should fade out one at a time, taking 1 second for each one to fade.
      •   The word 'Comics' should fade in as a whole word, taking 1 second to appear. It should stay on screen for 2 seconds, and then fade out one letter at a time (1 second for each fade).
      •   The words should be in a large white font, taking up the full height of the animation.
      •   The animation must be set to loop.
      •   All animations must be smooth.
      •   The animation must be exported in a suitable format for use on a website.   [13]

CONTINUED

   b Describe the differences and similarities between cel animation, stop motion animation and time-lapse animation. [3]

[Total 16]

2 Henry owns a property sales business named Henry's Homes.

You have been provided with the following file: **Henry logo.jpg**

   a Create a short animation to advertise Henry's property sales business.

The animation must meet the following requirements.

- The aspect ratio must be 16:9.
- The background should be pale blue.
- The image **20.1 Henry logo.jpg** should be on the left-hand side of the animation. It should start small and then increase in size, before decreasing again. This should repeat throughout the animation.
- A white ball should come in from the left to the right, revealing the sentence 'We take pride in selling your property', for example:

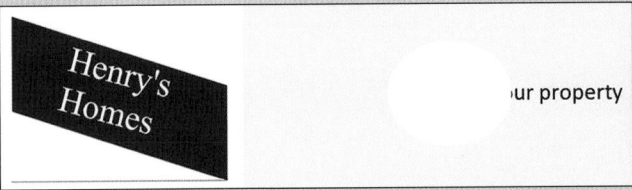

- When the ball disappears off the left-hand side of the animation, it should stay off for 1.5 seconds.
- When it returns, it should move from left to right. It should display the text 'No sale, no fee' (as a mask) as it passes over it before disappearing off to the right, for example:

- The animation should be set to loop.
- All animations must be smooth.
- Animation should be exported in a suitable format for viewing on a computer.

[19]

   b Describe what is meant by a frame and a key frame. [2]

[Total 21]

CONTINUED

3   Ying needs an animation for her independent film company: Films by Ying. Ying's logo is shown below.

Create a short animation for the logo.

The animation must meet the following requirements.

- The screen ratio should be 16:10.
- The background should be white with the green outline already displayed.
- The letters should bounce in from the left. The Y should appear first, then the B, then the F.
- When all the letters are on screen they should remain for 2 seconds, and then fade out.
- The animation should loop.
- All animations should be smooth.
- The file should be exported as an animation gif.   [12]

SUMMARY CHECKLIST

- ☐ I can configure the stage/frame/canvas for an animation by:
  - ☐ setting colour, size, aspect ratio
  - ☐ using rulers, guides and grid settings
  - ☐ setting snapping options.
- ☐ I can import and create vector objects including:
  - ☐ tracing bitmaps
  - ☐ adding text.
- ☐ I can control object properties including:
  - ☐ stroke and fill settings
  - ☐ size position and orientation
  - ☐ transparency.
- ☐ I can use inbetweening ('tweening') tools including:
  - ☐ show motion
  - ☐ show shape, size and colour changes.
- ☐ I can set paths for animation to follow.
- ☐ I can use layers.
- ☐ I can apply masks.

CONTINUED

- ☐ I can control animations by:
  - ☐ adjusting frame rates
  - ☐ looping or stopping animations.
- ☐ I know and understand the basic principles of animation including:
  - ☐ frames, key frames, property key frames, timings, coordinates
  - ☐ inbetweening and the effect it creates
  - ☐ morphing and the effect it creates.
- ☐ I know and understand different animation types and methods including:
  - ☐ cell animation, stop motion, time lapse, flip book, CGI, 2D, 3D.
- ☐ I know and understand the use of animation variables when creating animations including:
  - ☐ primary, for example graphical elements
  - ☐ secondary, for example sound, components of animation
  - ☐ the use of animation variables to control the position of an animated object or parts of an animated object.

PROJECT

Figure 20.46: When taking photos of students and/or their work to use in your animation, remember to ask for their permission.

In a pair, create an animation, using animation software on a computer, to advertise your school to potential students. Within your animation, you could include:

- images from the school, such as photographs of the buildings, facilities and student work and activities. You must get permission before taking any photos (see Figure 20.46).

- your own vector graphics, such as the school logo, or examples of extra-curricular activities.

Your animation should use a variety of animation techniques, such as:

- key frames

- layers

- paths

- motion tweening

- shape tweening.

Before starting your animation, carefully think about the primary components, such as the main characters or objects, secondary components, such as the sound and background, plus any other components, such as the frame rate.

> Chapter 21
Programming for the web

CONTINUED

- create functions to be executed
- use JavaScript timing events
- add comments to annotate and explain code
- understand a range of object-based JavaScript programming techniques and terms.

BEFORE YOU START

- Can you use the HTML scripting language to create web pages?
- Do you know how to add images, lists and tables to a web page?
- Have you used CSS (Cascading Style Sheets) to specify fonts and colours in a web page?
- Have you had experience of creating programs in a language such as Python using sequence, selection and iteration?

Introduction

The scripting languages, **HTML** and **CSS**, allow you to add elements to a web page and to style those elements by specifying font styles and colours. An HTML element is any object that has a start and an end tag, such as a heading `<h> </h>` or a paragraph `<p> </p>`.

HTML and CSS are often called the 'Content' and 'Presentation' layers of a website as they code what is on it and how it will look (see Figure 21.1).

To make a website interactive, a third layer is needed. The third layer allows users to enter information, select items to buy or to play a game. The third layer is called the 'Behaviour' layer because it refers to how **elements** will behave when users interact with them such as left or right clicking on them or moving the mouse pointer over them or pressing a particular key. The functionality of the third layer is provided by a programming language. Different languages can be used but JavaScript is the oldest and the one most used with the many different web browsers.

KEY WORDS

HTML: Hyper Text Markup Language is the code you use to create web pages

CSS: Cascading Style Sheets used to define the styles of different elements on the web page

KEY WORD

element: an object on a web page with an opening and closing tag

Your web browser reads and interprets the HTML and CSS scripts to display the web page correctly. The web browser also executes the JavaScript code. The JavaScript program runs on the user's computer and not on the web server that provides the web page. JavaScript uses the same basic constructs as other languages including sequence, selection and iteration and uses commands, loops and functions.

Figure 21.1: A software developer writes code.

21.1 Using JavaScript

The JavaScript code must be placed within the script tags `<script>` and `</script>` to notify the browser that this is the code it has to execute. The `<script>` and `</script>` tags can be placed within the `<head>` or `<body>` sections of the HTML document, although it is most often placed within the `<head>` section.

JavaScript can also be placed in an external document and then the name of the script and location is placed within the `<script>` tags. This makes the HTML document less cluttered and easier to read. External scripts will be looked at later in more detail.

JavaScript can create, change the properties of, or remove elements from the document.

For JavaScript to know which element to work on, each element must be given a Name or ID.

WORKED EXAMPLE 21.01

The code gives the paragraph the ID of `paragraph1`.

```
<!DOCTYPE html>

<html>

    <head>

    </head>

    <body>

    <h1>Making JavaScript work</h1>

    <h2>Some example text</h2>

    <p ID = "paragraph1">This text has
    been added using HTML in a paragraph
    with the ID of paragraph1.</p>

    </body>

</html>
```

Inserting JavaScript in HTML

To change any of the properties of paragraph1 some JavaScript code must be added to the webpage. The code is added within `<script></script>` tags.

WORKED EXAMPLE 21.02

The code changes the colour of `paragraph1` to red.

```
<!DOCTYPE html>

<html>

    <head>

    </head>

    <body>

    <h1>Making JavaScript work</h1>

    <h2>Some example text</h2>

    <p ID = "paragraph1">This text
    has been added using HTML in a
    paragraph with the ID of paragraph1.
    </p>

        <script>

            document.
            getElementById("paragraph1").
            style.color =  'red';

        </script>

    </body>

</html>
```

In the worked example, the statement `document.getElementById("paragraph1").style.color = "red";` tells JavaScript which element to work on, in this case element "paragraph1". Notice how the element ID is in speech marks.

The rest of the statement `.style.color = "red";` tells the code that it has to change one of the style properties, in this case the colour, to red. (In JavaScript colour is spelled 'color'.)

Notice that a semi-colon ; is placed at the end of each statement. This helps JavaScript to identify separate statements, as many can be placed on one line.

Figure 21.2 shows how the HTML and JavaScript will be interpreted by a browser.

Making JavaScript work

Some example text

This text has been added using HTML in a paragraph with the ID of paragraph1.

Figure 21.2: The web page displayed by a browser.

A browser always gives priority to `<script></script>` tags and stops interpreting the HTML to run the code. In Worked example 21.02, if the `<script>` had been placed in the `<head>` section, then the paragraph colour would have stayed black as the code would have run before the browser had created paragraph1 and so there was nothing to turn red. Therefore, place the `<script>` after the HTML instructions to create the element.

DID YOU KNOW?

JavaScript was invented in 1995 for use with the most popular browser of the time called Netscape. JavaScript was originally called Mocha. It took the US computer programmer Brendan Eich ten days to develop the language. JavaScript is now used in more than 90% of all websites.

Changing styles

Elements have different styles that can be set using JavaScript.

In Worked example 21.02, colour of the text was set using `.style.color = "red";`

- Other text styles include:

  `.style.fontFamily = "verdena, arial";`

  `.style.fontStyle = "italic";`

- Other styles include

  `.style.fontSize = "large";`

- Other font sizes include

  `xx-small, x-small, small, medium, large, x-large, xx-large`

Functions

As demonstrated in Worked example 21.02, the browser will carry out the code instructions as soon as it gets to them. But in an interactive webpage, the code must be run only when it is needed, and the code stopped from running immediately it is placed within functions.

A **function** is a set of instructions that perform a specific task such as multiplying a value by a particular number. It is independent code that only runs if it is 'called', either by an event such as clicking a button or by some other Javascript code.

Any function can be used as many times as you want when a program is running. Functions save time and space when writing a program.

KEY WORD

function: a self-contained module of code that completes a particular task; it can be used over and over again by being called from other code

Every function has a name or identifier. In the following example, we will name the identifier `turnitRed`.

```
function turnitRed() {

    document.getElementById("paragraph1").
    style.color =  'red';

}
```

Notice that the function name is followed by `()` and the commands are enclosed in curly brackets `{...}`. Curly brackets are also called braces or curly braces.

This function can be placed within script tags within the `<head>` or `<body>` sections of the HTML code.

WORKED EXAMPLE 21.03

The code to set the colour of paragraph1 to red can be placed in a function defined within script tags.

```
<!DOCTYPE html>t

<html>

    <head>

        <script>

            function turnitRed() {

            document.
            getElementById("paragraph1").
            style.color =  'red';

}

        </script>

    </head>

    <body>

    <h1>Making JavaScript work</h1>

    <h2>Some example text</h2>

    <p ID = "paragraph1">This text has
    been added using HTML in a paragraph
    with the ID of paragraph1.</p>

    </body>

</html>
```

The code will not be run until it is 'called' by something happening on the webpage.

The 'something' that calls the code is usually an **event**.

KEY WORD

event: something that happens to an HTML element

Events

There are many different events that will trigger a function to be called, such as when a mouse button is clicked when the pointer is over an element, or when the pointer moves over or out of element.

WORKED EXAMPLE 21.04

In this example, the event is a left-button click when the pointer is over a button.

```
<!DOCTYPE html>

<html>

    <head>

        <script>

            function turnitRed() {

            document.
            getElementById("paragraph1").
            style.color =  'red';

}

        </script>

    </head>

    <body>

    <h1>Making JavaScript work</h1>

    <h2>Some example text</h2>

    <p ID = "paragraph1">This text has
    been added using HTML in a paragraph
    with the ID of paragraph1.</p>

    <button id = "MyButton" onclick =
    "turnitRed()">Make it Happen</button>

    </body>

</html>
```

In Worked example 21.04, a button has been added to the webpage with the ID of "MyButton".

The button has been given an onclick event that will call the function "turnitRed()".

Whenever the mouse is clicked when the pointer is over the button, it will call the function.

When the page loads, the text in paragraph1 should be black, as shown in Figure 21.3, but the paragraph text should turn red when the button is clicked, as shown in Figure 21.4.

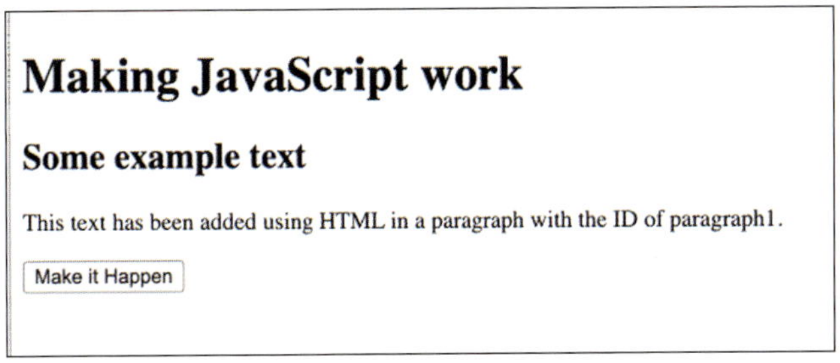

Making JavaScript work

Some example text

This text has been added using HTML in a paragraph with the ID of paragraph1.

[Make it Happen]

Figure 21.3: Paragraph1 in black.

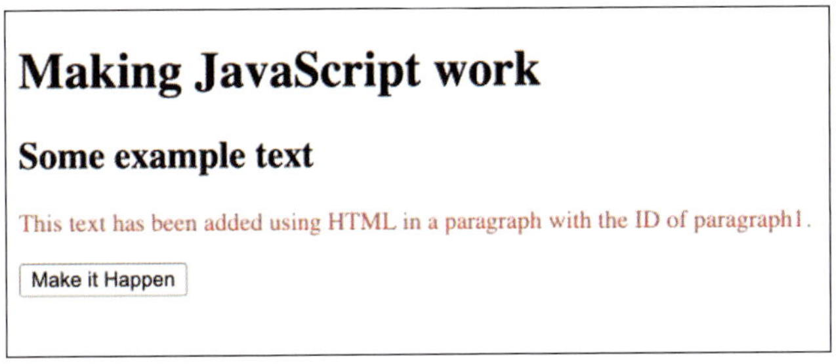

Making JavaScript work

Some example text

This text has been added using HTML in a paragraph with the ID of paragraph1.

[Make it Happen]

Figure 21.4: When the function is called, paragraph1 turns red.

DISCUSSION POINT

What are the advantages of using functions in computer programs?

Common HTML events

There are other element events in addition to onclick, including:

- onchange: when an HTML element is changed, e.g. when a user enters their name into a text box.
- onmouseover: when the mouse pointer enters an element.
- ommouseout: when the mouse pointer moves out of an element.
- onkeydown: when a key is pressed when an element is selected, e.g. in an input box.

onchange and onkeydown are very similar in how they work but onkeydown is triggered before the character is typed into the input box and onchange will only be triggered when a field has actually changed.

ACTIVITY 21.01

Open the file **21.01_EventsActivity.html**, which contains the code used in Worked example 21.04 New elements have been added.

Add actions to the elements that will change the colour of the text in the paragraph as a result of the following events to the elements:

onchange

onmouseover

onmouseout

onkeydown

Create new functions so that a different colour is used each time.

The onload event

More events than those occurring to elements can be responded to.

The web page itself has an 'onload' event. An 'onload' event occurs when the page loads.

A function linked to this event can be called from the `<body>` tag.

`<body onload = "makeitRed">` would call the function in the previous example.

A function called from the onload event can set up or initialise the styles of the elements on the page.

Parameters in functions

We have been defining functions with a name followed by some round brackets.

```
function message() {

}
```

The round brackets are important. The brackets can contain values to be used by the function.

These values, passed to the function, are called parameters.

For example:

`function message(part1, part2)` would use the values in these parameters to do something.

`function calculate(number1, number2)` would use the values stored in `number1` and `number2` to do something such as multiplying them together or comparing them.

Functions to be executed

When invoked from code

So far, we have been calling functions from events such as `onclick` or `mouseover` but functions can also be called (invoked) from JavaScript code.

The following function:

```
function calculate(number1, number2) {
var result = number1 * number2;
}
```

can be called from code and given the parameters at the same time.

The statement to call the function and give the parameters could be:

```
function calculate(9, 3);
```

The function is called and the numbers to be used as parameters are given in the brackets. The function would interpret the numbers 9 and 3 as `number1` and `number2`.

In the function, the variable result would have the value 27.

But nothing has been done with this result. It has not been displayed or used by the function.

When a function is called from code, the result is usually turned back to the code that called it by using the `'return'` command and stored in a variable.

For example:

`var answer = function calculate(9, 3)` would call the function and store the result in the variable answer when the function returns the result.

```
function calculate(number1, number2) {
var result = number1 * number2;
return result;
}
```

WORKED EXAMPLE 21.05

In this code, the parameters 9 and 3 are passed to the function calculate. The function uses them as number1 and number2.

```
<!DOCTYPE html>
<html>
<head>
    <script>
        function calculate(number1, number2) {
            var result = number1 * number2;
            return result;
        }
        var answer = calculate(9,3);
        alert(answer);
    </script>
    </head>
    <body>
    <h1>Functions with parameters</h1>
    </body>
</html>
```

The code

```
var answer = calculate(9,3);
alert(answer);
```

calls the function with the parameters 9 and 3. The result of the calculation is returned to the variable `'answer'` and then displayed in an alert box.

Create a web page that asks a user to enter the length and width of a rectangle and then uses a function to obtain the values entered. This then calls a function and provides the parameters for the calculation of the area. This is then returned to the function that called it and it is displayed in an alert.

Self-invoked functions

A self-invoked function does not have to be called. It runs automatically.

Self-invoked functions are anonymous: they do not have a name.

```
(function () {
    // body
})();
```

WORKED EXAMPLE 21.06

This code will show `"Hello"` in an alert box.

```
<html>
    <head>
        <script>
            (function () {
                alert("hello");
            })();
        </script>
    </head>
<body>
</body>
</html>
```

Self-invoked functions can be used for initialisation in the same way as the onload event.

Show/hide HTML elements using style.visibility and style.display

Two very useful properties allow elements to be hidden from the user until they are needed. This is often used in interactive games.

The visibility property allows elements to be visible or hidden.

`getElementById("paragraph1").style. visibility("hidden")` makes the element invisible to the user and `getElementById("paragraph1"). style.visibility("visible")` makes it visible again.

Even if an element such as a button is not visible, the user could still interact with it without knowing. The display property for an element can prevent this.

`getElementById("paragraph1").style.display = "none"` makes the element invisible and unable to be clicked on.

`getElementById("paragraph1").style.display = "block"` makes the element visible and interactive.

WORKED EXAMPLE 21.07

This code has two buttons, one to make the paragraph hidden and one to make it visible.

```
<!DOCTYPE html>

<html>

    <head>

        <script>

            function hide() {

                document.getElementById("paragraph1"). style.visibility =  'hidden';

            }

            function show() {

                document.getElementById("paragraph1"). style.visibility =  'visible';

            }

        </script>

    </head>

    <body>

        <h1>Making JavaScript work</h1>

        <h2>Some example text</h2>

            <p ID = "paragraph1">This text has been added using HTML in a paragraph with the
            ID of paragraph1.</p>

        <button id = "show" onclick = "show()">Show the paragraph</button>

        <button id = "hide" onclick = "hide()">Hide the paragraph</button>

    </body>

</html>
```

There are two buttons, each with an onclick event, one to hide and one to show the paragraph.

REFLECTION

Have you been entering the code given in the worked examples to help you practise and improve your programming skills?

Question

1   Explain the difference between the style.visibility and the style.display properties of an element.

ACTIVITY 21.03

The code in Worked example 21.07 is basic. You are going to make it look more professional. Open the file **21.02_VisibilityandDisplay Activity.html**. Edit the HTML code by changing and adding functions to allow the following to happen:

1   Hide the Show button when the page loads.

2   Make the Hide button and paragraph become invisible when the Hide button is clicked, as shown in Figure 21.5.

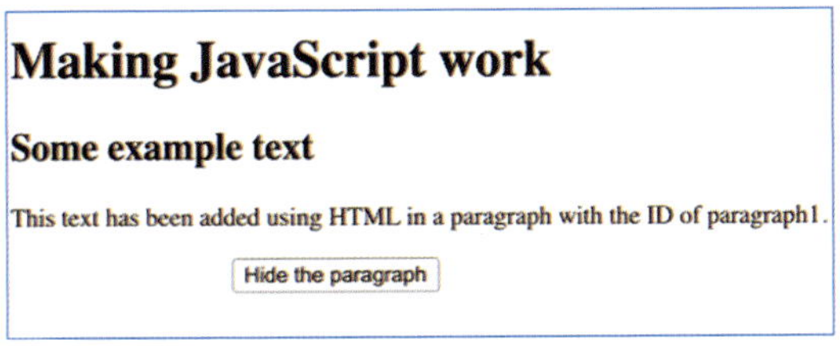

Making JavaScript work

Some example text

This text has been added using HTML in a paragraph with the ID of paragraph1.

[Hide the paragraph]

Figure 21.5: The web page when it loads.

3   Make the Show button become visible, as shown in Figure 21.6.

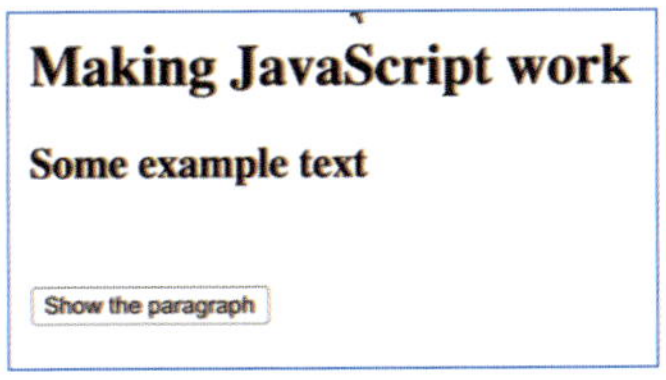

Making JavaScript work

Some example text

[Show the paragraph]

Figure 21.6: The web page after the 'Hide the paragraph' button has been clicked.

innerHTML

All the elements on a web page can have HTML within them and this is known as their **innerHTML**. innerHTML includes all text content of the element, including all spacing and inner HTML tags.

KEY WORD
innerHTML: the HTML content within an element

JavaScript can be used to change the HTML of any of the elements from paragraphs to buttons.

WORKED EXAMPLE 21.08

The following code adds different inner HTML text to a paragraph depending on which button is pressed.

```
<!DOCTYPE html>

<html>

    <head>

    <script>

        function happy() {

            document.
            getElementById("paragraph1").
            innerHTML =  'I am happy today.';

        }

        function sad() {

            document.
            getElementById("paragraph1").
            innerHTML =  'I am sad today.';

        }

    </script>

    </head>

    <body>

        <h1>Making JavaScript work</h1>

        <h2>How are you feeling?</h2>

        <button id = "HappyButton" onclick =
        "happy()">Happy</button>

        <button id = "SadButton" onclick =
        "sad()">Sad</button>

        <p ID = "paragraph1"; style="font-
        size:300%;"></p>

    </body>

</html>
```

Display data in different ways

Pop-up boxes can be used to display text or information. Pop-up boxes do not write text to the web page. The text appears in an extra box on top of the screen. Figure 21.7 shows an example of a pop-up box.

Figure 21.7: A pop-up box.

There are three types of pop-up box: alert, confirm and prompt.

Alert

An alert box displays text in a box over the top of a web page. It is usually used to alert (tell) the user of something. In this example, the text `"Hello World"` will be displayed in the alert box.

```
alert("Hello World");
```

You might sometimes see an alert with the word `window` in front of it. This gives exactly the same result. For example:

```
window.alert("Hello World");
```

Confirm

A confirm box has two options: OK and cancel. For example, this confirm box will display 'OK to proceed?'

```
confirm ("OK to proceed?");
```

The option chosen by the user is returned as a value that can then be used to decide what to do (see Figure 21.8). In this example, the value returned is stored in the variable answer (see Chapter 4 Algorithms and flowcharts).

```
var answer = confirm ("OK to
proceed?");
```

Figure 21.8: The confirm box asking a user whether they want to proceed.

Prompt

A prompt box allows a user to enter some text and gives them the option of OK and cancel.

```
prompt("What day is it?")
```

If OK is selected, then the text input can be stored into a variable. In this example, it will be stored in the variable answer.

```
var answer = prompt("What day is it?")
```

ACTIVITY 21.04

Open the file **21.03.html**.

Please change highlighted to:

The web page displays an alert box.

Amend the code so that a prompt box is then displayed asking the user to enter their name.

Another alert box should then be shown containing their name.

Using document.write

The code `document.write(theOutput)` will output the text inside the brackets to the web page. For example:

```
<script>
    document.write("Hello world");
</script>
```

This will display 'Hello world' in the web page.

ACTIVITY 21.05

Create a web page that displays the title:

My First JavaScript Web Page

at the top of the page.

First, put your basic HTML tags into the file you are using to create the website.

```
<HTML>
<BODY>
</BODY>
</HTML>
```

Inside the body tags, put your JavaScript tags.

```
<HTML>
<BODY>
    <SCRIPT>
    </SCRIPT>
</BODY>
</HTML>
```

Inside the JavaScript tags write your code to output My First JavaScript Web Page.

```
<HTML>
<BODY>
    <SCRIPT>
        document.write("My First JavaScript
Web Page");
    </SCRIPT>
</BODY>
</HTML>
```

Open your file in a web browser to check the result of the code.

TIP

In Activity 21.05, the text inside the brackets is in speech marks so that it is interpreted literally as text to be written on screen. If there aren't speech marks there, then the website would mistake the text for a command name or a variable name.

The browser console, using console.log()

Web browsers keep a list of all of their activities such as network requests, JavaScript, CSS, security errors and warnings, and messages logged by JavaScript code that do not appear on the webpage. In other words, it provides information on what is happening in the background and provides useful information if you are developing a webpage.

By default, the console is not shown to the user, but it can be seen by changing the settings.

This method works for the more widely used browers:

1 Press Ctrl+Shift+I to open the Developer Tools.
2 Click on the Console tab.
3 You should see the output of console.log() in the console

The command to write to the console is:

```
console.log()
```

WORKED EXAMPLE 21.09

The following code writes messages to the console log. The messages inform the developer of the webpage that the actions have been processed.

```
<HTML>
<BODY>
    <SCRIPT>
        alert("Welcome to the website");
        console.log("Alert")
        var confirmed = confirm("Are you
        sure you want to proceed?");
        console.log("Confirmation")
        var userAnswer = prompt("What is 10
        + 10?");
        console.log("Question asked")
    </SCRIPT>
</BODY>
</HTML>
```

Run the code and read the messages in the console log.

ACTIVITY 21.06

1 Create a web page that displays your name at the top of the page.

2 Create a web page that outputs a story as a series of alert boxes.

3 Add a console log to tasks 1 and 2 to confirm each box that has been successfully output.

4 Create a basic text web page using HTML. Edit the web page so that each element (for example, `paragraph`) has a name and display the text in JavaScript instead.

Questions

2 Which command(s) will output a box with a message?

3 Which command(s) will write data to the console?

4 Which command(s) will output a new box for a user to enter data?

5 What is the purpose of writing data to the console?

Images and image properties

An image can be added into a web page using the `<img>` tag in HTML.

The following code:

```
<img src="Riverside.jpg" width = "512">
```

would insert an image named 'Riverside.jpg' and resize the image to a width of 512 pixels.

The full HTML code would be:

```
<!DOCTYPE html>

<html>

    <body>

        <h1>Images</h1>

            <img src="Riverside.jpg" width =
            "512">

    </body>

</html>
```

This would load the image, as shown in Figure 21.9.

Figure 21.9: The Riverside.jpg displayed on the web page.

Changing images

If the image element is given an ID, then the image can be changed using JavaScript.

In the following code, the `img` is given the ID of `"PlaceHolder"` and a button and function have been added to change the image for another one.

WORKED EXAMPLE 21.10

Open the file **21.04_Images.html**. The images **21.05_Riverside.jpg** and **21.06_Saltburn.jpg** must be in the same folder as the code.

```
<!DOCTYPE html>

<html>

    <head>

      <script>

        function change() {

            document.
            getElementById("PlaceHolder").
            src =  'Saltburn.jpg';

        }

      </script>

    </head>

    <body>

        <h1>Images</h1>

        <img id = "PlaceHolder"
        src="Riverside.jpg" width = "512">

        <p></p>

        <p></p>

        <p></p>

        <button id = 'change' onclick =
        "change()">Change the image</button>

    </body>

</html>
```

CONTINUED

Click the button. The original image will be replaced by 'Saltburn.jpg', as shown in Figure 21.10.

Figure 21.10: The original image has been replaced.

If you do not want to have an image displayed when the web page loads, then you can leave the source of the image, the src statement, empty:

```
<img id = "PlaceHolder" src=""
width = "512">
```

ACTIVITY 21.07

Open the file **21.07_Images_Activity.html**. Using the four images, **21.08_Istanbul.jpg**, **21.09_Pisa.jpg**, **21.10_Rome.jpg** and **21.11_Venice.jpg**, edit the webpage so that it has four buttons that will each call a different function to load an image into the placeholder, as shown in Figure 21.11.

When a button of that city is pressed, the correct image should be shown.

Figure 21.11: The image displayed when the 'Picture of Istanbul' button is clicked.

Changing image properties

Javascript can also be used to change image properties such as height and width.

ACTIVITY 21.08

1   Open the file **21.12_ImageWidth.html**. Use the following JavaScript code to change the width of an image displayed on a webpage by using a button to call a function to resize the image.

```html
<!DOCTYPE html>

<html>

    <head>

        <script>

            function smaller() {

                document.
                getElementById("Riverside").
                width = "256";

            }

        </script>

    </head>

    <body>

        <h1>Images</h1>

        <img src="Riverside.jpg" id =
        'Riverside' width = "512">

        <p></p>

        <p></p>

        <p></p>

        <button id='smaller'
        onclick="smaller()">Make it
        smaller</button>

    </body>

</html>
```

2   Open the file **21.13_ImageWidthActivity. html.** Add another button that would return the image to its previous size.

Use the Display style property to hide the buttons and make them appear when needed, including when the page loads.

TIP

As the width changes, the height changes too, so that the image does not become distorted.

21.2 The structure and syntax of JavaScript code

JavaScript uses the same structure such as variables, loops, selection as other programming languages. In JavaScript, the commands are written slightly differently.

The syntax of the language consists of the rules that should be used when writing the code so that it can be understood and used by the web browser.

One of the rules that we have already used is the semi-colon. In the code you have already written, a ';' has been placed at the end of every command and rules for defining and calling functions have been used.

Variables and operators

A variable is a space in memory that is given an identifier (name), where you can store data that can change while the program is running.

For example, you could create a space in memory called name and you could store the name Luca in there. You could later change it and store Katerina. You can check what is stored there by asking what is stored in name. The computer would tell you Katerina.

TIP

The identifier must be one word (that is, no spaces) and start with a letter. It must not be any of the KWs that are used by JavaScript (these are known as reserved words). For example, var, return and if are KWs as they are part of the syntax of JavaScript.

Declaration

A variable **declaration** tells the program that you need a space in memory and what its identifier will be.

KEY WORD

declaration: tells the program that a space in memory is needed and what its identifier will be

An example variable declaration in JavaScript is:

```
var name;
```

var tells JavaScript that you are creating a variable.

name is the name of this variable.

Apart from 'var' there are two other methods of declaring variables. These are 'const' and 'let'.

A variable declared using var outside a function is global and can be used in any code in the webpage. If it is declared using var within a function, then it is limited to just that function.

A variable declared using let can be used only within a block of code, that is, a section of code within curly brackets or braces, {...}. It can be declared within a function or an if statement, but it is limited to those blocks and if it is used outside a block, an error message will be displayed.

The values of var and let declared variables can be changed within the code, but if it is declared using cons, then it is a constant and cannot be changed. A const variable cannot be updated or redeclared.

Throughout this chapter, var will be used.

Assignment

Assignment means adding a value to that variable. For example:

```
name = "Luca";
```

The "=" symbol that assigns the value is called the assignment operator.

Different assignment operators are used in other computer languages.

The name of the variable comes first and = can be read as the word 'becomes'. This is the assignment operator. Luca is what is being stored. Luca is in speech marks (" ") because it is a string. For example:

```
age = 18;
```

This time the variable is called age, and 18 has been put into it.

You can change the value in the variable. For example:

```
name = "Katerina";
age = 21;
```

These values have overwritten the previous data.

Variables are values that can change, e.g. X = 2 and then later X=X+3.

Literals are actual values, numbers or text.

For example, a variable is declared as:

```
var name;
```

When name is used in the code, the computer knows that it is a variable name and uses whatever value has been assigned to it.

If "name" in speech marks is included in the code, the computer knows that this is not a variable but actual, literal text.

Data types

The data stored in a variable will be of a set **data type**. Table 21.1 shows the main data types used in JavaScript.

KEY WORD
data type: the type of data being stored, for example a number, string (text)

Data type	Description	Example

Number	A numeric value.	```<pseudocode>age = 16```
		
		```score = 12.4```

String	Letters, characters and numbers. Any text string must start and end with either single or double quotation marks, for example <pseudocode> '...' or <pseudocode>"..."	```name = "Katerina"```
		
		```address = '24 Main Street'```
		
		```message = "Hello World"```

Boolean	True or False.	```correct = true```
		
		```correct = false```

Array	A series of values of the same data type (see Section 21.13 Arrays).	```numbers = <1,2,3>```

Data type	Description	Example
Object	A series of named values of a particular variable. For example, the variable <pseudocode> 'movie' has many properties such as title, genre, etc. Defining these creates an object.	`movie =` `{title:"The House Story",` `genre:"Drama",` `length:96,` `releaseYear:2013}`

Table 21.1: Data types.

If data types are not declared when declaring a variable; it is assumed when a value is given to the variable. For example:

```
var name;
```

`name` could be of any data type. But if instead you put:

```
var name = "";
```

`name` is now a string.

For example, in:

```
var age;
```

`age` could be of any data type. But if instead you put:

```
var age = 0;
```

`age` is now a number.

Type conversions

You can convert one type of data into a second data type.

To convert data to a string, use the command `toString()` method. For example:

```
var Number = 99;
Var stringNumber = Number.toString();
```

To convert data to an integer, use the function `parseInt()`. For example:

```
var numberString = parseInt("999");
```

A string can also be converted to a number by multiplying it by 1. For example:

```
var String = "999";
var numberString = String*1;
```

Boolean data can be converted to numbers; true is converted to 1, and false to 0. For example:

```
var numberBoolean = Number(true);
```

KEY WORD

Boolean: a data type, either true or false

Converting data to the correct form is important to make sure you get the data you expect. You will learn about addition in the next section. The + symbol can be used to add together two numbers (for example, 2 + 3 = 5), but it also joins together two strings (for example, the string "2"+ the string "3" = "23").

WORKED EXAMPLE 21.11

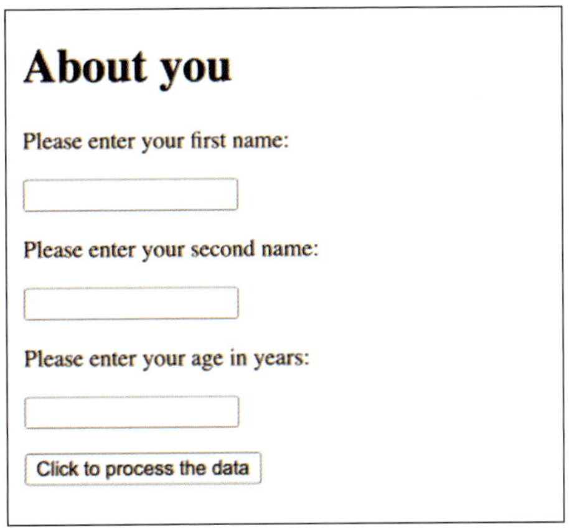

About you

Please enter your first name:

Please enter your second name:

Please enter your age in years:

Click to process the data

Figure 21.12: A web page that asks users to enter information.

In this example, we will create a web page that asks the user to input their first name, second name and age, and then writes the data, as shown in Figure 21.12.

Using HTML, paragraphs and input boxes are created for the data input. A button is added to call a function to process the data. Each input box is given an ID and the expected type of input is specified.

```
<body>
<h1>About you</h1>
<p>Please enter your first name:</p>
<p></p>
<input type = "text" id = "FirstName">
   <p>Please enter your second name:</p>
<p></p>
   <input type = "text" id = "SecondName">
<p></p>
   <p>Please enter your age in years:</p>
<p></p>
   <input type = "number" id = "Age">
<p></p>
<p></p>
   <button id="process" onclick = "process()">Click to process the data</button>
</body>
</html>
```

CONTINUED

Now, a function must be created to process and output the data.

```
<!DOCTYPE html>

<html>

    <head>

        <script>

            function process() {

            var first = document.getElementByld("FirstName").value;

            var second = document.getElementByld("SecondName").value;

            var age = document.getElementByld("Age").value;

            document.write("Your name is " + first + " " + second + " and you are " + age + "
            years old.");)

        </script>

    </head>
```

The function, called by the button, creates and assigns data to variables by reading the values in the input boxes.

It then writes to the document. This output consists of literal text enclosed in "" and the variables `first`, `second` and `age`. The separate elements are joined together or concatenated using the `'+'` symbol.

Be careful when joining literal text and variables that you leave a space at the end of the literal text before you add the variable, or before the text if it is coming after a variable.

The complete code is:

```
<!DOCTYPE html>

<html>

    <head>

        <script>

            function process() {

            var first = document.getElementByld("FirstName").value;

            var second = document.getElementByld("SecondName").value;

            var age = document.getElementByld("Age").value;

            document.write("Your name is " + first + " " + second + " and you are " + age + "
            years old.");)

        </script>

    </head>
```

CONTINUED

```
<body>

    <h1>About you</h1>

    <p>Please enter your first name:</p>

    <p></p>

    <input type = "text" id = "FirstName">

    <p>Please enter your second name:</p>

    <p></p>

    <input type = "text" id = "SecondName">

    <p></p>

    <p>Please enter your age in years:</p>

    <p></p>

    <input type = "number" id = "Age">

    <p></p>

    <p></p>

    <button id="process" onclick = "process()">Click to process the data</button>

</body>

</html>
```

Operators

An **operator** is a symbol, or set of symbols, that performs an action. Several types of operator are used in JavaScript. They include arithmetic, **comparison** and **logical operators**.

Arithmetic operators

Table 21.2 shows the **arithmetic operators**.

Operator	Function	Example
+	Addition	`x = 1 + 2;` `x` is now 3
-	Subtraction	`x = 5 - 1;` `x` is now 4
*	Multiplication	`x = 2 * 3;` `x` is now 6
/	Division	`x = 10 / 3;` `x` is now 3.33
++	Increment (increase by 1)	`x++;`
--	Decrement (decrease by 1)	`x--;`

Operator	Function	Example
%	Modulus (return the remainder part of a division)	`x = 11 % 5;` `x` is now 1
`Math. floor()`	Round down a calculation (remove the remainder)	`x = Math. floor(10/3;`

Table 21.2: Arithmetic operators.

In an arithmetic calculation you can use numbers (**literals**) or variables.

ACTIVITY 21.09

Open the file **21.14_Arithmetic operators.html** and look at the page source. Use the console log to show the results of some mathematical operations. An example is shown in Figure 21.13.

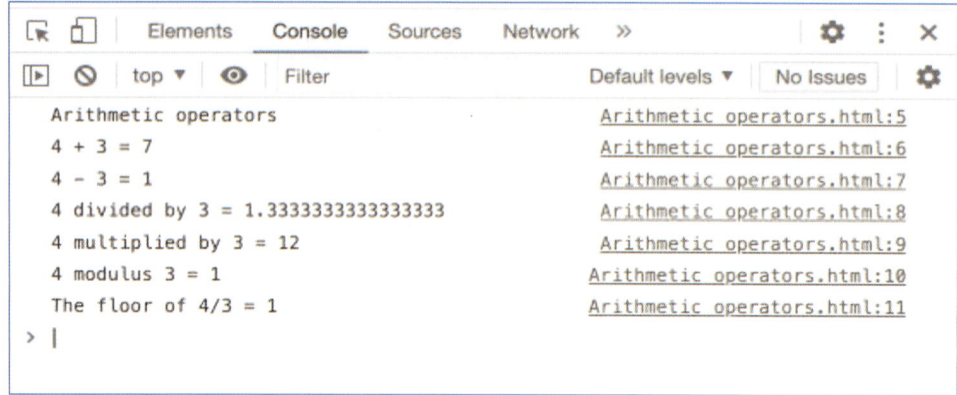

Figure 21.13: The results of calculations in the console log.

Comparison operators

Comparison operators are used to compare two values, as shown in Table 21.3. For example, they could see whether two values are equal to each other, or if one is greater than the other.

Operator	Function	Example
==	Equal to	5 == 6; This is false.
<	Less than	5 < 6; This is true.
>	Greater than	5 >=6; This is false.
<=	Less than or equal to	5 <= 5; This is true.
>=	Greater than or equal to	5 >= 6; This is false.
===	Equal to and of the same data type	5 === "5"; This is false because the first is a number and the second is a string.

Operator	Function	Example
!=	Not equal to	5 != 6; This is true.
!===	Not equal to or not of the same data type	5 !=== "5"; This is true, because they are not the same data type.

Table 21.3: Comparison operators used in JavaScript.

These operators compare values so that decisions can be made.

Questions

6   Explain what is meant by a variable.

7   Write down the comparison operators used in JavaScript for not equal to, greater than or equal to, less than.

Selection

Comparison operators are used with `if`, `else`, `else if` and `switch` statements so that a choice can be made if the comparison is true or false.

WORKED EXAMPLE 21.12

The following code asks a user to input a number and runs some code if the comparison is correct.

The user is asked to enter a number into an input box.

```
<body>
    <h1>Relational operators</h1>
    <p>Please enter a number between 1 and 10</p>
    <input type = "number" id = "question" oninput = "message()">
</body>
```

When the user enters a number, the `'oninput'` event occurs. It is similar to the `'onchange'` event but occurs before the user clicks outside the input box so that it loses the focus.

When a number has been input, the function `message() {` is called.

```
<html>
    <head>
        <script>
            function message(){
                var number = document.getElementById("question").value;
                if (number >5) {
                    alert("This number is greater than 5.");
                }
            }
        </script>
    </head>
```

CONTINUED

The function assigns the number entered to the variable `'number'`.

The `if` statement compares the number entered to 5 and if it is greater, it displays a message in an alert.

The complete code is:

```html
<html>
    <head>
        <script>
            function message(){
                var number = document.getElementByld("question").value;
                if (number > 5) {
                    alert("This number is greater than 5.");
                }
            }
        </script>
    </head>
    <body>
        <h1>Relational operators</h1>
        <p>Please enter a number between 1 and 10</p>
        <input type = "number" id = "question" oninput = "message()">
    </body>
</html>
```

The worked example clearly shows the syntax of the `'if'` statement. Notice that it also uses curly brackets or braces, like a function statement.

In the example, a user only gets a message if the number is greater than 5. So, if a user enters a number less than 5, they will just sit there, waiting for something to happen.

There should be two options, one for if it is true and one for if it isn't.

Fortunately, the `if` statement has an `'else'` option stating what should happen if the comparison is false.

ACTIVITY 21.10

Open **21.15_if1.html**. Change the `if` statement in the code to include an `'else'`.

```
Function message() {
    var number = document.
    getElementByld("question").value;
        if (number > 5) {
            alert("This number is greater
            than 5.");
        } else {
            alert("This number is 5 or less")
        }
    }
```

Notice that the `'else'` section has its own curly brackets or braces.

TIP

Checking that an acceptable number has been added is called error checking. Error checking should be used in all web pages where users are required to enter data. It can check that data has been entered and display an error message if an input box is left blank.

UNPLUGGED ACTIVITY 21.11

With a partner write down functions on paper for the following:

1   Compare two variables (number1 and number2) to see whether they are equal. Provide an alert saying they are equal and one saying they are not.

2   Compare the two variables to see whether number1 is greater than number 2. Provide two alerts for the two results.

ACTIVITY 21.12

A teacher would like to enter three test results and find the average. If the average is 50 or above, they would like an alert saying `"Pass"` and if it is below 50, the message should say `"Fail"`.

Code a web page that would allow them to do this, and show the average and the messages.

In this example, it may be better to provide a button to press after the teacher has entered the three test results.

Lots of ifs

In the previous examples there are only two options to choose between but there may be situations where there are more. To cope with this, the `'else if'` statement can be used.

WORKED EXAMPLE 21.13

A user is asked to enter a number between one and ten into an input box. If the number is greater than 10, the user should be told that it is too large and the input box should be cleared. If the number is 5 or less, they should be told it is a low number and if it is greater than 5, they should be told that it is a high number.

HTML is used to create the input box and a button to click after entering the number.

```
<body>
    <h1>Relational operators</h1>
    <p>Please enter a number between 1 and 10</p>
    <input type = "number" id = "question">
    <p></p>
    <button onclick = "message()">Click after entering number</button>
</body>
```

The button calls the function `message()`.

CONTINUED

The function uses `if`, `else if` and `else`.

```html
<!DOCTYPE html>

<html>

    <head>

        <script>

            function message() {

                var number = document.getElementByld("question").value;

                if (number > 10) {

                    alert("This number is too large.");

                    document.getElementByld("question").value = "";

                } else if (number <=5){

                    alert("This number is a low number");

                }

                else {

                    alert("This is a high number")

                }

            }

        </script>

    </head>
```

CONTINUED

The full code is:

```html
<!DOCTYPE html>
<html>
  <head>
    <script>
      function message() {
        var number = document.getElementById("question").value;
        if (number >10) {
          alert("This number is too large.");
          document.getElementById("question").value = "";
        } else if (number <=5){
          alert("This number is a low number");
        }
        else {
          alert("This is a high number")
        }
      }
    </script>
  </head>
  <body>
    <h1>Relational operators</h1>
    <p>Please enter a number between 1 and 10</p>
    <input type = "number" id = "question">
    <p></p>
    <button onclick = "message()">Click after entering number</button>
  </body>
</html>
```

ACTIVITY 21.13

Open the file **21.16_if4.html**. A teacher would like to enter a student's score out of ten.

If the score is less than five, the comment should be `'You must try harder next time.'`

If the score is five, the comment should be `'You have gained half marks.'`

If the score is greater than or equal to seven, the comment should be `'This is a good result.'`

If the score is greater than or equal to nine, the comment should be `'This is an excellent result.'`

You may have to experiment with the order of the `'else if'` statements.

Ternary operator

Using the **ternary operator** can make the code more concise.

> **KEY WORD**
>
> **ternary operator:** the only JavaScript operator that takes three operands: a condition followed by a question mark (?), then an expression to execute if the condition is true followed by a colon (:), and finally the expression to execute if the condition is false. This operator is frequently used as an alternative to an if ... else statement

The following code uses `'if'` and `'else'` to decide which message to display:

```
var age = 18;

var message;

if (age >= 16) {

    message = 'You can drive.';

} else {

    message = 'You cannot drive.';

}
```

The amount of code used can be reduced using the ternary operator.

```
var age = 18;

var message;

age >= 18 ? (message = 'You can drive.') :
(message = 'You cannot drive.');
```

The first message is displayed if the age is greater than 18 and the second if it isn't.

Switch

Another way of making decisions is to use the `'switch'` statement.

The switch statement takes a variable and compares it with various examples or cases. If it matches one of the cases, then something happens, for example the user is given an alert.

A default action can be given if the variable does not match any of the cases.

For example:

```
function checkAnswer() {

    season = document.
    getElementByld("answer").value

    switch(season) {

        case "Spring":

            alert("Things are starting to
            grow");

            break;

        case "Summer":

            alert("Lovely and warm");

            break;

        case "Autumn":

            alert("It's getting cooler");

            break;

        case "Winter":

            alert("It is cold");

            break;

        default:

            alert("You did not enter a season")

    }

}
```

Notice that the switch statement has braces or curly brackets.

After each case there is a colon `:`

After each case, `break;` is added so that searching will stop when that case has been matched to the variable.

> **ACTIVITY 21.14**
>
> Open the file **21.17_ifCase.html**. Ask a user to enter a day of the week. An alert should show that day number, for example `Sunday = day 1`.
>
> Add a default value in case a day of the week is not entered.

Logical operators

A logical operator is symbol or word to connect two or more expressions to produce a compound expression that can be used in a comparison.

There are three logical operations: AND, OR and NOT.

Three logical operators are shown in Table 21.4.

Operator	Function	Explanation	Example

&&	AND	Is true if the condition before and after are both true. If one is false, then it is false.	`(5 < 6) && (7 < 10)`
			 Both are true, so the result is true.
			 `(5 > 6) && (7 < 10)`
			 The first statement is false, so the result is false.

||	OR	Is true if one or both of the conditions are true. If both are true, it is true.	`(5 < 6) ||`
			 `(7 < 10)`
			 Both are true, so the result is true.
			 `(5 > 6) ||`
			 `(7 < 10)`
			 The second statement is true, so the result is true.

!	NOT	Replaces a true with false, or a false with true.	`!(5 < 6)` This is false because 5<6 is true, but the `!` will change this to false.

Table 21.4: Logical operators.

Look at the Venn diagram in Figure 21.14. The diagram shows the number of rainy and sunny days.

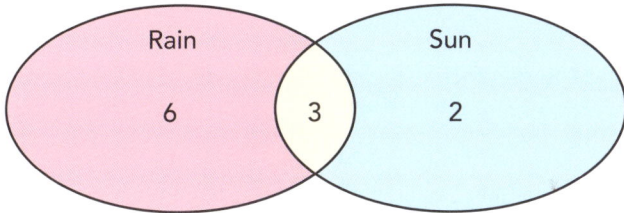

Figure 21.14: Venn diagram.

There were three days when there was RAIN AND SUN.

There were six days when there was RAIN AND NOT SUN.

There were two days when there was SUN AND NOT RAIN.

There were 11 days when there was SUN OR RAIN.

The words in bold code font in the sentences above are all logical operators.

WORKED EXAMPLE 21.14

A student would like to select a suitable T-shirt from a local store. The colour must be red, blue or white, the size should be medium and the store must be no more than 10 kilometres away. We will need to create and code a web page that would state whether a T-shirt was suitable or not.

HTML code is used for user entry in `<body>`

```
<body>
    <h1>Logical operators</h1>
    <p>Please enter the colour of the T-shirt</p>
    <input type = "text" id = "colour">
    <p></p>
    <p>Please enter the csize of the T-shirt. It should be S, M or L</p>
    <input type = "text" id = "size">
    <p></p>
    <p>Please enter the distance in kilometres to the shop</p>
    <input type = "number" id = "distance">
    <p></p>
    <button onclick = "message()">Click after entering the information</button>
</body>
</html>
```

Input boxes are used for data entry and a button is provided to run the function.

In words, the logic of deciding if the T-shirt is suitable would be:

IF the colour is red OR blue OR white AND the size is M and the distance is less than or equal to ten, the T-shirt is suitable.

This is written in JavaScript as:

```
if ((colour == "red" || colour== "blue" || colour == "white") && size == "M" && distance
<=10)
```

The items for colour selection are enclosed in brackets so that they are evaluated together.

```
<html>
    <head>
      <script>
         function message() {
         var colour = document.getElementById("colour").value;
         var size = document.getElementById("size").value;
         var distance = document.getElementById("distance").value;
         if ((colour == "red" || colour== "blue" || colour == "white") && size == "M" &&
         distance <=10) {
             alert("This T-shirt is suitable.");
           } else {
             alert("This T-shirt is not suitable.");
         }
         }
      </script>
    </head>
```

CONTINUED

The complete code is:

```html
<html>
   <head>
      <script>
         function message() {
            var colour = document.getElementByld("colour").value;
            var size = document.getElementByld("size").value;
            var distance = document.getElementByld("distance").value;
            if ((colour == "red" || colour== "blue" || colour == "white") && size == "M" &&
            distance <=10) {
               alert("This T-shirt is suitable.");
             } else {
               alert("This T-shirt is not suitable.");
            }
            }
      </script>
   </head>
<body>
      <h1>Logical operators</h1>
      <p>Please enter the colour of the T-shirt</p>
      <input type = "text" id = "colour">
      <p></p>
      <p>Please enter the csize of the T-shirt. It should be S, M or L</p>
      <input type = "text" id = "size">
      <p></p>
      <p>Please enter the distance in kilometres to the shop</p>
      <input type = "number" id = "distance">
      <p></p>
      <button onclick = "message()">Click after entering the information</button>
   </body>
</html>
```

ACTIVITY 21.15

Open the file **21.18_logicalActivity.html**. A high school would like you to design a web page to help with student administration. It should allow users to enter the first and second names of each student and their year group (7 to 13) and their tutor group. In each year there are four tutor groups named red, green, blue and yellow.

Create the code that would allow these items to be entered and display a message if all the data is acceptable, or another message if any of the year groups or tutor groups have been added incorrectly, for example a year group other than 7 to 13 and a colour other than those that are used.

ACTIVITY 21.16

1   Create a function for each of the arithmetic operators. Use a prompt to ask the users to enter two numbers, then call the function for each of the operators and output each result.

2   Items in a shop are reduced by 10%. Create a function to take a value as a parameter and return the reduced price. Ask the user to input the cost of an item using a prompt. Display the reduced price each time.

String operators and string manipulation

A **string** is a variable that stores text.

> **KEY WORD**
>
> **string:** a data type: data is stored as text which can be characters, numbers and symbols

```
var myString = "This is some text";
```

The string variable stores the text "This is some text".

Finding the length of a string

Like an array, a string has a length.

```
var len = myString.length;
```

The variable 'len' would be 17.

Extracting parts of a string

There are various ways of extracting parts of a string such as:

1   `slice()`

```
var sub =myString.slice(8, 11);
```

Here, '8' is the start position and '11' is the end position, but the tenth character is NOT included in the slice. The variable 'sub' would therefore contain characters 8 to 10.

The variable 'sub' would contain `'som'`.

Remember that string numbering starts at 0.

2   `substr()`

The first parameter specifies the start and the second parameter specifies the length of the extracted part.

```
var sub = myString.substr(8, 9);
```

sub would contain 'some text'.

Changing the case of the text

```
var text = myString.toUpperCase();
```

text would contain `'THIS IS SOME TEXT'`

```
var text = myString.to LowerCase:
```

text would contain `'this is some text'`.

Concatenating strings or joining them together

Strings can be joined together.

```
var text1 = "My first name";

var text2 = "My second name";

var text3 = text1.concat(text2);
```

text3 would be 'My first nameMy second name'

When concatenating strings, you must remember to add spaces where they are required.

```
text3 = text1.concat(" ", string2);
```

Finding the character at a particular position

You can use `charAt()` to find the character at a particular position.

```
var text = "My first name";
```

`var char = text.charAt(0);` would return the letter 'M'.

ACTIVITY 21.17

1   With a partner, carry out research to find other string manipulations. List them and give an example of how each can be applied.

2   Create a program that stores the first name, second name and age of a person. Output these in a sentence, for example, 'Bunmi Okon you are 20 years old'.

3   Create a form that takes a person's first name, second name and favourite number. Create a username for them in a function, using the first letter of their first name, their second name and their favourite number. Output their username in a sentence.

JavaScript Loops for iterative methods

Iteration is used a lot in programming. It sounds complicated but it means doing something over and over again until you get a desired result.

In a program it could be some code that keeps repeating until a variable reaches a certain value.

The code that does this is called a **loop**.

A loop is a code that repeats the code inside it a set number of times based on a condition.

It can be used when you want to perform the same action multiple times. For example, you may want to output a number ten times. Instead of writing the same line of code ten times, you can put it in a loop, which reduces the amount of code.

You may not know how many times some code needs to be run. For example, you want to multiply a number by itself until it is greater than 1000. You will not know, at the start, how many times this code needs to be run.

There are two types of loop: count controlled and condition controlled.

KEY WORDS

iteration: repeating steps or instructions over and over again

loop: a control flow statement specifying iteration

Count-controlled loops

A count-controlled loop repeats a set number of times. The number of times is set in the code.

For loop

This states that 'For a set number of times, do something'.

The for loop has to be told:

where it has to start, for example at 1

where it has to finish, for example at 10

how large the increments have to be each time, that is, does it count in increments of 1 so it would be 1,2,3,4,5, etc. or in increments of 3 giving 1,3,5, etc.

The following code:

```
for(count = 0; count < 10; count = count+1){

    alert(count);

}
```

would provide ten alert boxes containing the variable count. It would start at 0 and in the next loop it would be 1 and so on.

`count = count+1` shows that count has to increment by one each time. This can also be written as `count++`

So:

```
for(count = 0; count < 10; count = count++){
    alert(count);
}
```

would work exactly the same.

Count is a variable that is declared for the loop. It usually counts the number of times a loop is run, although it can be used in other ways. This statement can be excluded if, for example, you want to use a variable that already exists.

The second element, `count < 10`, is the condition. As long as this is true, the loop will run. This code can be excluded, but then the for loop will run continually unless you include a **break statement**. This is a line of code that tells the program to stop the construct it is currently in (that is, the loop) and go to the next line of code after the loop.

The third element is what happens each time the program gets to the end of the loop, and goes back to the beginning. In this case, the variable count increments (increases by one).

This for loop will output the first 12 square numbers:

```
for (count = 1; count <= 12; count++){
    alert(count * count);
}
```

KEY WORD

break statement: a statement that halts the processing of a section of code

---

For/in loop

If you have an object or string variable that you need to loop through to inspect each element, for example to output them all, you can use a for/in loop:

```
var movie = "A new movie";
    var count;
    for (count in movie){
        alert (movie[count]);
    }
```

This will display all the characters in the string `"A new movie"` one by one.

Condition-controlled loops

The number of iterations is not known before the loop is started. The iterations stop when a certain condition becomes true or false.

while loop

A while loop runs the code while a condition is true:

```
var count = 0;
while(count <= 12){
    alert(count);
    count++;
}
```

The variable used in the while loop must be declared before the loop is defined: `var count = 0;`

The condition is checked before the loop runs.

do/while loop

In a do/while loop the condition is checked at the end of the loop, which means the loop will always run at least once:

```
var count = 0;
do{
    alert(count);
    count++;
}
while(count <= 12);
```

In this example, 12 will also be output, as the value is not checked until the end of the loop.

ACTIVITY 21.18

Create a web page that will allow a user to enter a number three times, between 1 and 10, until they enter the magic number. You must decide what the magic number is in the code.

Here are some tips:

- Use a button to run a function.

- Use a `'while'` loop.

- You will need a variable to count the number of goes the person has had.

- Use the `'break'` command to break out of the loop if the user guesses the magic number.

- Provide alert boxes to tell the user.

  - if they have guessed the number

  - if they haven't guessed the number

  - that they have had three goes without guessing the number.

Question

8 Describe the difference between a count-controlled loop and a condition-controlled loop.

REFLECTION

How did you solve errors that you encountered while writing web pages?

Arrays

An **array** is a data structure that allows you to store multiple values under one name. Arrays were included in the table of data types, but they are studied now as loops are needed to manipulate them.

If you have similar items, instead of giving each one a variable name, they can be stored together in an array under one name.

This is often represented as a table, with each value given an index number with which to access it (known as the array index). For example:

```
var colours = ["orange", "purple", "green", "yellow", "grey"];
```

KEY WORD

array: a data structure that can store multiple items under one identifier; the items are of the same type

This code declares an array, called colours, with five elements. These are shown as a table, such as in Table 21.5.

Index	0	1	2	3	4
Value	orange	purple	green	yellow	grey

Table 21.5: An array.

Remember that counting starts at 0 and so the first item in the array has an index of 0.

Data can be extracted from this array. For example, this code would store purple in:

```
var myFavcolour = colours[1];
```

Data can be replaced in this array. For example, this code will replace yellow with pink:

```
colours[3] = "pink";
```

The length of the array can be found. For example, this code will return '5':

```
var arrayLength = colours.length;
```

This can then be used in a `'for'` loop to go through the array from beginning to end examining the data stored at each index.

Data can be added to this array. For example, this code will make a new index, '5', and put blue in it:

```
colours.push("blue");
```

WORKED EXAMPLE 21.15

In this example, we will store five words in an array. The web page will ask the user to enter a number between one and five to display the words.

First, set up the web page, declare an array and store the data in it.

```
[HTML]
[BODY]
Enter a number between 1 and 5.
[input type="number" id="wordToOutput"]
[button onclick="outputWord()"]Press me to see the word[/button]
    [SCRIPT]
        var words = ["One", "Two", "Three", "Four", "Five"];
    [/SCRIPT]
[/BODY]
[/HTML]
```

Remember that indexing starts at 0, and 1 has to be deducted from the number entered to find the index.

```
[HTML]
[BODY]
Enter a number between 1 and 5.
[input type="number" id="wordToOutput"]
[button onclick="outputWord()"]Press me to see the word[/button]
    [SCRIPT]
        var words = ["One", "Two", "Three", "Four", "Five"];
        function outputWord(){
            var inputNumber = document.getElementById("wordToOutput").value;
            inputNumber = inputNumber - 1;
            alert(words[inputNumber]);
        }
    [/SCRIPT]
[/BODY]
[/HTML]
```

CONTINUED

Only the numbers 1 to 5 can be entered, so the input can be checked and an error output given to the user if it is not valid.

```
[HTML]
[BODY]
Enter a number between 1 and 5.
[input type="text" id="wordToOutput"]
[button onclick="outputWord()"]Press me to see the word[/button]
   [SCRIPT]
      var words = ["One", "Two", "Three", "Four", "Five"];
      function outputWord(){
         var inputNumber = document.getElementByld("wordToOutput").value;
         inputNumber = inputNumber - 1;
if(inputNumber ]= 0 && inputNumber [ 5){
            alert(words[inputNumber]);
         } else {
            alert("Invalid number, it must be between 1 and 5");
         }
      }
   [/SCRIPT]
[/BODY]
[/HTML]
```

WORKED EXAMPLE 21.16

The following code asks users to enter colours and the onchange event triggers them being stored in an array. If the input box is left blank, the code shows the contents of the array in

```
[HTML]
    [head]
        [script]
            var colours = [];
            function check() {
                var entry = document.
                getElementById("wordinput").
                value;
                if (entry.length ] 0){
                    colours.push(entry);
        }
        else {
            functionList();
        }
        }
        function functionList(){
            var len = colours.length;
                for (let i = 0; i [ len;
                i++) {
                alert(colours[i]);
            }
        }
        [/script]
    [/head]
    [body]
[p] Enter a colour and press Enter- leave
blank and press Enter to finish.[/p]
    [input type="text" value =
    "Enter colour here" onchange =
    "check()"id="wordinput"]
[/body]
[/HTML]
```

ACTIVITY 21.19

Create an array with a series of numbers.

1   Create a function that will multiply each number in the array by two and output the result, but do not store it.

2   Create a function that will multiply each number in an array by ten, store the results and output them.

3   Create a function that will check if **any** of the numbers are greater than 20.

4   Create a function that will check if **all** the numbers are greater than 20.

5   Create a function that will return an array with all elements in that are greater than or equal to ten.

Comments to annotate and explain code

A comment is text that you add to your code, which the interpreter (the software that runs your program) does not run. Comments can be used to make notes about how your code works so other developers can understand what you have done.

To add a comment, write //, then anything after that will be a comment. For example:

```
var count = 0; //number to act as
    //   counter in loop
while(count <= 12){ //loop 0 to 12
    //displaying square numbers
        document.write(count * count);
    //output square numbers
count++; //increment counter
}
```

Comments can be single line, as previously, or they can be multi-line. You can make a comment go over several lines without having to put // in front of each line. Start the comment with /* and end it with */. For example:

```
/* This program will generate the username
It takes 3 characters from the last name
And 2 characters from the firstname */
```

ACTIVITY 21.20

For the following activities, add comments to all the code.

1 Create a web page that has a series of colours stored in an array. Use a loop to go through each element in the array and output it on a new line on the web page.

2 Create a web page that stores a number in a variable. Use a loop to output the 12-times-table for this number.

REFLECTION

What approach did you take to these activities? Did you plan the web page first, or start programming straight away? Why did you choose this approach?

JavaScript timing events

JavaScript has an inbuilt timer that lets you delay performing a task within a function, or perform an action at set intervals.

setTimeout

setTimeout() allows you to set a delay before something happens, for example before an output appears. It can cause a delay before a function is called.

```
<body>
    <p id = "para"></p>
    <script>
    var myTimeout = setTimeout(myFunction,
    5000);
    function myFunction() {
    document.getElementById("para").
    innerHTML = "It works";
    }
</script>
```

The code:

```
var myTimeout = setTimeout(myFunction,
5000);
```

sets a timeout of 5 seconds before the function myFunction is called.

The units used in setTimeout() are milliseconds and so 1000 of them are 1 second.

setTimeout() can also be used in an anonymous (unnamed) function.

```
<body>
    <p id = "para"></p>
    <script>
setTimeout(function(){
    document.getElementById("para").
    innerHTML = "It works";;
    }, 5000);
</script>
</body>
```

WORKED EXAMPLE 21.17

In this worked example, we will create a web page that after 2 seconds will display some text, after a further 2 seconds will show an image and then after the same time intervals some more text.

Using HTML, two empty paragraphs and two placeholders can be placed. A button will be needed to start the process.

```
<body>
    <h1>Using setTimeout</h1>
    <p></p>
    <p></p>
    <p id = "para1"></p>
    <p></p>
    <p></p>
    <img src="" id = "image1" width = 256>
    <p id = "para2"></p>
    <img src="" id = "image2" width = 256>
    <p></p>
    <p></p>
    <button id = 'change' onclick = "change()">Start the program</button>
    </body>
</html>
```

The button calls the function `change()`.

In the code there is a function named `change()`.

Within this function create `setTimeout` functions to insert the text and the images.

The first should have a delay of 2000, the second should have a delay of 4000 etc.

```
<html>
<head>
  <script>
    function change() {
      setTimeout(function(){
        document.getElementById("para1").innerHTML = "Here is the first image.";
        }, 2000);
      setTimeout(function(){
        document.getElementById("image1").src =  'Saltburn.jpg';
        }, 4000);
      setTimeout(function(){
        document.getElementById("para2").innerHTML = "Here is the second image.";
        }, 6000);
      setTimeout(function(){
        document.getElementById("image2").src = "Riverside.jpg";
        }, 8000);
      }
    </script>
    </head>
```

Remember that any images should be in the same folder as the web page.

setInterval

This allows you to make something happen repeatedly. For example, every 2 seconds you can output the same alert box.

The call follows the structure:

```
setInterval(function(){
    Event to repeat;
}, timeBetweenRepeats);
```

In this example, the alert appears every second:

```
setInterval(function(){
    alert("Hello");
},1000);
```

The following code declares a global variable, counter, and both outputs its value then increments its value every second:

```
var counter = 0;
    setInterval(function(){
        alert(counter);
        counter++;
    },1000);
```

You can only have one interval running at a time, because JavaScript is not designed to keep multiple threads running. Each interval will be one thread.

WORKED EXAMPLE 21.18

In this worked example, we will create a web page that will output a colour from an array every 2 seconds and will then go back to the beginning and start again.

First, we will create a paragraph where the colours can be displayed.

```
[BODY]
    [p id="para"][/p]
```

In the [script] section, the array and a variable to keep count must be declared.

```
var colours = ["Red", "Green", "Blue", "Pink", "Black", "Yellow"]
var counter = 0;
```

A function using setInterval can now be created.

```
setInterval(function() {
    document.getElementByld("para").innerHTML += colours[counter]
    counter++
    if (counter ] 5) {
        counter = 0}
    }, 2000);
```

CONTINUED

The colour at the index of the array indicated by `'counter'` is written to the inner HTML of the paragraph.

The counter is then incremented by one.

If counter is now greater than five, it is reset to zero.

```
<HTML>
<BODY>
   <p id="para"></p>
   <SCRIPT>
      var colours = ["Red", "Green", "Blue", "Pink", "Black", "Yellow"]
      var counter = 0;
      setInterval(function() {
         document.getElementByld("para").innerHTML += colours<counter>
         counter++
         if (counter > 5) {
            counter = 0}
      }, 2000);;
   </SCRIPT>
</BODY>
</HTML>
```

ACTIVITY 21.21

1   Create a web page that displays an image every few seconds, and if the user clicks on the image, they get a point and the image is hidden. When they have gained ten points, output a message telling them that they have won.

2   Create a program that asks a question in an alert. After a set time, the answer appears.

3   Create an array of JavaScript terms and definitions. Every 5 seconds, display another term and its matching definition.

Creating and using external scripts

You can write your JavaScript code in a separate document and then import it into your HTML document.

A separate document is created and the JavaScript code is written inside it. The file is saved with a sensible name with the extension `.js`.

Inside this document, the JavaScript code that would usually go within the script tags is written. For example:

```
var value1 = 5;
var value2 = 10;
document.write(value1 * value2);
```

This code can then be called from within the HTML document. The name of the file goes within the script tag, in this example the JavaScript file `javascriptparagraph.js` is being imported into this webpage:

```
<html>

    <script src="javascriptparagraph.js">
    x</script>

</html>
```

ACTIVITY 21.22

Open the file **21.19_array1.html**. Move the JavaScript code into an external text document and save it with a file name with the extension .js.

Add the source to the `<script>` tag. Make sure the external file is in the same folder as the HTML document.

REFLECTION

Did you find any extra code that was outside of the requirements? How did you learn how to use this code? Did you learn better through independent experimentation?

Question

9 Identify one advantage of using an external script.

PRACTICE QUESTIONS

1 The files required are:

21.20_ImageGallery.html

21.21_Gallery.js

21.22_D1.jpg, **21.23_D2.jpg**, **21.24_J1.jpg**, **21.25_J2.jpg**, **21.26_JE1.jpg**, **21.27_JE2.jpg**

Open **ImageGallery.html** in a browser and in a text editor.

The webpage must show six images in a continuous loop when the 'Start button' is clicked.

The images must be shown in the following order:

D1.jpg → J1.jpg → JE1.jpg → D2.jpg → J2.jpg→ JE2.jpg

Each image must be shown for 1 second (1000 milliseconds).

Examination Style Question

Programming for the web

An image gallery

Click the button to start the image display

Start

CONTINUED

a Open **Gallery.js** in a text editor.

Amend **ImageGallery.html** to use the **Gallery.js** script.

Complete the `Animate()` function and the `Timer()` function to cycle through the images displaying
them at the "ImageDisplay" bookmark in the html file.

Save your completed files as **ImageGallery** followed by your name and **Gallery** followed by your name. [8]

b Edit your solution to include a button under the *Start* button.

Add code so that clicking the button stops the animation.

Save your completed files. [2]

2 The file required is:

21.28_GuessingGame.html

Open **GuessingGame.html** in a browser and in a text editor.

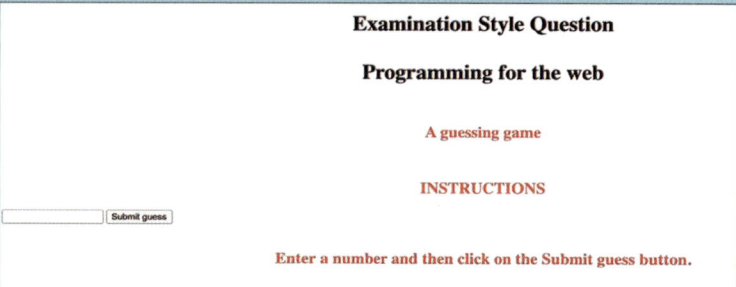

Examination Style Question

Programming for the web

A guessing game

INSTRUCTIONS

Enter a number and then click on the Submit guess button.

The code generates a random number between 1 and 10. The user has to enter their guess and then press the button to submit it. There are also instructions about entering a number and clicking the Submit guess button.

Inspect the HTML and JavaScript code in **GuessingGame.html** and develop it to produce the following:

a When the page loads the instructions, 'Enter a number and then click on the Submit guess button' are not visible.

They should become visible when the mouse pointer moves onto the word 'INSTRUCTIONS' and become hidden again when the mouse pointer moves off the word. [6]

b Create a function that compares the random number with the number that they have entered.

If they are the same, an alert should show the message 'Well done'.

If the guess is lower than the random number, the message should be 'Your guess was too low'.

If the guess is higher than the random number, the message should be 'Your guess was too high'.

Save the document as **GuessingGame1** followed by your name. [4]

c Add code that keeps track of the number of attempts and when they guess correctly, change the message to 'Well done! You got it on guess' followed by the number of attempts. [3]

SUMMARY CHECKLIST

- ☐ I can add interactivity to web pages.
- ☐ I can change HTML content and styles.
- ☐ I can show/hide HTML elements.
- ☐ I can display data in different ways.
- ☐ I can react to common HTML events.
- ☐ I can provide user interaction.
- ☐ I can create statements.
- ☐ I can create loops for iterative methods.
- ☐ I can create functions.
- ☐ I can use timing events.
- ☐ I can add comments to annotate and explain code.
- ☐ I can describe the structure and syntax of JavaScript code.
- ☐ I can describe a range of object-based JavaScript programming and terms.

PROJECT

Rock, paper, scissors is a game for two players who, at the same time, have to make a shape representing a rock, paper or scissors using one of their hands (see Figures 21.16 to 21.18).

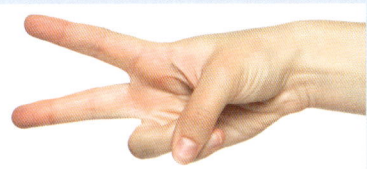

Figure 21.18: Scissors.

Figure 21.16: Rock.

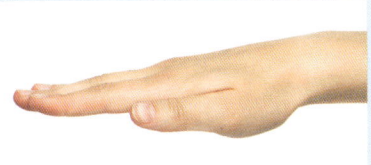

Figure 21.17: Paper.

The rules are:

- rock beats scissors because it will blunt them
- paper beats rock because it will wrap it up
- scissors beat paper because they will cut it up.

Your project is to create a game that allows a user to play against the computer.

This project will allow you to use the skills and techniques that you have learned.

CONTINUED

There is one additional command that you will need to use. This is generating a random number. The code for this is:

```
var variable name = Math.floor(Math.
random() * 3) + 1;
```

This statement would generate a random number between 1 and 3.

If you are confident in using HTML and CSS, and want to do it all yourself, download the images **21.29_Rock.jpg**, **21.30_Paper.jpg** and **21.31_Scissors.jpg**.

However, if you want to just do the JavaScript programming, download **21.32_Project.html**.

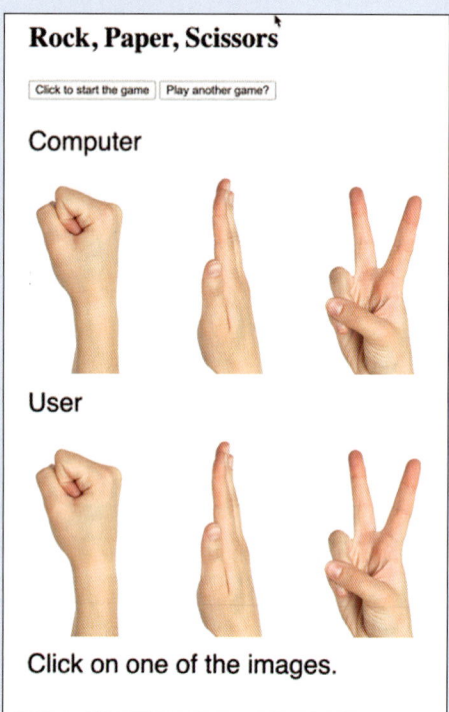

Figure 21.19: The web page for the game.

The heading, buttons, images and paragraphs have already been created.

Open **21.32_Project.html** in a text editor or suitable software and examine the HTML.

Check the IDs of all the images, buttons and the paragraph as you will need to use them in the JavaScript.

Specification

When the page loads:

- all the images should be visible

- only the 'Click to start the game' button should be visible

- the paragraph should be hidden.

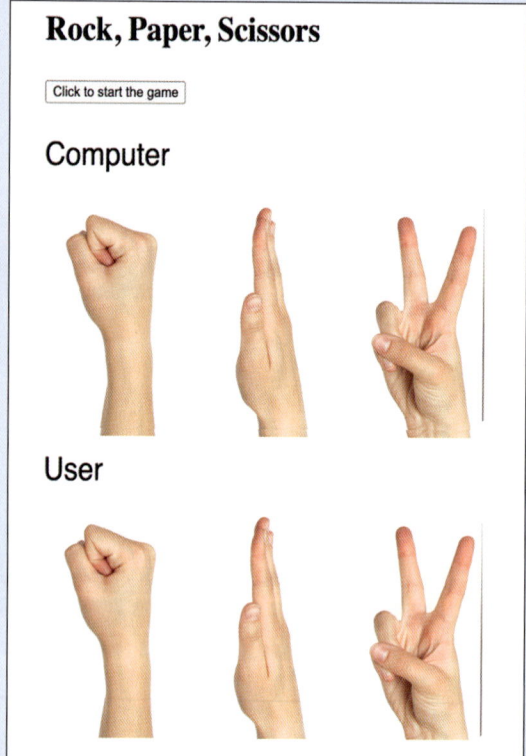

Figure 21.20: The opening screen.

When the user clicks the button to start the game:

- the three computer hand images should be hidden

- the paragraph should have the text, 'Click on one of the images'

- the 'Click to start the game button' should be hidden.

CONTINUED

Rock, Paper, Scissors

Computer

User

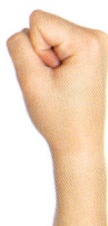

Click on one of the images.

Figure 21.21: The start of the game.

When the user clicks on one of the images:

- the other two images should be hidden

- the code should generate a random number between 1 and 3

- depending on the random number generated, the computer's image of rock or paper or scissors should be made visible

- a function should decide on whether it is a draw, or whether the computer or the user has won

- the result should be shown in the paragraph

- the 'Play another game?' button should be visible.

If the 'Play another game?' button is clicked the screen should be prepared for a new game:

- all computer's images should be hidden

- All the user's images should be visible

- the 'Play another game?' button should be hidden

- the paragraph should have the text 'Click on one of the images'.

Rock, Paper, Scissors

Play another game?

Computer

User

User win

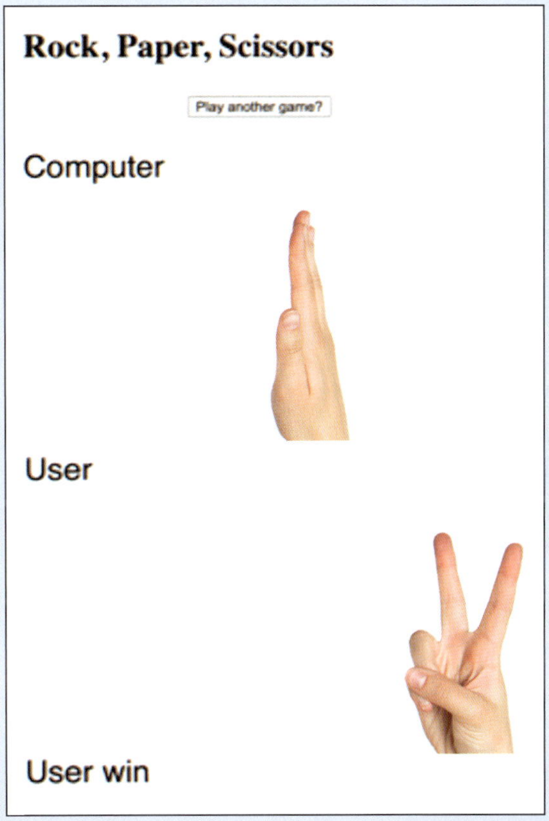

Figure 21.22: The result of the game.

> Glossary

2D (two dimensional): only on the *x* and *y* axes, for example a traditional cartoon

3D (three dimensional): has *x*, *y* and *z* axes, with objects having depth

absolute cell reference: a cell reference that does not change when it is copied into other cells

actuator: a type of motor that is used to move and operate another mechanism or device

aggregating information: combining data about an individual from multiple sources

algorithm: a set of instructions or steps to be followed to achieve a certain outcome

align: make objects line up along a set point

alignment: positioning text so that it is in line, for example on the left, right or centre

alpha testing: initial testing of the software by a limited group of people

analysis: the process of researching a given situation and finding out the requirements

animation: a series of images that are played one after another to simulate movement

anonymising information: changing data so the individual it relates to cannot be identified

anti-virus software: software that is used to check for and identify viruses on a computer and remove them

arithmetic operator: a symbol, or symbols, that performs a mathematical calculation; these often appear as algebraic operators that you will be used to using in mathematics

array: a data structure that can store multiple items under one identifier; the items are of the same type

artificial intelligence: the use of computer programs that can simulate human intelligence

aspect ratio: the proportion of a screen or video width to its height

assignment: giving a variable a value

attribute: a category of information within an entity

automation: the ability to operate automatically

autonomy: the ability to be independent; independence

avar: a hinge on a wire-model object that lets you manipulate its position

backward chaining: breaking a goal down into sub-goals that allows the system to work backwards from the goal

bandwidth: the range of frequencies available for a communication method, which determines the transmission rate

batch processing: sets of data processed all at one time without user interaction

beta testing: a sample of users test a pre-release version of the software

Bézier curve: smooth curves made of paths that can be scaled indefinitely

biometric: data related to a person's physical character, such as a fingerprint

bitmap: an image made up of small squares, called pixels; each individual pixel can only be one colour

bit rate: the rate at which bits can be transferred in data transmission

black box testing: testing of inputs and outputs to a system or part of a system that does not take into account the workings of the system

blockchain: a database that stores records of transactions across many different computers and systems

Boolean: a data type that can have two values, usually TRUE or FALSE

break statement: a statement that halts the processing of a section of code

bridge: a network component that connects segregated parts of a LAN

brute force attack: a hacking method that involves guessing passwords and obtaining manual access

bugs: errors within a system's software that mean it does not work correctly

calculated field: an arithmetic calculation on a field from the data source

calibration: the process of testing and modifying a device to make sure that it is taking accurate readings

canvas: the area in graphics software where graphics can be created and edited

cel animation: (also called cell animation) individual images are drawn on separate sheets, then layered on top of one another. The images are photographed, one frame at a time

cell: a single unit/rectangle of a spreadsheet formed at the intersection of a column and a row where data can be positioned; its reference (name/address) is based on its column and row

centralised system: a system (or process) controlled at one location or by one organisation

CGI: an abbreviation of computer-generated imagery; any image (still or moving) that is created using a computer

clean data: part of the data transforming process; it involves identifying and resolving issues such as missing values, duplicates, errors, inconsistencies and formatting problems

client: a computer in a network that is not a central point of control

clip: a short piece of a video or audio

cloud computing: using a network of servers hosted on the internet to store and manage data

CMYK: cyan/magenta/yellow/black colour system; all colours are a combination of these four colours

collaborate: work together

collaborative: working together to achieve a goal

colour depth: the number of colours that can be represented in the image

comment: human readable descriptions inside of computer programs detailing what the code is doing; they are not used by the computer

comparison: comparing two items of data resulting in true or false

comparison operator: a symbol, or symbols, that compares the two sides of the operator and the result is either true or false

compiler: translates high-level programming language into an executable file in machine code

compound key: two or more fields that form the primary key; each field that comprises the compound key is itself a key from another table

compression: reducing the size of a file, such as an image or video file

concatenate: to join two strings together

conditional branching: using comparison operators to make decisions in flowcharts, which affect the flow of logic

conditional fields: select records to use in a mail merge from a data source by using Boolean logic

condition-controlled loop: a loop that runs based on a condition, not the number of times it will run

connector symbol: a symbol used to show where part of a flowchart stops and where the flowchart starts again

construct: a control structure, such as a loop or a conditional statement

contiguous data: a range of cells that are next to each other, without any rows or columns between them

control system: a system that manages or regulates a process by physically changing aspects of the system depending on collected data

coordinates: the position (x and y) of an object on the stage

count-controlled loop: a loop where you know the number of times it will run

CPM: critical path method, also known as CPA (critical path analysis)

critical path: the tasks that must be completed on time for a project to complete on time

CSS: cascading style sheets used to define the styles of different elements on the web page

custom-written software: software that is written to meet the specific requirements of a client

data: numbers, letters, symbols, sounds or images without meaning

database: (in a database) a structured method of storing data

database management system: software used to manage a database

data dictionary: metadata (information) about the database

data driven: a system dependent on the data that it is provided with

data flow diagram (DFD): data flow diagram that shows how data moves around a system

data mining: the process of collecting large sets of data and analysing them to identify patterns and trends

data packets: units of data; when data is sent, it is broken down into smaller pieces or packets while it is sent; when it is received, it is put back together to make a cohesive piece of data

data redundancy: having the same data repeated in many records

data series: data used to represent data points on a graph

data type: the type of data being stored, for example a number, string (text)

data visualisation: the graphical representation of information and data

DDoS: a cyber attack that overwhelms websites with traffic to take them offline

decision: a comparison used to make a choice

demographic: a particular section of a population

dependency: when a task or activity relies on another task or activity being completed before the next task or activity can start

design: the stage in the life cycle when the design specification is produced

design documentation: gives a summary of how the system will be constructed

design specification: illustration of how the system will look, what the data structures will be and how the system will work

development: the stage in the system life cycle when different parts of the system are produced

device: hardware component of a computer system consisting of electronic components

digital currency: money that only exists in digital format

digital divide: the difference in ability to access modern technology

digital literacy: the skill level of a person to use digital technology to find and create information, and communicate with others using digital technology

direct data source: data that is collected and used for a specific purpose

distribute: make the space between objects the same

duty of confidence: an agreement between an organisation and an individual that data cannot be disclosed to others without an individual's consent

economic: considering a country in terms of their production and consumption of goods and services

element: an object on a web page with an opening and closing tag

embedding: importing data from a data source so that any changes to the data source are shown in the new document

emerging technologies: technologies that are still in development and their full potential has not yet been reached

encryption: scrambling data so it cannot be understood without a decryption key to make it unreadable if intercepted

entity: an object in the real world that we collect data on, for example a person, place, object or event; data about entities are stored in a table within a database

entity relationship diagram (ERD): a diagram that represents the relationships between entities

equalisation: the technique of increasing or decreasing different frequencies in sound

evaluation: a formal review to examine the suitability of the new system

event: something that happens to an HTML element

execution: the development stage of a project

explanation system: a component of an expert system that provides an explanation of how an outcome was reached

exported: to prepare data for use in another application

field: a common word for attribute

filter: a tool to select certain data and exclude other items of data

flat file: a database stored in a single table

flip book animation: each page of a book that has a different image drawn onit; when flicked through, they create an animation

float time: the spare time in a project before the next dependent task must be started

FLOPS: floating-point operations per second, used to measure the performance of supercomputers

flowchart: a set of symbols with commands used to represent a problem

flow line: the direction of logic in a flowchart

foreign key: a field in a table that refers to the primary key in another table

FOR loop: a count-controlled loop

formula: a mathematical calculation using +, −, × or ÷

forward chaining: a system that moves forward from rule to rule until it reaches a possible outcome

frame: a single image in a video file

frame rate: the number of consecutive frames shown each second, measured in frames per second (fps)

function: a ready-made formula used to perform a calculation

function: a separate piece of code that has an identifier and performs a task; it can be called from elsewhere in the code and returns a value

Gantt chart: a chart used for planning a project

gateway: a network component that joins different LANs together

geotags: an electronic tag that assigns a geographical location

goal driven: a system that is dependent on a finding a desired goal

goal seek: achieving a set target by adjusting other variables in a model

grid: a tool that displays a grid on the background of the screen to help with alignment

guides: lines that you can drag on the stage to help you position objects

hologram: a 3D image that is created using laser beams and mirrors

HSL: hue/saturation/lightness colour system; all colours are a combination of the hue saturation and lightness selected

HTML: Hyper Text Markup Language is the code you use to create web pages

hub: a network component that joins computers together and forwards units of data (data packets) to all connected devices

identifier: the name given to a variable, subroutine or function

implementation: the stage in the system life cycle when the system is installed for the user

imported: to bring in data from another application

increment: add one to something

incremental: creating a system or adding new functionality in small parts

index: a list of keys or KWs that identify a unique record and can be used to search and sort records more quickly

indirect data source: data that was collected for a different purpose (secondary source)

induction loop: a system that uses magnets to create an electrical current in a wire

inference engine: part of the expert system that makes judgements and reasoning using the knowledge base and user responses

information: data that has been given context by being processed, organised or structured in a meaningful and useful way, so that it conveys meaning and knowledge

infrastructure: the facilities that are needed for the operation of a society, such as roads, buildings and utilities

initiation: start of a project

innerHTML: the HTML content within an element

input: putting data into an algorithm

integer division: where only the whole number is given from a division

Internet of Things: connects devices over the internet, allowing them to share data; the IoT gives us the ability to connect objects that have historically not been connected, such as weather stations and phones, or mail boxes and watches

Internet Protocol (IP) address: a unique address for each node/device on a network

interpreter: translates and executes a high-level programming language one line at a time

iteration: repeating a section of code for a fixed number of times or until a required outcome is achieved

iterative: creating a system or adding new functionality in a repetitive cycle

kerning: changing the spacing between pairs of letters to improve the readability of text

key frame: a frame identifying the start or end point for an action within an animation

knowledge base: a component of an expert system that stores the knowledge provided by experts

knowledge base editor: a component of an expert system that is used to change or update the knowledge base

layer: a 'surface' onto which an image or object is placed; each object is placed on a separate layer and they are stacked on top of each other

library: a place that stores a list of images and objects/symbols in an animation

licensing: the rules on how you can use something, for example software

literal: the actual data being used (instead of a variable)

local area network (LAN): a relatively small network that is located within a single building or site

logical operator: symbols that represent the logical operations and, or, not

loop: allows code to be repeated

lossless compression: a method of compression where the decompressed image is identical to the original

lossy compression: a method of compression where the decompressed image is not identical to the original

MAC address (Media Access Control address): a unique address given to a device by the manufacturer

mail merge: the automatic insertion of data, such as names and addresses, from a source file into a master document, such as a letter or email

mainframe computer: powerful computer serving several terminals

maintenance: changes made to a system after its implementation

malicious actor (perpetrator): a group or entity whose mission is to affect or cause harm in the digital world; they perform malicious (deliberately hurtful) acts against individuals or organisations, usually with a personal agenda

malware: malicious software designed to gain unauthorised access to, or to disrupt or damage, a computer system

marketing documentation: materials to promote the benefits and functionality of a system

mask: a layer that involves shapes, or other components, that restrict what can be seen of the other layers

master document: the template that will be used for all records

master file: a table in a database containing information about one set of things, for example employees

measurement system: a way of measuring data, either at set times or continuously

microprocessor: an integrated circuit that is used in monitoring and control systems

MIPs: millions of instructions per second, used to measure the performance of supercomputers

mixed reference: a cell reference that uses both relative and absolute referencing

model: a representation of a process

modulus division: when the remainder is given from a division

monitoring system: a system that observes and often records the activities in a process

mono: an audio clip that has a single track which is played through the same channel

morphing: an object smoothly changing into another object

nested loops: a loop that exists inside another loop

nesting: a construct that exists inside of another construct

network: two or more computers or devices connected together so they can communicate and share data and resources

network architecture: the layout of a network, both logical and physical

network interface card: a network component required to attach a computer to a network

network protocols: a set of rules that determine how computers on a network communicate with each other

network topology: the arrangement or pattern in which all devices on a network are connected

non-atomic data: data items contain more than one item of data, for example 'Ushma Patel' is non-atomic as it contains the forename and surname

non-contiguous data: a range of cells that are not directly next to each other

normal form: the extent to which a database has been normalised

normalisation (databases): process of structuring data in a database

normalisation (audio): technique to edit an audio recording to increase the overall volume by a fixed amount

off-the-shelf software: general purpose software available to a large market

online processing: real-time processing using websites and digital forms

opacity: the lack of transparency of an image; at 0% opacity the image is fully transparent

operating system: specific software that manages the hardware within a computer system

operator: a symbol, or set of symbols, that performs an operation, for example arithmetic operators

orientation: the direction of text, for example horizontal or vertical

output: displaying data from an algorithm to the user

overdubbing: adding a new recording onto an existing audio clip

parallel processing: allows lots of instructions to be executed at the same time

parameter: a piece of data that is sent to a subroutine

partition: a section on a hard disk with a unique file system, where data can be stored

path: route a symbol takes when moving around the stage

peer: a computer of equal importance in a peer-to-peer network

peer review: assessment by other people who have a similar skill level

peer-to-peer: a type of network in which each computer on the network has the same level of importance: peer-to-peer networks have no central server

PERT: performance evaluation and review technique

pixel: a small square of one colour, which is combined to create a bitmap image

post-check loop: the condition controlling the loop is checked at the end of the loop, therefore the loop will always run at least one time

pre-check loop: the condition controlling the loop is checked at the start of the loop, therefore the loop might not run at all

primary component: the focus of the animation, such as the main characters

primary key: a field that contains the unique identifier for a record

procedure: a type of subroutine that does not return a value to the main program

process: an action performed on some data to make a change

prompt: a question asked to the user which requires a response

prototype: an early version of a software solution with limited functionality

pseudocode: a simple language used to write an algorithm

quarantined: files identified as possibly containing a virus that are being held in a temporary location

query: a tool used to search for data in a database

rapid application development (RAD): use of prototyping to develop a system in a very short time frame

real-time processing: data is processed as soon as it has been input and outputs are generated instantly

record: a common word for entity

redundancy: having spare components in readiness to take over in case another component fails

referential integrity: data in the foreign key of the table on the 'many' side of a relationship must exist in the primary key of the table on the 'one' side of a relationship

regulated: controlled by rules and laws

relationship: the way in which two entities in two different tables are connected

relative cell reference: a cell reference that changes when it is copied into other cells

repeater: a network component that is used to boost a signal in data transmission

REPEAT UNTIL loop: a condition-controlled loop that runs until the condition is true

requirements documentation: provides an overview of the functionality and needs of the new system

resolution: the number of pixels within a frame of video

resources: people, equipment, facilities or funding required to complete a project

reverberation: the repetition of sound, which creates a slight echo effect

RGB: red/green/blue colour system; all colours are a combination of quantities of red, green and blue

router: a network component that uses a computer's IP address to send data packets to a destination outside the current network

ruler: a tool that lets the position of items be viewed on the screen and helps draw them to the correct size

rules base: a part of the knowledge base that contains all the rules to be analysed by the expert system

sample rate: the number of times sound is sampled in a second

sample resolution: the number of bits that are used to represent each sound sample

secondary component: components that enhance the animation, such as backgrounds and sound

selection: use of a conditional statement to decide a course of action or which section of code to run

sensor: an input device that collects data from the surrounding physical environment

server: a computer in a network that is a point of control

server farm: a group of servers in the same location that have a huge amount of processing power

simulation: uses a computer model to predict real-life behaviour

snapping: a feature that will predict where you want objects placing, by aligning them to other objects, images or gridlines

social media: a range of software programs that allow users to interact and share information with other people via the internet

social networking: the use of websites and apps that allows users to communicate and interact

software: program that gives instructions to the computer

software developer: someone who designs and creates computer programs

source file: the file containing the data that will be merged into the master document

splicing: joining together two or more audio clips

spreadsheet: software that can organise, analyse and manipulate data, which is organised in a grid of rows and columns

SQL injection: an attack used to destroy, modify or retrieve data

SSL: Secure Socket Layer

stage: the area where the animation takes place; to be visible within the animation, the object must be on the stage

stereo: an audio clip that has two tracks which are played through different channels

stop motion animation: photographs are taken of physical objects; the objects are moved slightly each time and the photographs combined to create the animation

string: a data type: data is stored as text which can be characters, numbers and symbols

subroutine: a set of instructions that have an identifier and that are independent from the code; it is called from another part of the program and returns control when it has finished

supercomputer: large computer with parallel processing to complete highly complex tasks quickly

superimpose: to place something on top of something else (usually pictures or words) so that both can be seen at the same time

surveillance: the act of watching a person or place: this can be done in secret

switch: a network component that uses a computer's MAC address to send data packets to a destination within a network

switching: the process of transmitting data across a network

symbol: a component, such as an image, of an animation that has a name and is put in the library; multiple copies of the object can be created

system: a collection of components to form a whole system

system flowchart: a diagram showing an overview of how a system works

system software: software needed to operate a computer system

system specification: the hardware and software needed to run the system

table: a collection of related data, organised in rows and columns (for example, about people, places, objects or events)

technical documentation: an overview of the structure of the system, how it was put together and how it works

telecommunications: the transmission of information instantly over long distances, such as a phone call

ternary operator: the only JavaScript operator that takes three operands: a condition followed by a question mark (?), then an expression to execute if the condition is true followed by a colon (:), and finally the expression to execute if the condition is false. This operator is frequently used as an alternative to an if ... else statement

test data: data that will be used for testing a system

test plan: a detailed and structured plan of how testing should be carried out

time lapse: a camera automatically takes a photograph every set period, such as once a minute, and these are combined to create an animation

timeline: the place that controls the order the frames are run, along with timings and the positioning of the layers

TLS: Transport Layer Security

tracing bitmap: a way of converting a bitmap image into a vector graphic

track: a specific recording, for example of one instrument or voice: the tracks can be edited separately and combined to play concurrently

transaction file: data that is used to update a master file

transform: changing the dimensions, rotation, colour fill, opacity, etc. of an object over a certain number of frames between two key frames

transform data: the process of converting data from one format or structure to another, to make it more suitable for analysis or processing

transition: the method with which one video clip merges into a second clip

transparency: to what extent an object can be seen through

triangulation: the process of pinpointing the location of a device, using radio signals from a satellite

trimming: removing part of an audio clip, such as to delete unwanted sound

tunnelling: a protocol that allows data to be moved securely between networks; tunnelling repackages data into a different form, meaning the nature of the data can be obscured

tween: (inbetweening) an animation where the start and end points are set; the computer generates the images between the start and end points to produce the animation

two-factor authentication: an additional device is required to log on to a service

ultrasonic: sound waves that cannot be heard by humans

user documentation: a user guide giving instructions to the user on how to use the software

user interface: a way of communicating between the user and the computer system

user requirements specification: what a user needs a new system to do

utility software: software that performs maintenance on the computer system

validation: the process of checking data matches acceptable rules

variable: a space in the memory of a computer that has an identifier where you can store data; this data can be changed

vector: an image that uses geometric points and shapes; calculations are used to draw the image

verification: ensuring data entered matches the original source

virtual currency: digital currency that is decentralised

virtual private network: an encrypted connection that can be used to send data more securely across a network

waveform: a visual representation of sound within audio editing software

what-if analysis: experimenting with changing variables to see what would happen to the output if those variables changed

WHILE...ENDWHILE loop: a condition-controlled loop that runs while the condition is true

white box testing: testing the whole system in terms of structure and logic, covering all paths through the system

wide area network (WAN): a relatively large network that is normally two or more LANs that are linked

wireless access point: a network component that receives and transmits radio signals to allow wireless (Wi-Fi) connection to a network

workbook: a spreadsheet file, which contains one or more worksheets

worksheets: a collection of rows and columns of cells, used to store and manipulate data

⟩ Acknowledgements

The authors and publishers acknowledge the following sources of copyright material and are grateful for the permissions granted. While every effort has been made, it has not always been possible to identify the sources of all the material used, or to trace all copyright holders. If any omissions are brought to our notice, we will be happy to include the appropriate acknowledgements on reprinting.

Thanks to the following for permission to reproduce images:

Cover image: peepo/GI

Unit 1 CO Agsandrew/GI; Westend61/GI; Ratnakorn Piyasirisorost/GI; RichHobson/GI; Sinology/GI; PressureUA/GI; Subtik/GI; Blackwaterimages/GI; Andersen Ross Photography Inc/GI; EmirMemedovski/GI; Hello World/GI; Cavan Images/GI; Damircudic/GI; Drazen_/GI; Berezka_Klo/GI; Alistair Berg/GI; Kupicoo/GI; d3sign/GI; Witthaya Prasongsin/GI; Basak Gurbuz Derman/GI; Stocktrek Images/GI; Nikada/GI; **Unit 2 CO** Westend61/GI; The Mercury News/GI; Eclipse_images/GI; Grace Cary/GI; StefaNikolic/GI; PonyWang/GI; Morsa Images/GI; **Unit 3 CO** Sakis Mitrolidis/GI; Westend61/GI; Andriy Onufriyenko/GI; Dennis Galante/GI; Petri Oeschger/GI; Jacky Parker Photography/GI; Justin Paget/GI; Tunvarat Pruksachat/GI; Carol Yepes/GI; SasinT Gallery/GI; Seksan Mongkhonkhamsao/GI; Didier Marti/GI; Xia yuan/GI; **Unit 4 CO** Enot-poloskun/GI; Grace Cary/GI; Codrut Evelina/GI; Recep-bg/GI; **Unit 5 CO** Weerapatkiatdumrong/GI; Chesnot/GI; Nastasic/GI; Witthaya Prasongsin/GI; Twenty47studio/GI; Westend61/GI; d3sign/GI; Wwing/GI; GrLb71/GI; Image SourceGI; Boonchai wedmakawand/GI; John Lund/GI; Jamie Grill/GI; PonyWang/GI; Jasmin Merdan/GI; Rifka Hayati/GI; SDI Productions/GI; **Unit 6 CO** Imazins/GI; Ulisberg Alves/GI; Magnilion/GI; Athima tongloom/GI; Slobo/GI; Izusek/GI; Eternity in an Instant/GI; David C Tomlinson/GI; Morsa Images/GI; Avalon/GI; Aamir Qureshi/GI; Huntstock/GI; Wendy Stone/GI; Imazins/GI; **Unit 7 CO** Anthony Miller/GI; Jiang Yu/GI; AndreyPopov/GI; Nikola Ilic/GI; Stan Honda/GI; Tony Anderson/GI; Maskot/GI; Jonathan Knowles/GI; Mabus13/GI; Evgeniia Siiankovskaia/GI; **Unit 8 CO** Roberto_Z/GI; Courtneyk/GI; Roberto Machado Noa/GI; Onoky - Eric Audras; Ziga Plahutar/GI; **Unit 9 CO** Witthaya Prasongsin/GI; SeppFriedhuber/GI; Coberschneider/GI; Monty Rakusen/GI; Alan Schein/GI; MarioGuti/GI; Thomas_EyeDesign/GI; Laurence Dutton/GI; Lisa Kyle Young/GI; Cheunghyo/GI; Yongyuan Dai/GI; Orlando Sierra/GI; Songsak rohprasit/GI; Monty Rakusen/GI; **Unit 10 CO** enot-poloskun/GI; Image Source/GI; Tom Werner/GI(x2); Buena Vista Images/GI; Twenty47studio/GI; Arx0nt/GI; Philip Nealey/GI; Design Pics/GI; Courtneyk/GI; Jupiterimages/GI; **Unit 11 CO** Filo/GI; Amriphoto/GI; Patrick Daxenbichler/GI; Tetra Images/GI; Jacky Parker Photography/GI; Vithun Khamsong/GI; Mint Images/GI; AleksandarGeorgiev/GI; Songsak rohprasit/GI; **Unit 12 CO** d3sign/GI; Yasser Chalid/GI; Hobo_018/GI; Dev Images/GI; Tara Moore/GI; Jorg Greuel/GI; Image Source/GI; Pawel Libera/GI; Yuichiro Chino/GI; Jason Butcher/GI; Teera Konakan/GI; Witthaya Prasongsin/GI; Westend61/GI(x2); d3sign/GI; Vithun Khamsong/GI; Monty Rakusen/GI; Miljko/GI; Peter Cade/GI; EyeWolf/GI; Damircudic/GI; Alistair Berg/GI; Nitat Termmee/GI; **Unit 13 CO** Vladimir Vladimirov/GI; Piranka/GI; Gremlin/GI; Oscar Wong/GI; Krisada tepkulmanont/GI; Pekic/GI; Monty Rakusen/GI; Golero/GI; Charles O'Rear/GI; Westend61/GI; Dean Mouhtaropoulos/GI; Wladimir Bulgar/GI; Joseph Giacomin/GI; Guido Mieth/GI; Alvaro Medina Jurado/GI; FG Trade/GI; Richard Clark/GI; Westend61/GI; **Unit 14 CO** DAJ/GI; Vince Streano/GI; MoMo Productions/GI; AlonzoDesign/GI; SOPA Images/GI; Shannon Fagan/GI; Xijian/GI; Luxxtek/GI; VisualField/GI; Jelena83/GI; Vtls/GI; Thanasis/GI; Jasmin Merdan/GI; Maskot/GI; Mickey Cashew/GI; Kevin Jordan/GI; Zazamaza/GI; Chris Rogers/GI; Jose Luis Pelaez Inc/GI; Thanit Weerawan/GI; Bortonia/GI; Jordi Salas/GI; Luis Alvarez/GI; Oscar Wong/GI; Anton Petrus/GI; Imazins/GI; Erik Simonsen/GI; RicardoImagen/GI; Wang Yukun/GI; JodiJacobson/GI; PM Images/GI; Boonchai Wedmakawand/GI; Artur Debat/GI; **Unit 15** Andrewhoughton/GI; Maskot/GI; Simonkr/GI; Morsa Images/GI; MTStock Studio/GI; Peter Muller/GI; **Unit 16 CO** MimaCZ/GI; Kasayizgi/GI; Helen King/GI; LukaTDB/GI; Rudi_Suardi/GI; David Madison/GI; Patricia Marroquin/GI; AndreyPopov/GI; Luis Alvarez/GI; SDI Productions/GI; Mint Images/GI; Monty Rakusen/GI; Photo_Concepts/GI; Taiyou Nomachi/GI; Deepak Sethi/GI; **Unit 17 CO** Neustockimages/GI; Monty Rakusen/GI; Peter Cade/GI; Monty Rakusen/GI; **Unit 18 CO** Yagi Studio/GI; Kemal Yildirim/GI; Berenika_L/GI; Don Farrall/GI; **Unit 19 CO** Quelqun/GI; Yevheniia Rodina/Shutterstock; Yadid Levy/Alamy Stock Photo; DavidZydd/GI; Caterina Oltean/GI; Nancy C. Ross/GI; Nanette J.Stevenson-ebbystouch.com/GI; Khanh Bui/GI; Joe Regan/GI; ArtistGNDphotography/GI; **Unit 20 CO** Baac3nes/GI; Mike Turtle/GI; Photofusion/GI; N-Photo Magazine/GI; Science & Society Picture Library/GI; Jangeltun/GI; VasjaKoman/GI; Alistair Berg/GI; SolStock/GI; Unit 21 CO Best-Backgrounds/GI; MTStock Studio/GI; Peter Dazeley/GI; Ryasick/GI.

Key GI = Getty Images.

Screenshots from Microsoft Excel are used with permission from Microsoft.